THE OFFICIAL® GUIDE TO

FLEA MARKET PRICES

Second Edition

Harry L. Rinker

HOUSE OF COLLECTIBLES
THE RANDOM HOUSE INFORMATION GROUP
NEW YORK

House of Collectibles and colophon are registered trademarks of Random House, Inc. Originally published in different form in 2003 by House of Collectibles, a member of the Random House Information Group, a division of Random House, Inc.

This book is available for special discounts for bulk purchases for sales promotions or premiums. Special editions, including personalized covers, excerpts of existing books, and corporate imprints, can be created in large quantities for special needs. For more information, write to Special Markets/ Premium Sales, 1745 Broadway, MD 6-2, New York, NY, 10019 or e-mail specialmarkets@randomhouse.com.

Please address inquiries about electronic licensing of reference products for use on a network, in software or on CD-ROM to the Subsidiary Rights Department, Random House Reference, fax 212-572-6003.

Visit the Random House Web site: www.randomhouse.com

Manufactured in the United States of America

0 9 8 7 6 5 4 3 2 1

ISBN: 1-4000-4889-3

ISSN: 1533-211X

Cover photos by Rinker Enterprises, Inc.:

1) Purinton Pottery teapot, Apple pattern, $125
2) California souvenir snow globe, $10
3) 1933 RCA Victor advertising jigsaw puzzle, $175
4) Mae West carnival chalkware statue, $120
5) Flintstones molded vinyl banks, $45 each

Second Edition: April 2004

CONTENTS

Chapter 6: The Flea Market Scene Today

Part Two: FLEA MARKET PRICES – Categories A to Z

Part Three: REFERENCE SOURCES

PREFACE

Welcome to a somewhat unconventional price guide. It is designed to serve the non-traditionalist independent buyer and collector as well as the person collecting in "established" categories. The approach is informal. When you read the category introductions and carefully scan the listings, you will find a fair amount of humor. Do not be afraid to laugh. This book is about the pure fun and joy of collecting.

The flea market and garage sale markets are huge—far larger than the collector, dealer, and decorator markets to which over ninety percent of the books about antiques and collectibles cater. The more flea markets and garage sales I visit, the more I realize that seventy to eighty percent of the material found at flea markets cannot be researched in a general antiques and collectibles price guide. This title seeks to remedy that situation.

The Official Guide to Flea Market Prices contains dozens of unconventional categories. It offers the opportunity to test the waters by introducing new collecting categories and having a little fun at the same time. Some categories eventually work their way into established antiques and collectibles price guides while others fall by the wayside. Alas, some collecting categories only enjoy a brief moment in the sun. This is why there are dozens of new categories included in this book for the first time and why some categories found in previous editions are missing.

Criteria

Availability and affordability are the primary factors determining what collecting categories do and do not appear in this book. Objects do not have to be 25, 50, or 100 years old to be included. If it is collected and offered for sale in quantity at flea markets, I have tried to include it.

Because many objects appeal to multiple buyers, I urge you to become familiar with the index. The object you are attempting to research may be in this book. You simply are not looking in the correct collecting category.

Discounted contemporary merchandise, manufacturer and store overstock, and holiday remnants are not included. Tube socks, cheap Asian knockoffs, clothing odds and ends, cassette tapes, and handcrafted products, all too common at some flea markets, are not collectible. This book is not a price guide to junk.

The information in this book is solid, thorough, and fresh. If objects are repeated, it is because they are extremely common and provide a means for those individuals with an interest in tracking the market.

Ideal Companions

I recommend using ***The Official Guide to Flea Market Prices*** in conjunction with ***The Official Directory to U.S. Flea Markets, 8th Edition*** to locate the flea markets near you and in any area you plan to visit. You have to find treasures before you can buy them.

For a list of guides to American flea markets, see Chapter 2.

Credit Where Credit Is Due

Change is inevitable. As the eternal optimist, I welcome change. This is not true for everyone. But, as the twenty-first century dawns, it is far better to go with the flow than swim against the currents of change.

I now host my own television show, Home & Garden Televisions' "Collector Inspector." Thus far, I have taped fifty-two half-hour episodes of "Collector Inspector" and participated in two hour-long HGTV specials, "Collectibles Coast to Coast" and the "2003 Endless Yard Sale." In addition to my television commitments, I have greatly increased my personal appearance schedule.

The result is that I have less and less time to edit and write books. I still want to keep my hand in the publishing side of the trade as the new edition of this book demonstrates. However, the burden of preparing the books now resides exclusively with the Rinker Enterprises staff rather than with me.

Dana Morykan did the research, compilation, and page layout for this book. Simply put, she did almost all of it. Dana is my right arm. She is Rinker Enterprises when I am in the field. She is a jack of all trades and master of them as well. We have worked together for almost fifteen years. I have nothing but the highest praise for her and total confidence in her work.

Rinker Enterprises always has been a family affair. My employees are part of my extended family. Kristen Morykan, Dana's daughter, assisted with the research and compilation of the listings. Kristen currently is a sophomore at Temple University. Dena George, Dana's twin sister and a former Rinker Enterprises' Associate Editor, proofread the manuscript.

Dana was supported by Virginia Reinbold, the person responsible for the fiscal soundness of Rinker Enterprises, and Ronald "Ronnie" Kemp and Richard "Cap" Schmeltzle who see that the building is maintained and does not come crumbling down.

In the first edition of this title, we welcomed Dorothy Harris aboard as the in-house leader at House of Collectibles. Dorothy has weathered the storms of several in-house restructurings and an office move from one building to another, no small feat in New York City. Several assistants worked on this book with Lindsey Glass at the helm when the ship reached port.

As in the past, there are two groups that deserve special thanks. The first are those individuals associated with the operation of flea markets. We have seen firsthand how hard these individuals work. The second is you, the purchaser and user of this price guide. We thank you for your continued support and look forward to continuing to earn your vote of confidence.

Finally, the American flea market seen became international with the arrival of dmg media group. dmg media group acquired Metrolina and the West Palm Beach flea market and antiques show. We welcome our cousins from across the ocean and trust they find that it more than paid to get their feet wet in American waters.

March 2004

Harry L. Rinker
Emmaus, PA

Let Me Know What You Think

As much as I would like this book to be perfect, it is not. We all make mistakes. If you spot information that you believe is incorrect or have a suggestion to make that you think will improve the next edition, I encourage you to send your comments and/or criticisms to: Harry L. Rinker, Rinker Enterprises, Inc., 5093 Vera Cruz Road, Emmaus, PA 18049.

INTRODUCTION

GOOOOD MORNNNNNINGGGG, Flea Marketeers. Welcome to ***The Official Guide to Flea Market Prices.*** Today's specials are the very best goodies, tidbits, and knick-knacks found in every flea market throughout the good old U.S. of A. It's all here—neatly printed and organized for your use and reading pleasure.

Sound a bit like a carnival barker? It should. Going to a good flea market will produce as much fun, enjoyment, treasures, and memories as a visit to any carnival. Flea marketeering is a grand adventure. You have an idea of what to expect, but you know there will be a number of surprises. If you are lucky, you will grab a brass ring.

Find It Here First

The Official Guide to Flea Market Prices provides a first look at many potential collecting categories. Collectibility is tested at the flea market level. Dealers are continually offering material not seen previously. The successful sale of new groups of items immediately attracts the attention of other dealers. Their enthusiasm spreads. Before long, a new collecting category enters the established market.

Spotting these new categories before they appear as a regular entry in a general antiques and collectibles price guide is a challenge, one in which we think we excel. Expect to find a new category here first!

Not every hunt is successful. Some categories in this book may be dropped in subsequent editions. Not all efforts to establish a new collecting category succeed. For those that do not make it, may they enjoy their brief moment in the sun.

What good are price listings if you do not know how to use them? This book combines general information about flea marketeering and specific sources such as collectors clubs, periodicals, and reference books with price listings by category—all the tools necessary to enhance your flea marketing experience and further your education in your chosen areas of interest. Although new when you first buy it, this book will quickly become a much consulted friend, one with which you will look forward to spending a great deal of time.

Three Parts

The Official Guide to Flea Market Prices is divided into three principal parts.

PART ONE

The first part is a guide for flea marketeers. It helps you identify a "true" flea market, tells you how to find and evaluate flea markets, provides a list of the top thirty flea markets nationwide, gives tips for surviving the flea market experience and honing your shopping skills, and provides in-depth analysis of the current flea market scene.

Much of the information is duplicated from previous editions. You will find minor changes in the sections dealing with general guides to flea market locations, trade papers, and top thirty flea markets. Chapter 6, "The Flea Market Scene Today," has been totally rewritten to reflect changes within the flea market scene over the past three years.

In talking with individuals who purchased earlier editions of this book, I was surprised to learn how many "experienced" flea marketeers had skipped this first part. They made a mistake. Even the most experienced flea marketeer will find something of value.

One of the worst mistakes you can make in the antiques and collectibles field is to assume that you know all you need to know.

PART TWO

The second part of the book is devoted to price listings by category. Previous users are advised to thumb through the categories and not rely on the assumption that they know what the book contains. This edition of ***The Official Guide to Flea Market Prices*** contains numerous new categories.

You deceive yourself if you assume this book is just another antiques and collectibles price guide. Not true. This book was prepared using the premise that everything imaginable turns up at a flea market—from the finest antiques to good reusable secondhand items. ***The Official Guide to Flea Market Prices*** contains dozens of categories that are not found in any other antiques and/or collectibles price guide.

In a few categories you will not find specific priced items. Instead you are provided with general information that allows a broad understanding of the category. Occasionally, you are referred to specialized books on the subject.

One of the great joys about working on the categories in this book is that so many are supported with collectors' clubs, newsletters, and periodicals. You will find full addresses for these listed in the appropriate category before the price listing.

The Official Guide to Flea Market Prices provides the Rinker Enterprises, Inc., staff and me an opportunity to let our hair down. If you are comfortable with a formal traditionalist price guide approach this price guide is not for you. Category introductions range from serious to humorous to sublime. If the key to a great flea market is that it evokes these emotions and more within you, why should this book do any less?

PART THREE

Although I am not certain why, the third part of this book, which contains reference material for flea marketeers, including the "Flea Marketeer's Annotated Reference Library" and a list of "Antiques and Collectibles Trade Papers," is often completely overlooked by purchasers of this book. I strongly recommend that you become familiar with this section. The information not only helps you become highly proficient as a flea marketeer but also serves as your introduction to many other wonderful areas within the antiques and collectibles field.

Let's Go!

It is time to honor the cry of the circus ringmaster: "On with the show." Take a moment and read the program (the first section) before you watch the acts in the center ring (the second section) and then relive the memories (the third section). Most of all, don't forget—the entire purpose of the performance is for you to have fun.

Part One

A FLEA MARKET EDUCATION

Chapter 1
WHAT IS A FLEA MARKET?

It is difficult to explain the sense of excitement and anticipation felt by collectors and dealers as they get ready to shop a flea market. They are about to undertake a grand adventure, a journey into the unknown. Flea markets turn the average individual into an explorer in search of buried treasure. The search is not without adversity. Conditions ranging from a hostile climate to intense competition may be encountered. Victory is measured in "steals" and stories that can be shared at the end of the day.

Flea markets provide the opportunity for prospective collectors to get their feet wet in the exciting world of antiques and collectibles and for novice dealers to test their merchandise and selling skills at minimal expense. Many first contacts, some of which last a lifetime, are made between collectors and dealers there. More than any other environment in the antiques and collectibles trade, the flea market is the one forum where everyone is on equal footing.

Before you learn how to find, evaluate, and survive flea markets, it is important that you understand exactly what a flea market is, how it fits into the antiques and collectibles marketplace, and the many variations that exist. This is the first step to identifying the flea markets that are most likely to provide the greatest opportunities for you.

Defining a Flea Market

Few terms in the antiques and collectibles field are as difficult to define as "flea market." If you visit the Rose Bowl Flea Market in Pasadena, California, you will find discontinued and knock-off merchandise, crafts, clothing (from tube socks to dresses), home-care items, plants of all types, and specialty foods as much in evidence as antiques and collectibles. On the other hand, if you visit the Ann Arbor Antiques Market in Michigan, you will find primarily middle- and upper-level antiques and collectibles. Both are flea markets, yet they are light-years apart from one another.

The flea market concept is generations old. As it spread around the world, each country changed and adapted the form to meet its own particular needs. Regional differences developed. In New England, the Mid-Atlantic states, and the Midwest, the term generally is used to describe a place where antiques and collectibles are sold. In the South and Southwest, the term is more loosely interpreted to include craft, secondhand, and discounted goods.

It is not hard to see why this confusion exists. *Webster's Ninth New Collegiate Dictionary* defines a flea market as "a usually open-air market for secondhand articles and antiques." Individuals involved with antiques and collectibles do not equate secondhand (recycled or reusable) goods with antiques and collectibles. Although the dictionary may lump them together, collectors and dealers clearly differentiate one from the other.

The flea markets described in this book fit a much more narrow definition than the dictionary definition.

Flea market means a regularly scheduled market, held either indoors or outdoors, in which the primary goods offered for sale are those defined by the trade as antiques or collectibles. Occasionally, some handcrafted products and secondhand goods may be found among the offerings, especially in the seasonal and roadside flea markets where professional flea market dealers mix with individuals selling on a one-shot basis.

The problem with defining "flea market" with an antiques and collectibles perspective is that a multiplicity of flea market types exist. There are the seasonal flea markets such as Renninger's Extravaganza (Kutztown, Pennsylvania) and Brimfield's (Brimfield, Massachusetts), the monthlies such as the Metrolina Expo (Charlotte, North Carolina), and numerous weeklies scattered across the country.

One of the best ways to understand what an antiques and collectibles flea market encompasses is to discuss how it differs from three other closely related institutions in the antiques and collectibles trade: the antiques mall, the garage sale, and the antiques show. While the differences may appear subtle, they are significant to collectors and dealers.

Prior to the arrival of the antiques mall, there was a clearly defined ladder of quality within the antiques and collectibles community that progressed from garage sale to flea market to small show to major show or shop. This is how most goods moved through the market, and the route many dealers used to establish themselves in the trade. Two things changed the equation: Collectors recognized the role flea markets played as the initial source of goods and actively participated as a means of eliminating the "middleman," and the antiques mall came into existence.

Antiques malls arrived on the scene in the early 1980s. As the decade of the 1990s ends, the trend is toward the Super Mall, a mall with 300 plus dealers that offers a full range of services from direct sales to auctions. Malls developed because flea market sellers wanted a method to do business on a daily basis without the overhead of owning a shop. They also sought an indoor environment free from the vagaries of weather. Additionally, the buying public was delighted to find as many sellers as possible in one location.

Malls differ from flea markets in that they are open for business on a daily basis (a minimum of five and often seven days a week), the display and sales process is often handled by a manager or other mall representative, a more formal business procedure is used, and the quality of material is somewhat higher than that found at flea markets. The main drawbacks are that the buyer generally has no contact with the owner of the merchandise and price negotiation is difficult.

Garage sales are usually one-time events, often conducted by people with no pretensions of being antiques or collectibles dealers. They are merely attempting to get rid of items they no longer find useful. While it is true that some antiques and collectibles enter the market through this source, most individuals conducting garage sales have enough good sense to realize that this is the worst way to sell these items. Emphasis in a garage sale is on secondhand merchandise.

A recent development in the garage sale area is the annual or semiannual community garage sale. A promoter rents a large hall or auditorium and sells space to any individual wishing to set up. Usually there is a rule that no established antiques and collectibles dealers are allowed to take part. However, many dealers sneak in with friends or simply use a different name to rent a space in order to "pick" the merchandise during setup. Although community garage sales fit the dictionary definition of a flea market, the large volume of secondhand merchandise distinguishes them from the flea markets discussed in this book.

An antiques show consists of a number of professional dealers (weekend, full-time, or a combination of both) who meet in a fixed location on a regular basis, usually two to three times each year, to offer quality antiques and collectibles to collectors, interior decorators, and others. Once an antique or collectible reaches the show circuit, it is usually priced close to book value. Flea markets thrive on the concept that merchandise priced for sale is significantly below book value. While this is more myth than reality, it prevails.

Confusion arises because a number of monthly flea markets have dropped the term "flea market" from their titles. They call themselves "shows" or "markets." They do not use "flea" because of a growing list of problems, ranging from unscrupulous dealers to an abundance of unmarked reproductions, that plagued flea markets in the 1990s. Calling yourself something else does not change what you really are. Most monthly markets and shows are nothing more than flea markets in disguise.

Seasonal Flea Markets

Seasonal flea markets are those held a maximum of three times a year. Theoretically, they are held outdoors. However, many sites now provide either indoor or pavilion shelters for participants. Most have clearly established dates. For example, Renninger's Extravaganza is held the last weekend in April, June, and September.

If there is a Mecca in the flea market world, it is Brimfield. The name is magic. You are not an accomplished flea marketeer until you have been there. Actually, Brimfield is not a flea market, it is an event. In early May, July, and September over fifteen separate flea markets open and close. On Fridays the dealer count exceeds 1,500. Area motel rooms are booked over a year in advance. Traffic jams last hours.

For the past several years Renninger's has been promoting seasonal markets during the winter months at its Mount Dora, Florida, location. They are an important stop on the Southern winter circuit. Although there are a few seasonal markets in the Midwest, none are on a par with the Renninger's Extravaganzas and the Brimfield weeks.

Monthly Flea Markets

The monthly flea market's strength rests on a steady dealer clientele supplemented by other dealers passing through the area, a frequency that allows dealers enough time to find new merchandise, and a setting that is usually superior to the seasonal and weekly flea markets. The monthlies range from the upscale Ann Arbor Antiques Market to the something-for-everybody flea market (like the Kane County Flea Market in St. Charles, Illinois).

Most of the monthly flea markets have some outdoor spaces. The Kentucky Flea Market in Louisville, Kentucky, and the Fairgrounds Antiques Market in Phoenix, Arizona, are two exceptions. Flea markets with outdoor space operate only during warm weather months, generally April through November. A few of the larger operations (e.g., the Springfield Antiques Show & Flea Market in Springfield, Ohio) operate year-round. Double-check the schedule for any flea market you plan to visit between November and April, even those located in the South and Southwest.

Another strength of the monthly flea markets rests in the fact that they attract a large number of dealers who appear regularly. Collectors and dealers have time to cultivate good working relationships. A level of buying trust is created because the collector knows that he or she will be able to find the seller again if questions develop.

Weekly Flea Markets

The weekly flea markets break down into two types: those held on a weekday and those held on a weekend. The weekday markets are primarily for dealers in the trade. Monday flea markets at Perkiomenville, Pennsylvania, and Wednesday flea markets at Shipshewana, Indiana, are legends. These markets begin in the predawn hours. The best buys are found by flashlight as participants check merchandise as it is being unpacked. Most selling ends by 9:00 a.m. These markets appeal primarily to individuals actively involved in the resale of antiques and collectibles. Most collectors prefer something a bit more civilized.

Renninger's in Adamstown, Pennsylvania, shows the staying power of the weekend flea market. Within driving distance of several major population centers, yet far enough in the country to make the day an outing, Renninger's combines an ever-changing outdoor section with an indoor facility featuring primarily permanent dealers. Renninger's is open only on Sundays, except for Extravaganza weekends. Because buyers like to shop on Saturdays as well, Renninger's Promotions created Renninger's in Kutztown, Pennsylvania.

Weekend flea markets are now a fixture across the country and constitute the largest segment of the flea market community. It is common to find several in one location as each tries to capitalize on the success of the other. However, their quality varies tremendously.

The biggest problem with weekend flea markets is merchandise staleness. Many dealers add only a few new items each week. Collectors shop them on a four- to eight-week cycle. The way to avoid missing a shot at a major new piece is to maintain a close working relationship with several dealers. Most weekend flea market dealers shop the market. They can be your eyes when you are not there.

As with the monthly flea markets, you can buy from indoor dealers knowing that you are likely to find them if a problem develops later. Be much more careful when purchasing from the transient outside dealers. Get a valid name, address, and phone number from anyone from whom you make a purchase.

One of the things I like best about large weekend flea markets is that they feature one or more book dealers who specialize in antiques and collectibles books. I always stop at these booths to check on the latest titles. In some cases, I find a book I never saw advertised in the trade papers. Some of the dealers offer search services for out-of-print titles. Spending time getting to know these book dealers is something you will never regret.

Roadside Flea Markets

I have ignored roadside flea markets up to this point because the merchandise they offer is usually of garage sale quality. This is not to say that I have not found some great buys at roadside markets. However, when I consider the amount of time that I spend finding these few precious gems, I realize I can do much better at a traditional flea markets.

Chances are that you collect one or two specific categories. If so, not every type of flea market is right for you. How do you find the best markets? What type of evaluation can you do in advance to avoid the frustration of coming home empty-handed? These questions and more are answered in the next chapter.

Chapter 2
FINDING AND EVALUATING FLEA MARKETS

In order to attend a flea market, you have to locate one. It is not as easy as it sounds. In order to thoroughly research the available markets in any given area, you will have to consult a variety of sources. Even when you have finished, you are still likely to spot a flea market that you missed in your research along the way. I told you there was a strong sense of adventure in flea marketeering.

Flea Market Guides

There are four national guides to United States flea markets. Buy them all.

The Flea Market Shopper's Companion: A Complete Guide for Buyers and Sellers Coast to Coast by James Goodridge (Kensington Publishing, 850 Third Avenue, New York, NY 10022).

Prior to the publication of *The Flea Market Shopper's Companion*, James Goodridge edited four regional flea market guides published by Adams Publishing. Goodridge's title combines the information into a single volume, a concession to the fact that today's flea marketeer is as much a national shopper as a regional shopper. The book lists flea markets alphabetically and provides information about size, trading days, parking, and types of traders. The Flea Market Shopper also contains buying and selling tips. This paperback retails for $14.95.

The Original Clark's Flea Market U.S.A.: A National Directory of Flea Markets and Swap Meets (Clark Publications, 5469 Inland Cove Ct., Milton, FL 32583 / (850) 623-0794).

Clark's, issued quarterly, lists over 2,000 flea markets and swap meets. The guide is organized alphabetically by state. The secondary organization is city or town closest to the flea market within the state. You will find information on name, address, days and occasionally hours of operation and telephone number. Information provided about each market varies greatly. Completely missing are directions for hard-to-find markets. I buy an issue every year or two as a safety check against my regular sources. A one-year subscription is $38.00. Single copies are available from the publisher at $10.00, a price that includes postage and handling.

The Official Directory to U.S. Flea Markets, Eighth Edition, edited by Kitty Werner (House of Collectibles, Ballantine Division of Random House, 201 East 50th Street, New York, NY 10022).

The Official Directory under Kitty Werner's direction gets better with each edition. The book covers over 1,000 flea markets in the United States, Canada, and

Europe. Yes, Canada and Europe—it's time someone paid attention to our northern neighbor and our cousins abroad. Each listing contains information about a flea market's dates, hours, admission, location, a very detailed description of the type of merchandise found, dealer rates, and a telephone number and full address for the chief contact person. I especially like the list of "Other Flea Markets" found at the end of most state listings. These are markets that did not respond to the questionnaire. Werner advises users to "please call first" to make certain they are open. You can purchase a copy of this guide in most larger bookstores. It is a bargain at $14.00.

U.S. Flea Market Directory: Guide to the Best Flea Markets in All 50 States, Third Edition, edited by Albert LaFarge (Griffin Trade, St. Martin's Press, 175 5th Avenue, New York, NY 10010).

Designed to compete with *The Official Directory,* it provides detailed information that includes maps and travel directions, days and times, number of dealers, description of goods sold, dealer information, and other useful tidbits for approximately 1,000 flea markets nationwide. As one might expect, LaFarge covers many of the same flea markets that are found in *The Official Directory.* However, there are enough differences to make both books a must buy. *U.S. Flea Market* retails for $15.95 and is available at most bookstores. The most recent edition was published in 2000. Copies are still available on the Internet.

Antiques and collectibles flea markets are not unique to the United States. In fact, the modern flea market originated in Paris. Flea markets play a vital role throughout Europe, especially in France, Great Britain, and Germany.

Travel Keys (PO Box 160691, Sacramento, CA 95816) has published a separate flea market guide for France, Great Britain, and Germany, each edited by Peter B. Manston. Although badly in need of revision, the books still have value if you are traveling abroad. First, many of the flea markets are decades old—same time, same place. If possible, double-check before setting out. Once at a market, do not hesitate to ask dealers to recommend other flea market venues. Second, the introductory material is a must read, especially the section on export laws and regulations. This is information you will not find anywhere else.

National and Regional Shop Guides

NATIONAL GUIDES

In the late 1990s a day "antiquing" means visiting a variety of selling markets. A flea market stop is combined with a visit to nearby antiques and collectibles malls. For this reason, I recommend Judy Lloyd's *No-Nonsense Antique Mall Directory.* It covers 5,000 malls throughout the United States. The most recent edition was published in 2001 and it is sold out. The Lloyds have taken a two-year hiatus to raise two grandchildren in their care. The next edition is slated for Spring 2004. For more information write: FDS Antiques, PO Box 188, Higginsport, OH 45131. In the interim, check out the listings on their Internet site, www.antiqueguide.net.

Wilbert and Deanne Fuller's *Fullers' Best Antiquing U.S.A.: A Travel Guide To America's Greatest Places To Antique* (Debill Publishing Co., P.O. Box 783169, Wichita, KS 67278; $19.95 post paid) is helpful. The book provides information about 1,100 of the largest antiques and collectibles malls, 175 major antique markets and shows, and hundreds of antique auctions. The listings are selective. Directions are ballpark, not specific. Lloyd's guide is more comprehensive, but Fullers' is a good choice until the next edition of Lloyd's is available.

REGIONAL GUIDES

A number of specialized regional guides for locating antiques and collectibles flea markets, malls, and shops exist. Most are published by trade papers. A few are done privately. None focus solely on the flea market scene.

The *AntiqueWeek Guide To Antique Shops & Malls* (AntiqueWeek, PO Box 90, Knightstown, IN 46148 [800] 876-5133) is typical. Organization is by state, region, and by city and town within a region. Brief listings for each business are supplemented by display advertising. Each edition covers flea markets, malls, shops, shows, and more. The coverage gets better with each edition. The principal problem with this and similar guides is that you have to pay a fee to be listed. As a result, coverage is limited to those willing to pay. However, they are a great starting point and a bargain at $4.95 each.

When planning to visit a new area, contact some of the trade papers that serve the region and ask if they publish a regional guide or know of such a guide. Regional guides are inexpensive, ranging from $5 to $15. Many of the businesses listed in the guide sell it across the counter. I always pick up a copy. The storage pouch located behind the front driver's seat of my car is littered with road maps and regional guides, most of which show signs of heavy use.

Resource Directory

David Maloney Jr.'s *Maloney's Antiques and Collectibles Resource Directory, 7th Edition* (Krause Publications, 700 E. State St., Iola, WI 54990) contains category listings for antiques shops and flea markets. The listings include addresses and telephone numbers. Hopefully, you own a copy of Maloney's book. If you do not, you should. Make a resolution—right now—to buy a copy the next time you visit a bookstore or the stand of an antiques and collectibles book seller at a flea market. It is the best investment anyone in the trade can make. If you do not think so, I will give you your money back.

Trade Newspapers

The best source of flea market information is advertisements in trade newspapers. Some papers put all the flea market advertisements in one location, while others place them in their appropriate regional section. Most trade papers' events calendars include flea markets with the show listings. Once again, the problem rests with the fact that all advertising is paid advertising.

Not all flea markets advertise in every issue of a trade paper. Some advertise in papers outside their home area because the locals know where and when to find them. Flea markets that operate between April and September usually do not advertise in December and January. The only way to conduct a complete search is to obtain a four- to six-month run of a regional paper and carefully scan each issue. When doing this, keep your eyes open for reports and features about flea markets. As advertisers, flea markets expect to get written up at least once a year.

The following is a list of national and regional trade papers that I recommend you consult for flea market information. You will find their full addresses and phone numbers (when known) in the listing of trade newspapers at the back of this book.

This list is by no means complete. I am certain that I have missed a few regional papers. However, these papers provide a starting point. Do not be foolish and go flea marketeering without consulting them.

NATIONAL TRADE PAPERS

The Antique Trader Weekly, Iola, WI
AntiqueWeek, Knightstown, IN
Antiques and the Arts Weekly, Newtown, CT
Collectors News, Grundy Center, IA
Maine Antique Digest, Waldoboro, ME

REGIONAL TRADE PAPERS

New England

The Fine Arts Trader, Randolph, MA
The Journal of Antiques and Collectibles, Hudson, NY
New England Antiques Journal, Ware, MA
Northeast Journal of Arts & Antiques, Hudson, NY
Unravel the Gavel, Belmont, NH

Middle Atlantic States

Antiques Tattler, Adamstown, PA
Northeast Journal of Antiques & Art, Hudson, NY
Renninger's Antique Guide, Lafayette Hill, PA

South

The Antique Shoppe, Keystone Heights, FL
Cotton & Quail Antique Trail, Iola, WI
The Old News Is Good News Antiques Gazette, Hammond, LA
Southeastern Antiquing and Collecting Magazine, Acworth, GA
Southern Antiques, Decatur, GA

Midwest

The American Antiquities Journal, Springfield, OH
The Antique Collector and Auction Guide, Salem, OH
Auction Action Antique News, Shawano, WI
Auction World, Overland Park, KS
The Collector, Heyworth, IL
Collectors Journal, Vinton, IA
Discover Mid-America, Kansas City, MO
Great Lakes Trader, Williamstown, MI
Indiana Antique Buyer's News, Silver Lake, IN
The Old Times Newspaper, Maple Lake, MN
Yesteryear, Princeton, WI

Southwest

The Antique Register, Phoenix, AZ

West Coast

Antique & Collectables, El Cajon, CA
Antique Journal, El Cajon, CA
Old Stuff, McMinnville, OR
West Coast Peddler, Whittier, CA

NFMA (National Flea Market Association)

In 1997 Jerry Stokes founded the National Flea Market Association of Owners & Managers. It has evolved into the National Flea Market Association (NFMA) and is headquartered at 1951 W. Camelback Road, #445, Phoenix, AZ 85015. John R. Chism is its current president.

The Association issues a newsletter, offers educational programs, and holds conventions. Its Internet website (www.fleamarkets.org) lists its objectives and provides the opportunity to exchange ideas, co-advertise, and promote better flea market shopping.

The vast majority of the flea markets that comprise the membership of the NFMA are swap meets, places where you are more likely to find discounted new merchandise, farm produce, crafts, contemporary collectibles (many speculative), and blatant reproductions than antiques and collectibles. There will be an occasional jewel, but discovering it requires a great deal of hunting.

Which Flea Market Is Right for You?

The best flea market is the one at which you find plenty to buy at good to great prices. This means that most flea markets are not right for you. Is it necessary to attend each one to make your determination? I do not think so.

I am a great believer in using the telephone. If long distance rates jump dramatically as a result of the publication of this book, I plan to approach AT&T and ask for a piece of the action. It is a lot cheaper to call than to pay for transportation, lodging, and meals, not to mention the value of your time. Do not hesitate to call promoters and ask them about their flea markets.

What type of information should you request? First, check the number of dealers. If the number falls below one hundred, think twice. Ask for a ratio of local dealers to transient dealers. A good mix is 75% local and 25% transient for monthly and weekly markets. Second, inquire about the type of merchandise being offered for sale. Make a point not to tell the promoter what you collect. If you do, you can be certain that the flea market has a number of dealers who offer the material. Do not forget to ask about the quality of the merchandise. Third, ask about the facilities. The more indoor space available, the higher the level of merchandise is likely to be. What happens if it rains?

Finally, ask yourself this question: Do you trust what the promoter has told you?

When you are done talking to the promoter, call the editor of one of the regional trade papers and ask his or her opinion about the market. If they have published an article or review of the market recently, request that a copy be sent to you. If you know someone who has attended, talk to that person. If you still have not made up your mind, try the local daily newspaper or chamber of commerce.

Do not be swayed by the size of a flea market's advertisement in a trade paper. The Kane County advertisement is often less than a sixteenth of a page. A recent full-page advertisement for Brimfield flea markets failed to include J & J Promotions or May's Antique Market, two of the major players on the scene. This points out the strong regional competition between flea markets. Be suspicious of what one promoter tells you about another promoter's market.

Evaluating a Flea Market

After you have attended a flea market, it is time to decide if you will attend it again, and if so, how frequently. Answer the following nineteen questions "yes" or "no." In this test, "no" is the right answer. If more than half the questions are "yes," forget about going back. There are plenty of flea markets from which to choose. If twelve or more are answered "no," give it another chance in a few months. If seventeen or more answers are "no," plan another visit soon.

There are some flea markets that scored well with me, and I would like to share them with you. They are listed in the next chapter.

Flea Market Quick Quiz

1. Was the flea market hard to find? ___ Yes ___ No
2. Did you have a difficult time moving between the flea market and your car in the parking area? ___ Yes ___ No
3. Did you have to pay a parking fee in addition to an admission fee? ___ Yes ___ No
4. Did the manager fail to provide a map of the market? ___ Yes ___ No
5. Was most of the market in an open, outdoor environment? ___ Yes ___ No
6. Were indoor facilities poorly lighted and ventilated? ___ Yes ___ No
7. Was there a problem with the number of toilet facilities or with the facilities' cleanliness? ___ Yes ___ No
8. Was your overall impression of the market one of chaos? ___ Yes ___ No
9. Did collectibles outnumber antiques? ___ Yes ___ No
10. Did secondhand goods and new merchandise outnumber collectibles? ___ Yes ___ No
11. Were reproductions, copycats, fantasy items, and fakes in abundance? (See Chapter 5.) ___ Yes ___ No
12. Was there a large representation of home crafts and/or discontinued merchandise? ___ Yes ___ No
13. Were the vast majority of antiques and collectibles that you saw in fair condition or worse? ___ Yes ___ No
14. Were individuals that you expected to encounter at the market absent? ___ Yes ___ No
15. Did you pass out fewer than five lists of your "wants"? ___ Yes ___ No
16. Did you buy fewer than five new items for your collection? ___ Yes ___ No
17. Were more than half the items that you bought priced near or at book value? ___ Yes ___ No
18. Was there a lack of good restaurants and/or lodging within easy access of the flea market? ___ Yes ___ No
19. Would you tell a friend never to attend the market? ___ Yes ___ No

Chapter 3
TOP U.S. FLEA MARKETS

Deciding which markets will and will not appear on the list is not an easy task. There are thousands of flea markets throughout the United States.

Everyone has regional favorites that failed to make the cut. There simply is not room to list them all. In making my choices, I used the following criteria. I wanted to provide a representative sample from the major flea market groups—seasonal, monthly, and weekly. Since this guide is designed for the national market, I made certain that the selection covered the entire United States. Finally, I selected flea markets that I feel will "turn on" a prospective or novice collector. Nothing is more fun than getting off to a great start.

This list is only a starting point. Almost every flea market has a table containing promotional literature for other flea markets in the area. Follow up on the ones of interest. Continue to check trade paper listings. There are always new flea markets being started.

Finally, not every flea market is able to maintain its past glories. Are there flea markets that you think should be on this list? Have you visited some of the listed flea markets and found them to be unsatisfactory? As each edition of this guide is prepared, this list will be evaluated. Send any thoughts and comments that you may have to: Harry L. Rinker, Rinker Enterprises, Inc., 5093 Vera Cruz Road, Emmaus, PA 18049.

The "Top U.S. Flea Markets" list contains the following information: name of flea market, location, frequency and general admission times, type of goods sold and general comments, number of dealers, indoors or outdoors, special features, current admission fee, and address and phone number (if known) of manager or promoter.

Seasonal Flea Markets

1. "AMERICA'S LARGEST" ANTIQUE AND COLLECTIBLE SALE

Portland Expo Center, Portland, OR, Multnomah County Expo Center, Exit 306B off I-5; Saturday 8 a.m. to 6 p.m. and Sunday 9 a.m. to 5 p.m., early March, mid July, and late October; antiques and collectibles; 1,250+ dealers in March and October, indoors; 1,800+ dealers in July, indoors/outdoors; admission—$7; parking—$7; Palmer/Wirfs & Associates, 4001 N.E. Halsey, Portland, OR 97232, (503) 282-0877, www.palmerwirfs.com.

Also check out Palmer/Wirfs & Associates' Cow Palace Shows, San Francisco, CA, exit off Hwy. 101; Saturday and Sunday: late February and early October, Saturday 8 a.m. to 6 p.m.; Sunday 9 a.m. to 5 p.m; antiques and collectibles; 300 dealers; indoors; admission—$6; parking—$6.

2. BRIMFIELD

Rte. 20, Brimfield, MA 01010; six consecutive days, Tuesday through Sunday, in May, July, and September; antiques, collectibles, and secondhand goods; 5,000+ dealers; indoors/outdoors; includes more than 20 individually promoted antiques shows with staggered opening and closing dates, admission—varies according to field, ranging from free to $5; average parking fee—$3 to $6; www.brimfield.com.

Brimfield Acres North, (413) 245-9471; opens 1 p.m. Tuesday, 8 a.m. Saturday.

Brimfield Barn Antique Market, (413) 245-3209; opens at 7 a.m. Tuesday through Sunday.

Central Park Antiques Shows, (413) 245-4674 (during shows) or (413) 596-9257, www.brimfieldcentralpark.com; opens at 6 a.m. Tuesday through Sunday.

Collins Apple Bard; opens at daybreak Tuesday through Sunday.

Crystal Brook, (413) 245-7647; opens at daybreak, Tuesday through Sunday.

Dealers' Choice, (508) 347-3929; opens at 11 a.m. Tuesday and 9 a.m. Saturday.

Faxon's Midway, (508) 347-3929; opens at 7 a.m. Tuesday through Sunday.

Faxon's Treasure Chest, (508) 347-3929; opens at 9 a.m. Tuesday through Sunday

Francesco's Antique Show; opens at daybreak Tuesday through Sunday.

Green Acres, (413) 245-6118; opens at 6 a.m. Tuesday through Sunday.

Heart-O-the-Mart, (413) 245-9556, www.brimfield-hotm.com; opens at 9 a.m. Wednesday through Sunday.

J & J Promotions, (413) 245-3436 or (978) 597-8155, www.jandj-brimfield.com; opens at 6 a.m. Friday and 9 a.m. Saturday.

Jeanne Hertan Shows, (413) 245-9872 (during shows) or (860) 763-3760; opens at noon on Wednesday and 6 a.m. Thursday through Sunday.

Mahogany Ridge, (413) 245-0381 or (413) 245-3182; opens at daybreak Tuesday through Sunday.

May's Antique Market, (413) 245-9271, www.maysbrimfield.com; opens at 9 a.m. Thursday through Saturday.

New England Motel & Antique Market, Inc., (413) 245-3348 or (508) 347-2179, www.antiques-brimfield.com; opens at 6 a.m. Wednesday through Sunday.

Quaker Acres, (413) 245-9878; opens at daybreak Tuesday through Sunday.

Shelton Antique Shows, (413) 245-3591; opens at daybreak Tuesday through Sunday.

Sturtevant's, (413) 245-7458; opens at daybreak Tuesday through Sunday.

The Meadows, (413) 245-9427 or www.brimfieldantiqueshows. com; opens at 6 a.m. Tuesday through Sunday.

You can subscribe to the Brimfield Antique Guide from Brimfield Publications, P.O. Box 442, Brimfield, MA 01010; (508) 764-4920, www.brimfieldguide.com, email: brimfieldp@aol.com. Three issues for $15.95.

3. RENNINGER'S EXTRAVAGANZA

Noble Street, Kutztown, PA 19530; Thursday, Friday, and Saturday of last full weekend of April, June, and September. Open 10 a.m. to 5 p.m. Thursday and 8 a.m. to 5 p.m. Friday and Saturday; antiques and collectibles; 1,200+ dealers; indoors/outdoors; admission—$15 (three-day pass), $6 (one-day pass/Friday), $4 (one-day pass/Saturday); Renningers, 740 South Noble St., Kutztown, PA 19530; (877) 385-0104 or (610) 683-6848, www.renningers.com.

Monthly Flea Markets

4. ALAMEDA POINT ANTIQUES AND COLLECTIBLES FAIRE

Located at the former Naval Air Station, Alameda, CA, exit off Hwy. 880; first Sunday of every month, January through December, 6 a.m. to 3 p.m.; 800+ booths; antiques, collectibles and vintage furnishings—all items must be at least

20 years old, no reproductions; admission—VIP (6 a.m.) $15; early buyer (7:30 a.m.) $10; general admission (9 a.m.) $5, children 16 and under free; free parking; Antiques By The Bay, Inc., P.O. Box 2230, Alameda, CA 94501, (510) 522-7500, www.antiquesbybay.com.

5. ALLEGAN ANTIQUES MARKET

Allegan County Fairgrounds, Allegan, MI 49010; last Sunday of the month, April through September, 7:30 a.m. to 4 p.m; antiques and collectibles; 400+ dealers indoors/outdoors; admission—$3; free parking; Larry L. Wood, 2030 Blueberry Dr. N.W., Grand Rapids, MI 49504, (616) 735-3333, www.alleganantiques.com.

6. ANN ARBOR ANTIQUES MARKET

5055 Ann Arbor-Saline Rd., Ann Arbor, MI 48103; May through August and October (third Sunday of the month), April and September (Saturday and Sunday, weekend of third Sunday of month); November (first Sunday of the month); 7 a.m. to 4 p.m; antiques and select collectibles; 500+ dealers; all under cover; admission—$6; free parking; Nancy and Woody Straub, Managers, (850) 984-0122, www.annarborantiquesmarket.com.

7. BURLINGTON ANTIQUES SHOW

Boone County Fairgrounds, Burlington, KY 41005; third Sunday of the month, April through October, 8 a.m. to 3 p.m.; antiques and collectibles; indoors/outdoors; admission—$3, early buyers (5 a.m. to 8 a.m.) $5; Paul Kohls, Manager, P.O. Box 58367, Cincinnati, OH 45258, (513) 922-5265.

8. CENTREVILLE ANTIQUES MARKET

The St. Joseph County Grange Fairgrounds, M-86, Centreville, MI 49032; first Sunday in May; second Sunday in June, July, August, and October, 7 a.m. to 3 p.m.; antiques and collectibles, no reproductions; 300+ dealers, indoors/outdoors; admission—early buyer (Saturday dealer setup) $30; general $4; free parking; Robert C. Lawler Management, 1510 N. Hoyne, Chicago, IL 60622, (773) 227-4464, www.antiquemarkets.com.

9. FAIRGROUNDS ANTIQUE MARKET

Arizona State Fairgrounds, 19th Ave. & McDowell, Phoenix, AZ 85009; six+ times/year, third weekend, call for dates and times; antiques, collectibles, and crafts, antique glass and clock repairs; 100 to 200 dealers summer, 400 to 600 dealers winter; indoors; admission—$3; Robert and Wanda Jones, PMB 228, 23425 N. 39th Dr., Suite 104, Glendale, AZ 85310-4197, (602) 717-7337 or (623) 587-7488, www.azantiqueshow.com.

10. THE FLEA MARKET AT THE FAIRGROUNDS

Alabama State Fairgrounds, Birmingham, AL 35208; exit 120 off I-20, follow signs for Alabama State Fair Complex; first weekend of every month, year-round, Friday 3 p.m. to 7 p.m., Saturday 9 a.m. to 6 p.m., Sunday 9 a.m. to 5 p.m; antiques, collectibles, and new merchandise (somewhat swapmeet-like); 500 booths indoors, unlimited outdoor spaces; free admission; free parking; The Flea Market at the Fairgrounds, 27050 E. 14th St., Catoosa, OK 74015, 800-362-7538.

11. FLEA MARKET AT THE NASHVILLE FAIRGROUNDS

Tennessee State Fairgrounds, Wedgewood and Nolensville Rd., Nashville, TN 37204; fourth weekend of every month January through November, third weekend in December, Friday 12 p.m. to 5 p.m., Saturday 7 a.m. to 6 p.m., Sunday 7 a.m. to 4 p.m.; antiques and collectibles, crafts, and some new merchandise, indoors/outdoors; about 2,000 booths; free admission; parking—$2, overnight RV parking $30; Nashville Fairgrounds Flea Market, P.O. Box 40208, Nashville, TN 37204, (615) 862-5016, www.tennesseestatefair.org.

12. GORDYVILLE USA FLEA MARKET & AUCTION

Gifford, IL 61847: Rte. 136, 7.5 miles east of I-57; second full weekend of each month; Friday 4 p.m. to 9 p.m., Saturday 9 a.m. to 6 p.m., Sunday 9 a.m. to 4 p.m.; 250 to 500 dealers, antiques, collectibles, vintage items, arts and crafts, indoors/outdoors; auction every Saturday; free admission; Patty Frerichs, P.O. Box 490, Gifford, IL 61847, (217) 568-7117, Fax: (217) 568-7376.

13. KANE COUNTY FLEA MARKET

Kane County Fairgrounds, Rte. 64 & Randall Road, St. Charles, IL 60174; first Sunday of every month and preceding Saturday afternoon; Saturday 12 p.m. to 5 p.m. and Sunday 7 a.m. to 4 p.m.; antiques, collectibles, and some crafts (a favorite in the Midwest, especially with the Chicago crowd), indoors/outdoors; admission—$5, children under 12 free; free parking; Kane County Flea Market, P.O. Box 549, St. Charles, IL 60174, (630) 377-2252; www.kanecountyflea-market.com.

14. KENTUCKY FLEA MARKET

Kentucky Fair and Expo Center at junction of I-264 and I-65, Louisville, KY.; three- or four-day show, dates vary, Friday noon to 7 p.m., regular hours Saturday 10 a.m. to 7 p.m., Sunday 11 a.m. to 5 p.m.; antiques, collectibles, arts and crafts, and new merchandise, indoors (climate-controlled); 1,000+ booths (2,000+ Labor Day and New Years shows); free admission; Stewart Promotions, 2950 Breckinridge Ln., #4A, Louisville, KY 40220, (502) 456-2244, www.stewartpromotions.com.

15. LAKEWOOD ANTIQUES MARKET

Lakewood Fairgrounds, I 75/85 to Exit 243 East, Atlanta, GA; second weekend of every month, Thursday through Sunday, January through December, Thursday 8 a.m. to 6 p.m., Friday and Saturday 9 a.m. to 6 p.m., Sunday 10 a.m. to 5 p.m.; antiques and collectibles, 1,500+ dealers, indoors/outdoors; admission—$5 Thursday (early buyers day, good for the whole weekend), $3 Friday through Sunday (good for the whole weekend); free parking; Lakewood Antiques Market, 2000 Lakewood Ave., Atlanta, GA 30315, (404) 622-4488, www.lakewoodantiques.com.

16. LONG BEACH OUTDOOR ANTIQUE & COLLECTIBLE MARKET

Veterans Stadium, Lakewood Blvd. and Conant St., Long Beach, CA; third Sunday of each month, 8 a.m. to 3 p.m.; antiques and collectibles; 800+ dealers; admission—early (5:30 a.m. to 6:30 a.m.) $10, general $5, children under 12 free; free parking; Americana Enterprises, Inc., P.O. Box 69219, Los Angeles, CA 90069, (323) 655-5703, www.longbeachantiquemarket.com.

17. METROLINA EXPO

7100 N. Statesville Rd., Hwy. 21, Charlotte, NC; I-77 to Exit 16A; first full weekend of every month based on the first Saturday of the month plus the previous Thursday and Friday; Thursday (early buyers/dealer setup day) 8 a.m. to 5 p.m., Friday and Saturday 9 a.m. to 5 p.m., Sunday 10 a.m. to 5 p.m.; indoors/outdoors; antiques and collectibles; 2,000+ dealers; admission—four-day pass $10, Thursday one-day pass $5, Friday through Sunday $5 adult, $3 senior 62+, children under 12 free; free parking.

Metrolina hosts two Antiques Spectaculars yearly: April and November, Thursday through Sunday, 2,000 to 3,000 dealers; Spectacular admission—Wednesday 9 a.m. to 5 p.m. $50 (includes 5-day pass), Thursday 9 a.m. to 5 p.m. $12 (four-day pass $20), Friday and Saturday 9 a.m. to 5 p.m. and Sunday 10 a.m. to 5 p.m. $7 adult, $5 seniors; free parking; Metrolina Expo Center, P.O. Box 26652, Charlotte, NC 28221, (704) 596-4643 or (800) 824-3770, www.metrolinaantiqueshow.com.

18. PRIDE OF DIXIE ANTIQUES MARKET

North Atlanta Trade Center, Norcross, GA; fourth weekend of every month, Friday 9 a.m. to 5 p.m., Saturday 9 a.m. to 6 p.m., Sunday 11 a.m. to 5 p.m.; indoors (climate controlled); antiques and collectibles; 800+ dealer booths; admission—adults $4 (good all weekend), children free; free parking; North Atlanta Trade Center, 1700 Jeurgens Ct., Norcross, GA 30093, (770) 279-9899, www.northatlantatradecenter.com/dixie.html.

19. ROSE BOWL FLEA MARKET

Rose Bowl in Pasadena, CA at 1001 Rose Bowl Dr.; second Sunday of every month; antiques, collectibles, primitives, vintage clothing, jewelry, arts and crafts, and new merchandise; about 2,200 vendors; admission—VIP (5 a.m. to 7 a.m.) $20, early (7 a.m. to 8 a.m.) $15, express (8 a.m. to 9 a.m.) $10, regular (after 9 a.m.) $7, children under 12 admitted free with an adult, box office closes at 3 p.m., market closes at 4:30 p.m.; Canning Enterprises, P.O. Box 400, Maywood, CA 90270, (323) 560-SHOW (7469); www.rgcshows.com/rosebowl.asp.

20. RUMMAGE-O-RAMA

Wisconsin State Fair Park, Milwaukee, WI, I-94 to Exit 306; January through May and August through December (call for dates), Saturday and Sunday, 9 a.m. to 5 p.m.; indoors; general merchandise, sterling silver, fashion clothes and accessories, shoes, rummage items, antiques, collectibles, arts and crafts, new merchandise; varies between 450 to 750 dealers; admission—$2; free parking; Rummage-O-Rama, 84th St., Milwaukee, WI 53151, (414) 521-2111.

21. SANDWICH ANTIQUES MARKET

The Fairgrounds, State Rte. 34, Sandwich, IL 60548; third or fourth Sunday each month, May through October, 8 a.m. to 4 p.m.; indoors/outdoors; antiques and collectibles; 500+ dealers; admission—early buyer (Saturday dealer setup) $30; general $5; free parking; Robert C. Lawler, Sandwich Antiques Market, 1510 N. Hoyne, Chicago, IL 60622, (773) 227-4464, www.antiquemarkets.com.

22. SCOTT ANTIQUE MARKETS

Ohio Expo Center, Columbus, OH; Saturday 9 a.m. to 6 p.m. and Sunday 10 a.m. to 4 p.m., November through June (call for dates); indoors; antiques and collectibles; 1,200+ booths; free admission; parking—$4; Scott Antique Markets, P.O. Box 60, Bremen, OH 43107, (740) 569-2800, www.scottantiquemarket.com.

Scott conducts a second monthly flea market—The Scott Antique Market, Atlanta Exposition Centers, adjacent north and south facilities, I-285 to Exit 40 at Jonesboro Rd., three miles east of Atlanta airport—the second weekend of every month, Friday and Saturday 9 a.m. to 6 p.m., Sunday 10 a.m. to 4 p.m.; about 2,400 indoor booths and 500 outdoor booths per show; admission—$3 all weekend for both buildings.

23. SPRINGFIELD ANTIQUES SHOW AND FLEA MARKET

Clark County Fairgrounds, Springfield, OH, exit 59 on I-70; third weekend of the month, year-round, Friday 5 p.m. to 8 p.m., Saturday 8 a.m. to 5 p.m. and Sunday 9 a.m. to 4 p.m.; more than half the market is antiques and collectibles; 400 dealers indoors/900 dealers outdoors in warm weather; admission—$2.

Extravaganzas are held in May, July, and September, Friday noon to 6 p.m., Saturday 8 a.m. to 5 p.m., Sunday 9 a.m. to 4 p.m.; 2,500+ dealers; admission—regular $3, Friday morning early buyer's fee $10; Steven and Barbara Jenkins, P.O. Box 2429, Springfield, OH 45501, (937) 325-0053, www.jenkinsshows.com.

24. SUPER FLEA

Greensboro War Memorial Coliseum Complex Event Center, Greensboro, NC 27416; weekend dates vary (call for dates), Saturday 8 a.m. to 5 p.m., Sunday 10 a.m. to 5 p.m.; indoors, climate controlled; antiques, collectibles, arts and crafts, some new merchandise; about 300 dealers; Super Flea, P.O. Box 5447, Greensboro, NC 27435, (336) 373-8515, www.superflea.com.

Weekly Flea Markets

25. ADAMSTOWN

Rte. 272, Adamstown, PA 17517; antiques, collectibles, and secondhand material; free admission; three major markets:

Renninger's; Sundays, year-round, indoor market open 7:30 a.m. to 4 p.m.; outdoor market open sunrise to 4 p.m., 375+ indoor dealers, 400+ outdoor dealers; Renninger's, 2500 N. Reading Rd., Denver, PA 17517; (717) 336-2177, www.renningers.com.

Shupp's Grove; April through October, Saturday and Sunday, 7 a.m. to 5 p.m.; outdoors; Shupp's Grove, P.O. Box 892, Adamstown, PA 19501, (717) 484-4115, www.shuppsgrove.com.

Stoudtburg Antiques Mall, Sundays, year-round, 7:30 a.m. to 5 p.m.; 200+ indoor dealers, 100+ outdoor dealers; Carl Barto, 2717 Long Farm Ln., Lancaster, PA 17601, (717) 484-4385.

26. ANNEX ANTIQUES FAIR AND FLEA MARKET

Sixth Ave., between 24th and 26th Sts., New York City, 10116; year-round, Saturday and Sunday, sunrise to sunset; mostly outdoors with an indoor market in the bi-level garage on West 25th St. between 6th and 7th Aves.; variety of merchandise including antiques and collectibles; 700+ dealers; admission—$1 for indoor market, flea market is free; Annex Antique Fair, P.O. Box 7010, New York, NY 10111, (212) 243-5343.

27. ANTIQUE WORLD AND MARKETPLACE

10995 Main St., Clarence, NY 14031 (Main St. is Rte. 5), year-round, every Sunday, 8 a.m. to 4 p.m.; indoors/outdoors; eight-building complex with a capacity for 1,100+ dealers; free admission; parking—$1; Kelly's Antique World and Marketplace, 10995 Main St., Clarence, NY 14031, (800) 343-5399, www.antiqueworldmarket.com.

28. FIRST MONDAY TRADE DAYS

Canton, TX 75103 (two blocks from downtown square); year-round, Friday through Sunday (Friday before the first Monday of each month) 7 a.m. until dark; antiques, collectibles, new merchandise, crafts (Note: This belongs in the book—not because it is a great source for antiques and collectibles, but because it is the best known swap meet–flea market in the world); 3,000+ vendors; antiques and collectibles located on three-acre plot north of Courthouse; free admission; parking—$3; First Monday Trade Days, P.O. Box 245, Canton, TX 75103, (903) 567-6556, www.firstmondaycanton.com.

29. LAMBERTVILLE ANTIQUES FLEA MARKET

Rte. 29, 1.5 miles south of Lambertville, NJ 08530; Wednesday, Saturday, and Sunday, outdoors 8 a.m. to 4 p.m.; indoors 10 a.m. to 4 p.m.; antiques and collectibles only; 150 dealers; free admission; free parking; Heidi Cekoric, 1864 River Rd., Lambertville, NJ 08530, (609) 397-0456.

30. RENNINGER'S TWIN MARKETS

Hwy. 441, Mount Dora, FL 32757; Saturdays and Sundays (except Easter Sunday), 9 a.m. to 5 p.m.; free admission; free parking. Extravaganzas held on the third weekend of January, February, and November; opens Friday 8 a.m. indoors and 10 a.m. outdoors, Saturday and Sunday 8 a.m. to 5 p.m.; indoors/outdoors; antiques and collectibles; 1,400+ dealers; admission—Friday $10, Saturday $5, Sunday $3, three-day pass $15; free parking. Monthly Fairs held the third weekend of every month except December; outside dealers open by 7:30 a.m., inside dealers at 9 a.m.; Renninger's Twin Markets, Inc., P.O. Box 1699, Mount Dora, FL 32756, (352) 383-8393, www.renningers.com

31. SHIPSHEWANA AUCTION AND FLEA MARKET

On State Rte. 5 near the southern edge of Shipshewana, IN 46565; Tuesday 7 a.m. to 5 p.m., Wednesday 7 a.m. to 3 p.m., May through October; indoors/outdoors; antiques, collectibles, arts and crafts, new merchandise, and produce (you name it, they sell it); 1,000 booths; free admission; June, July, August parking—$2; Trading Place of America, P.O. Box 185, 345 S.Van Buren St. (S.R. 5), Shipshewana, IN 46565, (260) 768-4129, www.tradingplaceamerica.com.

Thus far you have learned to identify the various types of flea markets, how to locate them, the keys to evaluating whether or not they are right for you, and my recommendations for getting started. Next you need to develop the skills necessary for flea market survival.

Chapter 4
FLEA MARKET SURVIVAL GUIDE

Your state of exhaustion at the end of the day is the best gauge that I know to judge the value of a flea market—the greater your exhaustion, the better the flea market. A great flea market keeps you on the go from early morning, in some cases 5:00 a.m., to early evening, often 6:00 p.m. The key to survival is to do advance homework, have proper equipment, develop and follow a carefully thought-out shopping strategy, and do your follow-up chores as soon as you return home.

If you are a Type-A personality, your survival plan is essentially a battle plan. Your goal is to cover the flea market as thoroughly as possible and secure the objectives (bargains and hard-to-find objects) ahead of your rivals. You do not stop until total victory is achieved. If you do not have a Type-A personality it does not matter. You still need a survival plan if you want to maximize fun and enjoyment.

Advance Homework

Consult a flea market's advertisement or brochure. Make certain you understand its dates and time. You never know when special circumstances may cause a change in dates and even location. Check the admission policy. It may be possible to buy a ticket in advance to avoid the wait in line at the ticket booth.

Determine if there is an early admission fee and what times are involved. Admitting collectors and others to the flea market through the use of an early admission fee is a growing practice at flea markets. In most cases the fee is the cost of renting a space. The management simply does not insist that you set up. Actually, this practice had been going on for some time before management formalized it. Friends of individuals renting space often tagged along as helpers or assistants. Once inside, the urge to shop superseded their desire to help their friend.

Review the directions. Are they detailed enough to allow you to find the flea market easily? Remember, it still may be dark when you arrive. If you are not certain, call the manager and ask for specific directions.

Make certain of parking provisions, especially when a flea market takes place within a city or town. Local residents who are not enamored with a flea market in their neighborhood take great pleasure in informing police of illegally parked cars and watching the cars get towed away. In some cases, parking may be more of a problem than locating the flea market. Avoid frustration and plan ahead.

Decide if you are going to stay overnight either the evening before the flea market opens or during the days of operation. In many cases local motel accommodations are minimal. It is common for dealers as well as collectors to commute fifty miles each way to attend Brimfield. The general attitude of most flea market managers is that accommodations are your problem, not theirs. If you are lucky, you can get a list of accommodations from a local Chamber of Commerce. The American Automobile Association regional guidebooks provide some help. However, if you attend a flea market expecting to find nearby overnight accommodations without a reservation, you are the world's biggest optimist.

If possible, obtain a map of the flea market grounds. Become familiar with the layout of the spaces. If you know some of your favorite dealers are going to set up, call and ask them for their space numbers. Mark the location of all toilet facilities and refreshment stands. You may not have time for the latter, but sooner or later you are going to need the former.

Finally, try to convince one or more friends, ideally someone whose area of collecting is totally different from yours, to attend the flea market with you. Each becomes a second set of eyes for the other. Meeting at predesignated spots makes exchanging information easy. It never hurts to share the driving and expenses. Best of all, war stories can be told and savored immediately.

Flea Market Checklist

To have an enjoyable and productive day at the flea market, you need the right equipment. What you do not wear can be stored in your car trunk. Make certain that everything is in order the day before your flea market adventure.

CLOTHING

Most flea markets you attend will either be outdoors or have an outdoor section. If you are lucky, the sun will be shining. Beware of sunburn. Select a hat with a wide brim. I prefer a hat with an outside hat band as well. First, it provides a place to stick notes, business cards, and other small pieces of paper I would most likely lose otherwise. Second, it provides a place to stick a feather or some other distinguishing item that allows my friends to spot me in the crowd. Some flea marketeers advertise their collecting wants right on their clothing. Others use the band of their hat as a holder for a card expounding their collecting wants. Make certain that your hat fits snugly. Some flea market sites are quite windy. An experienced flea market attendee's hat looks as though it has been through the wars. It has.

I carry sunglasses, but I confess that I rarely use them. I find that taking them on and off is more trouble than they are worth. Further, they distort colors. However, I have found them valuable at windswept and outdoor markets located in large fields. Since I usually misplace a pair a year, I generally buy inexpensive glasses.

The key to dressing for flea markets is a layered, comfortable approach. The early morning and late evening hours are often cool. A light jacket or sweatshirt is suggested. I found a great light jacket that is loaded with pockets. Properly outfitted, it holds all the material I would normally put in my carrying bag.

You must assume that it is going to rain. I have never been to Brimfield when it was not raining. Rain, especially at an outdoor flea market, is a disaster. What is astonishing is how much activity continues in spite of the rain. I prefer a poncho over a raincoat because it covers my purchases as well as my clothing. Most flea markets offer ponchos for sale when rain starts. They are lightweight and come with a storage bag. Of course, you have to be a genius to fold them small enough to get them back into their original storage bag. One I purchased at Kane County lasted years. Mrs. Robinson, being a shrewd promoter, just happened to have them imprinted with information about her flea market. I had a great time there so I have never objected to being a walking bulletin board on her behalf.

The ideal footwear for a flea market is a well broken-in pair of running or walking shoes. However, in the early morning when the ground is wet with dew, a pair of waterproof work boots is a much better choice. I keep my running shoes in the car trunk and usually change into them by 9:00 a.m. at most flea markets.

Rain at outdoor flea markets equals mud. The only defense is a good pair of galoshes. I have been at Brimfield when the rain was coming down so fiercely that dealers set up in tents were using tools to dig water diversion ditches. Cars, which were packed in the nearby fields, sank into the ground. In several cases, local farmers with tractors handsomely supplemented their income by pulling out the stuck autos.

FIELD GEAR

I always go to a flea market planning to buy something. Since most flea market sellers provide the minimum packaging possible, I carry my own. My preference is a double-handled canvas bag with a flat bottom. It is not as easy an item to find as it sounds. I use one to carry my field gear along with two extra bags that start out folded. I find that I can carry three filled bags comfortably. This avoids the necessity of running back to the car each time a bag is filled.

If you are going to buy something, you have to pay for it. Cash is always preferred by the sellers. I carry my cash in a small white envelope with the amount with which I started marked at the top. I note and deduct each purchase as I go along. If you carry cash, be careful how you display it. Pickpockets and sticky-fingered individuals who cannot resist temptation do attend flea markets.

Since I want a record of my purchases, I pay by check whenever I can. I have tried to control my spending by only taking a few checks. Forget it. I can always borrow money on Monday to cover my weekend purchases. I carry a minimum of ten checks.

Most flea market sellers will accept checks with proper identification. For this reason, I put my driver's license and a major credit card in the front of my checkbook before entering the flea market. This saves me the trouble of taking out my wallet each time I make a purchase.

A surprising number of flea market sellers take credit cards. I am amazed at this practice since the only means they have of checking a card's validity is the canceled card booklet they receive each week. They wait until later to get telephone authorization, a potentially dangerous practice.

I buy as much material through the mail as I do at flea markets. One of the principal reasons I attend flea markets is to make contact with dealers. Since flea markets attract dealers from across the country, I expand my supplier sources at each flea market I attend.

The key is to have a wants list ready to give to any flea market seller that admits to doing business by mail. My wants list fills an 8½ inch by 11 inch sheet of writing paper. In addition to my wants, it includes my name, post office box address, UPS (i.e., street) address, and office and home telephone numbers. I also make it a point to get the full name and address of any dealer to whom I give my list. I believe in follow-up.

Not every dealer is willing to take a full-page wants list. For this reason, I hand out my business card. However, I am smart. The back of my business card contains an abbreviated list of my wants and a blank line for me to add additional information. Do not pass up this opportunity for free advertising by using only one-sided business cards. I have received quotes on a few great items as a result of my efforts.

I carry a simple variety-store ten-power magnifying glass. It is helpful to see marks clearly and to spot cracks in china and glass. Ninety-nine percent of the time I use it merely to confirm something that I saw with the naked eye. Jewelers loupes are overkill unless you are buying jewelry.

Years ago I purchased a good Swiss Army pocket knife, one which contains scissors as part of the blade package. It was one of the smartest investments that I made. No flea market goes by that I do not use the knife for one reason or another. If you do not want to carry a pocket knife, invest in a pair of operating room surgical scissors. They will cut through almost anything.

I am a buyer. Why do I carry a book of sales receipts? Alas, many flea market sellers operate in a nontraditional business manner. They are not interested in paper trails, especially when you pay cash. You need a receipt to protect yourself. More on this subject later.

I keep a roll of toilet paper in the car and enough for two sittings in my carrying bag. Do not laugh; I am serious. Most outdoor flea markets have portable toilets. After a few days, the toilet paper supply is exhausted. Even some indoor facilities run out. If I had five dollars from all the people to whom I supplied toilet paper at flea markets, I would be writing this book in Hawaii instead of Pennsylvania.

I carry a mechanical pencil (a ball-point pen works just as well). When I pick up someone's business card, I note why on the back of the card. Use the pencil to mark dealer locations on the flea market map. I do not always buy something when I first spot it. The map helps me relocate items when I wish to go back for a second look. I have wasted hours at flea markets backtracking to find an item that was not located where I thought it was.

Anyone who tells you they know everything about antiques and collectibles and their prices is a liar. I know the areas in which I collect quite well. But there are many categories where a quick source-check never hurts. Every general price guide is different. Find the one that best serves your needs and use it consistently. You know you have a good command of your price guide when you do not have to use the index to locate the value for the item you are seeking. I scored some major points with dealers and others when I offered to share information with them.

FROM THE CAR TRUNK

My car trunk contains a number of cardboard boxes, several of which are archival file boxes with hand inserts on the side. I have them because I want to see that my purchases make it home safe and sound. One of the boxes is filled with newspaper, diapers, and some bubble wrap. It supplements the field wrapping so that I can stack objects on top of one another. I check the trunk seals on a regular basis. A leaking car trunk once ruined several key purchases I made on an antiquing adventure.

A wide-brim hat may protect the face and neck from the sun, but it leaves the arms exposed. I admire those individuals who can wear a long-sleeved shirt year-round. I am not one of them. In the summer, I wear short-sleeved shirts. For this reason, I keep a bottle of sun block in the trunk.

I also have a first-aid kit that includes aspirin. The most used object is a Band-Aid for unexpected cuts and scratches. The aspirin comes in handy when I have spent eight or more hours in the sun. My first-aid kit also contains packaged cleaning towelettes. I always use one before heading home.

It does not take much for me to get a flea market high. When I do, I can go the entire day without eating. The same does not hold true for liquid intake. Just as toilet paper is a precious commodity at flea markets, so is ice. I carry a small cooler in my trunk with six to a dozen cans of my favorite beverage of the moment. The fastest way

Clothing Checklist

_____ Hat
_____ Sunglasses
_____ Light jacket or sweatshirt
_____ Poncho or raincoat
_____ Waterproof work boots or galoshes

Field Gear Checklist

_____ Canvas bag(s)
_____ Cash, checkbook, and credit cards
_____ Wants lists
_____ Business (Collector) cards
_____ Magnifying glass
_____ Swiss Army pocket knife
_____ Toilet paper
_____ Sales receipts
_____ Mechanical pencil or ballpoint pen
_____ This price guide

Car Trunk Checklist

_____ Three to six cardboard boxes
_____ Newspaper, bubble wrap, diapers, and other appropriate material
_____ Sun block
_____ First-aid kit
_____ Cooler with cold beverages

to seal a friendship with a flea market dealer is to offer him or her a cold drink at the end of a hot day.

How to Shop a Flea Market

After having attended flea markets for a number of years, I would like to share some suggestions for bagging the treasures found in the flea market jungle. Much of what I am about to tell you is simply common sense, but we all know that this is probably the most ignored of all the senses.

Most likely you will drive to the flea market. Parking is often a problem. It does not have to be. Most people park as close to the main gate as possible. However, since most flea markets have a number of gates, I usually try to park near a secondary gate. First, this allows me to get closer than I could by trying for the main gate. Second, I have long since learned that whatever gate I use is "my" main gate, and it serves well as home base for my buying operations.

As soon as I arrive at the flea market, I check three things before allowing my buying adrenaline to kick into high gear—the location of the toilets, the location of the refreshment stands, and the relationship between outdoor and indoor facilities. The latter is very important. Dealers who regularly do the flea market are most likely to be indoors. If I miss them this time around, I can catch them the next. Dealers who are just passing through are most likely set up outdoors. If I miss them, I may never see them again.

I spend the first half hour at any flea market doing a quick tour in order to understand how the flea market is organized, spot those dealers that I would like to visit later, and develop a general sense of what is happening. I prefer to start at the point farthest from my car and work my way back, just the opposite of most flea market shoppers. This method makes trips back to the car shorter each time and reduces the amount of purchases that I am carrying over an extended period of time.

Whenever I go to a flea market to buy, I try to have one to four specific categories in mind. If one tries to look at everything, one develops "antiques and collectibles" shock. Collectors' minds short-circuit if they try to absorb too much. They never get past the first aisle. With specific goals, a quick look at a booth will tell me whether or not it is likely to feature merchandise of interest. If not, I pass it by.

Since time is always at a premium, I make it a practice to ask every dealer, "Do you have any...?" If they say "no," I usually go to the next booth. However, I have learned that dealers do not always remember what they have. When I am in a booth that should have the type of merchandise that I am seeking, I take a minute or two to do a quick scan to see if the dealer is right. In about 25% of the cases, I have found at least one example of the type of material for which I am looking.

I eat on the run, if I eat at all. A good breakfast before the market opens carries me until the evening hours when dusk shuts down the market. I am at the flea market to stuff my bag and car trunk, not my face.

When I find a flea market that I like, I try to visit it at least once in the spring and once in the late summer or early fall. In many flea markets the same dealers are located in the same spot each time. This is extremely helpful to a buyer. I note their location on my map of the market.

When I return the next time, I ask these dealers if they have brought anything that fills my needs. If they say "yes," I take a quick look and decide immediately what I do and do not want to buy. I ask them if they mind holding the items I agreed to buy so that I can move on quickly. I make a commitment to stop back and pay in a few hours. Some agree and some do not. Those who have done business with me previously and know my buying pattern are more willing to accede to my wishes than those who do not. I do not abuse the privilege, but I do not hesitate to take advantage of it either.

GUARANTEES

There is an adage among antiques and collectibles collectors that "if you bought something at a flea market, you own it." I do not support this approach. I feel every seller should unconditionally guarantee his merchandise. If I find a piece is misrepresented, I take it back.

I try to get a receipt for every purchase that I make. Since many individuals who sell at outdoor flea markets are part-time dealers, they often are unprepared to give a receipt. No problem. I carry a pad of blank receipts and ask them to fill one out.

In every case, I ask the dealers to include their name, shop name (if any), mailing address, and phone number on the receipt. If I do not think a dealer is telling me the truth, I ask for identification. If they give me any flack, I go to their vehicle (usually located in their booth or just outside their indoor stand) and make note of the license plate number. Flea market dealers, especially the outdoor group, are highly mobile. If a problem is discovered with the merchandise I bought, I want to reach the dealer in order to solve the problem.

Whenever possible, the receipt should contain a full description of the merchandise along with a completeness and condition statement. I also ask the dealer to write "money back guaranteed, no questions asked" on the receipt. This is the only valid guarantee that I know. Phrases such as "guaranteed as represented" and "money back" are open to interpretation and become relatively meaningless if a dispute develops. Many flea market dealers are reluctant to provide this guarantee, afraid that the buyer will switch a damaged item for a good one or swipe a part and return the item as incomplete.

SHOPPING AROUND

I always shop around. At a good flea market, I expect to see the same merchandise in several booths. Prices will vary, often by several hundred if not several thousand percent. I make a purchase immediately only when the price is a bargain, i.e., priced way below current market value. If a piece is near current market value, I inspect it, note its location on my map, and move on. If I do not find another in better good condition, at a cheaper price, or both, I go back and negotiate with the dealer.

I take the time to inspect carefully, in natural sunlight, any piece that I buy. First, I check for defects such as cracks, nicks, scratches, and signs of normal wear. Second, if the object involves parts, I make certain that it is complete. I have been known to take the time to carefully count parts. The last two times that I did not do this, the objects that I bought turned out to be incomplete when I got them home.

I frequently find myself asking a dealer to clean an object for my inspection. Outdoor flea markets are often quite dusty, especially in July and August. The insides of most indoor markets are generally not much better. Dirt can easily hide flaws. It also can discolor objects. Make certain you know exactly what you are buying.

I force myself to slow down and get to know those dealers from whom I hope to make future purchases. Though it may mean that I do not visit the entire flea market, I have found that the long-term benefits from this type of contact far outweigh the short-term gain of seeing every booth.

Flea Market Food

Flea market food is best described as overcooked, greasy, and heartburn-inducing. I think I forgot to mention that my first-aid kit contains a roll of antacid pills. Gourmet eating facilities are usually nonexistent. Is it any wonder that I often go without eating?

Several flea markets take place on sites that also house a farmer's market. When this is the case, I take time to shop the market and purchase my food at one of its counters.

I do make it a point to inquire among the dealers where they go to have their evening meals. They generally opt for good food, plenty of it, and at inexpensive prices. At the end of the day I am hungry. I do not feel like driving home, cleaning up, and then eating. I want to eat where the clientele can stand the appearance and smell of a flea marketeer. I have rarely been disappointed when I followed a flea market dealer's recommendation.

The best survival tactic is probably to bring your own food. I simply find this too much trouble. I get heartburn just thinking about a lunch sitting for several hours inside a car on a hot summer day. No thanks; I buy what I need.

Mailing List/Newsletter

Many flea markets actively recruit names for promotional mailings. Several send monthly, bi-monthly, or quarterly newsletters to their customers. I always take a minute or two to fill out their request card. It is not my nickel paying for the mailing.

Follow-Up

Immediately upon returning home, or at worst the next day, unpack and record your purchases. If you wait, you are likely to forget important details. This is not the fun part of collecting. It is easy to ignore. Discipline yourself. Get in the habit. You know it is the right thing to do, so do it.

Review the business cards that you picked up and notes that you made. If letters are required, write them. If telephone calls are necessary, make them. Never lose sight of the fact that one of your principal reasons for going to the flea market is to establish long-term dealer contacts.

Finally, if your experiences at the flea market were positive or if you saw ways to improve the market, write a letter to the manager. He or she will be delighted in both instances. Competition among flea markets for dealers and customers is increasing. Good managers want to make their markets better than their competitors'. Your comments and suggestions will be welcomed.

Chapter 5
HONING YOUR SHOPPING SKILLS

Earlier I mentioned that most buyers view flea markets as places where bargains and "steals" can be found. I have found plenty. However, the truth is that you have to hunt long and hard to find them, and in some cases, they evolve only after intense bargaining. Shopping a flea market properly requires skills. This chapter will help shape and hone your shopping skills and alert you to some of the pitfalls involved with buying at a flea market.

With What Type of Dealer Are You Dealing?

There are essentially three types of dealers found at flea markets: the professional dealer, the weekend dealer, and the once-and-done dealer. Each brings a different level of expertise and merchandise to the flea market. Each offers pluses and minuses. Knowing which type you are dealing with is advantageous.

PROFESSIONAL DEALER

So many flea markets developed in the 1980s and 1990s that there are now professional flea market dealers who practice their craft full-time. Within any given week, you may find them at three or four different flea markets. They are the modern American gypsies. Their living accommodations and merchandise are usually found within the truck, van, or station wagon in which they are traveling. These individuals survive on shrewd-

ness and hustle. They want to turn over their merchandise as quickly as possible for the best gain possible and are willing to do whatever is necessary to achieve this end.

Buy from professional flea market dealers with a questioning mind; i.e., question everything they tell you about an object from what it is to what they want for it. Their knowledge of the market comes from hands-on experience. It is often not as great as they think. They are so busy setting up, buying, selling, and breaking down that they have little time to do research or read trade literature. More than any other group of dealers in the trade, they are weavers of tales and sellers of dreams.

The professional flea market dealer's circuit can stretch from New England to California, from Michigan to Florida. These "professionals" are constantly on the move. If you have a problem with something one of these dealers sold you, finding him or her can prove difficult. Do not buy anything from a professional dealer unless you are absolutely certain about it.

Judge the credibility and integrity of the professional flea market dealer by the quality of the merchandise he or she displays. You should see middle- and high-quality material in better condition than you normally expect to find. If the offerings are heavily damaged and appear poorly maintained, walk away.

Do not interpret what I have said to imply that all professional flea market dealers are dishonest. The vast majority are fine, upstanding individuals. However, as a whole, this group has the largest share of rotten apples in its barrel—more than any other group of dealers in the flea market field. Since there is no professional organization to police the trade and promoters do not care as long as their space rent is paid, it is up to you to protect yourself.

The antiques and collectibles field works on the principle of caveat emptor, "let the buyer beware." It is important to remember that the key is to beware of the seller as well as his merchandise. It pays to know with whom you are doing business.

WEEKEND DEALERS

Weekend flea market dealers are individuals who have a full-time job elsewhere and are dealing on the weekends to supplement their income. In most cases, their weekday job is outside the antiques and collectibles field. However, with the growth of the antiques mall, some of these weekend dealers are really full-time antiques and collectibles dealers. They spend their weekdays shopping and maintaining their mall locations, while selling on the weekend at their traditional flea market location.

In many cases, these dealers specialize, especially if they are in a large flea market environment. As a result, they are usually familiar with the literature relating to their areas of expertise. They also tend to live within a few hours' drive of the flea market in which they set up. This means that they can be found if the need arises.

ONCE-AND-DONE DEALERS

Once-and-done dealers range from an individual who is using the flea market to dispose of some inherited family heirlooms or portions of an estate to collectors who have culled their collection and are offering their duplicates and discards for sale. Bargains can often be found in both cases. In the first instance, bargains result from lack of pricing knowledge. However, unless you are an early arrival, chances are that the table will be picked clean by the regular dealers and pickers long before you show up. Bargains originate from the collectors because they know the price levels in their field. They realize that in order to sell their discards and duplicates, they will have to offer their merchandise at prices that are tempting to dealer and collector alike.

The once-and-done dealers are the least prepared to conduct sales on a business basis. Most likely they will not have a receipt book or a business card featuring their address and phone number. They almost never attempt to collect applicable sales tax. There is little long-term gain in spending time getting to know the individual who is selling off a few family treasures. However, do not leave without asking, "Is there anything else you have at home that you are planning to sell?"

Spend some time with the collector. Strike up a conversation. If you have mutual collecting interests, invite him or her to visit and view your collection. What you are really fishing for is an invitation to view his or her holdings. You will be surprised how often you will receive one when you show genuine interest.

What Is It?

You need to be concerned with two questions when looking at an object: What is it? and How much is it worth? In order to answer the second question, you need a correct answer to the first. Information provided about objects for sale at flea markets is minimal and often incorrect. The only state of mind that protects you is a defensive one.

There are several reasons for the amount of misidentification of objects at flea markets. The foremost is dealer ignorance. Many dealers simply do not take the time to do proper research. I also suspect that they are quite comfortable with the adage that "ignorance is bliss." As long as an object bears a resemblance to something good, it will be touted with the most prestigious label available.

When questioning dealers about an object, beware of phrases such as "I think it is...," "As best as I can tell," "It looks exactly like," and "I trust your judgment." Push the dealers until you pin them down. The more they vacillate, the more suspicious you should become. Insist that the sales receipt carry a full claim about the object.

In many cases misidentification is passed from person to person because the dealer who bought the object trusted what was said by the dealer who sold it to him. I am always amazed how convinced dealers are that they are right. There is little point in arguing with them. The only way to preserve both individuals' sanity is to walk away.

If you do not know what something is, do not buy it. The general price guide and any specific price guides that you have in your bag can point you in the right direction, but they are not the final word. If you simply must find out right that minute and do not have the reference book you need, check with the antiques and collectibles book dealer at the market to see if he has the title you need in stock.

Stories, Stories, and More Stories

A flea market is a place where one's creative imagination and ability to believe what is heard are constantly tested. The number of cleverly crafted stories to explain the origin of pieces and why the condition is not exactly what one expects is endless. The problem is that they all sound plausible. Once again, I come back to the concept upon which flea market survival is founded: a questioning mind.

I often ask dealers to explain the circumstances through which they acquired a piece and what they know about the piece. Note what I said; I am not asking the seller to reveal his or her source. No one should be expected to do that. I am testing the openness and believability of the dealer. If the dealer claims there is something special about an object (e.g., it belonged to a famous person or was illustrated in a book), I ask to see proof. Word-of-mouth stories have little credibility in the long run.

Again, there are certain phrases that serve as tip-offs that something may be amiss. "It is the first one I have ever seen," "You will never find another one like it," "I saw one a few aisles over for more money," "One sold at auction a few weeks ago for double what I am asking," and "I am selling it to you for exactly what I paid for it" are just a few examples. If what you are hearing sounds too good to be true, it probably is.

Your best defense is to study and research the area in which you want to collect before going to flea markets. Emphasis should be placed equally on object identification and an understanding of the pricing structure within that collecting category. You will not be a happy person if you find that although an object you bought is what the seller claimed it was, you paid far more for it than it is worth.

Period, Reproduction, Copycat, Fantasy, or Fake

The number of reproductions, copycats, and fantasy and fake items at flea markets is larger than in any other segment of the field. Antiques malls run a close second. In fact, it is common to find several dealers at a flea market selling reproductions, copycats, and fantasy items openly. When you recognize them, take time to study their merchandise. Commit the material to memory. In ten years, when the material has begun to age, you will be glad that you did.

Although the above terms are familiar to those who are active in the antiques and collectibles field, they may not be understood by some. A period piece is an example made during the initial period of production or an object licensed during a person's, group's, or show's period of fame or stardom. The commonly used term is "real." However, if you think about it, all objects are real, whether period or not. "Real" is one of those terms that should set your mind to questioning.

A reproduction is an exact copy of a period piece. There may be subtle changes in areas not visible to the naked eye, but essentially it is identical to its period counterpart. A copycat is an object that is similar, but not exactly like the period piece it is emulating. It may vary in size, form, or design elements. In some cases, it is very close to the original. In auction terms, copycats are known as "in the style of." A fantasy item is a form that was not issued during the initial period of production. An object licensed after Elvis's death would be an Elvis fantasy item. A Chippendale-style coffee table, a form which did not exist during the first Chippendale period, is another example.

The thing to remember is that reproductions, copycats, and fantasy items are generally mass-produced and start out life honestly. The wholesalers who sell them to dealers in the trade make it clear exactly what they are. Alas, some of the dealers do not do so when they resell them.

Because reproductions, copycats, and fantasy items are mass-produced, they appear in the market in quantity. When you spot a piece in your collecting area that you have never seen before, quickly check through the rest of the market. If the piece is mint, double-check. Handle the piece. Is it the right weight? Does it have the right color? Is it the quality that you expect? If you answer "no" to any of these questions, put it back.

The vast majority of items sold at any flea market are mass-produced, twentieth-century items. Encountering a new influx of never-seen-before items does not necessarily mean they are reproductions, copycats, or fantasy items. Someone may have uncovered a hoard. The trade term is "warehouse find." A hoard can seriously affect the value of any antique or collectible. All of a sudden the number of available examples rises dramatically. So usually does the condition level. Unless the owner of a hoard is careful, this sudden release of material can drive prices downward.

A fake is an item deliberately meant to deceive. They are usually one-of-a-kind items, with many originating in shops of revivalist craftspersons. The folk art and furniture market is flooded with them. Do not assume that because an object is inexpensive, it is all right. You would be surprised how cheaply goods can be made in Third World countries.

It is a common assumption that reproductions, copycats, fantasy items, and fakes are of poor quality and can be easily spotted. If you subscribe to this theory, you are a fool. There are some excellent reproductions, copycats, fantasy items, and fakes. You probably have read on more than one occasion how a museum was fooled by an object in its collection. If museum curators can be fooled, so can you.

This is not the place for a lengthy dissertation on how to identify and differentiate period objects from reproductions, copycats, fantasies, or fakes. Read the books suggested in the "Flea Marketeer's Annotated Reference Library" that appears on page 478.

What follows are a few quick tips to put you on the alert:

1. If it looks new, assume it is new.
2. Examine each object carefully, looking for signs of age and repair that should be there.
3. Use all appropriate senses—sight, touch, smell, and hearing—to check an object.
4. Be doubly alert when something appears to be a "steal."
5. Make copies of articles from trade papers or other sources that you find about period, reproduction, copycat, fantasy, and fake items and keep them on file.
6. Finally, handle as many authentic objects as possible. The more genuine items you handle, the easier it will be to identify impostors.

What's a Fair Price?

The best selling scenario at a flea market is a buyer and seller who are both extremely happy with the price paid and a seller who has made sufficient profit to allow him or her to stay in business and return to sell another day. Reality is not quite like this. Abundance of merchandise, competition among dealers, and negotiated prices often result in the seller being less than happy with the final price received. Yet the dealers sell because some money is better than no money.

Price haggling is part of the flea market game. In fact, the next section discusses this very subject in detail. The only real value an object has is what someone is willing to pay for it, not what someone asks for it. There is no fixed price for any antique, collectible, or secondhand object. All value is relative.

These considerations aside, there are a few points relating to price and value that the flea marketeer should be aware of. Try to understand these points. Remember, in the antiques and collectibles field there are frequently two or more sides to every issue and rarely any clear-cut right or wrong answer.

First, dealers have a right to an honest profit. If dealers are attempting to make a full-time living in the trade, they must triple their money in order to cover their inventory costs, pay their overhead expenses, which are not inconsequential, and pay themselves. Buy at thirty cents and sell at one dollar.

The problem is that many flea market dealers set up at flea markets not to make money but simply to have a good time. As a result, they willingly sell at much lower profit margins than those who are trying to make a living. It is not really that hard to tell which group is which. Keep the seller's circumstances in mind when haggling.

Second, selling is labor and capital-intensive. Check a dealer's booth when a flea market opens and again when it closes. Can you spot the missing objects? When a dealer has a "good" flea market, he or she usually sells between fifteen and thirty objects. In most cases, the inventory from which these objects sold consists of hundreds of pieces. Do not think about what the dealer sold, think about what was not sold. What did it cost? How much work is involved in packing, hauling, setting up, and repacking these items until the objects finally sell. Flea market sellers need a high profit margin to stay in business.

Third, learn to use price guide information correctly. Remember the prices are guides, not price absolutes. For their part, sellers must resist the temptation to become greedy and trap themselves in the assumption that they deserve book price or better for every item they sell. Sellers would do better to focus on what they paid for an object (which, in effect, does determine the final price) rather than on what they think they can get for it (it never sells as quickly as they think). They will make more on volume sales than they will trying to get top dollar for all their items.

Price guide prices represent what a "serious" collector in that category will pay provided he or she does not already own the object. An Elvis Presley guitar in its original box may book for over $500, but it has that value only to an Elvis Presley collector who does not already own one. Price guide prices tend to be on the high side.

Fourth, the IRS defines fair-market value as a situation where there is a willing buyer and seller, neither compelled to buy or sell, and both parties equally knowledgeable. While the first and second part of this equation usually apply, the third usually does not. There is no question that knowledge is power in the flea market game and sharing it can cost money. If money were the only issue, I could accept the idea of keeping quiet. However, I like to think that a sale involves transfer of information about the object as well as the object itself. If there were a fuller understanding of the selling situation by both sides, there would be a lot less grousing about prices after the deal is done.

Finally, forget about book value. The only value an object has is what it is worth to you. This is the price that you should pay. The only person who can make this judgment is you. It is a decision of the moment. Never forget that. Do not buy if you think the price is unfair. Do not look back if you find later that you overpaid. At the moment of purchase you thought the price was fair. In buying at a flea market, the buck stops in your heart and wallet.

Flea Market Haggling

Few prices at a flea market are firm prices. No matter what anyone tells you, it is standard practice to haggle. You may not be comfortable doing it, but you might as well learn how. The money you save will be your own.

In my mind there are only three prices: a bargain price, a negotiable price, and a ridiculous price. If the price on an object is already a bargain, I pay it. I do this because

I like to see the shocked look on a seller's face when I do not haggle. I also do it because I want that dealer to find similar material for me. Nothing encourages this more than paying the price asked.

If the price is ridiculous, marked several times above what it is worth, I simply walk away. No amount of haggling will ever get the price to where I think it belongs. All that will happen is that the dealer and I will become frustrated. Who needs it? Let the dealers sit with their pieces. Sooner or later, the message will become clear.

I firmly believe it is the responsibility of the seller to set the asking price. When an object is not marked with a price, I become suspicious that the dealer is going to set the asking price based on what he or she thinks I can pay. I have tested this theory on more than one occasion by sending several individuals to inquire about the value of an unmarked item. In every case, a variety of prices were reported back to me. Since most of the material that I collect is mass-produced, I walk away from all unpriced merchandise. I will find another example somewhere else. This type of dealer does not deserve my business.

I have too much to do at a flea market to waste time haggling. If I find a piece that is close to what I am willing to pay, I make a counter-offer. I am very clear in what I tell the seller. "I am willing to pay 'x' amount. This is my best offer. Will you take it?" Most dealers are accustomed to responding with "Let's halve the difference." Hard though it is at times, I never agree. I tell the dealer that I made my best offer to save time haggling, and I intend to stick by it.

If the flea market that I am attending is a monthly or weekly, I may follow the object for several months. If it has gone unsold at the end of four to five months, I speak with the dealer and call attention to the fact that he has been unsuccessful in selling the object for the amount asked. I make my counter-offer, which sometimes can be as low as half the value marked on the piece. While the dealer may not be totally happy selling the object at that price, the prospect of any sale is often better than keeping the object in inventory for several more months. If the object has been sold before I return, I do not get upset. In fact, I am glad the dealer received his price. He just did not get it from me.

In Summary

If you are gullible, flea markets may not be for you. While not a Darwinian jungle, the flea market has pitfalls and traps which must be avoided in order for you to be successful. The key is to know that these pitfalls and traps exist.

Successful flea marketeering comes from practice. There is no school where you can learn the skills you need. You fly by the seat of your pants, learn as you go. The tuition that you pay are the mistakes you make along the way.

You can lessen your mistakes by doing homework. Research and study what you want to collect before you start buying. Even the most experienced buyers get careless or are fooled. Buying from the heart is much easier than buying from the head.

Never get discouraged. Everyone else you see at the flea market has experienced or is experiencing exactly what is happening to you. When you become a seasoned veteran, you will look back upon the learning period and laugh. In the interim, at least try to smile.

Chapter 6
THE FLEA MARKET SCENE TODAY

What a difference three years make. The 2004 flea market scene differs significantly from the 2001 flea market scene, the one I wrote about in the first edition of *The Official Guide To Flea Market Prices*. The changes may not seem apparent on the surface. You have to dig deeper to see them. Once you discover and interpret them, you will recognize how profound the changes are. In the flea market scene, the twenty-first century actually did begin in 2001.

The introduction to this chapter in the first edition of this book stated: "Change is occurring; and, it is very noticeable. This is truer today than it was two years ago. In fact, it is accelerating. Fasten your seat belts, the terrain ahead appears rather rough." The terrain is not only rough—it is filled with potholes. In 2004 the ride is bumper than ever.

The Economy and September 11, 2001

America experienced a mild recession as the twentieth century dawned. The effects continue to linger. Collectors use disposable income to buy antiques and collectibles. When disposable income lessens, collector sales decrease. As we enter 2004, the economic recovery is sporadic. Collectors continue to buy sparingly.

The good news is that collectors no longer dominate flea market sales. The person buying a flea market treasure to use or for decorative purposes is the primary buyer in today's market. Flea market goods are cheaper than new. Individuals on a budget find they can buy well at flea markets, especially in the area of dinnerware, flatware, furniture, jewelry, and stemware. This is especially true if the buyer has patience and comparison shops.

September 11, 2001 had a positive effect on the flea market scene. Attendance at flea markets increased as individuals decided to stay home rather than travel. Flea market gates for 2002 and 2003 were steady at worst and showed a ten to thirty percent increase at best.

September 11th created a national need to feel warm and fuzzy. A nostalgia craze swept across America. Flea markets are loaded with objects that evoke this emotion. It was not until the summer of 2003 that the economic decline began to impact strongly on the flea market scene. The delay caused the impact to be minimal.

A New Breed of Shoppers

Today's young collectors and buyers are "me" focused. These individuals from the "X" and "Y" generations come from smaller, more mobile families. They marry later. The result is that they do not have the same associations with the nineteenth and first two-thirds of the twentieth century as do the older, more traditionalist collectors.

Young collectors and buyers are very trend focused. They will collect or buy something only if it is in vogue. When a collecting category falls out of favor, young collectors and buyers will abandon it immediately and move on to something else. As a result, few categories run hot for more than two or three years. The 1970s is the hot decade of the moment. It is the age of avocado, golden harvest, and rust. Those who grew up in the 1970s are now in their mid-forties or late thirties.

Condition continues to remain a primary motivating factor in purchasing any item. No one wants to buy damaged goods. Flea market shoppers want to take the item they bought home and put it to immediate use. Buyers have little interest in fix-it-uppers.

The Decline of Flea Market Chic

Each year I see less and less material I would classify as flea market chic. The charm of damaged goods is over. I would like to report that the reason for the decline is that buyers and sellers finally woke up and relegated these items to where they belong—the local landfill. However, this is not the case. Flea Market Chic items disappeared because those selling them found there were no customers for them.

Flea Market Chic is being replaced by Country Primitive and Formalized Chic. Country Chic has a weathered, more natural look than the artificially distressed look of Flea Market Chic. Formalized Chic involves painting an object white and not distressing it. It makes an old piece look new. No attempt is made to create an aged appearance.

Increase Competition for Customers

On any given weekend in any area of the United States, there are dozens of events and places to go. Saturday morning and afternoon sports practice keeps soccer moms and dads close to home. All this and more compete with the flea market for attendees.

In order to lure customers, flea market promoters must continually market and promote. The verbal appraisal clinic, a place where individuals can bring objects from home to be appraised, is becoming a standard feature at most flea markets. Promoters continue to search for piggyback shows and events. Palmer Wirfs' October Portland Expo now includes a specialized vintage costume show while its November Oregon Convention Center Show is supported by an antiquarian book show. Early buyer opportunities, discount admission promotions, and hourly giveaways have become standard fare.

The Corporatizing of Flea Markets

Bigger is not necessarily better. Although Krause emerged victorious from the battle of the giants for control of antiques and collectibles publishing and trade periodicals, it was unable to withstand its own acquisition by a larger publisher completely outside the antiques and collectibles field. It is sad to see the decline of what were once jewels in the crown in the antiques and collectibles field, e.g., *The Antique Trader, The Antique Journal,* and the Wallace-Homestead imprint.

In the late 1990s, dmg world media, a division of England's daily mail group, acquired Piccadilly Shows, the Miami Beach show, and Metrolina. Krause acquired a coin show, a collectors' edition show, and the Atlantique City show. dmg world media's goal is to apply its European show management expertise to the American scene. The results are mixed thus far.

Can a single entity consolidate a large block of flea markets and antiques shows and create a workable antiques and collectibles trade show division? The highly individualistic nature of the trade makes the task a daunting one. Several attempts to create antiques mall chains failed. Several owners bought their malls back. Will flea market and antiques show consolidation suffer the same fate? Time will tell.

The Continuing Growth of the Internet

As in the past, the Internet is dominated in the antiques and collectibles sector by a single site, eBay. Most flea market dealers are also eBay sellers. As a result, not all the merchandise they uncover finds its way to their flea market booths. Some of their best pieces are first offered on eBay. One sees less and less high-end merchandise at today's flea markets.

The Internet has turned the concept of scarcity upside down. The Internet has shown that the survival rate of pieces is far higher than collectors and dealers thought. Pieces once thought to be scarce are now common. The Internet has flooded dozens, perhaps even hundreds of collecting categories.

Flea market dealers are finding it more and more difficult to achieve the traditional "price guide" value for what they offer for sale. When they do hold the line, they do not sell. Prices are slowly moving downward in many categories. These downward price trends are reflected in categories throughout this book.

The Internet continues to increase the seller and buyer base. Slowly, ever so slowly Internet sellers are discovering that flea markets offer the opportunity to interact with an entirely different group of customers. Internet buyers who visit flea markets are discovering that not all goods are sold on the Internet and bargains abound.

A Final Note

Permit me one final thought. The key to having an enjoyable experience at a flea market does not rest with the manager, the dealers, the physical setting or the merchandise. The key is you. Attend with reasonable expectations in mind. Go to have fun, to make a pleasant day of it. Even if you come home with nothing, savor the contacts that you made and the fact that you spent a few hours or longer among the goodies.

As a smart flea marketer, you know the value of customers in keeping flea markets alive and functioning. When you find a good flea market, write or call the regional trade papers and ask them to do more stories about it. Share your news with friends and others. Encourage them to attend. There is plenty for everyone.

Happy Hunting from all of us at Rinker Enterprises, Inc.

PRICE NOTES

Flea market prices for antiques and collectibles are not as firmly established as those at malls, shops, and shows. As a result, it is imperative that you treat the prices found in this book as "guides," not "absolutes."

Prices given are based on the national retail price for an object that is complete and in fine condition. These are retail prices. They are what you would expect to pay to purchase the objects. They do not reflect what you might realize if you were selling objects. A "fair" selling price to a dealer or private collector ranges from 20% to 40% of the book price, depending on how commonly found the object is.

Prices quoted are for objects that show a minimum of wear and no major blemishes to the display surface. The vast majority of flea market objects are mass-produced. As such, they survive in quantity. Do not buy damaged or incomplete objects. It also pays to avoid objects that show signs of heavy use.

Regional pricing is a factor within the flea market area, especially when objects are being sold close to their place of manufacture. When faced with higher prices due to strong regional pricing, I offer the price an object would bring in a neighboring state or geographic area. In truth, regional pricing has all but disappeared due to the large number of nationally oriented antiques and collectibles price guides, magazines, newspapers, and collectors' clubs.

Finally, "you" determine price; it is what "you" are willing to pay. Flea market treasures have no fixed prices. What has value to one person may be totally worthless to another. Is it possible to make sense out of this chaos? Yes, but in order to do so, you have to jump in feet first: attend flea markets and buy.

Happy Hunting! May all your purchases turn out to be treasures.

ABBREVIATIONS

# = number
3D = three-dimensional
adv = advertising, advertisement
approx = approximately
C = century
c = circa
circ = circular
cov = cover(ed)
d = diameter, depth, deep
dec = decorated, decoration
dj = dust jacket
ed = edition, edited
emb = embossed
expo = exposition
ext = exterior, external
FH = flat handle
ftd = footed
gal = gallon
ground = background
h = height, high
HH = hollow handle
hp = hand painted
illus = illustrated, illustrator, illustration(s)
imp = impressed
int = interior, internal
j = jewels
K = karat
l = length, long
L = liter
lb(s) = pound(s)
litho = lithograph(ed)
MBP = mint in bubble pack
mfg = manufactured, manufacturing
MIB = mint in box
MIP = mint in package
MISB = mint in sealed box
MISP = mint in sealed pkg
mkd = marked
mm = millimeter
MOC = mint on card
MOP = mother of pearl
nd = no date
NIB = new in box
NIP = new in package
NMOC = near mint on card
No. = number
NOS = new old stock
NRFB = never removed from box
orig = original
oz = ounce(s)
pc(s) = piece(s)
pt = pint
pg(s) = page(s)
pkg(s) = package(s)
pr = pair
pt = pint
pub = published, publisher
qt = quart
rect = rectangular
ret = retired
sgd = signed
SP = silver plated
sq = square
SS = sterling silver
ST = stainless steel
unmkd = unmarked
unsgd = unsigned
Vol = volume
w = width, wide
yg = yellow gold
yr = year

Part Two

FLEA MARKET PRICES

Categories A to Z

ABINGDON POTTERY

The Abingdon Sanitary Manufacturing Co. began manufacturing bathroom fixtures in 1908 in Abingdon, Ill. In 1938, they began production of art pottery made with a vitreous body. This line continued until 1970 and included more than 1,000 shapes and pieces. Almost 150 colors were used to decorate these wares. Given these numbers, forget about collecting an example of every form in every color ever made. Find a few forms that you like and concentrate on them. There are some great ones.

Club: Abingdon Pottery Club, 210 Knox Hwy. 5, Abingdon, IL 61410.

Bookends, pr, horse head, black 40
Bookends, pr, horse head, blue 50
Bookends, pr, horse head, white 45
Casserole, cov, Rose 42
Console Bowl, #532, 2-handled, pink, 14.5" l 45
Cookie Jar, Little Bo Peep 185
Cookie Jar, Little Old Lady 60
Cookie Jar, Miss Muffitt, #662 150
Cookie Jar, Money Bag, #588 50
Cookie Jar, Pumpkin, #674 90
Cookie Jar, Three Bears, #696 90
Cookie Jar, Train, #651 65
Figure, Heron, #574 20
Figure, penguin 70
Jam Set, 7-pc set with 3 cov jam pots on 8" tray, robin's egg blue 100
Jardiniere, #560 30
Planter, Bowtie, burgundy 35
Planter, Daffodil 30

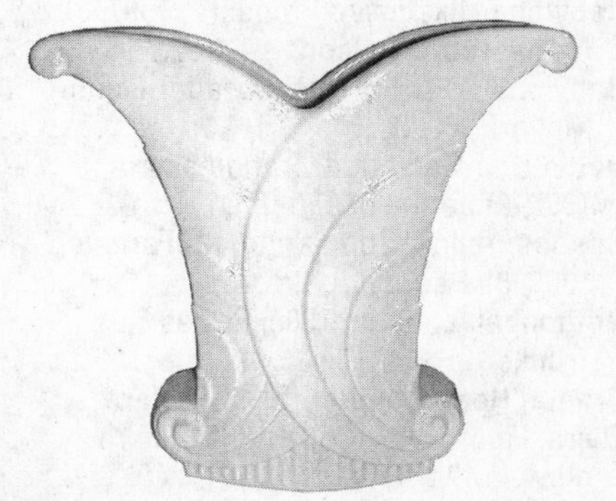

Planter, Donkey with Basket, yellow 50
Sconce Shelves, pr, blue 110
Vase, #116, 2-handled, white 28
Vase, #118, Classic, pink 30
Vase, #309, Neoclassic, gold on bronze 140
Vase, #325, pink 25
Vase, #417, Scroll, yellow, 8" h 105
Vase, #444, Fish 40
Vase, #486, Acanthus, white 40
Vase, #515, 2-tone .25
Vase, #522, white 40
Vase, #535, floral dec, gold trim 20
Vase, #597, yellow, 9.25" h 35
Vase, Art Deco design with fan-shaped top, white 55
Vase, Classic, yellow, 8" h 45
Vase, emb flower petals around base, dark rose color, 3.5" h 95
Vase, scroll handles, bead and rope design at shoulder, mint green, 13.5" h 150
Vase, scroll handles, bead and rope design at shoulder, white, 18" h 130
Vase, Ship, pink 20
Vases, pr, cornucopia shape, pink, 7" h . . .30
Window Box, #576 .25

ACTION FIGURES

Action, action, action! Action is the key to action figures. Action figures show action. You can recognize them because they can be manipulated into an action pose or are molded into an action pose. There is a wealth of supporting accessories for most action figures, ranging from clothing to vehicles, that is as collectible as the figures themselves. A good rule is the more pizzazz, the better the piece.

Emphasis is placed on pieces in mint or near-mint condition. The best way to find them is with their original packaging. Better yet, buy some new and stick them away. Unless noted, prices quoted are for action figures in their original packaging.

FIGURES

Aliens, Kenner, 1993, Series 2, Flying Alien Queen 10

Aliens, Kenner, 1997, Alien Resurrection, Newborn Alien 12
Antz, Playmates, 1998, Colonel Cutter 10
Antz, Playmates, 1998, General Mandible 10
Antz, Playmates, 1998, Princess Bala 15
Antz, Playmates, 1998, Weaver 10
Antz, Playmates, 1998, Z 15
Astro City, Future Confessor 8
Austin Powers, Equity Marketing, 1999, 7" Movie Headliners XL, Austin Powers 5
Austin Powers, McFarlane, 1999, 6", Austin Danger Powers, Would You Fancy a Shag 8
Austin Powers, McFarlane, 1999, 6", Austin Danger Powers, Very Shagadelic 8
Austin Powers, McFarlane, 1999, 6", Austin Powers, Crikey, I've Lost My Mojo 8
Austin Powers, McFarlane, 1999, 6", Dr Evil, One Million Dollars 8
Austin Powers, McFarlane, 1999, 6", Dr Evil, Why must I be surrounded by frickin idiots 10
Austin Powers, McFarlane, 1999, 6", Vanessa Kensington 10
Avengers, Toy Biz, 1997, 5", Iron Man Heroes Reborn 14
Avengers, Toy Biz, 1997, 5", Loki 15
Avengers, Toy Biz, 1997, 5", Scarlet Witch 15
Avengers, Toy Biz, 1999, 6", Ant-Man 16
Avengers, Toy Biz, 1999, 6", Falcon 15
Avengers, Toy Biz, 1999, 6", Hawkeye 15
Avengers, Toy Biz, 1999, 6", Tigra 10
Avengers, Toy Biz, 1999, 6", Wasp 10
Bone, ReSaurus, 1998, 7", Bone Phoney ...9
Bone, ReSaurus, 1998, 7", Thorn 7
Bride of Chucky, Little Big Heads, Chucky and Tiffiny 12
Bride of Chucky, Sideshow Toys, 17" 30
Broadway Joe Namath, Mego, 1970, 12" h 20
Captain Power, Mattel, 1987, Lord Dread 14
Captain Power, Mattel, 1987, Lt Tank Ellis 13
Captain Power, Mattel, 1987, Major Hawk Masterson 14
Casablanca, Exclusive Premiere, 1998, boxed set, Rick and Ilsa 30
Cavewoman, Rendition, 1998, Cavewoman 20
Coneheads, Playmates, Parental Unit Beldar in Suburban Uniform 10
Coneheads, 1991, Beldar, PVC 1
Congo, Kenner, 1995, Blastface 5
Congo, Kenner, 1995, Karen Ross 6
Congo, Kenner, 1995, Peter Elliot 5
Earth Worm Jim, Playmates, 1995, 6", Princess What's Her Name 10
Earth Worm Jim, Playmates, 1995, 6", Psycrow 8
Flash Gordon, Playmates, 1996, 5", Ming the Merciless 10
Flash Gordon, Playmates, 1996, 5", Princess Thunder 10
Ghost, Dark Horse Comics, 1998, Ghost, white outfit 15
Lady Pendragon, Action Toys, 1999, 6.5", Lady Pendragon 10
Mercy, Rendition, 1998, 7", Mercy 5
Babylon 5, Exclusive Premiere, 1997, 8", Ambassador Delenn 10
Babylon 5, WB Toy, Ambassador Londo Mollari 8
Battle Star Galactica, Trendmasters, 1996, Imperious Leader 10
Beatles, Yellow Submarine, McFarlane, 1999, 8", Paul 15
Dragonball Z, Irwin, 1999, Series 6, Trunks 6
Dragon Heart, Kenner, 1995, 4", Kara 6
Elvira, Figures Toy Co, 1998, 8", Elvira, glow-in-the-dark 20

Gargoyles, Applause, 3", Goliath, PVC 3
Gargoyles, Kenner, 1995, Series 1, 5", Demona 20
Gargoyles, Kenner, 1996, Series 2, 5", Elisa Maza 10
Generation X, Toy Biz, 1995, Series 1, 5", Emplate 6
Generation X, Toy Biz, 1995, Series 1, 5", Skin 9
Generation X, Toy Biz, 1996, Series 2, 5", Banshee 12
Generation X, Toy Biz, 1996, Series 2, 5", Mondo 7
Generation X, Toy Biz, 1996, Series 2, 5", White Queen, flesh legs 12
Generation X, Toy Biz, 1996, Series 2, 5", White Queen, white legs 7
Ghost Busters, Kenner, 1988, Series 3 Fright Features, 5", Egon Spengler 12
Ghost Busters, Kenner, 1989, Series 4 Monsters, 5", Mummy 12
Ghost Busters, Kenner, 1990, Series 5 Slimed Heroes, 5", Luis Tully 15
Hercules, Toy Biz, 1996, 5", Iolaus 12
Hercules, Toy Biz, 1996, 5", Salmoneus . . .10
Hercules, Toy Biz, 1996, 5", Xena 8
Iron Man, Toy Biz, 1995, Series 1, 5", Backlash 9
Iron Man, Toy Biz, 1995, Series 1, 5", Iron Man Hydro Armor 12
Iron Man, Toy Biz, 1995, Series 1, 5", Spiderwoman 7
Iron Man, Toy Biz, 1995, Series 2, 5", Iron Man Space Armor 11
Iron Man, Toy Biz, 1995, Series 3, 5", Century 9
Iron Man, Toy Biz, 1995, Series 3, 5", US Agent 45
Iron Man, Toy Biz, deluxe boxed figure, Agent Silver Dragon 12
Kiss, McFarlane, 1997, 8", set of 4 35
Mario Kart, Toy Biz, 1999, Series 1, Bowser 40
Masked Rider, 1995, Karate Kickin' Dex . . .6
Masters Of The Universe, Mattel, 1984, 5", Webstor 30
Mortal Kombat, Hasbro, 1994, 3.75", Sonya Blade 15
Mortal Kombat, Hasbro, 1994, 12", Scorpion 25
Mortal Kombat, Hasbro, 1998, 12", Jade . .15
Munsters, Side Show Toys, Little Big Head Marilyn 12
Nira, Skybolt Toyz, 1997, 6", Nira Platinum 6
Pee Wee Herman, 1985, King of Cartoons 20
Planet Of The Apes, 1998, 12", Cornelius . .15
Robotech, Matchbox, 1985, 3.75", Zor Prime 6
Robotech, Matchbox, 1985, 3.75", Robotech Master .4
Rocky & Bullwinkle, Exclusive Premiere, 1998, Boris & Natasha set 15
Rocky & Bullwinkle, Exclusive Premiere, 1998, Rocky & Bullwinkle set 15
Sailor Moon, Ban Dai, 1995, 6", Sailor Jupiter 4
Sea Quest, Playmates, 1993, Captain Nathen Hale Bridger 6
Sisters of Darkness, Skybolt Toyz, 1998, 6", Letha Demon Skin, autographed 6
Space Ghost, ReSaurus, Captain Terror . . .9
Space Ghost, ReSaurus, Pops Racer 12
Space Ghost, ReSaurus, Trixie 15
Spice Girls, Toymax, 1998, 3", Posh Spice, black outfit 4
Spice Girls, Toymax, 1998, 6", Sporty Spice, striped top .5
Star Trek, Classic Movie, Playmates, 1996, 5", General Chang 12
Star Trek, Deep Space Nine, Playmates, 1995, Series 3, 5", Dax 10
Star Trek, Playmates, mid-1990s, Scotty, "Where No Man Has Gone Before" 8

Star Trek, Playmates, 1996, Series 3, 5", Talosian Keeper .10
Star Trek, The Next Generation, Playmates, 1992, Series 1,5", Troi .15
Teenage Mutant Ninja Turtles, Playmates, 1993, 5", Don as Dracula .14
Tekken, Epoch, 1993, 7", Anna Williams .12
Terminator 2, Kenner, 1992, 5", Metal-Mash .10
Waterworld, Kenner, 1995, 5", Deacon .7
Xena, Toy Biz, 10", Zena .10
X Files, McFarlane, 1998, Series 1, Mulder, parka, alien corpse in chamber .6
X Files, McFarlane, 1998, Series 1, Scully, parka, attack alien .10
X-Men vs Street Fighter, Toy Biz, 1997, 5", Woverine vs Akuma .12
Zorro, Playmates, 1997, Evil Machete .7
Zorro, Playmates, 1997, Zorro Don Diego .15

ACCESSORIES

A Bug's Life, Mattel, 1998, Anthill Fortress, light-up, 22" .35
A Bug's Life, Mattel, 1998, Battle Bird .10
Alien, Electronic Hovertread Vehicle .12
Alien, Space Marine Power Loader .15
Avengers, Toy Biz, 2000, Sky Cycle .18
Bucky O'Hare, 1990, Toad Croaker .16
Cadillacs and Dinosaurs, Tyco, Hammer's Tribike .15
Cadillacs and Dinosaurs, Tyco, Jack Tenrec's Glider .15
Congo, Net Trap Vehicle .15
Congo, Trail Hacker .10
Crash Test Dummies, Crash Test Center .45
Ghost Busters, Ecto-3 .12
Ghost Busters, Fearsome Flush .8
Mighty Max, Mattel, 1992, Mighty Max Defeats Vamp Biter playset .5
Secret Wars, Mattel, Doom Cycle .15
Secret Wars, Mattel, Freedom Fighter .38
Secret Wars, Mattel, Tower Of Doom .40
Street Fighter, Hasbro, 1993, Karate Chopper .20
Street Fighter, Hasbro, 1993, Street Striker .25
Waterworld, Kenner, 1995, The Trimaran .25

ADVERTISING CHARACTERS

Many companies created advertising characters as a means of guaranteeing product recognition by the buying public. Consumers are more apt to purchase an item with which they are familiar and advertising characters were a surefire method of developing familiarity.

The early development of advertising characters also enabled immigrants who could not read to identify products by the colorful figures found on the packaging.

Trademarks and advertising characters are found on product labels, in magazines, as premiums, and on other types of advertising. Character subjects may be based on a real person such as Nancy Green, the original "Aunt Jemima." However, more often than not, they are comical figures, often derived from popular contemporary cartoons. Other advertising characters were designed especially to promote a specific product, like Mr. Peanut and the Campbell Kids.

Clubs: Camel Joe and his Friends, 2205 Hess Dr., Cresthill, IL 60435; Campbell Soup Collectors Club, 414 Country Ln. Ct., Wauconda, IL 60084, www.soupcollector.com; Campbell Soup Collectors International Assoc., 305 East Main St., Ligonier, PA 15658, www.soupkid.com/collect/collect.htm; Charlie Tuna Collectors Club, 7812 NW Hampton Rd., Kansas City, MO 64152.

Aunt Jemima, cloth sack, "Aunt Jemima Yellow Corn Meal," large color image of smiling Aunt Jemima, full unopened sack, 25 lbs, 20" h, 11" w .120
Aunt Jemima, toy string climber, die-cut cardboard, 2-pc, shiny emb bright color litho, 13.25" x 6" Aunt Jemima with "Le' Me To It! It's Worth Climbing For Aunt Jemima's Pancake Flour" on apron, hanging below 4" x 2.25" box of pancake flour .7,500
Black Cat, hanging match holder, litho tin, "Black Cat Shoe Dressing and Black Kitty Stove Enamel," Black Cat and young black girl, 5.5" h .1,750

Advertising Characters

Buddy Lee, doll, plastic, overalls, red and white plaid shirt 75

Buster Brown, clicker, Buster Brown Shoes, multicolor image of Buster and Tige 45

Buster Brown, match holder, litho tin, multicolor image of Tige next to Buster Brown carrying freshly baked loaf of bread to children waiting at table set for tea party, "The Secret of the Goodness of 'Buster Brown' Bread Is Care, Cleanliness and the Best Ingredients" on hanging basket, 7.75" h 1,975

Buster Brown, pocket mirror, "Buster Brown Shoes For Boys and Girls," Buster and Tige image, red, black, and white, 1.75" d 165

Campbell's Kids, pennant, red felt, "Campbell's Soups," Campbell's Soup kid image, 21" l, 8" h 125

Charlie Tuna, pin, diecut metal, contour of state of Wisconsin with center image of Charlie, fishing line sign "Sorry Charlie" and carrying case inscribed "Wisconsin Jaycees," 1970s 14

Crushy, Orange Crush soda, sign, round, Crushy above "Orange-Crush Carbonated Beverage," orange ground, 1940s .225

Dutch Boy, match holder, litho tin, emb die-cut Dutch Boy holding paint bucket match holder, "Dutch Boy Paints," 6.75" h 450

Gold Dust Twins, adv trade card, Fairbanks' Gold Dust Washing Powder, die-cut cardboard, Twins sitting in tub, adv text on back 50

Hamm's Bear, Hamm's Beer, backbar statue, plastic, figural bear holding calendar, complete with months and numbers, 16" h 85

Hamm's Bear, Hamm's Beer, salt and pepper shakers, bears standing with legs apart, Silver State Specialties, 1997, NIB 35

Hamm's Bear, stuffed toy, baseball bear, 21" h 65

Kool Penguin, cigarette lighter, plastic figural Mr Kool penguin, electric, 9" x 4" x 3.75" 325

Little Sergeant, clicker, Little Sergeant Shoes, orange, black, and white, Little Sergeant image 35

Michelin Man, ashtray, plastic, black and white Michelin man, mkd "Made in USA," 4.75" h, 5" w, 5.5" l 100

Mr Peanut, fan, cardboard, Planters Peanuts, Mr Peanut in peanut car, c1940, 5.25" x 8" 450

Nipper, watch fob, RCA, SS, detailed multicolor cloisonné enameled image of Nipper listening to RCA Victor phonograph, "His Master's Voice" below, 1.5" x 1.25" 1,150

Pep Boys, bank, litho tin 4-sided can, shows the boys in bank setting, 2.5" h, 2.25" w, 1" d 275

Reddy Kilowatt, pinback button, "Your Electric Servant,"red, white, and blue, 1950s 20

Reddy Kilowatt, token, plastic, blue, gold Reddy image on 1 side, reverse inscription "Reddy Kilowatt/The Mighty Atom," 1960s 18

Red Goose, neon clock, glass and metal, octagonal, "Red Goose Shoes, For Boys, For Girls," Red Goose in center, green frame, 18" w 1,750

Wise Owl, thermometer, painted wood, Wise Potato Chip Co, "Potato Storage Thermometer," Wise Owl logo, 8.25" h, 2.75" w 350

ADVERTISING ITEMS

Divide advertising items into two groups: items used to merchandise a product and items used to promote a product. Merchandising advertising is a favorite with interior decorators and others who want it for its mood-setting ability. It is often big, splashy and showy. Promotional advertising (giveaways) are primarily collector-driven.

Almost every piece of advertising appeals to more than one collector. As a result, prices for the same piece will often differ significantly, depending on who the seller views as the final purchaser. Most advertising is bought for the purpose of display. As a result, emphasize theme and condition. The vast majority of advertising collectibles are two-dimensional. Place a premium on large three-dimensional objects.

Clubs: Advertising Cup and Mug Collectors of America, P.O. Box 680, Solon, IA 52333; Antique Advertising Assoc. of America, P.O. Box 5851, Elgin, IL 60123; Inner Seal Collectors Club (Nabisco), 6609 Billtown Rd., Louisville, KY 40299; Porcelain Advertising Collectors Club, P.O. Box 381, Marshfield Hills, MA 02051; The Ephemera Society of America, P.O. Box 95, Cazenovia, NY 13035, www.signaturecoll.com; Tin Container Collectors Assoc., P.O. Box 440101, Aurora, CO 80044; Trade Card Collector's Assoc., P.O. Box 284, Marlton, NJ 08053, www.tradecards.com.

Advertising Tear Sheet, Remington, "His First Circus...His First Gun," 1948, 8.5 x 11" 4

Advertising Trade Card, Emersons Ginger-Mint Julep, 6 x 3" 10

Advertising Trade Card, Hills Bros Coffee, "Try this on your phonograph. Play with loud needle. Do not remove record from card," 3.25" x 5.75" 25

Advertising Trade Card, Prestone Anti-Freeze, "Don't let anyone monkey with your car," features Pontiac's winterizing program, 3.25 x 5.5" 5

Ashtray, Ernest A Brey, Quality Meats, Spinnerstown, PA, circ Bakelite base, center cigarette rest with adv medallion, 1955 12

Ashtray, General Electric Radiotrons-Hi Relief Tubes, Bakelite, 1930–40s, 4" x 6" 20

Ashtray, Kool Cigarettes, white milk glass, Kool penguin in 4 poses around tray, "Smoke Kools for that Kool taste" on rim, 4 rests, 5.5" d 5

Ashtrays, set of 3, Texaco Service, litho metal, pin-up images in center, 4.25" sq 200

Bank, Admiral Appliances, vinyl, figural George Washington, 1980s 25

Bank, Aylmer Cream of Corn Soup, litho tin canister, cap on bottom to empty coins, 4" h, 2.5" d 20

Bank, Bosco Chocolate Malt Flavor, litho tin round can, cartoons on sides, 3" h, 2.5" d 80

Bank, Howard Johnsons, plastic, replica restaurant, late 1950s, 3.5" h 28

Bank, Listerine, figural elephant, ceramic, bottom mkd "Free with Listerine Simmons Cream Offer, Made in the USA," 2.5 x 3.5" 10

Bank, Log Cabin Syrup, litho tin log cabin with mother at door and children around, other side shows banner nailed to cabin wall, 4.5" h, 3.5" w, 2.5" d 30

Bank, Wonder Bread, "I'm A Fresh Guy Bank!," 5" l, 3.5" h, 3.25" w 185

Bill Hook, celluloid button on wire hook, "The Busch Shoe Repair Co.," image of shoe-shaped automobile, 7.75" h . . .185

Blotter, Garl Electric Co, Akron, OH, "We own and control this entire system of connecting Poles and any Poles used that are not manufactured by us are an infringement upon our patents," black and white 20

Blotter, Morse & Rogers Shoes, celluloid button, round, black lettering, yellow ground, red and black felt, 3.25" d 15

Blotter, Morton Salt, 3.75 x 7.75" 7

Booklet, Kellogg's, 32 pgs, health information and diet tips, 7.5 x 5.25" 3

Bowl, Curries Ice Cream, mkd "Desert Ware, Wallace China" 60

Box, Beacon Brand Cheese Spread, wood, National Creamery Co, 11" x 3.75" x 3" 4

Box, Nabisco Barnum's Animals Cookies, cardboard, multicolored circus animals illus, 1940s, 5" x 2.5" x 1.75" 45

Brochure, Briggs & Stratton Power Charger, 4 pgs, 8.5" x 11" 40

Brochure, Planet Jr Tractor and Power Unit, 4 pgs, fold-out center, 8" x 11" 10

Brochure, Stover Pump Jacks, Stover Mfg & Engine Co, 21 pgs, 1930s, 9" x 4" . .8

Broom Holder, O N East, Dealer in Grain, Feed, Hard & Soft Coal, wooden rollers, 6" x 3" 10

Brush, wooden top, emb "Sage-Allen & Co, Hartford, Conn. Reliable Dry Goods," 2.25" x 8.25" 10

Calendar, 1922, US Cartridge Co, large image of standing grizzly bear carrying box of shells, 34.5" h, 15" w . .800

Calendar, 1931, Great Northern, "America's Longest Tunnel," American Indian illus, May sheet only, 10" x 12" 125

Calendar, 1952, Western Exterminating Co, 1023 12th Street NW, Washington DC, 12 different pin-up prints, sgd "Al Moore," ©1950 Esquire Inc, 6.25" x 5.5" 30

Calendar, 1954, Goodrich Hardware Co, Fayetteville, TN 10

Catalog, Eveready Battery, 12 pgs, 1960 . . .5

Catalog, Superior Match Co, 164 pgs, 1950s, 8.5" x 11" 20

Change Tray, Lamb's Navy Rum, porcelain, Lamb's Rum bottle inside blue porthole, 6" d .12

Cigar Box Opener, Orange Blossom 10 Cent Cigars, chrome plated steel, Meagher & Sons, Rochester, NY, 5" l, .75" w 25

Clip, Wyoming Automotive Co, celluloid, center logo forms tire 20

Clock, GE, "Appliances/Television," metal and plastic, light-up, 25" h, 14.5" w 50

Clock, Grant Batteries, light-up, 1950-60s, 15.5" x 15.5" 160

Clock, Gruen Jewelers, electric, silver colored panel at bottom, 1940s, 18.25" h, 15" w 30

Clock, Lee, "Clothes for Work and Leisure," light-up, 15" d 50

Clock, Monarch Foods, light-up, 15" d . . .240

Clock, Quaker State Motor Oil, "Ask For Quaker State Motor Oil," light-up, 16" sq 50

Clock, St Joseph Aspirin, light-up 110

Coaster, Ford 50th Anniversary 1903-1953, metal, glass over paper insert 10

Coin Holder, Walter's Brewing Co, Eau Claire, WI, plastic, "Beer That Is Beer," 1970s, 3" l 5
Corkscrew, E Alexander & Son Merchants, 5" l 18
Crock, Willow Farms, "Real Butter/Taste The Difference" 25
Decal, Butternut Bread, "Remember a Loaf of Butternut Bread," boy rubbing his belly, 7.5" x 4.5" 5
Display, Ohio Varnish Co, "Floor Enamel for any surface Interior or Exterior," cardboard, countertop, attached color samples, 1920-30s, 12 x 18" 66
Doll, Morton Salt, R Dakin, 1966 10
Door Push, "Reach For Bunny Bread" 80
Door Push, "Reach for Dreikorn's Bread," reverse "Thanks! Call Again!" 50
Fan, hand, Berwind Genuine Pocahontas Briquettes, cozy cottage scene with poem "Home Sweet Home" 8
Fan, hand, CZ Sherry, 7 x 13" 12
Fan, hand, Planters Peanuts, Mr Peanut in peanut car, c1940, 5.25 x 8" 465
Flask, emb "Smoke Ambrosia Cigars," 6.5" h, 4.5" w 115
Hang Tag, John Deere, heavy paper, Quality Farm Equipment logo with "No. 8 Forage Harvester," 1950s 14
Key, emb "Use Eclipse Soap/Key To Success," 10.25" l 25
Label, Boiled Mutton, sheep, cowboy on range chasing cow 8
Label, Campfire Coffee, coffeepot on campfire 8
Label, Coco-Milco, gypsy woman holding cup of hot milk 4
Label, Deer Head, 10-point buck, 2 apples 3
Label, Dinette Pork & Beans, 2 fancy bowls of beans 2
Label, Forest City Lima Beans, beans in pod, bright leaves 2
Label, Old East Maine Clams, 3 clams, red, blue, and yellow, 1929 12
Label, Old Fashioned Malt Syrup, family in patio, old German village, 1930 15
Label, Triumph Brand, man on horseback blowing trumpet 5
Label, Zodiac, zodiac calendar 3
Ladle, "Use Hansens Dairy Lime Soap," graniteware, 10.5" l 30
Lighter, American Kitchens, "Save a Thousand Steps a Day," orig box 60
Lighter, Wilderness Fruit Filling, 2.25" x 1.25" 40
Lighter, "Winona Wilson Colonial Yarns and Fabrics," Zippo 20
Marble, John Deere, green 5
Measuring Spoon, Frigidaire 5
Mirror, Miller High Life, woman sitting on moon crest toasting with glass of beer, Miller Brewing Co, Milwaukee, WI, 1979, 14.25" x 14.25" 10
Mug, Nestle, Farfel the dog, "Especially for you-Jimmy Nelson," red and black lettering, 1950s 15
Mug, VanHouten's Cocoa, 4" h 45
Needle Book, Swem Funeral Home, Buchanan, MI, front shows print of small child titled "Who's Afraid" 3
Paperweight, "Babcock Printing Press Mfg. Co., New London, Conn.," glass, rect, black and white engraving style illus of printing press titled "The Optimus," 1" x 2.5" x 4" 65
Paperweight, "John W Pechin & Bro Philadelphia, PA, Oak Belting," glass, rect, round black and white logo, 3" d, .75" h 30
Paperweight, "P. P. Van Vleet, President, Van Vleet Mansfield Drug Co., Memphis, Tenn.," glass, rect, black and white photo portrait, 1" x 2.5" x 4" 30
Pencil, mechanical, The Ohio Plaster & Supply Co, Steubenville, OH 15
Pinback Button, Ann Page Foods, center Good Housekeeping Seal, 1930-40s 18
Pinback Button, Maltex and Maypo Health Club, Marky Maypo illus, black and white, 1950s 12
Pinback Button, Mr Pikle, "Pikle-Rite" above Mr Pikle image, green and red on white ground, 1946 9
Pinback Button, Old Dutch Cleanser, "Clean-Up Week," red, white, and blue, 1930s 8
Pinback Button, Stephenson Underwear, South Bend, IN, multicolor image of man displaying red undershirt, black lettering on white ground, 1920s 32
Pitcher, spongeware, Hagen Oil Co, "Hi-Test Petroleum Products" 55

Plate, Boston Clothing House, West Chester, PA, dirt road and fence leading to house with pink flowered trees and buildings in background, gold lettering 10

Plate, George Urban Milling Co, Buffalo, NY, Urban's Liberty Flour, Hobnail, Hocking Glass, 8.5" d 10

Plate, Schuler Farm Supply Ltd, "Your Massey Ferguson and Morris Dealer," roses motif, Hycroft Pottery 30

Playing Cards, Oldham Batteries 20

Pocketknife, Silvo Silver Polish, Turner & Co, Sheffield, England, 3" l 5

Pocket Mirror, N Zelen Jewelers, outer birthstone images, center black and white text "N. Zelen Jeweler/Two Doors From Ridgewood Theatre/1679 Myrtle Ave," 1920s 25

Pocket Mirror, Old Reliable Coffee, man resting with foot on oversized box of coffee, multicolor, 1.75" d 50

Postcard, August Schell Brewing Co, New Ulm, MN, view of brewery and an elk, multicolored, adv text on back 50

Postcard, Hadley Co, Bridgeport, CT, "Freshman All Electric Radio, Table Model Q15, Hear It Today!," red, black, and white on government postal card 20

Postcard, Philadelphia Lawn Mower Co, woman pushes the Graham All Steel lawn mower, adv text on back, multicolored 65

Postcard, Smile-Lax Laxatives, smiling baby proclaims "No More Constipation. My Mama Gives Me Smile-Lax, The Laxative Candy Chip," multicolored 40

Postcard, Westmoreland Glass Co, Grapeville, PA, shows milk glass decorated with roses and bows, 1960-70s, 4.5 x 7" .10

Pot Scraper, King Midas Flour, litho tin, 2.75" x 3.5" 385

Pot Scraper, Sharples Tubular Cream Separator, multicolor, same image both sides, 3" x 2.25" 300

Pull Toy, Towle's Log Cabin Syrup, litho tin, log cabin on red wheels, "Towle's Log Cabin Syrup, Log Cabin Express," 5.75" h, 4.75" l 525

Recipe Book, Fleischman's Yeast, "The Quick Method and the Overnight Method," includes 2 recipes for white bread, and recipe for Tea Biscuit, 6" x 3.5" 6

Ruler, French's, colored aluminum,"Some Potatoes Don't Measure Up To French's" on front, "French's First In Quality, Sales, Advertising, Promotion and Sales Force" on reverse," 12" l 4

Ruler, Nebraska Blue Cross-Blue Shield, 1950 and 1951 calendar on back, 12" l . . .8

Salt and Pepper Shakers, pr, Groendyke Transport, Bakelite 5

Salt and Pepper Shakers, pr, Ken-L Ration, cat and dog 8

Screwdriver, Gene's Service Station, "See Gene for Gasoline & Oils/We serve you with a smile/Gene's Service Station, 2718 Elmwood Ave, Kenmore, NY" 2

Shoe Brush, Bluemling Bros Shoe Dealers, Sharpsburg, Etna, Millvale, PA, wooden 10

Sign, American Field Hunting Garments, cardboard, diecut, counter stand-up, jump-out mallard, 1940-50, 14" x 16" . . .140

Sign, Black-Draught Vegetable Laxative, pine frame, MA Thedford Co, Chattanooga, TN, 1930s, 42" x 10" 35

Sign, Creamsicle, tin, boy holding popsicle, "Enjoy This Delicious Treat...." 18" x 14" 10

Sign, Goody Root Beer, tin, 1940, 13.5" x 19.5" 95

Sign, Popsicle, tin, "Good 'N Cool," 14" x 20" 10

Sign, Sunbeam Bread, tin, "Bread With A Bonus/More Energy, More Nutrition, More Flavor," 12" x 16" 10

Sign, Surf Rider Hawaiian Pineapple Juice, tin, 16" x 14" 10

Sign, Woolrich Sportswear, cardboard, 13.5" x 17" 15

Spool Cabinet, "Clark's O.N.T., Spool Cotton, On White Spools, George A. Clark, Sole Agent," 6 drawers, walnut, ...1,500

Spoon, Banner Buggies, old buggy image, Wm Rogers & Sons, 6" l 20

Stamp, Remington UMC, white paper, center circular red and white maker's name, unused, 1930s 14

Stickpin, DeKalb Corn, plastic, figural ear of corn merging to green wings, 1950s 5

String Holder, Columbia Products, tin, beige and black, 4.75" d 15

Swizzle Stick, Magic Bar, Shreveport, LA, glass, 6" l 6

Tape Measure, John Deere, celluloid, Pariesan Novelty, Chicago, 1920s 30

Thermometer, David Harum Flour/David Harum Feed, wood, 1937, 3" x 12" 66

Thermometer, Lamb's Market, metal, "Full Line of Fancy Groceries & Meats, 676 Cass St, Joliet, Ill," 7.5 x 2.75" 5

Thermometer, Morton Salt, tin, "Morton Free Running Salt–When it Rains It Pours," 16" h, 6" w 40

Thermometer, Sprite, "Enjoy Sprite, Tart and Tingling!," green lettering and logo on white ground, gold trim, 1960s, 12" d 275

Thermometer, Taglang's Economy Store, Fancy Meats & Groceries, 738 Wyandotte St, Bethlehem, PA, metal, 4" x 8" 30

Thermometer, Whistle, tin, 2 elves carrying oversized bottle, "Thirsty? Just Whistle" above, 21" h, 9" w 1,000

Thermometer, Wise Potato Chip Co, painted wood, "Potato Storage Thermometer," Wise Owl logo, 8.25" h, 2.75" w 360

Thimble, Gulf Life Insurance Co, aluminum, "A Southern Tradition" 5

Thimble, Prudential Life Insurance 3

Tie Clasp, Philco-Ford, metal, 1.25" l, MIB . .5

Tin, Dr Scholl's Borolin Bandage, uses for the bandages on cov, directions inside lid, 1930s, 3.75" x 2.75" 50

Tin, Gre-Solvent, 1930s, 3.5" d 10

Tin, Moth-Ene, Den-Wal Mfg Co, Newark, NJ, "Kills Moths, Their Eggs and Larvae, Positively Guaranteed," 2.25" d 5

Tin, Weikel's Justrite Coffee, Weikel and Smith Spice Co, Philadelphia, litho tin, pry-lid, 1 lb, 5.75" x 4.25" 130

Token, Ford, metal, "Thirty Years of Progress" 10

Tray, Ben Franklin Life Insurance, bust profile of Franklin, 4" d 25

Tray, Davidson's Premier Stoves and Ranges, "The Range That Will Last A Lifetime," 4.25" d 40

Tray, Land O'Lakes Butter, 13.25 x 11.75" . .10

Tray, Marlboro Cigarettes, Metal Tray Mfg Co, London, England, 12" d 15

Tray, Miller Beer, "Miller High Life-The Champagne of Beers," woman sitting on moon holding beer, 13" d 15

Tray, Noakers Ice Cream, blue lettering with orange highlights on yellow ground, 15.25 x 10.5" 30
Tray, Olson and Matheson Produce, "Phone 20, Lake Mills, Iowa," 8.75" x 14.25" 20
Tray, Sears, Roebuck & Co Chicago, depicts company office and warehouse, "Originators Of The Guarantee That Stands The Test In The Scales Of Justice," 4.25" x 6" 20
Watch, Irish Spring Soap, 3-leaf clover on black ground, "Ladies Like It Too!" .10
Watch Fob, Curtis Publishing Co, dark luster brass, triangle symbol inscribed for publications *Saturday Evening Post, Country Gentleman,* and *Ladies Home Journal,* inscribed "Junior Member," reverse inscribed "Award of Merit" above Curtis name, 1920s 8
Whistle, Yellow Cab, 2 tubes, "Whistle for a Yellow Cab or Phone CHerry 4900," Kirchof 5
Yo-Yo, Tastee-Freez, orig red paint, gold logo, 2.25" d 10

AIRLINE & AVIATION

Airline mergers and bankruptcies have produced a wealth of obsolete material. There were enormous crowds at Eastern's liquidation sale in spring 1991. I have a bunch of stuff from Piedmont and Peoples, two airlines that flew into the sunset in the 1980s.

The wonderful thing about airline collectibles is that most of them initially were free. I try to make it a point to pick up several items, from bathroom soap to playing cards, each time I fly. Save the things most likely to be thrown out.

Club: Aeronautica & Air Label Collectors Club, P.O. Box 1239, Elgin, IL, 60121; Antique Airplane Assoc., 22001 Bluegrass Rd, Ottumwa, IA 52501, www.aaa-apm.org/aaa/; Aviation Relic Prints Club, 190 W. Dowling Rd., Dowling, MI 49050; Lighter-Than-Air Society, 1436 Triplett Blvd, Akron, OH 44306, http://spot.colorado.edu/~dziadeck/lta.html; Society of Antique Modelers, P.O. Box 528, Lucerne Valley, CA 92356, www.antiquemodeler.org/; World Airline Historical Society, 13739 Picarsa Dr., Jacksonville, FL 32225.

Badge, French aviator's, WWI 185
Book, *Aero Club of America Bulletin,* Jan 1912 275
Booklet, "Indian Aero Motor," c1910 575
Bowl, Delta Air Lines, Abco Tableware, NY, 4.625" d, price for set of 4 6
Broadside, American Airline Company, c1919 90
Catalog, "Flying Machines for the Chicago Aero Works," c1909-10 625
Children's Book, *Our Air Ship A.B.C.,"* dated 1912 275
Cigarette Lighter, Canadian Pacific Airlines, inscribed "Madison" on 1 side, mkd "Super Automatic Lighter Japan" on bottom 9
Cup and Saucer, US Air, china, Abco Tableware, NY, 2.375" h cup, 5" d saucer 10
Fan, BOAC Airlines, "Speedboat Routes Across The World" 7
Flatware, Pan American Airlines, International Silver, 1970s, price for 4 pcs . . .15
Goggles, aviator's, EB Meyrowitz, boxed 250
Flight Attendant's Wings, Western Airlines, goldtone, 1980 15
Handkerchief, cotton, black and white image of Lindbergh and "Lindy-So this is Paris!-Compliments of the Multistamp Co of NY" 125
Manual, Hall-Scott Big Four Type A77a Airplane Engine, c1918-20 115
Medallion, commemorating first flight of Colonial Western Airways, dated 1928 350

Passenger Towel, from the airship Graf Zeppelin LZ127, c1929 575
Pencil, oversized, image of Lindbergh and plane with "New York to Paris" . . .65
Pilot's Wings, Eastern Airlines, black felt with metal enamel center disk, 1955 95
Pilot's Wings, U.S. Airship, silver, c1920 450
Pinback Button, National Air Races, Aug 31 to Sep 3, Cleveland, undated . . .15
Postcard, first United Kingdom aerial post by sanction of HM Postmaster General, c1911 70
Poster, The Wright Brothers plane, by the Associated News Service, dated January 27, 1922 700
Sheet Music, *The Air Ship Waltz,* dated 1891 160
Souvenir Plate, Glenn Curtiss, c1910 400
Souvenir Spoon, commemorating Count von Zeppelin's historic flight, Aug 4, 1908, boxed 350
Timetable, Mohawk Airlines, 1954 10
Timetable, Northwest Airlines, Apr 30, 1978 2
Travel Bag, Air New Zealand, teal, white trim and piping, metal zipper, 1970s 10
Trophy, silver cup for the "2nd Annual Seaplane Convention," 1927 575
Trophy, silver cup for the "Rhode Island Aerial Pageant," October 1927 250
Uniform Patch, TWA, embroidered cloth, tan and red logo on white ground, 3" w 4

AKRO AGATE

When the Akro Agate Co., was founded in 1911, its principal product was marbles. The company was forced to diversify during the 1930s, developing floral-ware lines and children's dishes. Some collectors specialize in containers made by Akro Agate for the cosmetic industry.

Akro Agate merchandised many of its products as sets. Full sets that retain their original packaging command a premium price. Learn what pieces and colors constitute a set. Some dealers will mix and match pieces into a false set, hoping to get a better price.

Most Akro Agate pieces are marked "Made in USA" and have a mold number. Some, but not all, have a small crow flying through an "A" as a mark.

Club: Akro Agate Collector's Club, Inc., 97 Milford St., Clarksburg, WV 26301.

Bowl, #321, lemonade and oxblood marbleized, tab handles, 9" w handle to handle 30
Children's Dishes, Interior 18 Panel, 4 pcs, two 2.5" d saucers, creamer 1.25" h, tumbler 2" h 25
Children's Dishes, Stacked Disk, 16 pcs . .60
Children's Dishes, Stippled Band, 7 pcs, transparent green, 2 plates, 1 saucer, 2 cups, and cov teapot 15
Child's Creamer, Chiquita, cobalt 9
Child's Creamer, Interior Panel, opaque blue, large 40
Child's Cup, Concentric Ring, lavender, 1" h, 2" d 60
Child's Cup, transparent cobalt 14
Child's Cup and Saucer, green 50
Child's Demitasse Cup, J Pressman, green 8
Child's Demitasse Cup, J Pressman, pink 25
Child's Demitasse Cup and Saucer, J Pressman, green 8
Child's Dinner Plate, opaque green 8
Child's Pitcher and Cup, Stippled Band, 2.5" h pitcher, 1.25" h cup 10
Child's Plate, Concentric Rib, opaque green 3
Child's Plate, Interior Panel, opaque green, large 7
Child's Plate, Interior Panel, opaque green, small 6
Child's Plate, J Pressman, green 5
Child's Saucer, opaque yellow 12
Child's Teapot, Interior Panel, opaque green, large 55
Child's Teapot, marbleized blue, 2.5" h 8

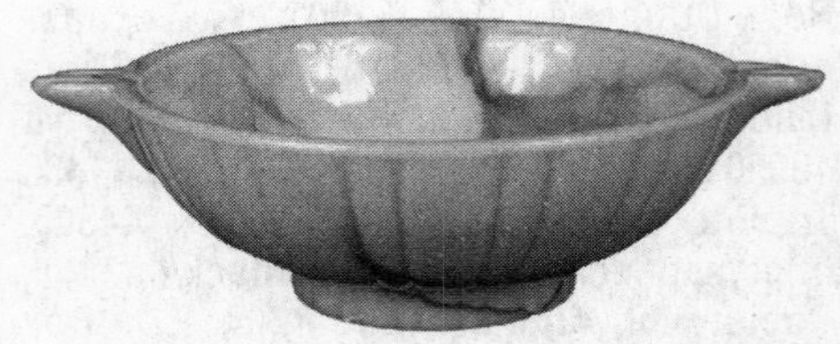

Child's Tea Set, 15 pcs, Gypsy, #234, octagonal, orig box, 1930s, ...100
Child's Tea Set, 15 pcs, Little American Maid, #360, octagonal, orig box, 1930s 160
Child's Tumbler, octagonal, yellow, 2" h ...10
Child's Water Pitcher, Stacked Disk, opaque green, small 10
Cigarette Holder, cobalt blue, 2.75" h 7
Cornucopia Vase, red, white, and blue, #7657 15
Demitasse Cup and Saucer, jadeite green 10
Dresser Jar, Colonial Lady, opaque white 45
Flowerpot, Ribbed Top, ivory, #292, 2.25" h 3
Flowerpot, Stacked Disc, 5" h, 5.75" d 20
Jar, brown and white, emb sleeping Mexican and cactus scene, sombrero shaped lid, 4.5" h, 3.5" d 30
Jardiniere, grayish blue, white, and dark blue swirl, #306, scalloped top 275
Lamp, urn shaped, jadeite and caramel ..50
Marble, oxblood swirl, .675" d 10
Planter, oval, ivory, #654, 6" d 8
Planter, rect, milk glass, #656, 6" l 5
Powder Box, Colonial Lady 50
Teacup, Stippled Band, transparent green 7
Toothpick Holder, slag, 2.25" h 4
Vase, marbleized, daffodil dec on both sides, 4.5" h 8
Vase, yellow and white, Art Deco style, 8.5" h 100

ALADDIN

The Mantle Lamp Co., of America, founded in 1908 in Chicago, is best known for its lamps. However, in the late 1950s through the 1970s, it also was one of the leading producers of character lunch boxes.

Aladdin deserves a separate category because of the large number of lamp collectors who concentrate almost exclusively on this one company. There is almost as big a market for parts and accessories as for the lamps themselves. Collectors are constantly looking for parts to restore lamps in their possession.

Club: The Aladdin Knights, 3935 Kelley Rd., Kevil, KY 42053, www.aladdinknights.org.

Note: All kerosene lamps are priced with complete burners.

Abacus Lamp, electric, M-476 60
Desk Lamp, electric, M-238, plastic shade 75
Floor Lamp, kerosene, B-293, Model B, antique ivory lacquer 225
Floor Lamp, kerosene, B-294, Model B, bronze and gold lacquer 250
Hanging Lamp, kerosene, Model 23, aluminum hanger and font, with white paper shade 75
Planter Lamp, electric, G-349, alacite ...150
Planter Lamp, electric, P-408 100
Table Lamp, electric, G-2, marble-like glass 350
Table Lamp, electric, G-141, moonstone ..80
Table Lamp, electric, ivory alacite mounted on cast metal antiqued gold base, fluted whip-o-lite shades, alacite scrolled finials, 23" h, price for pr 300
Table Lamp, electric, M-1, metal, bronze 150
Table Lamp, kerosene, 102, Model A, Venetian, peach 250
Table Lamp, kerosene, 107, Model B, Cathedral, clear crystal 150
Table Lamp, kerosene, B-30, Model B, Simplicity, white 175
Table Lamp, kerosene, B-40, Model B, Washington Drape, green crystal, round base, 1939 125

Table Lamp, kerosene, B-60, Model B, alacite 600
Table Lamp, kerosene, B-86, Model B, Quilt, green moonstone 350
Table Lamp, kerosene, B-122, Model B, Majestic, green moonstone 450
Table Lamp, kerosene, B-131, Model B, Oriental, green 200
Table Lamp, kerosene, B-139, Model C, aluminum font 50

ALUMINUM, HAND-WROUGHT

Most aluminumware was sold on the giftware market as decorative accessories. Do not be confused by the term "hand-wrought." The vast majority of the pieces were mass-produced. The two collecting keys are manufacturer and uniqueness of form.

Clubs: Hammered Aluminum Collectors Assoc., P.O. Box 1346, Weatherford, TX 76086; Hand and Hammer Collectors Club, 2610 Morse Ln., Woodbridge, VA 22192.

Bowl, cov, Buenilum 18
Box, Sailboat, Wendell August 50
Brooch, Bittersweet, Wendell August 30
Casserole, cascading flower stem and flowers ftd, Farberware 28
Casserole, Daisy band, Everlast 20
Casserole, Peapod, small, Everlast 25
Casserole, Rose and Forget-Me-Not, Everlast 30
Chafing Dish, Buenilum, small 15
Coasters, Daisy, Everlast 7
Coaster Set, 6 coasters and holder, Everlast 20
Coffee Set, urn, sugar, and creamer, Continental 175

Crumb Tray and Brush, Rodney Kent 5
Dresser Set, Rodney Kent 30
Ice Bucket, Buenilum 18
Ice Bucket, Mum, #504, stylized leaf handles 65
Letter Holder, Dogwood, Wendell August 30
Pitcher, Mum, Continental 15
Pitcher, plain, Everlast 30
Silent Butler, Canterbury Arts, unmkd 20
Silent Butler, Ivy, Everlast 15
Silent Butler, rect, Rodney Kent 5
Tray, #631, flower shape with daisies, Continental 12
Tray, #891, Water Lily, Wendell August 20

AMERICAN BISQUE

The American Bisque Company, founded in Williamstown, West Virginia, in 1919, was originally established for the manufacture of china head dolls. Early on the company expanded its product line to include novelties such as cookie jars and ashtrays, serving dishes, and ceramic giftware.

B. E. Allen, founder of the Sterling China Company, invested heavily in the company and eventually purchased the remaining stock. In 1982 the company changed hands, operating briefly under the name American China Company. The plant ceased operations in 1983.

American Bisque items have various markings. The trademark "Sequoia Ware" is often found on items sold in gift shops. The Berkeley trademark was used on pieces sold through chain stores. The most common mark found consists of three stacked baby blocks with the letters A, B, and C.

Bank, Casper the Friendly Ghost, 8.5" 225
Bank, pig, wearing jacket and bowtie, 5.25" 15
Cookie Jar, bell, "Ring For Cookies," 10" h 77
Cookie Jar, bunny in hat, 12.25" h 50
Cookie Jar, school bus, "After School Cookies," 11" h 110
Cookie Jar, space ship, "Cookies Out Of This World," 10.25" h 300

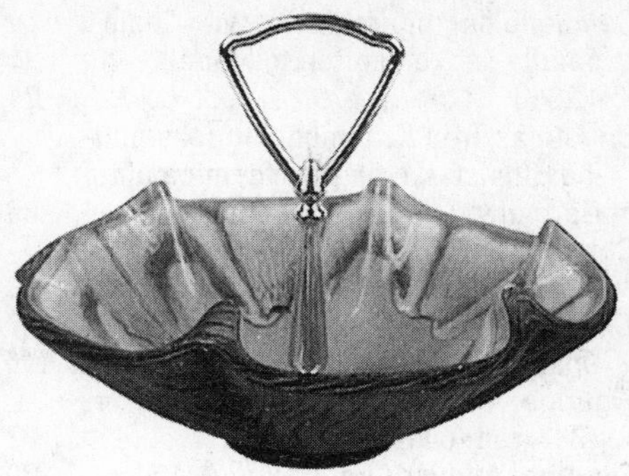

Cookie Jar, strawberry, 8.75" h 25
Creamer, pig, 5" 12
Nappy, Seuqoia pattern, #610, 7" d 4
Planter, circus elephant, pink and blue, 5.5" 8
Planter, circus horse, 7" 16
Planter, Cocker Spaniel and basket, 5.75" 12
Planter, Davy Crockett canoe, 2.75" x 8.25" 30
Planter, flying duck, 4.5" 10
Planter, kitten and shoe, blue, 3.5" x 6.5" ..10
Planter, smiling fish, pink and blue, 4.75" ..12
Salt and Pepper Shakers, Dumbo, 3.5" 20
Vase, rose, 6.5" 7

AMUSEMENT PARKS

From the park at the end of the trolley line to today's gigantic theme parks such as Six Flags Great Adventure, amusement parks have served many generations. No trip to an amusement park was complete without a souvenir, many of which are now collectible.

Prices are still modest in this collecting field. When an item is returned to the area where the park was located, it often brings a 20% to 50% premium.

Clubs: Historic Amusement Foundation, 4410 N. Keystone Ave., Indianapolis, IN 46205; International Assoc. of Amusement Parks & Attractions, 1448 Duke St., Alexandria, VA 22314; National Amusement Park Historical Assoc., P.O. Box 83, Mount Prospect, IL 60056.

Cow Creamer, "Dorney Park, Allentown, PA" label on side 65
Menu, Coney Island, Feltmans Arcade Restaurant, Schlitz Beer adv, 1943 50
Pinback Button, Atlantic City, "Ye Olde Mill," multicolored, amusemark park ride with people in boats going into and coming out of ride building, early 1900s, 1.25" d 15
Pinback Button, Dorney Park, Alfundo in center, "Dorney Park" above, "Alfundo 85th Year/Allentown, PA" below 16
Pitcher, Coney Island, ruby glass, clear base and handle, inscribed "From Jack to Suzie," 1907, 4.5" h 50
Postcard, Asbury Park, "Station and Park," postmarked Aug 24, 1909 3
Postcard, Coney Island, aerial view of the Half Moon Hotel, boardwalk, and beach 7
Postcard, Coney Island, players on stage at Midget City Opera House at Dreamland, used, 1907 20
Postcard, Dorney Park, Swiss Chalet eatery 5
Postcard, Hershey Park, Hershey Beach Park, swimming pool and bath house, postmarked 1938 3
Refrigerator Magnet, Coney Island, "The Swimming's Fine at Coney Island" 2
Ribbon, Coney Island, double, metal and celluloid top, red, white, and blue top ribbon with disk depicting profile of firefighter, bottom ribbon inscribed "21st Annual Convention N.Y.S.F. Asso'n Coney Island Aug. 15, 16, 17, & 18, 1893," heavy paper Whitehead & Hoag Co paper label on back, 8.25" l, 2.675" w 50

Souvenir Folder, Asbury Park and Ocean Grove, NJ, 18 color fold-out views, unused, 1938 9
Ticket Book, Dorney Park, dated 1968, printed by National Ticket Co, Shamokin, PA 20
Ticket Roll, Chesapeake Beach, MD, good for ride on carousel or coaster, 11¢ value 25
Token, Asbury Park 1
Toothpick Holder, Coney Island, ruby-stained pressed glass, Shamrock pattern 40

ANGELS

Angels were flying high in the mid-1990s. Angels and angel collectibles made the cover of Time and were the subject of a primetime network television series. Some saw it as divine provenance. Others argued it was nothing more than a decorating craze.

There will always be a heavenly chorus of angel collectors, albeit somewhat reduced in size at the moment. Christmas-theme angel collectibles sell well.

Clubs: Angel Collector Club, 14 Parkview Ct., Crystal Lake, IL 60012; Angels Collectors' Club of America, 12225 S. Potomac St., Phoenix, AZ 85044; National Angel Collectors' Club, P.O. Box 1847, Annapolis, MD 21404.

Candleholder, figural angel with "halo" candle socket, Lefton foil label, 4.25" h 24
Christmas Tree Ornament, angel standing atop star, emb plastic, mica glitter, Germany 35
Christmas Tree Ornament, figural angel, plastic, 1950s 3
Christmas Tree Ornament, scrap and tinsel, 1890-1910 15
Figurine, April Angel, Lefton, 4.25" h, #332, red foil label 32
Figurine, August Angel, Napco, 4.5" h 20
Figurine, Dreamsicle Angel Cherub with Kitty, #10343, 2.5" h 22
Planter, angel pulling cart, bisque, 4.75" h, 7" l 20
Planter, angel standing in front of planter box, 1950s, mkd "5B/401," Japan, 5.75" h 35
Platter, Christmas Angel, blue ground, scalloped edge, 9.75" sq 8
Postcard, star above 2 angels, emb, gold highlights, Belgium, used, 1908 5
Salt and Pepper Shakers, ceramic, Japan, 4" h 20
Shelf Sitter, mkd "Made in Japan," 2.75" h 5

ANIMAL FIGURES

Animal collectors are a breed apart. Collecting is a love affair. As long as their favorite animal is pictured or modeled, they are more than willing to buy the item. In many cases, they own real life counterparts to go with their objects. My son's menagerie includes a cat, dog, tarantula, lovebird, two rabbits, a Golden Ball python, and three tanks of tropical fish.

Note: See Breyer Horses and Cat, Cow, Dog, Elephant, Frog, Horse, Owl, Pig, and Turtle Collectibles for additional listings.

CERAMIC

Bird, stylized, frosted orange and brown glaze, Brayton Laguna, 7.75" 40
Colt, blue flambé glaze, American Encaustic Tile Co, mkd "12-201," 10.5" 160
Doe and Fawn, Japan, 3.5" h 10

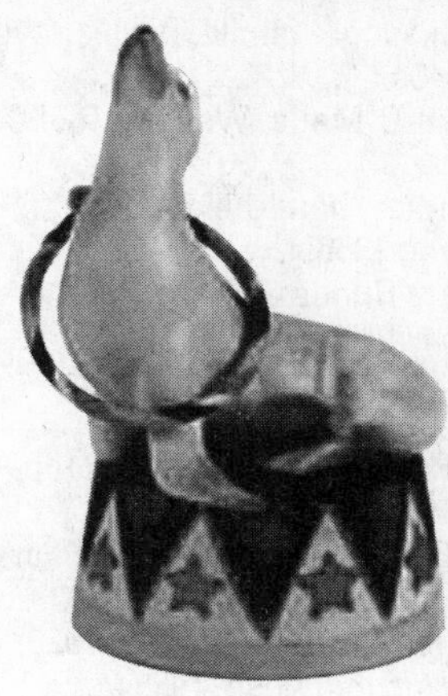

Dog, butterscotch and blue flambé glaze, Fulper, 8" .350
Dove, glossy white with gold highlights, Wayland Gregory script signature, 4.5" .25
Duckling, Cybis, 4" .50
Elephant, raised trunk, flambé glaze, Royal Doulton, 5.5" .175
Elephants, pr, glossy lemon yellow glaze, Volly Wieselthier, General Ceramics, 5.25" .175
Fledgling Kingfisher, Boehm, 6.5" .80
Kitten, white and gray, Boehm, 3.5" .90
Ostrich, *Fantasia* character, #28, Vernon Kilns, 6" .800
Pikin' Frog, frog strumming banjo, mottled glossy green glaze, titled around base, WA Flowers, 10.5" .60
Rooster, brown and ivory, Pennsbury, 12" .85
Rooster, salt-glazed, Billy Ray Hussey, incised "BH/32," 8.5" .100
Seal, multicolor, Cybis, 5.25" .140

GLASS

Baby Elephant, crystal, Swarovski, 1.25" .150
Barnyard Rooster, black, Dalzell/Viking (Paden City) .375
Bird, blue, Paden City, 5" .125
Cat, custard satin glass, #5165, Fenton .15
Centenary Swan, crystal, with stand, Swarovski, 2" h .150
Chanticleer, blue, Paden City .150
Circus Seal, ball on nose, New Martinsville, 7" .75
Dolphin, crystal, Heisey, 3-ftd .50
Dolphin, crystal, Swarovski .210
Elephant, green, Co-Operative Flint .125
German Shepherd, New Martinsville .55
Giraffe, crystal, Heisey .275
Goose, wings up, Haley Glass .125
Mice, 2 mice in shoe, mkd "Made in Japan," 3.5" l, 2.5" h .18
Pelican, New Martinsville .65
Plug Horse, crystal, Haley Glass .115
Rabbit, white milk glass, Imperial .20
Rooster, New Martinsville .60
Roosters, pr, Japan, 5.5" and 7" h .30
Sparrow, crystal, Heisey .100

APPLIANCES, ELECTRICAL

Nothing illustrates our ability to take a relatively simple task—e.g., toast a piece of bread—and create a wealth of different methods for achieving it quite like a toaster. Electrical appliances are viewed as one of the best documents of stylistic design in utilitarian form.

Collectors tend to concentrate on one form. Toasters are the most commonly collected, largely because several books have been written about them. Electric fans have a strong following. Waffle irons are pressing toasters for popularity. Modernistic collectors seek bar drink blenders from the 1930s through the 1950s.

Clubs: Old Appliance Club, P.O. Box 65, Ventura, CA 93002; Porcelier Collectors Club, 21 Tamarac Swamp Rd., Wallingford, CT 06492; Upper Crust: The Toaster Collectors Assoc., P.O. Box 529, Temecula, CA 92593.

Blender, white base, Kenmore by Sears, 1950s .30
Broiler, chrome, Manning Bowman, 1940 .30
Can Opener, pink and chrome body, Udico Electric Co, 1960 .40
Coffeepot, Coffeemaker, immersible, Presto, 1970 .15
Coffeepot, Coffeemaster, 2-tier, Sunbeam, 1940s .45
Coffeepot, Flavo Matic, silo shaped, colored aluminum, 1950s .35

Coffeepot, Porcelier Porcelain, #5007, wildflower decal on basketweave body, 13" h 60

Coffeepot, urn shaped, chromium on brass, Forman Family, 1920s 25

Cooker/Roaster, Dominion, attached cord, 1950s 35

Cooker/Roaster, Sunbeam, 1952 40

Crock Pot, avocado body, mushroom designs, Rival, 1970s 20

Deep Fryer, Fri-Well, Dormeyer, 1952 35

Defroster, adonized aluminum, wood handle, Shane Mfg Co, 1950s 10

Defroster, aluminum, plastic handle, Nu-Rod, 1960s 10

Egg Cooker, 4 pcs, plastic space age body, Westinghouse, 1950s 35

Egg Cooker, 4 pcs, Sunbeam, 1951 25

Food Processor, Little Pro, Cuisinart, 1980s 10

Frypan, colored aluminum, Century Enterprises, 1950s 50

Frypan, Controlled heat Automatic Frypan, Sunbeam, 1955 20

Frypan, electric skillet, glass top, turquoise base, GE, 1950s 50

Hot Plate, Automatic Heat-Rite Base, Sears, 1960s 10

Hot Plate, Buffet Queen, 2 burners, Bakelite handles, Cory Corp, 1940s 15

Hot Plate, Signature, white, chrome top, Montgomery Ward, 1940s 20

Hot Plate, Two Heater Electric Stove, Bakelite handle, Cory Corp, 1940s 10

Hot Plate, white porcelain enamel, Samson United Corp, 1950s 15

Iron, Royal, wood handle, Brock Snyder Mfg, 1940s 20

Iron, Steam-O-Matic, Waverly Tool Co, 1920s 20

Mixer, Dormey, hand-held model, Dormeyer, 1950s 10

Mixer, Mary Dunbar Handymix, Chicago Electric Mfg, 1930s 25

Mixer, Mixmaster, pink, Sunbeam, 1950s 80

Popcorn Popper, Fostoria, glass top, McGraw Electric Co, 1940s 15

Popcorn Popper, red and tan with crank, US Mfg Co, 1940s 20

Roaster, Heet-Wel, Welco Inc, 1930s 40

Roaster, Westinghouse, 1950s 40

Sandwich Grill, Samson, plain wood handles, Samson United Co, 1930s 45

Toaster, chrome and pink plastic body, GE, 1950s 50

Toaster, Fostoria, McGraw Electric Co, 1950s 35

Toaster, Model T-9, Sunbeam, 1940s 50

Toaster, Toast-O-Lator, Toastolator Co, 1930s 125

Waffle Iron, black Bakelite handles, Westinghouse, 1950s 30

Waffle Iron, chrome, white Bakelite handles, Manning Bowman & Co, 1924 50

Waffle Iron, White Cross, National Stamping and Electric Works, 1930s . . . 40

ART DECO

The famous 1925 Paris "Exposition Internationale des Arts Décoratifs Industriels Modernes" marked the culmination, not the beginning of the Art Deco movement. All the elements of the design style were in place by 1920.

The essential design elements are bold, simplistic geometric shapes based on traditional forms. Ornamentation is greatly simplified, surfaces are smooth, angles are crisp, and curves, when used, are highly controlled. Colors were bold and basic, often used in sharp contrast to one another. Themes were borrowed from ancient cultures such as Aztec, Egyptian, Japanese, Mayan, and sub-Saharan Africa.

Art Deco has a strong feminine quality, stressing luxury and refinement. It found a ready home in the bedroom (boudoir) and living room (parlor). Its American influence was strongest in architecture, jewelry, and Hollywood movies.

Many individuals use Art Deco to describe a wide range of design trends occurring between 1910 and 1940. This is a major mistake. Art Deco is at the periphery of the main evolutionary design style of the period, Modernism. It is modernism, particularly streamlined modern, that continued and expanded upon the design style advances of the Arts and Crafts movement.

Armchair, channeled fan back, fully reupholstered in pink and blue tapestry fabric, on laminated wood frame, 36" x 37" x 34" 115
Ceiling Fixture, aluminum, spherical, recessed, milk and clear glass lense, stamped "10-15-57," Henry Dreyfuss for Luminator/20th Century Limited," 8.5" d, price for pr 500
Ceiling Fixture, brushed aluminum, 3 flaring sections to shade, unmkd, 26" x 28" 115
Chaise Lounge, scalloped, channeled back, reupholstered in pastel tapestry, on large gilded ball feet, unmkd, 46" x 71" x 36" 150
Clutch Bag, tapestry in red, orange, and yellow geometric designs, repouse latch clasp and chain handle, 7" x 7" . . .50
Cocktail Shaker, silver-plated brass, Napier Co, Meriden, CT, 12" h 1,150
Coffee and Tea Service, pewter, bulbous teapot, coffeepot, sugar bowl and creamer, triangular finials and wrapped handles, stamped mark, Reed & Barton, 10" x 8.5" coffeepot 90
Coffeepot and Teapot, pewter, ebonized handle and finial, script mark "221," Lumning, 9 x 7.75" coffeepot, 6.25" x 8.5" teapot 100
Coffee Table, mahogany, circular top, bentwood legs, Watkins Bros tag, 19" x 28.25" 250
Compact, chrome, enameled blue stylized woman's face, orig silk applicators, Richard Hudnut, 2.25" d . . .60

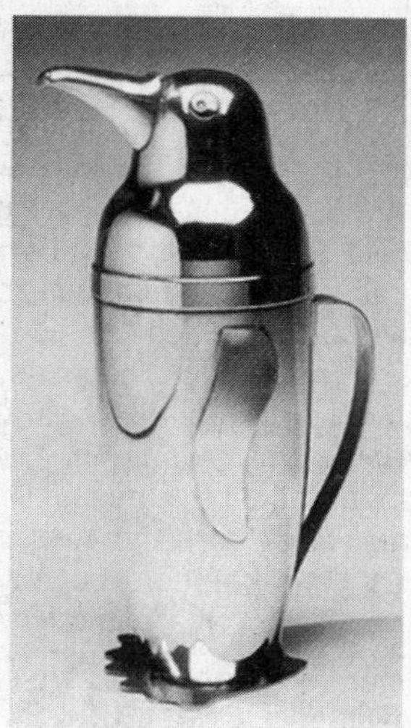

Compact, chrome, enameled red and black, with silk tassel, 3.75" x 2" 60
Desk Clock, chrome, circular crystal face and stepped base, Lux, 4.5" h 100
Desk Lamp, aluminum, Bakelite, and wood, tubular frame and rect base, Stanley Matthews, unmkd, 10" x 17" . . .400
Double Candleholders, pr, chrome, U-shaped tubular branch on ribbed circular base, Chase, 9.75" x 8.5" 225
Espresso Machine, brass, black Bakelite handle, stamped "Made in Italy," c1930, 12" x 7.5" .300
Floor Lamp, brushed chrome, tubular shaft, white plastic cylindrical shade, Von Nessen, 51 x 15" 225
Lamp Base, French, stylized buds and leaves in blue, brown, and green on mottled yellow ground, unmkd, 24" h . .175
Table Lamp, boomerang shaped, bright chrome stand with adjustable black enameled cylindrical shade, paper label, mkd "Made In Italy/Arredoluce Monza," 10" x 13.5" 625
Tea Set, teapot, creamer and cov sugar, 4 teacups, 6 saucers, and 6 dessert plates, concentric orange and black stripes on cream colored ground, N V De Sphinx and Petrus Regout & Co, Maastricht, Holland, c1925 60
Vase, spherical, black opaque glass, George Sakier for Fostoria, unmkd, 6" x 6.5" 150

ART POTTERY

Art pottery production was at an all-time high during the late 19th and early 20th centuries. At this time over one hundred companies and artisans were producing individually designed and often decorated pottery which served both utilitarian and aesthetic purposes. Artists often moved from company to company, some forming their own firms.

Condition, quality of design, beauty in glazes, and maker are the keys in buying art pottery. This category covers companies not found elsewhere in the guide.

Club: American Art Pottery Assoc., P.O. Box 525, Cedar Hill, MO 63016.

Arne Bang, dish, 3-lobed, 3 small ribbon handles, amber and green crystalline glaze, mkd "AB/206," 9" d 500

Bjorn Winbald, vase, figural woman, wearing bulbous hat, polychrome glazes, ink mkd "Denmark/64" with artist's cipher, 19.5 x 6.75" 225

Chelsea Keramics Art Works, pilgrim flask, flattened spherical body with raised rim, applied scroll handles and feet, glossy streaked blue green and brown glaze, base imp "CKAW," 9" h 625

Clewell, vase, flared rim tapering to bulbous foot, inscribed "Clewell 293-29," 7.75" h .575

Dedham, breakfast plate, Rabbit pattern, blue stamp with imp rabbit, 8.5" d 85

Dedham, breakfast set, bowl, cup and saucer, Duck pattern, 9" d bowl, 2.25" h cup, 6" d saucer 500

Dedham, charger, Rabbit pattern border, mkd "Dedham Pottery" with 2 imp rabbits, 12" d 275

Dedham, mug, rabbit and foliate border, 1968 exhibition mark, 2.75" h 95

Dedham, tea tile, circ Azalea pattern, blue registered mark, 5.5" sq 95

Harding Black, vessel, ovoid, sgraffito dec of X's and ridges on olive green semi-matte ground, incised "Harding Black/1952/DH," 9.5" x 6.5" 450

Harrison McIntosh, bowl, wax-resist, rays of mottled white glaze alternating with blue-green, stamped "HM," paper label, 2.25" x 8.5" 925

John Lessell, vase, possibly designed for Camark Pottery, oviform body, flared rim above tapered neck, stylized trees in landscape, white outlines, matte pearl gray glaze, sgd "Lessell" at side, c1926, 9.75" h 575

Ken Ferguson, bowl, incised abstract nude under gray semi-matte glaze, stamped "F," c1978, 5" x 12" 450

Rorstrand, vase, Gunnar Nylund, cylindrical, emb collared rim, ribbed body, speckled ochre matte glaze, unglazed base, incised "R" with crown mark and "GN," 8.75" x 3" 550

Saxbo, vessel, cylindrical base and corseted neck by E Sonne, terra cotta, celadon and indigo hare's fur matte glaze, stamped "Saxbo/ Denmark/Sonne," 7.5" x 7.25" 500

Scheier, bowl, round, tapering to ftd base, zig-zag dec on matte tan and brown glaze, c1965, 5" h 225

Scheier, vase, oval form body, flared rim on tapered neck, free form brown brush strokes on shaded pink, brown, and tan glaze, 6" h 275

Toshiko Takaezu, vessel, spherical, closed-in rim, gray, brown, and umber dipped glaze, incised "TT," 6" x 5" 550

Van Briggle, chamberstick, owl, electric 325

Van Briggle, compote, lotus leaf 50

ASHTRAYS

Most price guides include ashtrays under advertising. The problem is that there are a number of terrific ashtrays in shapes that have absolutely nothing to do with advertising. Ashtrays get a separate category from me.

With the nonsmoking movement in high gear, the ashtray is an endangered species. The time to collect them is now.

Advertising, Champion, ceramic Champion Ford plug in center, "Champion Sill – Manite" stamped on bottom, 3.5" h, 5" d 125
Advertising, Coca-Cola, ruby glass, set of 4 card suits (spade, heart, diamond, and club), orig box, 1950s . . .600
Advertising, Hamm's Beer, ceramic, figural Hamm's Bear wearing sign around his neck "Have a Hamm's" 95
Advertising, Phillips 66, rubber tire with glass insert, "Miller's Super Service Oakland, Iowa" on insert, "Phillips 66, Farm Service Deep Cleat" on tire, orig box, 6.5" d 130
Boomerang, ceramic, red speckled, small boomerang center design, c1950s, 12.5" l 15
Commemorative, Apollo XVII, ceramic, center full color image of emblem for lunar landing Dec 7-19, 1972, 5.5" d 10
Christmas Tree, ceramic, Holt-Howard 2
Collie, ceramic, Japan, 5.5" d 3
Donkey and Cart, ceramic, Japan, 4.5" h . . .4
Ducks, Royal Windsor, Royal Copley, 4.5" x 2.5" 8
Dutch Shoes, pr, Delft Porcelain, orig box, 1950s, 2" h, 5.25" l, 2.25" w 5
Genies, pr, chalkware, seated male and female, painted black, pink, and gold, circular depression between legs holds glass insert, 1940s 40
Oakland Raiders, ceramic, white, silver and black helmet in center, gold trim, 4.5" d 8
Oblong, gold tweed, mkd "Royal Haeger ©149-USA," 1967, 13" l 15
Occupied Japan, porcelain, emb floral dec, mkd, 2.75" d 2
Scottie Dog, pressed glass, frosted, 2.5" d 3

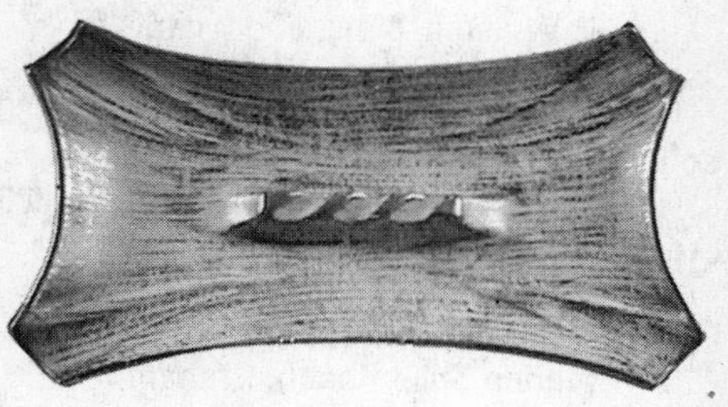

Souvenir, glass, "Duluth Minnesota," boat and lake scene, felt bottom, set of 4 in orig box, 3" d 5
Stacking, porcelain, Chintz pattern, set of 4 in holder, 4.5" w 15
Stacking, porcelain, elephant dec, Occupied Japan, set of 4, 3" x 2.25" 20

AUTOGRAPHS

Collecting autographs is a centuries' old hobby. A good rule to follow is the more recognizable the person, the more likely the autograph is to have value. Content is a big factor in valuing autograph material. A clipped signature is worth far less than a lengthy handwritten document by the same person.

Before spending big money for an autograph, have it authenticated. Many movie and sports stars have secretaries and other individuals sign their material, especially photographs. An "autopen" is a machine that can sign up to a dozen documents at one time. The best proof that a signature is authentic is to get it from the person who stood and watched the celebrity sign it.

Clubs: The Manuscript Society, 350 N. Niagra St., Burbank, CA 95105; Universal Autograph Collectors Club, P.O. Box 6181, Washington, DC 20044, www.uacc.org.

Barnum, PT, sgd letter to his tailor, dated Jan 8, 1865 690
Bryant, Paul "Bear," color photo, 8" x 10" 70
Capote, Truman, first ed book *Local Color*, dated Mar 27, 1952 400
Christie, Agatha, sgd letter, 1 pg, dated Sep 15, 1958 300

Churchill, Winston, black and white photo, sgd and dated "1946" on mat below image, 10" x 8" 3,000

Cobb, Ty, photo, wearing cuffed 3-pc suit, c1910, 4.75" x 6.5" 500

Crosby, Stills, Nash and Young, Fender Stratocaster electric guitar, sgd "David Crosby; Neil Young; Carry On, Stephen Stills; Teach, Graham Nash" 1,600

Cummings, EE, postcard, sgd "E. E. C.," dated Jul 9, 1964 175

Dr Seuss, color poster "And to Think That I Saw it on Mulberry Street," 18" x 14", matted and framed 375

Edison, Thomas, card, 1.75" x 3.5" 400

Gorbachev, Mikhail, color photo of Gorbachev hugging Reagan outside White House, 7.75" x 10" 350

Lennon, John, sgd in red felt pen on reverse of WFIL radio station competition form, matted with color xerox of obverse of form and WFIL "Helping Hand Marathon" handbill, 1975, framed, 20" x 16" 2,000

Lindbergh, Charles, unsgd note regarding a request for Air Force photos, 1 pg 200

Mack, Connie, sgd letter to aspiring minor league baseball player, 1 pg, dated Jan 28, 1936 345

Morse, Samuel, clipped signature on .75" x 3" sheet, mounted on larger card 225

Nightingale, Florence, clipped signature on 1.5" x 3" sheet, mounted on larger card 375

Nixon, Richard, program from 1957 Gala Inaugural Concert, sgd on front cov, with printed invitation to concert, dated Jan 20, 1957 200

Paige, Satchel, baseball, with letter of authenticity 550

Remington, Frederic, sgd card, 1.5" x 3" . .225

Ryan, Nolan, baseball, 300th win game ball, dated Aug 31, 1990, with letter of authenticity 1,200

Truman, Bess, sgd letter as First Lady, dated Oct 25, 1949 125

AUTOMOBILE COLLECTIBLES

An automobile swap meet is 25% cars and 75% car parts. Restoration and rebuilding of virtually all car models is a never-ending process. The key is to find the exact part needed. Too often, auto parts at flea markets are not priced. The seller is going to judge how badly he thinks you want the part before setting the price. You have to keep your cool.

Two areas that are attracting outside collector interest are promotional toy models and hood ornaments. The former have been caught up in the craze for 1950s and 1960s Japanese tin. The latter have been discovered by the art community, who view them as wonderful examples of modern streamlined design.

Clubs: Hubcap Collectors Club, P.O. Box 54, Buckley, MI 49620; Spark Plug Collectors of America, 14018 NE 85th St., Elk River, MN.

Note: See License Plates and Road Maps for additional listings.

Advertising Display, hanging mobile, die-cut cardboard, Sinclair, separate hangers in shapes of oil can, car chassis, tire, battery charger, and antifreeze can, 48" h, 28" w 225

Battery Charger, MoPar Trickle, metal, Chrysler Corp, 9" h, 4" w 65

Calendar, Stutz Bearcat, paper in wood frame, yellow roadster image, Brown and Bigelow, with Hawkinson Treads and Mohawk Tires adv, 1966, 26" h 18

Car Jack, Cadillac, Buckeye Jack Mfg Co, Alliance, OH, Cadillac logo on side, 11.5" h 60
Motor Oil Can, Star Aero-Flo, metal, white roadster and lettering on red ground, 2 gal, 11.25" h, 8.5" w 15
Print, 1930 Alfa-Romeo, paper in wood frame, 14" h, 18" w 15
Print, Unic Automobiles, paper in wood frame, centaur mascot rising from open convertible, 35.75" h, 26.75" w . . .150
Radiator Ornament, Art Deco lion's head with flowing mane, chrome-plated metal, 9" l 10
Showroom Sign, 1963 Chevrolet Impala Convertibles, cardboard, mounted in newer metal frame, 20.5" h, 34.5" w 40
Sign, Ford emblem, pressed wood, 20.75" h, 19" w 475
Sign, United Motors Service, light-up, metal and plastic, oval with automobile silhouette in center, 15.75" h, 25.25" w, NOS 2,200
Thermos Bottle, Esso, tin litho ext, glass int and plastic lid, trademark "Happy" character at various locations on US map, "Happy Motoring," 9.25" h 18

AUTO RACING

Man's quest for speed is as old as time. Automobile racing dates before the turn of the century. Many of the earliest races took place in Europe. By the first decade of the 20th century, automobile racing was part of the American scene.

The Indianapolis 500 began in 1911 and was interrupted only by World War II. In addition to Formula 1 racing, the NASCAR circuit has achieved tremendous popularity with American racing fans. Cult heroes such as Richard Petty have become household names.

Although interest in Indy 500 collectibles remains strong, the current market is dominated by NASCAR collectibles. Beware of paying premium prices for items made within the last 20 years. In addition, copycat, fantasy, and contemporary limited edition items are being introduced into the market as quickly as they can be absorbed. A shake-out appears to be years in the future. In the interim, check your engine and gear up for fast action.

Clubs: Auto Racing Memories, P.O. Box 12226, St. Petersburg, FL 33733; National Indy 500 Collectors Club, 10505 N. Delaware St., Indianapolis, IN 46280; The National Racing Club, 615 Hwy. A1A North, Ste. 105, Ponte Vedra Beach, FL 32082.

Autograph, Mario Andretti, photo 20
Avon Bottle, Stock Car Racer, Wild Country After Shave 12
Bobbing Head, Bill Elliott, Sports, Accessories and Memorabilia, Inc., 8" h 40
Collector Plate, Jeff Gordon, 6.5" d 30
Comic Book, Legends of Nascar, #7, Junior Johnson, Vortex Comics 4
Figure, Sterling Marlin, Racing Champions, 1991 .8
Game, NASCAR Daytona 500, Milton Bradley, 1990 20
Magazine, *Racing Pictorial,* Spring 1973 30
Magazine, *Sports Illustrated,* May 25, 1959, Indy 500 cars 10
Medallion, Ken Schrader, Mint Collectibles of Racing 35
Model Kit, 1930 Ford Yellow Jacket, #PC-76, 1962, MIB 75
Model Kit, 1989 Pontiac #42, Kyle Petty, Monogram, 1/24 scale 35

Pennant, "Souvenir of Indianapolis Speedway," felt, burgundy with yellow strip and streamers, 11.75" h, 30" w 45
Program, Indianapolis 500, May 30, 1953 20
Thermometer, Bobby Labonte, T-Series Racing Plaques, Inc 20
Toy, Hot Wheels Race Ace, No. 2620, die-cast metal, white, Mattel, 1986 20
Toy, race car, cast iron, nickel-plated driver, Hubley, 1960s, 4.75" l 60
Toy, race car, No. 3, litho tin wind-up, 6.5" 150
Toy, race car, rubber, Auburn, 1930s, 6" l 25

AUTUMN LEAF

The Hall China Co. developed Autumn Leaf china as a dinnerware premium for the Jewel Tea Co. in 1933. The giveaway was extremely successful. The "Autumn Leaf" name did not originate until 1960. Previously, the pattern was simply known as "Jewel" or "Autumn." Autumn Leaf remained in production until 1978.

Pieces were added and dropped from the line over the years. Limited production pieces are most desirable. Look for matching accessories in glass, metal and plastic made by other companies. Jewel Tea toy trucks were also made.

Club: National Autumn Leaf Collectors' Club, 62200 E. 236 Rd., Wyandotte, OK 74370.

Ball Jug, 7" h 30
Bowl, oval 30
Bowl, round, 9" d 25

Cake Plate, 9.5" d 20
Casserole, cov, round, 2-qt, 9" d 30
Coffeepot, 10" h 45
Creamer and Sugar Set, Rayed 35
Creamer, Sugar, and Cov Drip Jar, ruffled-D 45
Dish, cov, oval, 11.5" l, 6" w 55
Drip Coffeepot, china, 10.5" h 250
Drip Coffeepot, china and aluminum, 13" h 45
French Baker, fluted, 3-part 35
Gravy Boat, with underplate, 9" l 40
Irish Mugs, 6" h 40
Marmalade, cov, with 6" underplate 80
Mixing Bowls, nesting set of 3 60
Mustard Jar, cov, with underplate 60
Partial Service, 40 pcs, consisting of 7 dinner plates, 8 luncheon plates, 6 salad plates, 8 bread and butter plates, 3 cereal bowls, and 8 fruit dishes 225
Platter, oval, 11" l, 8.5" w 25
Platter, oval, 14.5" l, 10" w 30
Salad Bowl, 9" d 15
Salt and Pepper Shakers, range size 25
Salt and Pepper Shakers, small, ruffled-D 39
Soup Bowl, flat, 8.5" d 10
Teapot, Aladdin, 11" l 65
Teapot, Rayed, long spout, 8" h 65
Vase, 6" h 160

AVON

Avon products, with the exception of California Perfume Co. material, are not found often at flea markets any longer. The 1970s were the golden age of Avon collectibles. There are still a large number of dedicated collectors, but the legion that fueled the pricing fires of the 1970s has been hard hit by desertions. Avon material today is more likely to be found at garage sales than at flea markets.

Club: National Assoc. of Avon Collectors, Inc., P.O. Box 7006, Kansas City, MO 64113.

1951 Studebaker, Wild Country After Shave, 2 oz, orig box 6
1953 Buick Skylark, Everest After Shave. .10
1964 Ford Mustang, Tai Winds After Shave, orig box 25

Betsy Ross, Sonnet Cologne, July 4, 1976, 4 oz, 5.75" h 9
Bolt, Wild Country, #2214, 2 oz 14
Bride and Groom, pr, white, 7" h 12
Cat on Pillow, white milk glass, 3.25" h 9
Clock, white milk glass, gold cap, Regence Fragrance, 5 oz 5
Curious Kitty, #42399, 2.5 oz 7
Fire Alarm Box, Spicy After Shave, 4 oz, 4.75" h 15
Gay Nineties, 7.5" h 12
Golden Harvest Ear of Corn, hand lotion dispenser. 6
Indian Tepee, orig box 6
King Chess Piece, Oland After Shave, 5 oz, orig box 9
Little Bo Peep, white, Sweet Honesty Cologne, 5.5" h 16
NFL Chicago Bears .16
NFL Dallas Cowboys, Wild Country After Shave 10
Partridge, Somewhere, 5 oz, 4" h, orig box 7
Peacock, Moonwind Cologne 15
Pony Express, Wild Country After Shave, 5 oz, orig box 12
Rooster, white milk glass body, red plastic head, 6" h 9
Rosepoint Bell, blue, Roses, Roses Cologne, 1975, 7" h .6
Side Wheeler, Wild Country After Shave, orig box 6
Snoopy, 5.5" h 5
Strike, bowling pin, Wild Country After Shave, 4 oz, orig box 10
Sure Winner Racing Car, Wild Country After Shave, 5.5 oz, orig box 6
Swan, white milk glass, gold plastic crown cap, 3" h 6
Volkswagen Bug, 4 oz, orig box 6
Winnebago, #32130, 5.5" l, orig box 10

BADGES

Have you ever tried to save a name tag or badge that attaches directly to your clothing or fits into a plastic holder? We are victims of a throwaway society. This is one case in which progress has not been a boon for collectors.

Fortunately, our grandparents and great-grandparents loved to save the membership, convention, parade and other badges that they acquired. The badges' colorful silk and cotton fabric often contained elaborate calligraphic lettering and lithographed scenes in combination with celluloid and/or metal pinbacks and pins. They were badges of honor. They had an almost military quality about them.

Look for badges with attached three-dimensional miniatures. Regional value is a factor. I found a great Emmaus, PA, badge priced at $2 at a flea market in Florida: back home, its value is more than $20.

Borden's Premium, brass bow-shaped bar pin above die-cut plastic charm with emb Elsie the cow image, c1950, 1.5" h 15
Boy Scouts, fabric-cov bar pin above goldtone medallion with emb image of Eisenhower, "War Service 1945 Boy Scout Waste Paper Campaign, General Eisenhower," 1.75" h 20
Brooklyn Assemblyman Campaign, brass hanger bar name frame above ribbon with candidates' names and celluloid photo pinback button, 1930s . .25
Captain America Sentinels of Liberty, brass luster, shield shape, dark blue and red enameled accents, eagle above Captain America image, 1.5" h 500
Connecticut 1960 National Convention GOP, brass bar with dark blue enamel lettering, blue ribbon with die-cut brass state map hanger, 3.5" h 20

Fireman's Celebration, brass rope-twist frame with celluloid insert with fireman image, red, white, and blue ribbons, c1910, 1.25" d frame 20

GAR, die-cut brass, ear of corn hanger above star in circle, "Souvenir 1899, 33rd Nat'l Encampment Philadelphia Sept 4-9-1899," 2.75" h 35

Harrison Centennial Inauguration, silver bars with "Centennial Inauguration" joined by red, white, and blue ribbon, white metal medallion below with Washington image on 1 side, Harrison and Morton jugate on other, 1889 95

Indianapolis 500 Pit Crew, bronze, 1981 . . .40

Inspector Post's Detective Corps, silver luster with black inscription "Detective Post's J.D.C.," 1932-33, 1.5" 25

Junior G Man, die-cut brass, eagle across top, black text, 1930s, 1.5" h 25

New Bedford Semi-Centennial 1847-1897, metal frame hanger with "Committee," red, white, and blue flag ribbon with loop at bottom holding brass medallion with emb whaling ship on front and factory on back, 4.75" h 25

Radio Orphan Annie Decoder, emb brass, 1938, 2" d 50

Tom Mix, goldtone, built-in siren whistle at center, "Sheriff Dobey County, Tom Mix Ralston Straight Shooters," 2.25" h 75

War Service Ship Building, employee badge, steel, convex oval shape, silver colored with black lettering, 2.5" l 60

BAKELITE

This is a great example of a collecting category gone price-mad. Bakelite is a trademark used for a variety of synthetic resins and plastics used to manufacture colorful, inexpensive, ulitarian objects. The key word is inexpensive. That can also be interpreted as cheap. There is nothing cheap about Bakelite collectibles in today's market. Collectors, especially those from large metropolitan areas who consider themselves design-conscious, want Bakelite in whatever form they can find.

Buy a Bakelite piece because you love it. The market has already started to collapse for commonly found material. Can the high-end pieces be far behind?

Bangle Bracelet, multicolor stripes, 1" w 225

Beer Foam Scraper, Schmidt's Beer, adv both sides, 1940s 15

Cigar Holder, Whiz Mfg Co 8

Cuff Links, pr, figural dice, 1930s 25

Dress Clip, apple juice Bakelite reverse carved with 2 swimming goldfish accented with seaweed, reverse-painted detail 90

Electric Fan, Barber/Coleman (Barcol), airplane-style aluminum blade and guard, off-center motor, 1920-30s 30

Ice Tongs, Bakelite handles 12

Napkin Ring, yellow, elephant with green eyes balancing green ball on its head, 3" d, 2.25" w 50

Pin, bunch of currants, translucent carved green leaves above cluster of dark butterscotch currants, 2.75" h 275
Pin, Mexican man, butterscotch, bone, red, and green, painted details, 4" h . . .450
Pin, swimsuit-clad blonde under palm tree, translucent green, painted details, 2.5" h 500
Pocketknife, figural lady's shoe, 2" l 25
Radio, Fada 454, table-top model, Z-shaped grill, 1938 65

BANDANNAS

Women associate bandannas with keeping their hair in place. Men visualize stage coach holdups or rags used to wipe the sweat from their brows. Neither approach recognizes the colorful and decorative role played by the bandanna.

Some of the earliest bandannas are political. By the turn of the century, bandannas joined pillow cases as the leading souvenir textile found at sites, ranging from beaches to museums. Hillary Weiss's *The American Bandanna: Culture on Cloth from George Washington to Elvis* (Chronicle Books, 1990), provides a visual feast for this highly neglected collecting area.

The bandanna played an important role in the Scouting movement, serving as a neckerchief for both Boy Scouts and Girl Scouts. Many special neckerchiefs were issued. There is also a close correlation between scarves and bandannas. Bandanna collectors tend to collect both.

Benjamin Harrison, white muslin, printed red and blue patriotic themes border, eagle and shield design and campaign slogan "Tippecanoe And Morton Too" in center, 1888 90
Buffalo Bill, silk, Buffalo Bill portrait in corner, Indian designs around edges, c1910s, 27" x 28.5" 350
Buster Brown, multicolor printed cotton, Tige in center above signature "R.F. Outcault" and surrounded by text "Buster Brown At The Zoo, Permission N.Y. Herald.," 5 captioned scenes with Buster, Tige and zoo animals along sides, c1905, 12.75" sq 200
Farm Aid, white printing on navy blue ground, "Farm Aid – Keep America Growing!, Merle Haggard and George Dickel, Tennessee Sippin' Whiskey, ©1987," 21" sq 12
Goofy, multicolor image of Goofy on paint-spattered ground, "Goofy" in corners, mkd "The Walt Disney Company. Made by J.A. Woronowicz, S. River, NJ," polyester and cotton, 22" sq 12
Lone Ranger, images of Lone Ranger on Silver, shot gun, and lasso, "The Lone Ranger, Hi-Yo Silver!," corral fence bordered ground, Cheerios premium, 21.5" x 22.5" 18
Monkees, black and white, images of band members' faces and names and "Monkees" guitar logos, ©1967 Robert Productions, Inc 18
Rodeo motif, multicolor on yellow ground, 34" sq 25
Roy Rogers, images of Roy on Trigger, corral fence, and vignette portraits of Roy and Trigger, inscribed "King of the Cowboys" and "Many Happy Trails Roy Rogers & Trigger," yellow ground with red border, frayed corners 50
St John's Ambulance, images of wounded man and text detailing bandanna's uses for treating wounds, muslin, c1900, 58" x 38" 25
Tampa Bay Buccaneers, white "X" with Bucco Bruce image at center and "Buccaneers" along each side, orange ground 14

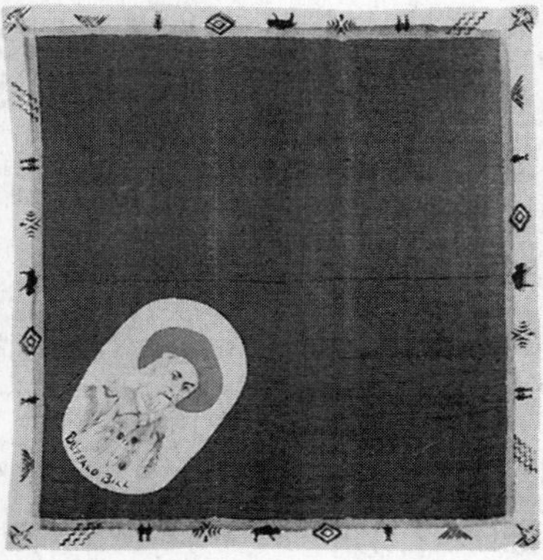

Tom Mix, image of Tom Mix on horse, "Best Wishes Tom Mix," 1920s, 15.75" x 17" 135

Woodrow Wilson, cotton, center portrait surrounded by double border of 48 state seals and eagles at corners, multicolor on white ground, c1916, 16.5" x 17" 85

BANKS

Banks are classified into two types—mechanical (action) and still (non-action). Most mechanical banks found at flea markets today are reproductions. If you find one that you think is real, check it out in one of the mechanical bank books before buying it.

The still or non-action bank dominates the flea market scene. There is no limit to the methods for collecting still banks. Some favor type (advertising), others composition (cast iron, tin, plastic, etc.), figural (shaped like something) or theme (Western).

Beware of still-bank reproductions. Most banks were used, so look for wear in places you would expect to find it. Save your money and do not buy if you are uncertain of a bank's authenticity.

Club: Still Bank Collectors Club of America, 4175 Millersville Rd., Indianapolis, IN 46205.

ADVERTISING

Atlantic, litho tin, figural oil barrel, 3.5" h, 2.5" d 30

Autocrat Coffee, litho tin canister, "Brownell and Field Co, Providence, R.I.," 2.25" h, 2.5" d 35

Aylmer Cream of Corn Soup, litho tin canister, 4" h, 2.5" d 20

Bab-o Cleaner, waxed cardboard canister with litho paper label and tin top and bottom, nursery rhyme Jack and Jill at the well, front says "Bab-o for Enamel and Porcelain/ B.T. Babbitt, Inc.," 3" h, 2" d 30

Biullups Premium, litho tin, figural gas pump, 4" h, 2.25" w, 1.75" d 65

Bosco Chocolate Malt Flavor, litho tin round can, cartoons on sides, 3" h 80

Calumet Baking Powder, waxed cardboard canister, tin top and bottom and litho tin topper stand-up character that slides in slot on top next to coin slot, mkd "Calumet Baking Powder Co. Chicago, U.S.A.," 4" h, 2.5" d 70

Canny Cook Thrift, litho tin canister, "National Canners Association Washington D.C.," shows little mechanical men stirring ingredients in bowls, 4" h, 2.5" d 25

HyGrade's Ham, litho tin figural canned ham, older style tab and key attached to open, 6" h, 4" w, 2.5" d 40

John Deere, litho tin canister, "John Deere Centennial 1837–1937" with plow logo on sides, 3.5" h, 2" d 110

Kendall Outboard Motor Oil, litho tin canister, "Kendall Refining Co. Bradford, PA" bottom back, 3.5" h, 2.5" d 45

Monarch Paint, litho tin, "The Martin Senour Co. Pioneers of Pure Paint," 2.25" h, 2" d 30

Northeastern Life Tower Bank, Seattle, WA, silver colored, #439, 5.25" h 65

Ocean Spray Cranberry Sauce, litho tin canister, "Packed by Cranberry Canners, Inc. South Hanson Mass.," 2.5" h, 2.75" d 25

Pabst Blue Ribbon, litho tin canister, "Brewed and Packed by Pabst Brewing Company Milwaukee, Wis. U.S.A.," 3.5" h, 2" d 20

Pure Premium, litho tin, figural gas pump, 5" h, 2.25" w, 1.75" d 40

RCA 8 Transistor Marathon Savings, cardboard canister with paper label, some scuffs, creases and soiling, 4.75" h, 3" d 15
Thermo Anti Freeze, litho tin canister, "Pubicker Industries Inc. Philadelphia, Penna.," 2.75" h, 2" d 50

FIGURAL

Baseball Bats on Rack 40
Billiken 85
Black Man, repair to foot, repaint and paint loss, 5.25" h 60
Cadet 285
Camel, small 140
Conestoga Liberty Bell 60
Deco Elephant 115
Dot Stove 30
Flat Top Auto "E" 1,000
Hall Clock 315
Horse Beauty 80
Indian on Log 40
Judd Building, 1885, small 160
Lion with Ears Back 60
Mosque, large, with combination 285
National Safe 50
Pagoda 400
Pirate on Chest, Wilton 60
PO Box, English, tin 45
Porthole Bank, 1908 80
Radio, tin 80
Register Basket, 1902 70
Safe (National) 150
Seal on Rock 315
Skyscrapers Six Posts, cast iron, 6.5" h . . .80

Tea Cup, brass 65
White City Barrel on Cart 460
WWI Soldier's Hat .90
Yellow Cab 1,000

BARBED WIRE

Barbed wire is a farm, Western or military collectible. It is usually collected in 18-inch lengths and mounted on boards for display. While there are a few rare examples that sell in the hundreds of dollars for a piece, the majority of strands are common types that sell between $2 and $5 per sample.

Club: American Barbed Wire Collectors Society, 1023 Baldwin Rd., Bakersfield, CA 93304.

BARBERSHOP & BEAUTY PARLOR

Let's not discriminate. This is the age of the unisex hair salon. This category has been male-oriented for far too long. Haven't you wondered where a woman had her hair done in the 19th century? Don't forget drug store products. Not everyone had the funds or luxury to spend time each day at the barbershop or beauty salon.

Club: National Shaving Mug Collectors Assoc., 320 S. Glenwood St., Allentown, PA 18104.

Globe, triangular, white milk glass with fired-on "Barber Shop" lettering and red and blue striped edges, 12" h, 9.5" w 825
Hair Dryer, electric, Shelton Electric Co., New York and Chicago, metal, 110 volts, patent number S104576, Oct 6, 1908 patent date, 9" h, 7.5" l 12
Hot Water Heater, The Superior, metal with milk glass globe, 110 volts, National Stamping and Electric Works, Chicago, IL, Aug 30, 1910 patent date, 17.5" h, 8" w 250
Latherizer, The Latherizer Corp, New York, NY, metal and rubber, patented Sept 15, 1925, 3" h, 5.25" l 40

Manual, *The Barber's Manual,* by AB Moler, illus, ©1910, hard cov, 210 pgs, 9" h, 6" w 18

Razor Kit, Army issue, metal razor, blade holder, and sharpening stone in canvas kit, engraved "Property of US Army," 2.25" w, 4.5" l 25

Razor Kit, Curvfit, Curvfit Sales Corp, 33 Jefferson St, Stamford, CT, woman's, gold-plated razor with 2 pkgs of razor blades, unopened, 2.25" w, 3.25" l 18

Razor Kit, Ever-Ready, metal, 3" chrome-plated razor and chrome razor blade box with 2 razors, metal kit box with felt int 25

Razor Kit, Rolls, Made in England, US. Pat Off, nickel-plated, orig box and instructions 12

Razor Kit, Schick Repeating Razor, Magazine Repeating Razor Co, 285 Madison Ave, New York, NY, metal and cardboard, orig box and instruction sheet, 1" w, 6.5" l 12

Razors and Box, wooden storage box with hinged lid, int fitted to hold 20 straight razors, contains 17 razors, each engraved with manufacturer names including Schmidt, Joseph Rodgers, Brandt, Bengall, and Superb, ivory and plastic handles, 9" h, 6.25" w 200

Shaving Kit, Heljestrand, leather and steel, 16" leather strop, razor mkd "Heljestrand Sweden," and 7 single-edge razor blades, orig directions in English and Swedish printed on fine tracing paper, leather-cov case, 4.5" w, 6" l, 1.5" d 25

Sign, "Beauty Shoppe," porcelain, 1-sided, 12" h, 24" w 415

Sterilizer, nickel-plated brass, 7.25" x 4.75" x 9.25" 125

Sterilizer, The Sun Steam Tight Hot Towel Sterilizer, stainless steel with porcelain stand, patented Apr 1, 1924, 63" h, 21" d 650

Sterilizer, tin with hinged lid, wood knob, spout on back for steam and to empty, 2 handles on side, spout on front to drain, 14" h, 11.25" d 30

Sterilizer, wood and glass, drawer above 2 glass doors, "Antiseptic Sterilizer" decal on upper door, lower door has glass shelf, 24" h, 11.5" w 200

Strop, Diamond, Lipshaw Mfg Co, Detroit, MI, leather and wood, 2 strops attached to wooden base, 3.25" w, 22.25" l 25

Strop, Traveler, leather and wood 8

BARBIE DOLL COLLECTIBLES

As a doll, Barbie is unique. She burst upon the scene in the late 1950s and has remained a major factor in the doll market for more than 40 years. No other doll has enjoyed this longevity. Every aspect of Barbie is collectible, from the doll to her clothing to her play accessories. Although collectors place the greatest emphasis on Barbie material from the 1950s and 1960s, there is some great stuff from the 1970s and 1980s that should not be overlooked. Whenever possible, try to get original packaging. This is especially important for Barbie material from the 1980s forward.

Clubs: Barbie Doll Collectors Club International, P.O. Box 586, White Plains,

NY 10603; Barbie Doll Lover's Club, 399 Winfield Rd., Rochester, NY 14622.

DOLLS

Barbie #1, blonde ponytail, MIB 7,000
Barbie #2, blonde ponytail, MIB 8,000
Barbie #4, blonde ponytail 350
Barbie #4, brunette ponytail 525
Barbie #5, redhead ponytail, orig box ...500
Barbie #6, blonde ponytail 275
Barbie #6, brunette ponytail 325
Barbie, black bubblecut 175
Barbie, brunette swirl, coral lips 400
Barbie, lemon blonde swirl, lemon lips, orig box 700
Chris, blonde, orig outfit, ribbons, and barrettes 125
Francie, short blonde hair, orig swimsuit 325
Ken, blonde crewcut, orig red swim trunks and sandals 75
Midge, blonde, MIB 225
Midge, redhead, freckles, orig swimsuit 100
Ricky, pink skin, orig 2-pc swimsuit 85
Skipper, redhead, orig swimsuit and shoes 125
Skooter, blonde, MIB 200
Skooter, blonde, orig swimsuit and shoes 75
Stacey, talking redhead 325
Talking Barbie, brunette, orig swimsuit and bows 300
Talking Ken, #1439 Suede Scene outfit ..125
Todd, orig outfit 100
Tutti, brunette, Jumpin' Rope outfit, MIB 125
Twist N Turn Barbie, blonde, 1966 400
Twist N Turn Barbie, redhead, 1966, MIB 1,000

OUTFITS

Barbie, After Five, #934 75
Barbie, Barbie Baby Sits, #953, MIP 125
Barbie, Barbie in Holland, #823, MIP 275
Barbie, Busy Morning, #956, MIP 250
Barbie, Career Girl, #954 130
Barbie, Commuter Set, #916, MIP 1,000
Barbie, Fashion Editor, #1635, MIP 400
Barbie, Friday Night Date, #979 100
Barbie, Guinevere, #873, MIP 175
Barbie, Holiday Dance, #1639, MIP 500

Barbie, Invitation to Tea, #1632, MIP 350
Barbie, Knit Hit, #1621, MIP 175
Barbie, Knitting Pretty, #957 300
Barbie, Little Red Riding Hood, #880 250
Barbie, Matinee Fashion, #1640, MIP 625
Barbie, Mood for Music, #940 190
Barbie, On the Avenue, #1644, MIP 500
Barbie, Orange Blossom, #987, MIP 125
Barbie, Patio Party, #1692, MIP 200
Barbie, Peachy Fleecy, #915 125
Barbie, Poodle Parade, #1643, MIP 550
Barbie, Red Flare, #939, MIP 125
Barbie, Skaters Waltz, #1629, MIP 225
Barbie, Ski Queen, #948, MIP 125
Barbie, Slumber Party, #1642, MIP 225
Barbie, Sophisticated Lady, #993, MIP ..210
Barbie, Stormy Weather, #949 55
Barbie, Suburban Shopper, #969, MIP ...250
Barbie, Winter Holiday, #975 150
Francie, Long on Looks, #1227, NRFB 300
Francie, Waltz in Velvet, #1768, NRFB ..225
Ken, American Airlines Captain, #779, MIB 275
Ken, Drum Major, #775, NRFB 200
Ken, Holiday, #1414, MIB 200
Ken, Ken in Holland, #777, MIB 165
Ken, Ski Champion, #798, MIB 125
Ricky, Saturday Show, #1502, NRFB 125
Skipper, Dreamtime, #1909, MIP 75
Skipper, Dress Coat, #1906, NRFB 150
Skipper, Learning to Ride, #1935, NRFB ..350
Skipper, Rain or Shine, #1916, MIP 65
Skipper, Super Slacks, #1736, NRFB 125
Skipper, Sweet Orange, #3465, NRFB 75
Skipper, Town Togs, #1922, MIP 140
Todd, Ring Bearer, #9480, NRFB 100
Tutti, Plantin' Posies, #3609, NRFB 125

ACCESSORIES

Alarm Clock, blonde swirl Barbie on face 325

Austin Healy Sports Car, red and white 3,000
Barbie's Scrapbook 150
Binder, 3-ring, black with Barbie, Midge, and Ken 600
Board Game, The Barbie Game, Queen of the Prom, Mattel, #450, 1960 50
Booklet, "Barbie and Ken and Barbie's Best Friend Midge," ©1962 5
Booklet, "The World of Barbie Fashions," 1966 10
Carrying Case, Skipper/Skooter, pink and white polka dot 400
Hallmark Keepsake Ornament, Enchanted Evening Barbie, 1996, MIB 10
Perk Up Case, black with redhead swirl and 2 Barbie figures 120
Pin, 35th Anniversary Festival, 1994, MIB 50
Thermos, ponytail Barbie, black ground, red lid and cup 55
Vanity Set, hand-held mirror and brush, blue plastic with Ballerina Barbie image, 1962 125
Wallet, black with red swirl Barbie and 2 other Barbie figures, red int 50

BARWARE

During the late 1960s and early 1970s it became fashionable for homeowners to convert basements into family rec rooms, often equipped with bars. Most were well stocked with both utilitarian items (shot glasses and ice crushers) and decorative accessories. Objects with advertising are usually more valuable than their generic counterparts.

Cocktail Set, Bottoms Up, Hazel Atlas, shaker with lid and built-instrainer, 6 matching glasses, mkd "HA" 165
Cocktail Set, Carousel, chrome top and carousel, horse and poodle glasses, orig box, 1950s .200
Cocktail Set, Model No K1570, Manning-Bowman & Co, chrome-plated metal and Catalin, shaker, 6 cups, and tray, teapot form shaker with Catalin handle, finial, and stopper, oval tray with green Catalin handles, all pcs mkd except tray, c1928, 13" h shaker 4,000
Cocktail Set, Park, Revere Copper and Brass Co, chrome-plated brass and Catalin, cylindrical Zephyr shaker with red Catalin finial, 4 Empire cups with red Catalin bases, round Viking tray, shaker and tray stamped "REVERE/ROME/NY," c1938-41, 10.75" h shaker 1,800
Cocktail Set, Shake A Leg, West Virginia Specialty Glass Co, ruby glass and chrome, ruby glass leg-shaped shaker and 6 cups with applied silver trim, c1937, 15.25" h shaker 2,000
Cocktail Shaker, bell-shaped, chrome . . .125
Cocktail Shaker, Chicago World's Fair, Aluminum Products Co, enameled aluminum "Happy Days at the Century of Progress," engraved with drink recipes, 11" h 500
Cocktail Shaker, clear glass with aqua and gold hexagonal design, goldtone lid and spoon, 1950s, 9" h 45
Cocktail Shaker, Cockatoo, figural, amber glass body, SS head and legs 400

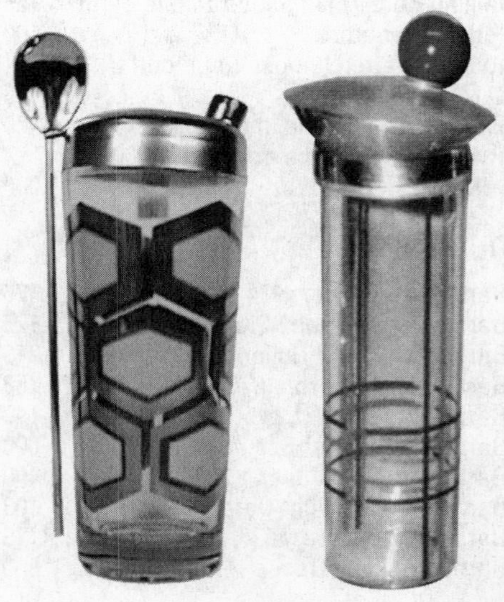

Cocktail Shaker, golf bag, Model No 439, Derby Silver Plate Co, SP metal with simulated cowhide grain, leather straps, and stitching, flat knob finial, 1925, 11" h 2,300

Cocktail Shaker, teapot style, chrome, red Catalin handle, 1930s 45

Cocktail Shaker, Tippler Tumbler, West Bend Aluminum Co, chrome, red plastic top, "Tipple Tips" booklet, c1934 65

Cocktail Shaker, Tam-O-Shanter, Seymour Products 200

Cocktail Shaker, Zeppelin, figural, chrome, 3-pc 125

Liquor Set, 4 chrome cups and cobalt blue glass tray, Lurelle Guild 200

Liquor Set, marbleized plastic bowling ball with gilded metal bowler finial opens to reveal center chrome dispenser surrounded by 6 shot glasses trimmed with red, green, and blue glass rings . .85

Shot Glass Set, 6 anodized aluminum shot glasses, 1 each in orange, purple, green, yellow, blue, and red, wire stand, 1950s 60

Traveling Bar, Zeppelin, Germany, chrome-plated brass, 9 components, c1928, 9.25" h .2,000

BASEBALL CARDS

Baseball cards date from the late 19th century. The earliest series are tobacco company issues dating between 1909 and 1915. During the 1920s American Caramel, National Caramel, and York Caramel issued cards.

Goudey Gum Co. (1933 to 1941) and Gum, Inc. (1939), carried on the tradition in the 1930s. When World War II ended, Bowman Gum of Philadelphia, the successor to Gum, Inc., became the baseball giant. Topps, Inc., of Brooklyn, NY, followed. Topps purchased Bowman in 1956 and enjoyed almost a monopoly in card production until 1981 when Fleer of Philadelphia and Donruss of Memphis challenged its leadership.

In addition to sets produced by these major companies, there are hundreds of other sets issued by a variety of sources, ranging from product manufacturers such as Sunbeam Bread to Minor League teams. There are so many secondary sets now issued annually that it is virtually impossible for a collector to keep up with them all. The field is plagued with reissued sets and cards, as well as outright forgeries. The color photocopier has been used to great advantage by unscrupulous dealers.

The listing below is simply designed to give you an idea of baseball card prices in good to very good condition and to show you how they change, depending on the age of the cards that you wish to collect. For detailed information about card prices, consult the following price guides: James Beckett, *Beckett Baseball Card Price Guide No. 24,* Random House, 2002; Bob Lemke, ed., *2003 Standard Catalog of Baseball Cards, 12th Edition,* Krause Publications; and *Sports Collectors Digest 2002 Baseball Card Price Guide, 16th Edition,* Krause Publications. Although Beckett is the name most often mentioned in connection with price guides, I have found the Krause guides to be more helpful.

Bowman, 1950, #68 Curt Simmons . . . 11.00
Bowman, 1952, #111 Hoot Evers 3.50
Bowman, 1953, #13 Joe Tipton 14.00
Bowman, 1953, #15 Johnny Mize 34.00
Bowman, 1954, #62 Enos Slaughter . . 12.00
Bowman, 1954, #90 Roy Campanella . 46.00
Bowman, 1955, #37 Pee Wee Reese . 18.00
Bowman, 1955, #88 Steve Bilko 2.50
Fleer, 1960, #47 Cy Young 3.00
Fleer, 1960, #72 Ted Williams 28.00
Fleer, 1960, #77 Pie Traynor 1.25
Fleer, 1963, #5 Willie Mays 52.00
Fleer, 1963, #22 Jim Kaat 5.75
Fleer, 1963, #61 Bob Gibson 16.00
Fleer, 1972, #33 Hank Gowdy 20
Fleer, 1975, #14 Ty Cobb 40
Goudey, 1934, #37 Lou Gehrig 875.00
Goudey, 1934, #44 Oscar Melillo 15.00
Milton Bradley, 1969, #197 Manny Mota .15
Milton Bradley, 1970, #76 Roberto Clemente 8.25
O-Pee-Chee, 1971, #118 Cookie Rojas .60
O-Pee-Chee, 1971, #640 Frank Robinson 15.00

O-Pee-Chee, 1973, #531 Ron Woods . 1.50
O-Pee-Chee, 1979, #107 Willie McCovey .70
O-Pee-Chee, 1979, #323 Mike Schmidt 2.50
O-Pee-Chee, 1979, #324 Ken Singleton .08
Post Cereal, 1963, #6 Lenny Green . . . 9.50
Post Cereal, 1963, #200 Roger Craig. . 1.00
Tip Top Bread, 1910, #22 John Flynn . 80.00
Topps, 1953, #106 Johnny Antonelli . . 6.00
Topps, 1954, #134 Cal Hogue 4.50
Topps, 1955, #95 Preston Ward 3.50
Topps, 1955, #210 Duke Snider 90.00
Topps, 1956, #52 Bob Grim 2.50
Topps, 1956, #150 Duke Snider 34.00
Topps, 1957, #2 Ed Lopat. 37.00
Topps, 1958, #40 George Kail. 4.50
Topps, 1958, #111 Stu Miller. 2.25
Topps, 1959, #3 Don McMahon 1.75
Topps, 1959, #10 Mickey Mantle 125.00
Topps, 1959, #111 Redlegs Team, Checklist 89-176. . . . . 4.50
Topps, 1960, #120 Duke Carmel 1.00
Topps, 1960, #343 Sandy Koufax 33.00
Topps, 1960, #350 Mickey Mantle. . . . 120.00
Topps, 1961, #12 Moe Thacker 70
Topps, 1962, #140 Gehrig and Ruth . . . 11.00
Topps, 1962, #240 George Altman. . . . 1.25
Topps, 1963, #377 Orioles team 2.75
Topps, 1966, #491 Dennis Bennett . . . 2.50

Topps, 1970, #234 Tommy Dean. 30
Topps, 1972, #200 Lou Brock 1.50
Topps, 1975, #545 Billy Leo Williams . .90
Topps, 1976, #104 Cincinnati Reds checklist 25
Topps, 1977, #365 Lou Brock 70
Topps, 1977, #468 Ramon Hernandez. .06

BASEBALL MEMORABILIA

What a feast for the collector! Flea market vendors often display caps, bats, gloves, autographed balls and photos of your favorite all-stars, baseball statues, regular and world series game programs and team manuals or rosters. Do not overlook secondary material such as magazine covers with a baseball theme. Condition and personal preference should always guide the eye.

Be careful of autograph forgeries. The general feeling among collectors is that more than 50 percent of the autographed baseballs being offered for sale have fake signatures. But do not let this spoil your fun. There is plenty of good stuff out there.

Clubs: Society for American Baseball Research, 812 Huron Rd. E. #719, Cleveland, OH 44115, www.sabr.org; The Glove Collector Club, 14057 Rolling Hills Ln., Dallas, TX 75240.

Autographed Baseball, signed by 22 members of 1950 Philadelphia Athletics team 700
Autographed Baseball, signed by John McGraw and Casey Stengel, 1949 785
Autographed Pass, 1934 All-American Tour of Japan pass, signed by tour manager Connie Mack, 4" x 3" 750
Badge, Gil Hodges, black and white photo on blue ground, early 1950s, 3.5" 40
Bobbing Head Doll, Cleveland Indians' Chief Wahoo, 1960s, gold base 250
Bobbing Head Doll, Detroit Tigers Mascot, 1960s, gold base 75
Bobbing Head Doll, New York Mets' Mr Met, 1960s 125
Bobbing Head Doll, New York Yankees, first series with colored base 125

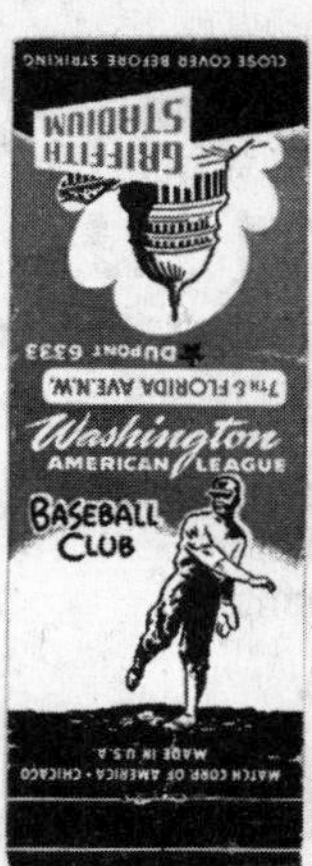

Bobbing Head Doll, Roberto Clemente, SAM Inc, #1,480 of limited edition of 3,000, certificate of authenticity, orig Cooperstown box, MIB 125

Bobbing Head Doll, Steve Carlton, Cooperstown, #191 of limited edition, MIB 150

Bobbing Head Doll, Willie Mays, 1960s, gold base 750

Figure, Barry Bonds, Starting Lineup, Kenner, 1990, MIB 20

Figure, Mark McGwire, Starting Lineup Classic Doubles, Kenner, 1997 10

Matchcover, Washington Senators, home game schedule, 1948 15

Miniature Bat, "White Sox Rooter," c1908, 3.5" l 60

Pennant, Los Angeles Olympic Stadium, dark blue felt, white spine, color image of stadium with football game in progress, "Los Angeles Calif.," 1930s, 3/4 size, 23" l 125

Pennant, Pittsburgh Pirates Championship, black felt, gold spine and streamers, color team photo framed within a gold pirate's hat and neckerchief, gold lettering "Pittsburgh Pirates," 1960, 29" l 325

Pennant, World Series Cleveland Indians, red felt, gold spine and streamers, color image of Indian chief, white scroll with players' names in black, white lettering "Cleveland Indians World Series 1948," 29.5" l 500

Premium, Armour Franks, Frankie Robinson emb plastic coin, red, 1959, 1.5" d 6

Program, 1987 World Series, color and black & white photos, 96 pgs, 8" x 11" 20

Scorecard Folder, Detroit Tigers vs Boston, 1936, 6.25" x 9.5" 12

Squeak Toy, Cleveland Indians mascot, vinyl, 6.75" h 95

Ticket, 1952 World Series, Game 7, Dodgers hosting Yankees at Ebbets Field, mint condition 850

BASKETBALL MEMORABILIA

As the price of baseball cards and baseball memorabilia continues to rise, collectors are turning to other sports categories based on the affordability of their material. Basketball and football are "hot" sport collecting fields.

Collecting generally centers around one team, as it does in most other sport collecting categories. Items have greater value in their "hometown" than they do "on the road." You know a category is gaining strength when its secondary material starts to bring consistently strong prices.

Autographed Magazine, *Beckett Basketball Monthly* signed by Dennis Rodman, cov image of Rodman in uniform 75

Board Game, Harlem Globetrotters Game, Milton Bradley, 1971 20

Card, Fleer, 1987-88, #11 Larry Bird 30

Card, Hoops All-Star Panels, 1990-91, set of 4 15

Card, Topps, 1970-71, #7 Bill Bradley 40

Cereal Box, Frosted Mini Wheaties, Team USA, Larry Bird, 1992 25

Cookie Jar, figural basketball, Treasure Craft 30

Figure, Jason Kidd, Starting Lineup, Kenner, 1995 6

Figure, Shaquille O'Neil, Starting Lineup, Kenner, 1997 10

Game, All-Star Basketball, Whitman No. 2005, fold-out basketball court, rubber balls, metal shooter 25

Game, Basketball, Transogram, 1969 30

Program, Magicians of Basketball, Harlem Globetrotters, 1965, 30 pgs, 8" x 10.5" 18

Punchboard, basketball theme, 1¢ punch, WH Brady Co, 1930s, 6.5" x 9" 18

Sticker Book, USA Basketball, Golden Book #2398, ©1992 4

BATMAN

"Galloping globs of bat guano, Caped Crusader!" and similar cries may be heard as the Dark Knight and his sidekick are summoned to restore peace to Gotham City.

The saga of the search for Batman and Robin-related items began with Batman's appearance in 1939 in issue #27 of Detective Comics. Today, Boy Wonder and Caped Crusader collectibles are found in almost every medium imaginable. Local flea markets offer a large variety of bat-goodies capable of making any bat collector go batty!

Club: Batman TV Series Fan Club, P.O. Box 107, Venice, CA 90294, www.batfanclub.com.

Action Figure, Animated Series, Kenner, 1992, Series 1, 5", Riddler 20

Action Figure, Animated Series, Kenner, 1993, Series 2, 5", Batman Infrared 9

Action Figure, Animated Series, Kenner, 1993, Series 2, 5", Catwoman 30

Action Figure, Animated Series, Kenner, 1994, Deluxe, 5", Batman Power Vision .20

Action Figure, Animated Series, Kenner, 1994, Series 3, 5", Killer Croc 10

Action Figure, Batman Knight Force Ninjas, Kenner, 1998, Riddler 12

Action Figure, Batman Returns, Kenner, 1992, 5", Batman Air Attack 18

Action Figure, Dark Knight, Kenner, 1990, Series 1, 5", Batman Iron Winch 10

Action Figure, Mask of the Phantasm, Kenner, 1994, 5", Phantasm 25

Bank, Batman head, plastic, 5" 5

Banner, Batman Returns, 12', MIP 6

Baseball Cap, Batman Forever logo, child's size 5

Batjet, Dark Knight, Kenner, 1990 25

Batmobile, Animated Series, Ertl, 1992, die-cast 18

Batski Boat, Batman Returns, Kenner, 1992, 5" 60

Binoculars and Telescope Set, Henry Gordy International, 1988 6

Bookmark, Batman Returns, Book Bites ...3

Bruce Wayne Street Jet, Animated Series, with Bruce Wayne action figure 45

Bubble Gum, Batman Forever, 1995, box of 24, MISB 10

Doll, Play By Play, 1999, 10", Batman 6

Earrings, Batman Returns, Rosecraft, 1991, logo, pierced style 5

Eraser, Batman Forever, Noteworthy, set of 3, Batman, Robin, and Riddler 9

Figure, Batman Returns, Ertl, die-cast, 1991, Batman 3

Figure, Batman Returns, Ertl, die-cast, 1991, Penguin 6

Hair Comb, Kid Care, 1991, MIP 5

Hallmark Keepsake Ornament, 1994, Batman 16

Handcuffs, Henry Gordy International, 1988, MOC 6

Hoverbat, Animated Series, with villain capture claw and launching missile ...28

Ice Hammer, Animated Series 26

Jokermobile, Animated Series, with launching missile, MIB 26

Key Chain, Batman Forever, Applause, 1995, Batman logo 4

Lunch Bags, paper, Crime Squad, pkg of 15 1

Night Flash Sparkle Gun, Henry Gordon International, 1988, MOC 6

Pencil Sharpener, Noteworthy, Catwoman 3
Print, Batman Forever, Zanart, 1995, Batmobile and Batcave, 11" x 14" 4
Refrigerator Magnet, Batman Forever, Applause, 1995, Robin 4
Refrigerator Magnet, Gift Creations, 1991, 2", Gotham City Public Works logo 2
Robin Dragster, Animated Series, MIB . .200
Salt and Pepper Shakers, Clay Art, 5", MIB 20
Snack Container, Fun Dimensions, flip-top lid 4
Tablecloth, Batman Returns, 1992, 54" x 84", MIP 6
Trading Cards, Batman Returns, Topps, box of 36 packs with 15 cards/pack 10
Two-Face Armored Car, Batman Forever, Kenner, 1995, die-cast 6
Wallet, Batman, red 4
Wallet, Batman & Robin, animated style art 4

BATTERY OPERATED TOYS

Battery operated "automata" toys originated as cheap Japanese import goods in the 1950s. They were meant for amusement only, many being displayed on shelves of bars in rec rooms of private homes. They were marketed through 5&10¢ stores and outlets.

During the golden age of battery operated toys, the late 1940s through the end of the 1960s, it is estimated that over 2,000 plus examples were sold in the American market. Approximately ninety-five percent were made in Japan. Battery operated toys were offered in a wide range of toy categories including robots, vehicles, and automata that simulated a wide range of animal and human behavior.

Unless noted otherwise, all toys listed are in working order and made in Japan.

Club: Battery-Operated Toy Collectors of America, P.O. Box 676, Tolono, IL 61880.

Baggage Handling Bear, TN, 7" h 35
Banana Eating Monkey, Alps, 9" h 80
Bartender, TN, MIB .90
Bear Boss, Linemar .75
Beethoven the Piano Playing Dog, TN, orig box 165
Blinkey the Cat, Alps, orig box 75
Bongo Playing Monkey, Alps, ...60
Bubble Blowing Monkey, Alps, orig box .100
Climbing Linesman, Toplay Ltd, orig box .500
Cymbal Playing Monkey 35
Dentist Bear, S&E .215
Dolly Dressmaker, TN 110
Fishing Polar Bear, Cragstan 175
Flying Circus, Tomiyama, orig box 550
Gino Neapolitan Balloon Blower, Rosko, orig box 130
Grandpa Bear, Alps, orig box 100
Happy Fiddler Clown, Cragstan, orig box 120
Happy the Clown Puppet Show, Yonezawa, orig box 225
Hungry Baby Bear, Yonezawa, orig box . .100
Hungry Cat, Linemar, orig box 200
Hy-Que the Amazing Monkey, TN, orig box, 17" h 550

Ice Cream Baby Bear, Modern Toys, orig box 400
Jolly Bambino the Eating Monkey, orig box 135
Jolly Pianist, orig box 125
Jolly Popcorn Vendor, TN, orig box 190
Jungle Trio 185
Knitting Grandma, Modern Toys, 9.75" h . .60
Magician Rabbit 65
McGregor Cigar Smoking Scotsman, TN, orig box, 13" h 135
Mickey Mouse Krazy Kar, Louis Marx & Co, orig box 75
Miss Friday the Typist, MIB 85
Musical Jolly Chimp, Korea, orig box 30
Ol' Sleepy Head Rip, Spesco, orig box . . .150
Photoing On Car, China, orig box 85
Piggy Cook, Yonezawa, 10.75" h 45
Roulette Man, Cragstan, orig box, 8.75" h 200
Sam the Shaving Man, Plaything, orig box 250
Sheriff, Cragstan, orig box 65
Shoeshine Joe, TN, orig box 65
Sleeping Baby Bear, Linemar, MIB 110
Smoking Papa Bear, Marusan 110
Speed Star Bumper Car, TN 95
Strutting My Fair Dance, Haji, orig box . .215
Teddy the Artist, Electro Toy, orig box . . .250
Teddy the Boxing Bear, Cragstan 50
Telephone Bear, Modern Toys, orig box, 10" h 165
Windy Juggling Elephant, TN, orig box . .115

BAUER POTTERY

J. A. Bauer established the Bauer Pottery in Los Angeles in 1909. Flowerpots were among the first items manufactured, followed by utilitarian items. Dinnerware was introduced in 1930. Artware came a decade later. The firm closed in 1962.

Gloss Pastel, mixing bowl, #18, light brown 30
Gloss Pastel, mixing bowl, #24, chocolate 20
Gloss Pastel, mixing bowl, #36, yellow 20
Hi-Fire, mixing bowl, #12, green 60
La Linda, coaster, turquoise 10
La Linda, fruit bowl, 5", pink 20
La Linda, saucer, blue 4
Monterey Modern, 3-tier tray, pink 45
Monterey Modern, bread and butter plate, 6.5", brown 10
Monterey Modern, coffee server, open, chartreuse 50
Monterey Modern, coffee server, open, cobalt 90
Monterey Modern, creamer, burgundy . . .20
Monterey Modern, coffee cup, green 15
Monterey Modern, coffee cup, yellow . . .15
Monterey Modern, dinner plate, 10.5", pink 20
Monterey Modern, divided bowl, yellow . .50
Monterey Modern, fruit bowl, 4.5", green .12
Monterey Modern, gravy boat, black 45
Monterey Modern, luncheon plate, 9.5", chartreuse 15
Monterey Modern, luncheon plate, 9.5", yellow 13
Monterey Modern, pitcher, 1 pt, brown . . .30
Monterey Modern, pitcher, 1 qt, chartreuse 40
Monterey Modern, rect platter, 12", chartreuse 25
Monterey Modern, salad plate, 7.5", black 20
Monterey Modern, saucer, gray 6
Ringware, ball jug, cobalt 125
Ringware, coffee cup, yellow 40
Ringware, coffeepot, blue speckleware . .30
Ringware, flower bowl, yellow 25
Ringware, mixing bowl, orange-red 75
Ringware, ramekin, orange-red 30
Ringware, salad plate, 9", light blue 40
Ringware, saucer, cobalt 20
Ringware, saucer, orange-red 20

BEANIE BABIES

While there is still an active secondary resale market for Ty's Beanie Babies, the market collapse is at hand. A year from now, sellers will thank their lucky stars if they can get these prices.

The items are priced each. Beanie Babies without tags have little or no value.

Ally Alligator, ret 10/97 10
Ants Anteater, ret 12/98 3
Baldy Eagle, ret 5/98 3
Bessie Cow, ret 10/97 11
Bongo Monkey, brown tail, ret 11/97 7
Britannia, UK flag bear, ret 7/99 30
Bubbles, black and yellow fish, ret 5/97 . .22
Bumble Bee, ret 6/96 250
Claude Crab, tie-dyed, ret 12/98 2
Crunch Shark, ret 9/98 2
Cubbie Bear, brown, ret 12/97 3
Echo Dolphin, blue, ret 5/98 5
Fetch Dog, ret 12/98 .6
Flash Dolphin, ret 5/97 32
Flip Cat, ret 10/97 12
Floppity Bunny, lavender, ret 5/98 3
Freckles Leopard, ret 12/98 2
Garcia Bear, ret 5/97 70
Glory Bear, ret 12/98 11
Goldie Goldfish, ret 12/97 6
Groovy Bear, ret 12/99 3
Hippity Bunny, ret 5/98 4
Hoot Owl, ret 10/97 .10
Iggy Iguana, no spikes, ret 3/99 2
Inch Inchworm, felt antennae, ret 7/96 . . .35
Inch Inchworm, yarn antennae, ret 5/98 . . .4
Kiwi Toucan, ret 1/97 34
Lucky Ladybug, 7 spots, ret 7/96 70
Lucky Ladybug, 21 spots, ret 7/97 150
Manny Manatee, ret 5/97 35
Mooch Spider Monkey, ret 12/99 5
Morrie Eel, ret 12/00 .2
Mystic Unicorn, tan horn, ret 11/97 5
Nana Monkey, ret 7/95 1,100
Nanook Husky, ret 3/99 3
Nuts Squirrel, ret 12/98 3
Peace Bear, pastel, ret 7/99 18
Pecan Bear, ret 12/99 3
Periwinkle Bear, ret 12/00 8
Pounce Cat, ret 3/99 .2
Puffer Puffin Bird, ret 9/98 2
Pugsly Pug Dog, ret 3/99 4
Roam Buffalo, ret 12/99 2
Slippery Snake, ret 12/95 500
Sly Fox, brown belly, ret 7/96 22
Sly Fox, white belly, ret 9/98 2
Smoochy Frog, ret 3/99 2
Spangle Bear, white face, ret 12/99 10
Spooky Ghost, ret 12/97 4
Spot Dog, ret 10/97 .12
Spot Dog, no spot, ret 7/94 850
Sweetheart Orangutan, ret 12/99 3
Tabasco Bull, ret 1/97 24
Waves Whale, black, ret 5/98 2
Weenie Dachshund, ret 5/98 8
Ziggy Zebra, ret 5/98 3

BEATLES

Ahhh! Look, it's the Fab Four! The collector will never need Help to find Beatle memorabilia at a flea market—placemats, dishes, records, posters and much more. The list is a Magical Mystery Tour. John, Paul, George and Ringo can be found in a multitude of shapes and sizes. Examine them carefully. They are likely to be heavily played with, so conditions will vary from poor to good.

Clubs: Beatles Connection, P.O. Box 1066, Miami, FL 33780; Working Class Hero Beatles Club, 3311 Niagara St., Pittsburgh, PA 151213.

Alarm Clock, chrome case and glass cov over clock face with black Beatles' image on silver ground, "The Beatles 4 Ever," 1988 45

Button, "I'm A (Official) Beatles Fan, litho tin, black and white portraits and names, 1964, 4" d .25

Charm Bracelet, metal link chain with 4 charms, each with celluloid photo insert, 1964, 7" l 85
Diary, color picture of Beatles in clear vinyl cov, 1965, 3" x 4.25" 35
Flicker Rings, blue plastic base with flicker insert image that changes from Beatle's portrait to name, set of 4 70
Necklace, black and white celluloid insert with Beatles image, brass frame and chain 45
Pin, enameled brass, Yellow Submarine, 1968, 1.5" l 20
Record, *Let It Be,* Capitol Records, 45 rpm, paper sleeve, 1969 40
Record, *Revolver,* Capitol Records, 33 1/3 rpm, mono, cardboard album cov, 1966 60
Record Player, 3-speed, blue case 550
Ring, brass, "The Beatles," celluloid insert with group photo, 1964 65
Token, commemorating Beatles' 1964 visit to US, brass, 1.25" d 20
Watercolor Set, The Beatles Yellow Submarine, boxed set with 6 pictures, 2 paint trays, and brush, 1967 165

BEER CANS

Beer can collecting was very popular in the 1970s. Times have changed. The field is now dominated by the serious collector and most trading and selling goes on at specialized beer can-ventions.

The list below contains a number of highly sought-after cans. Do not assume these prices are typical. Most cans fall in the 25-cent to 50-cent range. Do not pay more unless you are certain of the resale market.

There is no extra value to be gained by having a full beer can. In fact, selling a full can of beer without a license, even if only to a collector, violates the liquor laws in a large number of states. Most collectors punch a hole in the bottom of the can and drain out the beer.

Club: Beer Can Collectors of America, 747 Merus Ct., Fenton, MO 63026, www.bcca.com/index.html

Cone Top, Duquesne Pilsener Beer, with cap 175
Cone Top, E&B Special 75
Cone Top, Falstaff, with cap, new spout . .70
Cone Top, Krueger .200
Flat Top, Ace Hi Beer, top opened 85
Flat Top, Banner, rolled, bottom opened . .30
Flat Top, Best, top opened, lid stamp 25
Flat Top, Budweiser, top opened 30
Flat Top, Carling's Black Label, top opened 35
Flat Top, Crystal Rock, top opened 125
Flat Top, Finast Lager Beer, top opened .100
Flat Top, Genesee 12 Horse Ale, air sealed 135
Flat Top, Gluek Stite, 8 oz, bottom opened .25
Flat Top, Hampden Ale, bottom opened . . .15
Flat Top, Iron City, bottom opened 75
Flat Top, Lancers, top opened 20
Flat Top, Land of Lakes, top opened 30
Flat Top, Milwaukee's Best, bottom opened 15

Flat Top, National Bohemian Pale Beer, top opened 45
Flat Top, Old Dutch, bottom opened 50
Flat Top, Ortlieb's, bank top, drill hole in bottm lid 65
Flat Top, Rheingold Scotch Ale, top opened 75
Flat Top, University Club ML, bottom opened 35
Flat Top, Valley Forge, top opened, MD tax stamp 30
Flat Top, Valley Forge, top opened, PA lid stamp 75
Flat Top, Valley Forge Bock, black letters, top opened 225
Tab Top, Black Dallas, bottom opened 35
Tab Top, Del Dia, air sealed 85
Tab Top, Jet, bottom opened 35
Tab Top, Whitman & Lord, top opened, zip tab 125

BELLEEK

Belleek is a thin, ivory-colored, almost iridescent-type porcelain. It was first made in 1857 in Ireland. Production continued until World War I, was discontinued for a period of time, and then resumed.

The American Belleek era spanned from the early 1880s until 1930. Several American firms manufactured porcelain wares resembling Irish Belleek.

Club: The Belleek Collectors International Society, P.O. Box 1498, Great Falls, VA 22066, www.belleek.ie.

Bouillon Cup and Saucer, cream, gold banding, Lenox 95
Bouillon Cup and Saucer, eggshell china, pink int, gilded details, Ott & Brewer, 2.5" x 6" 130
Candlesticks, pr, black, Art Deco style, enameled flowers with raised gold accents, Lenox, 8.25" h 225
Cream Jug, Shell pattern, blue-glazed handle and coral relief, first black mark, Irish, c1880, 5.25" h 500
Cup and Saucer, hp Orient pattern, Morgan Belleek China Co 250
Cup and Saucer, Tea Ware, Hexagon pattern, pink-tinted, second black mark, Irish, early 20th C, 5.25" d 225
Loving Cup, 3-handled, 3 monograms on gilded lavender ground, inscription around rim, green ink stamp, artist's signature, Ceramic Art Co, 1904, 8" x 6" 120
Mug, hp Art Deco enameled flowers, sgd "HRM," Lenox, 7" h 150
Mug, hp bird, Lenox, 4.25" h 85
Pitcher, grapevines on blue ground, Ceramic Art Co, green ink stamp, 6" x 7.5" 175
Platter, Art Deco design, hp border, solid handles with gold trim, 16.5" l . . .125
Ramekin, pink roses on pastel ground, gilded details, Willets, stamped mark and signature, 3.75" x 3.5 35
Sugar Bowl, Shell pattern, pink-tinted edge and coral, first black mark, Irish, c1880, 4" h 575
Tea Cup and Saucer, molded, gilt-trimmed relief of horns on orange peel ground, first black and registry marks, Irish, c1870, 5.75" d saucer 175
Tea Kettle and Cover, Tea Ware, Grass pattern, enamel-decorated relief, first black mark, Irish, c1880, 6" h 225
Toothpick Holder, hp ravens seated on pine branches,straight sides, 2.25" h . .140
Urn, bulbous, women and cupids in neoclassical landscape, green stamp mark and artist's signature, Ceramic Art Co, 11" x 9" 625
Vase, cylindrical, hp bird on branch with flowers, 9.5" h, 3" d 250
Vase, tapered, daffodils in yellow on shaded ground, brown ink stamp, artist's signature, Willets, 8.5" x 4.5" . . .265

BELLS

Bell collectors are fanatics. They tend to want every bell they can find. Admittedly, most confine themselves to bells that will fit on a shelf, but there are those who derive great pleasure from an old school bell sitting on their front lawn.

Be alert for wine glasses that have been converted into bells. They are worth much less than bells that began life as bells. Also, collect Limited Edition bells only if you like them, not with the hope they will rise in value. Many Limited Edition bells do not ring true on the resale market.

Club: American Bell Assoc. International, Inc, 7210 Bellbrook Dr., San Antonio, TX 78227.

Cow Bell, Swiss, copper 140
Figural, lady, brass, 3.75" h 95
Limited Edition, Goebel, Annual Angel, 1991, 2.75" h 15
Limited Edition, Goebel, Annual Angel, set of 20, 1976 through 1995, MIB 225
Limited Edition, Hallmark, giraffe, bronze, sgd Todd Warner, 1970s, 5.25" h 150
Limited Edition, Hummel, 1989, Latest News 115
Limited Edition, Hummel, 1990, What's New 65
Limited Edition, Hummel, 1991, Favorite Pet 125
Limited Edition, Hummel, 1992, Whistler's Duet 80

Limited Edition, Lladro, Christmas 1994, #16139 80
Limited Edition, Lladro, Christmas 1995, #6206 75
Limited Edition, Lladro, Sounds of Summer #5953, 5" h 85
Limited Edition, Precious Moments, "You Have Touched So Many Hearts," 4.25" h .7
Locomotive, Amtrak, cast iron, F40PH with Graham-White air ringer and locomotive mounting bracket 210
Merchant's, metal bell suspended on flexible metal strap, bell rings when door is opened 15

BEVERAGE SETS

Mention the term "beverage set" and most people think of the familiar glass pitcher and tumblers made during the 1940s. However, beverage sets were also made from plastic, ceramic, and aluminum and in every design imaginable. Listed below is a small sampling of the various materials, manufacturers and motifs.

Anchor Hocking, Lido, aquamarine, ball-shaped pitcher and 6 glasses, late 1960s/early 1970s, MIB 40
Anchor Hocking, Lido pattern, avocado, ball-shaped pitcher and 6 glasses, late 1960s/early 1970s, MIB 25
Corelle, Farm Fresh, 2 qt jug with plastic lid and eight 16 oz tumblers, red and green checkerboard and fruit design on clear glass, MIB 60
Everlast, hammered aluminum, bar set, consisting of 6 glasses, 8 coasters with holder, ice bucket and tongs, and tray, dogwood pattern, cups mkd #987 40
Homer Laughlin, pitcher and 4 tankards, leaves and currants design, c1900s, 9" h pitcher, 4.25" h tankards 100
Indian Chiefs, enameled glass pitcher and 8 glasses, each decorated with a different Oklahoma Indian chief, rect handled wooden tray, 8.75" h pitcher, 5.25" h glasses, 27" x 7.25" tray 300
Inverted Thumbprint, ruby-flashed clear glass, gold trim, pitcher and 6 tumblers, 8" h pitcher, 4" h tumblers 60

Louie Glass Co, pitcher and 6 tumblers, iridescent blue, 1930s/40s, 9.5" h pitcher, 5.75" h tumblers 65

MacBeth-Evans, tomato juice set, pitcher and 2 juice glasses, 5.75" h pitcher, 3" h glasses 12

Souvenir, orange plastic bottle-shaped jug and 6 orange navel orange-shaped tumblers with green plastic caps, mkd "Florida's Weeki Wachee Spring of Live Memories" on 1 side and "Florida's Silver Spring Nature's Underwater Fairyland" on other, orig mesh bag 15

Swankyswig Type, pitcher and 6 glasses, floral design in yellow, pink, white, and green 45

Vacron, plastic 2 qt pitcher and 6 tumblers, white with multicolored bases 20

Virginia Glass, pitcher and 6 tumblers, frosted green and clear, gold rims, 13" h pitcher, 2.75" h tumblers 20

White Milk Glass, Hobnail pattern, pitcher and 6 pedestal glasses, c1960, 8" h pitcher, 5.5" h tumblers 35

BIBLES

The general rule to follow is that any Bible less than 200 years old has little or no value in the collectibles market. Many people have trouble accepting this argument. They see a large late 19th century family Bible filled with engravings of religious scenes and several pages containing information about the family. It is old and impressive. It has to be worth money. Alas, it was mass produced. The most valuable thing about it is the family data and this can be saved with the aid of a photocopier.

An average price for a large family Bible from the turn of the century is between $35 and $75, although there are Bibles that sell for a lot more.

BICENTENNIAL

America's 200th birthday in 1976 was PARTY TIME for the nation. Everyone and everything in the country had something stamped, painted, printed, molded, cast and pressed with the commemorative dates 1776-1976. The American spirit of "overdo" and "outdo" always puts our nation in a great mood. We certainly overdid it during the Bicentennial.

The average flea market will have a wide variety of Bicentennial goodies. Remember the Bicentennial was only a quarter century ago. This is one category where you only want to buy items in fine or better condition.

Charm, enameled brass, Peanut's Snoopy wearing tri-corner hat and carrying large Bicentennial flag 25

Cigarette Lighter, table model, Zippo Barcroft 110

Cookie Tin, oval, litho tin, "The Frigate Constellation" sailing ship on lid, ship's history inside lid, 14.5" x 11.5" x 3.5" 8

Dolls, Campbells Kids boy and girl in colonial costumes .50

Pocketknife, Case XX, stag handles, engraved bolsters, #3614, tang #5165, mkd "Case XX Stainless USA," orig box with wood base and glass dome 135

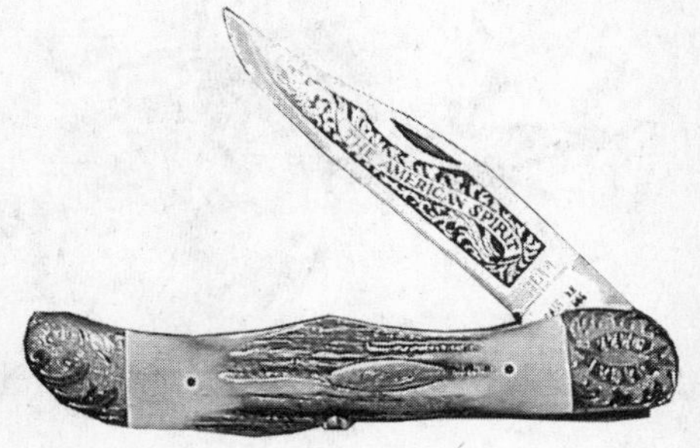

Proof Set, Franklin Mint, 50 coins, .925 silver, proof condition 275
Purse, tooled leather with crossed flags, laurel wreath, and banner with "1776-1976" 15
Stein, Budweiser, CSL8, 10.25" h 200
Train Set, Bachmann, N scale 80

BICYCLES

Bicycles are divided into two groups—antique and classic. Chances of finding an antique bicycle, such as a high wheeler, at a flea market are slim. Chances of spotting a great balloon tire classic are much greater.

Do not pay much for a bicycle that is incomplete, rusted, or repaired with non-original parts. Replacement of parts that deteriorate, e.g., leather seats, is acceptable. It is not uncommon to heavily restore a bicycle, i.e., to make it look like new. If the amount of original parts is less than half, question an extremely high price.

Clubs: Classic Bicycle & Whizzer Club of America, 35769 Simon Dr., Clinton Township, MI 48035; International Veteran Cycle Assoc., 248 Highland Dr., Findlay, OH 45840; Vintage Bicycle Club of America, 325 West Hornbeam Dr., Longwood, FL 32779; The Wheelmen, 63 Stonebridge Rd., Allen Park, NY 07042, www.thewheelmen.org.

Columbia, man's bike, 1950s, horn tank with horn button, rear rack, restored with some orig parts 500

Columbia, woman's bike, 1950s, horn tank with horn button, rear rack, restored with some orig parts 300
Fastback, 1971, orig and complete 300
Franklin Custom Tandem, 1982-83, TA cranks, Suntour drivetrain 950
Mead Crusader, leather seat, warped front wheel with wrong hub, 28" wood rims 250
Schwinn Cruiser, 1952, grip shift 6-speed, drum brake rear, Cro-Mo fork with cantilever brake, alloy rims, hubs, chain ring, and bars, BMX type pedals, all new parts 650
Schwinn Custom Paramont tandem, bronze color, orig manual and tools, 22.5" front wheel, 19.5" rear wheel . . .1,500
Schwinn Hollywood, restored, orig parts re-chromed, NOS Schwinn "S" pink and white seat, reproduction tires and hand grips 500
Schwinn Phantom, 1953, new tires, wrong seat and carrier, otherwise orig and good condition 1,400
Schwinn Phantom, black, later model frame, some orig parts, new paint, professionally pinstriped, drum brake front hub 1,000
Schwinn Stingray, 1977, mostly non-orig parts 75
Schwinn Stingray Low Rider, orig frame with high flange 68 spoke wheels, tufted velvet seat, seat shocks, dent in rear fender 500
Shelby Airflow, Delta Triple-Lite, 1950, professionally restored, chrome, high cushioned seat, 26" nylon tires, 35" h .700

BIG LITTLE BOOKS

The first Big Little Book was published by Whitman Publishing Co., in 1933. As with any successful endeavor, copycats soon appeared. Saalfield Publishing Co. was first with the introduction of its line of Little Big Books. Lesser known and less successful imitators include Engel-Van Wiseman, Lynn Publishing Co., Goldsmith Publishing Co., and Dell Publishing Co.

Condition and story content are the keys to determining value. Prices listed are for books in very good to fine condition.

Club: Big Little Book Collectors Club of America, P.O. Box 1242, Danville, CA 94526, www.biglittlebooks.com.

Apple Mary and Dennie Foil the Swindlers, #1130, 1936 25
Barney Baxter in the Air with the Eagle Squadron, #1459, 1938 25
Buck Rogers and the Doom Comet, #1179, 1935 75
Chester Gump at Silver Creek Ranch, #734, 1933 60
Chester Gump Pole to Pole Flight, #1402, 1937 40
Dick Tracy and the Stolen Bonds, 1944 45
Dick Tracy Out West, #723, 1933 80
Felix the Cat All Picture Comics, #1439, 1943 90
Frank Merriwell At Yale, #1121, 1935 20
In the Name of the Law, #1155, 1937 35
International Spy Doctor Faces Death at Dawn, #1148, 1937 30
Little Orphan Annie and Chizzler, #748, 1933 70
Little Orphan Annie and Sandy, #716, 1933 50
Lone Ranger and the Vanishing Herd, The, #1196, 1936 42
Snow White and the Seven Dwarfs, #1460, 1928 60
Tarzan's Revenge, #1488, 1938 65
Tom Beatty Ace of the Service Scores Again, #1165, 1937 25
Tom Mix and the Hoard of Montezuma, #1462, 1937 45

BISQUE

Every time I look at bisque figures, I think of grandmothers. I keep wondering why I never see a flea market table labeled "Only things a grandmother would love."

Bisque is pottery ware that has been fired once and not glazed. It is a technique that is centuries old and is still being practiced today. Unfortunately, some of today's figures are exact copies of those made hundreds of years ago. Be especially aware of bisque piano babies.

Collectors differentiate between Continental (mostly German) and Japanese bisque with premiums generally paid for Continental pieces. However, the Japanese made some great bisque. Do not confuse the cheap five-and-dime "Occupied Japan" bisque with the better pieces.

Doll, girl, molded and painted brown hair, painted eyes, nostrils, and lips, feet molded together, jointed arms, mkd "Made In Japan," orig dress, 5.25" h 95
Figurine, 17th C-style gentleman wearing pale blue jacket, metallic gold vest, and pale pink pants, mkd "Made in Germany," missing 1 finger, 12.5" h 15
Figurine, angel, European, 12.5" h 75

Figurine, Love Disarmed, incised "Falconnet," pseudo Sevres mark on bottom, 9.5" h 65

Figurine, woman carrying basket of fish, hp, 11" h 25

Figurine, woman in pink and pale green dress and wide-brimmed hat carrying handbag, mkd "100 22," France, 17.75" h 45

Figurine, woman wearing white blouse, and pink and green skirt and bonnet, mkd "Made in Germany," 7.5" h 12

Grouping, cookie seller ringing bell, young boy, and dog, hp, unmkd, 5.25" h 50

Grouping, well-dressed couple seated on lion head bench, gold and green accents, mkd "Germany 3812," 5.25" h .60

Inkwell, bisque figurine of a lady wearing pink and blue dress and bonnet and standing on shellwork base, 5.25" h ...40

Lamp Base, young boy, repaired right hand, Germany, late 19th C, 21" h 55

Pitcher Vase, hp floral dec, mkd "Hand Painted, Wales Chinaware, Made In Japan," 7" h, 4.5" w 25

Planter, young girl 45

Vase, girl wearing green and violet costume, green bow, molded house scene, bird with envelope, gilt trim, Unger Bros, 9" h 50

BIZARRE ART

There is some really great stuff made by senior citizen groups and community organizations that can be found at local bazaars, church rummage sales and so on. Of course, after a few years, these items often turn up at flea markets.

Some bazaar craftspeople also create unique decorative accessories that may hold some resale value. Most stuff is just "stuff" and can be had for pennies on the dollar. Perhaps some day this tacky stuff will catch a decorator's eye and skyrocket in value!

BLACK MEMORABILIA

The Black memorabilia category is viewed quite broadly, ranging from slavery-era items to objects showing ethnic stereotypes. Prices range all over the place. It pays to shop around.

Because Black memorabilia embodies a wide variety of forms, the Black memorabilia collector is constantly competing with collectors from other areas, e.g., cookie jar, kitchen and salt and pepper collectors. Surprisingly enough, it is the collectors of Black memorabilia who realize the extent of the material available and tend to resist high prices.

Reproductions, from advertising signs (Bull Durham Tobacco) to mechanical banks (Jolly Nigger), are an increasing problem. Remember—if it looks new, chances are it is new.

Club: Black Memorabilia Collector's Assoc., 2482 Devoe Ter., Bronx, NY 10468.

Ashtray, 2 natives pulling and pushing a die-shaped cart, ceramic, Japan, 3" h, 4.25" w 30

Bank, mechanical, Darkie and Cabin, man flips in doorway of cabin when coin is inserted, cast iron, orig paint 1,500

Bank, mechanical, Darktown Battery, baseball players, cast iron 7,425

Bookends, pr, African man's and woman's heads, wood, 8" h 28

Bootscraper, figural shoeshine boy seated atop bootscraper, 2 brushes mounted on an oval scalloped tray, cast iron, 12" h, 12.5" w 925

Cigarette Dispenser, figural man's face, wearing top hat and bowtie, paint decorated wooden box with spring mechanism that shoots cigarettes out man's mouth, 8.5" h 825

Clock, figural, in the form of a man seated atop a clock face and holding a whiskey jug and a guitar, with shifting eyes, cast iron and wood construction, paint decorated, 10" h 1,550

Dolls, set of 4, wax-coated, dressed as a woman with a chicken, a man with a bandanna, a man dancing, and a man with cotton, approx 7" h including wooden base 275

Dolls, set of 5, cloth "Poinsettia" dolls, dressed as a man with an ax and wood, a woman with broom and dustpan, a woman with a washboard, a man with a walking stick and flowers, and a woman with a carpet bag, ©1939, approx 9" h 415

Figure, man wearing shoeshine box on strap which reads "Depot Street Shine Parlor, Louisville, KY, 5 cents," papier mâché, 19" h 275

Marionette, plastic head and hands, wood feet and body, 14.5" h 90

Matchbox Holder, wire, figure riding bicycle, basket on front holds matches, 6" h, 5.5" l 65

Pincushion/Tape Measure, figural cloth Mammy, Japan, 5" h, MIB 75

Smoking Stand, figural butler with exaggerated long legs, wearing a long-tailed red coat and holding an ashtray with a match/cigarette holder, 36" h . . .385

Teapot, figural black woman, upper body is lid, ceramic, mkd "USA," 8" h 100

BLAIR CERAMICS

After a stint at Purinton Pottery where he was instrumental in designing several Purinton patterns, including Apple, William Blair moved to Ozark, Missouri, and opened his own pottery there in 1946. Reacting negatively to the traditional round dinnerware shape, Blair produced square, rectangular, and other geometric-shaped wares. Gay Plaid, with its horizontal forest green stripes and brown and chartreuse vertical stripes, is the most highly sought-after pattern.

At its peak, Blair Pottery employed thirty workers, produced as many as 3,500 pieces per week, and shipped to all forty-eight states, Canada, Cuba, and Hawaii. Neiman-Marcus and Marshall Field were among the department stores that carried Blair ceramics.

Bamboo, salt and pepper shakers, pr 18
Bamboo, sugar bowl, cov, stick handle . . .15
Gay Plaid, bowl, 5.5" 6
Gay Plaid, bowl, 9" 20
Gay Plaid, casserole, cov 25
Gay Plaid, coffee server 45
Gay Plaid, coffee server, individual size, 5" h 35
Gay Plaid, creamer 10
Gay Plaid, cream soup and saucer 24
Gay Plaid, cup and saucer 10
Gay Plaid, gravy boat, stick handle 18
Gay Plaid, jug, ice lip 18
Gay Plaid, mug 12
Gay Plaid, pitcher, 6.5" h 75
Gay Plaid, plate, 6.25" 5
Gay Plaid, plate, 7.25" 8
Gay Plaid, plate, 10" 12
Gay Plaid, platter, 14" 15
Gay Plaid, relish, 3-part 15
Gay Plaid, tumbler 18
Gay Plaid, vegetable bowl, divided 18
Gay Plaid, vegetable bowl, handled, 10" . .15

BLUE RIDGE

Southern Potteries of Erwin, Tenn., produced Blue Ridge dinnerware from the late 1930s until 1956. Four hundred patterns graced eight basic shapes.

Club: Blue Ridge Collectors Club, 208 Harris St., Erwin, TN 37650.

Angelina, plate, 9.5" 25
Anneliese, luncheon service, 4 each cup and saucer, 6.25" plate, 10.5" plate, 8" bowl, cov sugar, creamer, and 13" x 10" platter 95
Apple Pea, plate, 8.75" 10
Becky, berry bowl 4
Becky, creamer and cov sugar 28
Becky, cup and saucer 8
Becky, plate, 6.25" 5
Becky, plate, 9.25" 6
Becky, platter, 13.5" x 10.25" 15
Becky, tidbit, 2-tier, wooden handle 20
Becky, vegetable bowl, 9.5" 15
Bow Knot, plate, 10.25" 12
Chick, pitcher, 5.75" h 35
Chrysanthemum, creamer and sugar, no lid 40
Crab Apple, plate, 9.25" 25
Crab Apple, platter, 14" x 11" 20
Crab Apple, vegetable bowl, 9.25" 100
French Peasant, chocolate pot 450
Fruit, dessert plates, set of 6 30
Fruit, plate, cherries, 9.5" 10
Fruit Fantasy, plate, 7.5" sq 10
Grape, plate, 8.25" 10
Jane, pitcher, 7.25" h 65
Tulip, plate, 9" 25

BOBBING HEADS

The first bobbing head dolls appeared in the first decade of the twentieth century. These consisted of cartoon characters, e.g., Foxy Grampa, Happy Hooligan, and Palmer Cox Brownie characters, and generic types such as Black Minstrel, Keystone Cop, Policeman Rabbit, and Uncle Sam. These bobbing head dolls were produced in Germany and sell in the $150 to $350 range depending on condition.

Bobbing head dolls enjoyed a revival in the late 1950s. Beatles, Peanuts, and Sports Mascot series represent a few of the new entries. Early Sport Mascots were made of papier-mâché and imported from Japan by Sports Specialties. Plastic examples made in Hong Kong, Korea, and Taiwan quickly followed.

In the late 1990s and early 2000s, the bobbing head doll enjoyed another revival. Bobbing head dolls became popular giveaways at baseball and other sporting events. In 2003, one encounters bobbing heads almost everywhere one turns—from registering at a Red Roof Inn to buying a meal at a fast food restaurant.

Club: Bobbin' Head National Club, P.O. Box 9297, Daytona Beach, FL 32120.

Alfred E Neuman, orig "Certified Mod" tag around waist, 9" h 45
Beatles, ceramic, set of 4, "Made in Japan, Car Mascots, Inc, Los Angeles, 26, Calif USA" gold sticker, orig box, 8" h, orig box 500
Beatles, plastic, set of 4 in orig sealed bag, 1964, 4" h 80
Chicago Blackhawks, 1961-63, mini, "Japan" stamped on base, 4.5" h 75
El Diablo, gold suit, Funko, limited edition of 480, MIB, 7" h 40
Harpo Marx, SAM Inc, limited edition, certificate of authenticity, MIB 50
Lone Ranger and Tonto, 1996, SAM Inc, #432 in limited edition of 1,500, certificate of authenticity, MIB 165
Marilyn Monroe, Sam Inc, hp, #537 of limited edition of 5,000, with certificate of authenticity, NIB, 1996 30

Mickey Mouse, orig price tag from Walt Disney World ($1.50) on bottom, early 1970s 35
Monkees, Funko, PVC plastic, boxed set includes Davy, Mike, Mickey and Peter, 7" h 40
Mrs Beasley, Family Affair, Ashton-Drake, hp resin, certificate of authenticity, MIB 45
Pluto, "Walt Disney Productions, Made in Japan" foil label, 5.75" h 50
Roy Rogers, mkd 1962 on bottom 150
Three Stooges, playing golf, ceramic, Creative Imaginations, 1999, set of 3 includes Moe, Larry, and Curly 50
Underdog, Funko Wacky Wobbler Bobbing Head Doll, PVC plastic, collector's display box, limited edition, 7.5" h 65
Washington Senators, 6" h 450
Wayne Gretzky, 1994, SAM Inc, MIB 250
Yosemite Sam, 1993, Warner Brothers Looney Tunes, MIB, 7" h 40

BOOKENDS

Prices listed below are for pairs. Woe to the dealer who splits pairs apart!

Club: Bookend Collector Club, 4510 NW 17th Pl., Gainesville, FL 32605.

Afghan Dog, Art Deco, cast metal, mkd "Nuart Creations, NYC," c1920s-30s, 3.75" h 45
Children on Sled, clad brass, Jennings Bros, unsgd, c1930, 5" h 115
Cockatoo Perched on Book, clad copper, polychrome dec, unmkd, 1930s, 9.25" h 275
Dutch Boy and Girl, gilt metal, sgd "Frankart," Spelter, 5" h, 5.5" w 225
Elephants, seated, clad brass, unsgd Jennings Bros, c1930, 4.5" h 90
German Shepherd, bronze clad cast iron, Germany, 5.75" h 50
Hunting Dog, looking to side, 1 paw raised, bronze and green marble, Viennese, 1920-30, 4.5" h, 8" w 225
Indian Brave, cast bronze, unsgd Bradley & Hubbard, cast "bronze 9683," 1920-30, 5.5" h 175
Indian on Horseback, both with bowed heads, cast iron with bronze patination, 6" h, 5" w 35
Liberty Bell, Sesquicentennial, 1926, bronze, mkd "Design Pat. Appld," 6.25" h 60
Man and Woman, frolicking through woods, bronze, ©1926 Gifthouse Inc, 6.5" h, 4.75" w 120
Man Riding Horse, cast iron, 5.75" h, 4.75" w 15
Pirate, metal, celluloid face, onyx base, c1925, 6.5" h 110
Rooster, metal, 7.75" h, 6.5" w 15
Sailing Ships on Waves, cast iron, Bradley & Hubbard mark, 5.5" h 45
Shepherd, cast iron, 5.5" h, 5" w 20
Styllized Flowers, hammered copper, Roycroft, 3.5" h, 2" w 170
Two Dogs at Gate, bronze, stamped "B & H," 1920, 5.25" h 465
Two Horses and Coach, metal, imp "Judd 9653," 6.25" l, 2.75" h 25
Two Owls Seated on Log, metal, 6" h 8
Two Scottish Terriers, clad brass, probably Jennings Bros, 192030, 4" h 104
Victorian Couple, porcelain, white with gold trim, Japan, c1950, 7.25" h 25
Washington Crossing the Delaware, cast brass, mkd "solid brass ©1930" with Jennette & Sons stamp, 6" h 90

BOOKMARKS

Don't you just hate it when you lose your place in that book you've been reading? Bookmarks can help keep your sanity and they're easy to find, easy to display and fun to own.

Bookmark collecting dates back to the early 19th century. Bookmarks have been made from a wide variety of materials, including celluloid, cloth, cross-stitched needlepoint in punched paper, paper, sterling silver, wood and woven silk. Heavily embossed leather markers were popular between 1800 and 1860. Advertising markers appeared after 1860.

Woven silk markers are a favorite among collectors. T. Stevens of Coventry, England, manufacturer of Stevensgraphs, is among the most famous makers. Important U.S. companies that made woven silk bookmarks include John Best & Co., Phoenix Silk Manufacturing Co., J. J. Mannion, and Tilt & Son.

The best place to search for bookmarks is specialized paper shows. Be sure to check all related categories. Most dealers file them under subject headings, e.g., Insurance, Ocean Liners, World's Fair and so on.

Club: Antique Bookmark Collector's Assoc., 2224 Cherokee, St., Louis, MO 63118.

Advertising, Maltine Products, celluloid owl, Whitehead & Hoag, 1890s, 3.75" l . . 28

Advertising, Wisner Pianos, diecut, pink and red carnation on green stem, black text, white ground, early 1900s 8

Brass, machine-cut design with woman's portrait above ornate scrollwork, 4.25" l .6

Celluloid, girl wearing ruffled dress and hat and holding a tasseled bag at top, 5" l, 1" w 18

Sterling Silver, Easter motif, emb "Easter," lilies, and chick emerging from egg above a cross, Alvin, 3.5" l 55

Stevensgraph, "May Health and Happiness Be Thine," tasseled end, 10.5" h . .50

Victorian, Berlin work (embroidered punched paper), motto "To My Dear Mama" in red and green 18

Victorian, machine-embroidered, "For A Good Boy," dog howling as boy plays fiddle, Welch & Kenton, Coventry, 19th C, 7.5" l 260

BOOKS

There are millions of books out there. Some are worth a fortune. Most are hardly worth the paper they were printed on. Listing specific titles serves little purpose in a price guide such as this. By following these 10 guidelines, you can quickly determine if the books that you have uncovered have value potential.

1. Check your book titles in *American Book Prices Current,* which is published annually by Bancroft-Parkman, Inc., and is available at most libraries, as well as *Huxford's Old Book Value Guide,* published by Collector Books. When listing your books in preparation for doing research, include the full name of the author, expanded title, name of publisher, copyright date and edition and/or printing number.
2. Examine the bindings. Decorators buy handsomely bound books by the foot at prices ranging from $40 to $75 per foot.
3. Carefully research any children's book. Illustration quality is an important value key. Little Golden Books are one of the

hottest book areas in the market today. In the late 1970s and early 1980s, Big Little Books were hot.

4. Buy all hardcover books about antiques and collectibles that you find that are less than $5. There is a growing demand for out-of-print antiques and collectibles books.
5. Check the edition number. Value, in most cases, rests with the first edition. However, not every first edition is valuable. Consult *Black's Bibliography of American Literature* or *Tannen's How to Identify and Collect American First Editions.*
6. Look at the multi-faceted aspects of the book and the subject that it covers. Books tend to be collected by type, e.g., mysteries, westerns, etc. Many collectors buy books as supplements to their main collection. A Hopalong Cassidy collector, although focusing primarily on the objects licensed by Bill Boyd, will want to own the Mulford novels in which Hopalong Cassidy originated.
7. Local histories and atlases always have a good market, particularly those printed between 1880 and 1930. Add to this centennial and other celebration volumes.
8. Check to see if the book was signed by the author. Generally an author's signature increases the value of the book. However, it was a common practice to put engraved signatures of authors in front of books during the last part of the 19th century. The Grant signature in the first volume of his two-volume memoir set is not original, but printed.
9. Book-club editions have little or no value with the exception of books done by George and Helen Macy's Limited Editions Club.
10. Accept the fact that the value of most books falls in the 50¢ to $2 range and that after all your research is done, this is probably what you'll get.

Club: Antiquarian Booksellers Assoc. of America, 50 Rockefeller Plaza, New York, NY, 10036, www.abaa.com.

BOOTJACKS

Unless you are into horseback riding, a bootjack is one of the most useless devices that you can have around the house. Why do so many individuals own one? The answer in our area is "just for nice." Actually, they are seen as a major accessory in trying to capture the country look. Cast iron reproductions are a major problem, especially for "Naughty Nellie" and "Beetle" designs.

Aluminum, steer head, "101 Ranch," 11.5" l 90
Cast Iron, beetle, painted black, 9.25" l . . .45
Cast Iron, closed loop 75
Cast Iron, cut-out scrollwork, "Downs & Co," 13.5" l 200
Cast Iron, devil, cut-out circular eyes and stomach, painted white horns and arms, red mouth, c1880-90, 10.5" l 300
Cast Iron, double-ended, filigree center, patented May 18, 1869, 12" l 50
Cast Iron, emb flower, "ACME," 10" l 10
Cast Iron, forked end, heart and keyhole cutouts, painted gold and white, 9.5" l .175
Cast Iron, lyre form, 10.25" l 75
Cast Iron, Naughty Nellie, naked woman, painted black on top, white on bottom, 10" l 60
Cast Iron, nickel-plated, "American Bulldog" hinged six shooter 125
Cast Iron, open heart and circle, scalloped sides, 13" l 225
Cast Iron, pair of pheasants, 19" l 200
Cast Iron, V-shaped, ornate 50
Wood, pistol, hand-carved, brass hinges and pins, c1860-70, 10" l 350
Wood, Shaker, natural "Y" shape with chamfered edges, old red finish, 20.5" l 100

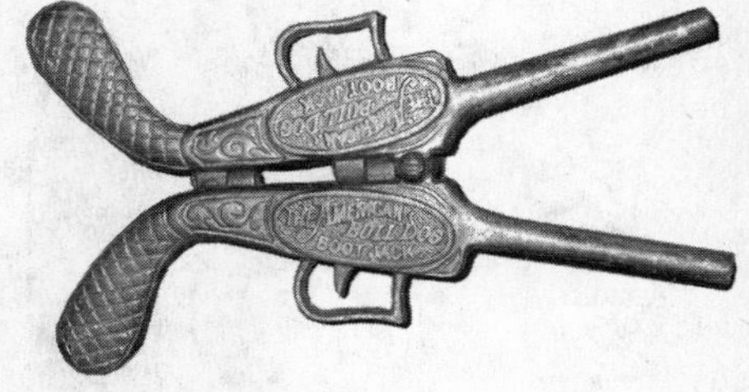

BOTTLE OPENERS

Although cast iron figural bottle openers are the most sought-after type of bottle openers, do not forget the tin advertising openers. Also known to some as church keys, the bulk still sell for between $2 and $10, a very affordable price range.

Clubs: Figural Bottle Opener Collectors Club, 9697 Gwynn Park Dr., Ellicott City, MD 21042, http://members.aol.com/JohnF129/index.htm; Just For Openers, P.O. Box 64, Chapel Hill, NC 27514, www.just-for-openers.org.

ADVERTISING

ABC Beer, San Diego Brewing, San Diego, CA, 1930s 3
Ballantine, Ballantine Brewing, Newark, NJ, 3-ring logo, 1950s 11
Berlin Brewing, Berlin, WI, 1910s 6
Champagne Velvet Beer, Terre Haute Brewing, Terre Haute, IN, engraved bottle, 1930s 4
Chief Oshkosh Special Old Lager, Oshkosh Brewing, Oshkosh, WI, 1910s 17
Cleveland & Sandusky Brewing Co, Cleveland, OH, opener/screwdriver, 1910s 67
Cold Spring, Cold Spring Brewing, Cold Spring, MN, 1900s 26
Congress Beer, Derby Cream Ale, Haberle Congress, Syracuse, NY, opener/penknife 20
Daeufers Beer, Daeufer Brewing, Allentown, PA, slide out, 1930s 10
Deppen Queen Quality, Deppen Brewing, Reading, PA, bottle shaped, 1910s 10

Ebling's, Ebling Brewing, New York, NY, bottle shaped, 1930s 9
Fehr's X/L Beer, Fehr Brewing, Louisville, KY, wooden, bottle shaped 12
Flocks, Flocks Brewing, Williamsport, PA, 1910s 11
Gluek Root Beer, Gluek Beverages, Minneapolis, MN, 1920s 7
Golden Glow Beer, Milwaukee Brewing, Oakland, CA, 1930s 3
Koerbers Beer, Koerbers Brewing, Toledo, OH, 1930s 3
Miller High Life, Miller Brewing, Milwaukee, WI, bottle shaped, 1940s . . .3
Miller High Life, Miller Brewing, Milwaukee, WI, can shaped, pop-out opener, 1950s 10
Narragansett Lager, Narragansett, Cranston, RI, bottle shaped 8
Pabst Blue Ribbon, Pabst Brewing, Milwaukee, WI, engraved bottle, 1940s 3
Phoenix Beer, Phoenix Brewing, Buffalo, NY, enameled, yellow ground, 1910s . . .22
Pickwick Ale/Stout, Haffenreffer, Boston, MA, printed, 2-sided, 1910s 23
Piels, Piel Bros, New York, NY, slide out, 1930s 10
Storz, Storz Brewing, Omaha, NE, opener/corkscrew, 1930s 4

FIGURAL, CAST IRON

Alligator and Black Boy 30
Amish Man's Head .32
Bear Head 24
Black Face 45
Bulldog Head 35
Chipmunk 70
Cocker Spaniel 60
Cowboy and Cactus 205
Crab 38
Dragon 145
Fish 80
Foundryman 45
Jackass 35
Monkey 85
Mouth 75
Nude, Art Deco 35
Parrot, Hubley 75
Pelican 80
Ram 45
Rooster 28
Seagull 60

BOTTLES

Bottle collecting is such a broad topic that the only way one can hope to survive is by specialization. It is for this reason that several bottle subcategories are found elsewhere in this book. Bottles have a bad habit of multiplying. Do not start collecting them until you have plenty of room. I know one person whose entire basement is filled with Coca-Cola bottles bearing the imprint of different cities.

There are many bottle categories that are still relatively inexpensive to collect. In many cases, you can find a free source of supply in old dumps. Before getting too deeply involved, it pays to talk with other bottle collectors and to visit one or more specialized bottle collector shows.

Club: Federation of Historical Bottle Collectors, 2230 Toub St., Ramona, CA 92065, www.fohbc.com.

Note: Consult Maloney's Antiques & Collectibles Resource Directory, by David J. Maloney, Jr., at your local library for additional information on regional bottle clubs.

Barber, Acme Hair Vigor, label under glass, emb Wildroot top, 9.25" h, 3" d . . 465

Flask, Eagle – Eagle, c1865-75, deep bluish aqua pint, smooth base, applied mouth . 90

Flask, Eagle / "Louisville, KY. / Glass-works," aqua quart, smooth base, applied mouth, c1860-70, 8.5" h 160

Flask, "For Pikes Peak" / Traveler, aqua half-pint, smooth base, applied mouth, c1865-75 145

Flask, "Liberty" / Eagle – "Willington / Glass Co / West Willington / Conn," medium yellowish olive green half-pint, smooth base, applied double collar mouth, c1860-70 200

Flask, Sheaf of Wheat above Star – "Westford Glass Co / Westford / Conn," deep smoky olive amber pint, smooth base, applied double collar mouth, c1860-70 180

Flask, "Union" / Clasped Hands / "F.A. & Co." – Cannon, bluish aqua pint, smooth base, applied mouth, c1865-75 145

Ink, barrel form, "SI Comp," deep bluish aqua, smooth base, tooled mouth, c1870-90, 2.25" h 110

Ink, igloo form, "Moore's Excelsior School Writing Ink Manufactured by J & IE Moore, Warren Mass," aqua, smooth base, ground lip, c1875-90, 1.5" h 175

Ink, umbrella form, medium blue green, 8-sided, open pontil, rolled lip, hand carved wooden stopper, 2.5" h 165

Medicine, "Dr. Townsend's Aromatic Hollands Tonic," medium amber, smooth base, applied sloping collar mouth, c1865-75, 9" h 225

Medicine, "Germ, Bacteria Or Fungus Destroyer, Wm Radam's Microbe Killer, Registered Trade Mark Dec. 13, 1887, Cures All Diseases," man killing skeleton, golden amber, smooth base, tooled mouth, c1890-1900, 10.5" h 325

Medicine, "Lediards – Morning Call," deep olive green, smooth base, applied sloping collar mouth, c1865-75, 9.75" h 360

Medicine, "L Q C Wishart's – Pine Tree Tar Cordial, Phila, Patent 1859," pine tree image, medium emerald green, smooth base, applied mouth, c1860-70, 8" h 175

Medicine, "Primley's Iron & Wahoo Tonic, Jones & Primley Co, Elkhart, MD," medium tobacco amber, smooth base, applied sloping double collar mouth, c1875-80, 8.5" h 110

Medicine, "Puritana, WT & Co, USA," deep cobalt blue, smooth base, tooled mouth, about perfect, c1890-1910, 6.75" h 100

Poison, medium cobalt blue coffin, smooth base, tooled mouth, c1890-1910, 3.5" h 80

Poison, Mercury Bichloride, Upjohn Co, Kalamazoo, MI, "Poison – Poison," golden yellow amber, smooth base, tooled lip, orig label, c1890-1910, 3.25" h 95

Poison, skull and crossed bones, "Poison, Tinct, Iodine," cobalt blue, smooth base, tooled mouth, c1890-1910, 3.25" h 75

Poison, Tinct Iodine, Owl Drug Co, 2-winged owl on mortar and pestle, deep cobalt blue, smooth base, tooled mouth, orig label, c1910-20, 4" h 110

BOYD CRYSTAL ART GLASS

The Boyds, Bernard and his son, purchased the Degenhart Glass Factory in 1978. Since that time, they have reissued a number of the Degenhart forms. Their productions can be distinguished by the color of the glass and the "D" in a diamond mark. The Boyd family continues to make contemporary collectible glass at its factory in Cambridge, Ohio.

Bell, doll, Louise, lemon vaseline 28
Bell, owl, vaseline 25
Doll, Melissa, peacock blue 10
Figurine, airplane, lemon vaseline 45
Figurine, Artie penguin, black carnival ...22
Figurine, Artie penguin, columbus white ..20
Figurine, bear, cobalt blue 75
Figurine, Katie butterfly, moss green 12
Figurine, Kewpie doll, cobalt blue 20
Figurine, Lucky unicorn, alpine blue 25
Figurine, Patrick balloon bear, windsor blue 14
Figurine, praying angel, lemon vaseline ..25
Figurine, Sly fox, moss green 22
Figurine, Taffy carousel horse, cobalt blue 24
Figurine, Teddy bear, peacock blue, dated "98" 18
Hand Mirror, yellow vaseline 45
Salt Dip, bird, yellow vaseline 22
Salt Dip, bunny on nest, rosie pink 20
Salt Dip, hen on nest, peacock blue 20
Salt Dip, lamb, vaseline 24
Salt Dip, turkey on nest, moss green 24
Train Set, mustard, 6 pcs 45
Train Set, pink opalescent, 6 pcs 55

BOYD'S BEARS & FRIENDS

Gary and Tina Lowenthal of McSherrytown, Pennsylvania, began the Boyd plush toy line in 1979. The Boyd name came from Boyd, Maryland, the location of the Lowenthal's antiques business.

An active secondary market, especially on the Internet, has developed for discontinued Boyd plush toys and cast resin collectibles. Prices should be viewed as highly speculative. Like many collectibles of this type, their primary appeal is to the buyer's heart, not head. Boyd does not release production numbers. Scarcity is more related to speculative hoarding than actual lack of product.

Bearstone, Bailey, Home Sweet Home ...15
Bearstone, Bailey, The Night Before Christmas 50
Bearstone, Bailey's Birthday 32
Bearstone, Clarence & Raphael, Angels Fly High 30
Bearstone, Clarisse Growsalot 50
Bearstone, Eddie, Proud To Be A Bearmerican 20
Bearstone, Edmund and Bailey, Gathering Holly 48
Bearstone, Elliot & Snowbeary 30
Bearstone, Elliot & The Tree 32
Bearstone, George & Gravie, Forever 15
Bearstone, Grace Z Beartique 50
Bearstone, Lefty On The Mound 30
Bearstone, Marlowe with Kinsey, Egg Detectives 20
Dollstone, Laura with Jane, First Day of School 25
Dollstone, Mark with Luke, The Prayer ...16
Dollstone, Mia, The Save 25
Dollstone, Tami with Doug, Half Time 20
Folkstone, Arabella & Oscar, Icy 25
Folkstone, Birdie Holeinone, NOGA of Golfers 28
Folkstone, Chester Birdbreath, pin 6
Folkstone, Cram, The Study Faerie 20
Folkstone, Flake & Melton 6
Folkstone, Giselle 14
Folkstone, Honker T Flatfoot 25
Folkstone, Illumina, Angel of Light 34

Plush, Alexis Berriman 80
Plush, Amy Z Sassycat 48
Plush, Ariela Angelfrost 18
Plush, Aunt Becky Bearchild 40
Plush, Aunt Yvonne Dubeary 30
Plush, Baldwin 16
Plush, Bear in Bunny Suit with Carrot Marlowe 26

BOY SCOUTS

Collecting Boy Scout memorabilia is a mature field with well-established subcategories. Books have been published detailing at least seventeen of these subs.

Most collectors focus mainly on cloth patches. There are many kinds and each has devotees. Merit badges, Cub Scout insignia, High Adventure patches, Jamboree patches, Council patches, and Order of the Arrow are just a sampling.

Because OA (Order of the Arrow) patches were issued locally in small quantity and collectors all over the country are seeking them, prices on scarce issues have been driven up to thousands of dollars. Prices for old insignia and handbooks and pre-1940 uniforms have also risen.

Boy Scout collectors buy, sell and trade at Trade-O-Rees. Most are held annually under the management of local collectors and attract from 50 to 200 collectors. These events are great learning opportunities as experienced collectors willingly help out those with less knowledge.

Clubs: American Scouting Traders Assoc., P.O. Box 210013, San Francisco, CA 94121; International Badgers Club, 2903 W. Woodbine Dr., Maryville, TN 37803; National Scouting Collectors Society, 806 E. Scott St., Tuscola, IL 61953.

Bandanna, blue and yellow, with a brass fleur-de-lis pin mkd "Capitol Washington D.C.," 1938, 28" sq 15
Binoculars, Official Boy Scout 20
Bolo Tie, Region 7 "Big Ten" 15
Book, *Handbook for Patrol Leaders,* 1933 .18
Book, *Songs Scouts Sing,* 1935 8
Book, *The Hickory Ridge Boy Scouts,* 1912 10
Council Patch, Aloha S1a 2
Council Patch, Grayback Council T1 55
Council Patch, Sir WM, Johnson Council CSP S1 20
Council Patch, Westmoreland Fayette Council RWS 8
First Day Cover, 1950 National Jamboree . .6
Flashlight, Cub Scout 25
Handbook, 1935 10
Insignia, Eagle Scout patch type 4A, 1972-75 20
Insignia, hat patch, Explorer CAW 4
Insignia, TH Foley Tenderfoot pin, 1910s 250
Jacket Patch, Camp Soule, 1978 5
Knife, Fork and Spoon Kit, Imperial, plastic case 14
Medal, bronze, Firemaking 185
Membership Card, 1916 Series, 1917 95
Neckerchief Slide, Broad Creek, 1970 15
Neckerchief Slide, Camp Incawanis, metal 20
Patch, Camp Bert Adams, 1949 50
Patch, Camp Winnebago 24
Pillow Case, 1950 National Jamboree 38
Pinback Button, "We're Backing Scouting" 8
Pocket Patch, 1960 Cub Scout Jubilee . . .10
Scarf, 1935 National Jamboree, red 140
Scarf, 1964-65 World's Fair Scout Service Corp 32
Scarf, Camp Twin Echo, staff 15
Scarf, Ten Mile River Scout Camps 10
Souvenir Pin, 1957 National Jamboree . . .25
Tie Clasp, Explorer 5
Vitt-L-Kit, BSA #1387, vinyl case, orig box .15

BRASS

Brass is a durable, malleable and ductile metal alloy, consisting mainly of copper and zinc. It appears in this guide because of the wide variety of objects made from it.

Bookends, Arts & Crafts, sliding, cut-out pine trees and log cabin backed with green glass, sgd "Bradley and Hubbard," 6.25" h, 12.5" w 150

Bookmark, enameled geometric Art Deco design, 4.5" h 5

Book Stand, hinged, ornated cut-out scrollwork, 9" x 7.25" 95

Candle Snuffer, brass tray, sgd "Bradley & Hubbard" 15

Ewer, engraved and painted bands, India, 12" h 20

Inkwell, brass beehive, ceramic well, GB & Sons, c1869, 4.5" h, 5.5" sq 350

Letter Opener, emb Hermes portrait on handle, Townshend and Co, 8" l 18

Picture Frame, oval, easel back, stamped "Stern Brothers New York," 4.5" h, 2.5" w 40

Platter, oval, engraved monogram within a wreath, dated "June 8-78" 15

School Bell, turned wood handle mkd "#4," 6" h 18

Sleigh Bells, set of 4 graduated bells on 13.5" l metal strap 25

Statue, eagle, turned oak base, 10" h 50

Tea Caddy, Art Deco motif, mkd "NMK," Germany 1920, 5.5" h 40

Trivet, cut-out scrollwork, 8.5" l, 3.5" w 12

Vase, Arts & Crafts style, mkd "Beldray," c1900, 10" h, 7" d 55

BREWERIANA

Beer is a liquid bread, or so I was told growing up in Pennsylvania German country. It is hard to deny German linkage with the brewing industry when your home community contained the Horlacher, Neuweiler and Uhl breweries.

Brewery signs and trays, especially from the late 19th and early 20th centuries, contain some of the finest advertising lithography of the period. Three-dimensional advertising figures from the 1930s through the 1970s are no slouches, either. Brewery advertising has become expensive. Never fear. You can build a great breweriana collection concentrating on barroom accessories such as foam scrapers, coasters and tap knobs.

Clubs: American Breweriana Assoc., Inc., P.O. Box 11157, Pueblo, CO 81001, www.americanbreweriana.org; National Assoc. of Breweriana Advertising, 2343 Met-To-Wee Ln., Wauwatosa, WI 53226, www.nababrew.org/.

Note: See Barware, Bottle Openers, and Steins for additional listings.

Clock, "Old Drum Brand / Blended Whiskey / 90 Proof 75% Grain Neutral Spirits / Calvert Distillers Corp, NYC," electric, tin clock face illus with marching drummer, 12" d 230

Clock, "Pearl Lager Beer," neon light-up, octagonal, Neon Products Inc., Lima, OH, 18.25" w 385

Decanter, 1929 Model T Police Car, china, plastic, and rubber, "James B. Beam Distilling Co., Clermont, Beam, Kentucky," contains Jim Beam Kentucky Bourbon Whiskey, 7" h, 6.5" w, 15.5" l 65

Menu Sheet, All American Beer, Brackenridge Brewing, Brackenridge, PA, 1930s 12

Menu Sheet, Arrow Beer, Globe Brewing, Baltimore, MD, 1930s 35

Menu Sheet, Budweiser and Busch Ginger Ale, Anheuser Busch, St Louis, MO, 1920s 8

Menu Sheet, Ehrets Extra Beer, Ehret Brewing, New York, NY, 1940s 10

Neon Sign, Ballantine, arched "BALLANTINE" above "ALE (3-ring logo) BEER," pink, green, and white, no transformer, back of tubes repainted, 1960s, 27" w 180

Neon Sign, Burger Beer, "Light BURGER ON TAP" in oval, orange, red, and white, 1960s, 18" h, 27" w 75

Neon Sign, Hamm's Beer, script "Hamm's," red, 1960s, 10" h, 26" w 55

Neon Sign, Lucky Lager, script letter "L" above "Lucky On Tap," red and white neon tubes, 1960s, 16" h, 18" w 40

Neon Sign, Miller Genuine Draft, neon "Miller," plastic "Genuine Draft," 1980s 18

Neon Sign, Rolling Rock Beer, "Rolling Rock" in rounded rectangle, red and green, 1960s 150

Neon Sign, Script "Schlitz" on an angle within a slanted rectangle, pink, 1970s 20

Neon Sign, Steg Beer, "STEG" in outline lettering, pink, 1960s 75

Picture, "Custer's Last Stand, Presented by Budweiser," cardboard picture and frame, graphic illustration of Little Big Horn battle, sgd "O. Berkey, Anheuser – Busch, Inc. – St. Louis, MO," 24" h, 41" w 120

Poster, "Budweiser – King of Beers / Anheuser-Busch, Inc., St. Louis, MO," cardboard, 8 Clydesdales pulling beer wagon, 20" h, 47.25" w 55

Salt and Pepper Shakers, Hamm's Beer, figural slim bears with eyes closed, heads turned to left 125

Sign, Blatz Brewing, Lacrosse, WI, "Blatz, The Three Best Beers," metal and plastic, light-up, 1970s, 7.25 x 10" ..20

Sign, Horlacher Brewing, Allentown, PA, "Hugo Says: Drink Horlacher's," plastic and metal, light-up, 1950s, 6.5" x 6.5" 115

Sign, "Kingsbury Pale Beer / Manitowoc Products Co. / Manitowoc, Wis.," emb tin, beer bottle image, red ground, 19.5" h, 27.5" w 145

Sign, Latrobe Brewing, Latrobe, PA, "Rolling Rock Beer,"plastic and metal, light-up, 1960s, 26.5 x 11.5" 60

Sign, Ortliebs Brewing, Philadelphia, PA, "Ortlieb's, Philadelphia's Favorite Beer," 100th Anniversary, metal and plastic, light-up, 1960s, 5 x 11.5" ...40

Sign, Peter Hand Brewing, Chicago, IL, "People's Beer, Hits the Spot!," plastic and metal clock/light, 1960s, 12.5 x 6.5" 85

Sign, Stegmaier Brewing, Wilkes-Barre, PA, "Stegmaier's Gold Medal Beer, Brewed to the Taste of the Nation," register light, plexiglass and metal, 1940s, 12.5 x 5.5" 130

Sign, "Trommer's White Label in Bottles," register light, reverse glass and metal, 1940s, 13 x 10" 125

Statue, chalkware, man's head and shoulders atop glass bottle of "John Wieland Extra Pale Lager Beer," bottle cap is hat, "Pacific Brewing and Malting Co., San Jose, California," 9" h, 3" d 45

Statue, Hamm's Beer, plastic, figural Hamm's Bear holding sign "Good Friends Meet Here," 16" h 95

Tap Knob, Altes Lager, plastic, enamel insert, 1950s 75

Tap Knob, Brumaster Beer, chrome, copper insert, 1940s 85

Tap Knob, Dutch Club Beer, chrome, enamel insert, 1940s 115

Tap Knob, Hamm's Beer, Bakelite, enamel insert, 1940s 140

Tap Knob, Koch's, silver painted, enamel insert, 1930s 40

Tap Knob, MC Pilsener Deluxe, chrome, printed enamel insert, 1930s 75

Tap Knob, Pabst Breweries, chrome, enamel insert, 1930s 32
Tap Knob, Plymouth Beer, Bakelite, printed metal insert, 1940s 50
Tap Knob, Schmidt Beer, chrome, enamel insert, 1950s 90
Tap Knob, Tam O Shanter, Bakelite, enamel insert, 1940s 60
Tray, "Edelweiss Beer," litho metal, round, pretty smiling girl wearing flowered dress, "The Peter Schoenhofen Brewing Co, Chicago – Copyright 1913," 13.5" d 165
Tray, Utica Club West End Brewing Co, Utica, NY, 12" d 20
Tumbler, Enterprise Brewing Co, etched "Yosemite, Lager, Enterprise Brewing Co, San Francisco, Cal," 3.5" h 85

BREYER HORSES

The Breyer line of plastic model horses has been on the market since the 1950s. During the past five decades the company has not only produced a line of horses but also dogs, wildlife, and farm animals. In 1984 Breyer Molding Company was sold to Reeves International and moved from Chicago to New Jersey. The Breyer company is still in business today.

Breyer consists of four lines that are differentiated by height. *Traditional* (horses and animals in separate categories), which average around nine inches; *Classic,* which average six inches; *Little Bit,* which stand around four inches; and *Stablemates,* which average three inches.

Club: Breyer Collectors Club, 14 Industrial Rd., Pequannock, NJ 07440.

#5, Hope, Family Arabian Mare, matte palomino 20
#20, Four-eyed Misty, glossy palomino pinto 200
#41, Western Pony, glossy black pinto 55
#46, Pacer, semi-gloss liver chestnut, 4 socks 45
#51, Commander, Five Gaiter, glossy alabaster 275
#59, Morganglanz, matte chestunut 35
#85, Azteca, Foundation Stallion, matte dapple gray 35
#96, Shire Mare, semi-gloss honey sorrel 40
#99, Two Bits, Quarter Horse Gelding, glossy bay, eyewhites 100
#110, Western Prancer, semi-gloss dark smoke 55
#117, Project Universe, Five Gaiter, matte chestnut pinto 45
#124, Sugar, Running Mare, matte bay . . .45
#127, Running Stallion, semi-gloss black appaloosa 50
#166, Lying Foal, matte buckskin 35
#213, Proud Arab Stallion, matte dapple gray 60
#426, Prancing Arabian Mare, Lady Roxana, matte light sorrel 40
#435, Secretariat, matte chestnut 30
#445, John Henry, Famous Race Horse, semi gloss dark bay 45
#470, Misty's Twilight, matte chestnut pinto 48
#497, Wimpy, Ideal Quarter Horse, matte golden chestnut 165
#703, Blanket Appaloosa, San Domingo, matte gray appaloosa 35
#704, Tennessee Walker, matte red bay . .55
#711LE, Breezing Dixie, Lady Phase, matte dark bay appaloosa 90
#758, Roy Rogers' Trigger Gift Set, Western Horse, matte palomino 42
#769, Morgan Mare, Marabella, matte liver chestnut 30
#807, Paint Horse Stallion, Stock Horse Stallion, matte liver chestnut pinto 40
#809, Paint Horse Foal, Stock Horse Foal, matte liver chestnut pinto 24
#835, Prancing Morgan, Sherman Morgan, semi-gloss black 185

#843, Selle Francais, Touch of Class, semi-gloss liver chestnut 35
#854CE, Memphis Storm, Tennessee Walker, glossy charcoal 75
#861, Family Appaloosa Foal, Stock Horse Foal, semi-gloss bay appaloosa 25
#881, Wild American Horse, Phar Lap, matte 35
#907, Family Arabian Stallion, semi-gloss wood grain 65
#926, Sergeant Pepper, Haflinger, matte black leopard 50
#946, Diamondot Buccaneer, Performance Horse, matte blue roan appaloosa 65
#971LE, Iron Metal Chief, Missouri Foxtrotter, semi-gloss black 55
#993, Shenandoah, Smoky, matte buckskin 40
#SR410592, Turbo, the Wonder Horse, Mustang, matte palomino 200
#SR494092, Sears Future Champ Show Set, Saddlebred Weanling, matte bay pinto 70
#SR700397, Sirocco, Indian Pony, matte chestnut pinto 70
#SR700994, Dressage Domino, Roemer, matte black pinto 120
#SR702697, Toys R' Us Brown Sugar, Justin Morgan, matte medium bay 45
#SR710196, Joy, JC Penny Pride and Joy Set, Nursing Foal, matte light sorrel 23
#SR710295, JC Penny Race Horses America Set, Phar Lap, matte medium dapple gray 35
#SR710493, JC Penny Wild Horses of America Set, Mustang, semi-gloss black 85

BRITISH ROYALTY

This is one of those categories where you can get in on the ground floor. Every king and queen, potential king and queen and their spouse is collectible. Buy commemorative items when they are new. I have a few Prince Harry items. We may not have royal blood in common, but...

Most individuals collect by monarch, prince, or princess. Take a different approach—collect by form, e.g., mugs, playing cards, etc. British royalty commemoratives were made at all quality levels. Stick to high-quality examples.

As in any modern collectible category, prices are speculative. This is especially true for limited edition Princess Di commemoratives. It is common to find recent issues at flea markets selling for much less than their original price.

Club: Commemorative Collector's Society, Lumless House, Gainsborough Rd., Winthrope, Near Newark, Nottingham NG24 2NR, U.K.

Cup and Saucer, swirl design, salmon pink, gold trim, white int with portrait and oak leaves, commemorates 1959 Queen Elizabeth II visit to Canada, Aynsley Bone China, England, 1959 35
Postcards, Prince Charles, Andrew, Edward, and Princess Anne, set of 5 5
Print, litho, HRH Prince Edward of Wales, pub in *Illustrated London News,* Jan 10, 1885 10
Spoons, set of 6 metal spoons with celluloid insert in handle, set consists of Princess Diana, Charles, Prince Phillip, the Queen, the Queen Mother, and the wedding of Fergie and Andrew, mkd "Waratah" on handle, outline of Australia and "Randa" on back 15
Toffee Tin, Bluebird Assorted Toffees, commemorates George VI 1939 visit to Canada and US, mkd "Harry Vincent Ltd Hunnington Worcestershire England," 3.75" x 1.25" 40
Trade Cards, "Kings and Queens of England," Kings of York Laundry, descriptions on back, 1954, set of 30 ...12

BRUSH POTTERY

J.W. McCoy founded the J.W. McCoy Pottery in Roseville, Ohio, in 1899. George Brush became general manager in 1909. After merging with several other small potteries in 1911 the company became the Brush-McCoy Pottery Company. The McCoy family sold its interests in 1925 and the pottery was renamed The Brush Pottery Company.

Ashtray, Onyx, green, 5" 14
Bowl, Onyx, brown, 5" 17
Bowl, Onyx, green, 7.25" 22
Cookie Jar, bear 65
Cookie Jar, Cinderella's coach 200
Cookie Jar, circus horse 295
Cookie Jar, clock 235
Cookie Jar, cow, kitten finial 160
Cookie Jar, Davy Crockett 75
Cookie Jar, donkey and cart 165
Cookie Jar, elephant with ice cream cone 110
Cookie Jar, Goldilocks 65
Cookie Jar, hillbilly frog 215
Cookie Jar, Humpty Dumpty 115
Cookie Jar, Peter Pan, 11.75" h 300
Flower Frog, Onyx 6
Pitcher, ribbed, jade green, 6" h 25
Planter, crouching dog, white, early 1950s, 3.75" h, 5.5" l 25
Planter, elephant, blue, 1939, 3.5" h 18
Planter, elephant, yellow, 1939, 3.5" h 15
Planter, frog, 1950s, 2.75" h, 5.75" l 18
Planter, pig, pink, 1952, 5.5" l 25
Planter, Princess, ftd, 3" h, 13.5" l 15
Planters, turtles, #205A male and #204A female, pink, 1940s 38

Stick Vase, #070, cobweb, pink, mid-1950s, 7.25" h 20
Urn, Onyx, brown, 6" h 17
Urn, Onyx, green, 6" h 45
Vase, #074, cobweb, pink, mid-1950s, 8" h .24
Vase, Onyx, brown 20

BURMA SHAVE

The famous Burma Shave jingle ad campaign was the brainstorm of Allan Odell, son of Burma-Vita's founder, Clinton M. Odell. The first sets, six signs placed 100 feet apart, appeared in 1926 on a stretch of road from Minneapolis to Albert Lea. Success was instantaneous and the Burma Shave name was fixed in the minds of drivers across the country. If You...Don't Know...Whose Signs These Are...You Haven't Driven...Very Far...Burma Shave.

Bank, glass jar, emb "Burma Shave" and vertical ribs, metal screw-on lid with coin slot, 2" h 28
Jar, glass, emb "Burma Shave" and vertical ribs, blue and white metal screw-on lid 30
Road Sign, blue lettering, yellow ground, 2-sided, "Burma Shave / Half A Pound," 1930s, 11" x 40" .140
Road Sign, blue lettering, yellow ground, 2-sided, "Burma Shave / Your Budget," 1930s, 11" x 40" .225
Road Sign, white lettering, red ground, 2-sided, "Burma Shave / Free," 9.5" x 35" 165
Road Sign, white lettering, red ground, 2-sided, "Burma Shave / Near and Far," 1960s, 17.25" x 40" .90
Road Sign, white lettering, red ground, 2-sided, "Burma Shave / That Folks," 1960s, 17.25" x 40" .90
Shaving Cream, "Brushless with Lanolin," red, white, and yellow tube and box . . .12
Shaving Mug and Brush, white china mug with red "Burma-Shave" logo, brush with red and white handle 25
Toy Truck, diecast, American Highway Legends, "If You / Don't Know / Whose Signs / These Are / You Can't Have / Driven Very Far / Burma Shave" on side, Hartoy Trucks, 1/64 scale, MIB . . .40

CALCULATORS

The Texas Instruments TI-2500 Datamath entered the market in the early 1970s. This electronic calculator, the marvel of its era, performed four functions—addition, subtraction, multiplication, and division. This is all it did. It retailed for over $100. Within less than a decade, calculators selling for less than $20 were capable of doing five times as many functions.

Early electronic calculators are dinosaurs. They deserve to be preserved. When collecting them, make certain to buy examples that retain their power transformer, instruction booklet, and original box. Make certain any calculator that you buy works. There are few around who know how to repair one.

It is a little too early for a category on home computers. But a few smart collectors are starting to stash away the early Texas Instrument and Commodore models.

Club: International Calculators Collectors Club, 14561 Livingston St., Tustin, CA 92780, www.oldcalcs.com.

Addimult, mechanical 15
Bohn Contex, dust cover 12
Bowmar MX40, red LED 24
Bowmar MX55, red LED 18
Calfax Data Brain II 18
Canon Palmtronic 10M 28
Casio 8M 16
Casio CM-607 20
Casio CP-803 Personal 8 20

Casio Melody 80 85
Chadwick Magic Brain 12
Corvus 312, red LED 12
Curta II, SN558708, plastic case 1,000
Hewlett Packard 27 285
Hewlett Packard 38e, financial 100
Hewlett Packard 46 160
Hewlett Packard 55 185
Hewlett Packard 71b 125
Hewlett Packard 80, 1972 110
Kings Point KP-460A, LED 15
Monroe Model 1610 68
Montgomery Ward P8F, LED 15
Novus Mathematician 24
Olivetti Tetractys 24 55
Otis King, Model K 120
RCA Model 1212, spherical 110
Rockwell 64 RD, scientific 16
Sharp EL-8024, electronic 15
Sperry-Remington 661-D 15
Texas Instruments Exactra 19 55
Texas Instruments Little Professor, 1976 . . .35
Texas Instruments SR-10 18
Texas Instruments SR-50, slide rule 30
Texas Instruments TI-30 25
Texas Instruments TI-58 25
Texas Instruments TI-68, scientific 70
Texas Instruments TI-340 15
Texas Instruments TI-1200 18
Texas Instruments TI-1500 15
Unisonic 1011, slip case 12

CALENDAR PLATES

Calendar plates are one of the traditional, affordable collecting categories. A few years ago, they sold in the $10 to $20 range; now that figure has jumped to $35 to $50.

Value rests with the decorative motif and the place for which it was issued. A fun collection would be to collect the same plate and see how many different merchants and other advertisers utilized it.

Club: Calendar Plate Collectors Club, 710 N. Lake Shore Dr., Tower Lakes, IL 60010.

1906, Indian with calendar in headdress, mkd "Imperial China" 60
1907, Order of Elks 50
1908, dog portrait .35

1908, flowers .35
1908, Gibson-type girl portrait, "Peock's Pharmacy, Edgewood, IA" adv .40
1908, John A Bock, Farmington, W VA, 'Square Deal' Store .45
1909, horsehead .22
1909, Queen Louise portrait .26
1909, Santa flying in zeppelin, dropping presents to children .50
1910, boxer dog .45
1910, high school center, bell border .32
1910, lighthouse scene .35
1910, Niagara Falls .15
1910, peacock .30
1911, cherub, "Cash Grocery Store, WC Vanderberg, Hoopstown, IL"adv .40
1911, Lincoln's portrait .75
1911, red touring car, Buffalo Pottery .45
1912, biplane, Cincinnati, OH grocery adv .65
1912, hot air balloons .75
1912, Sunbonnet Babies getting acquainted .75
1913, boy in rags beneath arch .24
1913, owl on book, "Hanover Ohio" adv .25
1914, Betsy Ross, "Norfolk, VA" adv .35
1914, Washington's tomb, artist sgd "A. Smith" .32
1915, Panama Canal with American flag .50
1916, American flag and eagle with shield .32
1918, violets and 21 clocks from cities around the world .28
1919, ship scene center .25
1920, American Eagle & Victory, Great World War .28
1921, dove and 5 allied flags .38
1922, dog flushing birds .45

1924, flowers and holly .30
1928, deer in field, Williamsville, IL adv .50
1930, Dutch boy and dog, Saunemin, IL adv .50
1954, Fiesta ware, ivory .35
1962, Merry Christmas, Gately's .15
1964, Pebbleford, pink, adv .8
1969, God Bless Our House, Meakin .8

CALENDARS

The primary reason calendars are collected is for the calendar art. Prices hinge on quality of printing and the pizazz of the subject. A strong advertising aspect adds to the value.

A highly overlooked calendar collecting area is the modern art and photographic calendar. For whatever reason, there is little interest in calendars dating after 1940. Collectors are making a major mistake. There are some great calendars from this later time period selling for less than $2.

"Gentlemen's" calendars did not grace the kitchen wall, but they are very collectible. Illustrations range from the pinup beauties of Elvgren and Moran and the Esquire Vargas ladies in the 1930s to the Playboy Playmates of the 1960s. Early Playboy calendars sell in the $50 plus range.

But what's the fun of having something you cannot display openly? The following list will clear corporate censors with no problems.

Club: Calendar Collector Society, 18222 Flower Hill Way #299, Gaithersburg, MD 20879.

1920, Chevrolet Motor Cars, farm scene with car and family above, full pad, 16" x 31" .145
1920, Globe Feeds, children and chicks, full pad .110
1922, Sunshine Biscuits, girl in yellow and pink gown, June sheet, 9" x 15" .5
1922, Texaco, star logo, full pad, 25" x 13" .185
1922, Western & Southern Life Insurance, girl in bonnet with flowers, 9" x 9" .20

1923, Mount Airy Tire & Battery Co, paper in wood frame, "S Mile S," pretty woman framed within large tire, 19.25" h, 10.75" w 145

1926, Socony, cardboard, Soconny logo above map of New York and New England, 24.75" h, 13" w 90

1927, GE Packard Mazda Lamps, paper in wood frame, "Twilight," woman wearing swimsuit and robe, Hayden artist, "Copyright 1926 GE Co" in lower right, 20.5" h, 9" w 145

1928, Iroquois Brewery, profile of young squaw with feathers and beads in hair, full pad, framed .850

1929, De Laval Cream Separators, paper in wood frame, boy sitting on steps, feeding scraps to puppy, sgd "Norman Price," "Copyright, The De Laval Separator Co, Printed in USA" at bottom of print, 24.5" h, 13.25" w 100

1934, Wrigley's Spearmint Gum, paper in wood frame, Myrt and Marge radio stars, Dec calendar page only, 14.75" h, 8.75" w 100

1940, Hood's Mild, happy baby face with bottle, Oct pad, 10" x 14" 35

1947, Gilmore Gasoline, red lion logo, 7" x 17" 20

1948, Armwall Machine Co, paper with metal edging, "In Full Swing, " girl on swing, apple blossoms overhead, painted by Walt Otto, "Copyright Shaw Barton, Coshocton, Ohio" across bottom of print, 32.75" h, 16" w 18

1949, Royster Fertilizers, baby girl with wooden doll, sgd "Charlotte Becker," full pad, 4.75" x 8" .15

1952, Blue Ridge Lines, paper in wood frame, stagecoach and bus image, sgd "Harper Goff," "Shaw-Barton, Coshocton, Ohio, Printed in USA" at bottom right, 26" h, 16" w 35

1955, John Deere, wildlife book, full pad . .35

1960, Sinclair Petroleum Products, paper with metal ends, woman wearing ballgown, Thomas Oil Co, Greensburg, PA adv, 33.5" h, 16" 28

1961, NAPA Herminie Motor Co, paper with metal edging, racing scene with pinup girl leaning against red convertible, sgd "Medcalf," 33.75" h, 16" w 35

1966, Stutz Bearcat, paper in wood frame, yellow convertible at beach, Hawkinson Treads and Mohawk Tires adv, "Created by Brown and Bigelow Div of Standard PackagingCorp, USA," at lower left,26" h, 17.5" w

1969, Elvgren pin-up, "Swingin' Sweetie," folding punch-out, orig envelope, 4.75" x 10" 15

1979, Ruger Firearms, 30th anniversary, hunting moose in canoe scene, full pad 65

CALIFORNIA POTTERIES

California pottery collectors divide into three distinct groups—art pottery, dinnerware, and figurine collectors. California art pottery is trendy and expensive. Dinnerware prices are stable. Figurine prices are cooling following a major price run in the mid- and late 1990s.

California pottery collectors focus on firm, pattern, or period within their adopted specialty. Over a dozen checklist books dealing with a specific manufacturer have been published in the last ten years. Each was followed by a short speculative period in the company's product.

Brad Keeler, figure, crouching jaguar on rocky base, 4.5" h, 10.5" l 210

Brad Keeler, figures, pair of flamingoes, black and white, 10" h (standing upright) and 7.5" h (bending) 110

Brad Keeeler, planter, swan, pale pink ground, 7.5" h, 8"l .85

Brad Keeler, platter, lobster, #869, 17" l . . 135

Brayton Laguna, beverage set, pitcher and 4 mugs, brown glaze, band of pretzels around center of each pc, figural pretzel handles, mkd "Brayton Laguna Beach Calif. Designed by F. Horvath," 7.5" h pitcher, 5" h mugs, price for set 225

Brayton Laguna, cookie jar, grandma, 11" h 115

Brayton Laguna, figure, cowboy, 9.5" h . .200

Brayton Laguna, pitcher, Little Miss Muffet, 5" h 80

Brayton Laguna, salt and pepper shakers, figural Dutch boy and girl, 5" h 60

California Faience, bowl, cuence technique on rim, sky blue, yellow, and matte black glaze, red clay body, mkd "California Faience," 2.5" h, 12" d 350

California Faience, flower frog, pelican, matte green 275

California Faience, flower frog, pelican, turquoise 300

California Faience, tile, sky blue glaze, red clay body, mkd "Califormia Faience," 4" sq 120

California Faience, vase, sky blue glaze, red clay body, mkd "California Faience," 8" h, 4.5" d 550

Claire Lerner, figurine, pair of cranes, chartreuse, 9.5" h 24

Claire Lerner, vase, tropical motif with emb bird and palm tree, CL22, dark green, 12" h 25

Freeman-McFarlin, figure, black cat, 10" h 60

Freeman-McFarlin, figure, gold lion, reclining, 811, 12.5" h, 19.5" l 350

Freeman-McFarlin, figures, pair of gold rabbits, #114 and #115, 11" h (sitting up), 6" h (reclining) 150

Garden City, salt and pepper shakers, cylindrical with fluted lower half, yellow, 5.25" h 80

Garden City, vase, flattened bowl shape with pedestal base, yellow 210

Garden City, vase, fluted cylinder form with slightly flaring rim and pedestal base, white, mkd "USA," 11" h 70

Gilner, planter, native figure with metal earrings standing beside spear and shield propped against foliage planter, 6.75" h, 5" w 35

Gilner, planter, pixie and log, chartreuse, 6" h 60

Gilner, salt and pepper shakers, pixie 45

Hedi Schoop, candleholders, pr of ladies, each holding a basket on her hip, pink and purple with gold dec, #486 and #487, 9.5" h 325

Hedi Schoop, figure, minstrel, pink and green with gold highlights, 12.5" h 25

Hedi Schoop, planter, lady wearing blue and white dress dec with yellow roses and yellow and blue trim and holding a parasol, 13" h, 7.25" w 150

Miramar of California, ashtray, oblong, cigarette rests on flattened rim, dark green, metal stand, #174, 7" x 5" 30

Miramar of California, planter, 4-sided bowl form with rope twist rim, metal stand, #616, turquoise, 8" q 35

Sascha Brastoff, dinner service, Surf Ballet, 54 pcs 400

Sascha Brastoff, figurine, elephant, S8, 8" h 160
Sascha Brastoff, figurine, rooster, pink and gold, 16.75" h 150
Sascha Brastoff, jar, egg-shaped, quail dec, 044A, 8" h 135
Sascha Brastoff, sculpture, fish, 2F, 7.75" h, 20.5" l 95
Sascha Brastoff, vase/candlelabra, figural woman, upraised arms hold candles, open hat is a bud vase, 13" h . 265
Twin Winton, figurine, black girl holding lollipop, #T-9, mkd "Twinton" on front of base, 5.5" h 50
Twin Winton, planter, squirrel with nut, 8" h 50
Twin Winton, wall pocket, lamb's head, 5" h, 7.5" w 45
Weil Ware, vase, woman pushing flower cart, floral dec on dress and cart, 8" h . 40
Weil Ware, wall pocket, lady wearing flowered scarf and blouse holding cornucopia, 9" h, 5" w 50

CAMARK POTTERY

Camark pottery derives its name from its location in Camden, Arkansas. The company was organized in 1926 and produced decorative and utilitarian items in hundreds of shapes, colors, and forms. The pottery closed in 1986.

Ashtray, figural stork on ashtray base, green matte glaze, 7.5" h, 7" x 4" base . . 65
Basket, Nor-so, flower form with large scrolling handles, light green with gold fleck dec, 4" h 40

Bowl, rope design, burgundy, paper label and stamp, 2" x 4.25" 25
Console Bowl, lotus leaf, off-white matte glaze, #140, 11" x 8.5" 30
Console Set, basket and pair of candleholders, Morning Glory II, 9.75" h basket, 5.25" h candleholders 80
Console Set, bowl and pair of candleholders, Iris, 6" h x 15" w bowl, 5.5" h candleholders 85
Cornucopia Vase, green, 7" h 28
Fan Vase, burgundy and pale yellow, ring handles at base, 6" h, 6.5" w 45
Figure, black cat gazing into clear glass fishbowl 65
Figure, cat, black, 16" l 40
Figure, dachshund, turquoise, 3" h, 4.5" l . . 55
Figure, elephant, blue, 2.5" h 25
Flower Bowl and Frog, Nor-So, pansy, green, gold highlights, 4" 35
Flower Frog, double swan, yellow, 8" h . . 125
Flower Frog, flying bird, yellow, 5.5" h 30
Pitcher, Nor-So, spherical with large scrolling handle, black with gold fleck dec, 4.5" h 40
Pitcher and Bowl, miniature, Nor-So, pink with gold handle and rims, 3" h pitcher, 5.5" d bowl 35
Planter, rooster, #501, green, 9" h 35
Salt and Pepper Shakers, figural letters "S" and "P", pink, Mackinac Island souvenir sticker 25
Vase, #831, fan shape with emb purple clematis, pedestal base, 8.25" h 90
Vase, pitcher form with diamond-shaped body, green, 9.5" h 60

CAMBRIDGE GLASS

The Cambridge Glass Company of Cambridge, Ohio, began operation in 1901. Its first products were clear tableware. Later color, etched, and engraved pieces were added to the line. Production continued until 1954. The Imperial Glass Company of Bellaire, Ohio, bought some of the Cambridge molds and continued production of these pieces.

Club: National Cambridge Collectors, Inc., P.O. Box 416, Cambridge, OH 43725, www.cambridgeglass.org.

Bonbon, Caprice, #133, low, ftd, moonlight blue, 6" sq .65
Bonbon, Caprice, #148, oval, moonlight blue, 4.5" w .40
Bonbon, Caprice, #154, moonlight blue, 6" sq .45
Bonbon, Caprice, #155, oval, moonlight blue, 6" w .60
Bowl, Caprice, #49, 4-ftd, moonlight blue, 8" d 200
Bowl, Caprice #50, moonlight blue, 8.5" sq 100
Bowl, Caprice, #52, crimped, moonlight blue, 9.5" d 150
Bowl, Caprice, #54, belled, 3-ftd, moonlight blue, 10.5" d 175
Bowl, Caprice, #58, moonlight blue, 10.5" sq 135
Bowl, Caprice, #61, crimped, moonlight blue, 12.5" d .95
Bowl, Caprice, #62, belled, 3-ftd, moonlight blue, 12.5" d 150
Bowl, Caprice, #62, belled, 4-ftd, moonlight blue, 12.5" d .95
Bowl, Caprice, #65, oval, moonlight blue, 10" w .90
Bowl, Caprice, #81, low, 4-ftd, moonlight blue, 11.5" d 100
Bowl, Caprice, #82, shallow, 4-ftd, moonlight blue, 13.5" d 135
Bowl, Caprice, #151, 2 handles, ftd base, moonlight blue, 5" w .40
Cabaret Plate, #32, 4-ftd, moonlight blue, 11" d .45
Candy Dish, cov, #165, moonlihgt blue 125
Candy Dish, cov, #167, moonlight blue 150
Candy Dish, cov, #168, 2-part, moonlight blue 250
Cigarette Box, cov, #207, moonlight blue, small .45
Cigarette Box, cov, #208, moonlight blue, large 110
Compote, #130, low, ftd, moonlight blue .24
Cup and Saucer, #17, moonlight blue .15
Oil, #101, blue stopper, moonlight blue, 3 oz .85
Plate, #30, moonlight blue, 16" d 110
Plate, #131, low, ftd, moonlight blue, 8" d .40
Relish, #120, 2-part, moonlight blue, 6.75" d .25
Relish, #124, 3-part, moonlight blue, 8.5" d 20
Relish, #126, 4-part, moonlight blue, 12" d 250

Rose Bowl, #235, 4-ftd, moonlight blue, 6" d 120
Rose Bowl, #236, 4-ftd, moonlight blue, 8" d 250
Salad Bowl, #80, cupped, moonlight blue, 13" d 250
Salad Bowl, #82, moonlight blue 325
Salt and Pepper Shakers, pr, #97, moonlight blue, 3 pcs 125
Sherbet, #300, moonlight blue, low .28
Sherbet, #300, moonlight blue, tall .12
Tumbler, #10, ftd, moonlight blue, 10 oz .35
Tumbler, #12, ftd, moonlight blue, 3 oz .70
Tumbler, #300, ftd, moonlight blue, 5 oz .30
Tumbler, #300, ftd, moonlight blue, 12 oz .40
Tumbler, #310, flat, moonlight blue, 5 oz .85
Tumbler, #310, flat, moonlight blue, 10 oz .60
Tumbler, #310, flat, moonlight blue, 12 oz 115

CAMERAS

Just because a camera is old does not mean it is valuable. Rather, assume that the more examples of a camera that were made the less likely it is to be of any value. Collectors seek unusual cameras or examples from companies that failed quickly.

A portion of a camera's value rests on whether it works. Check bellows cameras by shining a strong light over the outside surface while looking at the inside. Also check the seating on removable lenses.

Collectors have begun to focus on 35mm cameras. A collection can be built of early models at a modest cost per camera. There is also a growing market in camera accessories and ephemera.

Plastic cameras depicting cartoon characters Mickey Mouse, Bugs Bunny, Punky Brewster, Holly Hobbie, Teenage Mutant Ninja Turtles, etc., are a fun collecting area that can really brighten up a shelf. The most striking are the "face" cameras resembling some of these characters, clowns, bears, or Santa Claus, and even a full-figure Charlie Tuna.

Early 1930s Kodak box and folding cameras can be found in red, blue, brown, green, pink, and some even more exotic colors. The challenge exists in finding an example of each model in each color.

The Art Deco crowd will want both sizes of the Beau Brownies and the diamond, lightning bolt, and step patterns of the folding Petites.

Collecting cardboard covered disposable cameras is the new craze. Rewrapped and reloaded models advertising products such as Winchester bullets, Playboy, Budweiser, college sports teams, cereals, etc., are the most desirable.

Unless noted otherwise, cameras listed are in very good to excellent working condition.

Clubs: American Society of Camera Collectors, 7415 Reseda Blvd., Reseda, CA 91335; Photographic Historical Society, Inc., P.O. Box 39563, Rochester, NY 14604.

VINTAGE CAMERAS

Argoflex Em, metal body, 1948 40
Argus, Super Seventy-five, 1954-58 20
Asahi Pentax Spotmatic, c1964 75
Bell & Howell Agat 18, c1984-89 50
Bell & Howell Autoload 342, 1970-72 10
Birdseye Flash, plastic, c1954 10
Bolsey Jubilee, 35mm, c1955-56 60
Braun Paxette I, c1952 50
Canon Pellix, 1965-66 175
Collegiate Camera No. 3 60
Coronet Ambassador, c1955 25
Coronet Crystarflex, c1953 85
Eastman Anniversary Kodak, special edition of No. 2 Hawk-Eye Model C, 1930 35
Eastman Baby Brownie, New York World's Fair model, 1939 300
Eastman Boy Scout Brownie Six-20 175
Eastman Hawkette No. 2, folding Kodak, brown Bakelite body, 1930s 100
Eastman Jiffy Kodak Vest Pocket, black plastic, 1935-42 40
Eastman Kodak Brownie 44A, 1959-66 15
Eastman Kodak Duaflex Model IV 10
Eastman Kodak Pony 828, 1949-59 15
Eastman Six-20 Kodak B, folding, 1937-40 50
Fokaflex, black Bakelite, TLR-style box camera, Czechoslovakia, 1950s 100
Graflex Century 35 Model N 50
Graflex Graphic 35 Electric, c1959 60
Imperial Deluxe Six-Twenty Twin Lens Reflex, plastic TLR box 10
Impulse Ltd Voltron Starshooter 110, c1985 50
Leitz Leica III F, chrome body 350
Macy M-16, black box, 1930s 25
Metropolitan Industries Cardinal 120, metal box, Art Deco faceplate 25
Minolta A3, 35mm rangefinder, 1959 75
Minolta Six, collapsible folding camera, 1935 150
Miranda Automex II, 1963 125
Olympic Junior, Bakelite, c1934 150
Olympus 36 IV, c1950 85
Olympus Focaflex Automatic, c1962 225
Orion No. 142, plastic 10
Polaroid 110A Pathfinder, c1957-60 75
Polaroid Swinger Model 20 5
Sears Colorado, gray plastic 60
Sears Marvel S016, box camera, Art Deco faceplate, c1940 10
Sears Tower One-Twenty, box, 1950s 10
Spartus Vanguard, plastic box, c1962 12
Spartus Vest Pocket, folding 30
Universal Mercury Rapid winder, c1939 . .75
Voigtlander Baby Bessa, c1930 175
Voigtlander Vitomatic II, c1960 85
Zeiss Ikon Contina 1C, 1958-60 50
Zeiss Ikon Super Ikonata A 530, 1935-37 .250

NOVELTY CAMERAS

Bazooka Joe, Cardinal Camera Corp, metal and black plastic case, orig box, 1957 40
Bugs Bunny, Helm Toy Corp, c1978 75
Clown Head, Kiddie Camera 75
Davy Crockett, Herbert George Co, box camera, black plastic, Crockett and rifles on metal faceplate 60
Donald Duck, Herbert George Co, black plastic, relief images of Donald, Huey, Dewey, and Louie on back, late 1940s . .50
Encore De Luxe, cardboard, Encore Camera Co, Hollywood, 1940s-50s 50
GEC Transistomatic Radio Camera, combination transistor radio/camera, c1964 225
Hopalong Cassidy, plastic box camera, with flash, c1950 200
Indiana Jones Safari, orig box 35
Marlboro Cigarettes, plastic cigarette box shape, c1989 .75
Masters of the Universe, Mattell, Castle Grayskull-shaped green plastic case, c1985 15
Mick-A-Matic, Child Guidance Products, c1971 60
Police Academy 6, Fujicolor Quicksnap, disposable, c1989 .30
Punky Brewster, Helm Toy Corp, red plastic, c1984 20
Roy Rogers & Trigger, Herbert George Co, black plastic, Roy and Trigger on aluminum faceplate 35
Santa Claus, Kiddie Camera 60
Snoopy-Matic, Helm Toy Corp, doghouse shape 175

CANDLEWICK

Imperial Glass Corporation issued its No. 400 pattern, Candlewick, in 1936 and continued to produce it until 1982. In 1985 the Candlewick molds were dispersed to a number of sources, e.g., Boyd Crystal Art Glass, through sale.

Over 650 items and sets are known. Shapes include round, oval, oblong, heart, and square. The largest assortment of pieces and sets were made during the late 1940s and early 1950s. Watch for reproductions!

Clubs: Candlewick Club, 275 Milledge Terr., Athens, GA 30606; National Candlewick Collector's Club, 6534 South Ave., Holland, OH 43528; National Imperial Glass Collectors Society, P.O. Box 534, Bellaire, OH 43906, www.imperialglass.org.

After Dinner Cup 16
Ashtray, oblong, 4.5" .8
Bon-Bon, heart shape, handled, 5" 40
Bouillon Cup, 2 handles 80
Bowl, 7" 50
Bowl, 9" 55
Bowl, 13" 150
Bowl, fluted, 5.5" 75
Bowl, round, ribbed, 4 toes, 8.5" 125
Bread and Butter Plate, 6" 10
Bud Vase, large mouth, 4" 75
Bud Vase, low ftd, large beads, 5.75" 65
Cake Stand, 3-bead stem, 11" 140
Candleholder, handled 80
Centerbowl, 11" 25
Coaster, 5 spokes 85
Coaster, 10 spokes .12
Cocktail, 3.5 oz 140
Coffee Cup 12
Compote, 4.5" 45
Compote, 4-bead stem, 5.5" 30
Compote, low, 2-bead stem 35
Creamer and Sugar, beaded foot 85
Cream Soup Bowl 65
Cruet, handled, with stopper, 6 oz 165
Deviled Egg Tray 200
Dinner Plate, 10" 55
Fan Vase, 6" 85
Float Bowl, 10" 20
Icer Bowl 75
Jelly Bowl, 4" 15
Luncheon Plate, 9" 18
Marmalade Ladle 18

Mayonnaise Set, 3 pcs 60
Mint Tray, center handle 35
Mustard Jar, cov, with spoon 100
Mustard Spoon 35
Pitcher, 1 pt 325
Pitcher, 80 oz 225
Plate, 2 handles, 7.5" 15
Punch Ladle 75
Relish, 2 sections, 2 handles, 6.5" 20
Relish, 3 sections, 10.5" 50
Relish, 5 sections, 13" 90
Salad Plate, crescent shape, 8.5" 90
Salt and Pepper Shakers, 9-bead base . . .30
Salt Dip, 18 beads, 2" 12
Saucer 4
Sherbet, 6 oz 75
Teacup 8
Torte Plate, 14" 50
Tray, oblong, 6.5" .20
Tray, oval, 9" 35
Vase, straight sides, 10" 300
Water Tumbler, 9 oz 120

CANDY COLLECTIBLES

Who doesn't love candy? Forget the chocoholics. I'm a Juicy Fruit man. Once you start looking for candy related material, you are quickly overwhelmed by how much is available. Do not forget the boxes. They are usually discarded. Ask your local drugstore to save the more decorative ones for you. Today's garbage is tomorrow's gold.

Note: See Candy Containers for additional listings.

Box, Pinocchio Chewing Gum, Dietz Gum Co, image of Pinocchio with tree branch nose supporting a nest with 2 birds, Jiminy Cricket below, cardboard, ©1940, 6.25" x 8.5" x 2" 350

Box, Squirrel Brand Peanut Bars, image of squirrel eating peanut bar, cardboard, 5.75" x 10.25" x 3" 385

Display, Adams Chicklets Candy Coated Gum, litho metal over wood countertop display with divided compartments for individual pkgs, litho metal adv change dish in front, 2.75" x 12.25" x 16" 250

Display Box, Curtiss Baby Ruth Peppermint Gum, cardboard, red and white diagonal stripe design, 20 unopened orig packs, 5" x 6" x 4.25" 2,850

Display Box, Florida Brand Peppermint Chewing Gum, Southern Chicle Co, full box with 20 unopened packs, back insert display, and orig lid, 1920s, 5" x 6.25" x 4.25" 3,100

Display Rack, Life Savers, litho tin countertop rack, orig paper label intact, 16.5" x 9.5" x 9.75" 325

Jigsaw Puzzle, Curtiss Candy Co, "Singing in the Rain," double-sided, reverse shows Curtiss 1¢ candies, 6" x 7" 45

Pail, Rabbits Candy, Lovell & Covel Co, Peter Cottontail graphics all around, 3" h, 3" d 550

Pail, Schraffts Candy, litho tin, nursery rhyme graphics all around, bail handle, 3.75" h, 4" d 1,000

Pocket Mirror, Beeman's Pepsin Gum, celluloid, gentleman's (Beeman?) portrait above slogan "Good for Digestion," 2.25" d 250

Pocket Mirror, WJ White Chewing Gums, celluloid, red and white product image on white ground, white lettering on dark blue rim, 2.25" d 130

Sign, Fleer's Pepsin Gum, litho cardboard, string hanger, round, product image on front, white lettering on red rim text on back, 4.25" d 175

Tin, Parkinson's Butter-Scotch, litho tin, image of 3 horses wearing blankets "Parading In The Paddocks, Racecourse Doncaster" on lid, red and gold on dark blue ground, 2.5" x 7.5" x 1" 85

Tin, Pulver's Kola Pepsin Chewing Gum, litho tin, images of Yellow Kid gum machines on back, 3" l 500
Tin, Schrafft's Kiddyland Candy, litho tin cylinder with multicolor cartoon character images, 5.25" h, 3.25" d 675

CANDY CONTAINERS

Candy containers were produced in shapes that appealed to children and usually sold for ten cents. They remained popular until the 1960s when they became expensive to mass produce.

Candy containers with original paint, candy, and closures command a high premium, but be aware of reproduced parts and repainting. The closure is a critical part of each container; its loss detracts significantly from the value.

Club: Candy Container Collectors of America, P.O. Box 352, Chelmsford, MA 01824.

COMPOSITION

Banty Rooster, black body with red head and comb, painted yellow metal feet, 5.5" h, 3.75" l 375
Belsnickle, orange robe with applied beads, black boots and base, missing feather tree, 8" h 325
Chick, glass eyes, wire legs, 4.5" h 300
Chick Nodder, wearing bright blue jacket and orange pants, 6" h 130
Chicks on Nest, 2 chicks (1 hatching) and 2 eggs on wicker nest, 3.25" h,4.25" d . .300

Daisy Duck, long billed, wearing red dress and black hat, 6.5" h 250
Drake, polychrome painted, bottom bill flaps, glass eyes, painted pink metal feet, 7.5" h, 9" l .475
Elephant, walking, glass eyes, 5.75" l 200
Hen on Nest, hen with red highlights on woven straw nest, 5" h 300
Hen on Stump Nest, 2 chicks under wing, browns, red, yellow and white 140
Pheasant on Tree Stump, polychromed pheasant on spring legs, mica and painted stump, 3.75" h 150
Rabbit, standing upright, glass eyes, holding a white clover in mouth, gray and white paint, 7.75" h 415
Rabbit, white fur covering, hide feet and ears, pink glass eyes 125
Rabbit, white with black spots, seated, carrot in mouth, glass eyes, 7.25" h . . .200
Rooster, black body with yellow and white hightlights, painted metal feet, 6.75" h, 6.5" l 250
Turkey, painted, lead feet, 3.75" h 150

GLASS

Army Bomber, 5.5" l .18
Bulldog, brown body, gold collar 65
Candlestick Phone, Victory Glass Co, 4.75" h 25
Clown on Rocking Horse, white clown with red hat, red reins on horse 275
House, green roof and gable ends, orange eaves, red foundation and fireplace, replaced closure 200
Locomotive, Stough's E3S Narrow Cab, c1940, screw-on closure, 1.5" h, 4" l 25
Pistol, Kolt Candy 50
Radio, emb "Tune In," 3 radio dials, black and gold serpentine radio horn, mkd "USA," 4.5" h, 2.5" w 100

SPUN COTTON

Crane, glass eyes, red wood beak, real feathers, spring-loaded wings, red paper twist legs, 12" h 50
Duck, glass eyes, yellow wood bill, yellow metal feet and legs, "Whitmans Philadelphia" label, 8" h 165
Goose, glass eyes, wood bill flaps, spring loaded wings, real feathers, orange composition feet, 10" h 150

CAP GUNS

Classic collectors collect the one-shot, cast iron pistols manufactured during the first third of the 20th century. Kids of the 1950s collect roll-cap pistols. Children of the 1990s do not know what they are missing. Prices for roll-cap pistols are skyrocketing. Buy them in working order only. Ideally, acquire them with their original accessories, e.g., holsters, fake bullets, etc.

Club: Toy Gun Collectors of America, 312 Sterling Way, Anaheim, CA 92807.

Circle, A Brand, Oh Boy series, 1922 patent date .65
Cowboy, Hubley, white grips, 11" l .125
Cowboy King, Stevens, 1948 .140
Derringer, Hubley, chrome plated, white plastic grips, 3.25" l .8
Dick Tracy, miniature .35
Eagle Single Shot, cast iron, 1890s, 7.5"l .100
Echo Single Shot, 4.5" l .50
Hopalong Cassidy, Wyandotte, nickel silver finish, ivory plastic grips, brown leather holster with steer conch, 1950s .300
Hubley #210, roll caps, 4.25" l .50
Pal, Hubley, single shot, 6" l .8
Paratrooper, Zee Toys, 1972, MIP .25
Pet, nickel plated, 6" l .20
Pirate, double barrel, silver-toned metal, ivory grips, 9.75" l .95
Pony Boy, leather holster and belt, 1950s, 9.5" l .45

Rodeo Series, Hubley, Bakelite handle, engraved barrel and stock, leather holster .100
Roy Rogers, crossed pistols with pearl grips on buckle of tooled leather, 2 cap guns with "RR," horseshoe, and "Trigger" on grips, gilt hammers, guns mkd "Los Angeles Calif. Made in USA," 10" l guns, 31" l belt .1,200
Roy Rogers, Pal, 5.5" l .90
Shoot the Hat, cast iron .700
Smoky, 1950s .30
Sneaky Pete, #605, uses Shark strip caps, with key chain, 1960s, MIP .6

CARNIVAL CHALKWARE

Carnival chalkware is my candidate for the kitsch collectible of the 1980s. No one uses quality to describe these inexpensive prizes given out by games of chance at carnivals, amusement parks, and ocean boardwalks.

The best pieces are those depicting a specific individual or character. Since most were bootlegged (made without permission), they often appear with a fictitious name, e.g., "Smile Doll" is really supposed to be Shirley Temple. The other strong collecting subcategory is the animal figure. As long as the object comes close to capturing the appearance of a pet, animal collectors will buy it.

Air Raid Warden, c1940, 14" h .110
Betty Boop, c1930-40, 15" h .250
Black Kewpie, c1935-45, 12" h .110
Buffalo, bank, c1950, 10.5" l .30
Charlie McCarthy, c1938, 16" h .60
China Boy, JY Jenkins, 1948, 13" h .115
Clown, bank, c1950, 13" h .40
Corn in Hand, Iowa Centennial, 1838-1938, 12" h .30
Crying Pig, c1940-50, 7" .12
Devil's Head, bank, c1950, 6.5" h .75
Donald Duck, c1934, 13" h .85
Donald Duck, c1942-50, 7" h .6
Elephant, c1960, 10.5" h .35
Fat Kewpie, c1935-45, 13" h .50
Ferdinand the Bull, bank, c1940-50, 9" h .50
Fish Bowl Stand, nude figure peering over fish bowl (missing), c1930, 15" h .100

George Washington, c1940, 11" h 40
Horse 'N Saddle, c1940-50, 10.5" h 30
Hula Girl, c1947, 15" h 150
Indian with Drum, c1940-50, 12.5"h 75
Junior Pig, bank, c1940-50, 9.5" h 28
King Kong, c1930-40, 7" h 35
King Kong, 12.5" h 60
Majorette, c1940-50, 15.5" h 40
Piggy Bank, c1950, 11" l 55
Pinocchio, c1940, 15" h 95
Porky Pig, bank, c1945, 12" h 35
Rider on Horse, c1940, 9" h 82
Sailor Boys, pr, c1934, 9" h 40
Sailor Girl, c1930-40, 14" h 55
Skull, c1950, 6" h 50
Skull with Snake, c1960, 6" h 50
Small Pig, c1935, 6" h 18
Snow White, c1937, 14" h 50
Tom Boy, c1940, 15.5" h 60
Uncle Sam, c1935, 15" h 60
Wolf, c1934, 17" h 28

CARNIVAL GLASS

Carnival glass is iridized pressed glass. "Classic" carnival glass was produced between 1905 and 1930 by manufacturers in Australia, Czechoslovakia, England, Finland, France, Germany, Sweden, and the United States. Leading American manufacturers include Dugan, Fenton, Imperial, Millersburg, and Northwood.

Carnival glass has been made continuously since its introduction. American manufacturers of carnival glass in the post-1945 period include Boyd, Fenton, Imperial, Mosser, and L. G. Wright. The Jain Glass Works in India made carnival glass from 1935 until 1986.

Period molds survive and are occasionally used to create reproductions.

Clubs: American Carnival Glass Assoc., P.O. Box 235, Littlestown, PA 17340; Collectible Carnival Glass Assoc., 2360 N. Old SR 9, Columbus, IN 47203; International Carnival Glass Assoc., Box 306, Mentone, IN 46539.

Beverage Set, Crackle, pitcher and 6 tumblers, marigold, Imperial, pre-1930, 8" h, pitcher, 4.75" h tumblers 165
Bowl, Basket Weave, ruffled, red Fenton, pre-1910, 2.25" h, 5.5" d 650
Bowl, Captive Rose, amethyst, Fenton, c1910, 7.5" d 125
Bowl, Grape pattern #473, ruffled, Helios (pale green), Imperial, pre-1920, 8" d . . .50
Bowl, Windmill, amethyst, pre-1970, 8" x 4.5" 40
Compote, Peacock at the Urn, marigold, clear foot, Fenton, pre-1920, 5.5" h, 4.5" d 55
Compote, Strawberry Wreath, amethyst, Millersburg, pre-1920 425
Console Set, sleigh and 2 candleholders, cobalt, Westmoreland, pre-1970, 9" x 6" sleigh, 4.5" h candleholders 150
Covered Dish, duck, amethyst, mkd "WG," Westmoreland, 1970s, 8.5" l 45
Covered Dish, turkey, amethyst, LE Smith, pre-1970 55
Ice Cream Bowl, Peacock at the Urn, white, pre-1920, 10" h 650
Master Salt, figural swan, ice green, 4" x 3.75" x 3" 95

Mug, Orange Tree pattern, blue, Fenton, c1910, 3.5" h, 4" w .60
Mug, Robin, ruby, mkd "IG," Imperial 35
Rose Bowl, Horse Medallion, sapphire blue, Fenton, pre-1920, 3.5" h, 4,5" d . .2,750
Toothpick Holder, elephant head at each end, amethyst, pre-1950 25
Toothpick Holder, emb flowers, scalloped rim, 4 feet, amethyst, 2.5" h 20
Vase, Venetian, pale amethyst, Dugan, c1906, 6" h 165

CARTOON & COMIC CHARACTER COLLECTIBLES

This is a category with something for each generation. The characters represented here enjoyed a life in comic books and newspaper pages or had a career on movie screens and television.

Every collector has a favorite. Buy examples that bring back pleasant memories. "That's All Folks!"

Note: For information on collector clubs/fan clubs for individual cartoon characters, refer to *Maloney's Antiques & Collectibles Resource Directory* by David J. Maloney, Jr., published by Antique Trader Books.

Andy Panda, movie film, #481 Crow Crazy, Castle Films, fits 8mm or 16mm sound projector, orig box .15
Archie, jelly glass, Archie Comics Series, "Fashion Show," 1971 7
Baby Huey, drinking glass, Pepsi Collector Series .15
Beetle Bailey, salt and pepper shakers, figural Beetle and his locker, hp, 2.75" MIB 12
Betty Boop, apron, 2 large pockets on front, adjustable shoulder straps, Betty cooking on barbecue grill 70
Betty Boop, bathroom set consisting of toothbrush holder, soap dish, and mug .55
Blondie & Dagwood, jigsaw puzzle, diecut stiff board, uncut, 49 pcs, 1 of a series of 5 cartoon theme puzzles used as supplements in the Philadelphia Sunday Inquirer, ©1933 King Features Syndicate, Forbes-Boston, 10" x 8" 20
Blondie & Dagwood, memo holders, figures include Blondie, Dagwood, and Daisy, 1974, MOC 50
Bullwinkle, toy musical instruments, Bullwinkle's Musical Band, 3 plastic instruments, 1969, MOC 50
Casper the Friendly Ghost, AM transistor radio, LS Sutton, Ltd., 1972 75
Casper the Friendly Ghost, inflatable Bop Bag, Pizza Hut premium, 1995, 36" h, MIP 25
Casper the Friendly Ghost, Viewmaster set, Casper's Ghostland #B545, 3 reels and 16 pg booklet, 1969, MIP 12
Dennis the Menace, book, Dennis the Menace, A.M., Ambassador of Mischief, 1960 12
Garfield, alarm clock, Big Ben style, battery operated, Sunbeam, 1978 115
Gumby, jigsaw puzzle, color photo of approx 50 Gumby figures and 1 Pokey figure at center, Springbok/Hallmark Card, Inc, ©1984 Art Clokey, 100+ pcs, 7" x 10.5" 15
Henry, coloring book, 1956, 1 pg colored . .30
Henry, magnetic memo holders, figures include Henry, Blimp, Dusty, and Henrietta, MOC 50
Little Iodine, jigsaw puzzle, plastic, image of Little Iodine and her father, sealed in King Features Syndicate, orig wrapping, 1969, 5.75" x 5.75" 35
Little LuLu, bank, vinyl, 10" h 20
Little LuLu, chalkware figure, red hat, dress, and shoes, holding ice cream cone 25
Maggie and Jiggs, adv postcard, Maggie and Jiggs image, "Yale Tires for the Pure Oil Company," ©1912 85

Mighty Mouse, stationery kit, 1983, unused 12

Mighty Mouse, stickers, 21" x 10.25" card with 3-D stickers of Mighty Mouse and other Terrytoon figures, card dated 1979, stickers dated 1978, made in Taiwan . . .40

Pink Panther, movie poster, Pink Phink, 1964 175

Popeye, spinach can 10

Popeye, toy, Bluto Dippy Dumper, windup, litho tin dump truck with full-figure celluloid Bluto driver, stop and go, spin, and rear-up action, Marx, c1930s, 9.25" l 800

Popeye, toy, figure, jointed wood, enamel finish, flexible arms and legs, c1930s, 11.5" h 500

Popeye, toy, Floor Puncher, windup, litho tin, Popeye punches floor-mounted punching bag, Chein, c1930s, 7.5" h . . .675

Popeye, toy, Popeye Hauling and Construction Set, 1970, MOC 25

Popeye, toy, Popeye Heavy Hitter, windup, litho tin, Popeye swings mallet to ring carnival game's bell, Chein, c1920s-30s, 11.5" 3,800

Popeye, toy, Popeye in a Barrel, windup, litho tin, Popeye waddles back and forth, Chein, c1930s, 7" h 550

Popeye, toy, Popeye/Olive Oyl Jigger, windup, litho tin, dancing Popeye jiggles up and down, seated Olive Oyl plays accordion and rocks back and forth, house-shaped base, Marx, c1930s, 6.5" h 797

Popeye, toy, Popeye Overhead Puncher, windup, litho tin, Popeye punches suspended punching bag, orig box, Chein, c1920s-30s, 9.5" h 5,000

Popeye, toy, Popeye the Pilot, windup, litho tin, oversized Popeye head protrudes from cockpit, red, white, and blue airplane, erratic-type action, Marx, c1930s, 8" wing span 700

Skeezix, toothbrush holder, litho tin, die-cut Skeezix with "Prophylactic Listerine" on his shirt, orig box with comic strip panel, 6" h, 3" w 450

Scooby Doo, plush toy, Scooby in night-clothes, slipper in his mouth, 13" h 15

Simpsons, night light, figural Bart Simpson, dated 1990, MOC 20

Skippy, notebook, Skippy cartoon characters on cov, 1935, 9" x 11" 25

Tom & Jerry, cookie cutters, red plastic, 1956, MIP 85

Tom & Jerry, jelly glass, Welch's, Tom chasing Jerry running with football 10

Tom & Jerry, mug, ceramic, Jerry tying a bomb to Tom's tail, 1970, 3.25" h 30

CASH REGISTERS

If you want a cash register be prepared to put plenty of money in the till. Most are bought for decorative purposes. Serious collectors would go broke in a big hurry if they had to pay the prices listed below for every machine they buy.

Beware of modern reproductions. Cash registers were meant to be used. Signs of use should be present. Many machines have been restored through replating and rebuilding. Well and good. But when all is said and done, how do you distinguish a modern reproduction from a refurbished machine? When you cannot, it is hard to sustain long-term value.

Club: Cash Register Collectors Club of America, P.O. Box 20534, Dayton, OH 45420.

National, brass, marble shelf, emb front lift-top panel, orig "Gilbertson & Son" marquee, 16" h, 23" w, 19.5" d 225

National, candy store model, brass, marble, glass, and wood, 20.5" h 1,500

National, nickel finish, emb case, "The Amount Of Your Purchase" marquee, restored, c1893, 18" h, 8.5" w, 15" d 1,000

National, No. 7, detail adder 300
National, No. 317, brass, "Amount Purchased" marquee, 21" h, 10" w, 16" d 500
National, No. 35, nickel plated, ornate emb vine design, c1935, 17" h 500
National, No. 332, brass, ornate emb design, marble tray, 1913, 16.5" h, 16.5" w 375
National, No. 542-5E, standing model . . .405
Western, Verdic-Corbin Co, Detroit, barbershop, plated cast iron, heavily emb, 5¢ to $1, restored, castings replated, marquee and number tabs replaced, 21" h, 9" w, 15" d 750

CASSETTE TAPES

Flea markets thrive on two types of goods—those that are collectible and those that serve a secondhand function. Cassette tapes fall into the latter group. Buy them for the purpose of playing them.

The exception is when the promotional pamphlet covering the tape shows a famous singer or group. In this case, you may be paying for the paper ephemera rather than the tape, but you might as well have the whole shooting match.

Several times within recent years there have been a number of articles in the trade papers about collecting eight-tracks. When was the last time you saw an eight-track machine? They are going to be as popular in thirty years as the wire tape recorder is today. Interesting idea—too bad it bombed.

Average price $1 to $2.

CAST IRON

This is a category where you should be suspicious that virtually everything you see is a reproduction or copycat. Even cast iron frying pans are being reproduced.

One key to spotting newer material is the rust. If it is orange in color and consists of small pinpoint flakes, forget it. Also check paint patina. It should have a mellow tone from years of exposure to air. Bright paint should be suspect.

Note: See Banks, Bookends, Bottle Openers, Doorstops, and Griswold for additional listings.

Ashtray, drunk leaning against palm tree, Wilton, 4.5" h 70
Bathtub, clawfoot, c1900s 750
Bookends, pr, each is a pirate holding a gun and resting his foot on a treaure chest, 5.75" h, 4" w 40
Bookends, pr, RCA Nipper dogs, black and white 25
Clock, figural skillet, Pioneer 15
Door Knocker, flower basket, orig white, green, and pink paint, early 1900s, 4" h, 3" w 85
Door Knocker, lion's head 25
Door Knocker, parrot, red and yellow with blue wings, perched on leafy branch, green and white oval back plate, 4.5" h 65
Dutch Oven, cov, oval, mkd "Hadrich, Montenegro, RS290X170," 3.5" h, 14" l, 7" w 45
Egg Timer, Wilton 12
Figures, pr, cocker spaniels, brown with red collars, Hubley, 4.5" h, 7" l 250
Figures, set of 3, Popeye, Olive Oyl, and Wimpy, some paint loss, 3.25" h 200
Flower Frog, Art Deco, painted green, 13 adjustable wire flower holders, mkd "J.R.O. patd.," 1930s, 5" h, 3.25" d . .25
Hardware, pocket door handles, 1880s-90s, 7.5" h, price for pr 35
Heat Register, arched top, ornate scroll design, working louvers, 1880s, 14.5" h, 11" w 80
Kettle, mkd "Warpak 7," bail handle, 6" h, 9" d 45

Meat Grinder, Universal #1 10
Oil Lamp Bracket, wall mount, mirrored back 50
Sad Iron, miniature, with trivet 8
Shooting Gallery Target, 3 birds and 2 stars mounted in a row, red and blue paint, Coney Island, early 1900s, 7.5" h, 18" l 140
Stove, Ekco #11, lined with fire bricks, double ring gas burner, 3 ornate cast iron legs, early 1900s, 6" exhaust, 26" h, 30" w 250
Trivet, Descoware, some pinholes in red enameling, 1960s .40

CATALINA POTTERY

The Catalina Pottery, located on Santa Catalina Island, California, was founded in 1927 for the purpose of making clay building products. Decorative and functional pottery was added to the company's line in the early 1930s. A full line of color-glazed dishes was made between 1931 and 1937.

Gladding, McBean and Company bought Catalina Pottery in 1937, moved production to the mainland, and closed the island pottery. Gladding, McBean continued to use the Catalina trademark until 1947.

Ashtray, figural fish, #550, Toyton red, 4.5" l 150
Bowl, flared sides, white, 9.5" x 14" 150
Bowl, oval, pearly white glaze, 17.5" l . . .200
Bud Vase, #300, Descanso green, 5" h . . .100
Candleholders, pr, #380, seafoam 200
Candleholders, pr, Descanso green 150
Carafe, cov, handled, Toyton red 125
Charger, rolled edge, Toyton red, 14.5" d .225
Chop Plate, Toyton red, 12.5" d 70
Flower Bowl, white ext, blue int, mkd "Catalina Pottery," 4" h, 18" w 175
Flowerpot, Toyton red, 4.5" h 65
Fruit Bowl, ftd, blue, 13" d 175
Pitcher, Toyton red, 7.5" h 350
Relish Tray, handled, clover shaped, seafoam 650
Salt and Pepper Shakers, pr, figural cactus 65
Tile, saracen, cuerda seca technique, polychrome glaze, 6" sq 450
Tumbler, blue 35
Vase, #503, tan, 5.5" h 100
Vase, #600, tan, 5.5" h 135
Vase, #601, sawtooth edges, turquoise, 7.25" h 200
Vase, #612, handled, Mandarin yellow, 5" h 125
Vase #627, blue, 7.75" h 135
Vase, #636, turquoise, 7" h 145
Vase, futuristic shape, matte white 300

CATALOGS

Catalogs are used as excellent research sources. The complete manufacturing line of a given item is often described, along with prices, styles, colors, etc. Old catalogs provide a good way to date objects.

Many old catalogs are reprinted for use by collectors as an aid to identification of their specialities, such as Imperial and The Cambridge Glass Co.

Collecting Hint: The price of an old catalog is affected by condition, data, type of material advertised, and location of advertiser.

1882, DM Ferry & Co, Detroit, MI, Seed Annual, 4 litho color plates, black and white illus, 168 pgs, 5.75" x 8.75" 40
1920, Leich Electric Co, Genoa, IL, 8 pgs, telephones, 4.25" x 6" 20
1924, BL Gilbert Magic Co, Chicago, IL, 48 pgs, 5.75" x 8.5" 20
1925, Acme Chair Co, Reading, MI, #40, 24 pgs, 7.75" x 10.5" 40
1927, Chase & Sanborn, Chicago, IL, 61 pgs, 6" x 9" 15

1929, General Electric Co, Schenectady, NY, 20 pgs, 8" x 10.75" 40
1929, Pennsylvania Sugar Co, Philadelphia, PA, 16 pgs, 4" x 9" 14
1933, Charles B Knox Gelatine, 70 pgs, desserts, salads, candies and frozen dishes, 4.5" x 6.75" 12
1933, Lane Bryant, New York, NY, 76 pgs, clothing, 8.5" x 11" 24
1935, Daniel Low & Co, Salem MA, 64 pgs, jewelers and silversmiths, 6.75" x 9.5" . . 34
1936, Armstrong Cork Products, Lancaster, PA, 60 pgs, 5" x 8" 14
1940, Martin-Senour Co, 16 pgs, 6" x 9" . . . 12
1940, Montgomery Ward & Co, Chicago, IL, 32 pgs, 8" x 10.5" 32
1941, Greenlee Tool Co, Rockford, IL, 47 pgs, 6" x 9" 20
1942, Browning Arms Co, St Louis, MO, 60 pgs, 6.75" x 9.25" 58
1949, Edward Barnard Co, Rome, NY, 40 pgs, saddlery and riding equipment, 8.5" x 11" 50
1950, Kohler Co, Kohler, WI, 24 pgs, plumbing fixtures, 7.25" x 10" 18
1953, Montgomery Ward & Co, Inc, Chicago, IL, 104 pgs, photography equipment, 7.75" x 11" 18
1953, US Trading Stamp Co, Houston, TX, 32 pgs, 5.5" x 8.5" 10
1958, Albert Constantine & Son, New York, NY, 130 pgs, woodworking, 7" x 10.25" 20
1958, Miller Stockman Supply Co, Denver, CO, #115, 64 pgs, ranch and cowboy needs, 8" x 10.5" 24
1961, James Bliss & Co, Inc, Boston, MA, 24 pgs, Fall and Winter, nautical gifts, sports, hunting, 6" x 9" 12

1961, Wilson Sporting Goods Co, River Grove, IL, 72 pgs, 6.5" x 9.5" 25
1964, Indian Craft Mfg Co, Jamaica, NY, 5.5" x 8.5" 14
1964, Maher & Grosh Cutlery Co, Clyde, OH, #66, 22 pgs, 7" x 10" 30
1965, Oneida, Ltd, Oneida, NY, 38 pgs, 8.5" x 11" 24
1967, Sears, Roebuck & Co, Chicago, IL, 1064 pgs, Spring/Summer, 8" x 11" 32
1968, Martin's Flag Co, Fort Dodge, IA, 36 pgs, 7" x 10.25" 15
1969, Parker Distributors, New Rochelle, NY, 192 pgs, hunting, 8.25" x 10.75" 28
1970, Lionel Toy Division, Clemens, MI, 16 pgs, 8.5" x 11" 42
1973, Selmer, Elkhart, IN, 42 pgs, drums and accessories, 8.5" x 11" 42
1979, Topstone Ind, Inc, Danbury, CT, 4 pgs, Halloween supplies, 8.5" x 11" . . . 15
1983, Bally Gambling Equipment Corp, Bensenville, IL, 11 pgs, 8.5" x 11" 20

CAT COLLECTIBLES

It is hard to think of a collecting category that does not have one or more cat-related items in it. Chessie the Cat is railroad oriented; Felix is a cartoon, comic, and toy collectible. There rests the problem. The poor cat collector is always competing with an outside collector for a favorite cat item.

Cat collectors are not nearly as finicky as their pets. I have never seen a small cat collectibles collection. In addition, unlike most dog collectibles collectors, cat collectors are more willing to collect objects portraying breeds of cats other than the one that they own.

Clubs: Cat Collectors, P.O. Box 150784, Nashville, TN 37215, www.catcollectors.com; Cat's Meow Collectors' Club, 2163 Great Trails Dr., Wooster, OH 44691, www.catsmeow.com.

Ashtray, Holt-Howard style Siamese cat head, ceramic head with metal fittings, meows when knob is pushed to open metal top and empty ashes, paper label, Japan, 4.5" w 125

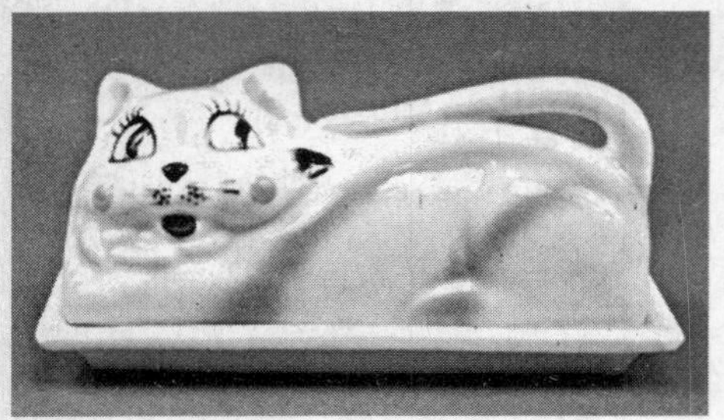

Bank, cat in basket, Goebel, 1974, 4.5" h, 5" w 95

Butter Dish, figural cat, ceramic, mkd "52/724," 1950s, 6.5" x 3" 15

Clicker, Felix the Cat, black, red, and white, "I'm Surprised At You Felix" 65

Cookie Jar, cat head, mkd "Made in Poppytrail CA Metlox," 9" h 275

Creamer, figural cat, American Pottery Co, 1940s, 4.75" h 50

Earrings, cat face on oval enamel plaques, screw back, 1960s, 1" w 30

Figurine, cat with ball of yarn, lead crystal with frosted accents, mkd "Lenox," 2.5" h, 5" l 145

Figurine, white Persian, Goebel, 3.5" h 125

Lamp, cat and fiddle, ceramic, American Bisque Co, 1950s, 8" h 65

Lunchbox, Heathcliff, metal, Aladdin, dated 1982 45

Planter, figural Siamese cat and kitten, pink and green, Hull, 6" h, 11.5" l 150

Planter, fluffy kitten sitting next to cup, pink, Hull 40

Soaky Bottle, Top Cat, 10" h 45

String Holder, Felix the Cat head, chalkware, orig paint 300

Teapot, cat head, foil label "Chase, Japan," 5.5" h 125

Teapot, figural cat, incised "Copyright 9520," Erphila, Germany, 7.5" h 200

Tray, brass, 3 emb kitttens, mkd "#1640," 7" x 5" 165

TV Lamp, 2 Siamese cats, mkd "Kron" on back, base mkd " Texans Inc, Bang Texas," 1950s, 13.5" h, 8.5" w 100

Wall Plaque, Siamese cat, paper label "Gifts From Around The World, Handcrafted in Japan For McCrory Corp, York, PA," 5.25" h 55

CELLULOID

Celluloid is the trade name for a thin, tough, flammable material made of cellulose nitrate and camphor. Originally used for toilet articles, it quickly found a use as inexpensive jewelry, figurines, vases, and household items. In the 1920s and 1930s, it was used heavily by the toy industry.

Examine ivory or tortoise shell pieces before buying. Both were well imitated by quality celluloid.

Club: Victorian Era Celluloid Collectors Assoc., P.O. Box 470, Alpharetta, GA 30239.

Belt, faux tortoiseshell, rect celluloid plaques connected to form a chain, 48" l 45

Cuff Box, Art Nouveau woman on lid, 6.75" h, 7.5" w 225

Doll, celluloid clown face, stuffed cloth body with musical chime, wearing red and white checked overalls, 1940s, 24" h 25

Dresser Set, box mkd "Toilet" on lid, brass ormolu corners and clasp, contents include a mirror, brush, comb, nail buffer, nail file, button hook, 2 rouge pots, and cuticle pusher 275

Dresser Set, pyralin, faux tortoiseshell, Arlington Co, LaBelle pattern, includes beveled glass hand mirror, comb, natural bristle brush, nail buffer with case, hair receiver, powder box, and oblong pin tray, all pcs mkd "LaBelle, Shell, Pyralin," c1923 125

Fan, child's, hp design on pierced sticks, 44" l attached celluloid chain, 4.25" h, 7.25" w open size 50

Figure, cat, 1940s, 5.25" l 10

Figurine, pig, pink with white stomach and red lips, 2" h, 3.5" l 10
Hair Comb, Victorian, high back black comb set with clear rhinestones 150
Necklace, graduated sizes of autumn leaves, yellow, orange, and brown, center leaf 2" x 1.2", 16" l 85
Nodder, Scottie dog, windup, tail spins, mkd "Made In Occupied Japan" 125
Opera Glasses, unmkd, c1920, 2.75" h, 4.25" w 95
Photo Album, celluloid cov with floral design on green patterned velvet, metal clasp, 10.75" x 8.75" 175
Photo Album, velvet-cov cardboard, celluloid panel on lid with cameo-type woman's profile in relief, metal trim . . .150
Pin, figural, 3 parrots on a branch, glass eyes, mkd "Japan," 1.25" h, 3" l 65
Pocketknife, 2 blades, 3.25" l 15
Straight Razor, Imperial, bamboo motif case, mkd "Extra Hollow Ground, Fully Warranted" 90
Tape Measure, figural bear, mkd "Made In Japan" 75

CEREAL BOXES

There is no better example of a collectible category gone mad than cereal boxes. Cereal boxes from the first half of the twentieth century sell in the $15 to $50 range. Cereal boxes from the 1950s through the 1970s can sell for $50 and up. Where's the sense?

The answer rests in the fact that the post–World War II cereal box market is being manipulated by a shrewd speculator who is drawing upon his past experience with the lunch box market. Eventually, the bubble will burst. Don't get involved unless you have money to burn.

Club: Sugar-Charged Cereal Collectors, 5400 Cheshire Meadows Way, Fairfax, VA 22032.

Count Chocula, Canada, free personalized sports poster offer, flat, 1982, sample size 25
Cream of Rice, "Introductory Size 4 to 5 servings," Grocery Store Products Co, West Chester, PA, 3 oz, 3.25" h, 2.25" w .35
Freakies, Ralston, Freakmobiles offer, 1975 275
Kellogg's C-3PO, empty, 1984 25
Kellogg's Corn Flakes, 1920s-30s 40
Kellogg's Frosted Flakes, NHL premiums offer, flat, 1984-85 .15
Kellogg's Homer's Cinnamon Donut, The Simpsons, Springfield Shopper on back, full, 12 oz 20
Kellogg's Rice Krispies, cut-out mask on back panel, 1953 25
Kellogg's Sugar Pops, Sugar Pops Pete on front, action cut-out on back, missing top flaps, 1959, 9.5" x 7.25" 25
Kellogg's Sugar Smacks, variety pack size, early Quick Draw McGraw on front, empty, 1960s, 4" h, 3" w 10
Kellogg's Triple Snack, 1960s 35
Kellogg's Multigrain Team, Ron Lancaster 20
Post Corn Crackos, 1960s 35
Post Sugar Crisp Corn Flakes, Canada, Mickey Mouse image and cutouts for Disney movie *Three Little Kittens* on back, dated 1936 215
Post Sugar Crisp Corn Flakes, Canada, text for Disney movie *The Return of Toby Tortoise* on back 160
Post Tens, variety pack, includes 2 each Frosted Rice Krinkles, Super Sugar Crisp, Toasties, and Suger Sparkled Flakes, 1 each Grape Nuts Flakes, Raisin Bran, and Alpha Bits, full, 1972, 4" x 14" x 3" 30
Post Toasties, full, 1950s, 1 oz free sample size, 4" x 3" x 2" 28
Quaker Puffed Wheat, Columbus in the West Indies series, c1940 45
Quaker Puffed Wheat "Sparkies," Boeing Flying Fortress on back panel, 1940s, 8.5" x 6.5" 42

Springfield Shopper

Springfield Power Plant Now Safer Than Ever

Principal Skinner Changes Home Phone Number Again

Quaker Quisp, Quisp Zoo on Planet Q on back, 1970s 150

Teenage Mutant Ninja Turtles, flattened . .10
Wheaties, Bruce Jenner, flat, 1978 90
Wheaties, Dale Earnhardt, full 20
Wheaties, Michael Jordan, full, 1989 25
Wheaties, model city series, 1946, 4" x 3" x 2" 80
Wheaties, Peter Garagin, flat, 1987 80
Wheaties, Ramone's Joey Ramone, 10.5" x 8.5" 38
Wheaties, Walter Payton, flat, 1987 55

CEREAL PREMIUMS

Forget cereal boxes. The fun rests with the non-edible goodies found in the box. Premiums have changed a great deal over the past decade. No self-respecting manufacturer in the 1950s would have offered a tube of toothpaste as a premium. Yuck!

Collectors draw a distinction between premiums that came with the box and those for which you had to send away. The latter group is more valuable because the items are often more elaborate and better made.

Club: Sugar-Charged Cereal Collectors, 5400 Cheshire Meadows Way, Fairfax, VA 22032.

Badge, Dick Tracy Junior Secret Service, brass shield with Tracy profile, Quaker, 1930s 65
Cavalry Hat, Rin-Tin-Tin and Rusty Fighting Blue Devils, black felt with gold cord, blue, silver, and gold patch with Rusty and Rinty on front, Arlington Hat Co, NY, medium, Nabisco, 1954, 11" d 70
Figure, Screaming Yellow Zonkers, vinyl, bright yellow, Zonkers, 1970s, 1.5" h 15
Flicker Image, Honeycomb Kid, Kid with lasso/Kid riding a pair of buffalo, green plastic base, Post Honeycomb .125
Key Chain, Lone Ranger 17th Anniversary 1933-1950, silvered brass, Lone Ranger riding Silver on front, "Official Seal/The Lone Ranger Lucky Piece" and Lone Ranger, Tonto, and silver bullet surrounded by horseshoe design on back, General Mills Cheerios, 1950 . .28
Pinback Button, Buck Rogers in the 25th Century member, Buck, rocket pistol, and spaceship on blue ground with yellow rim, with back paper, Cream of Wheat, 1935, 1" d 75
Puzzle, cardboard, photo image of smiling Roy holding 2 collie puppies against western mountain background, ©1952 Frontiers Inc, unpunched, Post, 4" x 5" 25
Ring, Casper, tin, Post Toasties Corn Flakes, 1949, 2.5" l 35
Secret Decoder, Apple Jack Kid, red vinyl, Kellogg's Apple Jacks, 1983, 2.25" h 18
Secret Decoder, Toucan Sam, blue vinyl with movable circular wheel at center and small cut-outs that reveal letter and number combinations, Kellogg's Fruit Loops, 1983, 2.25" h 18
Tab, litho tin, Wild Bill Hickok, image in black on red, blue, and yellow ground, Post Raisin Bran, 1950s, 1.75" h 20
Toy, flying saucer, plastic, battery operated, Quaker Quisp, 1966 300

CHARACTER BANKS

These lovable creatures just beg for your money. Although pre-1940 bisque, cast iron, and tin character banks exist, this form reached its zenith in the age of injection molded vinyl plastic. Post-war examples are bright, colorful, and usually large in size. They make a great display collection.

Watch out for contemporary banks, especially ceramic models. Any bank less than ten years old should be considered garage sale fodder—worth $1 to $2 at most.

Batman Electronic Talking Bank, Batman standing on glowing ice, battery operated, plastic, plays theme music, Batman talks, turns, eyes and chest plate light up, cape flutters, orig box, 14" h 75

Big Boy, Big Boy Restaurants, vinyl, mkd "Taiwan," 8.5" h 10

Cap'n Crunch, vinyl, 1972, 7" h 45

Casper the Friendly Ghost, holding money bag and coin, American Bisque, mkd "USA," 1940s, 8.5" h 375

Colonel Sanders, Kentucky Fried Chicken, vinyl, green, Margaret Co, Los Angeles, 1962, 10" h 25

Donald Duck, plastic, unmkd, c1970, 11" h 45

Flintstones, "Fred Loves Wilma," Fred and Wilma holding hands, ceramic, early 1960s, 8.25" h 125

Galen, Planet of the Apes, plastic, mkd "Play Pal Plastics, Inc 1974 APJAC Productions, Inc, Twentieth Century Fox Film Corporation," 10.5" h 35

Garfield, wearing helmet and holding football, ceramic, Enesco, mkd "Garfield, 1976, 1981, United Feature Syndicate, Inc Licensee Enesco," 5.5" h 40

General Douglas MacArthur, bust, composition, gold painted, "Save For Freedom" on base, 7" h 65

Hush Puppy, Hush Puppies Brand Shoes, vinyl, 8.5" h 25

Mickey Mouse, glass, mkd "Walt Disney Productions" on base and "Mickey Mouse Club" on back, 7" h 50

Miss Piggy, wearing blue gown and gloves, purple shawl, red corsage, ceramic, "Sigma" sticker, c1979, 8" h . .25

Pinocchio, sitting on stack of books, vinyl, Play Pal Plastics, 1981, 11" h 45

Porky Pig, bisque, red jacket, yellow bow tie, mkd "Japan," late 1930s, 5" h 65

Porky Pig, composition, late 1930s, 6.5" h .50

Quick Draw McGraw, Purex bottle, orange vinyl, blue and white accents, Knickerbocker, 9.5" h 25

Rocky and Bullwinkle, "Rocky & His Friends," Rocky, Mr Peabody, and Bullwinkle carrying flags and signs, ceramic, 1960, 4.25" h, 6.25" w 300

Scarecrow, Wizard of Oz, sitting on log, pointing to his brain, ceramic, orig box, 9" h 60

Six Million Dollar Man, wearing orange suit and breaking through a brick wall, vinyl, Animals Plus, Inc, 1976, 10" h 20

Snow White and Seven Dwarfs Dime Register, pictures Snow White and forest animals, litho tin, 1938, 2.5" x 2.5" x .75" .125

Sonic Hedgehog, sitting on stump, blue plastic, 7" h 10

Spider-Man, Marvel Comics, plastic gumball machine, Hasbro, 1980 18

Sylvester the Cat, vinyl, Warner Bros, Dakin, 1976, 6" h 15

Woody Woodpecker, plastic, 1977, 9.75" h 35

Yosemite Sam, standing on strongbox, vinyl, Warner Bros, Dakin, 1971, 7" h . . .40

CHASE CHROME & BRASS

The Chase Chrome and Brass Company was founded in the late 1870s by Augustus S. Chase and some partners. Through numerous mergers and acquisitions, the company grew and grew. The mergers helped to expand the product line into chrome, copper, brass, and other metals. Several name changes occurred until the company was sold as a subsidiary of Kennecott Corp. in its merger with Standard Oil in 1981.

Most items are marked.

Club: Chase Collectors Society, 2149 W. Jibsail Loop, Mesa, AZ 85202.

Bookends, pr, Art Deco, Walter Von Nessen, patinated metal, circ brass within copper patinated bars with brass-finished accents, imp Chase mark on base, 5.25" h, 5" w 115

Candelabra, pr, Art Deco, chrome, each with 3 candle cups and scallop-edge drip plates, 2 cups on angled and curved armature, tapered cylindrical shaft with flower blossom motif on lower shaft, weighted round disk base, raised mark on base, 13.5" h, 12" w 225

Candy Dish, cov, glass liner, 3" h, 5.5" d . . .40

Cocktail Set, Blue Moon, designed by Howard F Reichenback, 1935, chrome, glass, and Catalin "shot measure ball" finial, 8 cobalt blue glass cups with chrome ftd bases, round tray, all pcs mkd, 12" h shaker 1,150

Cocktail Set, Doric, designed by Howard F Reichenbach, c1938-41, chrome and Catalin, Blue Moon shaker with ribbed white Catalin finial, 6 Doric cups with ribbed white Catalin disc feet, round tray, all pcs mkd, 11.75" h, shaker 450

Cocktail Set, No. 90114, chrome, 6 cordials with flared rims on cylindrical vessels dec with horizontal ribbing on cobalt blue resin ftd bases, decanter dec with similar ribbing, coordinating blue stopper, circ tray with etched rings radiating to center, all with imp Chase mark, decanter also imp "PAT.D 95925," 3" h cordials, 12" h decanter, 11" d tray 285

Doorstop, Angry Cat, brass and copper, arched tubular copper body with brass head, tail, and base, 8.5" h, 4.5" w 175

Ice Bowl and Tong Set, Arctic, designed by Russell Wright, stainless 125

Lamp, chrome and glass, ribbed ring-form standard suspending a swirl chrome socket with square frosted glass shade, on a round chromed base with concentric ring dec, imp Chase mark., 14" h 115

CHENILLE

Collector interest in chenille bedspreads, curtains, and rugs has increased dramatically over the past decade. While the great majority of bedspreads feature a generic floral design, the most sought after are those with western motifs or unusual multicolor patterns.

Bedspread, 3 sprays of pink and yellow flowers with green stems and leaves tied with a white ribbon bow, white vining pom-pom borders, single pink flower at center top, yellow flower on pillow area, light green ground, 102" x 72" 70

Bedspread, 4 pink and yellow flowers arranged in a circle at center, surrounded by pink and blue flowers and green vines, green and white leafy vine border, double size 60

Bedspread, allover geometric 4-petal floral design in pink and white, pink and white fringe, 100" x 95" 80

Bedspread, Annie Oakley on rearing horse at center, red-lettered "Annie" above and "Oakley" below, green cactus at bottom corners, red and green bull's-eye target at top, green rope border, light beige ground, twin size 100

Bedspread, baseball theme, baseball player in a batting stance within a diamond frame, "The Champ" and a baseball above diamond, "Big League" below, twin size, 104" x 68" 75

Bedspread, Buffalo Bill on rearing horse at center, red-lettered "Buffalo" above and "Bill" below, green cactus and teepees in corners, charging buffalo at top, green rope border, light beige ground, twin size 60

Bedspread, green stylized flowers and 3-line zigzag borders on yellow ground, double size 40

Bedspread, Hopalong Cassidy with lariat on rearing Topper, brown picket fence behind, red-lettered "Hopalong Cassidy" below, "Bar 20" sign on pillow area, light beige ground, 102" x 75" 160

Bedspread, large central heart comprised of yellow flowers and green leaves surrounded by rect yellow sprialling frame with a yellow flower in each corner, yellow spiralling border, white ground, twin size .60

Bedspread, pr of facing peacocks with pink and yellow flowers behind, smaller pr of peacocks on pillow area, pink and yellow vining floral border, blue cotton ground, 29" x 88" 200

Bedspread, pink flower basket with blue, pink, and yellow flowers, double pink twining ribbon border, 98" x 87" 90

Bedspread, pink, peach, and yellow flowers with green leaves, pink ribbon bows, and blue scrolls and ribbons on white ground, 98" x 80" 60

Bedspread, pink, yellow, and blue flowers and purple accents on white ground, 96" x 84" 35

Bedspread, Roy Rogers on rearing Trigger at center, framed within "Double R/R Ranch" gate with alternating red and brown letters on sign, script "Roy Rogers" on pillow area, 112" x 83" 250

Bedspread, swan swimming on pond within double ring in center, diagonal striped background, pink on white, crib size, 1950s, 59" x 39" 60

Bedspread and Curtain, western motif, cowboy on rearing horse within a red twining rope frame with a horseshoe and 2 cowboy boots, matching curtain panel with a horseshoe and a cowboy boot on red twining rope, c1950, 98" x 72" spread, 63" x 34" curtain 300

Rug, 2 sprays of blue and white flowers with green stems and leaves tied with a burgundy ribbon bow on rose-colored ground, 53" x 29" 30

Rug, Hopalong Cassidy, Topper's head with green and red bridle and dark brown reins in front of a section of brown picket fencing, "Hopalong" and "Cassidy" in alternating brown and red letters at top and bottom, light beige ground, 36" x 24" 110

Rug, Roy Rogers, multicolor double "R" brand surrounded by a green rope border, horseshoe in upper right corner, steer head in lower left corner, white ground, 36" x 24" 90

CHILDREN'S BOOKS

Children's books are collected in a variety of ways: by series, theme, character, author, or illustrator.

The baby boomer generation learned to read while following the antics of Dick and Jane and their assorted relatives, friends and pets. See if you can find your favorite among the list.

Note: Books listed are in very good or better condition.

Basic Pre-Primer, Dick and Jane, ***red, green, and black soft cov with Dick pushing Jane on swing, 1936, 4th printing, stitched binding, 40 pgs 290***

Fun Wherever We Are, blue and white illus wraps, Dick and Jane on cover playing with beach ball in water, 1962, 2nd ed, 80 pgs 80

Fun With John and Jean, green and brown illus boards, same story and cov as *Fun With Dick and Jane,* Catholic version of Dick and Jane, 1952, later printing, 160 pgs 65

Fun With Our Friends, yellow and white illus boards, Sally ringing doorbell on cover, 1962, later printing, 160 pgs 60

Good Times With Our Friends, orange illus boards, image of Sally throwing a ball for Spot on cov, 1941, 1st ed, 128 pgs 145

Guess Who, Basic Reader series, peach and red illus boards, 1951, later printing, 96 pgs 65

New Fun With Dick and Jane, The, ***New Basic Reader Series, aqua and red illus boards, Spot watching Dick and Jane stacking blocks on cov, 1951, 1st ed, 160 pgs 275***

New Guess Who, The, illus boards, pink cov, introduces Mike, Pam, and Penny (3 new black characters), 1965, 2nd printing, 96 pgs 200

New Our New Friends, The, orange and red illus boards, Book 1, Level 2, 1956, 5th printing, 192 pgs 55

New We Work and Play, The, yellow and red illus wraps, Dick painting a chair on cov, 1956, later printing, 64 pgs 65

Now We Read, green and white illus wraps, Sally on cov with 2 black girls and their dolls, 1965, 6th printing, 48 pgs 100

Our New Friends, blue illus boards, Dick, Jane, and Spot walking under umbrella on cov, 1946, 7th printing, 192 pgs 100

Sally, Dick, and Jane, green and white illus wraps, Sally, Dick, and Jane on cov, 1962, 6th printing, 48 pgs 165

Think-And-Do Book, accompanies *New Our New Friends,* yellow and red wraps, 1952, later printing, 80 pgs 40

Think-And-Do Book, accompanies *We Look and See,* red illus wraps, Spot and Puff investigating a duck pull toy on cov, 1956, later printing, 82 pgs 35

We Come and Go, paperback, blue illus wraps with blue cloth spine, 1946, 6th printing, 72 pgs 85

CHINTZ CHINA

Chintz patterned goods owe their origin to Indian chintes, fabrics decorated with richly hued flowers and brightly plumed mythical birds, that were imported to England from India in the 17th century. Although English Staffordshire potters produced chintz patterned ceramics as early as the 1820s, the golden age of chintz decorated ceramics dates from 1920 through 1940. While dozens of post-World War II patterns were made, collectors prefer prewar examples.

Clubs: The Chintz China Collector, P.O. Box 6126, Folsom, CA 95630; Chintz Chums, 600 Columbia St., Pasadena, CA 91105; Chintz Connection, P.O. Box 222, Riverdale, MD 20738; US Chintz Collectors Club, P.O. Box 50888, Pasadena, CA 91115, www.chintznet.com.

Aynsley, cup and saucer, chintz band 95

Barker Brothers, cake plate, Royal Tudor Ware, 11.25" d 185

Barker Brothers, cakestand, Lorna Doone, Royal Tudor Ware, c1937 180

Barker Brothers, tea tray, Royal Tudor Ware, c1937, 8.75" d 170

Crown Bone China, cup and saucer, Maytime pattern, c1950 100

Crown Ducal, teapot, Primula pattern, 5" h 260

Czechoslovakia, bowl, Portland pattern, 9" x 7.25" 130

England, cup and saucer, Rosina pattern .85

H&K Tunstall, bowl, 9" w 110

Haltonware, Japan, butter dish, cov, Hazel pattern, 1930s, 6.25" x 4.25" 125
James Kent, bon-bon plate, Old Foley pattern, c1935 70
James Kent, bowl, Marigold pattern, fluted edge, 13" x 6.5" 120
James Kent, cake plate and server, Old Foley, 10.5" d plate, 9.5" l server 175
James Kent, dish, Rosalynde pattern emb shell design, 1940s 125
James Kent, relish tray, Rosalynde pattern, 13" l, 6.5" w 135
James Kent, sugar bowl, cov, Du Barry pattern, 3.5" h 120
James Kent, teapot, Du Barry pattern, 4.5" h, 9.5" w 525
Johnson Brothers, pitcher, Rose Chintz pattern, 6" h 200
Johnson Brothers, plate, Old English pattern, 10" d 80
Johnson Brothers, plate, Rose Chintz pattern, 9.25" d 65
Lawley Ware, bowl, blue pansy pattern, c1932, 2.5" h, 4.5" d 60
Lefton, tidbit tray, 2 tiers, metal center handle, 9.5" h 75
Lord Nelson, cake plate, Marina pattern, 6-sided, 10.75" w .125
Lord Nelson, creamer and sugar, Anemone pattern, 2.25" h 100
Lord Nelson, creamer and sugar, Marina pattern 65
Lord Nelson, creamer and sugar, Royal Brocade 200
Lord Nelson, cup and saucer, Rosetime pattern, 1930s 110
Lord Nelson, divided dish, Royal Brocade pattern, 7.75" d 125

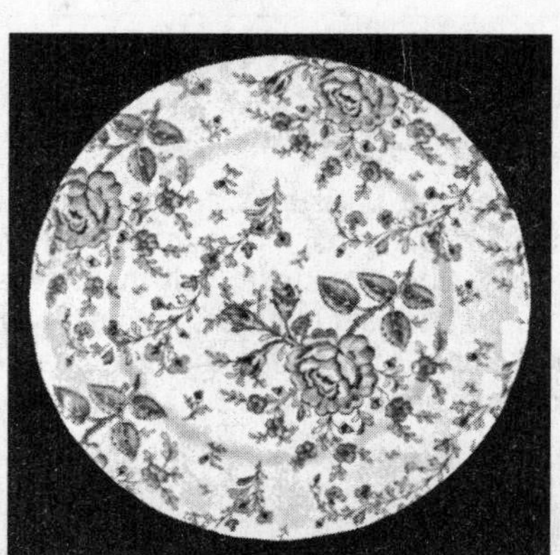

Lord Nelson, jam set, Heather pattern, jar, lid, spoon, and plate, 4.5" h jar 190
Lord Nelson, tea set, Royal Brocade pattern, 8 pcs, cov teapot, creamer, sugar, and 2 cups and saucers, 1930-55 800
Rosina China Co, demitasse cup and saucer, paisley pattern 100
Royal Albert, snack set, cup and plate, Petit Point pattern 55
Royal Crown Melody, plate, Pasadena pattern, 9" d 215
Royal Doulton, plate, Persian pattern, c1949 60
Sampson Smith, cup and saucer, Yellow Chintz pattern 55
Shelley, cup and saucer, Daisy pattern, c1949 60
Shelley, cup and saucer, Primrose pattern, Richmond shape, 1930-40 120
WR Midwinter, tidbit tray, Lorna Doone pattern, aluminum center handle, c1937 100

CHRISTMAS

Of all the holiday collectibles, Christmas is the most popular. It has grown so large as a category that many collectors specialize in only one area, e.g., Santa Claus figures or tree ornaments.

Anything Victorian is "hot." The Victorians popularized Christmas. Many collectors love to recapture that spirit. However, prices for Victorian items, from feather trees to ornaments, are escalating.

Learn to distinguish turn-of-the-century ornaments from modern examples. Moderately priced boxes of old ornaments can still be found. Happy hunting, Ho! Ho! Ho!

Clubs: Golden Glow of Christmas Past, 6401 Winsdale St., Minneapolis, MN 55427; Treasury of Christmas Ornaments Collectors' Club, P.O. Box 277, Itasca, IL 60143.

Book, *A Christmas Memory,* Capote 45
Bubble Light Tree, 18 lights, green 100
Candy Container, basket, paper with foil trim, Santa on airplane lithograph 165
Candy Container, belsnickel, white robe and base with mica flecks and green glitter trim, red pipe cleaner trim, black boots, green feather tree, 9.25" h 650
Candy Container, belsnickel, white robe, with mica flecks, black boots and base, red pipe cleaner trim, and remnants of green feather tree, 11.25" h 825
Candy Container, boot, papier-mâché, German, 5" h 45
Candy Container, cornucopia, gold paper, angel lithographs 145
Christmas Tree, retro, aluminum, 201 branches, self-leveling stand, rotating color light, instructions, 1950s 7' h 200
Cookie Cutter, gingerbread man, 1940s ...35
Cookie Cutter, Santa, tin 100
Creche, German, 4" figures, 1930s 125
Figure, reindeer, celluloid, white, 1950s, 4" h 10
Figure, Santa in sleigh, celluloid, red and white, 4.125" h. 6.5" l, 2.25" w 145

Garland, .5" silver, 72" l 40
Garland, 1" silver, 84" l 55
Garland, beaded chain, indents, 36" l 145
Garland, beaded chain, round, Japan, 48" l 20
Ornament, angel, cotton, gold paper wings, 3" h 50
Ornament, automobile, glass, pink, pearl, 4" 150
Ornament, baseball bat, glass, red, white, and blue, 6" 225
Ornament, bird, glass, blue and pink, 6" ...50
Ornament, clown, glass, green and yellow, 4" 50
Ornament, frog, glass, on clip, 3" 245
Pin, Christmas tree, multicolor rhinestones, gold tone setting, sgd "Eisenberg Ice," 2.25" h 35
Pin, Christmas tree, multicolor rhinestones, 5 candles, sgd "Weiss" in block letters within a circle on back, 2.125" h 340
Snow White Melodee Bells, Criterion Bell and Specialty Co, NY, 1960s-70s ...12
Toy, Santa in sleigh, celluloid, windup ...165
Tree, aluminum, gold, 72" h 65
Tree, aluminum, silver, 48" h 50
Tree, aluminum, silver and blue, 96" h ...125
Tree, aluminum, silver and green, 72" h ..100

CHRISTMAS & EASTER SEALS

Collecting Christmas and Easter Seals is one of the most inexpensive "stamp" hobbies. Sheets usually sell for between 50¢ and $1. Most collectors do not buy single stamps, except for the very earliest Christmas seals.

Club: Christmas Seal and Charity Stamp Society, P.O. Box 18615, Rochester, NY 14618.

CIGARETTE LIGHTERS

Cigarette lighters come in all shapes and sizes. Collections could be assembled focusing on several different categories, i.e., flat advertising lighters, figural lighters, or even figural advertising lighters. The possibilities are endless. Buy lighters in good condition only. Scratches and/or missing parts greatly detract from a lighter's value. Remember, cigarette lighters were mass-produced and are therefore plentiful.

Clubs: International Lighter Collectors, P.O. Box 17333, Quitman, TX 75783, www.vintagevault.com; Pocket Lighter Preservation Guild & Historical Society, Inc., 380 Brooks Dr., Suite 209A, Hazelwood, MO 63042, www.studioshowroom.com/zippo/; SPARK International, P.O. Box 1656, Olten, 4600 Switzerland, http://members.aol.com/intspark.

Advertising, Amoco, windproof, Barlow, Japan 55
Advertising, Economy Savings and Loan Co, windproof, Barlow, Japan 15
Advertising, Kent cigarette emblem on front, 2" h 16
Advertising, Little-Deutag Drilling, windproof, Barlow, Japan, 2.25" h 14
Advertising, Salem cigarettes, Zenith, 1.75" h 50
Advertising, Sarah Coventry, silver lettering on black ground, Japan, 1960s-70s 25

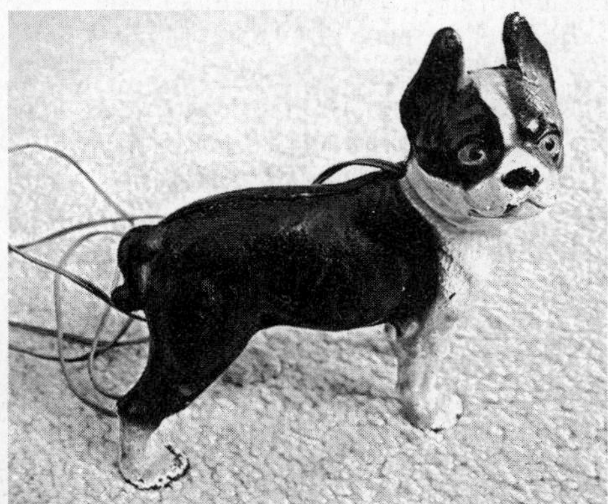

Advertising, Winchester Inn, 2300 South Alameda, Long Beach Calif, Scripto Vu .55
Chadwick Projection Lighter, Japan, 1950s 55
Eclydo, Swiss jeweled watch mounted on front, green enamel ground, 2.5" h . .60
Figural, beer can, Duke Beer, 4.75" h 15
Figural, book, brass with copper trim, monogram, and dated "1918" on 1 side, Scottish thistle and Greek cross on other side 200
Figural, boot, metal, Occupied Japan, 4" h 80
Figural, Boston terrier, cast iron, electric, push button on dog's belly and area below tail glows, 6" h, 5" l 160
Figural, bottle, playing cards around bottom, mkd "Pat. Applied For, Kem Co, Detroit MI, Made In USA" 25
Figural, coin, Japan, 5.5" d 45
Figural, donkey, Amico, Japan, 2" h, 2.5" . 140
Figural, golf cart, table model, white metal, black and tan leather inserts, red Bakelite knob on cart handle 60
Figural, hand grenade, Combat Table Lighter, orig box and tag, 4.5" h 50
Figural, horse head, brown with gold trim, Japan 28
Figural, kiwi bird, metal bird on wood base, Japan, 3.5" h 60
Figural, lantern, hp floral design, mkd "Weston, USA," 5.5" h 30
Figural, monkey, Prince Mfg Co 55
Figural, pistol 25
Figural, rearing stallion, Japan, 6.5" h 45
Figural, Scottie dog, syroco, attached ashtray 42
Figural, vintage phonograph, gold tone . . .65
Hollywood, front has multicolor rhinestones on textured silver-colored ground, striped chrome back 50
Pinup Vu, mkd "Japan" 55
Prince, enameled logo and "Defense Academy Japan Obaradai" on front, mkd "Prince Rocky Pat. 234754 Prince Mfg Co," 2.125" h .18
Rogers, Ballerina Vu 45
Rogers, etched leaf pattern 20
Ronson, coin mounted on either side, 1941 2-shilling on 1 side, 1932 half-penny on other side 75
Ronson, Imari, Royal Crown Derby 100
Scripto Vu, 1960s Ski-Doo snowmobile . . .45

Scripto Vu, Greek key design, table model 45
Scripto Vu, state of Oregon, mountain on 1 side, building on the other 40
Zenith, hp rowboat image on both sides . .85
Zippo, "1932-1997" anniversary model 15
Zippo, bowling logo, gold letters, orig black plastic box .90
Zippo, brushed chrome, 2.25" h 18
Zippo, cowboy on bucking bronco on front, mkd "Marlboro Country Store" on back, gold tone 40
Zippo, fishing lure, view lighter, MIB 130
Zippo, Farmhand, MIB 225

CIRCUS

Traveling tent circuses were an exciting event in rural towns across the country—evidence the large amount of memorabilia left behind.

Every circus collector should make it a point to see the great annual circus parade held in Milwaukee. It features equipment from the Circus World Museum in Baraboo, Wisconsin.

Clubs: Circus Fans Assoc. of America, P.O. Box 59710, Potomac, MD 20859, www.circusfans.org; Circus Historical Society, 4102 Idaho Ave., Nashville, TN 37209.

Activity Book, *3 Ring Circus,* coloring and cut-out book, Saalfield Pub Co, 1945, 10.75" x 14" 12
Book, *Ringling Bros and Barnum & Bailey Circus,* 1932, illus info about acts, animals, and performers, with old adv, 10" x 7" 70

Book, *Toby & Flip Action Toy Book,* Whitehall, 1947 40
Figurine, circus elephant, Dresden, 5.25" h 160
Game, Circus Boy, Harlett Gilmar, 1956 . . .65
Glasses, Circus Carousel, set of 6, each with a different carousel animal on frosted ground, Libbey, 7" h, 2" d 65
Little Golden Book, *Little Peewee, Circus Dog,* #52, G edition, 1948 35
Movie Poster, *Circus World,* John Wayne, Rita Hayworth, 1964 155
Movie Poster, *The Big Circus,* Victor Mature, Red Buttons, Rhonda Fleming, 1959 95
Pin, Barnum & Bailey Circus, gold tone elephant attached by chain to enameled Barnum & Bailey logo, .75" x .75" elephant 70
Planter, circus elephant, teal, 1930s-40s, 4" h 20
Postcard, German Circus Krone, shows Cilly holding a tiger on her shoulders, unused 32
Postcard, linen, Winter Quarters of the Barnum & Bailey Circus and Monkey Island, FL, 1954 8
Poster, Hunt Bros Circus, growling tiger .100
Poster, Ringling Bros and Barnum & Bailey Circus, paper litho, 28" x 41" . . .165
Program, Ringling Bros and Barnum & Bailey Cicus, 1969 20
Program, Ringling Bros and Barnum & Bailey Circus Bicentennial Edition, 1976 20
Ring, emb gray metal, "Al Tomaini Giant" .55
Salt and Pepper Shakers, figural, performing lion (salt) on polka-dotted base (pepper), 5.5" h 75

Sheet Music, *Circus Parade,* circus ring on cov, c1904 65
Sheet Music, *Laugh Clown Laugh,* Lon Chaney, clown on cov 12
Toy, Comic Car Circus, friction, litho tin, orig box, Modern Toys, Japan, 6.75" l 85
Toy, Man on the Flying Trapeze, litho tin, windup, 9" h 275

CLARICE CLIFF

Clarice Cliff (1899-1972) joined A. J. Wilkinson's Royal Staffordshire Pottery at Burslem, England, in the early 1910s. In 1930 she became the company's art director.

Cliff is one of England's foremost 20th-century ceramic designers. Her influence covered a broad range of shapes, forms, and patterns. Her shape lines include Athens, Biarritz, Chelsea, Conical, Iris, Lynton, and Stamford. Applique, Bizarre, Crocus, Fantasque, and Ravel are among the most popular patterns.

In addition to designer shape and pattern lines, Cliff's signature also appears on a number of inexpensive dinnerware lines, such as Tonquin, manufactured under the Royal Staffordshire label.

Clubs: Clarice Cliff Collector's Club, Fantasque House, Tennis Dr., The Park, Nottingham NG7 1AE, UK, Clarice Cliff Official Assoc., www.claricecliff.org.

Ashtray, Tonquin, brown, 4.5" d 20
Berry Bowl, Tonquin, blue 6
Berry Bowl, Tonquin, brown 7
Berry Bowl, Tonquin, mulberry 15
Berry Bowl, Tonquin, red 8
Bone Dish, Tonquin, crescent, blue 14
Bone Dish, Tonquin, crescent, brown 15
Bone Dish, Tonquin, crescent, green 11
Bone Dish, Tonquin, crescent, mulberry . .12
Bone Dish, Tonquin, crescent, red 14
Bowl, Crocus, ftd, flaring sides, Bizarre ware, stamped mark, 6.5" d, 3" h 550
Bread and Butter Plate, Tonquin, blue 8
Bread and Butter Plate, Tonquin, brown . .10
Bread and Butter Plate, Tonquin, mulberry .8
Bread and Butter Plate, Tonquin, red 10
Bud Vase, Tonquin, ftd, brown, 5" h 26
Bud Vase, Tonquin, ftd, mulberry, 5" h 26
Butter, cov, Crocus, wide shallow base, shallow cov with slightly domed top and flat button finial, Bizarre ware, 2.75" h .550
Candle Sconce, Tonquin, blue, 9" h 85
Candlesticks, pr, Tonquin, red, 10" h, 4.5" sq base, red 250
Chamberstick, Tonquin, brown, 2" h, 5.5" d 25
Creamer, Tonquin, blue, 3" h 9
Creamer, Tonquin, brown, 3" h 13
Creamer, Tonquin, green, 3" h 14
Creamer, Tonquin, red, 2" h 36
Creamer and Sugar, Aurea, Bizarre ware 200
Cup and Saucer, Tonquin, blue 14
Cup and Saucer, Tonquin, brown 15
Cup and Saucer, Tonquin, red 8
Dinner Plate, Tonquin, blue 10
Dinner Plate, Tonquin, brown 16
Dinner Plate, Tonquin, mulberry 17
Dinner Plate, Tonquin, multicolor 24
Dinner Plate, Tonquin, red 15
Gravy Boat and Underplate, Tonquin, black 40
Luncheon Plate, Tonquin, blue 10
Luncheon Plate, Tonquin, brown 18
Luncheon Plate, Tonquin, mulberry 21
Mayonnaise Set, Tonquin, bowl, ladle, and underplate 46
Pitcher, Melon, Fantasque line, wide conical body, solid triangular handle, mkd, c1930, 5.75" h 875
Pitcher, My Garden, bulbous base, wide cylindrical body, arched bumpy branch handle, Bizarre ware, 7.5" h . . .415

Pitcher, Tonquin, brown, 6.25" h 25
Pitcher, Tonquin, red, 6.25" h 46
Plate, Blue Chintz, Bizarre ware, 8" d 600
Plate, Forest Glen, mkd "Clarice Cliff, Newport Pottery, England," 9.75" d . . .950
Plate, Melon, Fantasque line, 9" d 775
Plate, Pansies Delicia, mkd "Pansies, Bizarrre by Clarice Cliff, Hand Painted, England," imp "83," 10" d 120
Platter, Tonquin, rect, blue, 11.5" x 9.5" 40
Platter, Tonquin, rect, brown, 11.5" x 9.5" . .25
Platter, Tonquin, rect, mulberry, 11.5" x 9.5" 56
Platter, Tonquin, rect, red, 11.5" x 9.5" 59
Salt and Pepper Shakers, Tonquin, blue, 3" h 108
Sauce Boat, Tonquin, blue, 5.5" l 16
Sauce Boat, Tonquin, brown, 5.5" l 26
Soup Bowl, Tonquin, flat, blue, 8" d 8
Soup Bowl, Tonquin, flat, brown, 8" d 21
Soup Bowl, Tonquin, flat, mulberry, 8" d . .20
Sugar, cov, Tonquin, red, 5" h 26
Sugar Shaker, Nasturtium, Bonjour shape, Bizarre ware, 5" h, 1.75" w 550
Teapot, Tonquin, brown, 5" h 74
Tumbler, Sunray, conical form, 3" h 600
Vegetable Bowl, Tonquin, brown, 8" d 26
Vegetable Bowl, Tonquin, mulberry, 8" d . .17

CLICKERS

If you need a clicker, you would probably spend hours trying to locate a modern one. I am certain that they exist. You can find a clicker at a flea market in a matter of minutes.

Although most clickers were produced as advertising promotions, I believe their principal purpose was to drive parents crazy.

Bonnie Laddie Shoes, purple, emb boy . . .25
Buster Brown Shoes, multicolor, Buster and Tige 45
Castles Ice Cream, blue and white, "I'm Chirping For Castles Ice Cream" and bird 34
Cleo Cola, red, white, and green, "Healthy Size" 38
Crackin' Good, red and white, lightning bolt and "Crackin' Good Cookies and Crackers" 24
Dairylea Ice Cream, red and white, "Always Clicks, Delicious Dairylea Ice Cream" 28
Felix the Cat, black, red, and white, "I'm Surprised At You Felix," 2 cats 68
Forbes Coffee, red, white, and blue, "Forbes Quality Brand Coffee" and trademark logo 45
Fort Pitt Brewing Co, Sharpsburg, PA, litho tin, green and red on yellow ground 18
Godman Shoes, black and yellow, "For Boys, For Girls" and "Godman Shoes" in shield 28
Green Duck, green and white, "Green Duck 100% Union Made Buttons Badges Emblems" 16
Gunther's Beer, red and white, "Just Click For Gunther's Beer, The Beer That Clicks" 22
Halloween, witch on a flying broom with another witch kneeling on her shoulders, silhouetted against a full moon, 2 bats flying above, c1930s-40s, 1.75" 25
Jack and Jill, multicolor, Jack and Jill walking arm in arm, "Instantly Prepared Gelatin Dessert, Jack and Jill, At Your Grocer" 42
Little Sergeant Shoes, orange, black, and white, Little Sergeant image 34
Maxwell House, blue and gray, "Drink Maxwell House Coffee" 52
Menges for Sheriff, multicolor, man with sandwich board sign stating "I Am Chirping For Menges For Sheriff" 16

New & True Coffee, multicolor, coffee cup 30
Purity Salt, multicolor, product image 38
Red Goose Shoes, red goose on yellow ground 15
State Insurance, Indianapolis, Pennsylvania, red, white, and blue, "Assets Over A Million Dollars, Harrisburg, PA" and logo 30
Steelco Stainless Steel, blue and white, "4450 Ravenswood Chicago, The Greatest Name in Fine Cookware" 25
Stroehmann Bread, red, white, and yellow, 2 clowns holding "Stroehmann Bread" banner, 4.5" l 42
Sun Dial Shoes, multicolor, "Sundial all leather Shoes" and clown 28
Water, multicolor, frowning man holding bottle labeled "Water" 22

CLOCKS

Look for clocks that are fun (have motion actions) or that are terrific in a decorating scheme (a school house clock in a country setting). Clocks are bought to be seen and used.

Avoid buying any clock that does not work. You do not know whether it is going to cost $5, $50, or $500 to repair. Are you prepared to risk the higher numbers? Likewise, avoid clocks with extensively damaged cases. There are plenty of clocks in fine condition awaiting purchase.

Club: National Assoc. of Watch and Clock Collectors, Inc., 514 Poplar St., Columbia, PA 17512, www.nawcc.org.

Advertising, Atlas Tires Batteries Accessories, white neon light-up, metal body, face, and hands, 18.5" x 18.5" 775
Advertising, Buy St Joseph Aspirin, light-up clock, metal with glass face and front, Pam Clock Co, New Rochelle, NY, body stamped "Sep 1954," 14.5" d .275
Advertising, Camel Cigarettes, wall mount, purple and yellow with Camel logo on top half of face, 28.5" w 135
Advertising, Cities Service, light-up, metal with glass face and front, 15" d .450

Advertising, Drink Coca-Cola, counter light-up clock, metal with reverse painted glass, "Lunch With Us" on base, 9" h, 19.5" l, 5" d 1,000
Advertising, Dr Pepper, light-up, metal body, glass front, plastic face, 15.5" h, 15.5" w 150
Advertising, Hennessy Liquor, figural bottle topped with clock face, all clock numerals are "5"x, mkd "Stylus Brand Made In USA" 250
Advertising, Raid bug spray, radio alarm clock, bug leaning on Raid radio dial, 7.25" h, 7" w 375
Advertising, Royal Crown Cola, orange neon light-up, metal and plastic with glass insert at top, 34" h, 37" w 1,100
Advertising, Sauer's Flavoring Extracts, Richmond, VA, pendulum clock, black painted wood case, reverse painted glass door with 29 gold metallic medallions around perimeter, tin face, mkd "New Haven Clock Co New Haven, Conn," 42" h, 15" w, 5" d 1,650
Advertising, Sinclair HC Gasoline, white neon light-up spinner clock, metal with tin face and glass front, black and red double spinner, 21" d 1,500
Alarm, General Electric, model 7H182, round dial in square brown plastic case, electric, 5.5" sq 50
Alarm, Westclox Baby Ben, Style 6, Model 61V, circ ivory case with gold tone trim, 1950 70
Alarm, Westclox Moonbeam, Art Deco style yellow plastic case 135

Black Forest Cuckoo, carved pine case, leaf and branch motif, gabled crest with standing bird, hp double wooden cuckoos, round face with applied Roman numerals, 30-hour movement with strike mechanism mkd "Kuehl Clock Co, Germany," pine cone-shaped weights and pendulum, late 19th-early 20th C, 18.5" x 13.25" x 8.5" case 300

Black Forest Cuckoo, carved pine case, leaf and branch motif with game bag, rifle, rabbit, and bird around front, gabled crest with antlered deer, hp double wooden cuckoos, round face with Roman numerals, 30-hour movement with strike mechanism mkd "Emil Schmenckenberg, Germany," pine cone-shaped weights and pendulum, mid-20th C, 29" x 17.5" x 13.5" case 400

Black Forest Cuckoo, wood case, arched-top face with hp house with cuckoo door front, black and orange striping around edge, and Roman numerals, hand carved and painted cuckoo and bellows, 30-hour movement with strike mechanism, cast iron pine cone-shaped weights, wood pendulum bob, 19th C, 11.75" x 8.25" x 5" case 825

Character, Garfield, alarm, Big Ben style, Sunbeam, 1978, 17" h, 12" w 125

Character, Gargoyles Defenders of the Night, alarm, quartz movement, plastic case, oval face, orig box, 5" h, 4" w 20

Character, Hopalong Cassidy, alarm, US Time, 5.5" h 250

Character, Mickey Mouse, alarm, Big Ben style, Phinney-Waler, West Germany, 1969, 4" h 100

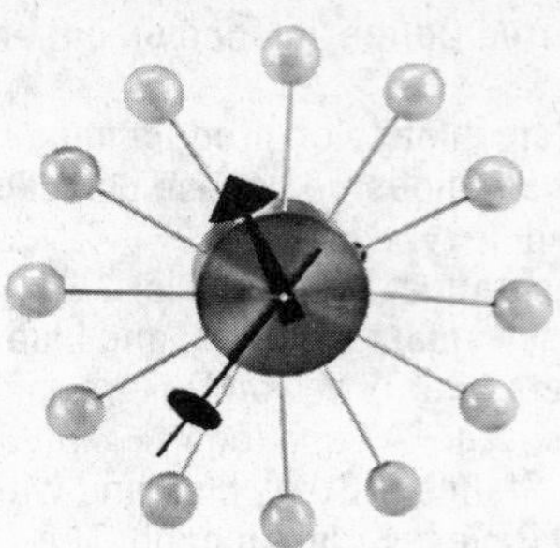

Character, Mickey Mouse, alarm, Big Ben style, The Bradley Co, West Germany, 6" h, 3.5" w 28

Howard Miller, Ball Clock, designed by George Nelson, spun brass center, enameled hands, spherical walnut numeral markers, unmkd, 13" d 600

Howard Miller, brass circular frame with clear plexiglass face and brass numeral markers, pendulum, and weights, Howard Miller decal, 15" d . .200

Howard Miller, brushed chrome frame, rosewood face and chrome numeral markers and hands, designed by George Nelson, Howard Miller tag, 13" d 550

Howard Miller, ceramic, orange, yellow, and brown matte glazes, white enamel hands, Howard Miller paper label, 13.5" d 450

Howard Miller, cork frame with printed graphic circ face and enamel hands, designed by George Nelson, Howard Miller tag, 11.5" sq 475

Howard Miller, oak frame with cork face, wood hour markers, and enameled hands, designed by George Nelson, paper label, 13" d 120

Howard Miller, sq black and white face with spun brass center and numeral markers, built-in model, orig box with installation instructions, designed by George Nelson 385

Howard Miller, Starburst Clock, black rays, white face, black hands terminating in orange and yellow, Howard Miller Clock Co label, 19" d . . .500

Howard Miller, white enamel case with black face, white hour and minute markers, and red hands, electric, Howard Miller Clock Co decal, 14" d . .120

Novelty, figural horse standing beside circ clock, bronze-finished metal, hard plastic base, United Clock Corp, Brooklyn, NY, 1950s, 11.5" h, 17" w 125

Novelty, golf theme, figural golfer with putter in front of oval plaque with inset clock face, 1950s, 8" h, 11" w 250

Pillar, Mitchell & Adkins, triple arched crest, reverse painting of church on lower half of door, ebonized and gilt columns, double weight-driven, 16" x 32" 425

Pillar, Pond & Barnes, Boston, MA, double glass door, reverse painting of squirrel, double weight-driven, 27" h,14" w 300

Porcelain, American, miniature, dark green, "#213" on case, 30-hour movement, 5.5" h .225

Porcelain, American, pink with hand-colored transfer floral scenes, partial paper label on rear reads "China No. 28 The ??? Clock Co," date on rear door reads "1899," c1910, 11.5" h 225

Porcelain, Ansonia, Peconic model, ivory case with light green and gilt borders and hp flowers, c1900, 12" h . .605

Porcelain, Ansonia, Royal Bonn, La Cantal model, bright blue case with hp floral motif and gilt highlights, American sash dial with perforated gilt mask over silvered dial, 8-day gong strike, c1900, 12.25" h 415

Porcelain, Ansonia, Royal Bonn, La Clair model, light blue and ivory with hp floral and gilt dec sgd case, Rococo sash enamel dial, c1895, 13" h 385

Porcelain, Ansonia, Waco model, hp floral and gilt dec on green case sgd "Waco," 8-day movement sgd "Ansonia Clock Co New York," 4.5" enamel dial with Ansonia trademark, c1900, 11.75" 225

Porcelain, German, miniature, Capo Dimonte style, c1920, 8.5" 65

Porcelain, New Haven, miniature, floral painted green case, enamel dial, cast bevel, case mkd "207," c1915, 6" h 110

Porcelain, New Haven, miniature, purple and white floral case, seconds bit, c1915, 5.5" h 110

Porcelain, New Haven, white with hp flowers, time/strike on a coiled gong, c1900, 13.5" h 140

Porcelain, Sessions, Holly model, miniature, green case, 30-hour movement, c1915, 5.75" h 250

Porcelain, Waterbury, white with painted roses, 30-hour movement, 9" h 225

Shelf, Forestville, column, mahogany case, 8-day time and strike movement, carved fruit basket crest, painted wood dial 375

CLOTHES SPRINKLERS

Before steam irons, clothes requiring ironing had to be manually dampened with water. Some housewives used soda pop bottles or other common bottles, with sprinkler caps attached, while others owned more decorative figural bottles made especially for this task. These are the bottles that are now sought after by collectors willing to pay $20 and up for the more common examples and as much as several hundred dollars for the extremely rare bottles. It is estimated that close to 100 different sprinkler bottles were manufactured.

Baker, Flour Fred, Spillers Flour of England adv, hard plastic, 7" h 110

Bottle, clear hard plastic with aqua cap and base, mkd "Columbus Plastic Patent Pending," 6.5" h 25

Bottle, plastic, "Laundry Sprinkler" in black lettering on white ground, black lid, mkd "A Lucky Wish Product, pat pen, Made in USA," 7" h 35

Chinaman, ceramic, hp, blue buttons on white jacket, blue shoes, metal cap, Cleminson, CA, 8.5" h 125

Chinaman, ceramic, yellow and green, metal cap, 9" h 45

Clothespin, ceramic, yellow, 1940s-50s, 7.75" h 275

Dutch Boy, ceramic, 8.25" h 300

Elephant, ceramic, smiling, looped trunk forms handle, American Bisque, 6.25" h 650

Elephant, ceramic, water sprinkles from upraised trunk 165

Iron, ceramic, white, souvenir, "Wonder Cave, San Marcos, Texas," 1950s 300

Iron, ceramic, white with emb rooster on flat surface, 6.5" h 145

Iron, ceramic, white with green ivy 125

Merry Maid, red with white apron, 6.75" h 85

Poodle, ceramic, pink, mkd with patent number, 8.25" h, 3.25" w 350

Rooster, ceramic, green, yellow, and white, red plastic stopper, 10" h 145

Rooster, ceramic, multicolor feathers, metal stopper 125

Siamese Cat, ceramic, metal cap, 8.5" h .215

Sprinkler Kate, Cleminson, CA, 6.5" h 40

CLOTHING

Decide from the outset whether you are buying clothing and accessories for use or display. If you are buying for use, apply very strict standards with respect to condition and long-term survival prospects. If you only want the items for display, you can be a little less fussy about condition.

Clubs: Kollectors of Nasty Old Ties (K.N.O.T.), 1860 Greentree Dr., Plover, WI 54467, www.geocities.com/RodeoDrive/4026; Textile & Costume Guild, c/o Fullerton Museum Center, 301 N. Pomona Ave., Fullerton, CA 92632; The Costume Society of America, P.O. Box 73, Earleville, MD 21919, www.costumesocietyamerica.com.

Afternoon Dress, woman's, ivory tulle with embroidery and lace insertions, lace trim, c1920 135

Afternoon Dress, woman's, pale green silk over rose silk, detailed with black velvet buttons, elaborate braid and fringe, c1870 150

Afternoon Dress, young woman's, 2-pc, floral printed lawn, bodice lined with cotton, ruching on bodice, c1865 185

Bathing Suit, woman's, black cotton blouse trimmed with fuchsia piping, matching bloomers, fuchsia stockings, c1890 85

Bell Bottom Pants, men's, white corduroy with yellow and orange "Lilly" and jungle print, labeled "Lilly Pulitzer Men's Stuff," late 1960s, size medium 115

Bodice, blue silk with black tulle overlay, lined with linen, c1900 28

Christening Gown, white lawn with lace collar and trim, lace insertion, c1920 45

Cocktail Ensemble, 2-pc, silk jersey printed with green, pink, peach, lavender, and white geometric and floral design, fitted top with long sleeves and jewel neckline, ankle length semi-full skirt, elasticized waist, labeled "Emilio Pucci" at neckline, 1970s, size 6 625

Dress, child's, ivory batiste with lace insertions, tucks, and embroidery, c1885 150

Dress, young girl's, red plaid linen, c1870 90

Dress, young girl's, 2-pc, burgundy silk with lace cuffs and trim, lined with brown polished cotton 230

Ensemble, black and white wool crepe with op-art geometric-pattern, sleeveless knee-length dress with fitted bodice and bell-shaped skirt, matching knee-length long-sleeved coat with center front button closure, follows silhouette of dress, black silk lining, 1960s, size 6 250

Ensemble, striped dress with matching coat, black wool knee-length shift with horizontal stripes in hot pink, green, and orange, black wool coat with fitted bodice, flared skirt, 2 large patch pockets, oversized buttons and matching striped shawl collar and lining, labeled "Pauline Trigére" at neckline, 1964, size 6-8 850

Evening Coat, knee-length satin-weave fabric printed with Eastern-inspired pattern in pale aqua, blue, and orange, narrow silhouette with Nehru collar, long fitted sleeves, and center front button closure, pale aqua lining, labeled "Christian Dior – New York" near closure, 1960s, size 8 300

Gown, black lace with fur-trimmed jacket, c1930 165

Gown, ivory and tan silk with elaborate lace trim and underpinnings, silver metallic lace sash, labeled "B. Altman Co., Paris, New York," c1915 250

Gown, lavender lightweight wool flannel detailed with embroidered net, crochet cov satin buttons, surface embroidery and rat-tail braid, ivory silk lining, labeled "Madame P. Blanc Robes, 2116 Arch St. Phila," c1900 325

Jacket, black, fully beaded with velvet beaded fringe, c1890 50

Jacket, velveteen, ivory, navy blue, pink, red, black, and green floral print with center front button closure and wide lapel collar, labeled "Emilio Pucci Florence Italy" at neckline, 1970s, size 8 525

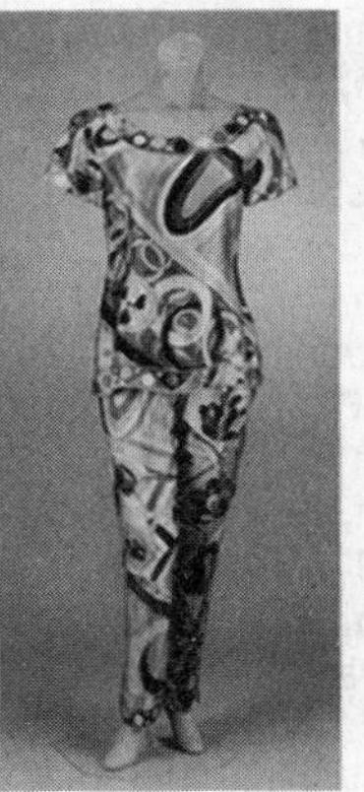

Mini Dress, beaded orange silk chartreuse A-line sleeveless dress with round neckline, Native American-inspired multi-colored embroidery at neckline, armholes, and hem, beading cosists of faux blue and green gems, gold bugle beads, faux pearls, and silver, blue, gold, and turquoise appliqué, orange silk lining, labeled "Sara Fredericks" at neckline, 1960s, size 8-10 225

Mini Dress, fitted, sleeveless, white cotton with pastel green, aqua, purple, and pink psychedelic design, slit neckline, narrow collar, labeled "Emilio Pucci" at neckline, 1960s, size 4 300

Mini Suit, white mod vinyl, hip length cap-sleeved jacket with sq neckline and double-breasted closure with op-art black and white buttons, matching A-line mini skirt, white polyester lining, labeled "Samuel Roberts" at neckline, 1960s, size 6-8 . .225

Pantsuit, multi-colored pink, blue, orange, black, and white, short-sleeved silk top with round neckline and matching slip pants, labeled "Emilio Pucci" at neckline, 1970s 275

Rain Coat, brown plastic, A-line, knee length, large round side pockets with welted seams and band collar that fastens to side with round goldtone and silvertone button, black wool jersey lining, labeled "Pierre Cardin Paris New York" at neckline, 1960s, size 8 625

Shoes, go-go boots, silver metallic fabric, ankle high, zipper on side, square toe, "After Five by Sophia" label, 1960s, size 7-7½ 70

Skirt, floor-length linen cotton wrap with Peter Max psychedelic print in orange, green, blue, yellow, and pink, "Peter Max" printed on fabric, 1970s, size 6 . . .60

Smock, Nixon campaign, white cotton mini-dress with self-tie neckline, blue trim, "Nixon" printed in bold block letters slightly off-centered down the front, c1968 90

Walking Suit, 2-pc, pale blue/green wool flannel trimmed with velvet and lace, embroidered buttons, capelet, ivory silk lining, labeled "Redfern Newport RI," c1900 55

Wedding Gown, 2-pc, ivory silk brocade with lace trim, buttons and silk ribbon, handmade Battenberg lace, c1846 415

COCA-COLA

John Pemberton, a pharmacist from Atlanta, Georgia, is credited with creating the formula for Coca-Cola. Less than two years later, he sold out to Asa G. Candler. Candler improved the formula and began advertising. By the 1890s America was Coca-Cola conscious.

Coke, a term first used in 1941, is now recognized worldwide. American collectors still focus primarily on Coca-Cola material designed for the American market. Although it would take a little effort to obtain, a collection of foreign Coke advertising would make a terrific display. What a perfect excuse to fly to the Orient.

Clubs: Coca-Cola Collectors Club, PMB 609 4780 Ashford Dunwoody Rd., Ste. A, Atlanta, GA 30338, www.cocacolaclub.org; Coca-Cola Collectors Club International, P.O. Box 49166, Atlanta, GA 30359; The Cola Club, P.O. Box 392, York, PA 17405.

Advertising Display Bottle, plastic, with orig cap and plain box, 1953, 20" h 650

Ashtray Set, ruby glass, set of 4 card suits (spade, heart, diamond, and club) in orig box, 1950s 600

Calendar, "Boy Scouts of America," Norman Rockwell artwork, Jamestown Bottling Co, Jamestown, NY, complete 1941 pad, 46" h, 22" w 4,000

Clock, spinner neon clock with "Ice Cold Coca-Cola" above silhouette girl logo, paper care tag on back, 1940, 22" d 4,400

Door Plates, pair, aluminum, 1 "Push," 1 "Pull," red lettering "Drink Coca-Cola Delicious and Refreshing 5¢" on both, c1905, 8" h, 2.25" w 925

Kick Plate, "Drink Coca-Cola" button, soda bottle, and "things go better with Coke," white ground, 1963, 12" h, 32" w 275

Mirror, red button with "Delicious, Drink Coca-Cola, Refreshing" and bottle, metal sleeve frame, 1930s, 12" x 3.5" . .325

Serving Tray, boy leaning against tree and holding bottle and sandwich, dog watching, 1931 .1,500

Serving Tray, woman leaning against green car, talking to female driver, 1942 187

Sign, celluloid over tin over cardboard, "Pause Refreshed" in yellow, glass of soda, "GO" in green circle, and yellow rim stripe on red ground, 1950s, 9" d .2,400

Sign, neon counter top sign, cast aluminum silhouette lettering with "Coca-Cola" neon letters floating in front, sandblasted glass panel that reads "In Bottles" surrouded by red neon on base, Neon Products, Lima, OH, orig paper care tag on back, c1939, 12" h, 24" w 6,825

Sign, tin, diecut 6-pack of bottles, 1954, 11" h, 13" w 1,000

Sign, tin, woman extending arm holding glass of Coke, "Coca-Cola" behind her in large red oval, 1927, 8" h, 11" w 375

Straws, full box, 1940s, 8.5" h 385

Thermometer, cigar-shaped, metal, "Drink Coca-Cola, Sign of Good Taste, Refresh Yourself," red and white, 1950s, 30" h 450

Tip Tray, oval, pretty girl seated at table with glass of Coke, 1909 450

Toys, set of 4 animals, duck, bear, elephant, and terrier, painted wood, each with rect logo "drink Coca-Cola in bottles," 1930s, 4" h, 5" l 2,300

Toy Truck, yellow and white, battery operated, orig box, 1950s 385

COINS, AMERICAN

Just because a coin is old does not mean that it is valuable. Value often depends more on condition than on age. This being the case, the first step in deciding if any of your coins are valuable is to grade them. Coins are graded on a scale of 70 with 70 being the best and 4 being good.

Start your research by acquiring Marc and Tom Hudgeons' *The Official Blackbook Price Guide to United States Coins* (House of Collectibles). Resist the temptation to look up your coins immediately. Read the hundred-page introduction, over half of which deals with the question of grading.

Do not overlook the melt (weight) value of silver content coins. In many cases, weight value will be far greater than collectible value.

Club: American Numismatic Assoc., 818 N. Cascade Ave., Colorado Springs, CO 80903, www.money.org; Young Numismatists of America, 2315 Poplar Ln., Anderson, SC 29621, http://members.aol.com/TheYNA/.

COINS, FOREIGN

The foreign coins that you are most likely to find at a flea market are the leftover change that someone brought back from their travels. Since the coins were in circulation, they are common and of a low grade. In some countries, they have been withdrawn from circulation and cannot even be redeemed for face value.

If you are a dreamer and think you have uncovered hidden wealth, use Chester L. Krause and Clifford Mishler's Standard Catalog of World Coins (Krause Publications). This book covers world coinage from 1701 to the present.

Avoid ancient coinage. There are excellent fakes on the market. You need to be an expert to tell the good from the bad. Coins are one of those categories where it pays to walk away when the deal is too good. Honest coin dealers work on very small margins. They cannot afford to give away anything of value.

Club: Ancient Numismatic Society, 8713 Caminto Abrazo, La Jolla, CA 92037.

COLLEGE COLLECTIBLES

Rah, rah, rah, sis-boom-bah! A college education is respectable again. Alumni tout their old alma mater and usually have a souvenir of their college days in their office at home or work.

You will not find a Harvard graduate with a room full of Yale memorabilia and vice versa. These items have value only to someone who attended the school. The exception is sport-related college memorabilia. This has a much broader appeal, either to a conference collector or a general sports collector.

Apron, Christ Church College, Oxford, England, bib type 25

Beer Stein, Siena Heights College, Adrian, MI, gold seal, Hull Pottery Mirror Brown with Ivory Foam liner, 5" h 28

Book, *Hilltop Heritage, Shippensburg State's First Hundred Years,* by John E Hubley, 1st printing, 1971, 85 pgs 24

Book, *Murder Goes to College,* by Kurt Steel, World Pub Co, Tower Books Edition, Second Printing, Jan 1943, ©1936, dj, 342 pgs 16

Cigar Label, College Ribbon, inner label, 9" x 6.5" 12

Class Ring, Pace University, NY, 10kt yellow gold, green stone, 1951 325

Cuff Links, Vassar College, gold tone 50

Diploma, Wiley College, Marshall, TX, 1939, in purple leather folder, tissue paper insert held in place with purple and white ribbon .55

Drinking Glass, Boston College, red and yellow logo on 1 side, "Ten Years of Big East Basketball" on other, 4" h 8

Game, College Basketball, Cadaco Ellis, 1954 38

Handbook, *1950 Esso Football Handbook,* college schedules and national football league schedule 18

Life Magazine, college couple from Bowdoin and Lasell in sleigh on cov, Jan 8, 1940 28

Lunch Box, oval with double bail handles, litho tin, multicolor college pennants all around, Ohio Art, 1950s 40

Movie Poster, *Animal House,* John Belushi, Tim Matheson, John Vernan, Verna Bloom, 1978 165

Movie Poster, *Get Yourself A College Girl,* Chad Everett, Nancy Sinatra, Mary Ann Mobley, Dave Clark Five, The Animals, 1964 110

Pinback Button, black and white jugate pictures of Johnson and Humphrey on facing pages of an open book, red, white, and blue "College Young Democrats for Johnson and Humphrey The Choice is Clear," 1.5" 15

Pin Tray, Kings College Cambridge, image of building, Coalport China, 4" d 25

Plate, College of Agriculture, University of Wisconsin, multicolor image on white ground, reticulated rim, 4" d 25

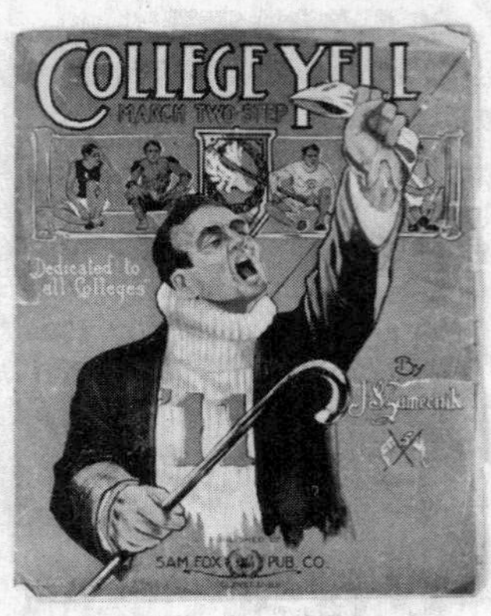

Plate, Harvard College, Celtic China series, pictures Harvard Hall, Hollis Hall, Holworthy Hall, Holden Chapel, and Stoughton Hall, Enoch Wood & Sons, blue, 10.5" d 400

Plate, Phelps Stokes Chapel, Berea College of Kentucky, 10" d 30

Plate, Yale University, New Haven, CT, Timothy Dwight College, Wedgwood, 1949 25

Postcard, Christian College, Columbia, MO, linen, unused 12

Postcard, Middlebury College, VT, linen, 1907 postmark 5

Program, Iowa State College, graduation, 1949 15

Records, *College Marching Songs,* Russ Morgan and his Orchestra, Decca Records, 45 rpm, boxed set of 4 65

Ruler, Central Iowa Business College, Marshalltown, IA, wood, school emblem and list of courses on reverse, early 1900s, ...12

Scrapbook, assembled by alumnus of Iowa State College, Ames, IA, includes photos and ephemera,1920s 100

Sheet Music, *College Life March & Two-Step,* by Henry Frantzen, cover image of college grad reading book, smoking pipe, 1905 18

Sheet Music,* College Yell, *by JS Zamecnik, pub by Sam Fox Pub Co, 11 x 13.75" 5

Soda, 6-pack of Coca-Cola bottles in cardboard carrier, "1990 National Football Champs Ga. Tech," 10 oz 45

Tape Measure, College At Buffalo, State University of NY, enameled brass, 1948, 1.75" d 25

Tile, Woman's Medical College of Pennsylvania, 1850-1950 Centennial commemorative, mkd "Mosaic" in an oval above "Made In USA" on back . . .20
Tobacco Silk, Columbia University, College Pennants series, felt, American Tobacco Co, 1908, 5" x 8" 10
Watch Fob, Indiana Vocational Tech College, gold tone, 1963, .75" w 10

COLORING BOOKS

The key is to find these gems uncolored. Some collectors will accept a few pages colored, but the coloring had better be neat. If it is scribbled, forget it.

Most of the value rests on the outside cover. The closer the image is to the actual character or personality featured, the higher the value. The inside pages of most coloring books consist of cheap newsprint. It yellows and becomes brittle over time. However, resist buying only the cover. Collectors prefer to have the entire book.

Africa, A Missionary Color Book For Children, Paul Hubartt, 1951, 10.75" x 7.5", few pgs colored 154
Barbie, Ken and Midge, Whitman, #1640, 1963, 12 pgs colored, 108 pgs 38
Batman, Whitman, unused, 1974, 8" x 11" .20
Bunny, diecut cov and pgs in shape of rabbit, Southfield Pub Co, unused, 1950, 7.75" x 8.25" 12
Bunny Boo, Whitman, 1954, flocked rabbit on cov, 9.25" x 8.5" 10
Easter, 2 bunnies on front, illus by Myers, Whitman, unused, 1956 28

GI Joe, coloring and activity book, c1982, few pgs used 12
Henry, 1956, 1 pg colored 32
JFK Coloring Book, 1962 35
Jimmy Carter, Vol. 1, 1976, 33 pgs 35
Lil Abner, 1941, 8.25" x 11", colored 38
Make Believe, A Coloring Book For Paints or Crayons, Children at Work and Play #968, Samuel Lowe, unused, 1955, 34 pgs 15
Mask, unused, 1986, 8" x 10.75" 10
Mister Magoo, Whitman, #1137, 1965, 128 pgs 48
Monkey Shines, few pgs colored, 1953, 8.25" x 11.25" 15
Ollie North, saluting North against American flag background, distributed by Andrews and McMeel, Kansas City, MO, 1987 12
Princess Diana, World International Pub Ltd, Finland, unused, 1986 20
Superman World Without Water, Whitman, 1980 18
Surprise!, drawings by Mary Alice Stoddard, Whitman, all pgs colored 6
Tonto, Whitman, 1 pg colored, 1955, 8.25" x 11" 25
Union Pacific Railroad, give-away, 1954, 29 pgs, 8" x 10", unused 24
Winnie Winkle, 1953 80

COMBS

A comb's value rests in its design and the material from which it is made. The more elaborate the comb—the higher the price.

An interesting collection can be built inexpensively by collecting giveaway combs. It is amazing how many individuals and businesses, from politicians to funeral parlors, use this advertising media.

Club: Antique Ornamental Comb Collectors Club International, 413C Broadway, Alexandria, MN 56308.

Comb, Bakelite, mottled brown and yellow, gold design, 7.5" l 25
Comb, clear plastic with emb brass edge, 8" l 12
Comb, faux tortoise shell, emb silver plated holder, c1940s, 5" l 32

Comb, folding, lime green Bakelite, mkd Japan 28
Comb, lucite, double row of teeth arranged in a wavy pattern, orange, mkd "Perm O Comb. Pat No.2348339" . .15
Comb, plastic, faux tortoise shell, brass case, West Germany, 5.25" l 20
Comb, tortoise shell, removable SS back with emb floral design, Amerith, 8.25" l . 18
Dresser Set, hand mirror, brush, and comb, marbleized pearl gray celluloid, c1920s 25
Dresser Set, hand mirror, brush, and comb, metal handles with pale gray marbleized backs, orig box, 1950s 60
Mirror and Comb, silver plated, ornate emb design, 9.5" l hand mirror 50

COMIC BOOKS

Comic books come in all shapes and sizes. The number that have survived is almost endless. Although there were reprint books of cartoon strips in the 1910s, 1920s, and 1930s, the modern comic book originated in June 1938 when DC issued Action Comics No. 1, marking the appearance of Superman.

Comics are divided into Golden Age, Silver Age, and Contemporary titles. Before you begin buying, read John Hegenberger's *Collector's Guide to Comic Books* (Wallace-Homestead, 1990) and D. W. Howard's *Investing in Comics* (The World of Yesterday, 1988). The dominant price guide for comics is Robert Overstreet's *The Overstreet Comic Book Price Guide.*

Most comics, due to condition, are not worth more than 50¢ to a couple of dollars. Very strict grading standards are applied to comics less than 10 years old. The following list shows the potential in the market. You need to check each comic book separately.

Note: Prices listed are for comic books in good condition.

Archie at Riverdale High, #1 6
Barney Google & Snuffy Smith, #3 8
Battle Action, #2 13
Betty and Me, #16 3
Black Black Jack, #20 9
Blue Ribbon Comics, #2 135
Captain America Comics, #5 535
Casper the Friendly Ghost, #10 20
Classic Comics, Robin Hood, #28 15
Classic Comics, Westward Ho!, #15 55
Classics Illustrated, Macbeth, #143 2
Comics on Parade, #12 45
Creatures on the Loose, #21 2
Dell Giants, #24, Woody Woodpecker's Family Fun 7
Dennis the Menace, #2 25
Diary Loves, #15 10
Dippy Duck, #1 9
Dracula, #2 4
Eerie Adventures, #1 40
Egbert, #15 5
Everthing's Archie, #3 4
Fairy Tale Parade, #3 35
FBI, The, #1 3
Flame, The, #2 135
Gang Busters, #6 25
Garrison's Gorillas, #2 3
Girl Comics, #3 20
Green Lantern, #3 .460

Harvey Hits, #3, Richie Rich 75
Hercules Unbound, #1 1
Heroic Comics, #31 6
Incredible Hulk, The, #6 150
Jeanie Comics, #14 12
Judge Parker, #2 5
Jughead, E132 3
Keen Detective Funnies, Vol 2, #7 235
Kewpies, #1 45
Leave It To Beaver, #5 18
Legend of Custer, The, #1 3
Lone Ranger, The, #22 10
Mad Follies, #4 10
Mad House, #100 1
Marge's Little LuLu, Dell Pub, #21 50
Marvel Mystery Comics, #7 975
Marvel Super Heroes, #13 5
Master of Kung Fu, #18 2
Meet Miss Bliss, #3 10
Mickey Mouse Magazine, Vol 3, #2 55
Miss America Comics, #1 150
Mother Goose and Nursery Rhyme Comics, #59 20
Navy Heroes, #1 12
Patsy & Hedy, #10 10
Popeye, #2 30
Public Enemies, #7 15
Punch & Judy Comics, Vol 2, #2 25
Red Rabbit Comics, #18 8
Roy Rogers Comics, #5 20
Rudolph the Red-Nosed Reindeer, #1, 1950 24
Scary Tales, #18 2
Shanna, The She-Devil, #5 2
Shazam!, #8 4
Sparkler Comics, 1st Series, #2, Frankie Doodle 30
Strange Worlds, Avon Periodicals, #3 ...200
Strange Worlds, Marvel Comics, #1 85
Tales From the Crypt, Eerie Pub, #10 3
Terrors of the Jungle, #18 35
Terry and the Pirates, #6, large feature ...62
Tom Terrific!, #5 18
Uncle Scrooge, #24, Christmas 12
United States Marines, #2 35
Voyage to the Bottom of the Sea, #6 4
Walt Disney Comics Digest, #44 5
Weird Science, Fantasy Annual, 1952 ...200
Wendy Witch World, #1 12
Wonder Comics, #6 50
Wonder Woman, #2 350
Yogi Bear, Dell Pub, #30 3
Young Love, #40 3

COMMEMORATIVE MEDALS

From the late nineteenth century through the 1930s, commemorative medals were highly prized possessions. The U.S. Mint and other mints still carry on the tradition today, but to a far lesser degree.

Distinguish between medals issued in mass and those struck for a limited purpose, in some cases in issues of one for presentation. An old medal should have a surface patina that has developed over the years causing it to have a very mellow appearance. Never, never clean a medal. Collectors like the patina.

In most medals, the metal content has little value. However, medals were struck in both silver and gold. If you are not certain, have the metal tested.

Club: Token and Medal Society, P.O. Box 366, Bryantown, MD 20617.

Anniversary, Israeli 25th, 10 lira coin, "Yom Haatzmaoot Tuf Shin Lamed Gimel" 100
Apollo 11, 1969, 2.5" d 60
Bicentennial, National Bicentennial Medal, bronze, MIP 25
Coronation, King Edward VIII at Westminster Abbey, May 12, 1937, red, white, and blue ribbon, c1937, 1.5" d 50
Coronation, King George VI, King and Queen's heads 1 side, "Fear God, Honor The King" other side, orig silk ribbon and pin, silvered aluminum, 1" d 20
Exposition Universelle, Paris, 1889, 2.5" d 125
Inauguration, emb profile and "Nelson Aldrich Rockefeller" on front, eagle and "Vice President of the United States of America, Inaugurated December 19, 1974" on back, orig box, bronze, 3" d 70

Inauguration, emb profile and "President of the United States, Harry S. Truman," White House, eagle, and "Inaugurated April 12, 1946, January 20, 1949" on back, 3" d 150

Inauguration, emb profile of Eisenhower, bronze, portrait on front, eagle on back, mkd "Medallic Art Co NY Bronze," 1953, 2.75" d 85

John Paul Jones, bronze, name and profile on front, 3-mast ship on back, 2.125" d 235

New York City Letter Carriers, emb image of a postman, made by Dieges & Clust, RI, 14k gold, c1890, 1.25" d 150

Service, Canada WWII Voluntary Service, SS, 1.325" d 60

Service, Heinz Co, 14k gold, 1.25" d 150

Service, Statue of Liberty, Boy Scout emblem, and "War Service, Every Scout To Save a Soldier," back reads "Presented on Behalf of the US Treasury Department For Service in Liberty Loan Campaign Boy Scouts of America June 1917," red, white, and blue ribbon, 1.25" d 85

Sicilian Earthquake, Italian silver, Victor Emmanuel image, c1910 150

Silver Jubilee of King George V and Queen Mary, 1910-1935, 1.25" d 8

Sports, Los Angeles Olympic Games souvenir, "World Class Boxer," 1984, orig box 12

Sports, red and black enameled dartboard on front, engraved "Warley & District Darts League Div A Runners Up 1948," SS 1.25" d 30

Sports, South American Championship Basketball, Games held in Montevideo, Uruguay, 1953, 1.5" h 20

Washington, praying, Freedom Foundation Valley Forge, PA, mkd "Medallic Art Co, NY," bronze, 3" d 35

Wm F Cody (Buffalo Bill), profile and "Col Wm F Cody, 1845-1917" on front, mkd "Metal Arts Co, Roch, NY" on back, blue and white ribbon, 3" h 400

COMPACTS

Compacts are small portable cosmetic makeup boxes that contain powder, mirror, and puff. The vanity case is the more elaborate compact. It contains multiple compartments for powder, rouge, and/or lipstick. Compacts that were used up until the 1960s, when women opted for the "au naturel" look, are considered vintage.

Vintage compacts were made in a variety of shapes, sizes, combinations, and in almost every conceivable natural or man-made material. Many are also multipurpose, such as the compact/watch, compact/purse, and compact/lighter and appeal to both compact collectors and collectors of the secondary accessory.

Club: International Compact Collectors Club, P.O. Box 40, Lynbrook, NY 11563.

Coty, "Envelope," gold tone, sgd case, puff with logo, framed mirror, 3.5" x 2.625" x .5" 75

Evans, clutch carryall, geometric brushed and polished gold tone case, snake chain, black silk coin purse, cigarette compartment behind swinging metal mirror, compartments for powder, comb, and lipstick, 3" h, 5.5" w, 1" w 150

Evans, gold tone armor mesh vanity bag, translucent royal blue enameled oval-shaped lid centered with raised white and pink flowered enameled dec, metal mirror, powder and rouge compartments, lined int, snake carrying chain, 5.25" h, 2.75" l 275

Flato, gold tone compact with etched cat with green cabochon stone eyes on lid, lipstick sleeve in maroon velvet case, c1950s 325

Gold-Washed Continental Silver, enameled dec on lid, allover bright-cut fern and floral design, .800 silver content, 4" x 3.125" 300

Gwenda (UK), white metal, loose powder, coved case, lid with blue foil ground and plastic cov, transfer scene, "New York World's Fair" enameled in black on reverse, sgd case, polished int lid as mirror 200

Henriette, ball-shaped, brass compact, c1930 75

Illinois Watch Case Co, gold tone, loose powder vanity case, hand-chased scrolled lid bands with cut-out case for viewing int watch, puff with logo, sgd case, triangular framed mirror, 2.75" sq 200

Italian, cat-shaped textured gold tone compact, faux sapphire, emerald, and diamond eyes, int beveled framed mirror 300

Langlois, case sgd "Cara Nome," white metal vanity case, cut-out flower basket circular logo lid with blue celluloid ground, engine-turned vertical lines, pressed powder, rouge compartment behind hinged double metallic mirror, 2" sq x 1.5" 75

Lindy, Charles Lindbergh photo on lid, "Lindy" powder puff label, 2" d 325

Mondaine, multicolored tooled leather vanity case designed to resemble a book, spine with logo, framed mirror, rouge and powder compartments 100

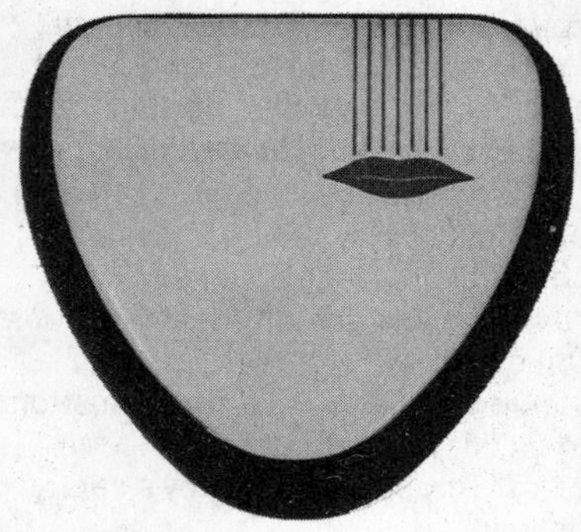

Revlon, #9508, gold tone, demitasse hand mirror compact, plastic floral dec, designed by Van Cleef & Arpels 50

White Lid, with stylized red lips and black trim, blue base, int wells for lipstick, powder, and rouge cases, patent #D-128-188, 5" x 5" 100

Yardley, gold tone vanity case with red, white, and blue emb design on lid, powder and rouge compartments, c1940s 75

CONDOM TINS

Condom tins have finally come "out of the closet!" Referred to by Playboy as "Sin Tins," there was a time when people were too embarassed to collect them or admit they owned one. Now it's agreed these tins are little works of art!

The earliest tins (1920s) are round and made of aluminum, all embossed with no color. Later tins (1940s) with colorful lithography are more collectible. Condoms were also marketed in paper and cardboard containers, from the early 1920s to the present. These are also collectible, but not nearly as desirable as the tins.

The five most common condom tins are the aluminum 3 Merry Widows and lithographed Ultrex Platinum, Ramses, Sheik, and Dean's Peacocks. In fact the Dean's Peacocks (pretty as it is) has been named "The 'Prince Albert' of condom tins!" (And the Ultrex Platinum, is the "Edgeworth.")

Note: The following tins are rectangular unless noted otherwise. Prices are for tins in pristine condition.

Apris, leaping stag, pink and white on black ground, Killian 175

Blue Ribbon, German Shepherd, American Hygienic Co, Baltimore, MD 1,000

Caravan, multicolor camel caravan in desert landscape, cactus in foreground, yellow ground, Tiger Skin Rubber Co 225

Carmen Brand Latex, circ, Rolf Armstrong girl on lid, yellow ground 600

Derbies, "Three" above jockey's cap and whip 200

Drug Pak, blue and white, mortar and pestle image, Nutex Co 185

Genuine Liquid Latex, red, white, and green, Shunk Latex Co 100

Golden Pheasant, multicolor pheasant on branch, red lettering, white ground, Reed & Co 150

Kamels, brown and white, sheik and camel in desert landscape, palm trees and palace in background, Frank Aaronoff 145

Optimus, cardboard box with 3 tins (4th tin missing), product image on box, orange, black, and white tins, 3.5" x 2.25" x .625" box 500

Patent Superior Liquid Latex, lift-off lid, red lettering on yellow ground 470

Shadows, sq, black-shadowed green lettering on white panel, green ends, Youngs Rubber Co 150

Sheik, small white silhouette of sheik on galloping horse on red in center of lid, red lettering on white ground, Julius Schmid Co .30

Smithies, white and blue lettering, 2 bands of red, white, and blue vertical stripes, red ground, Allied Latex Co . . .550

Thins Service Packet, dark blue and white, Youngs Rubber Co 350

Three Cadets, circ, "Carefully Tested 100% Perfect" variation, yellow, orange, and blue 385

Three Cadets, blue lettering on gold band at top, 3 saluting blue cadets on red ground, Julius Schmid 100

3 Pirates, cartoon female pirates on ship's deck, green tones 850

Town and Country, Art Deco design, Nelson Products, New York City 1,900

White Nutex, litho tin, black and white, 1.625" x 2.125" 575

CONSOLIDATED GLASS

The Consolidated Glass Company was founded in 1893, the result of a merger between the Wallace and McAfee Company and the Fostoria Shade & Lamp Company. In the mid-1890s, the company built a new factory in Corapolis, Pennsylvania, and quickly became one of the largest lamp, globe, and shade manufacturers in the United States.

The Consolidated Glass Company began making giftware in the mid-1930s. Most collectors focus on the company's late 1920s and early 1930s product lines.

Consolidated closed operations in 1932, reopening in 1936. In 1962 Dietz Brothers acquired the company. A disastrous fire in 1963 during a labor dispute heralded the end of the company. The last glass was made in 1964.

Club: Phoenix & Consolidated Glass Collectors' Club, 41 River View Dr., Essex Junction, VT 05452.

Banana Boat, Love Birds, hp, pink, brown, and blue-green on white milk glass, 6" h, 15" w .725
Candlesticks, pr, Catalonian 135
Comport, Line 700, #717, flared, ftd, powder blue wash 165
Cookie Jar, Con-Cora, purple violets on white milk glass, 6.5" h 85
Lamp, Chrysanthemum, 3-color wash on white satin milk glass, 12" h 125
Plate, Catalonian, russet, 6" d 100
Plate, Dancing Nudes pattern, 12 female figures, clear and frosted, 8.25" d 70
Rose Bowl, pink with white flowers, 6.75" h, 7" d 175
Shaker, Beaded Dahlia, opaque blue milk glass, 2.625" h .75
Shaker, Overlapping Leaf, opaque blue milk glass, 1.875" h .65
Spooner, Shell & Seaweed, enameled florals and scrolls, metal rim and handles 120
Tumbler, iced tea, Catalonian, emerald green, 12 oz 25
Tumbler, juice, Ruba Rombic, smokey topaz 65
Vase, Dogwood pattern, semi-ovoid, molded flowers and branches, brown and green highlights on custard ground, 10.5" h 860
Vase, Line 700, spherical, molded stems and small flowers, frosted with crystal highlights, 7" h 115

Vase, Owl, Martele line, salmon and green wash on white satin milk glass, 1928 165
Vase, Seagull pattern, flattened oval form, molded flying seagulls in red on green ground, 10" h 115

CONSTRUCTION SETS

Children love to build things. Building block sets originated in the nineteenth century. They exist in modern form as Legos and Lego imitators.

The Erector Set was popular with aspiring engineers. Alfred Carlton Gilbert, Jr., began his business by producing magic sets as the Mysto Manufacturing Company. With the help of his father, he bought out his partner and created the A. C. Gilbert Company located on Erector Square in New Haven, Connecticut.

Clubs: A. C. Gilbert Heritage Society, 1440 Whalley, Ste. 252, New Haven, CT 06515; Anchor Block Foundation, 1670 Hawkwood Ct., Charlottesville, VA 22901.

AC Gilbert, Erector Set, Amusement Park 350
AC Gilbert, Erector Set, Automatic Radar Scope No. 10042, 1960s 70
AC Gilbert, Erector Set, No. 6½, Electric Engine 200
AC Gilbert, Erector Set, No. 10057 55
AC Gilbert, Erector Set, Type B 350
American Model Builder Set, painted wood box, instructions 25
Halsam, American Logs Add On Set 15
Halsam, American Plastic Bricks #745 . . .75
Kenner, Motorized Girder, Panel, Bridge, and Turnpike Building Set, 1960 125
Lionel, Construction Kit #232, Erector-style, orig box and booklets, 1948 125
Meccano, Junior Set B, 1985 75
Noveltoy Corp, Block-Stix, 50 wooden blocks, 1930s 35
Playschool, Lincoln Logs #887 20
Questor, Super Transit Tinkertoy #146, 180 pcs 15
Spalding, Circus Tinker Zoo #747 25
Spalding, Tinkertoy Curtain Wall Builder #640 50

COOKBOOKS

Eighteenth and nineteenth century cookbooks are expensive, very expensive. The cookbooks that you are most likely to find date from the twentieth century. Most were promotional giveaways. A fair number came with appliances. Some were associated with famous authors. A few years ago, you could buy them in the 50¢ to $1 range and had a large selection from which to choose. No longer. These later cookbooks have been discovered. Prices now range from $5 to $20 for most of them.

Cover art affects price. Many cookbooks are bought for display purposes. Seek out the ones that feature a recognizable personality.

Clubs: Cook Book Collector's Club, 4756 Terrace Dr., San Diego, CA 92116; Cookbook Collectors Club of America, Inc, P.O. Box 56, St. James, MO 65559.

American Everyday Cookbook, The, Agnes Murphy, Random House, 1955, hard cov, dj 18

Beany Malone Cookbook, The, Lenora Mattingly Weber, Crowell, c1972, dj . . .150

Better Homes & Gardens Encyclopedia Of Cooking Volume 1: Special Edition, Meredith Pub, 1957, 1973 16

Betty Crocker's Cooking Calendar: A Year-Round Guide To Meal Planning With Recipes And Menus, Betty Crocker, Golden Press, spiral bound hard cov, illus, 1st ed, 176 pgs, 1962 15

Betty Crocker's Dinner For Two Cookbook, Betty Crocker, Simon and Schuster, spiralbound hard cov, 1st ed, 207 pgs, 1958 15

Blueberry Hill Menu Cookbook, Elsie Masterton, Thomas Y Crowell Co, 1963, dj, 373 pgs, black & white drawings 6

Brennan's New Orleans Cookbook, Hermann B Deutsch, Robert L Crager, 1964, dj, illus by Deirdre Stanforth, 14th ed 5

Electric Refrigerator Menus and Recipes, Recipes Prepared Especially For The General Electric Refrigerator, Alice Bradley, General Electric Co, 1927, hard cov 5

Fondue Cookbook, The, Ed Callahan, illus by Howard Sanders, Nitty Gritty Productions, 1968, paperback, no dj, 1st ed, 120 pgs 9

Good Housekeeping Book Of Meals Tested, Tasted, And Approved, Good Housekeeping, 1933, dj, 256 pgs 10

Graham Kerr Cookbook, The, Galloping Gourmet, Doubleday, 1969, 5th printing, hard cov, 284 pgs 8

Gun Club Drink Book: Being a more or less discursive account of alcoholic beverages, their formulae and uses, together with some observations on the mixing of drinks, Charles Browne, Charles Scribner's Sons, 1939, 1st ed, sgd by author 225

Hotel St Francis Cook Book, The, V Hirtzler, Chicago Hotel Monthly Press, 1919, 1st ed, 430 pgs 115

How Famous Chefs Use Marshmallows, Angelus Campfire, 1930, paperback 18

How To Cook A Pig And Other Back-To-The-Farm Recipes, Betty Talmadge with Jean Robitscher and Carolyn Carter, Simon & Schuster, 1977, hard cov, 1st ed, sgd by authors, 272 pgs . . .150

Larkin Housewives' Cook Book, Larkin Co, 1915 7

Mary Ann's Gilligan's Island Cookbook, Dawn Wells with Ken Beck and Jim Clark, Rutledge Hill, 1993, illus, ring bound, 3rd printing 18

Mary Frances Cook Book Or Mary Frances Among The Kitchen People, Jane Eayre Fryer, illus by Margaret G Hays and Jane Allen Boyer, John C Winston, 1912, hard cov, no dj, 1st ed, 1st printing 100

Modern Family Cook Book, Meta Given, J Ferguson, 1942, 1st ed, hard cov, no dj, 938 pgs 75
Pennsylvania Dutch Cookery, J George Frederick, Favorite Recipes Press, 1966, pictorial cloth hard cov reprint of 1935 orig, 275 pgs 8
Philadelphia National Cook Book, The, by a Lady of Philadelphia (Hannah Mary Bouvier Peterson), George W Childs, 1863, cloth, no dj, later ed 225
Pillsbury's Cook Book, The, ***Pillsbury Flour Mills Co, 1923, soft cov, color litho recipe and Mills illus 25***
Pocket Purity Cook Book, Harlequin, 1950, paperback 250
Practical Cook Book, Florence Austin Chase, Chase Pub, 1915, oilcloth, no dj, 1st ed, 294 pgs, 2-pg adv for Fleishmann's Yeast and Calumet Baking Powder 60
Simple Italian Cookery, ed by Edna Beilenson, illus by Ruth McCrea, Peter Pauper Press, 1959, hard cov, 60 pgs ...9

COOKIE CUTTERS

When most individuals think of cookie cutters, they envision the metal cutters, often mass-produced, that were popular during the nineteenth century and first third of the twentieth century. This is too narrow a view. Do not overlook the plastic cutters of recent years. Not only are they detailed and colorful, they also come in a variety of shapes quite different from their metal counterparts.

If you want to build a great specialized collection, look for cutters that were give-away premiums by flour and baking related businesses. Most of these cutters are priced in the $10 to $40 range.

Club: Cookie Cutters Collectors Club, 1167 Teal Rd. SW, Dellroy, OH 44620.

Baker, tin, flat back, strap handle, c1930, 5" x 3" 28
Bridge Set, tin, 5-part, heart, star, fluted circle, club, and diamond shapes, mkd "DRGM Made In Western Germany" ...25
Bunny, aluminum, c1920s, 2.625" l 25
Cartoon Set, red plastic, includes Tom & Jerry, Lucky Ducky, Barney Bear, Droopy, and Tuffy, with display box and orig adv, Quaker Oats premium, ©Loew's Inc, 1956 90
Chick, tin, flat back, strap handle, c1930, 3.75" x 5" 24
Chicken, aluminum, riveted red strap handle, Holey Tole 12
Christmas Set, metal, includes gingerbread man, Santa, Christmas tree, angel, reindeer, and star, Veritas, c1945 40
Cookie Press, 11 wheels including dog, camel, pinwheel, sun, star, and geometric shapes, 4 tips, Mirro 50
Diamond, aluminum, scalloped edge, green wood handle, 3.375" x 2.25" 15
Donald Duck Head, yellow plastic, Hallmark, 1970s, 4.5" h 20
Doughnut, aluminum, red wooden handle, 2 vent holes, 2" d 5
Doughnut, tin, scalloped edge, wire handle, 2.5" d.........................70
Gingerbread Man, red plastic, Betty Crocker, 3.875" h 16
Gingerbread Man, tin, 7.5" x 5" 60
Goofy, blue plastic, Disney, Hallmark, 1970s, 3.5" x 3", MIP 25
Halloween Set, orange plastic, includes witch head, owl, cat head, and pumpkin, Hallmark, 1973 28
Holiday, set of 4 including Santa, turkey, birthday cake, and pumpkin, red plastic, Tupperware 6
Horse, Davis Baking Powder, 3.75" x 3" ...38
Man, tin, mkd "Made in Germany," 5.75" h 48
Oval, tin, large outer band with center Christmas tree flanked by a praying child, St Nick, heart, angel, lamb, and star, 7.5" x 11" 400

Reddy Killowatt Head, red plastic, orig mailing box .40
Republican Elephant, tin, straight handle, 2" h, 3" l, orig box mkd "Campaign Cookie Cutter – Vote Republican" .30
Santa, aluminum, green wooden handle, 3.5" h .18
Snowman, aluminum, 5" h .10
Turkey, aluminum, 3" x 4" .8
Twelve Days of Christmas, set .30
Witch on Broom, copper-colored aluminum, 5.25" h, 5" w .18

COOKIE JARS

Talk about categories that have gone nuts over the years. Thanks to the Andy Warhol sale, cookie jars became the talk of the town. Unfortunately, the prices reported for the Warhol cookie jars were so far removed from reality that many individuals were deceived into believing their cookie jars were far more valuable than they really were.

The market seems to be having trouble finding the right pricing structure. A recent cookie jar price guide lowballed a large number of jar prices. Big city dealers are trying to sell cookie jars as high ticket art objects rather than the kitsch they really are. You be the judge. Remember, all you are buying is a place to store your cookies.

Clubs: American Cookie Jar Association, 1600 Navajo Rd., Norman, OK 73026, http://cookiejarclub.com; Cookie Jarrin', 1501 Maple Ridge Rd., Walterboro, SC 29488.

Apple, Red Wing .115
Asparagus, McCoy .95
Baseball Boy, California Originals .65
Big Apple, Hull, unmkd .45
Big Bird, California Originals .125
Black Scottie, Metlox .55
Bluebird on Pinecone, McCoy .135
Castle, Twin Winton .285
Chef with Spoon, Japan .45
Circus Horse, McCoy .200
Circus Wagon, California Originals .75
Clown, DeForest .65
Clown, Maurice Ceramics .125
Clown Riding Elephant, California Originals .185
Clown with Drum, Pfaltzgraff .595
Cookie Barn, Treasure Craft .25
Cookie Monster, California Originals .110
Cookie Time, Twin Winton .50
Cowboy Boots, American Bisque .90
Cow Jumped Over the Moon, Doranne .250
Crooked Shack, Twin Winton .65
Davy Crockett, Red Wing .525
Elephant with Ice Cream Cone, Brush .575
Flat Cook Stove, Twin Winton .75
Fred Flintstone, Vandor .125
Grandma's Cookies, Twin Winton .65
Hobby Horse, Twin Winton .295
Human Bean, Enesco .75
Humpty Dumpty, Abingdon .385
Humpty Dumpty, Metlox .385
Indian, McCoy .300
Kittens on Churn, Twin Winton .135
Lamb on Cylinder, McCoy .350
Little Boy Blue, Brush .700
Nabisco Oreo Cookie Truck .85
Noah's Ark, Metlox .325
Panda Bear, Metlox .95
Polka Dot Witch, Fitz & Floyd .225
Raggedy Ann, California Originals .175
Sailor Jack, Robinson-Ransbottom .200
Santa, standing, Treasure Craft .145
Seal on Igloo, American Bisque .375
Sheriff Pig, Robinson-Ransbottom, 12.5" h .125
Snoopy on Doghouse, McCoy .325
Teddy Bear, flat green hat, American Bisque .135
Teddy Bear, Twin Winton .225
Train Engine, Maurice of California .100

WC Fields, McCoy .175
Wheat, Shawnee, 7.75" h 60

COPPER PAINTINGS

Copper paintings, actually pictures stamped out of copper or copper foil, deserve a prize as one of the finest "ticky-tacky" collectibles ever created. I remember getting a four-picture set from a bank as a premium in the late 1950s or early 1960s. It is one of the few things that I have no regrets about throwing out.

However, to each his own—somewhere out there are individuals who like this unique form of mass-produced art. Their treasures generally cost them in the $15 to $50 range depending on subject.

COSTUMES

Remember how much fun it was to play dress-up as a kid? Seems silly to only do it once a year at Halloween. Down South and in Europe, Mardis Gras provides an excuse.

Collectors are beginning to discover children's Halloween costumes. While you may be staggered by some of the prices listed below, I see costumes traded at these prices all the time.

There doesn't seem to be much market in adult costumes, those used in the theater and for theme parties. Costume rental shops are used to picking them up for a few dollars each.

African Cannibal, orig box, c1930 35
Archie, Ben Cooper, 1977 16
Ariel, Disney 25
Astronaut, 1970s 25
Batman, Ben Cooper, 1970 18
Beatles Yellow Submarine 200
C-3PO, Star Wars, Ben Cooper, 1977 40
Cabbage Patch Kid, Tiny Tot 20
Car Hop Girl, 1950s 25
Casper the Friendly Ghost, Ben Cooper . . .15
Clown, Halco, 1960 15
Creature From The Black Lagoon, Collegeville, 1980 40
Darth Maul, Star Wars, with battery operated light saber, adult size 18

Donny Osmond, Collegeville, 1977 35
Ernie, Sesame Street, Ben Cooper 12
Evel Knievel, 1974 35
Fairy Princess, Collegeville 50
Fonzie, Ben Cooper, 1964 30
Frankenberry, cereal premium 120
Frankenstein, Ben Cooper 50
Fred Flintstone, 1973 15
Frosty O Bear, cereal premium, 1960 65
Garbage Pail Kid 30
Girl From UNCLE, 1967 275
Glitter Glo Fairy, Ben Cooper 55
Goofy, Disney 30
Groovie Goolies Wolfie 80
Gus the Ghost, Ben Cooper 20
Herman Munster, Ben Cooper 100
I Dream Of Jeannie, Ben Cooper 40
Jester, c1940 20
Josie and the Pussycats 65
King Kong, Ben Cooper 15
Laverne, Laverne & Shirley 30
Lurch, Addams Family 100
Marie Osmond, 1970s 15
Man From UNCLE, 1960s 105
Molly American Girl 42
Monster, Woolworth's, 1970s 25
Mr Ed, Ben Cooper, 1960s 60
Rat Fink, Ed Roth, 1964 200
Robin, Batman & Robin, adult 45
Rose Petal Place, 1983 12
She-Ra, Ben Cooper 12
Six Million Dollar Man, Ben Cooper, 1974 .15
Skeleton, Collegeville 15
Sully, Monsters Inc .18
Top Cat, 1960s 55
Twinkles, Collegeville 40
Underdog, 1974 20

Witchiepoo, HR Puf N Stuf 30
Wolfman, Ben Cooper, 1960s 40
Wonder Woman, 1976 20

COUNTRY STORE

There is something special about country stores. My favorite is Bergstresser's in Wassergass, Pennsylvania. There is probably one near you that you feel as strongly about. Perhaps the appeal is that they continue to deny the present. I am always amazed at what a country store owner can dig out of the backroom, basement, or barn.

Country store collectibles focus heavily on front counter and back counter material from the last quarter of the nineteenth century and first quarter of the twentieth century. The look is tied in closely with Country. It also has a strong rural small town emphasis.

Drop in and prop your feet up on the potbelly stove. Don't visit a country store if you are in a hurry.

Bottle Holder, Whistle Soda, heavy cast iron figural wall mount hand shaped bottle holder complete with unopened soda bottle, 3" x 10" x 2.5" 1,200

Box, Red Star Cleaning Powder, cardboard, paper label with detailed color graphics, unopened, c1880s, 5" x 3.5" x 1.25" 350

Cabinet, Dr Daniels' Veterinary Medicines, wooden with colorful graphics on tin door insert, 27" x 21" x 7.5" 6,700

Cabinet, Milward's Celebrated Needles, wooden 3-drawer cabinet with reverse glass labels on drawers, 10.375" x 14.75" x 8.75" 875

Counter Top Jar, glass, Shepp's Cocoanut, emb lettering, figural coconut finial on lid, 6.5" x 5.5" 500

Display, None-Such Mince Meat, diecut figural cardboard display sign, early, 11" x 8.75" 550

Display Bin, Beech-Nut Chewing Tobacco, blue variation Lorillard's store bin, 8.625" x 9.875" x 8.125" 465

Display Bin, Flake Merc Co Spices, counter top, lift-up door in bottom, color image of 1890's American battleship, 12.5" x 9" x 9.375" 715

Display Bin, Gladiator Blend Coffee, Brewster, Crittenden & Co, Rochester, NY, store size bin with roll-up door at top, elaborate gold and red stenciling on front and top, 21.5" x 13.25" x 13.25" 1,540

Display Bin, Sweet Cuba Fine Cut Tobacco, counter top, litho tin, red and white on yellow ground, 8" x 8" x 10" 450

Display Box, Argo Corn Starch, cardboard oversize counter top display box, c1920s, 18" x 9.625" x 5.625" 385

Display Box, Aunt Lydia's Thread, wooden counter top display box with stenciled and painted advertising, complete with 4 full boxes of colored thread (with 12 large spools each), 9" x 9.75" x 11.25" 250

Display Box, Blue Bird Handkerchiefs, counter top, litho metal, hinged top with glass insert displays early product boxes, c1920s, 6.75" x 11.5" x 8" 550

Display Box, Blue-jay Corn and Bunion Plasters, colorful graphics of hobos on railroad tracks, 8.75" x 18.25" x 3.75" . . .185

Display Box, DM Ferry & Co Flower Seeds, oak seed box with multicolored litho paper label inside lid, early, 9.75" x 11.5" x 6.75" 450

Door Push, Ox-Heart Brand Dutch Process Cocoa, heavy porcelain, white and red on green ground, early, 6.5" x 4" 575

Soda Dispenser, wooden Howe's Root Beer barrel with porcelain sign on back, metal taps on front, c1920s, 26" x 17" . .450

Thermometer, Moxie, litho tin over wood, oversize hanging outdoor thermometer, 38.25" x 12" 6,925

Tin, Puck Brand Black Pepper, Puck Foods, NY, cardboard sides, tin top and bottom, colorful graphics, 2 oz, 4.125" x 2.25" x 1.25" 225

Tin, Roosevelt Brand Allspice, Karasik Brothers Co, Chicago, IL, litho tin, colorful image of Teddy on both sides, 2 oz, 3.75" x 2.25" x 1.25" 825

Tin, Wan-Eta Cocoa, paper label over tin, colorful graphics of Indian girl both sides, early, 1/5 lb, 4.125" x 2.5" x 1.5" . .150

COWAN POTTERY

R. Guy Cowan founded the Cowan Pottery in 1913 in Cleveland, Ohio. It remained in almost continuous operation until financial difficulties forced it to close in 1931. Initially, utilitarian redware was produced. Cowan began experimenting with glazes, resulting in a unique lusterware glaze.

Club: American Art Pottery Assoc., P.O. Box 525, Cedar Hill, MO 63016.

Bookends, pr, boy and girl, special ivory glaze, stamped "Cowan," 6.254" x 4" . .385

Bookends, pr, elephant, semi-matte green glaze, stamped "Cowan," 7.5" x 5" 775

Bookends, pr, flying fish, antique green glaze, stamped "Cowan," 8.5" x 6" 550

Figurine, Pierrette, old ivory glaze, stamped "Cowan," 8" h 275

Flower Frog, Debutante, special ivory glaze, stamped "Cowan/S," 10.25" x 4.25" 935

Flower Frog, Duet, original ivory glaze, stamped "Cowan," 7.75" x 6.25" 495

Flower Frog, Heavenward, original ivory glaze, stamped "Cowan," 7.75" x 4.25" .195

Flower Frog, Pan, special ivory glaze, stamped "Cowan," 10" x 5.25" 275

Match Holder, ivory, 3.5" h 60

Paperweight, elephant, special ivory glaze, stamped "Cowan," 4.5" x 3.25" . .325

Snack Set, 6-sided cup and tray, light blue 100

Vase, spherical, ribbed, feathery vermillion glaze, stamped "Cowan," 10" x 10" 140

COWBOY HEROES

The cowboy heroes in this category rode the range in movies and on television. In a way, they were larger than their real life counterparts, shaping the image of how the west was won in the minds of several generations. The contemporary westerns may be historically correct, but they do not measure up in sense of rightness.

The movie and television cowboy heroes were pioneers in merchandise licensing. If you were a child in the 1949 to 1951 period and did not own a Hopalong Cassidy item, you were deprived.

Clubs: Cowboy Collector Network, P.O. Box 7486, Long Beach, CA 90807; Cowboy Collector Society, 4248 Burningtown Rd., Franklin, NC 28734; Westerns & Serials Fan Club, 527 S. Front St., Mankato, MN 56001, www.angelfire.com/biz2/normankietzerpubs/clubinfo.html#serials.

Note: For information on fan clubs for individual cowboy heroes, refer to *Maloney's Antiques & Collectibles Resource Directory* by David J. Maloney, Jr., published by Antique Trader Books.

Bonanza, game, Bonanza Michigan Rummy Game, Parker Bros, #810, ©1964 NBC, 14.25" x 14.25" x 1" box 35

Bonanza, matchcover, color photo of Lorne Greene as Ben Cartwright waving, reverse has brown text for Bonanza Sirloin Pit Restaurant in Bethesda, MD, unused, 1960s, 1.5" x 1.75" 15

Bonanza, record, Bonanza Ponderosa Party Time, 33 1/3 LP, #LPM/LSP2583, color photo of cast members, reverse text "They Sing, They Play Banjo, Fiddle, Guitar!," 1962 30

Cheyenne, Little Golden Book, *Cheyenne Starring Clint Walker*, #318, 1958 18

Cisco Kid, comb/shoe horn, hard plastic, white, side of handled mkd "The Cisco Kid On Television/Sponsor's Imprint Here," 1.25" x 5.5" 75

Cisco Kid, comic book, #41, Oct-Dec 1958, front cov depicts Cisco with gun climbing up porch of building 45

Cisco Kid, postcard, black and white, laughing Cisco Kid reigning his horse with SSS Club logo to right, unused, 1950s, 3.5" x 5.5" 40

Cisco Kid, poster, paper, Duncan Renaldo as Cisco Kid holding wrapped loaf of Nolde's American Made Enriched Bread, 1950s, 17" x 21" 75

Dale Evans, comic book, Dale Evans Comics, #22, Mar-Apr 1952, cov depicts Evans trying to calm down 2 fighting horses 25

Dale Evans, photograph, Evans on Trigger, black and white, 1950s, 8" x 10" 5

Daniel Boone, comic book, Fess Parker Daniel Boone, Gold Key, #12, Feb 1968 . .9

Daniel Boone, pencil case, "Fess Parker Pencil Case From the Daniel Boone TV Show," brown vinyl, zipper closure, 1964, 3.25 x 8" 35

Daniel Boone, TV Guide, #647, Fess Parker on cov, Aug 21, 1965 15

Davy Crockett, bandanna, purple rayon fabric, left side depicts colorful image of coonskin cap, long-barreled rifle, powder horn, Indian shield, and arrow, right side depicts full figure image of Crockett holding rifle with Indian campground in background, with 1.25" white metal figural tie slide, 1950s 30

Davy Crockett, belt buckle, diecast metal, "Pioneer King Davy Crockett," profile image of Crockett with rifle and powder horn surrounded by braided edge, 1950s, 1.75" x 33/8" 30

Davy Crockett, figure, plastic, yellow, rifle in right hand, Peco, c1955, 3.5" h . .12

Davy Crockett, patch, cloth, red, bright yellow smiling Crockett image, 1950s, 4.5" x 6" 20

Davy Crockett, pocketknife, plastic, 1 side of grip depicts color image of Crockett in brown outfit holding up rifle with fort in background, reverse grip dark brown, 3.5" l .35

Davy Crockett/Kit Carson, lunch box 90

Fury, neckerchief slide, emb brass, head of Fury on wagon wheel design, fabric bandanna and photo of Fury and Joey with facsimile signature, c1955 40

Gabby Hayes, arcade card, pinktone photo of Hayes in costume with gun drawn, white facsimile signature "Best Wishes From Geo 'Gabby' Hayes," 1940s, 3.25" x 5.25" 18

Gene Autry, comic book, Gene Autry Comics, #55, Sep 1951 12

Gene Autry, guitar, plastic, 16-pg songbook, Emenee Industries, c1955, 31" l . .50

Gene Autry, lobby card, Boots and Saddles, full color photo of Autry wearing red shirt and blue Levis, punching outlaw as girl holds his right arm, Republic Pictures, 1937, 11" x 14" . .20

Gene Autry, pinback button, "Gene Autry & Champ," black and white photo image on bright yellow ground, 1950s . .18

Gene Autry, ranch outfit, leather holster, 8" l composition toy gun, lariat cord, fabric bandanna with metal tie slide, M A Henry Co, NY, 1941 175

Gene Autry, record, Gene Autry's Melody Ranch Official Radio Broadcast, LP, #5012, cellophane cov sleeve depicts inset photo of smiling Autry on back of Champion on brown and yellow pebble ground, green and blue border, Golden Age, 1977 12

Gene Autry, song folio, Gene Autry's Deluxe Edition of Famous Original Cowboy Songs & Mountain Ballads, 98 pgs, inset photo of smiling Autry, ©1938 MM Cole Publishing Co, 9" x 12" .35

Hopalong Cassidy, badge, litho tin, Post Raisin Bran premium, 1950s 75

Hopalong Cassidy, ice cream carton, "Hopalong Cassidy's Favorite," Cloverlake Mellorine Vanilla, waxed blue carton, orange image of smiling Hoppy with guns drawn, Cloverlake Dairy Foods, Plainview Lubbock, TX, 1950s, 3.5" x 4.75 x 6.75" 85

Hopalong Cassidy, milk bottle cap, waxed stiff paper, red image of smiling Hoppy with name in red, Superior Dairies, Statesville, NC, 4" d 45

Hopalong Cassidy, party plate, cardboard, Hoppy on Topper riding down hillside, red, white, blue, and green, hat and boot designs in roped border, unused, 1950s, 8.5" x 8.75" 24

Hopalong Cassidy, pencil, wooden, orange, white stripes, Hoppy name in silver, unused, 1950s, 7" l 15

Hopalong Cassidy, Savings Club membership card, brown printing on simulated wood grain ground, reverse "Secret Code" for use by club members, 1950, 2.5" x 4" 35

Lone Ranger, atomic bomb ring, bright brass luster, Kix premium 75

Lone Ranger, badge, metal, silver luster, dark blue silhouette of Lone Ranger on Silver, 1938 35

Lone Ranger, key chain, silvered brass, "The Lone Ranger 17th Anniversary 1933-50," Lone Ranger riding Silver on front, Lone Ranger, Tonto, and silver bullet surrounded by horseshoe design on back, inscribed "Official Seal/The Lone Ranger Lucky Piece," Cheerios premium, 1950s 32

Lone Ranger, watch fob, silvered metal disk, dark blue and red accent paint around Lone Ranger image and "The Lone Ranger Hi-Yo Silver" 65

Maverick, frame tray puzzle, Whitman, #4427, ©1959 Warner Bros, 11.25" x 14.5" 45

Rex King, book, *Rex King of Wild Horses The Famous Movie Horse,* Whitman, W696, 20 pgs, 1928, 6.5" x 9" 28

Roy Rogers, autograph, sgd card, sepia-tone smiling image of Rogers standing beside Trigger, black facsimile signature "Many Happy Trails Roy Rogers & Trigger," dated May 1946, 3.5" x 5" 35

Roy Rogers, card, Roy Rogers Straight Shooters Serial Club, blue, black text, inset photo of Rogers on back of Trigger, numbers around sides to punch out for free admissions, text promotes "Man Hunt in Darkest Africa" for Arcade Theater, Oct 29, c1940s, 2.5" x 4" 38

Roy Rogers, necktie, child's, fabric, pre-tied, inscription at bottom "Many Happy Trails/Roy Rogers and Trigger," 1950s, 10" l 75

Roy Rogers, sheet music, **Along the Navajo Trail, *1942-45* *15***

Straight Arrow, bandanna slide, gold plastic, rect segment with name printed on side, top with raised arrow image . .30
Tom Mix, belt buckle, brass, diamond shaped checkerboard inset foil logo, red and blue Tom Mix brand on metallic gold 38
Tom Mix, playing card, Three of Clubs, black and white, Mix photo, white facsimile signature, 1920s, 1.75" x 2.5" . . .9
Tom Mix, Straight Shooters Telegraph Set, red, white, and blue checkerboard design box, metal tapper key on top, Morse Code instructions on lid, Skymasters Corp, Cincinnati, 1940, 2.25" x 4.25" x .75" box 65
Wild Bill Hickok, thermos, metal, red plastic cup, litho scene of Wild Bill and Jingles preparing for western street gunfight, Aladdin, 1955, 6.5" h . . .50
Will Rogers, bookends, pr, emb leather, green and gold on white ground, mkd "Durand, Chicago" 75
Wyatt Earp, coloring book, Saalfield, #1131, 1957, 11" x 14" 38

COW COLLECTIBLES

Holy cow! This is a moovelous category, as entrenched collectors already know.

Club: Cow Observers Worldwide, 240 Wahl Ave., Evans City, PA 16033.

Bank, cowboy parrot and cow, multicolor plastic, mkd "Serfin" on side, plug mkd "Niagara Plastics Erie PA," 8" h 15
Bank, Elsie, hard plastic, 1950s, 10" h 300
Bank, Elsie, metal, Master Caster Mfg Co, 1940s, 7" h .175
Button, Elsie, orig card, 1949, 4" x 3" 65
Calendar, Elsie, 1941 100
Cookbook, *Elsie's Cook Book,* by Elsie the Cow with the aid of Harry Botsford, 374 pgs, 1952 40
Cookie Jar, Beulah the cow, moos when lid is removed, 1950s, 11" h 350
Cookie Jar, Cow Jumped Over the Moon, cow finial, Robinson-Ransbottom, #317, c1940 110
Cookie Jar, Elsie, Pottery Guild of America, 1950s .350
Creamer, black and white Holstein, mkd "Made In Japan," 6.5" l 12
Creamer, Elsie, 1950s 100
Creamer, seated cow, mkd "Made in Czecho-Slovakia," 4.5" h 100
Cow Bell, copper, cast iron clapper, leather strap and buckle, 5" x 3.25" 125
Doll, Elsie Dutch Chocolate, orig box, 1950s 400
Doll, Elsie the Borden Cow, stuffed, plush, soft rubber face, moos when tipped over, My-Toy Creation, 13" h 75
Lamp, Elsie, orig box 450
Mask, Elmer, rubber, Stone Rubber Toy Co, 1950s 100
Milk Bottle, Borden's, red pyroglaze, wide mouth, 1 gal 450
Mug, green plastic, Purina Foods "Beautena" adv, Apco, 4.75" h 20
Napkin Ring, SP, 2.875" h, 3.25" l 275
Paperweight, reclining cow, chocolate slag glass, Boyd Crystal Art Glass Co, 2.25" h, 4" l 24
Postcard, "Elsie and Beauregard in Person," Borden's premium 20
Rattle, Beauregard, makes squeaking sound 250
Toothbrush Holder, cow, porcelain, mkd "Made In Japan," 3.5" h 165

CRACKER JACK

You can still buy Cracker Jack with a prize in every box. The only problem is that when you compare today's prizes with those from decades ago, you feel cheated. Modern prizes simply do not measure up. For this reason, collectors tend to focus on prizes put in the box prior to 1960.

Most Cracker Jack prizes were not marked. As a result, many dealers have Cracker Jack prizes without even knowing it. This allows an experienced collector to get some terrific bargains at flea markets. Alex Jaramillo's *Cracker Jack Prizes* (Abbeville Press, 1989) provides a wonderful survey of what prizes were available.

Club: Cracker Jack Collectors Assoc., P.O. Box 16033, Philadelphia, PA 19114.

Activity Book, Cracker Jack Painting & Drawing Book, 96 pgs, 1917, 9.5" x 11" . .35
Bookmark, diecut metal, cocker spaniel head at top, 2.75" l .35
Magazine Tear Sheet, Cracker Jack and his Sweetheart in home port, sharing a box of Cracker Jacks, illus by NP, c1919, 9" x 12" 15
Postcard, Cracker Jack Bears No. 6, 2 bears dancing with Cracker Jack vendor, Rueckhelm Bros & Eckstein, Chicago 40
Prize, Auto Race Spin Toy 14
Prize, bugle, 1920s, 1.25" l 8
Prize, clown figure, white plastic, 1950s . . .5
Prize, cup, tin, 1920s 10

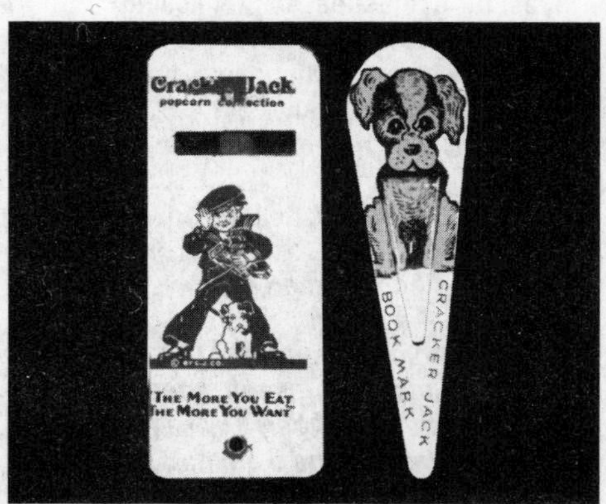

Prize, delivery truck, litho tin, .875" h, 1.5" l 80
Prize, equestrian, litho tin, 1920s 20
Prize, fireman's helmet, 1950s 5
Prize, fire truck, litho tin, mkd "FD," 1930s, 1.75" 45
Prize, ladderback chair, 1920s, .875" h 10
Prize, monkey figure, yellow plastic, 1950s, 1.75" h 5
Prize, palm puzzle, clown face, 2 metal balls, cardboard back, 1.25" d 12
Prize, pilot's wings, Cracker Jack Air Corps, lapel stud on back 80
Prize, spinner toy, image of Cracker Jack box and "Always On Top," red, white, and blue 100
Prize, spoon and fork, tin, 1930s, 2" l 12
Prize, teapot, 1930s, 1.125" h 10
Prize, telescope, 1920s 12
Prize, trowel, 1920s, 1.375" l 9
Prize, turtle charm, 1920s, 1" l 8
Prize, whistle, flat, red and blue Cracker Jack and "Cracker Jack popcorn confection, 'The More You Eat The More You Want'" on white ground, 2.625" x 1" 110
Prize, whistle, man with large mouth, gold-colored tin, 2.25" 45
Salt and Pepper Shakers, figural saluting Cracker Jack and Bingo 40
Thimble, bone china, red and blue adv on white ground, 22K gold rim, England 6

CRACKLE GLASS

If crackle glass catches your fancy, beware! It is still being produced by Blenko Glass Company and in foreign countries such as Taiwan and China. Examine prospective purchases carefully. Cracks are often hard to distinguish from the decorative "crackles."

Club: Collectors of Crackle Glass, P.O. Box 1186, N. Massapequa, NY 11758.

Creamer, orange, applied amber handle, 3.75" h 25
Jug, tangerine with applied amber crackle glass handle, Pilgrim, 7" h 75
Mug, miniature, amber, Pilgrim, 3" h 18
Perfume Bottle, clear over gold, atomizer top, DeVilbiss 65

Pitcher, amber, miniature, hourglass form, applied amber handle, pontil scar, 3.5" h 28
Pitcher, amber, miniature, left-handed handle applied to side, 3.75" h 30
Pitcher, amber, miniature, tankard form, applied clear handle, 4" h 25
Pitcher, amberina, miniature, applied clear handle, Kanawha, 3.25" h 25
Pitcher, amberina, mold blown, long spout, straight-sided, applied handle, Kanawha, 12.5" h 75
Pitcher, amberina, tri-fold top, mold-blown, applied amber handle, Hammond, 6.5" h 75
Pitcher, amberina, wide tri-fold top, 5.25" h 45
Pitcher, amethyst, applied clear handle, 3.5" h 65
Pitcher, amethyst, miniature, applied amber handle, 3.75" h 75
Pitcher, green, miniature, applied clear handle, 4.75" h 25
Pitcher, green, miniature, applied green scroll handle, pontil scar, orig label, Kanawha, 3.25" h .30
Pitcher, green opalescent, applied clear handle, pontil scar, 5.5" h 35
Pitcher, lemon-lime, straight-sided, pontil mark, Pilgrim, 13" h 100
Pitcher, light blue, applied blue handle, 1950s-60s, 4.5" h 35
Pitcher, light blue, overshot, applied clear reeded claw handle, Sandwich, c1870-1887, 5" h .325
Pitcher, orange, applied amber handle, large spout, 5" h .45
Pitcher, orange, miniature, applied clear handle, 3.5" h 25
Pitcher, pale amber, miniature, applied clear reeded handle, 4.5" h 30
Pitcher, ruby, miniature, applied clear handle, pontil scar, 3.75" h 25
Sugar and Creamer, vaseline, pear and leaf finial 150
Vase, clear with 3 applied green leaves, straight tapered sides, Blenko, 1940s-50s, 10" h .150
Vase, iridescent green, spherical with flaring rim, Loetz, 4.75" h 225

CRECHE COLLECTIBLES

Once primarily a religious holiday decoration, creches have increasingly become a year-round collectible, with many collectors keeping their sets on display in the non-holiday months.

The practice of displaying the Christmas Nativity figures is an ancient one, popularized by St. Francis of Assisi in thirteenth-century Italy. By the eighteenth century, the development of the creche figures in Naples had become a fine art.

Creche collectors look for all forms of the Nativity display, from the three-dimensional figures to paper cutouts. Pre–World War II European-made figures are especially desirable, although examples of well-known brand names such as Hummel or Anri in excellent condition will command a good price.

Creche, Berta Hummel, miniature 30
Creche, Precious Moments 25
Figure, Baby Jesus in manger, chalkware, mkd "Italy," 1.5" h, " l 20
Figure, Christ Child, chalkware, blue glass eyes, fur eyelashes, some missing fingers, c1930s, 8.5" l 125
Figure, cow lying down, hollow, hp, coiled wire horns, mkd "Italy," 5" l 15
Figure, donkey lying down, hollow, hp, mkd "Italy," 4.5" l 15
Figure, kneeling Mary, hollow, hp, mkd "Italy," 4" h 10
Figure, kneeling wiseman, hollow, hp, mkd "Italy," 4.125" h 8
Figures, hp composition, set of 13 including kneeling Joseph, kneeling Mary, Jesus in manger, 3 wise men, shepherd, angel, and 5 animals, mkd "Italy," 1950s-60s 65

Figures, molded plaster, 4 sheep, mkd "Germany," 1.5" to 2" l in size 18

Nativity Set, creche and 15 figures including Joseph, Madonna, Jesus, Wise Man Standing, Wise Man Nubian, Wise Man Kneeling, Shepherd Boy, Little Tooter, We Congratulate, Serenade, 2 Goodnight Angels, Angel with Trumpet, oxen lying, and donkey lying, Hummel, 11.75" x 17.25" stable . .975

Nativity Set, metal with silver tone finish, 11 pcs including stable, Joseph, Mary, Jesus, 3 wise men, shepherd, and 3 animals, 1" to 4.25" h figures, 7.5" x 5.625" stable, orig box, made in China . .15

Nativity Set, wooden stable and 13 hp lead figures including Joseph, Mary, Jesus, 3 wise men, kneeling shepherd, heralding angel, camel, elephant, shepherd, and 2 trees, gold highlights, 2.5" h wise men, 3.25" h tree 175

CUFF LINKS

Many people consider cuff links to be the ideal collectible. They have been around for centuries and have always reflected the styles, economics, and technologies of their era. Cuff link collecting can be profitable. Rare or unusual finds can be worth substantial dollars. Most serious collectors have had the thrill of buying a pair for "pennies" that turned out to be worth a great deal.

Many cuff link collectors specialize. Areas of specialization include size, shape, and closure type. Other collectors specialize by subject. Examples of this are cuff links that show animals, sports, advertising logos, cars, boats, etc.

Club: National Cuff Link Society, P.O. Box 5700, Vernon Hills, IL 60061.

Cuff Link Box, celluloid, rect, emb deer on front, sgd "Hickok," 3.75" x 3.75" x 1.5" 18

Cuff Links, pr, 10k yellow gold filled, sq plaque with chevron above a bar with 3 stars alternating with 2 small diamonds, Chevron gas station dealer's 40-year service award, c1930s-40s 85

Cuff Links, pr, adv, figural Miss Reingold Beer, gold tone metal with white enameled skirt, holding tray with beer and mug, orig box 40

Cuff Links, pr, oval, gold and silver tone metal set with a clear rhinestone, .75" x .5" 35

Cuff Links, pr, rect tiger eye plaque, gold tone setting, .875" l 16

Cuff Links, pr, sepia tone picture of Fess Parker as Davy Crockett in gold tone picture frame, c1950s 40

Cuff Links, pr, sq, dark blue turquoise set with rhinestones, silver tone metal, sgd "Snap Link," .5" 50

Cuff Links, pr, SS, oval plaques with emb scrollwork borders 20

Set, matching cuff links and 4 shirt studs, black stone in white metal setting, .5" cuff link, .325" stud, unmkd 20

Set, matching cuff links and collar button, silver tone circle set with black cabochon, .25" d 20

Set, matching cufflinks and tie bar, adv, Ballantine Beer logo 75

Set, matching cuff links and tie bar, adv, mkd "Yale & Towne Mfg Co Yale," key-shaped tie bar, lock-shaped cuff links . .18

Set, matching cuff links and tie bar, black bowling ball and 2 gold bowling pins on gold tone metal setting, sgd "Anson," c1960s .40

Set, matching cuff links and tie bar, gold filligree metal with tan colored stones capping the ends, sgd "Krementz USA" 25

Set, matching cuff links and tie bar, gold tone metal, glass cov inset picture of a horse, sgd "Anson" 25

Set, matching cuff links and tie bar, gold tone metal with mother-of-pearl discs, unmkd, 75" d cuff links 28

Set, matching cuff links and tie bar, ivory Buddha face, silver tone metal setting, mkd "Pat. 503655," 1" x .75" 150

Set, matching cuff links and tie bar, Knights of Columbus, K of C insignia on gold tone metal .50

Set, matching cuff links and tie tack, brushed and polished SS, braided leather button design, sgd "Anson" 25

Set, matching cuff links and tie tack, domed rect set with crushed red jade, gold-plated frame, sgd "Danté," orig box, 1.125" x .625" cuff links 55

CUPIDS

Be suspicious of naked infants bearing bows and arrows. It is not clear if their arrows are tipped with passion or poison.

Club: Cupid Collectors Club, 2116 Lincoln St., Cedar Falls, IA 50613, www.cupidcollectors.com.

Button, ivory, hp Cupid 75

Button, silver tone metal, emb "Over the Wall" image with 2 cupids climbing over a brick wall, 1.5" d 25

Calendar Plate, Cupid in center, 1910 35

Compact, center heart surrounded by 4 cupids, England, 3" d 60

Creamer, souvenir of "Cupid's Cave, Tenn, VA, KY," cold-painted floral dec, 2" h 12

Pin Box, metal, emb cupids, floral swags, and cornucopia, pink enameling, red felt lining, mkd "Japan," 1.25" x 2.5" x 1.75" 15

Planter, oblong, emb cupids, Imarco, Japan 16

Sheet Music, *For Me and My Gal,* cupids and photo of Carrie Lillie on cov, illus by Barbelle, ©1917 12

Thimble, silver, emb Cupid and swags, Simons 75

Valentine, emb and diecut, 2-tier, large heart with girls, Cupid, and roses, "With love and esteem – Loves Offering," Germany 25

Valentine Postcard, Raphael Tuck & Sons Cupids Series, No. 1, emb cupid and heart, "My dearest wish, Sweet Valentine, is that you may be mine" 12

Vase, ceramic, emb cupids, ferns, grapes, and grape leaves, pink and ivory, 8" h . .15

CURRENCY

People hide money in the strangest places. Occasionally it turns up at flea markets. Likewise early paper money came in a variety of forms and sizes quite different from modern paper currency. Essentially, paper money breaks down into three groups—money issued by the federal government, by individual states, and by private banks, businesses, or individuals. Money from the last group is designated as obsolete bank notes.

As with coins, condition is everything. Paper money that has been heavily circulated is worth only a fraction of the value of a bill in excellent condition. Proper grading rests in the hands of coin dealers. Krause Publications (700 East State Street, Iola, WI 54990) is a leading publisher in the area of coinage and currency. *Bank Note Reporter,* a Krause newspaper, keeps collectors up-to-date on current developments in the currency field. There is a wealth of information available to identify and price any bill that you find. Before you sell or turn in that old bill for face value, do your homework. It may be worth more than a Continental, which by the way, continues to be a real "dog" in the paper money field.

Clubs: Ancient Numismatic Society, 8713 Caminto Abrazo, La Jolla, CA 92037; Numismatic Assoc., P.O. Box 98, Homer, MI 49245.

CUSPIDORS

After examining the interiors of some of the cuspidors for sale at flea markets, I am glad I have never been in a bar where people "spit." Most collectors are enamored by the brass cuspidor. The form came in many other varieties as well. You could build a marvelous collection focusing on pottery cuspidors.

Within the past year a large number of fake cuspidors have entered the market. I have seen them at flea markets across the United States. Double-check any cuspidor with a railroad marking and totally discount any with a Wells Fargo marking.

Advertising, brass, imp Pony Express Chewing Tobacco Cut Plug logo, 9.875" h, 5" d 100
Advertising, brass, Redskin Brand logo, 10" h, 9" d 160
Bennington, mottled brown and yellow Rockingham glaze, late 1800s 300
Brass, vase-shaped, weighted bottom, 8" d 125
Brush-McCoy, shape #13, green band inside rim and on shoulder, green wreath dec, ivory ground, c1917, 5.5" h, 7.25" d 100
Cambridge Glass, green, pontil scar, 5" h, 4" d 75
Ceramic, dark green ext, ivory int 25
Ceramic, lady's, green and white with gold trim, 7.75" d 60
Copper, straight tapered sides, 5.5" h, 8" d 50
Glass, clear, lady's hand-held 50

Graniteware, brown mottled, 2-pc, 5.5" h, 11" d 35
Graniteware, gray mottled, 8.5" d 60
Hall China Co, green and white 95
Hull, Mirror Brown, Indian Aztec design, 3.5" h, 7.5" d 65
Ironstone, c1900s, 4.5" h, 7.25" d 35
Majolica, bamboo design, 2.75" h, 8.5" d .400
Milk Glass, 6-sided bowl, gold trim, 7" d .100
Railroad, emb "Hannibal and St Joseph" on 2 sides, weighted bottom, 10" h, 9" d .80
Railroad, Union Pacific, brass, 10" h, 9" d .95
Roseville, Fern Trail, early 1900s, 5" h, 7.5" d 150
Royal Doulton, porcelain, monk dec, 6.875" h, 7.625" d 300
RS Prussia, lady's, 2-handled, hp pink, purple, blue, and white floral dec, Erdmann Schlegelmilch mark, 5" h, 7.75" d 425
RS Prussia, lady's, hp yellow, pink, blue, and red flowers, gold highlights, unmkd 200
Stoneware, brown Albany glaze, c1940s . .45
Tin, turtle-shaped, cast iron head and legs, mkd "Pat Applied for 1891," 13" l, 10" w 525
Vaseline Glass, Albany Glass Co, Wreath & Shell pattern, lady's, 4.5" h 150
Yellow Ware, emb seashell pattern, scalloped rim, Rockingham glaze 175
Yellow Ware, green, brown, and black sponge dec, late 19th C, 4.5" h, 7" d 75

CUT GLASS

Collectors have placed so much emphasis on American Brilliant Cut Glass (1880 to 1917) that they completely overlook some of the finer cut glass of the post–World War I period. Admittedly, much cut glass in this later period was mass-produced and rather ordinary. But, if you look hard enough, you will find some great pieces.

The big news in the cut glass market at the end of the 1980s was the revelation that many of the rare pieces that had been uncovered in the 1980s were of recent origin. Reproductions, copycats, and fakes abound. This is one category where you had better read a great deal and look at hundreds of pieces before you start buying.

Condition is also critical. Do not pay high prices for damaged pieces. Look for chips, dings, fractures, and knife marks. Sometimes these defects can be removed, but consider the cost of the repair when purchasing a damaged piece. Of course signed pieces command a higher dollar value.

Club: American Cut Glass Assoc., P.O. Box 482, Ramona, CA 92065, www.cutglass.org.

Automobile Vase, floral design, nickel-plated hardware, first half 20th C, 11.5" l 165

Basket, brilliant cut Harvard, strawberry diamond, and 4 large cut daisies with leaves, double notched handle, large star-cut base, 22" h, 14" w 325

Bottle, gravic cut thistle and flower pattern, first half 20th C, 9.5" h 80

Bowl, brilliant cut hobstar and arches design, first half 20th C, 9" d 200

Bowl, etched pear and leaves, inscribed "Clark," last half 20th C, 12" l 185

Bowl, Waterford, large waffle pattern, sgd, last half 20th C, 8" d 140

Box, cov, Hawkes, hobstar and horizontal rib designs, sgd "Hawkes," first half 20th C, 4" d 140

Cake Stand, domed top wheel cut with floral designs, first half 20th C, 11.5" d 125

Candlesticks, pr, zipper and diamond point cutting, early 20th C, 10" h 250

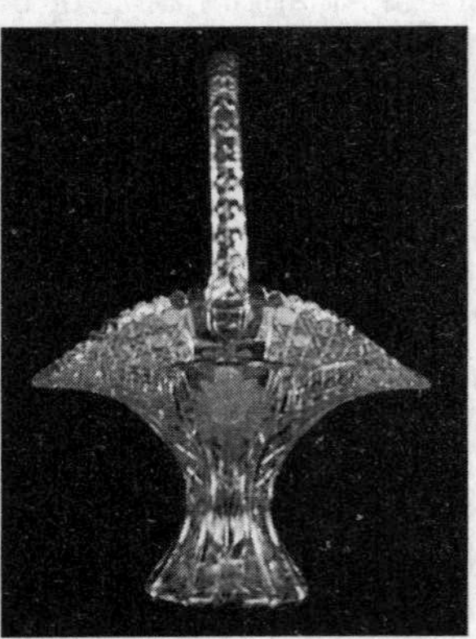

Celery, hobstar and buzzsaw designs, first half 20th C, 12" l 115

Celery, hobstar and fan designs, early 20th C, 11.5" l 35

Charger, Libbey, scrolling thistle and flower design, sgd "Libbey" in circle, c1900, 12" d 375

Compote, scalloped rim, fan design, mid-20th C, 9" h 95

Compote, thumbnails and stars on blown hollow base, 19th C, 10" h 35

Compote, Waterford, Glandore pattern, sgd, last half 20th C, 6.5" d 125

Console Bowl, acid etched pear dec, last half 20th C, 9" d 150

Cruet, gravic cut floral dec, silver overlay, early 20th C, 6" h .70

Dresser Bottle, etched sunflower pattern, first half 20th C, 5.5" h 60

Dresser Bottle, silver mounted, button and diamond pattern, worn hallmarks, early 20th C, 7.5" h 75

Dresser Box, cov, buzzsaw dec, first half 20th C, 5.5" d 145

Dresser Box, cov, Pitkin and Brooks, 6-sided box, circ lid, hobstar and paneled designs, sgd "P&B" in triangle, c1900, 5.5" w 260

Juice Pitcher, Waterford, Glandore pattern, sgd, last half 20th C, 6.5" h 165

Nappy, center handle, buzzsaw designs, first half 20th C, 6.25" d 95

Nappy, handled, divided 4-part, hobstar designs, first half 20th C, 11" l 125

Pitcher, button and daisy and rosette pattern, last half 20th C, 10" h 125

Pitcher, etched floral blossoms, first half 20th C, 10" h 150

Pitcher, etched floral design, first half 20th C, 10" h 60

Plate, hobstar and paneled arches, early 20th C, 7" sq 125

Sandwich Tray, button and etched floral dec, first half 20th C, 10" d 175

Server, Victorian, ribbed thumbprint pattern, resilvered basket, 10.5" l 140

Table Lamp, diamond point and floral designs, first half 20th C, 21" h 1,150

Vase, buzzsaw and floral design, first half 20th C, 12" h 150

Vase, buzzsaw dec, first half 20th C, 10" h .95

Vase, engraved floral designs, early 20th C, 12" h 115

Vase, florals and spiral ribs, c1925, 10" h . .60
Vase, gravic cut flowers, last half 20th C, 12" h 70
Vase, gravic cut florals and scrolls, ground pontil, early 20th C, 13" h 70
Vase, hobstar band and engraved florals, last half 20th C, 12" h 140
Whiskey Jug, hobstar and fan designs, first half 20th C, 7.25" h 175
Wine Jug, buzzsaw pattern, early 20th C, 11.5" h 225
Wine Set, Waterford, stoppered decanter and 6 stems, Kenmare pattern, sgd, last half 20th C, 12.5" h decanter 375

CZECHOSLOVAKIAN

Czechoslovakia was created at the end of World War I out of the area of Bohemia, Moravia, and Austrian Silesia. Although best known for glass products, Czechoslovakia also produced a large number of pottery and porcelain wares for export.

Czechoslovakia objects do not enjoy a great reputation for quality, but I think they deserve a second look. They certainly reflect what was found in the average American's home from the 1920s through the 1950s.

Club: Czechoslovakian Collectors Guild International, P.O. Box 901395, Kansas City, MO 64190.

Bowl, glass, melon-ribbed, ftd, mottled red and yellow, 8" d 75

Bowl, glass, shallow, ftd, mottled red and blue, 7" d 45
Candleholders, pr, ceramic, Art Deco, candlecup on arched base, white with blue cup int, mkd "Made in Czechoslovakia," 2" h, 3.5" w 25
Candlestick, glass, orange with cobalt blue band below socket, 8" h 20
Candlestick, glass, yellow with black bands above and below socket, mkd "Czechoslovakia," 9.75" h 55
Center Bowl, glass, flared rim, orange with black band at rim, applied black ball feet, 11.5" d .165
Compote, glass, red spattered under dark waves, black pedestal foot, mkd "Made in Czechoslovakia," 6.25" h 100
Dish, canoe-shaped, ceramic, white ext, blue int, mkd "Erphila Czechoslovakia 7742," 2" h, 12" l 35
Dish, rect, ftd, ceramic, white ext, blue int, mkd "Royal Crown Made In Czechoslovakia 7507," 2" h, 9.5" l, 5.5" w 50
Ewer, glass, crimped rim, mottled yellow shading to brown, applied cobalt blue handle, 9.5" h 85
Ewer, glass, crimped rim, orange with cobalt blue band at rim and applied cobalt blue handle, 10" h 125
Liquor Set, glass, egg-shaped, clear blue with white floral design, top opens to reveal a tray with 6 slots for glasses and center hole for liquor bottle 75
Pop-up Book, *Snow White*, dated 1983 . . .15
Trophy Cup, glass, yellow with white splashes and applied clear handles, 9.5" h 28
Vase, glass, baluster form, ftd, red with black base and pulled spikes, mkd "Czechoslovakia," 9" h 115
Vase, glass, baluster form, mottled green, yellow, and red over a pale blue ground under a paperweight finish, mkd "Made in Czechoslovakia," 10" h 115
Vase, glass, bulbous body, mottled red, orange, yellow, and blue, iridized finish, 8.5" h 130
Vase, glass, classic shape with flaring rim and ftd base, red shading to orange with applied black rim, mkd "Made in Czechoslovakia," 7" h 100
Vase, glass, corseted form, blue spotted over red, 10.25" h 100

Vase, glass, flared rim, bulbous body, ftd, yellow, red, and orange mottling over white, 7.75" h 25
Vase, glass, flared rim, ovoid body, black with red rim and 2 spiral strands, ground base, 10.5" h 45
Vase, glass, flared rim above 3 horizontal ribs, ftd, mottled blue base over large yellow, red, and orange mottling, 10" h 115
Vase, glass, ftd, cobalt blue with moonstone mottling, 10" h 80
Vase, glass, ftd, large and medium mottled red, orange, blue, yellow, and green, 10" h 100
Vase, glass, horizontal ribs, ftd, mottled white and blue over red, satin finish, 9.5" h 80
Vase, glass, ovoid, cased yellow with applied coiled black snake dec, 5.5" h . .75
Vase, glass, ruffled rim, red with applied black snake handles, mkd "Czechoslovakia," 10.5" h 115
Vase, glass, ruffled rim, stick neck, ovoid body, mottled green, yellow, and red with black rim, mkd "Made in Czechoslovakia," 8.5" h 80
Vase, glass, shouldered cylinder form, internally mottled colors of blue over yellow, 9.75" h 115
Vase, glass, shouldered tapering form, ftd, large mottled red, yellow, blue, and green, 11" h 75
Vase, glass, slightly flaring rim, ftd, streaks of blue and yellow over orange mottling, 10" h 75
Vase, glass, stick neck on bulbous body, mottled tortoise shell colors, 10" h 80
Vase, glass, stick neck on ovoid body, internally streaked colors in red, orange, and yellow, clear feet, 12" h . . .60
Vase, glass, trumpet form, red with black rim and coil stem under a paperweight finish, ground pontil, 9.25" h 100
Vase, glass, trumpet form neck on squatty body, opalescent green with applied black rim, mkd "Czechoslovakia," 12.5" h 95
Vase, glass, urn form, red with 2 black handles and base, iridized finish, 6.5" h 125
Wine Barrel, glass, orange with enameled vintage dec, 4 matching mugs with applied clear handles, 8" l 30

DAIRY COLLECTIBLES

For decades, the dairy industry has been doing a good job of encouraging us to drink our milk and eat only real butter. The objects used to get this message across, as well as the packaging for dairy products, have long been favorites with collectors.

Concentrate on the material associated with a single dairy, region, or national firm. If you try to collect one example of every milk bottle used, you simply will not succeed. The amount of dairy collectibles is staggering.

Clubs: Dairy & Creamers Assoc., Rt. 3, P.O. Box 189, Arcadia, WI 54612; National Assoc. of Milk Bottle Collectors Inc., 4 Ox Bow Rd., Westport, CT 06800.

Broom Holder, De Laval Cream Separators, litho tin, images of cream separators, orig adv envelope, 3.5" d . .650
Butter Print, curly maple, leaf, chip-carved edge, lollipop type, good patina, 8.75" l 325
Butter Print, wood, acorn and leaf design, rope twist border, cased, dark patina, oversized, 4.625" d case 140
Butter Print, wood, cow, simple carving, screw-in handle, 4.375" d 110
Butter Print, wood, pomegranate, inset handle, good patina, 3.5" d 50
Can, Borden's Malted Milk, metal, 25 lbs, 1920s 50
Egg Carton, Borden's Selected Fresh Ranch Eggs 45
Paper Hat, worn by employees at Borden's milk plants, 1950s 20
Pocketknife,"De Laval Cream Separators" 1 side, "World's Standard Nearly 2,000,000 In Use" other side, metal, mfg by Miller Bros, Meriden, 3.5" l closed size 175

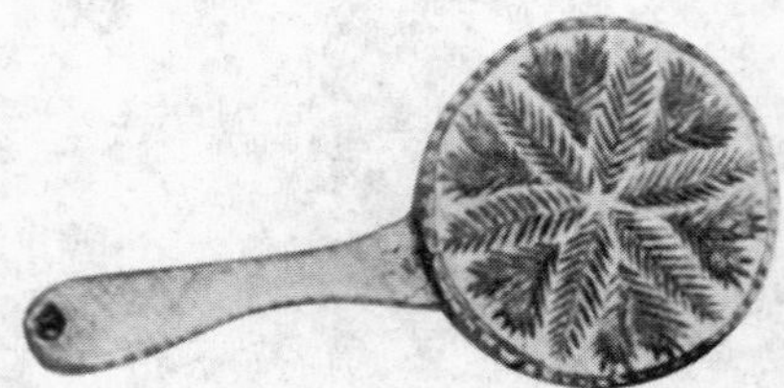

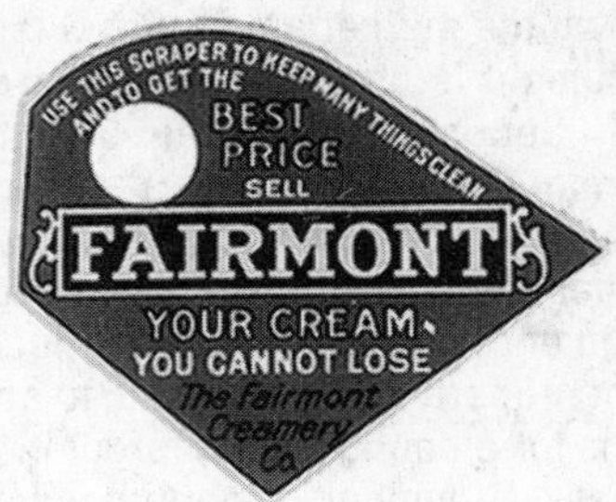

Pot Scraper, Fairmont Creamery, red, white, yellow, and black, "Use This Scraper To Keep Many Things Clean – And To Get The Best Price Sell Fairmont – Your Cream – You Cannot Lose – The Fairmont Creamery Co," 2.75" x 3.25" 300

Tip Tray, "Mount Vernon Evaporated Milk, Fresh Cream Flavor," litho tin, multicolor product image, mkd "Chas W Shonk Co Litho, Chicago," 3.375" x 4.625" 90

DAKIN FIGURES

The term "Dakin" refers to a type of hollow, vinyl figure produced by the R. Dakin Company. These figures are found with a number of variations—molded- or cloth-costumed, jointed or nonjointed and range in height from 5" to 10".

As with any popular and profitable product, Dakin figures were copied. There are a number of Dakin-like figures found on the market. Produced by Sutton & Son Inc., Knickerbocker Toy Company, and a production company for Hanna-Barbera, these figures are also collectible and are often mistaken for the original Dakin products. Be careful when purchasing.

Daffy Duck, late 1960s, 8" h 20
Donald Duck, orig label, 1960s-70s, 8" h . . .65
Little Miss Justrite, Justrite Denim Jeans, 1969, 8" h 30
Mickey and Minnie Mouse, pr, 1960s-70s, 8" h Mickey, 7" h Minnie 65
Pink Panther, 1971, 8" h 20
Pinocchio, feather in hat, 1972-73, 8" h . . .75
Pluto, orig string tag, 1960s-70s, 6" h, 12" l 35
Popeye, c1970, 8" h .45
Road Runner, 9" h 60
Smokey Bear, late 1970s, 8" h 35

DEARLY DEPARTED

I know this category is a little morbid, but the stuff is collected. Several museums have staged special exhibitions devoted to mourning art and jewelry. Funeral parlors need to advertise for business.

I did not put one in the listing, but do you know what makes a great coffee table? A coffin carrier or coffin stand. Just put a piece of glass over the top. It's the right size, has leg room underneath, and makes one heck of a conversation piece.

Ashtray, copper-colored metal, "Geo E Snyder Funeral Home, Snyders, Pa, New Ringgold, Pa" 15
Business Card, Taylor & Hancock, mourning goods, printed black and white, 1890s, 3.625" x 2.125" 8
Cabinet Card, funeral flowers 15
Casket, wood, missing lid, pre-1950, 5' l .125
Fan, cardboard, tri-fold, image of family in church on front, "Presented for your comfort by Wm J Schlup Funeral Home, 'The Home of Sincerity in Service,' Sherwood 1212, Akron, OH" on back . . .18
Fan, cardboard, wood stick handle, adv for Hawkins Funeral Home, Sarasota, FL on back, Cypress Gardens image on front, 11.75" h, 7" w 25
Fan, cardboard, wood stick handle, adv for "M Eichhorn Funeral – Undertaking. Courteous, Distinctive Funeral Service. Ambulance Day or Night...Lonaconing, MD," scripture verses on back, 13.5" h, 7.75" w 30

Life Magazine, Apr 19, 1968, cov image of Mrs Martin Luther King in mourning veil at husband's funeral 20
Memorial Card, for 1976 funeral of Mayor Richard J Daley, photo, name, and dates on 1 side, prayer of Saint Francis of Assisi on other, 3.75" x 5.5" 25
Newspaper, *The Commercial Appeal,* Aug 17, 1977, color photos and articles about the death of Elvis Presley 125
Newspaper, *The Zanesville Signal,* Aug, 1923, picture of President Harding on front page, articles include "Coolidge Plans Harding Funeral," "Hearts Ache on Funeral Train for Mrs Harding," and "Caravan of Sorrow Speeding Homeward Crowds are Silent," 2 pgs . .40
Postcard, Chinese funeral procession, view of Peking with funeral procession in front of shops, rickshaws, peddlers, printed in Brussels 30
Stereoview, President McKinley's Funeral, Kilburn Stereoview No. 14570, shows Presiden't body being taken into the Court House in Canton, OH, ©1901 18
Thermometer, Murphy's Funeral Home, Cleveland, OH, religious theme, small thermometer inset at upper right, 5" x 7" 15
Toy Train Building, Lastop Funeral Home, HO Scale, Kit #5739, AHM, late 1970s, NIB 40
Vase, black carnival glass, cone-shaped, Dugan Glass Co, 8.25" h 250

DEEDS & DOCUMENTS

A document is any printed paper that shows evidence or proof of something. Subject matter ranges from baptismal certificates to stocks and bonds. Flea markets are loaded with old documents. Though they generally have minimal value and are usually copies of the original forms, it makes good sense to check before discarding. It may be of value to its original owner or to a paper-ephemera collector.

Many eighteenth and early nineteenth century deeds are on parchment. In most cases, value is minimal, ranging from a few dollars to a high of $10. First, check to see if the deed is the original document. Most deeds on the market are copies; the actual document is often on file in the courthouse. Second, check the signatures. Benjamin Franklin signed a number of Pennsylvania deeds. These are worth a great deal more than $10. Third, check the location of the deed. If it is a city deed, the current property owner may like to acquire it. If it is for a country farm, forget it.

Finally, a number of early deeds have an elaborate wax seal at the bottom. When framed, these make wonderful display pieces in attorneys' offices.

Bond Certificate, New York News Bureau Assoc, 1911, 1000 Dollar Bond, coupons #37-60 attached .150
Certificate, ROTC Military Training, Senior Division, issued in 1929 at College of City of New York, basic infantry course 35
Deed of Lease, indenture dated 1750, hand-written in copperplate on thick vellum, wax seals by signatures, 30" x 13.5" 65
Farm Deed, Cuyahoga County, OH, includes note of oil acreage from National Gas & Oil Corp now under Natol Corp, dated 1954, orig envelope . .15
Mortgage Deed, Tuscarawas Building and Loan Co, New Philadelphia, OH, $300, hand-written in ink, 1907 8
Receipt, capital stock purchase for the Columbus & Zenia Rail Board Co, dated Apr 8, 1848, 5" x 7" 18
Receipt, newspaper adv, printed and filled out in ink, dated Jan 7, 1895 10
Receipt, Orange Memorial Hospital, maternity patient care, 1927 10
Receipt, Transcontinental & Western Air passenger receipt, 1929 12
Receipt Postcard, Standard Oil Co, dated Feb 1900, 5.5" x 3.5" 15
Stock Certificate, Cloverdale Water Co, 1908, eagle, gold seal, three $100 shares 45
Stock Certificate, Dean's Jewelry & Drug Store, vignette of Indians and skyscrapers 50
Stock Certificate, Missouri, Kansas, and Texas Railway Co, dated July 23, 1891, vignette of engine leaving round house, 10 shares 70

Trust Deed, property sale in Cedar County, MO, dated 1896, 68.5 acres sold for $500 12
Warranty Deed, Tuscarawas County, OH, 1912 8

DEGENHART GLASS

Degenhart pressed glass novelties are collected by mold, by individual color, or by group of colors. Hundreds of colors, some nearly identical, were produced between 1947 and 1978. Prior to 1972 most pieces were unmarked. After that date a "D" or "D" in a heart was used.

Do not confuse Kanawha's bird salt and bow slipper or L. G. Wright's mini-slipper, daisy and button salt, and 5" robin-covered dish with Degenhart pieces. They are similar, but there are differences. See Gene Florence's *Degenhart Glass and Paperweights: A Collector's Guide to Colors and Values* (Degenhart Paperweight and Glass Museum: 1982) for a detailed list of Degenhart patterns.

Club: Friends of Degenhart (Degenhart Paperweight and Glass Museum, Inc.) 65323 Highland Hills Rd., P.O. Box 186, Cambridge, OH 43725.

Boot, Daisy and Button, amber, 4.75" h, 3.75" w 50
Figurine, owl, Chad's Blue, sgd, 3.5" h 50
Figurine, owl, cobalt carnival, sgd, 3.625" h 130
Figurine, owl, Dark Rose Marie, sgd, 3.5" h 50
Figurine, owl, red carnival, sgd, 3.5" h . . .115
Figurine, owl, Seafoam Green, sgd, 1973, 3.5" h 20
Figurine, pooch, April Green, 1977, 3" h . . .25
Figurines, pr, Bernard and Eldena, amethyst carnival, sgd, 2.75" h 20
Figurines, pr, Bernard and Eldena, crystal, sgd, 2.75" h 20
Portrait Dish, amethyst, emb, Elizabeth Degenhart name and "First Lady of Glass," 5.5" d 55
Rooster Dish, cov, pink, 3" x 4" 60
Slipper, Colonial, Daisy and Button, blue, 1947, sgd, 2.5" h, 5.75" l 80

Slipper, Kat, Daisy & Button, pink 40

Tomahawk, cobalt carnival, sgd, 3.75" x 2" 20
Toothpick Holder, baby shoe, Nile Green, sgd, c1947, 2" h, 3" w 55
Toothpick Holder, baby shoe, white opalescent, sgd, c1947, 2" h, 3" w 55
Toothpick Holder, Forget-Me-Not, mint green slag, sgd, 1970s, 2.5" h 30

DEPRESSION GLASS

Depression Era Glass refers to glassware made between the 1920s and 1940s. It was mass-produced by a number of different companies. It was sold cheaply and often given away as a purchasing premium.

Specialize in one pattern or color. Once again, there is no way that you can own every piece made. Also, because Depression glass was produced in vast quantities, buy only pieces in excellent or better condition.

A number of patterns have been reproduced. See Gene Florence's *The Collector's Encyclopedia of Depression Glass* (Collector Books, revised annually) for a complete list of reproductions.

Clubs: 20-30-40's Society, Inc., P.O. Box 856, La Grange, IL 60525; Canadian Depression Glass Assoc., 119 Wexford Rd., Brampton, Ontario, L6Z 2T5 Canada; The National Depression Glass Assoc., P.O. Box 8264, Wichita, KS 67208.

AVOCADO, NO. 601, INDIANA

Bowl, 1 handle, 7" d, green 34
Bowl, 1 handle, 7" d, pink 28
Bowl, 2 handles, 5.25" d, pink 28

Bowl, 2 handles, oval, 8" l, green 34
Bowl, ftd, 6" d, green 33
Creamer and sugar, green 75
Cup, ftd, pink 35
Iced Tea Tumbler, pink 190
Pickle Dish, 2 handles, 8" d, green 36
Plate, 6.25" d, green 18
Plate, 8.25" d, green 22
Plate, 8.25" d, pink 19
Plate, 2 handles, 10.25" d 45
Relish Dish, ftd, 6" d, green 35
Salad Bowl, 7.5" d, green 65
Salad Bowl, 7.5" d, pink 50
Saucer, pink 24
Sherbet, green 70
Sugar, green 35

COLONIAL BLOCK, HAZEL ATLAS

Bowl, 4" d, crystal 6
Bowl, 7.5" d, crystal 16
Butter, cov, crystal 30
Milk Pitcher, 20 oz, 5.75" h, crystal 18
Sherbet, crystal 6
Water Goblet, green 12

CORONATION, HOCKING

Berry Bowl, closed handles, 4.25" d, pink ..5
Berry Bowl, closed handles, 8" d, pink 12
Berry Bowl, open handles, 4.25" d, ruby red 5
Berry Bowl, open handles, 8" d, ruby red .12
Berry Set, 1 large and 4 small bowls, ruby red 48
Cup, pink 5
Luncheon Plate, 8.5" d, pink 10
Nappy, handled, 6.5" d, ruby red 8
Nappy, no handles, 8" d, ruby red 14
Saucer, 6" d, pink 2
Sherbet, pink 5
Tumbler, 10 oz, 5" h, pink 22

CREMAX, MACBETH-EVANS

Bread and Butter Plate, 6.25" d, fired-on pink trim 4
Bread and Butter Plate, 6.25" d, fired-on yellow trim 4
Cup and Saucer, fired-on yellow trim 6
Dinner Plate, fired-on pink trim 8
Dinner Plate, fired-on yellow trim 8
Plate, 11.5" d, fired-on pink trim 13

FLORENTINE NO. 1, HAZEL ATLAS

Bowl, 6" d, pink 59
Bread and Butter Plate, 6" d, crystal 13
Cup, crystal 8
Cup, pink 9
Cup and Saucer, pink 23
Nut Bowl, ruffled handle, pink 25
Pitcher, 6.5" h, yellow 45
Pitcher, flat, 48 oz, crystal 70
Plate, 8" d, crystal 8
Plate, 8.5" d, crystal 17
Plate, 10" d, crystal 36
Salt and Pepper Shakers, no lids, crystal .30
Saucer, crystal 4
Shaker, crystal 32
Sherbet, crystal 17
Sherbet, pink 17

GEORGIAN / LOVEBIRDS, FEDERAL

Bowl, 4.5" d, green 9
Bowl, 5.75" d, green 26
Bowl, deep, 6.5" d, green 75
Bread and Butter Plate, 6" d, green 7
Butter, cov, green 85
Creamer, green 15
Cup and Saucer, green 15
Iced Tea, flat, green 150
Nappy, 4.5" d, green 12
Plate, 8" d, green 11
Saucer, green 7
Sherbet, green 15
Sherbet Plate, green 10
Sugar, cov, green 55
Tumbler, 9 oz, 4" h, green 65
Vegetable Bowl, oval, green 75

MADRID, FEDERAL

Bowl, deep, 9.5" d, amber 32
Bread and Butter Plate, 6" d, amber 5
Butter, cov, amber 70

Cake Plate, pink 15
Console Bowl, low, 11" d, amber 15
Cookie Jar, cov, amber 45
Creamer, amber 9
Cream Soup Bowl, amber 16
Cup and Saucer, amber 13
Grill Plate, crystal 9
Hot Plate Coaster, crystal 25
Jello Mold, amber 12
Pitcher, 60 oz, square, 8" h, amber 50
Plate, 7.5" d, blue 25
Plate, 8.75" d, amber 10
Plate, 10.5" d, amber 85
Platter, amber 15
Salt and Pepper Shakers, amber 55
Saucer, blue 10
Shaker, amber 28
Sherbet, amber 8
Sugar, amber 8
Tumbler, 9 oz, 4.25" h, amber 17
Tumbler, 9 oz, 4.25" h, blue 36

MISS AMERICA, HOCKING

Candy Dish, cov, crystal 60
Candy Dish, cov, 11.5" d, pink 175
Celery Dish, oblong, 10.5" d, pink 175
Cereal Bowl, 6.25" d, pink 28
Coaster, 5.75" d, crystal 15
Compote, 5" d, pink 32
Creamer, pink 22
Cup, pink 22
Cup and Saucer, pink 35
Dinner Plate, 10.25" d, crystal 20
Grill Plate, 10.25" d, pink 25
Iced Tea Tumbler, flat, orig label, pink ...130
Pitcher, no ice lip, orig label, pink ...130
Plate, 5.75" d, pink 12
Platter, 12.25" d, pink 35
Relish Dish, 4-part, crystal 10
Saucer, pink 8
Sherbet, pink 16
Vegetable Bowl, oval, 10" d, pink 40
Water Goblet, pink 55
Water Tumbler, flat, pink 40
Wine Goblet, pink 165

OLD CAFE, HOCKING

Bowl, closed handles, 9" d, pink 30
Bowl, tab handles, 6.25" d, pink 20
Candy Dish, low, 8" d, crystal 7
Candy Dish, low, 8" d, pink 8
Candy Jar, ruby lid, 5.5" h, crystal 18

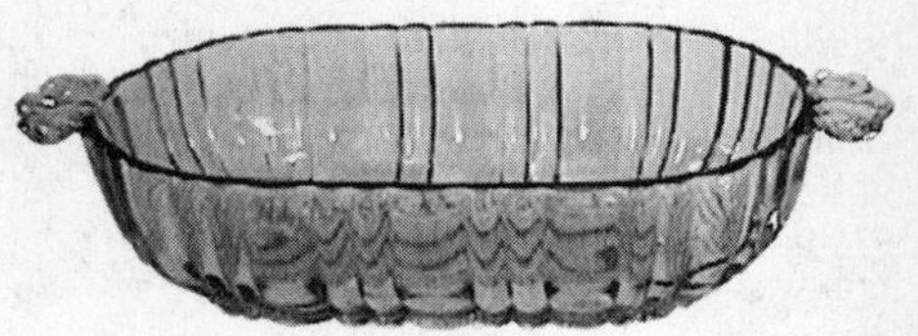

Cereal Bowl, tab handles, 5.5" d, crystal ...9
Cereal Bowl, tab handles, 5.5" d, royal ruby ...24
Cup, pink 5
Dinner Plate, 10" d, pink 52
Olive Dish, oblong, 4.5" l, pink 7
Olive Dish, oblong, 6" l, crystal 6
Olive Dish, oblong, 6" l, pink 8
Pitcher, go-with, crystal 18
Sherbet, 6" d, pink 15
Sherbet, flat, pink 15
Tumbler, 3" h, royal ruby 22
Tumbler, 4" h, pink 21
Tumbler, 4" h, royal ruby 24
Vase, 7.25" h, crystal 10

OLD COLONY, HOCKING

Bowl, plain, 9.5" d, pink 26
Bowl, ribbed, 9.5" d, pink 30
Butter, cov, pink 68
Candlesticks, pr, pink 270
Cereal Bowl, 6.25" d, pink 24
Comport, cov, ftd, 9" d, pink 50
Cookie Jar, cov, pink 75
Creamer, pink 22
Cup, pink 25
Cup and Saucer, pink 36

Dinner Plate, 10.5" d, open lace, pink 32
Flower Bowl, crystal frog, pink 25
Grill Plate, open lace, 10.5" d, pink 21
Luncheon Plate, open lace, 8.25" d, pink ..48
Plate, 4-part, solid lace, 13" d, pink 48
Plate, solid lace, 13" d 48
Platter, 5-part, solid lace, 12.75" l, pink 31
Platter, solid lace, 12.75" l, pink 38
Relish, 3-part, open lace, 10.5" d, pink 25
Salad Bowl, open lace, 7.25" d, pink 25
Salad Bowl, ribbed, 7.75" d, pink 30
Saucer, pink 12
Sherbet, ftd, pink 110
Sugar, pink 23
Tumbler, flat, 9 oz, 4.5" h, pink 20
Tumbler, ftd, 10.5 oz, 5" h, pink 85

PETALWARE, MACBETH-EVANS

Berry Bowl, 9" d, cremax, gold trim 18
Berry Bowl, 9" d, monax 19
Berry Bowl, 9" d, pink 20
Cereal Bowl, 5.75" d, monax 9
Cereal Bowl, 5.75" d, monax, gold trim 8
Cereal Bowl, 5.75" d, monax florette 13
Cereal Bowl, 5.75" d, pink 12
Cream Soup Bowl, 4.5" d, cremax 12
Cream Soup Bowl, 4.5" d, cremax, gold trim 12
Cream Soup Bowl, 4.5" d, pink 13
Creamer, monax florette 10
Creamer, pink 15
Creamer and Sugar, cremax 15
Creamer and Sugar, monax 12
Cup and Saucer, cremax 5
Cup and Saucer, cremax, gold trim 9
Cup and Saucer, monax florette 12
Cup and Saucer, pink 11
Dinner Plate, 9" d, cremax 9
Dinner Plate, 9" d, cremax, gold trim 9
Dinner Plate, 9" d, monax 9
Dinner Plate, 9" d, monax florette 15
Dinner Plate, 9" d, pink 14
Lamp Shade, 8.5" h, cremax 7
Mustard, no lid, cobalt 12
Platter, oval, 13" l, pink 20
Salad Plate, 8" d, cremax 5
Salad Plate, 8" d, cremax, gold trim 7
Salad Plate, 8" d, monax, fruit dec, gold trim 10
Salad Plate, 8" d, monax florette 9
Salad Plate, 8" d, pink 13
Salver, 11" d, cremax 10
Salver, 11" d, monax 17
Salver, 11" d, pink 16
Saucer, monax florette 3
Saucer, pink 2
Sherbet, 6" d, monax 3
Sugar, open, cremax, gold trim 11
Sugar, open, monax florette 10
Tidbit, center handle, monax 18

PRINCESS, HOCKING

Ashtray, 4.5" d, green 99
Berry Bowl, 4.5" d, green 30
Berry Bowl, 4.5" d, pink 33
Bowl, hat-shaped, 9.5" d, green 51
Bowl, hat-shaped, 9.5" d, pink 75
Cake Stand, 10", green 28
Cake Stand, 10", pink 50
Candy Dish, cov, green 63
Candy Dish, cov, pink 75
Cereal Bowl, 5" d, green 40

Cereal Bowl, 5" d, pink 41
Coaster, green 65
Cookie Jar, cov, green 56
Creamer, topaz 20
Creamer and Sugar, open, green 32
Cup, green 8
Cup, pink 10
Dinner Plate, 9.5" d, green 30
Dinner Plate, 9.5" d, pink 32
Dinner Plate, 9.5" d, topaz 15
Grill Plate, 9.5" d, pink 13
Pitcher, 37 oz, 6" h, pink 52
Pitcher, 60 oz, 8" h, pink 78
Platter, 12" d, green 25
Platter, 12" d, pink 29
Relish, divided, green, 7.5" 27
Salad Bowl, octagonal, 9", green 45
Salad Plate, 8" d, green 14
Salad Plate, 8" d, pink 17
Salt and Pepper Shakers, green 74
Salt and Pepper Shakers, pink 62
Salt and Pepper Shakers, topaz 92
Sandwich Plate, handled, 10.25" d, pink ..33
Saucer, 5.5" d, green 10
Saucer, 5.5" d, pink 12
Sherbet, green 20
Sherbet, pink 21
Sugar, cov, green 35
Sugar, cov, pink 45
Tumbler, 5 oz, flat, 3" h, pink 33
Tumbler, 9 oz, flat, 4" h, pink 29
Tumbler, 9 oz, flat, 4" h, topaz 25
Tumbler, 10 oz, ftd, 5.25" h, green 32
Tumbler, 10 oz, ftd, 5.25" h, topaz 25
Tumbler, 13 oz, flat, 5.25" h, topaz 33
Vase, 8" h, green 43
Vase, pink 62
Vegetable Bowl, oval, 10" d, green 25

PYRAMID, INDIANA

Berry Bowl, large, yellow 80
Berry Bowl, small, yellow 50
Bowl, 4.75" d, pink 65
Bowl, oval, green 45
Creamer and Sugar, pink 125
Creamer and Sugar, with tray, pink 235
Ice Bucket, bail handle, yellow 165
Luncheon Plate, 9" d, yellow 14
Pitcher, yellow 750
Tumbler, 5 oz, flat, 3" h, yellow 32
Tumbler, 8 oz, yellow 60
Tumbler, 10 oz, ftd, 4.25" h, yellow 22
Tumbler, 13 oz, flat, 5.25" h, yellow 35

THISTLE, MACBETH-EVANS

Bowl, 5.5" d, pink 28
Cake Plate, 13" d, pink 300
Cereal Bowl, pink 22
Cup and Saucer, pink 34
Grill Plate, pink 45
Plate, 8" d, green 19
Plate, 8" d, pink 14

DINNERWARE

There is a growing appreciation for the thousands of dinnerware patterns that graced the tables of low-, middle-, and some upper-income families during the first three-quarters of the twentieth century. Some of America's leading industrial designers were responsible for forms and decorative motifs.

Collectors fall into three groups: those who collect the wares of a specific factory or factories, often with a strong regional emphasis; individuals who are reassembling the set they grew up with; and those who are fascinated by certain forms and motifs. The bulk of the books on the subject appeared in the early 1980s.

Several of the companies have become established collecting categories in their own right. This is why you will find companies such as Blue Ridge and Hall elsewhere in this book.

AMERICAN LIMOGES

Bridal Bouquet, dinner plate, 10.25" d 26
Candle Light, Golden Wheat, dinner plate, 10" d 18
Candle Light, Meadow Rose, cup 14
Candle Light, Meadow Rose, plate, 7.75" d 16
Candle Light, New Princess, dinner plate . .6
Casino, cup and saucer 18
Norway Pink, bread and butter plate, 6.5" d 12
Triumph, Abstract Flower, vegetable bowl 10
Triumph, Bermuda, bread and butter plate 18
Triumph, Bermuda, dinner plate 20
Triumph, Blue Daisy, vegetable bowl 18
Triumph, Greta, creamer and cov sugar . .16
Triumph, Greta, dinner plate, 10" d 22

Triumph, Greta, platter, tab handles 20
Triumph, Greta, salad plate, 7.25" d 25
Triumph, Greta, serving bowl, 9" d 16
Triumph, Greta, soup bowl, 8.25" d 26
Triumph, Hollywood, dinner plate, 11" d 20
Triumph, Hollywood, platter, 12" l 32
Triumph, Oslo, platter 24
Triumph, Rosalie, platter, 12" x 9.5" 24
Triumph, Vermilion Rose, dinner plate, 11" d 16
Triumph, Vermilion Rose, soup plate, ...4

HARMONY HOUSE

April Flower, luncheon set, plate, cup, and saucer 25
Betsy Rose, chop plate, 13.5" d 25
Harvest Time, platter, parchment beige . . .32
Marshland, bread and butter plate, 6.25" d 28
Mount Vernon, creamer 20
Mount Vernon, cup, ftd 18
Pink Arbor, 5-pc place setting, dinner plate, bread and butter plate, soup bowl, and cup and saucer 10
Pink Arbor, creamer and cov sugar 12
Pink Arbor, platter, 13.25" x 11" 10

Pink Arbor, serving bowl, 8.5" d 12
Rosebud, cup and saucer 15
Rose Petite, dinner plate 10
Starfire, berry bowl, 5.5" d 15
Virginia, vegetable bowl, 9" d 25
Wheat, platter, parchment beige, 13" l 20

IROQUOIS

Garland, bread and butter plate 2
Garland, creamer 10
Garland, cup and saucer 8
Garland, dinner plate 10
Garland, salt and pepper shakers 16
Garland, sugar, cov .15

MIKASA

Academy, dinner plate 20
Annette, coffee mug 16
Cambridge, 4-pc place setting, dinner plate, ftd cup and saucer, and salad plate 35
Cambridge, creamer and cov sugar 32
Cambridge, rim soup, 8.375" d 15
Cambridge, vegetable bowl, 9.125" d 35
Cavalier, cup and saucer, ftd 15
Charisma Black, dessert plate, 7.5" d 10
Country Scene, dinner plate, 11" d 20
Dewdrop, serving bowl, 9.25" d 16
Duplex, saucer 10
Elite, gravy bowl, underplate 16
Fernflower, 4-pc place setting, dinner plate, bread and butter plate, and cup and saucer 15
Fernflower, cereal bowl, 5.25" d 10
Fernflower, chop plate, 12.5" d 20
Fernflower, dinner plate 18
Fernflower, soup bowl, 6.25" d 10
Garden Harvest, cake server 16

Heather Blossoms, cup and saucer 22
Heritage, butter dish, 8.25" x 4.5" 30
Hyde Park, cup 15
La Flora, dinner plate, 10.5" d 18
La Flora, luncheon plate, 8.25" 10
Lorraine, platter, 15.375" x 10.75" 130
Lydia, rim soup, 9.375" d 15
Margaux, rim soup, 9.375" d 15
Margaux, salad plate, 8.25" d 15
Mediterrania, creamer and cov sugar 18
Montclaire, snack plate 20
Nature's Garden, coffeepot, 9.375" h 25
Parisienne, cereal bowl, 6.5" d 14
Quilt, platter, 12" d .25
Quilt, serving bowl, 9.75" d 18
Rosemont, bread and butter plate, 6.5" d . .15
Rosemont, dessert plate, 7.5" d 12
Rosemont, fruit bowl, 5.5" d 15
Rosemont, platter, 14.75" l 90
September Glory, salad plate, 8" d 7
Serenade, cup and saucer, ftd 15
Serenade, soup bowl, 9.125" d 15
Silk Flowers, cup and saucer 18
Summer Setting, cake plate, 1950s 25
Wheat, creamer and cov sugar 20
Windsor Castle, bread and butter plate, 6.375" d 15
Windsor Castle, dessert bowl, 5.875" d . . .18
Windsor Castle, salad plate, 7.825" d 25

SALEM CHINA

Bird of Paradise, dinner plate, 10" d 16
Century, casserole, cov, gold trim, 10.5" d .32
Century, creamer 18
Century, serving bowl, 10" d 20
Coronet, soup bowl, 8" d 15
English Village, berry bowl 10
English Village, cup and saucer 18
English Village, dinner plate, 9.75" d 20
Georgetown, dinner plate, 10.25" d 30
Georgetown, saucer 12
Mandarin, dinner plate, 10.25" d 4
Princess Jane, platter, 13" l 20
Southwind, bread and butter plate 12
Southwind, creamer and cov sugar 16
Southwind, saucer .14
Symphony, dinner plate, 9.5" d 18
Tricorne Mandarin Red, dinner plate, 9" d .18
Wheat, gravy boat .12

W.S. GEORGE

Lido Canarytone, Peach Blossom, cup and saucer 15
Lido Canarytone, Peach Blossom, fruit bowl, 5.5" d 5
Lido Canarytone, Peach Blossom, gravy boat 18
Lido Canarytone, Peach Blossom, luncheon plate, 9.5" d 12
Lido Canarytone, Peach Blossom, platter, 13" x 10.375" 28
Lido Canarytone, Peach Blossom, salad plate, 7.375" d 6
Lido Canarytone, Peach Blossom, serving bowl, 9.125" d 25
Lido White, bowl, 6.5" d 6
Petalware/Georgette, soup bowl, 7.75" d . .10
Pussywillow, bowl, 4" d 10
Ranchero, Shortcake, creamer 22
Ranchero, Shortcake, plate, 6" d 15
Ranchero, Shortcake, plate, 9" d 18
Ranchero, Shortcake, platter, 11" d 34
Ranchero, Shortcake, platter, 15.5" x 13" . .40
Ranchero, Shortcake, salt and pepper shakers 34
Ranchero, Shortcake, sugar, cov 28
Ranchero, Shortcake, vegetable bowl, oval, 9.5" l 18

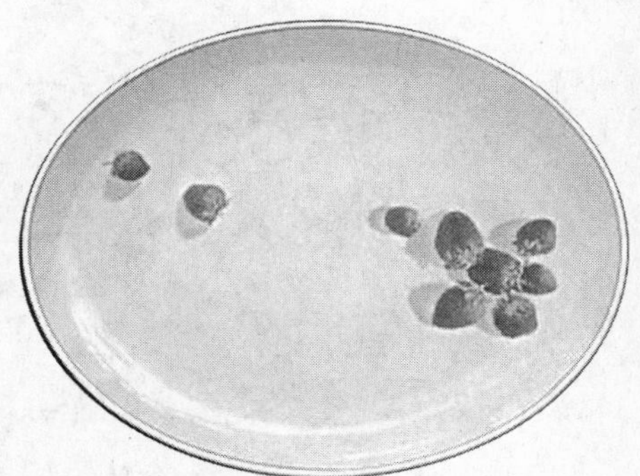

DIONNE QUINTUPLETS

On May 28, 1934, on a small farm in Callander, Ontario, Canada, five baby girls weighing a total of ten pounds, one and one quarter ounces were delivered into this world with the help of Dr. DaFoe and two midwives.

Due to their parents' poor financial circumstances and the public's curiosity, the quintuplets were put on display. For a small fee, the world was invited to come and see the quints at play in their custom-built home or to buy a souvenir to mark their birth.

The field of collectibles for Dionne Quintuplets memorabilia is a very fertile one!

Club: Dionne Quint Collectors, P.O. Box 2527, Woburn, MA 01888.

Baby Book, "Dionne Quintuplet Baby Book," infants wearing pink and white jumpers on cov, 16-pg booklet printed by Brown & Bigelow, pages inside for entering baby's statistics and history, growth charts, parenting tips, ©1935 NEA Service, Inc, 8.75" x 5.75" 60

Book, *Here We Are Three Years Old, The Dionne Quintuplets,* by Willis Thornton, Whitman Pub, 1937 35

Book, *Story of the Dionne Quintuplets,* 1935, 40 pgs 28

Book, *The Dionne Quintuplets We're Two Years Old,* by Willis Thornton, Whitman Pub, 1936, 40 pgs 35

Book, *The Dionne Years,* by Pierre Berton, 1st American ed, 1977 25

Dish, aluminum, image of Marie in center, 4.5" d 15

Dish, emb faces in center, names on rim, platinum trim, 6" d 90

Dolls, Madame Alexander, set of 5 babies, orig dresses with labels, 8" h 1,500

Fan, cardboard, wooden stick handle, Quints at the beach, mkd "1936 NEA Service, Inc, 17000 CB&B St Paul Minn," San Fernando Laundry adv on back "Don't kill your wife, let us do the dirty work," 14" h 20

Fan, cardboard, wooden stick handle, sepiatone image of 1-year-old Quints seated in chairs, "Use Linco Gasoline Motor Oil" adv on back 35

Magazine, *Look,* Dionne Quints on cov, 1938, 14" x 11" 25

Magazine Tear Sheet, Karo Syrup, picture of Yvonne, 13.5" x 10.5" 8

Picture Album, *Dionne Quintuplets Picture Album,* Dell Pub, 1936, 34 pgs 18

Spoon, full image of Quint above emb name on handle, Calton Silverplate, 1930s 15

Wall Plaque, chalkware, emb Quint heads, "Souvenir From Quintland Callander, Canada, Souvenir de Oliva Dionne Aug 6/37," 4.25" d 80

DISNEYANA

"Steamboat Willie" introduced Mickey Mouse to the world in 1928. Walt and Roy Disney, brothers, worked together to create an entertainment empire filled with a myriad of memorable characters ranging from Donald Duck to Zorro.

Early Disney items are getting very expensive. No problem. Disney continues to license material. In thirty years the stuff marketed in the 1960s and 1970s will be scarce and eagerly sought. Now is the time to buy it.

Clubs: Disney Once Upon A Classic Collectors Club, 1443 Dulcet Ave., Northridge, CA 91326; Imagination Guild, P.O. Box 907, Boulder Creek, CA 95006; National Fantasy Fan Club for Disneyana Collectors & Enthusiasts, P.O. Box 19212, Irvine, CA 92713, www.nffc.org; The

Mouse Club, 2056 Cirone Way, San Jose, CA 95124.

Ashtray, Three Little Pigs, set of 4, 3 pigs and wolf, each figure posed standing beside a different card suit, lusterware, stamped "Made in Japan," 2.25" h, 3" w, 1.5" d 45

Ashtray, Three Little Pigs, playing musical instruments, seated on triangular ashtray, lusterware, ©Walt Disney, made in Japan, 3" h, 3.375" w, 3" d 75

Bowl, *Fantasia,* Satyr, #124, hp, flower petal shape with 6 panels, each featuring a different satyr raised in bas-relief and painted in earthtones, Vernon Kilns, 3" h, 6.5" d 1,250

Bowl, *Fantasia,* Sprite, #125, hp, flattened spherical form with 4 sprites on blue clouds with yellow highlights, Vernon Kilns, 3" h, 10.5" d 1,500

Bowl, *Fantasia,* Winged Nymph, #122, hp, flattened spherical form, features 5 earthtone nymphs and multicolored flowers, Vernon Kilns, 2.5" h, 12" d . . .1,375

Calendar, adv for Morrell's meat products, 12 different Disney cartoon images, never used, in orig shipping tube, 1942, 30" x 14" 400

Chewing Gum Box, Pinocchio Chewing Gum, Dietz Gum Co, cardboard, Pinocchio images on lid, mkd "1940 Walt Disney Productions," 6.25" x 8.5" x 2" 325

Console Set, *Fantasia,* mushroom bowl #120, hp, rect, shallow, emb mushroom figures from Nutcracker Suite sequence, glazed finish, with pair of Hop Low salt and pepper shakers #35 and #36, Vernon Kilns, 2" x 12" x 7" bowl 700

Figurine, Alice in Wonderland, ceramic, 1960, 5" h 40

Figurine, Bambi, celluloid, mkd "© Walt Disney," c1940s, 4" h 75

Figurine, Cinderella's Jacques the mouse, mkd "Disney, Japan," 2.75" h 12

Figurine, Donald Duck playing fiddle, mkd "Japan," 2.5" h 20

Figurine, *Fantasia,* Centaur #31, Vernon Kilns, 10" h 1,750

Figurine, *Fantasia,* ostrich #28, Vernon Kilns, 6" h 900

Figurines, *Fantasia,* Centaurettes #18 and #22, Vernon Kilns, 7.5" to 8.5" h . .1,425

Figurines, *Fantasia,* elephants #25, #26, and #27, Vernon Kilns, 5" to 6" h, ...865

Figurines,* Fantasia, *hippos #32, #33, and #34, Vernon Kilns, 5" to 5.5" h 1,850

Figurines, *Fantasia,* Nubian Centaurettes #23 and #24, Vernon Kilns, 7.5" h to 8" h 1,175

Figurines, *Fantasia,* set of 6 sprites, #7, #8, #9, #10, #11, and #12, Vernon Kilns, 3" to 4.5" h 1,300

Figurines, Lion King, Simba and Timon 6

Figurines, Three Little Pigs, hp bisque, each pig dancing and playing a musical instrument, mkd "Japan" on back, 3.5" h 40

Figurines, Three Little Pigs, hp bisque, each pig playing a musical instrument, ©Walt Disney, debossed "Made in Japan" and numbers "570," "571," or "572" on back, stamped "Japan" on bottom, 4.5" h 50

Figurines, Three Little Pigs and the Big Bad Wolf, hp bisque, ©Walt Disney, George Borgfeldt Corp, made in Japan, orig cardboard box with paper cov and label "Who's Afraid of the Big Bad Wolf, Three Little Pigs," 3" to 3.5" h 210

Jumper Toys, Three Little Pigs, litho tin, pig with house, Line Mar Toys, Japan, ©Linemar Co, Inc and Walt Disney Productions, orig box with cellophane front, 4" h 650

Movie Film, *Mickey's Arabian Fight,* #2136-C, 1950s-60s, MIP 20

Movie Poster, *101 Dalmatians,* 1961 450

Mug, Disneyland, "Disneyland Hotel/ Stromboli's Ristorante," restaurant logo on front, Disneyland Hotel logo with Tinkerbell on back, mkd "Homer Laughlin China," 1980s, 3.5" h 50

Pin, figural Snow White and 2 dwarfs, multicolor celluloid, mkd "Occupied Japan," 1.5" h, 2" w 35

Pinback Button, Disneyland, "Walt Disney World 15 Years," red, blue, and yellow on white ground, castle and Epcot Center surrounded by confetti, 3" d 8

Pincushions, Three Little Pigs, lusterware, pig playing fiddle, posed next to pincushion, stamped "Made in Japan" and debossed "Japan" on base 20

Pull Toy, Mickey Mouse Xylophone, No. 748, paper on wood, Fisher-Price, 9" l 350

Sand Pail, Donald Duck, litho tin, Ohio Art, c1939 35

Sand Pail, Mickey, Minnie, and Pluto, litho tin, Ohio Art 375

Sand Pail, Mickey Mouse, Donald Duck, and Goofy, Ohio Art, c1930-40s 135

Sign, Donald Duck Soft Drinks, round, Donald's face in center, red and blue rim lettering, white ground 350

Stuffed Toy, Mickey Mouse, probably Dean's Rag Book Co, velveteen, felt ears, hands, and shoes, plastic cov metal eyes with floating pupils, printed toothy grin, velveteen shorts with red buttons, 1932-35, 9" h 350

Toothbrush Holder, Three Little Pigs, pigs playing musical instruments, slot for toothbrush behind, ceramic, mkd "Three Little Pigs! 5165, Made in Japan, ©Walt Disney" on bottom, 4" h, 4" w . . .55

Toothbrush Holder, Three Little Pigs, pigs standing in front of chimney, 2 pigs playing instruments, 1 with bricks and trowel, hp bisque, ©Walt Disney, made in Japan, 4" h, 4.5" w, 1.75" d 110

Toy, carpet sweeper, litho tin, Donald Duck, play wear, c1940s, 7.5" w sweeper base, 27" l handle 125

Toy, Disneyland Ferris Wheel, clockwork motor, bell, and 6 gondolas, litho tin, Disney characters and fairground scenes, Chein, 16.75" h 350

Toy, Donald Duck, Huey, Dewey, and Louie Marching Soldiers, clockwork motor, litho tin, rubber rifles, Linemar .375

Toy, drum, litho tin and metal, Mickey Mouse, c1930s, 6.5" d, 3.75" h 235

Toy, drum set, litho tin, Mickey and Minnie Mouse, Donald Duck, and Pluto, with orig drum sticks, drum heads have been punched and repaired, c1940s, 6.25" d 100

Toy, Mechanical Mickey Mouse with Xylophone, litho tin, clockwork motor, black, red, and yellow Mickey, foliate dec on xylophone, Linemar, 7" h 750

Toy, Mickey and Minnie Mouse, Fun-E-Flex painted wood figures, 3.75" h 250

Toy, sand sifter, litho tin, Mickey Mouse, Horace Horse Collar, and Clarabelle Cow, Ohio Art, c1930, 8" d 200

Toy, snow shovel, litho tin, Donald Duck, c1930-40s, 10" x 7" shovel, 27" l handle .350

Toy, wash tub, litho tin tub wrap, Mickey and Minnie using similar wash tub, light rust inside, c1930s, 7.75" h 25

Toy, water sprinkler can, litho tin, 2 images of Donald Duck, light rust on inside, c1938 110

Vase, *Fantasia,* Goldfish Bowl, #121, hp, spherical, 3 purple, yellow, orange, and green goldfish on white ground, Vernon Kilns, 6" h, 8" d 540

Vase, *Fantasia,* Pegasus, #127, hp, 8" h, 12" w, 5" d 1,400

Wristwatch, Mickey Mouse, Ingersol, orig instructions, guarantee, and box .350

DOG COLLECTIBLES

The easiest way to curb your collection is to concentrate on the representations of a single breed. Many collectors focus only on three-dimensional figures. Whatever approach you take, buy pieces because you love them. Try to develop some restraint and taste and not buy every piece you see. Easy to say, hard to do!

Clubs: Canine Collectors Club, 10290 Hill Rd., Erie, IL 61250; Wee Scots, P.O. Box 450, Danielson, CT 06239.

Note: See Poodle Collectibles for additional listings.

Ashtray, chromed metal, round dish with Mack bulldog at center, 6" h, 7" d 60

Bank, Rival Dog Food can, metal, 2.75" h, 2" d 30

Bookends, pr, poodles, sitting up, black with gold highlights, Japan, c1950, 6.25" h 25

Bookends, pr, Scottie, sitting up, blue bow collar, orange base, ceramic, mkd "Made In Japan" 85

Candy Container, dog wearing top hat, clear glass, mkd "T H Stough Co Jeannette PA," 3.5" h 75

Carnival Statue, chalkware, white with black spots, 10" h 95

Condiment Set, 1 large and 2 small bulldogs, lusterware, small dogs are salt and pepper shakers, large dog is jar and holds a spoon in its mouth, Japan 65

Cookie Jar, dog in basket, American Bisque, 13" h 65

Creamer, pug, figural, brown and white, mkd "Japan," c1940s, 4.5" h 70

Cuff Links, pr, oval with transfer of a springer spaniel's head, SS, sgd "Leonore Doskow" 100

Dish Towels, set of 7, muslin, each with an embroidered Scottie head and day of the week, 34" sq 100

Doorstop, Pekingese, cast iron, mkd "357," 5" h, 5.5" w 125

Figurine, Afghan, Lefton, #H7328, 5" h 35

Figurine, Pekingese, Josef Originals, pink ribbon on head, black and gold sticker, 3" h 35

Fingernail Brush, Scottie, amber Bakelite, mkd "Sterilized, Made In USA," 2.25" h, 3" l 85

Planter, Boston Terrier, brown and white, 5" h 30

String Holder, Westie head, chalkware .. 200

Stuffed Toy, sheepdog, straw stuffing, jointed head, 10" h, 11.5" l 125

Table Runner, embroidered Scottie dogs on white linen, fringed ends, c1930s, 48" x 15.5" 55

Tie Rack, setter's head, syroco, holds 8 ties, 6" h, 8" w 18

Toothbrush Holder, collie, porcelain, mkd "Goldcastle, Made In Japan," 1940s-50s, 6" h 165

Toy, Space Dog, KO, Japan, litho tin, barks, ears flap, eyes roll, 1950s 200

TV Lamp, boxer, chalkware, burgundy, 1950s-60s 40

DOLL HOUSES & FURNISHINGS

Doll houses and doll house furnishings have undergone a current craze and are highly collectible. Many artists and craftsmen devote hours to making scale furniture and accessories. This type of artist-oriented doll house furnishing affects the market by offering the buyer a choice of an old piece versus a present-day handmade piece.

Petite Princess, Plastic Art Toy Corporation, Tootsietoy, and Renwal are just four of hundreds of major manufacturers of machine-made doll house furniture. Materials range from wood to injection molded plastic. This furniture was meant to be used, and most surviving examples were. The period packaging is its supporting literature and can double the value of a set.

Club: Dollhouse & Miniature Collectors, P.O. Box 159, Bethlehem, CT 06751.

HOUSES

Combination Dollhouse, Stirn & Lyon, patented 1881, stenciled wood building sections dec with crayons, litho paper illus on cov, 15" h .175

Dolly's Playhouse, McLoughlin Bros, late 19th C, litho paper on board, folding, 2 rooms, folding printed paper furniture, orig box, 18.5" h house 375

Japanese House, 20th C, scale model, copper accents, soft wood, 1 room, sliding glass and cloth solji screen doors, 28" h, 36.75" w, 27.25" d 500

Victorian Cottage, early 20th C, wood, yellow with red trim, green shingled roof, 2 rooms downstairs, 1 upstairs, with 3/4 to 1" scale wood, pressed board, and Tootsietoy furniture and accessories, 23" h, 26" w, 23.75" d 450

Victorian Mansion, late 19th C, mansard roof and belvedere, sq lawn, mustard yellow with brown trim, gray roofs with red accents, 2 rooms downstairs, 2 upstairs, attic, staircases, cast iron fence and lions on wood plinths, wood outhouse, 36" h, 25" w, 49" sq base 2,875

FURNISHINGS & ACCESSORIES

Dolls, set of 3, German, all bisque, molded and painted hair and features, crocheted outfits, 1.375" h 90

Dolls, set of 5, German, bisque shoulder heads, cloth bodies, bisque limbs, young woman, man with mustache, older woman, man in uniform, and maid, 5.125" to 6.25" h 300

Furnishings, 6 pcs, cast iron, highchair, baby carriage, wheelbarrow, carpet sweeper, step ladder, and Star kitchen range, early 20th C, 1" scale 200

Furnishings, 8 pcs, metal gas stove, sewing stand, marble-top table, radiator, dressing mirror, fish tank, and 2 chandeliers, 1" scale 475

Furnishings, 13 pcs, metal trunk, tray, document box, serving tray, 2 castor sets with glass bottles, tea set and tray, picture frame, bottle carrier and 2 bottles, mantel clock, castle, and kitten in basket, wood owl, 1 to 1 1/2" scale 525

Highboy, 4 drawers, Plasco, 4.5" h 10

Ironing Board and Iron, Renwal 25

Kitchen Set, table and 2 chairs, Renwal . .20

Lawn Chair, Marx 8

Perambulator, German, metal with fancy scrollwork design and sunshade, 6" l, with 3.75" h bisque doll with stationary brown glass eyes and mohair wig 175

Refrigerator, Ideal, 2 doors, pull-out vegetable bins, rotating shelves, ice tray, turkey, Jell-O mold, MIB 150

Sewing Machine, cabinet, Renwal 35

Vanity and Bench, Superior, 2" h 8

DOLLS

People buy dolls primarily on the basis of sentiment and condition. Most begin by buying back the dolls they remember playing with as a child.

Speculating in dolls is risky business. The doll market is subject to crazes. The doll that is in today may be out tomorrow.

Place great emphasis on originality. Make certain that every doll you buy has the complete original costume. Ideally, the box or packaging also should be present. Remember, you are not buying these dolls to play with. You are buying them for display.

Clubs: Chatty Cathy Collector's Club, P.O. Box 4426, Seminole, FL 33775; Doll Doctor's Assoc., 6204 Ocean Front Ave., Virginia Beach, VA 23451; Doll Family Collector's Club, 1301 Washington Blvd., Belpre, OH 45714; Liddle Kiddles Klub, 3639 Fourth Ave., La Crescenta, CA 91214; Madame Alexander Doll Club, P.O. Box 330, Mundelein, IL 60060; National Doll & Teddy Bear Collector, P.O. Box 4032, Portland, OR

97208; United Federation of Doll Clubs, 10920 N. Ambassador Dr., Ste. 130, Kansas City, MO 64153.

Note: The dolls listed date from the 1920s through the present. For information about antique dolls, see Jan Foulke's *14th Blue Book Dolls and Values* (Hobby House Press: 1999) and Dawn Herlocher's, *200 Years of Dolls* (Antique Trader Books: 1996).

DOLLS

Arranbee, Nancy Lee, vinyl, blue sleep eyes, auburn hair, wearing smocked dress, 1954, 15" h 125

Arranbee, Nannette Bride, brunette, wearing ivory satin bridal gown with cord trim around bodice and matching headpiece with attached veil, separate slip, rayon socks, snap leather shoes, carrying a bouquet, 1950s, 17" h 300

Arranbee, Nannette Skater, hard plastic, blonde, pearly white satin outfit with fur trim, white and silver skates, mkd "R&B," 1949-56, 17" h 235

Effanbee, American Child, composition socket head, brown sleep eyes, real upper lashes, painted lower lashes, short feather brows, blonde human hair wig, 5-pc jointed body, pink organdy dress, pink cotton slip and panties, leatherette shoes, "Effanbee Durable Dolls" metal heart bracelet, 1939, 19.5" h 800

Effanbee, Dy-Dee, heart tag, 1967, 18" h .125

Effanbee, Fluffy, vinyl, wearing Brownie uniform, 8 h 115

Effanbee, Honey, hard plastic, walker, head turns from side to side, orig dress, 1950s, 18" h 300

Effanbee, Patsy, composition, sleep eyes, orig outfit, green dress and bonnet, white socks, black shoes, metal heart bracelet, 1920s, 14" h 400

Effanbee Patsyette, composition, replaced outfit, 1930s, 9" h 425

Effanbee, Patsy Joan, composition, molded hair, sleep eyes, real lashes, orig dress with matching bonnet and panties, metal heart bracelet, 1946 . . .425

Effanbee, Pun'kin, plastic, rooted hair, orig tag, 1969, 11.5" h 150

Horsman, B147, soft plastic head and arms, hard plastic legs, bottle mouth, sleep eyes, 1968, 12" h 20

Horsman, H14, soft vinyl, sleep eyes, dark brown wig, orig outfit, 15" h 35

Horsman, Ruthie, #21, vinyl, blonde hair, blue sleep eyes, 2-pc red outfit, 13" h . .50

Ideal, Betsy McCall, hard plastic body, arms, and legs, vinyl head, dark brown hair, brown sleep eyes, orig yellow dress and socks, replaced slip and shoes, early 1950s, 14.5" h 100

Ideal, Betsy Wetsy, hard plastic face, soft vinyl body, caracul wig, sleep eyes with tear ducts, wearing christening gown, bonnet, undershirt, and diaper, 1950s, 15.5" h 300

Ideal, Flatsy, brunette hair, blue dress, white stockings and shoes, with turquoise and white carriage, late 1960s . .45

Ideal, Little Miss Revlon, red ponytail hair, vintage dress, underwear, shoes, and earrings, 1950s, 10.5" h 175

Ideal, Shirley Temple, sleep eyes, wearing tagged Shirley dress with attached slip, panties, replaced shoes, 1958, 12" h 175

Ideal, Tammy, orig tagged hooded sweater, clam-digger jeans, white tennis shoes, 1960s, 12" h 80

Ideal, Toni, P-92, hard plastic with vinyl head, rooted brunette hair, sleep eyes, lashes, replaced outfit and skates, early 1950s, 18" h 165

Madame Alexander, Miss United States, International Series, #559, plastic, Wendy Ann face, blonde curly hair, blue sleep eyes, blue satin dress with pantaloons, layered organdy slip, lace shawl, matching hat, cameo necklace, black shoes, orig box, 1974-75, 8" h 50
Madame Alexander, Scarlett O'Hara and Rhett Butler, Portrait Children Series, plastic, orig outfits, hang tags, and boxes, 1981-85, 12" h 175
Mattel, Charmin Chatty, talker, wearing Let's Play Together tagged outfit, with 1 record, c1963 .200
Mattel, Cheerful Tearful, blonde hair, orig box with bottle, brush, booklet, and outfit, 1966-67, 7" h 90

DOORSTOPS

Cast-iron doorstops have gone through a number of collecting crazes over the past twenty years. The last craze occurred just a few years ago, raising the prices to such a level that doorstops are more likely to be found at antiques shows than at flea markets.

Reproductions abound. A few helpful clues are: check size (many reproductions are slightly smaller than the period piece); check detail (the less detail, the more suspicious you need to be); and check rust (bright orange rust indicates a new piece).

Club: Doorstop Collectors of America, 2413 Madison Ave., Vineland, NJ 08630

Note: Doorstops listed are cast iron unless otherwise noted.

Afghan, full figure, white with red collar, 8" h, 12" l 175
Bathing Beauties, 2 seated women wearing swimsuits and sharing an umbrella, hollow flat back, sgd "C Fish," mkd "250," c1980, 11.5" h 125
Bulldog, seated, chocolate slag glass, Summit Glass Co, 7" h 350
Cat, sitting, full figure, black, Albany Foundry, NY, mid-1920s, 6.75" h, 3.375" w 230
Cat, sitting, full figure, wearing bow, 8" h, 6" w 260
Clipper ship, flat back, orig paint, c1930, 11.25" h 75
Duck, lead, full figure, 1920-40 175
English Setter, pointing, full figure, black and white, Hubley, 8.5" h, 15" l 275
English Setter, pointing, full figure, green patina, Hubley, c1900, 9" h, 13" l 250
Flower Basket, gilded brass, 9" h, 6.5" w .130
Frog, screw holes in feet 70
German Shepherd, sitting, 5.75" h, 4" w . . .75
German Shepherd, sitting, pot metal, 9" h, 6.5" w 95
German Shepherd, standing, looking straight ahead 200
German Shepherd, standing, looking to side, Hubley, 9" h, 9" l 200
Gnome, sitting on tree stump, chalkware, orig paint, 11" h .150
Horse, with saddle and blanket, Hubley, 10.5" h, 12" l 6525
Kittens, 3 kittens in a yarn basket, mkd "B Taiwan," 6" h, 8" w 30
Lady, wearing ruffled dress, flat back, oval base, stamped "12 47," orig paint, c1850s, 6" h, 4.5" w 425
Pansy Bowl, orig paint, Hubley, #256, 7" h, 6.5" w 100
Puppy, crouching, chalkware, 1960s, 4.5" h, 8" l 40
Scottie, sitting, full figure, Hubley, c1940, 5" h, 6.5" w 125
Siamese Cat, seated, yellow and brown with turquoise eyes, ceramic with hard plastic door wedge tail, repaired ears, American Bisque, early 1940s, 8" h 70
Southern Belle, wearing ruffled dress, orig paint, late 1800s, 5" h, 3.5" w 200
Sun Bonnet Baby, wearing yellow dress and bonnet, c1900, 6.25" h 250

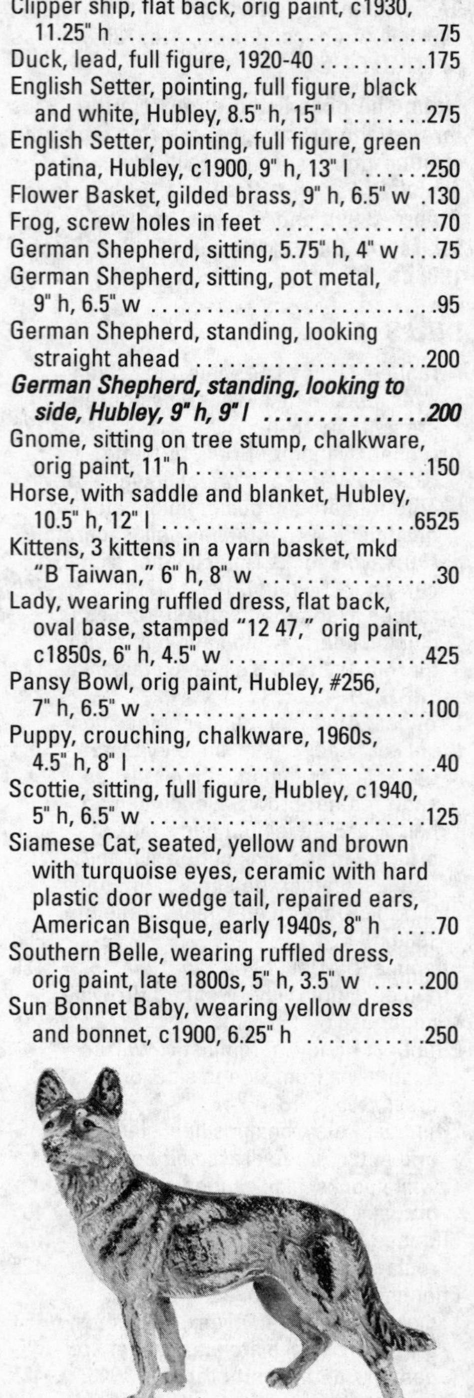

DRINKING GLASSES

It is time to start dealing seriously with promotional drinking glasses given away by fast-food restaurants, garages, and other merchants. This category also includes drinking glasses that start out life as product containers.

Most glasses are issued in a series. If you collect one, you better plan on keeping at it until you have the complete series. Also, many of the promotions are regional. A collector in Denver is not likely to find a Philadelphia Eagles glass at his favorite restaurant.

Just a few washings in a dishwasher can cause a major change in the color on promotional drinking glasses. Collectors insist on unused, unwashed glasses whenever possible. Get the glass, and drink your drink out of a paper cup.

Club: Promotional Glass Collectors Assoc., 2654 W.E. 23rd, Albany, OR 97321.

7-Up, Indiana Jones & the Temple of Doom, High Priest Mola 4
1962 Seattle World's Fair, US Science Pavillion, frosted, 6.5" h 5
Al Capp, Sneaky Pete's Hot Dog, Mammy, 1970s 73
All Star Parade, Disney, Big Bad Wolf and Three Little Pigs, 1939 50
Arby's, Bicentennial, Underdog Saves the Day, 5" h 5
Batman Forever, McDonald's, mug 4
Borden, Little Lola, cow and sun on front, rhyme on reverse, red and black, 3.5" h 20
Bosco, Bosco Bear being attacked by crabs, orange, 3.25" h 20
Bosco, Mickey Mouse, 3.25" h 50
Bozo the Clown, Bozo's head around top in red, Bozo in action in yellow, blue lettering, 1965, 5.5" h 12
Broom Hilda, Sunday Funnies 65
Care Bears, Bedtime Bear, American Greetings, 1985 3
Chinatown Toys, Milwaukee, WI, red, 4" h 10
Cincinnati Bengals, Super Bowl XXIII, orange and black 3
Clarabelle Cow, Disney, 1942 40
Compliments of Humbolt Flour Mills, yellow, 3.25" h 12
Domino's Pizza, Dick Tracy 185
Dr Pepper, Happy Days, The Fonz 4
Dunkin Donuts, Wizard of Oz, cast holding hands, orange, brown, and tan, 1970s 85
Freehold Raceway, Terrapin Stakes, Great Nero, Robert Myers, 1983 5
Holly Farms, Rocky & Bullwinkle, Boris Badenov, 1975 25
Keebler, 135th Anniversary 3
Kentucky Fried Chicken, featuring Col Sanders' recipe, 1954, 3.5" h 7
Lady and the Tramp, Peg, ©Walt Disney, 1960s 55
Lenders Bagels, 3 men with bagels, 3" h . . .3
Margo Bonded Root Beer, red, with syrup line, 4.25" h 6
Mountain Dew, Wisconsin Badgers hockey schedule 1981-82 4
Neil Armstrong Museum, Offical Grand Opening, July 1972 .4
PAT Ward Collector Series, Dudley Do-Right, late 1970s, 5" h 8
Pizza Hut, All-Time Greatest Denver Broncos 10
Polomar Jelly, Superman, in action, red and gray, 1964, 4.25" h 28
Prince of Wales Stakes, Second Jewel of Canada's Triple Crown, 1984 10
Pure Oil, 1914 Packard, Historic Auto Series 4
Sour Puss and Gandy Goose, Terrytoons, 1940s 385
Spiderwoman, Marvel Comics 215
Sugar Free Fresca, green and yellow 4
Sunday Funnies, Smilin' Jack 10

Swartz Peanut Butter, WWF Jake the Snake 4
Tru Treat Grapefruit Drink, red and yellow with syrup line, 5" h 10
Welch's, Flintstones, Pal at Work, Pebbles, green 6
Welch's, Howdy Doody: Our Favorite Treat, Clarabell, red, 1953 18
WLW Radio 7, hockey, Cincinnati Stingers, yellow and black, 5.5" h 4
Wolfman, Universal Pictures, 1960s 85

DRUGSTORE COLLECTIBLES

Corner drugstores, especially those with a soda fountain, were major hangouts in almost every small town in the United States. Almost all of them dispensed much more than medically related products. They were the 7-11's of their era.

This category documents the wide variety of material that you could acquire in a drugstore. It barely scratches the surface. This is a new collecting approach that has real promise.

Advertising Trade Card, Hire's Cough Cure, "They Must Be Very Hoarse," pub by Charles E Hires Co, 3" x 5" 10
Advertising Trade Card, Merchant's Gargling Oil, "A Close Affair. Hugging the Bat," multicolor, baseball catcher, adv text on back 45
Dispenser, counter top, Alka-Seltzer, heavy chrome base with litho tin sign on top, dispenses tablets into cobalt blue drinking glass, 14.625" h, 5" w 450

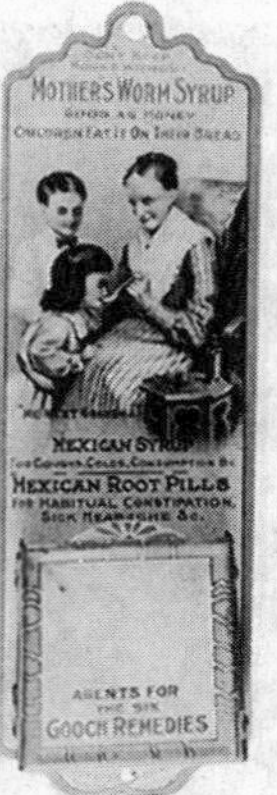

Display Case, Genco Razors, litho tin counter top case with hinged glass lid encasing 6 straight razors on velvet backing, 8" x 14.75" x 6.75" 325
Door Push, adv, porcelain, Ex-Lax, multicolor product image, 8" x 4" 400
Letter Opener, adv, celluloid, black and white, "Maryland Glass Corporation, Blue Glass Bottles, Baltimore" 40
Match Holder, adv, Mother's Worm Syrup, litho tin, multicolor image of grandmother feeding syrup to grandchildren, "Don't Keep House Without Mother's Worm Syrup, Good As Honey, Children Eat It On Their Bread," Mexican Syrup and Mexican Root Pills adv on back 6.875" h, 2.25" w 1,000
Match Holder, adv, wall mount, Dr Shoop's Health Coffee, litho tin, product image on yellow ground, 5" h, 3.5" w 300
Medicine Bottle, "C W Snow & Co, Druggists, Syracuse, NY," emb eagle above mortar and pestle inside shield, cobalt blue, smooth base, tooled mouth, c1880-90, 8.125" h 500
Medicine Bottle, "Swaim's Panacea Philada," olive green, pontil scarred base, applied sloping double collar mouth, c1845-60, 7.75" h 300
Medicine Bottle, "W C Montgomery's Hair Restorer, Philada," dark purple amethyst, smooth base, applied double collar mouth, c1865-75, 7.625" h 275
Sign, diecut cardboard, Johnson & Johnson's Talcum Powder, baby in crib holding talcum powder tin, 8.125" h, 14.125" w 625
Spinner, adv, celluloid, "Save the Baby, Lee's for Coughs, Colds, Croup," red and white 40

Spool Cabinet, oak, J&P Coates Best Six Cord, Spool Cotton, Assorted Colors, 4 drawers 475

Tin, American Baby Bouquet Borated Talcum Powder, litho tin, image of unhappy "before" and happy "after" naked baby on front and back, 4.75" h, 2.625" w, 1.375" d 600

Tin, Cadette Baby Talc, litho tin, toy soldier shape with silver cap, full, 7.375" h, 2.25" w, 1.25" d 230

Tin, McKesson's Baby-Powder, litho tin, multicolor image of 2 naked children warming themselves in front of fireplace, 6.125" h, 2.625" w, 1.375 200

Tin, Mulford's Toilet Talcum, sample size, litho tin, color portrait of beautiful woman in circle, ivory ground, 2.125" h, 1.25" w, .75 230

Tin, Peter Rabbit Baby Powder, litho tin, multicolor images on both sides of rabbit family in meadow and insects pulling and driving a chariot, 3.75" h, 4.25" w 450

Tin, Royal Violet Borated Talcum, litho tin, image of young girl's face in center, "The Best Toilet Powder," cylindrical, 4.125" h, 1.75" d 100

Tip Tray, adv, litho tin, rect, "Laxol, Castor Oil, Like Honey, Laxol," multicolor Laxol bottle, mkd "Chas W Shonk Co Litho Chicago," 3.375" x 4.625" 150

EASTER COLLECTIBLES

Now that Christmas and Halloween collectibles have been collected to death, holiday collectors are finally turning their attentions to Easter. The old Easter bonnet still hangs in the Clothing Collectibles closet, but chicken and rabbit collectors now have to contend with Easter enthusiasts for their favorite animal collectible.

Bank, chalkware, standing rabbit holding Easter basket, 12.5" h 65

Candy Container, rabbit, composition, front legs holding a green cabbage, gray and white, glass eyes, mkd "Whitmans Philadelphia" 35

Chocolate Mold, tin, rabbits playing drums, hinged, mkd "Anton Reiche, Dresden, #26024," 6" h, 10.625" w 150

Cookie Cutter, tin, rabbit, strap handle, early 20th C 25

Covered Dish, rabbit on egg, white milk glass, 5.25" l 275

Covered Dish, rabbit on eggs, basketweave base, white milk glass, 4.5" l 80

Diecut, rabbit heads, 4 intact sheets, printed in Germany, mkd "K&L 4780" . . .30

Doll, rabbit, jointed head with composition face and painted features, wearing a mohair hood with bunny ears, mohair straw-stuffed rabbit body, 12.5" h 110

Easter Basket, wicker, oval, high foot, multicolor weave, 31" h 350

Easter Egg, alumunim, emb "Easter Greetings," decorative borders 12

Easter Egg, paper litho, free-standing on a tubular insert which slides out, scene of rooster with eggs, stamped "Germany" on base of tube, 5.5" h 165

Easter Egg, paper litho, gnome on top of egg playing fiddle with other dancing gnomes, rabbits and chicks surrounding egg, mkd "Germany," 4" h 65

Easter Egg, paper litho, Humpty Dumpty in various comical costumes, 6.5" h . . .325

Easter Egg, white milk glass, emb "Easter Greeting," 4" h 30

Easter Egg, white milk glass, gild emb lettering with applied floral decal, 6" h .35

Greeting Card, stand-up rooster, emb, Raphael Tuck & Sons 40

Postcard, dressed rabbit family painting Easter eggs, hold-to-light illuminates eggs, lantern, and light rays 75

Toy, mother duck pulling ducklings in basket topped with a spinning umbrella and balloons, litho tin and celluloid, windup, 6.5" h, 5" l .75

Toy, multicolor rooster pulling a green and red cart with tin wheels, wood, windup, 9.5" l 200

EGGCUPS

Where modern Americans would be hard-pressed to recognize, let alone know how to use, an eggcup, their European counterparts still utilize the form as an everyday breakfast utensil. Their greatest period of popularity in America was between 1875 and 1950—long before cholesterol became a four-letter word.

Collectors place a premium on character eggcups. You can make a great collection consisting of eggcups from breakfast services of hotels, railroads, steamships, or restaurants. As tourists, many of our ancestors had a bad case of sticky fingers.

Club: Eggcup Collectors' Corner, 67 Stevens Ave., Old Bridge, NJ 08857.

Blue Ridge, Becky pattern, 3.25" h, 3.25" d 40
Chintz, allover multicolor flowers in red, orange, blue, yellow, and pink with green leaves 100
Figural, donkey pulling "egg" cart, black and gold, Italy, 2.5" h, 4.5" l 35
Figural, pink and white poodle holding cup on its back, Japan, late 1940s, 2.5" h 50
Figural, pink boot, Royal Art Pottery, England, 1.75" h, 2.25" l 25
Germany, peach luster ext, white int 10
Hankscraft, #740, porcelain, silver Art Deco design on white ground, 3" h 20
Holt-Howard, rooster on white ground, red band at base, 1968, 3.75" h, 2.75" w .30
Italy, hp brown, red, orange, white, and blue horizontal stripes, 3.5" h 20
Japan, dark pink, 2.5" h, 1.875" d 10
Japan, hp yellow daffodil on white ground, pale green int, 3.75" h 18
Japan, porcelain, white with gold trim . . .15
Japan, wild rose decal on white ground, scalloped rim, gold trim, 2.25" h, 1.75" d :12
Porcelain, hp cherries and grapes at rim, peach luster ground, mkd "Foreign," 2.25" h, 1.75" d 25
Stangl, Festival 16
Villeroy & Boch, Burgenland pattern, blue transfer, 2.25" h 25
Villeroy & Boch, Burgenland pattern, red transfer, 2.25" h .20

ELEPHANT COLLECTIBLES

Public television's unending series of documentaries on African wildlife has destroyed the fascination with wild animals. By the time parents take their children to the zoo or circus, elephants are old hat, blasé. Boo, hiss to public television—those pompous pachyderms. We want the mystery and excitement of wildlife returned to us.

Things were different for the pre-television generations. The elephant held a fascination that is difficult for us to comprehend. When Barnum brought Jumbo from England to America, English children (and a fair number of adults) wept.

There are a few elephant-related political collectibles listed. It is hard to escape the G.O.P. standard bearer. However, real elephant collectors focus on the magnificent beasts themselves or cartoon representations ranging from Dumbo to Colonel Hathi.

Clubs: Elephant Collectors Club, P.O. Box 680565, Franklin, TN 37068; Elephant Collector's Club: c/o Enchanted Elephant, 12650 Overseas Hwy., Arathon, FL 33050; The National Elephant Collector's Society, 380 Medford St., Somerville, MA 02145.

Bank, cast iron, 2-pc, bronzed finish, 2.5" h, 3.25" l 165
Bank, Grapette adv, clear glass, 7" h 45
Bank, gray elephant standing on pedestal base, American Bisque, 6" h . .90

Bank, seated baby elephant, brown with hp features and 3 flowers on stomach, 6" h 35
Bookends, pr, cast iron, bronze finish, 4.5" h, 5" w 75
Charm, blue plastic, full figure, 1" h, 2" l . . .20
Child's Plate, emb tin, Jumbo in center, alphabet rim, 5.5" d 125
Comb Holder, elephant balancing on hind legs, hp, white with pink ears and toenails, blue flower on sides, porcelain, 4.5" h 16
Creamer, Shawnee, 1940s, 4.5" h 75
Figure, celluloid, mkd "VCO USA," 2" h . . .15
Ink Blotter, amethyst glass, LJ Houze Convex Glass Co, 3.625" h, 3.5" l 35
Match Holder, copper, striker below upturned trunk, mkd "Japan," 2" h, 2.75" l 50
Movie Poster, *Elephant Walk,* Elizabeth Taylor, Dana Andrews, Peter Finch, Abraham Sofaer, 1954 140
Mug, Frankoma, 1973 Nixon/Agnew campaign, 4" h, 5" w 40
Pin, clear lucite elephant head with red ears and blue eyes, 3" h, 4" w 75
Pin, faux tortoise shell, 1.75" h, 2.75" l 15
Planter, chintz-style dec on white ground, Lefton 18
Planter, circus elephant holding 2 multicolor balls, Napco #K1857, 4.5" h 20
Planter, Republican elephant holding top hat with American flag design, mkd "Japan, 5160," 5.75" h 25
Razor Bank, figural elephant, white china, 2.75" h, 3" w 30
Squeak Toy, rubber, Edward Mobley, 1963 45

ELONGATED COINS

Although the elongation of coinage first began in 1893 at the Columbian Exposition in Chicago as souvenirs of that event, the revival of producing and collecting elongated coins began in earnest in the early 1960s. Initially available to the hobbyists and souvenir collectors from a few private roller/producers, the elongation of coins advanced by way of commercial enterprises beginning in 1976 during the Bicentennial celebration. Automated vending rolling machines producing souvenirs are all over the United States and abroad, from historical sites to national parks and amusement areas.

Elongated coins are now on the Internet. Most of the coins are trading and since so many are being produced, there is little value in them. The more serious collectors still deal with "Classic" specimens and the older productions.

The values for older antique specimens, such as the Lord's Prayer and Masonic emblem, range from $50 upwards to $350. Both are over 125 years old.

For further information on elongated coins, old and modern, contact the advisor listed below.

Club: The Elongated Collectors, 203 S. Gladiolus St., Momence, IL 60954, www.tecnews.org.

ELVIS

Elvis Presley was hot, is hot, and promises to be hot well into the future. Elvis collectibles are bought from the heart, not the head. A great deal of totally tacky material has been forgiven by his devoted fans.

Elvis material breaks down into two groups: (1) items licensed while Elvis was alive and (2) items licensed after his death. The latter are known as "fantasy" items. Fantasy Elvis is collectible but real value lies in the material licensed during his lifetime.

Beware of any limited edition Elvis items. They were manufactured in such large numbers that the long-term prospects for appreciation in value are very poor. If you love an item, fine. If you expect it to pay for your retirement, forget it.

Club: Elvis Forever TCB Fan Club, P.O. Box 1066, Miami, FL 33780.

Belt, blue vinyl with images of Elvis playing guitar and singing, stars, musical notes, and song titles, goldtone metal buckle, 1956, 2" w, 31" l 250

Flicker Button, black and white photos, changes from *Love Me Tender* title and playing guitar to portrait with facsimile signature, blue metal backing mkd "Vari-Vue," c1956, 2.5" d 20
Flip Book, *John's Pocket-Movie, Elvis Presley,* ©1957 EPE, 3" x 4" 165
Lobby Card, *King Creole, #3*, orange tone photo of Elvis fighting with another man, 1958, 11" s 14" 25
Magazine, *Elvis Presley Speaks,* Rave Pub, 1956, 8" x 10.25" 25
Membership Card, Elvis Presley National Fan Club, 2.25" x 4" 75
Necklace, Elvis Presley Love Me Tender, 13.5" l metal chain with 2" h heart-shaped pendant, MOC 300
Pinback Button, litho tin, 3/4 image of Elvis and music notes, issued by "The Green Duck Co, ©1956 EPE," .875" d ...20
Postcard, color photo, brown border, ©1987 Elvis Presley Ent, 4" x 6" 8
Postcard, multicolor image of Elvis wearing blue shirt and white lei, Christmas greeting "Aloha From Elvis And The Colonel," holly leaves and berries border with Santa in 1 corner, 3.25" x 5.5" 60
Record, *Elvis Presley Love Me Tender,* 45 rpm, RCA Victor label, EPA-4006, 1956, 7" x 7" cardboard cov 50
Scarf, pink silk rayon, 2 drawings of Elvis and guitar and 1 of him posing, images of records and a dog, song titles *I Want You, I Love You, Love Me Tender, Don't Be Cruel,* and *You're Nothing But A Hound Dog,* and "Best Wishes, Elvis Presley," 1956, 32" sq ...100
Sheet Music, *Jailhouse Rock,* large image of Elvis and smaller image of Elvis dancing behind bars, 1957, 9" x 12" 18

ENESCO

Enesco's product line includes more than 12,000 gift, collectible, and home accent items including the Precious Moments and Cherished Teddies collection. It also markets licensed gifts and collectibles such as Lilliput Lane and David Winter Cottages.

Enesco became a wholly-owned subsidiary of Westfield, Massachusetts-based Stanhome, Inc., a multinational corporation, in 1983. In 1997 The Bradford Group entered into a long-term licensing agreement to market the product lines of Stanhome's subsidiary, Enesco Giftware Group. In 1998 Stanhome, Inc., changed its name to Enesco Group, Inc. Today, Enesco products are distributed in more than thirty countries including Japan, Mexico, and Germany.

Note: Enesco sponsors collector clubs for Cherished Teddies, Christmas ornaments, David Winter Cottages, Memories of Yesterday, and Precious Moments.

Bank, figural chicken wearing blue bandanna, 6.25" h, 6" l 12
Christmas Angel, wearing red coat with spaghetti trim, holding a dec Christmas tree and wreath, 5" h 25
Christmas Dish, poinsettia leaf, 6.5" x 4.5" .15

Cup and Saucer, pink roses on pearl luster ground, gold handle, 2.75" h ftd cup 20
Figurine, owl perched on leafy branch, 1979, 5.25" h 18
Figurine, Umbrella Girl, seated girl feeding seagull beneath large beach umbrella, seashells scattered on sand, pastel colors, 1989, 5" h 20
Figurine, white kitten on large brown shoe, 2.5" h, 3.5" l .10
Music Box, plays "Toy Symphony," key wind, #550094, 1986, 6.5" h 65
Nappy, double, chintz pattern, gold trim and center handle, 8.5" x 4.5" 30
Ornament, Precious Moments, Angel On A Cloud, E5628, 1981-85, 3" h 75
Pillow Vase, Precious Moments, "May God's Blessing Be Upon You," 1985, 4.5" h, 4.5" w 15
Pitcher and Bowl, miniature, strawberry pattern, 4" h pitcher, 5.25" d bowl 15
Planter, hp Hummel-style girl holding a log, bird on tree stump beside her, E6202, 4.25" h, 4.75" w 50
Plate, multicolor peacock and flowers on white ground, 8.25" d 18
Salt and Pepper Shakers, Grandma and Grandpa, "You and Your One More Time" on Grandma's apron 40
Salt and Pepper Shakers, rooster and hen 15
Toothpick Holder, egg-shaped, hp violets on ivory ground, gold trim, 2" h 25
Vase, pitcher-shaped, miniature, hp geraniums on white ground, gold trim, 3.5" h 28

ERTL BANKS

This is another of those highly speculative areas that are addressed as the need arises. The 1980s and 1990s saw a surge in the number of cast-iron banks produced by several companies, Ertl being the most dominant. These banks were often made to commemorate special events or used as promotions or fundraising efforts for local charities.

Most of the Ertl banks were recently manufactured in Hong Kong. They should only be purchased if in fine condition or better and only if the original packaging is included. All of the banks are marked and numbered. Avoid any that are not marked. The serial numbers and series numbers are important in cataloging and pricing these items.

Club: Ertl Collectors Club, P.O. Box 500, Dyersville, IA 52040.

1905 Truck, Jewel Tea, MIP 75
1913 Ford Model T Delivery Truck, Hills Department Store logo, 1988, MIB 35
1913 Ford Model T Delivery Van, Pet Milk logo 45
1914 Chevrolet Run-About, Hershey's Chocolate Co logo 30
1920s Ford Delivery Truck, Pez, orig box, 1994 285
1923 1/2 Ton Truck, Wheels Of Time Jamboree, Macungie, PA, 1994 150
1929 Lockheed Airplane, Wings of Texaco Series #1, orig box 200
1930 Air Model Mystery Ship, airplane, Wings of Texaco Series #5, orig box . . .50
1931 Hawkeye Flatbed, Farmall 350 tractor on back 50
1932 Ford Van, Anheuser Busch logo, 1991 45
1932 Northrop Gamma, airplane, Wings of Texaco Series #2 65
1938 Chevy Panel Truck, Wheels Of Time Jamboree, Macungie, PA, orig box, 1993 100
1939 Dodge Airflow, Texaco Series #10, orig box, 1993 35
1953 Coca-Cola Truck, orig box 40
1954 GMC Series 950 Cab and Trailer, Ace Hardware logo 85

FANS, ELECTRIC

Many people think they have a gold mine when they come across a brass bladed fan. This is most often not the case. Plenty of common mass-produced brass bladed fans are still available. Condition determines price. If the paint is very good and the brass is polished, the price may jump up 50% compared to a similar fan in tarnished/rusty condition.

The most desirable fans are older and rarer models with features such as Art Deco design, exposed coils, a light bulb mounted on top of the motor, and use of an alternate power source.

Club: American Fan Collectors Assoc., P.O. Box 5473, Sarasota, FL 34277.

Akro Agate, oxblood base, 4 blades, 13" h 200
Art Deco Style, Bakelite motor housing, 7.5" blades 300
Century, #K-3, model 56, oscillator, 10" blades 15
Century, model 152, missing blade cage, 16" brass blades 20
Chicago Electric Mfg Co, Handybreeze, 8-879-E, SN3, 4 blades, olive drab cast iron base and enameled motor housing and blades, push button switch, 12" h, 9" d cage 65
Colonial Fan and Motor Co, style P16, 8" blades 465
Deluxe Casco 12
Diehl Mfg Co, J16912, 4 blades, oscillator, 1950s, 21" h, 20" d cage 125
Domestic Electric Co, S#2660, 30" h, 14.75" blades 110
Dominion, 5197, 4 aluminum blades, light brown cast iron base, steel cage, 12" h 9" d cage 60
Emerson, 4 blades, oscillator, 1930s, 24" h, 18" d cage 90
Emerson, type 11646, #118187, 12.5" blades 200
Emerson, type 19646, #135795, oscillator, 12.375" blades 75
Emerson, type 21546, #291125, oscillator, 12.5" blades 65
Emerson, type 21666, #781180, 13" brass blades 110

Emerson, type 27646, #A19253, oscillator, 12.5" brass blades 35
Emerson Trojan, type 53644, 8" blades 385
Eskimo, model 1100J, black enamel and chrome housing, 11" h, 8" blade d 30
General Electric, type AUU, #1223535, oscillator, 12" brass blades 30
Gilbert, Polar Club, P1849, 10" h 80
H Frost & Co, England, 3 blades, pink motor housing, ivory blades and forked base, 1950s 45
Hunter, style #V45780, type 10, oscillator, repainted 10" blades 25
Jandus, #448592, 8" blades 300
Luminaire, floor model 550
Menominee, oscillator, 8" blades 465
Northwind, type 44A, 8" blades 10
Northwind, type 444C, 8" blades 20
Robbins & Myers, list #2410, oscillator, 11.75" brass blades 15
Robbins & Myers, list #3500, 8" blades 15
Robbins & Myers, list #4504, 12" brass blades 20
Robbins & Myers, list #559435, oscillator, 16" blades 10
Victor Airplane, 110 volts, 50-60 cycles, alternating current, 12.25" blades 18
Vidrio Trojan, green agate base, 8" blades 130
Westinghouse, 6 brass blades, 3-speed, 16" h, 13" d cage 150
Westinghouse, style #164851, oscillator, 16" blades 20
Westinghouse, style #177109D, 16.125" brass blades 110
Westinghouse, style #803681, 4 blades, black base, 10.5" h 30
Westinghouse, style #1013812, 12" brass blades 100

NON-ELECTRIC

National Enameling and Stamping Co, Baltimore, MD, 20th Century Fly Fan, clockwork mechanism, patented 1893, 29" h 1,325
Jost Patent Radio Fan, 36.5" h, 21.5" brass blades 3,850
Lake Breeze, alcohol powered 2,000
New Thermo, Waukee, IA 1,000
Sterling Cycle Hot Air Floor Fan, very ornate, 45" h, 20.75" brass blades 7,150
Heat Generated, nickel plated, 21.5" h, 14" blades 875

FARM COLLECTIBLES

The agrarian myth of the rugged individual pitting his or her mental and physical talents against the elements remains a strong part of the American character in the 1990s. There is something pure about returning to the soil.

The Country look heavily utilizes the objects of rural life, from cast-iron seats to wooden rakes. This is one collectible area in which collectors want an aged, i.e., well-worn, appearance. Although most of the items were factory-made, they have a handcrafted look. The key is to find objects that have character—a look that gives them a sense of individuality.

Clubs: Antique Engine, Tractor & Toy Club, 5731 Paradise Rd., Slatington, PA 18080; Farm Machinery Advertising Collectors, 10108 Tamarak Dr., Vienna, VA 22182.

Bank, John Deere, litho tin canister, "John Deere Centennial 1837-1937" with plow logo on sides, 3.5" h, 2" d . . .110
Blueberry Rake, 11.5" w with 2.75" teeth, 8' l wooden handle 85
Buggy Wrench, "Joys Patent Feb 1 '98," nickel-plated, 10" l 75
Cabinet, wood, glass door, "Dr Lesure's Warranted Veterinary Medicines" on marquee, orig key, c1890s, 28.5" h, 15.75" w 1,500
Calendar, 1927, De Laval Cream Separators, boy sitting on steps, feeding scraps to puppy, sgd "Norman Price," ©1926 GE Co, 20.5" h, 9" w 100
Change Tray, Dr AC Daniel's Horse & Cattle Medicines, litho tin, scalloped rim, 3 white stallions in center, 4.25" d 1,700
Cigar Cutter, table top model, figural detailed frame with painting of cows, farmhouse, stream, and wildlife, frame emb "HA Schneck Allentown Cigars of Quality Maker," 7.5" h 1,500
Crumb Scraper and Tray, "CF Berquist & Co Lumber, Hardware, Farm Implements and Machiner," litho tin, image of kittens at table, 6.5" x 9.25" tray, 3" x 7" scraper 750
Knife Sharpener, "Sharpen Up Your Weed Control, Use Du Pont Lorox In Soybeans," multicolor soy field image, celluloid top, 2.25" d 30
Paperweight, Hartley Grain Co, glass, rect, black and white photo of farm grain service structure and office building, 1" x 2.5" x 4" 40
Plow Blade, Stanley #41, Millers patent adjustable, fillister bed and extra fence, type 4, with 9 cutters 950
Pocket Mirror, Sycamore Wagon Works, Sycamore, IL, celluloid, oval, image of Clover Leaf Dairy milk wagon, 2" x 2.75" 575
Tip Tray, "Success Manure Spreader, Kemp & Burpee Mf'g Co, Syracuse, NY USA," multicolor image of man driving a horse-drawn spreader, 4.875" x 3.375" 225
Windmill Weight, cast iron, Barnacle-eye rooster, Elgin, 18.5" h, 17.75" w 3,000
Windmill Weight, cast iron, Boss bull, Dempster, 13" h, 13.75" w 1,500
Windmill Weight, cast iron, bull, full-bodied, Simpson Windmill & Machine Co, 12.75" h, 13.5" w 1,000
Windmill Weight, cast iron, crescent-tail horse, Dempster, 15" h, 16" w 800
Windmill Weight, cast iron, cylinder, raised 5-point star on either end, mkd "BR4," 9.5" d 925
Windmill Weight, cast iron, horseshoe, 10.25" h, 8.75" w 925
Windmill Weight, cast iron, Hummer rooster, long-stem, Elgin, 13.25" h, 10" w 865
Windmill Weight, cast iron, letter "W," Althouse-Wheeler, 9" h, 16.5" w 975

Windmill Weight, cast iron, long-tail horse, flat, Dempster, 18.5" h, 17.5" w . . 925

Windmill Weight, cast iron, Mogul rooster, Elgin, 18" h, 20.5" w 5,000

Windmill Weight, cast iron, rainbow-tail rooster, Elgin, 19.25" h, 18.5" w 5,750

Windmill Weight, cast iron, squirrel, Elgin, 19.5" h, 13.5" w 3,750

Windmill Weight, cast iron, star, Halladay Standard, 15" h, 15" w 1,250

Windmill Weight, cast iron, warship *Monitor,* Baker Mfg Co, 7.5" h, 28.5" w 2,000

FARM TOYS

The average age of those who play with farm toys is probably well over thirty. Farm toys are adult toys. Collectors number in the tens of thousands. The annual farm toy show in Dyersville, Ohio, draws a crowd in excess of 15,000.

Beware of recent "limited" and "special edition" farm toys. The number of each toy being produced hardly qualifies them as limited. If you buy them other than for enjoyment, you are speculating. No strong resale market has been established. Collectors who are not careful are going to be plowed under.

Club: Antique Engine, Tractor & Toy Club, Inc., 5731 Paradise Rd., Slatington, PA 18080; Ertl Collectors' Club, P.O. Box 500, Dyersville, IA 52040.

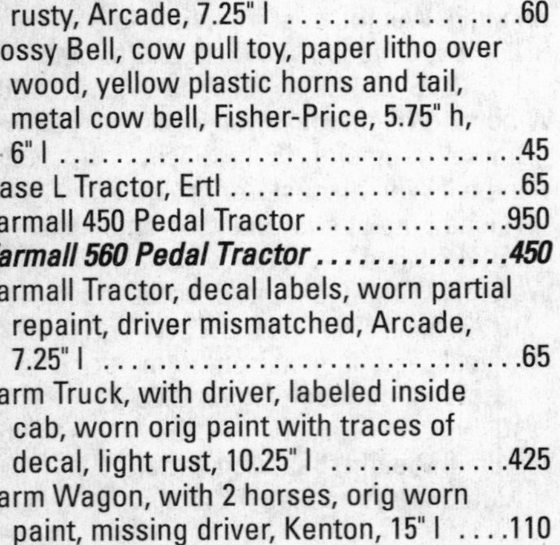

Allis-Chalmers Tractor, decal labels, rusty, Arcade, 7.25" l 60

Bossy Bell, cow pull toy, paper litho over wood, yellow plastic horns and tail, metal cow bell, Fisher-Price, 5.75" h, 6" l 45

Case L Tractor, Ertl 65

Farmall 450 Pedal Tractor 950

Farmall 560 Pedal Tractor 450

Farmall Tractor, decal labels, worn partial repaint, driver mismatched, Arcade, 7.25" l 65

Farm Truck, with driver, labeled inside cab, worn orig paint with traces of decal, light rust, 10.25" l 425

Farm Wagon, with 2 horses, orig worn paint, missing driver, Kenton, 15" l 110

Farm Wagon, with driver, 2 horses, and 2 wooden kegs, wagon wheels mkd "Arcade," 11" l 350

Fordson Tractor 17, with driver and visible engine, Craftoy 12

Ford Tractor, with dump wagon, worn old paint, Arcade, 15.25" l 225

International Harvester 856 Pedal Tractor 750

International Harvester 1026 Pedal Tractor 600

John Deere 10 Pedal Tractor 750

John Deere 20, D65 Pedal Tractor 475

John Deere 30 Pedal Tractor 325

John Deere 620 Pedal Tractor 900

John Deere 6600 Combine, Ertl 100

John Deere A Farm Tractor, Auburn Rubber 45

Loadster Grain and Cattle Stake Truck, Ertl 90

McCormick-Deering Farm Wagon, with 2 horses, decal label, orig paint with minor wear, Arcade, 12.5" l 250

McCormick-Deering Plow, decal label, orig paint with minor wear, Arcade . . . 225

McCormick-Deering Thresher, decal label, orig red paint, Arcade, 9.5" l 275

McCormick-Deering Tractor, worn decal, traces of orig paint, mismatched driver, Arcade, 7.25" l 60

Plow, "AC" monogram, old worn paint and nickel finish trim, Arcade, 5.75" l . . 110

Row Crop Tractor, decal labels, black rubber tires mkd "Arcade Balloon," orig paint, 5.25" l 40

Sulphide Marble, chicken, standing 115

Sulphide Marble, cow, standing, bubble around figure, surface abrasions 145

Sulphide Marble, sheep, standing, bubble around body, surface wear . . . 175

Tractor and Wagon, 8600, Ertl 65

FAST-FOOD COLLECTIBLES

If you haunt fast-food restaurants for the food, you are a true fast-food junkie. Most collectors haunt them for the give-aways. If you stop and think about it, fast-food collectibles are the radio and cereal premiums of the second half of the twentieth century. Look at what you have to eat to get them.

Whenever possible, try to preserve the original packaging of the premiums. Also, save those things which are most likely to be thrown out. I see a great many Happy Meals toys and few Happy Meals boxes.

Club: Fast Food Collectors Express, P.O. Box 221, Mayview, MO 64071; McDonald's Collectors Club, 1153 S. Lee St., Ste. 200, Des Plaines, IL 60016.

Burger King, action figures, set of 4 Archie wind-up racers, Archie in Model T, Veronica in Corvette, Betty in '57 Chevy, Jughead in Beetle, 1990 10
Burger King, figure, Creature From The Black Lagoon, 1997 4
Burger King, figure, Scooby & Shaggy, 1996 3
Burger King, key chain, Scooby Doo, plush, MIP 3
Burger King, Mystery Machine, glow-in the-dark, wind-up, 2000 3
Carl Jr's, DC Heroes Toy Set, Wonder Woman Spinner 20
Carl Jr's, Hercules Xena Mini Disc Launcher, 1996 3
Jack In The Box, figure, Wolfman, 1999 4
Kentucky Fried Chicken, Incredible Hulk Pencil Twirler, 1997 3
Kentucky Fried Chicken, Spiderman Wall Walker, 1997 3
McDonald's, Batman Returns, Batman in Batrocket, 1992, MIP 4
McDonald's, figure, Bugs Bunny wearing Superman suit, 1991 3
McDonald's, Hot Wheels Duracell Racer #88, 1992, MIP 2
McDonald's, Hot Wheels Mac Tonight NASCAR #6, 1998 2
McDonald's, Hot Wheels Police Car #8, 1997 2

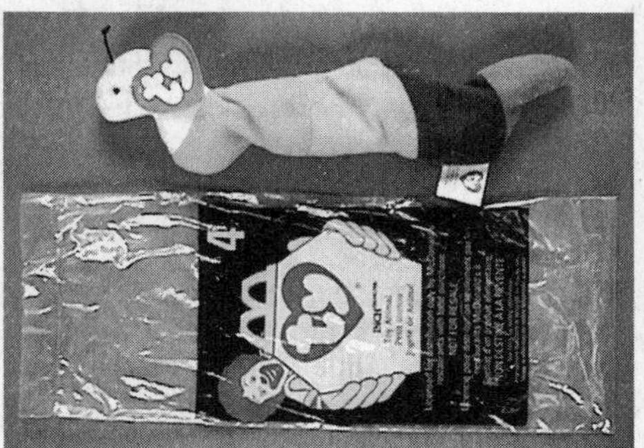

McDonald's, Teenie Beanie Baby, Inch the Worm, 1997 5

Taco Bell, Batman & Robin Animated Series, Batmobile, 1997 5
Taco Bell, Batman & Robin Animated Series, Mr Freeze Sleet Shooter 5
Wendy's, Felix the Cat Fortune Spinner 4
Wendy's, figure, Scooby hiding in a tree stump, 1998, MIP 3
Wendy's, Pinky & The Brain Brain-O-Vision, 1997, MIP 3

FENTON GLASS

Frank L. Fenton founded the Fenton Art Glass Company in Martins Ferry, Ohio, in 1905. Production began in 1907 and has been continuing ever since.

Early production included carnival, chocolate, custard, pressed, and opalescent glass. In the 1920s stretch glass, Fenton dolphins, and art glass were added. Hobnail, opalescent, and two-color overlay pieces were popular in the 1940s. In the 1950s Fenton began reproducing Burmese and other early glass types.

Throughout its production period, Fenton has made reproductions and copycats of famous glass types and patterns. Today these reproductions and copycats are collectible in their own right.

Clubs: Fenton Art Glass Collectors of America, Inc, P.O. Box 384, Williamstown, WV 26187, www.collectoronline.com/club-FAGCA.html; National Fenton Glass Society, P.O. Box 4008, Marietta, OH 45750.

Basket, Daisy & Button, Colonial Green, Olde Virginia Glass, 6" 25

Basket, Hobnail, amber, c1960s 32
Basket, Hobnail, Colonial Blue, c1960s . . .50
Basket, Hobnail, topaz opalescent, 1941-43, 4.5" 150
Basket, Hobnail, turquoise, c1936 50
Basket, Vasa Murrhina, autumn orange, 6435AO, 1965-68, 7" 85
Bell, Medallion, cameo satin with daisies, hp by Kay C, 1978-83 35
Bonbon, Dolphin, aquamarine blue, wheel cut, c1928, 6.5" 35
Bonbon, Persian Medallion, blue carnival glass, double handled, c1911 165
Bonbon, Silver Crest, ftd, c1948 38
Bowl, Basketweave, vaseline 65
Bowl, Black Rose, ruffled, 1953-54 225
Bowl, Blue Overlay, ruffled, c1943, 10" 55
Bowl, Hobnail, emerald opalescent, #3974, 1959-61, 9" 125
Bowl, Hobnail, ruby, 3-ftd, 7" d 30
Bowl, Jade Green, cupped rim, 3-ftd, c1932, 6" 36
Bud Vase, Hobnail, amber, 10.5" h 15
Bud Vase, Hobnail, emerald green opalescent, #3756, 1959-61, 8" 55
Bud Vase, Thumbprint, Colonial blue, 11" h 25
Candleholder, Hobnail, white milk glass, 1970s 20
Candlesticks, pr, Gold Crest, cornucopia shape, c1940s 95
Candlesticks, pr, Silver Crest, 6" h 75
Candy Dish, cov, Valencia, orange, c1970-74 50
Candy Dish, Silver Crest, ftd 48
Compote, Cactus, white milk glass, Olde Virginia Glass, 1967 30
Compote, Pinwheel, custard, 5" h, 6.5" w . .35
Compote, Stream of Hearts, Persian Medallion ext, marigold, ftd, c1925 120
Compote, turquoise milk glass, late 1950s, 3.5" h, 7" d 35
Condiment Set, white milk glass, chrome trim, glass spoon 185
Dresser Tray, Opal Mist, oval, tab handles, 12.5" 45
Epergne, Hobnail, 3-lily, white milk glass, 1960s, 3.5" h, 7.5" d 75
Fan Vase, Hobnail, topaz opalescent, 6" . .75
Fan Vase, Mongolian Green, #847, 1934-35, 5.5" 110
Fan Vase, Silver Crest, hp flowers, c1948 .48
Figure, butterfly on twig, custard 25
Figures, pr, birds, blue satin 60
Flower Box, custard, 1970s, 4" sq 25
Hurricane Candle Lamp, Snowcrest Swirl Optic, c1949 165
Ivy Ball, Hobnail, topaz opalescent, #3726, ftd 100
Jug, Hobnail, blue opalescent, #3865, 5.25" h 125
Jug, Hobnail, cranberry opalescent, #3964, 4.5" 95
Perfume Bottle, Willow Green, 7.5" h 40
Pitcher, Fern Optic, Dusty Rose Overlay, 1983-85, 5.5" h 65
Princess Slipper, Lavender Petals, hp by S Hopkins 21
Rose Bowl, custard, 4.5" h, 5.5" d 30
Rose Bowl, Hobnail, Colonial Blue, ftd, c1962 22
Toothpick Holder, Strawberry, custard . . .24
Top Hat Vase, Rose Crest, 1945, 4" h 45
Trumpet Vase, Aqua Crest, c1948, 6.5" h . .55
Vase, daisies on custard, 6.5" h, 6.5" d 50
Vase, Hobnail, blue opalescent, 4" 25
Vase, Hobnail, ruby, ftd 20
Vase, Jacqueline, vaseline, c1960, 6" 75
Vase, Mandarin, custard with Burmese highlights, satin finish ext, glossy int, 9.25" h, 5" d 165
Vase, Rose Mist, c1965, 9.5" 150
Vase, Vasa Murrhina, rose with adventurine green, c1964, 4" 75

FIESTA WARE

Fiesta was the Melmac of the mid-1930s. The Homer Laughlin China Company introduced Fiesta dinnerware in January 1936 at the Pottery and Glass Show in Pittsburgh, Pennsylvania. It was a huge success.

The original five colors were red, dark blue, light green (with a trace of blue), yellow, and ivory. Other colors were added later. Fiesta was redesigned in 1960, discontinued about 1972, and reintroduced in 1986. It appears destined to go on forever.

Values rest in form and color. Forget the rumors about the uranium content of early red-colored Fiesta. No one died of radiation poisoning from using Fiesta. However, rumor has it that they glowed in the dark when they went to bed at night.

Club: Fiesta Collectors Club, P.O. Box 471, Valley City, OH 44280.

Bowl, 4.75" fruit, medium green 425
Bowl, 5.5" fruit, medium green 65
Bowl, 12" salad, ftd, yellow 225
Bud Vase, red 110
Candleholders, pr, bulb, yellow 75
Candleholders, pr, tripod, yellow 400
Carafe, turquoise .220
Casserole, ivory 150
Chop Plate, 15", light green 40
Creamer, stick handle, cobalt 70
Cream Soup, red 65
Cup and Saucer, rings, medium green 50
Deep Plate, cobalt .70
Demitasse Cup and Saucer, chartreuse .530
Demitasse Cup and Saucer, cobalt 90
Lid, #4 mixing bowl, ivory 1,400
Nested Mixing Bowl, #1, turquoise 240
Nested Mixing Bowl, #4, ivory 180
Nested Mixing Bowl, #4, light green 100
Nested Mixing Bowl, #5, turquoise 90
Nested Mixing Bowl, #7, turquoise 60
Platter, oval, 12" l, light green 32
Relish Tray, ivory .185
Relish Tray, turquoise 300
Salt and Pepper Shakers, cobalt 30
Sauceboat, red 60
Teapot, medium, rose 275
Tumbler, juice, 5 oz, gray 200
Tumbler, water, 10 oz, turquoise 50
Vase, 10", turquoise 900
Vase, 12", cobalt 1,100
Water Pitcher, disk, chartreuse 275
Water Pitcher, disk, cobalt 125
Water Pitcher, disk, rose 190

FIGURINES

Looking for a "small" with character? Try collecting figurines. Collecting interest in the colorful figurines has grown considerably during the past ten years. Pieces are starting to become pricey. However, there are still bargains to be found at garage sales and flea markets.

Club: Ceramic Arts Studio Collectors Assoc., P.O. Box 46, Madison, WI 53701.

Note: See Angels, Animal Figurines and specific manufacturers for additional listings.

American Art Clay Co, Art Deco style bust of woman, glossy caramel glaze, ink stamp mark, 8" h 120
Bing & Grondahl, Adam, #2231, 6.5" h 85
Bing & Grondahl, Bears, #1825, 7.5" h . . .300
Bing & Grondahl, Boy with Crab, #1870, 7.5" h 180
Bing & Grondahl, Clown, hands in pockets, #2510, 4.25" h 55
Bing & Grondahl, Great Dane, #2190, 2.75" h 80
Bing & Grondahl, King Fisher, #1619, 4.5" h 100
Bing & Grondahl, Owl, #1800, 4.5" h 90
Bing & Grondahl, Polar Bear, #1629, 4.5" h 130
Boehm, baby crested flycatcher, stamp mark, 5.25" h, 3.25" l 80
Bosch-Freres Keramis, rooster, beige, blue, and green crystalline matte glazes, stamped "BF/K201," 6.25" h 70
Cybis, Little Red Riding Hood, wearing white cape and red gloves, 6.5" h 140
Cybis, Wendy, young girl in nightgown holding doll, sgd, 6.5" h 125
Cordey China, blonde hair in ringlets, bust of a lady, #5011/17, 6" h 260
Dresden, lady, wearing lacy green ruffled dress and bonnet, holding flower basket, 3.5" h 285
Florence Ceramics, Louise, 5.5" h 260
Homer Laughlin, Maverick Lamb, gold . . .55
Italy, Irish setter puppy, 3.5" h, 6.25" l 60
Italy, white poodle, 3.375" h, 6.5" l 65
Japan, birds, pr, pink with gold highlights, 6" h, 16" l 45

Japan, Chinese couple, hp porcelain, man holding mandolin, woman holding fan, 7" h 36
Japan, man in chair, porcelain, wearing 18th C costume 8
Keramous, young maiden, wearing bonnet and holding floral bouquet, polychrome glazes, ink stamp, 8" h 40
Lefton, Bloomer Girl, bisque, 4" h 50
Lenox, Tea At The Ritz, 8.5" h 285
Overbeck, colonial woman wearing pink and blue striped dress, incised "OBK," 5" h 300
Ram Pottery, black woman laundering clothes with washboard, brown, yellow, and ivory glazes, incised signatures, Nan Dean and Sally Langford, dated 8/23/95, 9" h 110
Royal Copenhagen, 2 children with dog, #707, 6" h 285
Royal Copenhagen, beagle puppy, #565R, 3.5" h 175
Royal Copenhagen, black-headed gull, #1468, 2.5" h 90
Royal Copenhagen, blacksmith, #4502, 8.75" h 375
Royal Doulton, Autumn Breezes, ink stamp, 7.75" h 125
Royal Worcester, Grandmother's Dress, young girl in yellow dress, ink stamped, small chip to base, 6.5" h 30
Wayland Gregory, Rooster, white glossy glaze, silver leaf details, script signature, 14" h, 13.5" w 225
Weller, Pop-eye Dog, black and brown features on white ground, incised mark, 3.75" h 400
Zsolnay, peasant girl carrying platter, lustered green and yellow glazes, medallion mark, 8.5" h 110

FIRE-KING

Remember those great coffee mugs you used to find at diners? Those nice big warm cups filled to the brim by a smiling waitress, not the Styrofoam of this decade. Chances are they were Fire-King mugs. Fire-King dinnerware and ovenware was sold in sets from the 1940s through the 1970s. The company guaranteed to replace broken pieces and their colorful wares were quite popular with housewives. While Fire-King has been around for many years, collectors are now discovering quantities at flea markets and many are enjoying this new collecting area.

Club: Fire-King Collectors Club, 1406 E. 14th St., Des Moines, IA 50316.

Alice, cup and saucer, jade-ite 70
Apple, mixing bowl, 9.5" d, jade-ite 42
Charm, berry bowl, 4.75" d, jade-ite 17
Charm, bowl, 4.75" d, azur-ite white 9
Charm, cup and saucer, azur-ite white 5
Charm, luncheon plate, azur-ite white 7
Charm, soup bowl, 6" d, jade-ite 36
Charm, sugar, cov, jade-ite 20
Jade-ite, ashtray, 4.25" d 35
Jade-ite, batter bowl, 7.5" d 20
Jade-ite, skillet, 1 spout 135
Jade-ite, skillet, 2 spout 190
Jane Ray, creamer and sugar, jade-ite 35
Jane Ray, platter, 12" d, jade-ite 25
Jane Ray, salt and pepper shakers, pr, jade-ite 60
Jane Ray, soup bowl, 7.5" d, jade-ite 30
Jane Ray, sugar, cov, jade-ite 35
Jane Ray, vegetable bowl, 8.25" d, jade-ite 43
Red Dot, grease jar 35
Red Dot, salt and pepper shakers, pr 40
Restaurant Ware, after dinner cup and saucer 112

Restaurant Ware, bowl, 5" d 47
Restaurant Ware, bread and butter plate, 5.5" d 15
Restaurant Ware, cup and saucer, 6 oz . .105
Restaurant Ware, eggcup 60
Restaurant Ware, grill plate 25
Restaurant Ware, luncheon plate 60
Restaurant Ware, milk pitcher, 20 oz 88
Restaurant Ware, platter, 8.75" d 95
Restaurant Ware, platter, 9.5" d 60
Restaurant Ware, soup bowl, flat 125
Sapphire, cereal bowl 23
Sapphire, nurser, 4 oz 15
Tulip, mixing bowl, 7.5" d, white 30
Tulip, mixing bowl, 9.5" d, white 40
Turquoise, plate, 7" d 12
Wheat, cup and saucer 95

FISHER-PRICE TOYS

In 1930 Herman Guy Fisher, Helen Schelle, and Irving R. Price founded the Fisher-Price Toy Company in Birmingham, New York. From that year forward, Fisher-Price toys were built with a five-point creed: intrinsic play value, ingenuity, strong construction, good value for the money, and action. With these principles and manufacturing contributions, the Fisher-Price Toy Company has successfully maintained quality and creativity in the toy market.

The collectibility of Fisher-Price toys is a direct reflection upon their desirability due to their unique characteristics and subject matter.

Club: Fisher-Price Collectors Club, 1442 N. Ogden, Mesa, AZ 85205.

Note: Listings for toys in good condition.

Amusement Park, #932 18
Big Bill Pelican, #794 15
Buzzy Bee, bumble bee, 6" h, 5.5" w 45
Change-A-Tune Carousel, #170 30
Chug-Chug Train, #168 20
Circus Train, #991 .35
Donald Duck, #765, 8" h, 6" l 110
Duck Family, #777 .18
Farm Animal House, #1005 4
Fred Flintstone Xylophone, #712 90
Granpa Frog, 5.5" h, 6" l 55

Happy Apple Chime, #435 3
Huffy Puffy Train 15
Jalopy, #724 3
Jolly Jumper, frog, #450, 4.5" h, 6" l 65
Lady Bug 5
Little People Barn Farm, #915 35
Little People Hospital 15
Merry Mousewife, #662 10
Molly Moo Cow, #132 15
Music Box Record Player, with 2 records 30
Nosey, #445, 6.5" h, 6" l 45
Parrot, 6" h, 5.5" l 70
Pelican, #794, 8" h, 9" w 50
Pony Chimes, #758, 6.5" h, 13.5" l 60
Record Player, #995 50
Roly Poly Chime Ball, #165 5
Seal, 7" h, 5" l 45
Snoopy, #180, basset hound, 5.5" h, 16" l . .45
Teddy Zilo, #752, c1948, 11" h, 9" w 85
Three Men In A Tub, #142 15
Timmy Turtle, #125, 6.5" h, 12.5" l 50
Tiny Tim, turtle, 3.75" h, 6.5" l 45
Toot-Toot Train, #643 5

FISHING COLLECTIBLES

A lot has been written recently about the increasing value of fishing tackle of all types. What has not been said is that high-ticket items are limited in number. Most sell for less than $5.

Fishing collectors emphasize condition. If a rod, reel, lure, or accessory shows heavy use, chances are its value is minimal. Original packaging is also important, often doubling value.

Collectors seek wooden plugs made before 1920 (most that survive were made long after that date), split bamboo fly rods made by master craftsmen (not much value for commercial rods), and reels constructed of German silver with special details and unique mechanical action. Advertising and other paper ephemera round out a collection. Find a pile of this material and you will have made a good catch.

Clubs: American Fish Decoy Assoc., 624 Merritt St., Fife Lake, MI 49633; American Fish Decoy Collectors Assoc., P.O. Box 252, Boulder Junction, WI 54512; National Fishing Lure Collectors Club, H.C. #33, Box 4012, Reeds Spring, MO 65737; Old Reel Collectors Assoc., 160 Shoreline Walk, Alpharetta, GA 30022.

Bait Tin, handmade, oval, copper bottom, hinged lid with screened cut-out heart, 2 tin belt loops on back, painted star and dots on side and bottom, some old green paint, 4.25" l .... .465

Book, *The Fly-Fisher's Entomology,* Alfred Ronalds, 6th ed, 1862, 20 color plates, with accompanying 47-pocket leather fly wallet with parchment pgs .415

Bootjack, maple, stamped "Thomas Rod Co., 170 Park Street, Bangor Maine," 2 swiveling wood legs, hole in end for hanging, 11" l 110

Bottle, Meek Reel Oil, cork stopper, partial contents, label has slight wear on 1 side 525

Brook Trout, mounted by David Footer, Lewiston, Maine, caught early 1970s in Moose Head Lake, Maine, 5 lb, 19" l, mounted on 11" x 24" rect pine board with scalloped edges 550

Calendar Print, Off Limits, Ralph Crosby Smith, fisherman with leaping trout, mother bear and cubs watching, shrink wrapped, 22" x 29" 110

Candy Container, fish-shaped, Victorian, papier mâché, large glass eye, painted silver with red mouth and tail accents, dark olive colored back with flap opening, 8.5" l 415

Fish Grabber, spring loaded, mkd "Norlund's Patent," 45" l 110

Fly Box, Hardy Neroda, with large clips and approx 2 dozen flies, 4" x 6" 300

Lobster, wood, realistically carved, old red paint, 16" l lobster mounted on 19" oval plaque 250

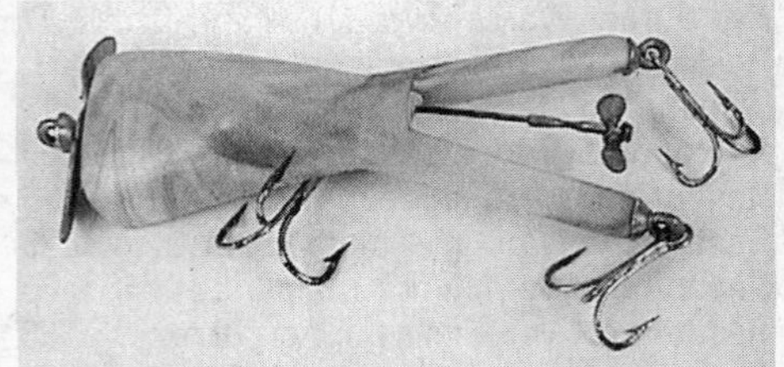

Lure, Bakelite frog, green marbleized 85

Lure, Heddon Musky Minnow #700, 3 hooks, cup hardware, marked props, glass eyes, green crackleback with hp gill marks, 4 belly weights, 5" l ...2,425

Minnow Bucket, Abbey & Imbrie, galvanized, lift-out liner, 9" x 12" multicolored oval paper label with image of large mouth bass and "Abbey & Imbrie/ Fishing Tackle/New York" 400

Minnow Trap, green glass, 6-sided jar with slight funnel opening on one end, Mason jar lids on both ends (1 solid for carrying bait, 1 perforated for water flow), 4" x 7" 275

Pitcher, Royal Doulton, "The Poacher Copr 1954," fisherman's head, trout handle, 7" h 300

Salmon Rod, "The Wye," Hardy, 3-pc, 2-tip, rubbed ball butt button, sliding screw locking band reel seat, thread locking ferrules, agate stripper, turned walnut ferrules, plugs and intermediate winds, orig canvas case with reel seat wrench, 10.5' l 415

Sculpture, wood, hand carved, detailed, bass hooked on Heddon crackleback minnow lure leaping from roots of tree stump and cattails, sgd "MB Fox 1988," 26" h 200

Sign, "Fishing Tackle," painted yellow and black with orange trim, green frame, signed "Herb Blackburn 1936" on back, 25" x 37" 450

Tackle Box, mahogany, mortise and tenoned corners, 4 divided lift-out trays, 2 brass-plated latches, worn leather handle, 20" x 12" x 10" h 350

Weather Vane, figural fish, hollow copper body, raised scale and gill details, on 43" iron shaft with iron flange, with round copper ball ornament and directionals, 25" l 300

FLAGS & FLAG COLLECTIBLES

A basic rule of collecting—the more made, the lower the value—holds true for flags as well; ask anyone who owns a 48-star flag.

Old flags are fragile and can be difficult to display. Hanging them often leads to deterioration. If you own flags, you should be aware of flag etiquette as outlined in Public Law 829, 7th Congress, approved December 22, 1942.

Many collectors do not collect flags themselves but items that display the flag as a decorative motif. A flag-related sheet music collection is one example.

Club: North American Vexillological Assoc., 1977 N. Olden Ave., PMB 225, Trenton, NJ 08618.

ABC Blocks, wood, lithographed paper, American flag style letters on 1 side, animal figures on reverse, set of 20 75
Advertising Trade Card, William's Yankee Soap, draped American flag, finely ruled beige-lined ground 110
Candy Box, Dresden type, top hat shaped, red and white diagonal stripes, star band, 2" h 50
Child's Book, *Yankee Doodle,* Uncle Sam riding horse and American flag motif drapes on cov, printed by McLoughlin Bros, NY 110
Christmas Ornament, Dresden, paper body with Dresden skirt and halo, flag border around skirt, 5" l 230
Christmas Ornament, scrap, diecut lady draped with American flag and wearing cotton batting dress, red and blue ribbon with gold tinsel, 12" l 135
Doll, boy, composition, dressed in an American flag costume, 11.5" h 135
Figure, Mama Katzenjammer wearing American flag outfit, black hair, painted eyes and brows, composition hands and feet, 10" h 275
Flag, 7 stars, linen, 5.25" x 3.25" 10
Flag, 39 stars, silk, hand stitched, 24" x 14", framed 175
Flag, 45 stars, 90" x 56", faded stars and white stripes, top and bottom red stripes replaced, 5 small mended holes 50
Flag, 48 stars, flown on US LCT 1181 Flotilla 33, WWII, crew members' names on flag, heavily battered and torn, missing approx 1/4 of stripe area on right, blue field punctuated with holes 80
Flag, 48 stars, rough linen material, 3.5" x 6", 10" stick 5
Flag, 49 stars, cotton, "Best 2 x 2 ply; 100% cotton-bunting; Valley Forge Flag Co., Spring City, Pa" label, 60" x 108" . . . 60
Flag Banner, Dresden, 12 Dresden stars, Dresden border with swags, printed on back "Hellig Olav 4/June 1910," 5" l, 2.25" w 465
Horn, tin, red, white, and blue flag motif, 23" l 100
Parasol, American flag material with red tassels, metal frame with bamboo shaft, tip of shaft jagged, 11" d open size, 17.5" l 140

FLAMINGOS

Flamingos offer a wide range of collectibles, from lovely art glass vases to pink plastic yard birds. The most popular flamingos are the graceful ceramic figurines produced en masse in the late 1940s and early 1950s. These were usually sold in pairs with one standing upright and the mate standing in a head-down pose. Measurements for pairs always refer to the upright flamingo.

Raised wing or in-flight flamingos, TV lamps, and planters are more difficult to find. White flamingos were produced, but they hold little interest to collectors. Also highly prized are mirror-framed air-brushed prints produced by Turner and copycats from that period.

Ashtray, ceramic, Florida souvenir, flamingos and palm trees on shore, leaping sailfish in distance, 1950s 15
Ashtray, metal, map of Florida with alligator, swordfish, palm tree, and flamingo, metallic paints, 1950s 15
Automobile License Plate, large wading flamingo, palm tree in background, "Boost Pan-American Exposition, Official, Miami" 18

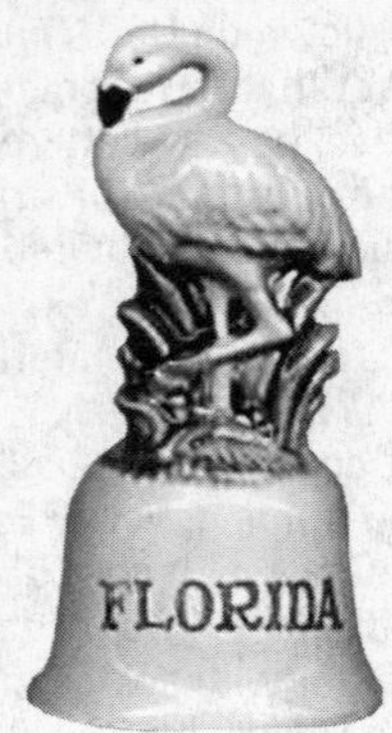

Bell, Florida souvenir, figural flamingo, 4.25" h 10

Beverage Set, insulated plastic, flamingos on pitcher and 6 tumblers, HJ Stotter, NY, 1950s, 11" h pitcher, 6" h tumblers . .20

Fan, hp paper, Florida souvenir, flamingos, alligator, palm trees, 18 sticks, 1950s . . .30

Figure, hand-blown glass, shaded pink and white body, yellow legs, 1950s 20

Figures, pr, ceramic, 1 standing upright, 1 with head down, Will George 150

Lawn Ornament, plastic, metal wire leg . .20

Pin, lucite, pink and white body with black accents 100

Salt and Pepper Shakers, thimble shape, hp palm tree on 1, flamingo on other . . .20

Snow Dome, Florida souvenir, plastic, palm trees, 2 flamingos, and setting sun 12

Swizzle Sticks, glass, pink flamingo tops, set of 8 10

TV Lamp, flamingo and seashells, 1950s .125

FLASHLIGHTS

The flashlight owes its origin to the search for a suitable bicycle light. The Acme Electric Lamp Company, New York, NY, manufactured the first bicycle light in 1896. Development was rapid. In 1899 Conrad Hubert filed a patent for a tubular hand-held flashlight. Two years later, Hubert had sales offices in Berlin, Chicago, London, Montreal, Paris, and Sydney.

Conrad Hubert's American Eveready company has dominated the flashlight field for the past century. National Carbon purchased the balance of the company in 1914, having bought a half-interest in it in 1906. Aurora, Chase, Franco, and Ray-O-Vac are other collectible companies.

Collectors focus on flashlights from brand name companies, novelty flashlights, and character licensed flashlights.

Club: Flashlight Collectors of America, P.O. Box 4095, Tustin, CA 92681.

Aurora, tubular, nickel case, 2 C batteries 30

Beacon, tubular, vulcanite case, nickel ends, 2 C batteries, 1919 18

Bond, tubular, nickel-plated brass case, 2 D batteries, 1930 15

Boy Scout, right angle, olive drab painted case, official BS emblem above switch 25

Bright Star, penlight, 2 AA batteries 10

Burgess, vest pocket, #2, Art Deco checkerboard pattern, 1928 12

Chase, vest pocket, nickel-plated, hinged bottom, slide switch, 3" x 1.5" x .75" 25

Eveready, candle, #1654, Art Deco nickel-plated case, opaque milk glass lens, 2 C batteries, 1932 35

Eveready, tubular, #2602, vulcanite case, nickel-plated ends, small bull's-eye lens, 2 C batteries, 1912 20

Eveready, tubular, #2632, nickel-plated case and ends, small bull's-eye lens, 3 D batteries, 1915 25

Eveready, tubular, #2660, black painted case, nickel ends, beveled lens, 2 D batteries, 1924 35

Eveready, vest pocket, #6662, nickel-plated case, ruby push button switch, 3 AA batteries, 1904 25

Eveready Daylo, tubular, #2616, vulcanite case, nickel ends, large bull's-eye lens, 2 D batteries, 1917 20

Eveready Daylo, tubular, #2630, nickel-plated, small bull's-eye lens, 2 C batteries, 1917 15

Eveready Lantern, #4708, round, nickel case, large bull's-eye lens, 1915 45

Eveready Liberty Daylo, box lantern, #3661, gun metal finish, 1919 30

Eveready Masterlite, table model, #2238, nickel-plated case, opaque milk glass globe, 2 C batteries, 1935 35

Eveready Masterlite, tubular, #2354, 3 D batteries, 1935 .28
Franco, tubular, vulcanite case, nickel ends, 3 D batteries, 1918 .20
Franco, vest pocket, green glass button switch .25
Jack Armstrong Light, black, 1 D battery .28
Kwik-lite, tubular, nickel, case unscrews in middle of tube, 2 C batteries .15
Military, right angle, olive drab, interchangeable lenses, 2 D batteries .18
Olin, tubular, chrome case, orig box, 7.5" l .50
Ray-O-Vac, tubular, Captain Ray-O-Vac, 2 D batteries .200
Ray-O-Vac, tubular, Space Patrol, 2 D batteries .35
Stewart Browne, Bakelite case, 2 D batteries .30
Yale, 3-Way Signal, 3 bulbs, 3 D batteries .30
Yale, tubular, #3302, double-ended, flood lens 1 end, spot lens other end, 3 D batteries .24

FLATWARE

Flatware refers to forks, knives, serving pieces, and spoons, There are four basic types of flatware: (1) sterling silver, (2) silver plated, (3) stainless, and (4) Dirilyte.

Sterling silver flatware has a silver content of 925 parts silver per thousand. Knives have a steel or stainless steel blade. Silver plating refers to the electroplating of a thin coating of pure silver, 1,000 parts silver per thousand, on a base metal such as brass, copper, or nickel silver. While steel only requires the addition of 13% of chromium to be classified stainless, most stainless steel flatware is made from an 18/8 formula, i.e., 18% chromium for strength and stain resistance and 8% nickel for a high luster and long-lasting finish. Dirilyte is an extremely hard, solid bronze alloy developed in Sweden in the early 1900s. Although gold in color, it has no gold in it.

Most flatware is purchased by individuals seeking to replace a lost or damaged piece or to expand an existing pattern. Prices vary widely. The listings represent what a replacement service quotes a customer.

SILVERPLATE

1847 Rogers, Legacy, c1928

Berry Spoon .40
Butter Knife, master, flat .7
Butter Spreader, individual, flat-handled .10
Cocktail Fork .10
Cold Meat Fork .15
Dessert Spoon .10
Dinner Fork .10
Dinner Knife, French blade .10
Flat Server .40
Gravy Ladle .30
Pickle Fork .20
Pie Server, flat-handled .40
Salad Fork .10
Sugar Tongs .30
Teaspoon .10

Community Plate, Evening Star, c1950

Berry Spoon .50
Butter Knife, master, flat .5
Butter Spreader, individual, flat-handled .12
Carving Set, 2-pc, steak size .80
Cocktail Fork .10
Cold Meat Fork .20
Cream Soup Spoon .10
Dessert Spoon .6
Flat Server .80
Gravy Ladle .35
Jelly Server .15
Luncheon Fork .9
Luncheon Knife, modern blade .10
Pie Server, flat-handled .80
Pie Server, hollow-handled, cake style .50
Salad Fork .10

Soup Ladle, hollow-handled 195
Soup Spoon, round bowl 10
Sugar Spoon 5
Tablespoon 12
Tablespoon, pierced 30
Teaspoon 6

Holmes & Edwards, Lovely Lady, c1937

Berry Spoon 45
Butter Knife, master, flat-handled 5
Butter Spreader, individual, flat-handled 10
Cocktail Fork 9
Cold Meat Fork 30
Dessert Spoon 7
Dinner Fork 10
Dinner Knife, modern blade 10
Gravy Ladle 30
Ice Tea Spoon 10
Jelly Server 20
Pie Server, flat-handled 119
Pie Server, hollow-handled 79
Salad Fork 7
Soup Spoon, oval 7
Soup Spoon, round bowl 12
Sugar Spoon 5
Tablespoon 10
Tablespoon, pierced 30
Teaspoon 6

Nobility Plate, Windsong, c1955

5 O'Clock Spoon 10
Carving Set, 2-pc, steak size 70
Cocktail Fork 10
Cold Meat Fork 30
Cream Soup Spoon 7
Dessert Spoon 10
Flat Server 30
Gravy Ladle 25
Pie Server, flat-handled 45
Sugar Spoon 10
Tablespoon 10

STERLING SILVER

International, Wild Rose, c1948

Berry Spoon 175
Butter Spreader, individual, flat-handled 30
Butter Spreader, individual, hollow-handled, paddle blade 30
Cold Meat Fork, small 90
Cream Soup Spoon 35

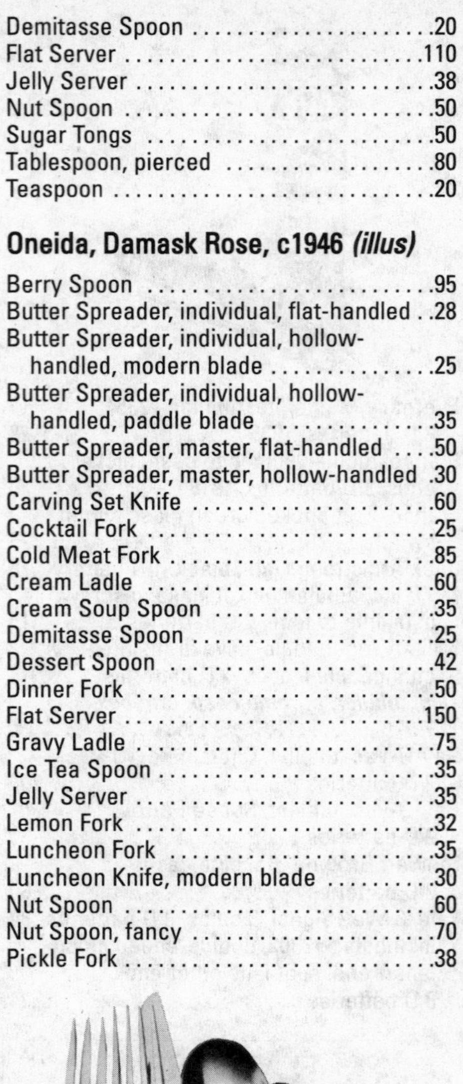

Demitasse Spoon 20
Flat Server 110
Jelly Server 38
Nut Spoon 50
Sugar Tongs 50
Tablespoon, pierced 80
Teaspoon 20

Oneida, Damask Rose, c1946 *(illus)*

Berry Spoon 95
Butter Spreader, individual, flat-handled 28
Butter Spreader, individual, hollow-handled, modern blade 25
Butter Spreader, individual, hollow-handled, paddle blade 35
Butter Spreader, master, flat-handled 50
Butter Spreader, master, hollow-handled 30
Carving Set Knife 60
Cocktail Fork 25
Cold Meat Fork 85
Cream Ladle 60
Cream Soup Spoon 35
Demitasse Spoon 25
Dessert Spoon 42
Dinner Fork 50
Flat Server 150
Gravy Ladle 75
Ice Tea Spoon 35
Jelly Server 35
Lemon Fork 32
Luncheon Fork 35
Luncheon Knife, modern blade 30
Nut Spoon 60
Nut Spoon, fancy 70
Pickle Fork 38

Pie Server, hollow-handled, cake style . . .60
Salad Fork 32
Sugar Spoon 35
Sugar Tongs 60
Tablespoon 75
Tablespoon, pierced 85
Teaspoon 25

Reed & Barton, Classic Rose, c1954

Butter Spreader, individual, flat-handled . .30
Butter Spreader, individual, hollow-handled, paddle blade 30
Cheese Server 45
Cocktail Fork 35
Cream Ladle 45
Demitasse Spoon 30
Gravy Ladle 85
Jelly Server 38
Lemon Fork 35
Nut Spoon 50
Pickle Fork 35
Salad Set, spoon and fork, flat-handled .375
Soup Spoon, oval bowl 45
Sugar Spoon 35
Tablespoon 85
Tablespoon, pierced 100
Teaspoon 28

Towle, Contessina, c1965

Butter Spreader, individual, hollow-handled, modern blade 25
Cocktail Fork 25
Cream Ladle 38
Jelly Server 30
Nut Spoon 28
Pickle Fork 25

Westmoreland, George & Martha, c1940

Butter Knife, master, flat-handled 38
Butter Spreader, individual, flat-handled . .25
Butter Spreader, individual, hollow-handled, paddle blade 28
Cocktail Fork 25
Cold Meat Fork 85
Cream Soup Spoon .35
Dessert Spoon 45
Gravy Ladle 60
Luncheon Fork 30
Luncheon Knife, French blade 30
Luncheon Knife, modern blade 30
Pie Server, hollow-handled, drop blade . . .55
Salad Fork 35
Salt Spoon 20
Sugar Spoon 30
Tablespoon 65
Tablespoon, pierced 75
Teaspoon 20

FLORENCE CERAMICS

Florence Ward of Pasadena, California, began making ceramic objects as a form of therapy in dealing with the loss of a young son. The products she produced and sold from her garage workshop provided pin money during the Second World War.

Florence Ceramics is best known for its figural pieces, often costumed in Colonial and Godey fashions. The company also produced birds, busts, candleholders, lamps, smoking sets, and wall pockets. Betty Davenport Ford joined the company in 1956, designing a line of bisque animal figures. Production ended after two years.

Scripto Corporation bought Florence Ceramics in 1964. Production was shifted to advertising specialty ware. Operations ceased in 1977.

Club: Florence Collector's Club, P.O. Box 122, Richland, WA 99352.

Ava, 10.5" h 200
Blue Boy, 11.75" h 500
Chinese Boy and Girl, pr, 8.5" h 100
Delia, 7.5" h 185
Girl, seated, planter, 5.25" h, 4.75" w 90

Her Majesty, 7" h 150
Irene, 6" h 80
June, planter, 7" h 40
Matilda, 8.5" h 165
Mimi, 6.25" h 100
Oriental Children, pr, 8.5" h 100
Our Lady of Grace, 9.5" h 300
Patricia, 7.25" h 140
Patsy, planter, 6" h 40
Polly, planter, 6" h 45
Scarlett, *Gone With the Wind,* 8.75" h . . .200
Vivian, 10" h 275
Wynkin' & Blynkin', pr, 5.5" h 375

FOOTBALL CARDS

Football cards are hot. Baseball card prices have reached the point where even some of the common cards are outside the price range of the average collector. If you cannot afford baseball, why not try football?

Football card collecting is not as sophisticated as baseball card collecting. However, it will be. Smart collectors who see a similarity between the two collecting areas are beginning to stress Pro-Bowlers and NFL All-Stars. Stay away from World Football material. The league is a loser among collectors, just as it was in real life.

Note: The prices listed below are for cards in very good condition.

Bowman, 1948, #21, Bill Chipley 90.00
Bowman, 1950, #10, Larry Craig 20.00
Bowman, 1953, #58, Harley Sewell. . . 40.00
Bowman, 1954, #127, Joe Koch. 6.00
Bowman, 1955, #87, Rick Casares . . . 16.00
Bowman, 1991, #7, Rob Moore 06
Bowman, 1991, #113, Troy Aikman 40
Bowman, 1992, #95, Clyde Simmons . .12
Bowman, 1993, #41, Eric Metcalf 10
Bowman, 1994, #295, Brett Favre 1.25
Bowman, 1995, #34, Ray Childress 04
Bowman, 1995, Bowman's Best Refractors, #V59, Trent Dilfer 7.25
Fleer, 1962, #62, Bill Mathis 1.75
Fleer, 1976, #41, Minnesota Vikings (Fran Tarkenton, Chuck Foreman; The Running Guards) 3.00
Fleer, 1979, Team Action, #39, Oakland Raiders (Pulling Out the Stops). 20
Fleer, 1985, Team Action, #38, Houston Oilers (Warren Moon, Earl Campbell; Retreating Into the Pocket) 2.40
Fleer, 1990, All-Pro, #40, Emmit Smith 14.00
Fleer, 1991, Ultra, #257, Gary Anderson .02
Philadelphia, 1964, #11, Dick Szymanski .50
Philadelphia, 1964, #124, YA Tittle 6.00
Topps, 1958, #23, Zeke Bratkowski . . . 1.25
Topps, 1958, #129, George Blanda . . . 10.50
Topps, 1959, #40, Bobby Layne 7.50
Topps, 1959, #55, Raymond Berry 4.50
Topps, 1959, #98, Green Bay Packer Pennant Card 70
Topps, 1959, #140, Bobby Mitchell . . . 10.50
Topps, 1960, #22, Milt Plum 70
Topps, 1960, #23, Jim Brown 25.00
Topps, 1960, #71, Los Angeles Rams . 1.50
Topps, 1961, #28, Dallas Cowboys . . . 3.00
Topps, 1961, #39, Bart Starr 9.00
Topps, 1961, #97, Billy Barnes 60
Topps, 1962, #72, Henry Jordan. 2.00
Topps, 1962, #151, Bill Kilmer. 4.50
Topps, 1962, #176, checklist. 30.00
Topps, 1964, #15, Don Oakes 1.75
Topps, 1964, #68, George Blanda 18.00
Topps, 1964, #96, Len Dawson. 22.00
Topps, 1964, #115, Gene Heeter 90
Topps, 1967, #100, Paul Rochester 70
Topps, 1967, #107, Fred Biletnikoff . . . 9.00
Topps, 1968, #25, Don Meredith 6.25
Topps, 1968, #89, Ron Mix 25
Topps, 1968, #127, Dick Butkus 11.00
Topps, 1969, #25, Johnny Unitas 7.50
Topps, 1969, #44, Dave Wilcox 30
Topps, 1969, #163, Jim Otto 1.25
Topps, 1972, #110, Gale Sayers 6.50
Topps, 1973, #268, Rufus Mayes 20
Topps, 1982, #302, Walter Payton 1.50
Topps, 1984, #191, Marcus Allen. 1.00
Topps, 1987, #340, Dan Fouts 20
Topps Stickers, 1961, complete set of 48 50

FOOTBALL MEMORABILIA

At the moment, this category is heavily weighted toward professional football. Do not overlook some great college memorabilia. Local pride dominates most collecting. Taking an item back to its hometown often doubles its value. Because of their limited production and the tendency of most individuals to discard them within a short time, some of the hardest things to find are game promotional giveaways. Also check the breweriana collectors. A surprising number of beer companies sponsor football broadcasts. Go Bud Light!

Bobbing Head, Holy Cross Crusaders, 1960s, made in Japan 106
Bobbing Head, Washington Redskins, "1962" stamped on bottom 500
Book, *Bear,* 3rd ed, 342 pgs, hard cover, dj boldly personalized and dated Dec 16, 1975, inside facing page autographed "To Tom Moon – Best Wishes, Bear Bryant" 125
Bookends, pr, figural busts of Knute Rockne, bronze, pale green, 7" h 150
Figure, Eddie George, Starting Lineup, Kenner, 1998 8
Figure, Jerry Rice, Starting Lineup, Kenner, 1995 6
Game Jersey, Efren Herrera, Dallas Cowboys team issue home jersey, "Dallas Cowboys by Sand-Knit" label with size "medium," player number "1" on front, "Herrera" and number "1" on back, game used, c1976 110

Game Ticket and Team Yearbook, unused ticket for Dec 26, 1960 championship game at Philadelphia's Franklin Field and 1960 Eagles team yearbook 700
Magazine,* The Saturday Evening Post, *Nov 15, 1913, sepia and red football theme cov by JC Leyendecker, 10.25" x 14" 35
Photograph, Bear Bryant, color, sgd boldly in black felt tip "To Gerald Plant – Best Wishes, Paul 'Bear' Bryant," 8" x 10" 70
Program, Dec 26, 1960 Philadelphia Eagles NFL championship game at Franklin Field in Philadelphia between Eagles and Green Bay Packers 525
Program and Ticket Stub, Super Bowl V, Jan 17, 1971 at the Orange Bowl in Miami, FL, program, full ticket stub . . .260
Ticket, unused, Dec 29, 1968 AFL championship game between NY Jets and Oakland, 3.5" x 11" 245
Ticket and Lineup Brochure, Knute Rockne Memorial Game, played Sep 26, 1931, at Notre Dame Stadium between Notre Dame "Players" and "Reserves," both ticket and brochure with Rockne photograph 435
Ticket Stub, Dec 27, 1964 championship game at Cleveland Stadium between Browns and Baltimore Colts 265
Ticket Stub, Dec 28, 1958 NFL championship game at Yankee Stadium between NY Giants and Baltimore Colts, staple mark near center 225

FOSTORIA GLASS

The Fostoria Glass Company was founded in Fostoria, Ohio, in 1887 and moved to Moundsville, West Virginia, in 1891. In 1983 Lancaster Colony purchased the company but produced glass under the Fostoria trademark.

Fostoria is collected by pattern, with the American pattern the most common and sought after. Other patterns include Baroque, Georgian, Holly, Midnight Rose, Navarre, Rhapsody, and Wister. Hazel Weatherman's *Fostoria, Its First Fifty Years,* published by the author about 1972, helps identify patterns.

Clubs: Fostoria Glass Assoc., 109 N. Main St., Fostoria, OH 44830; Fostoria Glass Collectors, P.O. Box 1625, Orange, CA 92856, www.fostoriacollectors.org; Fostoria Glass Society of America, P.O. Box 826, Moundsville, WV 26041.

American, crystal, bowl, handled, 9" d 45
American, crystal, candlesticks, pr, 3" h . .45
American, crystal, creamer, 3" h 15
American, crystal, creamer and cov sugar 45
American, crystal, decanter, stopper, 9.25" h 125
American, crystal, hat vase, 3" 25
American, crystal, ice tub, metal tongs . .100
American, crystal, mayonnaise bowl, flat top, 2.75" h, 6.25" d 25
American, crystal, nappy, tri-cornered, handled 10
American, crystal, oyster glass 18
American, crystal, platter, oval, 12" l 65
American, crystal, sugar cuber, metal lid and tongs 300
American, crystal, vase, sq ft, 9" h 65
Arlington, white milk glass, salt shaker and pepper mill, 5" h 75
Century, crystal, bowl, triangular, 3-ftd, 7.125" 15
Century, crystal, crescent salad plate, 7.5" 45
Century, crystal, cup and saucer 18
Century, crystal, divided relish, 2-handled, 7.375" l 20
Coin, amber, cigarette box, cov, 5.75" l . . .400
Coin, amber, oil lamp, 16.625" h 150
Coin, amber, salt and pepper shakers, 3.25" h 85
Coin, blue, cake plate, ftd, 6.5" h, 10" d . . .325
Coin, blue, compote, cov, ftd, 8.5" h 300
Coin, crystal, shaker, 3.25" h 35
Coin, olive green, cake plate, 6.5" h, 10" d 165
Coin, red, candy jar, cov, pedestal ft, 8.5" h 75
Colonial Dame, juice glass, green bowl, crystal stem, 4.75" h 18
Colony, crystal, bowl, 2-handled, 5" d 15
Colony, crystal, bowl, oblong, 8" l 30
Colony, crystal, bread and butter plate, 6" d 8
Colony, crystal, candlesticks, pr, 9" h 90
Colony, crystal, cocktail stem, 3.5 oz, 4" h .12

Colony, crystal, cup and saucer 16
Colony, crystal, goblet, ftd, 9 oz 20
Colony, crystal, individual creamer and sugar and tray 35
Colony, crystal, plate, 7" 12
Colony, crystal, sherbet stem, 5 oz 10
Colony, crystal, water goblet, 9 oz 18
Fairfax, green, butter dish, cov 125
Fairfax, green, compote, ftd, 7" 40
Fairfax, green, creamer and sugar 65
Fairfax, pink, creamer and sugar 65
Fairfax, pink, cup and saucer 22
Fairfax, pink, platter, oval, 12" 65
Fairfax, topaz, creamer and sugar 65
Hermitage, azure blue, icer bowl 40
Hermitage, topaz, sherbet 18
Horizon, cinnamon, coaster 12
Horizon, cinnamon, salad plate, 7" d 15
Horizon, spruce green, candy jar, cov, 5" d 50
Horizon, spruce green, creamer and sugar 40
Horizon, spruce green, salad plate, 7" 15
Horizon, teal green, console bowl, 2-handled, 12" l .48
Jamestown, blue, goblet, 9 oz, 5.875" h . . .25
Jamestown, pink, juice tumbler, ftd, 4.75" h 25
Jamestown, pink, salt and pepper shakers 95
Jamestown, pink, wine goblet, ftd, 4 oz . . .25
June, topaz, bouillon, ftd 25
June, yellow, plate, 6" 15
Lido, crystal, cup and saucer 45
Line 2183, pink milk glass, bowl, openwork rim, 9" sq 55
Oriental Etch, crystal, sherbet stem 25
Oriental Etch, crystal, tumbler, 5" 45
Oriental Etch, crystal, tumbler plate, 5" . . .18
Priscilla, amber, creamer and sugar 45
Priscilla, amber, custard, handled 20
Priscilla, amber, jug, ftd, 3 pt 145
Priscilla, amber, tumbler, handled, ftd 35

Priscilla, green, tumbler, handled, ftd, 6" h 45
Romance Etch, champagne stem, 5.5" h . .25
Royal, amber, flat soup, 7.75" d 30
Sun Ray, crystal, centerpiece bowl, double handled, 3" h, 14" x 9" 45
Trojan, topaz, #5000, pitcher 525
Tut, black, vase, 2-handled, 6.5" h 125
Vernon Etch, amber, compote, ftd, 5.5" h . .65
Versailles, blue, claret, 4 oz, 6" h 155
Versailles, blue, tumbler, ftd, 5.25" h 45
Versailles, pink, berry bowl, 5" 30
Victory Etch, crystal, sherbet stem, 5.25" h 18

FRANCISCAN

Charles Gladding, Peter McBean, and George Chambers organized the Gladding, McBean and Company pottery in 1875. Located in California, the firm's early products included sewer pipes and architectural items. In 1934 the company began producing dinnerware under the Franciscan trademark. The earliest forms consisted of plain shapes and bright colors. Later, the company developed molded, underglaze patterns such as Desert Rose, Apple, and Ivy.

Franciscan ware can be found with a great variety of marks—over 80 were used. Many of the marks include the pattern name and patent dates and numbers.

Club: Franciscan Collectors Club, 8412 5th Ave. NE, Seattle, WA 98115.

Autumn Leaves, ashtray, triangular 50
Coronado, burgundy gloss, bowl, 10.5" . . .45
Coronado, burgundy gloss, cup and saucer 18
Coronado, burgundy gloss, fruit bowl, small 15
Coronado, burgundy gloss, plate, 6.25" . . .12
Coronado, burgundy gloss, plate, 9.25" . . .18
Coronado, burgundy gloss, plate, 10.5" . . .30
Coronado, yellow gloss, bowl, 7.5" 16
Coronado, yellow gloss, creamer 15
Coronado, yellow gloss, cup and saucer .15
Coronado, yellow gloss, fruit bowl, small .15
Coronado, yellow gloss, plate, 6.25" 10
Coronado, yellow gloss, plate, 9.25" 15
Coronado, yellow gloss, platter, 13" 30
Coronado, yellow gloss, sugar, cov 20
Coronado, yellow matte, bowl, 7.5" 16
Coronado, yellow matte, cereal bowl 15
Coronado, yellow matte, cup and saucer .15
Coronado, yellow matte, flat soup 25
Coronado, yellow matte, plate, 11.5" 25
Coronado, yellow matte, plate, 6.25" 10
Coronado, yellow matte, plate, 9.25" 15
Coronado, yellow matte, salt and pepper shakers 20
Desert Rose, bread and butter plate 6
Desert Rose, cereal bowl 16
Desert Rose, creamer 20
Desert Rose, cup .12
Desert Rose, cup and saucer 15
Desert Rose, dinner plate, 10.5" 18
Desert Rose, flat soup 35
Desert Rose, mug, 10 oz 55
Desert Rose, mug, 7 oz 35
Desert Rose, platter 14.5" 65
Desert Rose, salad plate, 8" 12
Desert Rose, salt and pepper shakers, tall 65
Desert Rose, sugar, cov 45
Desert Rose, vegetable bowl, round, 9" . . .45
Madeira, cup and saucer 18
Madeira, dinner plate 20
Madeira, platter, oval 55
Madeira, salad plate, 8" 15
Madeira, saucer 10
Madeira, shaker, 3-hole 10
Starburst, ashtray, individual 40
Starburst, TV plate 95
Wildflower, ashtray 95

Wildflower, bread and butter plate 50
Wildflower, casserole, cov 800
Wildflower, chop plate, 12" 375
Wildflower, chop plate, 14" 450
Wildflower, creamer 150
Wildflower, cup and saucer 100
Wildflower, dinner plate 100
Wildflower, gravy boat 425
Wildflower, relish, oval 400
Wildflower, salad bowl, 10" 65
Wildflower, salad plate 60
Wildflower, sherbet 325
Wildflower, sugar 200
Wildflower, vegetable bowl 225
Wildflower, water pitcher 900

FRANKART

Every time there is an Art Deco revival, Frankart gets rediscovered. Frankart was founded in the mid-1920s by Arthur Von Frankenberg, a sculptor and artist.

Frankart figures were mass-produced and are identified through form and style, not specific features. While nudes are the most collectible, do not overlook other human figures and animals.

Almost every piece is marked with the company name followed by a patent number or "pat. appl. for." Avoid unmarked pieces. Frankenberg's wares were frequently copied during the late 1920s and early 1930s.

Bookend, nude woman, standing with arms at her side, one knee raised, 11" h 225
Bookends, pr, cocker spaniel, mkd, c1934, 6.5" 215
Bookends, pr, gazelle, sgd "Frankart Patent Applied For," orig felt on bases, 6.25" h, 7.25" l 150
Bookends, pr, nude startled by frog, Jap brown, paint loss, mkd "©1922," 10" h 325
Bookends, pr, nude startled by frog, verde, mkd "©1922," 10" h 685
Bookends, pr, sailing ships, mkd "Frankart Inc Pat Applied For," 7" h, 5" w 150
Bookends, pr, Scottie dogs, mkd "Frankart," 7" 200
Sculpture, nude, acrobatic pose, balanced on her upper back with legs straight up in the air, green and white marble base, mkd, 10.5" h 450

FRANKOMA

In 1933 John N. Frank, a ceramic art instructor at Oklahoma University, founded Frankoma, Oklahoma's first commercial pottery. Originally located in Norman, it eventually moved to Sapulpa, Oklahoma, in 1938. A series of disastrous fires, the last in 1983, struck the plant.

Look for pieces bearing a pacing leopard mark. These were produced earlier than items marked "FRANKOMA."

Club: Frankoma Family Collectors Assoc., 1300 Luker Ln., Sapulpa, OK 74066, www.frankoma.org.

Ashtray, inverted pyramid shape, green, individual size 25
Ashtray, "Oklahoma," #461, prairie green, 3.5" l 18
Beverage Set, #81 pitcher, 7.75" h, four #51c tumblers, and #91 round tray, 10" d, green, price for 6-pc set 90
Butter Dish, green, #4K 45
Christmas Plate, 1968, Flight into Egypt . . .25
Mug, donkey, autumn yellow, 1975 35
Mug, donkey, terra cotta, 1980 40
Mug, elephant, black, 1971 60
Mug, elephant, terra cotta, 1980 40
Salt and Pepper Shakers, pr, Art Deco design, peach 40
Vase, V-1 85
Vase, V-2 65
Vase, V-3 75
Wagon Wheels, creamer, prairie green . .20
Wagon Wheels, cup and saucer, prairie green 25

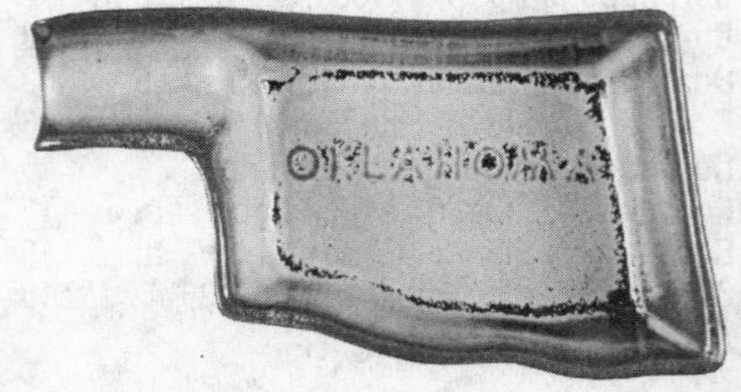

Wagon Wheels, dinner plate, prairie green 20
Wagon Wheels, fruit bowl, prairie green 12
Wagon Wheels, platter, prairie green 40
Wagon Wheels, salt and pepper shakers, prairie green 25
Wagon Wheels, sugar, prairie green 20
Wagon Wheels, teapot, prairie green, 2 cup 50
Wagon Wheels, vegetable bowl, prairie green 35

FRATERNAL ORDER ITEMS

Today, few people understand the dominant societal role played by fraternal orders and benevolent societies between 1850 and 1950. Because many had membership qualifications that were prejudicial, these "secret" societies often were targets for the social activists of the 1960s.

Many fraternal and benevolent organizations have disbanded. A surprising amount of their material has worked its way into the market. Some of the convention souvenir objects are downright funky. Costumes are great for dress-up. Do not pay big money for them. Same goes for ornamental swords.

Benevolent & Protective Order of Elks, card case, SS, c1930 45
Benevolent & Protective Order of Elks, whiskey decanter, Jim Beam, "Elks Club Centennial," 1968 65
Brotherhood of Railroad Trainmen, souvenir booklet, Ninth Biennial Convention held in Columbus, OH, May 1909 32
Eastern Star, boot, white china, gold emblem, 3.25" h, 3" l 10
Eastern Star, calendar towel, linen, printed emblem above calendar, 1966 15
Eastern Star, sewing kit, aluminum, blue enameled band on screw-off thimble lid, white cross and gold star on white enameled case, 1937 35
Independent Order of Odd Fellows, miniature urn, multicolor transfer on white china depicts OOF Home in Springfield, OH, made in Germany, 4.5" h 16

Knight Templar, postcard, black and white photo of "Knight Templar Parade, Michigan Avenue, Passing the Grand Stand," unused 5
Masonic, earrings, enameled Masonic emblem, gold-filled, screw backs, .25" d 28
Masonic, lapel pin, blue enameled emblem, 14K 15
Masonic, medal, 50-year award, copper pin bar, navy blue ribbon with copper caliper symbol pin, suspended medal emb "The Grand Lodge of Manitoba Ancient Free & Accepted Masons," c1937 35
Masonic, occupational shaving mug, carpenter and mason, 3.5" h, 2.5" d 175
Masonic, program, "Pittsburgh Commandery No. 1, KT, Monongahela House, January 29, 1891," gold-lettered satin cov 10
Masonic, souvenir spoon, Chicago skyline handle, Masonic Temple building in bowl, "Masonic Temple, Chicago, Ill," 5.25" l 85
Shriner, drinking glass, clear, red and black enameled names of officers and members of Murat Temple Lodge, IN, hobnail base, 1964 15
Shriner, fez, red, "Nemesis" and emblem in brass threading on front, black tassel, orig label reads "Made by Haller & Haller 'The Fez House' of Columbus, Ohio, exclusively for the 'Jap' Fuller Toggery Shop of Parkersburg, W VA," size 7 1/8 45
Shriner, hand fan, cardboard with wooden handle, fez shape with adv for "Moolah Shrine Circus," 7" x 8" 50

Shriner, ironstone platter, oval, York design made for the Mecca Temple, New York City, NY, by Shenango, 8.25" l 10
Shriner, plate, white china, Medinah Temple Ladies Night, Oct 25, 1901, emblem in center, gold trim, Syracuse China, 8" d 40
Shriner, postcard, Shriners Hospital, Philadelphia, c1940s 8

FROG COLLECTIBLES

A frog collector I know keeps her collection in the guest bathroom. All the bathroom fixtures are green also. How long do you think it took me to find the toilet? Thank goodness I have good bladder control.

In fairy tales frogs usually received good press. Not true for their cousin, the toad. Television introduced us to Kermit the Frog, thus putting to rest the villainous frog image of Froggy the Gremlin. I am willing to bet Froggy's "magic twanger" would not get past today's TV censors.

Club: The Frog Pond, P.O. Box 193, Beech Grove, IN 46107.

Advertising Trade Card, large frog eyeing a box of J&P Coates thread 5
Ashtray, figural frog, open mouth holds ashes, green glaze 5
Ashtray, figural frog perched on rect tray, matte green glaze, base imp with logo and "American Encaustic Tiling Co, New York," c1930s, 3" h, 5" l 375
Christmas Tree Light Bulb, figural frog, painted clear glass, German, c1920 75
Cigarette Lighter, table model, figural frog, pewter 30
Clicker, litho tin, Japan, 1960s, 2.25" l 6
Dish, figural frog, flow blue, 2" h, 5" w 80
Doorstop, figural frog, cast iron, 3" h, 6" l .70
Figure, chalkware, 4.5" h, black highlights on green and ivory body 30
Figure, reclining frog, wearing red bow, Lefton, dated 1985, 2" h, 3.125" l 30
Mug, Kermit the Frog, Muppet Show, mkd "Kiln Craft, Tableware, Made in England, Staffordshire Potteries Limited, Dishwasher Safe, English Ironstone," 1978 .10

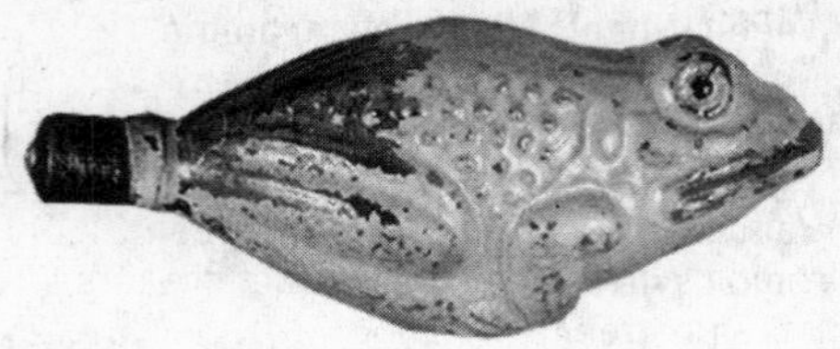

Mug, white china, green frog and cattails, sgd "Hildi," Fire-King 12
Paperweight, figural bullfrog sitting on a stump, cast iron 150
Pin, figural frog encrusted with 20-22K gold nuggets, green enamel eyes 150
Pin, green enameled tree frog wearing rhinestone bow on left leg, green cabochon eyes, gold plated, sgd "Florenza" 50
Plate, white china, multicolor transfer of gnome and frog prince, Germany, 8.5" d 65
Salt and Pepper Shakers, unmkd 20
Souvenir Spoon, figural frog holding umbrella mkd "OREGON" handle, emb frog holding umbrella in downpour and "Webfoot Salem Or" in bowl, SS 275
Planter, figural frog and lily pad, matte glaze, c1940, 3.5" h, 4" w 25
Souvenir Spoon, "Frog Town, Toledo, OH," frog on pumpkin handle, emb Soldier's Memorial Hall in bowl, SS 65
Teapot, figural frog standing on hind legs and holding a seashell, yellow porcelain, arms form spout, gold foil "Mann" label on bottom, c1970s, 8.5" h 40
Toothpick Holder, figural black frog holding a red flower on its head, ceramic, c1940s, 2" h 20

FRUIT JARS

Most fruit jars are worth less than $1. Their value rests in reuse for canning rather than in the collectors' market. Do not be fooled by patent dates that appear on the jar. Over 50 different types of jars bear a patent date of 1858 and many were made as long as 50 years later.

However, there are some expensive fruit jars. A good price guide is Douglas M. Leybourne, Jr.'s *The Collector's Guide to Old Fruit Jars: Red Book No. 8,* published privately by the author in 1997.

Clubs: Ball Collectors Club, 497 Fox Dr., Monroe, MI 48161; Federation of Historical Bottle Collectors, Inc., P.O. Box 1558, Southampton, PA 18966; Midwest Antique Fruit Jar & Bottle Club, P.O. Box 38, Flat Rock, IN 47234.

Atlas, green, pt, zinc lid and rubber seal, 5.75" h 9
Atlas E-Z Seal, aqua, qt 8
Ball Ideal, aqua, qt 5
Ball Ideal, clear, qt, glass cap, wire bail, 7" h 14
Ball Ideal, pale aqua, pt, Jul 14, 1908 patent date, glass lid, wire bail, 5.5" h . .12
Ball Mason, aqua, 1/2 gal, zinc lid with milk glass insert 20
Ball Perfect Mason, aqua, qt, sq, zinc lid . .6
Clarke Fruit Jar Co, Cleveland, O, aqua, 1/2 gal, glass lid, wire bail 50
Crown, aqua, qt, screw-on zinc lid, clear glass insert, mkd "2A," 6.75" h 15
Improved Corona, clear, qt, zinc lid and glass insert 1-
Kerr Economy, clear, pt, glass lid, wire bail 15
Lightning, clear, qt, glass lid with rubber seal, wire bail 15
Porcelain Lined Pat Nov 26 73 and Pat Feb 4 73, aqua, 1/2 gal, screw-on zinc lid, rubber seal 20
Queen, clear, pt, emb "Queen Trademark (2 stars) Wide Mouth Adjustable" on front and the number 13 surrounded by "Kivlan, Onthank, Boston, Smalley" on bottom, glass lid, wire bail 12

Smalley, aqua, qt, Dec 13, 1892, Apr 7, 1896, and Dec 1, 1896 patent dates, sq, threaded lid 8
Swayzee's Improved Mason, avocado green, qt, threaded lid, 6.5" h 35
The Marion Jar, aqua, 1/2 gal, Nov 30, 1858 patent date, zinc lid with rubber seal 18

FULPER POTTERY

Fulper Art Pottery was made by the American Pottery Company, Flemington, New Jersey, beginning around 1910 and ending in 1930. All pieces were molded. Pieces from the 1920s tend to be of higher quality due to less production pressures.

Pieces exhibit a strong Arts and Crafts and/or oriental influence. Glazes differed tremendously as Fulper experimented throughout its production period.

Club: Stangl/Fulper Collectors Club, P.O. Box 538, Flemington, NJ 08822.

Basket, embossed rose and rope handle, blue matte glaze, ink racetrack mark, 7.25" x 8.25" 130
Bookends, pr, book-shaped, ocher and green crystalline flambé glaze, rect ink mark, chips to both, 5" x 4.75" 130
Bowl, 3 ribbon handles, mirrored black crystalline glaze, die-stamped mark "859," restoration to chip and line on 1 handle and rim, 5.25" x 10.75" 100
Bowl, low, Chinese blue flambé glaze, ink racetrack mark, 2" x 9" 90
Bowl, low, emb rim, int with Flemington green glaze, ext with Chinese blue flambé glaze, rect ink mark, 10.5" d . . .160
Bowl, low, scalloped rim, cat's eye flambé glaze, ink racetrack mark, 13" d 160
Bowl, low, scalloped rim, ivory crystalline and Chinese blue flambé int, mottled blue and green ext, incised racetrack mark, 12.5" d 170
Bud Vase, cylindrical, cat's eye flambé glaze dripping over matte mustard ground, rect ink mark, 5.75" x 2" 325
Flower Frog, figural swan, ivory and Chinese blue flambé glaze, stamped "Fulper," 6.5" x 4.5" 200

Lamp, figural Southern belle, porcelain, polychrome glazes, imp racetrack mark, short firing line and inner chip to edge of dress, second firing line higher on skirt, 11.5" h 310
Urn, Colonial Ware, mottled green and yellow glaze, ink racetrack mark, hairline to one handle, 8.75" x 6.5" 80
Vase, 3 angular handles, Chinese blue crystalline glaze, ink racetrack mark, 4.25" x 5" 250
Vase, 3-sided, corseted, cat's eye flambé glaze, ink racetrack mark, rim chips, 8" x 3.25" 100
Vase, barrel-shaped, closed-in rim, cat's eye flambé glaze, ink racetrack mark, 2 rim chips, burst bubbles to body, 7.25" x 5" 110
Vase, bottle-shaped, green matte and cobalt flambé glaze, racetrack mark and paper label, 8.25" x 5" 310
Vase, buttressed with squat base, Chinese blue flambé glaze, rect ink mark, small grinding chip to base, 8.25" x 5.75" 325
Vase, Chinese form, black, ivory, and Chinese blue flambé glaze, raised racetrack mark and paper label, drilled hole to bottom, 12" x 9" 525
Vase, Chinese form, faceted with collared rim, umber and yellow microcrystalline flambé glaze, incised racetrack mark, some fine glaze bubbling to rim, 7.5" x 6.5" 375
Vase, Colonial Ware, 3-handled, mottled green and gunmetal glaze, ink racetrack mark, 7.25" x 5" 90
Vase, ovoid, Chinese blue crystalline flambé glaze, raised racetrack mark, 6.75" x 3.75" 250

Vase, ovoid, moss-to-rose flambé glaze, ink racetrack mark, small glaze miss to body, grinding chip to base, 5.75" x 3.5" 190
Vase, ribbed with applied rose dec, white semi-matte glaze, ink racetrack mark, couple small nicks to flower, tight line to shoulder, 6.5" x 5.75" 30
Vessel, 3 angular handles, turquoise crystalline glaze, mark obscured by glaze, 4.25" x 5.25" 175
Vessel, spherical, 2 buttressed handles, Chinese blue crystalline flambé glaze, ink racetrack mark, 6.5" x 7" 350
Vessel, spherical, 3 handles at rim, Chinese blue crystalline flambé glaze, incised racetrack mark, glaze inconsistency to rim, chip and glaze miss to foot ring, 6.75" x 7.75" 300
Vessel, squat, 2 angular handles, leopard skin crystalline flambé glaze, rect ink mark, minor bruise to glaze in making, 4.75" x 6.25" 200

FURNITURE

Much of the furniture found at flea markets is of the secondhand variety.

Armchair, Art Deco style, chrome tubing, black upholstery, 31" h, 24" w, 31" d . . .350
Armchair, rustic, 4 vertical spindles in back, slightly flared front posts, woven splint seat, orig weathered finish, loose damage to seat, 37" h, 24" w, 21" d 50
Beds, pr, Sheraton style, mahogany, tall post 575
Blanket Chest, Country style, pine with old worn red paint, dovetailed case and applied base lid edge moldings, turned feet, till with 2 hidden dovetailed drawers, repairs at lock and hinges, 23.5" h, 37.75" w, 20.5" d 475
Bookcase, Arts & Crafts style, oak, stacking, 5 sections, top 2 sections slightly recessed, 4-leg base, orig finish, plywood added to connect bottom 4 sections, 84" h, 34" w, 14" d . .800
Cabinet, Arts & Crafts style, oak, shaped 3/4 crest with upper shelf, single drawer above 2 paneled doors, base shelf, orig finish, 53" h, 20" w, 13" d 450

China Cabinet, Art Deco style, burl walnut, 2 doors, glass shelves, electrified int, 50" h, 44.5" w, 11.25" d . . 600

Desk, Empire, mahogany, slant-front, fitted int, 3-drawer base, carved support columns, claw feet 550

Dinette Set, Retro, metal Formica-top table with red and white geometric and flower design and chrome legs, chrome chairs with red and white vinyl backs and seats, 1950s 650

Dining Table, Duncan Phyfe style, mahogany, oval with 2 pedestals, crossbanded top with 4 leaves, Henkel-Harris 1,500

Dining Table and Chairs, Art Deco style, light burl walnut veneer with inlaid light walnut, chairs recovered with light mocha colored fabric, 9.5" l scratch to table top, ... 925

Footstool, Arts & Crafts style, oak, rect overhanging top, bootjack ends, base shelf with keyed-through tenons, orig finish, 15" h, 15.5" w, 9" d 400

Footstool, Arts & Crafts style, oak, sq, woven split reed top, sq legs, flat box stretchers, orig finish, 14" h, 16" sq 300

Hanging Cabinet, Arts & Crafts style, oak, hanging, long shelf above single cupboard door flanked by side shelves, cut corners on shelves, ring pull, 20" h, 20.5" w, 4" d 225

Highboy, Atlas Furniture Co, broken arch top, 3 over 7 drawers 715

Highboy, bonnet top with center flame finial, top has 3 over 3 drawers with center drawer, carved base has 1 over 3 drawers, Queen Anne cabriole legs, Henkel-Harris 1,325

Hoosier Cabinet, shaped crest, 2 paneled doors above recessed pie shelf with tambour sliding door, porcelain slide-out work surface, base with paneled cupboard door beside 2 short drawers, shaped apron, painted white, with flour sifter, on casters 700

Kitchen Cupboard, 2 glass doors with black-painted scallop and flower trim, 2 short drawers beside 1 deep short drawer, 2 paneled cupboard doors below, shaped apron, shelved int, painted white, chrome handles, 1940s-50s 575

Kitchen Cupboard, shaped crest, 2 glass doors with scrolling fretwork, 2 short drawers above 1 long drawer, 2 cupboard doors, shaped apron, shelved int, painted yellow, 1940s-50s, ... 525

Lamp Table, rustic, round top, 4-legged splayed base with "X" stretcher, orig overcoated finish, Old Hickory branded mark, seam separations in top, 30" d top, 30" h 550

Love Seat, Federal style, mahogany, camel back, carved arm supports, tapered carved legs 415

Lowboy, Queen Anne style, mahogany, 1 over 3 drawers, Treasure House 650

Music Cabinet, mahogany, single door with fancy brass hinges, shelf below . 275

Parlor Set, settee, armchair, and slant-seat armchair, settee and armchair with flared front posts, slant-seat armchair with high back, all with tightly woven split reed backs and seats and stretchers, orig overcoated finish . . . 2,250

Plant Stand, Arts & Crafts style, oak, sq top, diamond cutouts in frieze, sq legs, base shelf, 29" h, 14" sq 400

Rocker, Arts & Crafts style, oak, shaped crest, 3-splat back, shaped arms, flat side stretchers, leather upholstered seat, refinished, 39" h, 28" w, 23" d 400
Secretary, Federal style, mahogany, 3 drawers over 4 doors 650
Sewing Rocker, Arts & Crafts style, oak, tapered high back with shaped crest and 2 splats, upholstered low seat 250
Sideboard, Contemporary, birch plywood construction, 2 doors and drawer cabinet, molded birch legs, Thaden/Jordan, 55" h, 49" w, 18" d 200
Sideboard, Federal style, small, 3 drawers over 4 doors 635
Smoking Stand, Arts & Crafts style, oak, rect top shelf supported by sq posts, shaped ends on center shelf with holes drilled for pipes, single door, sq legs, refinished, 27" h, 13" w, 9" d . . .115
Stand, Empire style, mahogany, 2 drawers, center carved post, 4 claw feet 200
Student Desk, Contemporary, designed by Russel Wright, single pedestal, 3 graduated drawers, light finish, Conant Ball, 29.5" x 40" x 22.5" 200
Tea Table, Queen Anne style, mahogany, 2 candle slides 385
Vanity, mahogany, triple mirror, center drawer flanked by 2 drawers on each side, tall cabriole legs 550
Wardrobe, late Victorian, mahogany, 2 burl veneer doors, cyma-curved top with center carving, Queen Anne banty legs 450
Wing Chair, Chippendale style, mahogany, red brocade upholstery, claw and ball feet 475

GAMBLING COLLECTIBLES

Gaming devices, gaming accessories, and souvenirs from gambling establishments—from hotels to riverboats—are all collectible.

Gambling collectors compete with Western collectors for the same material. Sometimes the gunfight gets bloody. With the price of old (late nineteenth- and early twentieth-century) gambling material skyrocketing, many new collectors are focusing on more modern material dating from Las Vegas in the 1950s and 1960s and today's casinos.

Club: Casino Chip & Gaming Tokens Collectors Club, P.O. Box 340345, Columbus, OH 43234.

Ashtray, Casino de Macau, green glass, 1960s 25
Ashtray, metal, working roulette wheel . . .45
Ashtray, Monte Carlo, black amethyst 12
Mug, Harvey's Casino, Lake Tahoe, NV, emb tiki and torch image on carved-woodgrain dec ext, 4.25" h 10
Poker Chip, Apache Nugget Casino, Dulce, NM, $1, white, Langworthy mold, green edge inserts 150
Poker Chip, Club Greyhound, Jeffersonville, IN, black, hub mold, no edge inserts 40
Poker Chip, Desert Diamond Casino, Tucson, AZ, $5, red, Chipco mold, dark center 50
Poker Chip, Gold Shore Casino, Biloxi, MS, roulette, hat and cane mold 8
Poker Chip, Harrah's, Kansas City, MO, red, reverse hat and cane mold, brown and lavender edge inserts, "$5 Grand Opening" .20
Poker Chip, Pink Pussy Cat Topless Club, Reno, NV 30
Poker Chip, Smith's North Shore Club, Lake Tahoe, NV, $100 32
Postcard, Casino and Beach, Bayville, Long Island, NY, 1920s 5
Slot Machine, Caille, Superior Jackpot, 25¢, 4-reel, c1930, 15" x 24" 1,600
Slot Machine, Jennings, Rockola front with Sheffler strip, 1¢, 3-reel, c1923, 16" x 24" 1,350

Slot Machine, Jennings, Tic-Tac-Toe Chief, 10¢, chrome front, visible jackpot in oak case, post-1945, 16" x 27" x 16" 1,200
Slot Machine, Jennings, Wild Indian, 25¢, 3-reel, chrome front, oak cabinet, 17" x 18" 1,000
Slot Machine, Keeney, Egyptian pyramid-type stand, 25¢, floor model, 32" x 61" x 18" 2,500
Slot Machine, Keeney, Operator Bell, 25¢, counter top model, oak and metal cabinet, 16" x 25" x 16" 1,500
Slot Machine, Keeney, Twin, 5¢/10¢, multiple denomination console model, electric, dec wooden cabinet with silk-screened glass, 31" x 57" x 23" 100
Slot Machine, Mills, COK, 5¢, side vendor with future payout, c1930, 16" x 24" . .1,450
Slot Machine, Mills, Diamond, 50¢, 3-reel, chrome front, c1950, 15" x 25" 950
Slot Machine, Mills, Fruit/1776 Spearmint, 5¢, 3-reel, emb, c1930, 16" x 24" 1,000
Slot Machine, Mills, Horse Head Bonus, 5¢, Art Deco with "bonus" attachment, late 1930s, 16" x 26" x 16" 1,500
Slot Machine, Mills, Judge, 5¢, 1-reel, upright, oak cabinet, c1899, 22" x 65" 7,000
Slot Machine, Mills, Silent Mystery, 5¢, oak cabinet, metal casings, gold award feature, c1930s, 16" x 24" x 16" 1,100
Slot Machine, Mills, Silent Sales, 5¢, emb, side vendor, c1925, 19" x 24" . . .1,500
Slot Machine, Mills, Skyscraper, 5¢, 3-reel, c1933, 16" x 20" 850
Slot Machine, Olympia, Bunny XO, metal and plastic, electric, "0101803" and "039348" at corner, 32" h, 19" w, 13" d .325

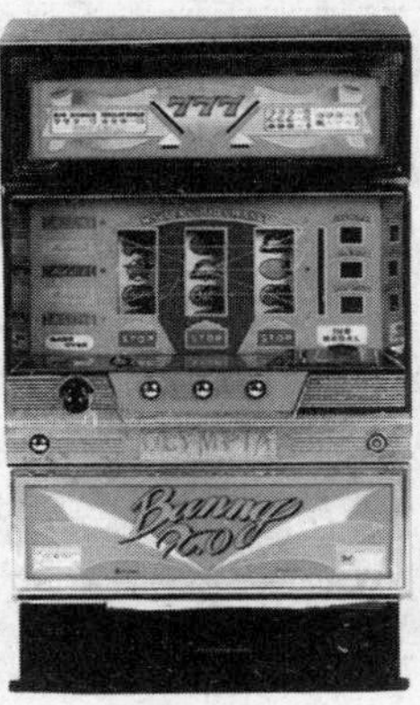

Slot Machine, P&H, Uncle Sam, 5¢, 1-reel, Roll-A-Top coin entry, emb cast iron case, 17" x 24" x 14" 2,000
Slot Machine, Victor, 25¢, upright, c1904 6,500
Slot Machine, Watling, Roll-A-Top, 5¢, counter model, ornate coin front castings, oak cabinet, double jackpot, 1930s, 17" x 26" x 16" 2,600

GAMES

Avoid common games, e.g., "Go to the Head of the Class," "Monopoly," and "Rook." They were produced in such vast quantities that they hold little attraction for collectors.

Most boxed board games found are in heavily used condition. Box lids have excessive wear, tears, and are warped. Pieces are missing. In this condition, most games fall in the $2 to $10 range. However, the minute a game is in fine condition or better, value jumps considerably.

Clubs: Assoc. of Game and Puzzle Collectors, P.O. Box 44, Dresher, PA 19025, www.chaichart.com; Gamers Alliance, P.O. Box 197, East Meadow, NY 11554; Gametimes, 49 Brooks Ave., Lewiston, ME 04240.

$64,000 Question, Lowell, 1956 20
Alan Sherman's Camp Granada, Milton Bradley, 1965 50
Animal Twister, Milton Bradley, 1967 15
Beat The Buzz, Kenner, 1958 15
Brain Waves, Milton Bradley, 1977 15
Clean Sweep, Schaper, 1967 30
Clue, Parker Brothers, 1963 10

Doc Holliday Wild West Game, Transogram, 1960 .45
Domino's Pizza Delivery Game, Wortquest USA, 1989 .10
Eliot Ness and The Untouchables Game, Transogram, 1961 .60
Emergency Game, Milton Bradley, 1973-74 .15
Flying Nun, Milton Bradley, 1968 .25
Flying The Beam, Parker Brothers, 1941 .75
Fonz Hanging Out At Arnold's, Milton Bradley, 1978 .15
Game of General Hospital, Cardinal, 1982 .18
Game of Tom Sawyer, Milton Bradley, c1937 .75
Game of Yertle, Revell, 1960 .50
Gardner's Championship Golf, 1950s .30
Hey Pa, There's A Goat On The Roof, Parker Brothers, 1965 .30
Hialeah Horse Racing Game, Milton Bradley, 1940s .35
Howdy Doody's Electric Doodler Game, Harett-Gilmar, 1951 .40
How To Succeed In Business Without Really Trying, Milton Bradley, 1963 .12
Journey To The Unknown Game, Remco, 1968 .95
Jungle Hunt Game, Rosebud Art Co, c1940s .15
Leave It To Beaver Rocket To The Moon, Hasbro, 1959 .35
Let's Drive, Milton Bradley, 1967 .15
Lost Gold, Parker Brothers, 1975 .15
Lost In Space, Milton Bradley, 1965 .60
Lot The Calf, Brown Games, 1964 .20
McHale's Navy Game, Transogram, 1962 .40
Meet The Presidents, Selchow & Righter, 1950 .20
Merv Griffin's Word For Word Game, Mattel, 1963 .15
Mr Machine Game, Ideal, 1961 .55
Mr Magoo's Maddening Misadventures, Transogram, 1970 .50
Mr Novak Game, Transogram, 1963 .35
Mr T Game, Milton Bradley, 1983 .10
NBC The Home Stretch, Hasbro, 1970 .15
Newlywed Game, Hasbro, 1967 .10
Our Defenders, Master Toy Co, c1944 .35
Parcheesi, Selchow & Righter, 1940s .30
Pitchin' Pal, Cadaco-Ellis, 1953 .20
Planet of The Apes, Milton Bradley, 1974 .25
Pollyanna, Parker Brothers, 1950s .18
Ring My Nose, Milton Bradley, c1926-28 .45
Rin-Tin-Tin, Transogram, 1955 .40
Ripcord, Lowell, 1962 .55
Rummy Royal, Whitman, 1959 .10
$ale of The Century, Milton Bradley, 1969 .15
Skittle Pool, Aurora, 1972 .30
Smitty Game, Milton Bradley, c1930s .110
SOS, Durable Toy and Novelty, c1947 .55
Stocks and Bonds, 3M, 1964 .10
Stoney Burke, Transogram, 1963 .35
Stop and Go, Shell Oil, c1930s .40
Stop Thief, Parker Brothers, 1979 .10
Stratego, Milton Bradley, 1926 .15
Three Chipmunks Big Record, Hasbro, 1960 .35
Three Men In A Tub, Milton Bradley, c1935-36 .35
Ticker Tape, Cadaco, 1963 .20
Tiddledy Winks, Milton Bradley, c1905 .15
Tiddly Winks, Whitman, 1950s .5
Toss Across Game, Ideal, 1969 .15
Touché Turtle, Transogram, 1962 .60
Track & Trap, Whitman, 1969 .15
Track Meet, Sports Illustrated, 1972 .12
Uncle Wiggily Game, Milton Bradley, 1920s .35
Uncle Wiggily Game, Milton Bradley, 1954 .20
Uranium Rush, Gardner Games, 1950s .60

Voodoo Doll Game, Schaper, 1967 30
Vox Pop, Milton Bradley, 1938 20
Walt Disney's Tiddly Winks, Whitman, 1963 10
What's My Line, Lowell, 1954-55 40
Wild Life, ES Lowe, 1969-71 20
Winnie-The-Pooh Game, Parker Brothers, 1933 65
Wonderbug, Ideal, 1977 12
Woody Woodpecker Game, Milton Bradley, 1958 40
Wow Pillow Fight Game For Girls, Milton Bradley, 1964 20
Wrestle Around Game, Ideal, 1969 15
Yahtzee, ES Lowe, 1975 10
Yahtzee Score Pads, ES Lowe, 1956 4
Yogi Bear Go Fly A Kite Game, Transogram, 1961 35
You Don't Say Game, Milton Bradley, 1964-69 10
Zorro Game, Whitman, 1965 20

GARDEN-RELATED ITEMS

Are there valuable collectibles in your garden shed or basement? Chances are the answer is yes. Garden-related collectibles are hot. They are featured regularly in illustrations in Country and decorating magazines.

Cast iron garden furniture and cast statuary led the parade a decade ago. Now, watch out for lawn sprinklers, watering cans, and even lawn mowers. Collectors currently prefer pre-1940 examples, but expect this to change.

Is there any hope for old garden hoses? Absolutely not! Send them to the landfill.

Ash Stand, metal, cylindrical container mounted on 3 vertical rods, large round base, old red paint, mid-1900s, 23" h 25
Fencing, cast iron, single panel, 3 posts, extra finials and hardware 225
Figure, frog, cast iron, c1900, 6" l 175
Hand Cultivator, 5 spring tines, hardwood handle, 12" l, 2.25" w 40
Hanging Planter, Adirondack twig, Arm & Hammer crate board bottom, alligatored surface, early 1900s, 20" h, 20" l, 11" w 250
Pitchfork, 3-tined 15
Statues, pr, cranes, 1 upright, 1 with head lowered, cast brass, 15" h upright crane 500
Sundial, cast iron, gold painted highlights, "Grow Old Along With Me The Best Is Yet To Be," mkd "Griswold Mfg Co Erie PA USA 357," pointer broken at tip, 1930s, 10.25" d 125
Wagon Wheel, wood, metal hub, painted white 50
Wall Plaque, terra cotta, man in the moon 16
Watering Can, #10, galvanized metal 20
Water Pump, cast iron, painted red 65
Wheelbarrow, child's toy, metal body and handles, hard rubber tire, painted red, mkd "Hy-Speed Made in the USA," 27.5" l 100

GAS STATION COLLECTIBLES

Approach this from two perspectives—items associated with gas stations and gasoline company giveaways. Competition for this material is fierce. Advertising collectors want the advertising; automobile collectors want material to supplement their collections.

Beware of reproductions ranging from advertising signs to pump globes. Do not accept too much restoration and repair. There were hundreds of thousands of gasoline stations across America. Not all their back rooms have been exhausted.

Almanac, "1938 Flying Red Horse Almanac," 9.5" h, 6" w 12
Chalkboard, Capitol Motor Oil, fiberboard, 15" h, 17" w 18
Clock, Dunlop Tires, tire frame, metal with plastic lettering, 2-sided, Brille clock works, 37" h, 50" w, 9.5" d 825

Cups and Saucers, 6 each, china, floral pattern with BP logo, mkd "D.V. Sarreguemines, France," 2.5" h cup, 2.75" d saucer 75

Gas Globe, Capitol Gasoline in red and white on 1 side, Kerosene Gas in green and yellow on other side, 13.5" d 325

Gas Globe, Indian Gas, blue lettering around red center circle, white ground, 13.5" d 250

Gas Globe, moving truck image with Majors Regular on 1 side, Majors Ethyl on other side, 13.5" d 3,000

Grease Can, metal, Chevrolet Gredag for "Cups, Hubs & Steering, No. 3," yellow, 4" d 165

Jigsaw Puzzle, Sohio premium, radio stars Gene and Glenn and Jake and Lena in "Just Breezin' Along," 300 pcs, ©1933, with puzzle picture and Sohio and Atlas Tire adv, 8" x 6.25" box 12

Kite, Zephyr Motor Oil/Gasoline, paper and wood, Top Flite, 33" h, 27.25" w 28

License Plate Attachment, flags on Shell logo, self-framing tin, 5.25" h, 3.25" w 15

Magazine, *The Texaco Star,* Oct 1931 issue, Vol XVIII, No. 8, 32 pgs, 11.25" h, 8" w 15

Oil Bottles and Rack, eight 1-qt glass bottles painted "HEP, Imperial Refineries, Clayton, MO" and emb state approvals, replacemnt lids, repainted wire rack, 14" h bottles 350

Penknife, Esso, figural "Happy" character, metal, 3.75" l 65

Poster, "Go Places With Chevron," red Chevy driving through western landscape, 55" h, 41" w 45

Premium, Shell, Franklin Mint Presidential Coin set, 35 bronze coins, cardboard display, "Presidential Profiles" booklet, and envelope, 1" d coins, NOS 10

Pump Sign, Texaco Fire Chief Gasoline, logo and fireman's helmet image, 1-sided porcelain, mkd "9-40 Made in U.S.A." at bottom, 12" h, 8" w 100

Salt and Pepper Shakers, Conoco, figural gas pumps, 2.75" h 55

Sign, "Clean Rest Rooms – Windshield Service – A Sinclair Dealer Service," 2-sided, porcelain, 37.25" h, 30" w 100

Snow Globe, Skelly and Hood Tires, glass and plastic, billboard in background, tire leaving deep imprint in snow, red base, 4" x 3" x 3" 150

Thermometer, Texaco, figural old-time gas pump, plastic, "Abby's Texaco Service" printed at bottom, orig box 50

GAUDY ITALIAN

While not all items marked "Made in Italy" are gaudy, the vast majority are. They are collected for their kitsch, not aesthetic value.

The Mediterranean look was a popular decorating style in the late 1950s and early 1960s. Etruscan-style pieces, reproduction and copycats of Etruscan antiquities painted in light yellows and greens, often relief decorated with sea motifs including mythical sea creatures, and featuring a high gloss, majolica-type glaze, were the most popular. Production values were crude.

The Mediterranean look fell out of favor by the mid-1960s. Those gaudy Italians that did not wind up in the garbage dump were relegated to basements, attics, and other damp and foreboding places. Some wish they had stayed there.

Vases are the most commonly found form. The modestly decorated examples sell in the $15 to $25 range. A large elaborate example fetches $40 or more. The gaudiness of the piece affects its value—the more gaudy, the higher the perceived value.

GAY FAD GLASSWARE

In the late 1930s Fran Taylor and her husband, Bruce, founded the Gay Fad Studios, a firm that decorated glass and metal wares for sale in the tabletop market. The business flourished. In 1945 the Taylors transferred their operations from Detroit to Lancaster, Ohio, just across the street from the Anchor Hocking Glass Co.

Gay Fad glassware is found in hundreds of different designs. Many appeared as sets, e.g., the eight-glass Gay Ninety Family Portrait series. Look for decanters, juice sets, tea and toast sets, and waffle sets. Gay Fad glassware is usually marked with an interlocking "G" and "F" or "Gay Fad."

Cake Pan, hp fruits on white ground, Fire-King, Anchor Hocking, 10" x 8.5" . . .18
Casserole, hp fruits on white ground, Fire-King, Anchor Hocking, 1 pt, 2" h, 6.75" w 15
Cocktail Shaker, clear with multicolor stripes, aluminum cap, 11" h, 4.5" d 18
Cookie Jar, barrel shape, hp fruits on white ground, gold highlights, Bartlett Collins, 1940s 35
Creamer and Sugar, hp fruits on clear glass, 3" h 8
Cruet, Outlined Fruit, satin glass, 5" h 10
Drinking Glass, hp apple and grapes on clear glass, 3.75" h, 3" d 10
Ice Tub, fired-on cranberry and gilt grapes, decanters, tumblers, and citrus wedges, gilt studio name, paper label . .30
Mixing Bowl, hp fruits on white ground, Fire-King, Anchor Hocking, 3.5" h, 7.375" d 18
Pitcher, hp orange on frosted ground, Federal Glass, 36 oz, 5.75" h 15
Plate, clear glass with textured ground and gold leaf dec, 7.75" sq 15
Punch Bowl Set, bowl, 12 cups and cup hangers, stand, and ladle, hp pine branches with pine cones and holly berry accents 650
Refrigerator Dish, hp fruits on white ground, Fire-King, Anchor Hocking, 2.25" h, 4.125" sq 10
Refrigerator Dish, rect, hp fruit on white ground, clear glass lid, Fire-King, Anchor Hocking, 8.375" x 4.25" 25
Souvenir Glass, pink and black on frosted ground, Mount Shasta, Drive-Thru Tree, Hollywood, and Mt Wilson Observatory, 9 oz .10
Souvenir Glass, yellow and black on frosted ground, features NY and Canadian landmarks, 10 oz 9
Tumbler, hp fruit on frosted ground 20
Tumblers, set of 8, Currier & Ives scenes on frosted glass, 16 oz, 5.75" h, 3" d 75

GEISHA GIRL

Geisha Girl porcelain is a Japanese export ware whose production began in the last quarter of the nineteenth century and still continues today. Manufacturing came to a standstill during World War II.

Collectors have identified over 150 different patterns from over one hundred manufacturers. When buying a set, check the pattern of the pieces carefully. Be on the lookout for "complete" sets with mix-and-match pieces.

Beware of reproductions that have a very white porcelain, minimal background washes, sparse detail coloring, no gold, or very bright gold enameling. Some of the reproductions came from Czechoslovakia.

Biscuit Jar, 5.5" h 20
Bowl, scalloped edge, 1940s, 10" d 65

Butter Pat, 1930s 25
Chocolate Pot, Parasol B, cobalt ground, 10" h 110
Cocoa Pot, 10" h 80
Cup, 2 geishas by lamppost, 1 in background with buildings, 1.375" h 8
Cup and Saucer, blue trim, red mark 24
Demitasse Cup and Saucer, lithophane geisha head in bottom of cup 55
Dresser Tray, Rendevous, Kutani, 9.5" x 7.25" 50
Egg Cup, 2.25" h, 1.75" d 32
Hair Receiver, 2.25" h, 3.5" d 20
Hatpin Holder, Parasol J, red border, gold stars on top, 4" h 35
Nut Bowl, melon shaped, 3-ftd, scalloped rim, 3.5" h, 7" d 15
Plate, Bamboo Tree, 7.25" d 10
Plate, lanterns hanging in trees, orange border, 7.25" 18
Powder Jar, 2.25" h, 3.25" d 18
Salt and Pepper Shakers, 2.5" h 12
Salt and Pepper Shakers, Waterboy, cobalt blue border, gold leaf design on top, 2.375" h 15
Saucer, Flower Gathering, 5.25" d 10
Saucer, Footbridge, 5.375" d 10
Saucer, Lantern, 5.5" d 10
Tea Set, includes 4.5" h teapot, 5.125" h creamer, 5.625" h cov sugar, and 4 each 7.375" d luncheon plates, 2.875" d cups, and 4.25" d saucers, unmkd 80
Tea Set, teapot, creamer, sugar, 5 cups and saucers, Imari, 7" h teapot 275
Vase, red handles, 5.5" h 18

GEORGES BRIARD

Georges Briard, born Jascha Brojdo, was an industrial designer who worked in a wide range of materials—ceramics, glass, enameled metals, paper, plastic, textiles, and wood. Brojdo emigrated from Poland in 1937. He earned a joint Master of Fine Arts degree from the University of Chicago and the Art Institute of Chicago. In 1947 Brojdo moved to New York where he chose the name Georges Briard as his designer pseudonym.

Columbian Enamel, Glass Guild (The Bent Glass Company), Hyalyn Porcelain, and Woodland were among the early clients of Georges Briard Designs. In the early 1960s Briard designed Pfaltzgraff's Heritage pattern. In 1965 he created sixteen patterns for melamine plastic dinnerware in Allied Chemical's Artisan line, marketed under the Stetson brand name.

Briard continued to create innovative designs for the houseware market through the end of the 1980s. Responding to changing market trends, many of Briard's later products were made overseas.

Do not confuse Briard knockoffs, many made in Japan, with licensed Briard products. A high level of quality and the distinctive Briard signature are the mark of a Briard piece.

Barware Set, goldtone cylinder holds chrome corkscrew, bottle opener, double shot glass, and ice tongs, 8.25" h, 4.5" d, orig box 25
Chafing Dish, graniteware, Ambrosia pattern, pineapple and strawberry on white ground, gold border, brass wire frame half-round handles, X stretcher, and ball feet, 12" x 7.5" dish 30
Chip and Dip, 22" x 13" divided tray with 3 sections and four 6" sq serving dishes, Persian Garden pattern 35
Coffeepot, graniteware, Ambrosia pattern, pineapple and strawberry on front, white ground, 7" h 10
Dish, amber glass, Forbidden Fruit pattern, black stylized grapes and leaves, gold signature, 7.25" sq 32

Fondue, 2 qt gold-specked Fire-King casserole, enameled metal lid with gold butterflies on white ground, goldtone metal stand, orig box 28
Fondue Pot, cov, graniteware, Ambrosia pattern, with metal stand, 4" h pot 32
Highball Tumblers, set of 6, glass, Marsh Weed pattern, 1970s, orig box, 5.75" h . .30
Ice Bucket, spun aluminum, green glass lid with gold sunburst pattern around brass and wood finial, small wood and brass handles, white glass lining, 7" h, 7.5" d 50
Plate, clear glass, Coin and Crown pattern, 8" d 8
Popcorn Bowl, #408, enameled porcelain, Melange pattern, black on white ground 28
Relish Dish, clear glass, leaf-shaped, divided, hp pear and apple, 9.25" x 5.5" . .8
Sandwich Tray, gold medallions with leaf design on rect frosted glass tray, gold border, wood handles, 17" x 7" 30
Server, Forbidden Fruit pattern, gold pears, apples, and signature on white ground, Bent Glass, 15" sq 40
Serving Tray, clear glass liner on gold-colored graniteware base, 2 pockets, teak and brass handles, Sonata pattern, 14" x 13" 45
Swizzle Sticks, glass, Christmas tree tops, orig box mkd "Holiday Glass Stirrers, Georges Briard, Inc" 6
Tray, clear glass, sq with cut corners, pink and gold Egyptian motif, gold rim, 11" sq 20
Tray, Sunflower pattern, Glass Guild 12
Tumbler, smoky glass with gold and white time zones, clocks, etc, 4.125" h, 4" d 15
Vegetable Dish, cov, graniteware, oval, Ambrosia pattern, white with gold band on rim and small fruits on lid, chip on underside of lid 25

G.I. JOE

The first G.I. Joe 12" tall posable action figures for boys were produced in 1964 by the Hasbro Manufacturing Company. The original line was made up of one male action figure for each branch of the military. Their outfits were styled after World War II, Korean Conflict, and Vietnam Conflict military uniforms.

The creation of the G.I. Joe Adventure Team made Joe the marveled explorer, hunter, deep-sea diver, and astronaut, rather than just an American serviceman. Due to the Arab oil embargo in 1976, the figure was reduced in height to 8" and was renamed the Super Joe. In 1977 production stopped.

In 1982 G.I. Joe made his comeback—with a few changes. "The Great American Hero" is now a posable 3.75" tall plastic figure with code names corresponding to the various costumes. The new Joe must deal with both current and futuristic villains and issues.

Clubs: G.I. Joe Collectors Club, 225 Cattle Baron Parc Dr., Fort Worth, TX 76108, www.mastercollector.com; G.I. Joe: Steel Brigade Club, 8362 Lomay Ave., Westminster, CA 92683.

ACTION FIGURE

Action Soldier, 1964 350
Action Soldier, 1965-66 250
Adventure Team, Air Adventurer with Kung Fu Grip, #7282 125
Adventure Team, Hurricane Spotter, #7343, 1971 200
Adventure Team, Man of Action, #7500, orig box, 1970-73 250

Adventure Team, Mike Powers Secret Outpost, #8040, 1975 100
Adventure Team, Sea Adventurer with Kung Fu Grip, #7281 250
Adventure Team, Secret Mission to Spy Island, #7411, 1970 200
Commemorative Collection, 1994, 3.75", Air Force Fighter Pilot 12
Commemorative Collection, 1994, 3.75", Navy Sailor 12
Deep Freeze, 1967 250
First Issue, 1964 200
Green Beret, #5978, 1966 200
Green Beret, #7536, 1966 250
Jungle Fighter, #7732, 1967 600
Landing Signal Officer, #7621, 1965 200
Military Police, #7521, 1964 250
Mortal Kombat, Hasbro, 1994, 3.75", Sonya Blade Movie Edition 15
West Point Cadet, #7537, 1967 250

CLOTHING AND ACCESSORIES

Action Man Bazooka, MOC 100
Adventure Team Helicopter, 1970s, NRFB 250
Adventure Team Training Center Slide for Survival, #7495, 1974 250
Adventure Team Vehicle, #7005, 1970 65
Arctic Assault Mission Gear, Hasbro, 1993 12
Battle Corps Cobra Scorpion, Hasbro, 1993 20
Battle Corps Ice Snake, Hasbro, 1992 12
Battle Corps Manta Ray, Hasbro, 1993 20
Beachhead Field Pack Set, #7713 110
Hovercraft, 1984 45
M-1 Garand Rifle, 1960s 35
Ocean Enforcer Mission Gear, Hasbro, 1993 12
Rubber Boots, brown, 1st issue, 1960s 150
Star Brigade Astronaut Mission Gear, Hasbro, 1993 13
Star Brigade Cobra Invader, Hasbro, 1993 10
Star Brigade Starfighter, Hasbro, 1993 15
Street Fighter Karate Chopper, Hasbro 20
Street Fighter Street Striker, Hasbro 25

GIRL SCOUTS

Juliette Gordon Low of Savannah, Georgia, began the Girl Scout movement in 1912. It grew rapidly. The 1928 Girl Scout manual suggested selling cookies to raise money. Today the annual Girl Scout cookie drive supports local troops and councils.

Girl Scout collectibles enjoy limited collector interest. There is a ready market for flashlights and pocketknives, primarily because they cross over into other collecting fields.

Book, *Girl Scout Pocket Songbook,* 1956, 48 pgs 8
Book, *Leadership of Girl Scout Troops – Intermediate Program,* ©1943, 365 pgs 15
Calendar, 1967, orig envelope, 10" x 17" 22
Canteen, aluminum, plaid and green canvas cov, Girl Scout insignia snaps, cotton straps, spout cov, 1960s 15
Commemorative Coin, "Girl Scout 50th Anniversary, 1912-1962," 1" d 8
Compass, metal and glass, pocket watch style, US Gauge Co, NY, 2" d 20
Cookie Cutter, Brownie, red plastic, mkd "Brownie" on uniform hem, 4.5" h 16

Doll, Effanbee, Punkin, vinyl, wearing Brownie uniform, 10" h 85
Handbook, Brownie, 1951 25
Handbook, Brownie, 1957 10
Handbook, Girl Scout, 1932, hardcover, 404 pgs 10
Handbook, Girl Scout, 1953, cloth cover, 510 pgs, 5.75" x 8.5" 18
Handbook, Girl Scout, 1958 14
Handbook, Girl Scout, 1961 32
Handkerchief, "Girl Scouts Have Fun," 12" sq 20
Insignia, Brownie pin, brass, 1st issue, post-1938, 30mm 15
Marbles, green and yellow glass, 20, MIP 30
Pocketknife, stainless steel, Geo Schrade, 2.75" l blade, 3.5" l closed 20
Presentation Statue, spelter, copper coated, designed by Marjorie Daingerfield, 1953, 6" h 125
Sash, Lake Erie Council Troop 1007, gold star pin, wings, 17 badges 25
Tear Sheet, *American Girl* magazine, 1954, pocketknife adv, black and white ..5
Uniform Button, dark green plastic, emb Girl Scout insignia, 1960s-70s 4

GLASS SHOES

Glass shoe is a generic term for any figural shoe (or slipper, boot, ice skate, etc.). Some examples are utilitarian in nature, e.g., the Atterbury shoe night lamp or the ruby glass cocktail shaker in the shape of a leg and foot wearing a metal sandal. Most were made for purely decorative purposes.

Shoes were extremely popular during the Victorian era, when household bric-a-brac from toothpick holders to pincushions to salt cellars were made in the form of footwear. Once the glass shoe entered the form vocabulary, it never went out of production. There was a lull during the Depression, when few families had money for non-essential items.

Several contemporary companies including Boyd, Degenhart, Fenton, and Mosser have reproduced early designs and introduced new ones. Thanks to several new books on the subject, glass shoes are enjoying a collecting renaissance.

Club: Miniature Shoe Collectors Club, P.O. Box 2390, Apple Valley, CA 92308.

Amber, Daisy & Button, sandal, c1880, 1.375" h, 4.5" l 85
Blue Milk Glass, riding boot, 4.5" l 6
Boyd, lavender, pink, and blue slag, Daisy & Button, cat slipper, 3" h, 6" l ...22
Boyd, rubina, Daisy & Button, slipper, 2.5" h, 5.5" l 16
Boyd, vaseline, bow slipper, 6" 25
Boyd, vaseline, cat slipper, 6" 28
Chocolate Slag, 3/4 boot, 2.5" h, 3.5" l, price for pr 10
Clear, beaded edge, plastic red rose at toe, 3" h, 7" l 9
Czechoslovakian, crystal, diamond pattern, fitted with matching salt and pepper shakers, 2.75" h, 3" l 45
Degenhart, blue, Daisy & Button, colonial bow slipper, 2.5" h, 5.75" l 75
Degenhart, blue, skate boot, beaded top edge, introduced 1967, 4.125" h 40

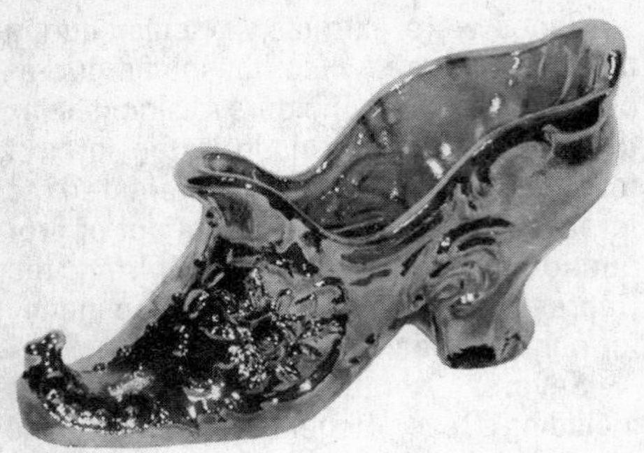

Degenhart, nile green, baby shoe, 2" h, 3" l 50
Degenhart, white opalescent, baby shoe, 2" h, 3" l 50
Fenton, amber, Hobnail, kitten slipper, 3" h, 6" l 20
Fenton, blue milk glass, Daisy & Button, slipper 45
Fenton, cobalt and white slag, cat slipper 20
Fenton, cobalt blue, roller skate, 3" h, 4.5" l 8
Fenton, green, Hobnail, kitten slipper, 3" h, 6" l 32
Fenton, pale green with hp flowers, slipper, sgd by "J Peyon," orig sticker .15
Fenton, topaz vaseline, rose slipper, 1997 Historical Collection, 6" 40
Fenton, white milk glass, high top boot, 4.25" h 35
Green, beaded and scroll pattern, 2.25" h, 4.25" l 14
Mosser, aqua opalescent, bow slipper . . .12
Mosser, emerald green carnival, slipper, turned-up toe, 5" 14
Mosser, milk glass carnival, bow slipper, 3.5" 12
Mosser, vaseline, beaded and scrolled pattern, 2.5" h, 4.5" l 10
Murano, goldstone flecks in ruby with clear heel, sling-back shoe, 5" l 35
Murano, green and clear satin glass, sling-back shoe, 4.25" l 78
Oneida Crystal, pink, slipper, 2.5" h, 5.5" l . . .5
Opalescent Vaseline, slipper 22
Vaseline, Daisy & Button, high top boot . .24
Vaseline, slipper, Victorian Rose 20
Vaseline, Texas boot, shot glass 18
White Milk Glass, Hobnail, cat slipper 6
White Milk Glass, pr of baby shoes, pink bow, 2" h, 4" w 45

GOEBEL FIGURINES

In addition to Hummel figurines, Goebel made thousands of other ceramic figurines and decorative accessories. There are Goebel figurines based upon artwork by Charlotte Byj, Disney, Harry Holt, Schaubach, and Norman Rockwell. Occasionally one will find pieces bearing the signature of a master sculptor, e.g., Frobek, Schrobek, or Unger. It is estimated that Goebel made over 40,000 non-Hummel items.

Club: Goebel Networkers, P.O. Box 396, Lemoyne, PA 17043.

A Child's Prayer, Charlotte Byj, unmkd, 5.75" 50
A Child's Prayer – Blonde, Charlotte Byj, 1964-72, 5.5" 95
Angel Ringing Bell, 1979-90, 4.25" 30
Angel with Mandolin, 1991-2000, 2.75" 10
Angel with Violin, 1991-2000, 2.75" 10
Awakening, sgd, Laszlo Ispunky, 1979-90, 8" 100
Baby Crawling, 1979-90, 2.75" 40
Blowing His Horn, 1979-90, 3.5" 25
Bowler, Phillip Kracikowski, 1972-79, 6" . . .50
Boy At The Beach, 1979-90, 4.75" 35
Boy Carrying Eggs, Lore, 1979-90, 4.75" . . .60
Boy Picking Mushrooms, Lore, 1979-90, 3.5" 55
Boy Watering Flowers, Lore, 1979-90, 5.25" 60
Boy With Apples, Lore, 1979-90, 4.75" 60
Boy With Bag of Fruit, 1979-90, 4.5" 45
Boy With Dog, Norman Rockwell, 1960-63, 4.5" 350
Boy With Dog And Ball, Nasha, 1950-59, 5.25" 350
Boy With Fish, Lore, 1979-90, 4.5" 60
Boy With Flowers For Girl, Nasha, 1935-49, 5.5" 400
Boy With Honey Pot, Lore, 1972-79, 5.25" 150
Boy With Horse, Lore, 1972-79, 7.75" 200
Brown Bunny, 1979-90, 2.25" 50
Brown Puppy, 1979-90, 2" 25
Brown Puppy, 1979-90, 4" 50
Bunnies At Play, Disney, 1950-59, 4" 350
Cactus Blues, Harry Holt, 1972-79, 6.25" 70

Cold Ol' Swimming Hole, Harry Holt, 1972-79, 5.5" .... .65
Cupid On Heart Base, 1972-79, 4.75" 55
Curiosity, Harry Holt, 1979-90, 4.5" .... .65
Festive Lady Tree Topper, 1964-72, 7.5" .. 125
Fish For Two, Harry Holt, 1972-79, 5.75" ... 75
Girl And Angel, 1972-79, 5.25" .... .60
Girl Eating Apples, Lore, 1972-79, 5.75" ... 150
Girl Walking, Lore, 1979-90, 4.75" .... .60
Girl Washing Clothes, Lore, 1979-90, 4.75" .... .60
Girl Watering Flowers, Lore, 1964-72, 6.25" 125
Girl With Bird On Stump, Nasha, 1950-59, 5.25" 350
Girl With Flowers, Lore, 1979-90, 4.5" ..... .60
Hallmark Child Praying, Betsey Clark, 1972-79, 4" 110
Hallmark Child With Flowers, Betsey Clark, 1972-79, 4.5" 110
Holy Family, 1960-63, 5" .... .60
Hush-A-Bye, Irene Spencer, 1979-90, 6.25" .... .75
Indian Chief, Harry Holt, 1972-79, 6.5" 85
King Standing, 1964-72, 6.5" .... .60
Little Girl Bell, 1964-72, 5.5" .... .50
Little Miss Coy, Charlotte Byj, 1964-72, 4.5" 140
Lore Sign, Lore, 1979-90, 4.75" 100
Madonna Bust, 1964-72, 6.5" .... .75
Please, Harry Holt, 1972-79, 4.5" .... .65
Puppy, 1972-79, 2" .... .40
Rise And Shine, Irene Spencer, 1979-90, 6.5" .... .55
Rocking Horse Candle Holder, 1979-90, 3.25" .... .35
Schnauzer, 1964-72, 4.875" 50
Soldier, 1979-90, 3.75" .... .30
Springtime Suitor Plaque, Lore, 1979-90, 5.875" .... .35
The Suitor, Harry Holt, 1979-90, 5.5" ...... .65
Tightrope Walker, A Ruiz, 1979-90, 8" 125
Tinkerbell, Disney, 1979-90, 8.5" 195
Touchdown Flyer – Amerikids, Harry Holt, 1979-90, 7.25" .... .70
Traveler, Bochmann, 1972-79, 8.25" 100
Trouble Shooter, Charlotte Byj, 1964-72, 5.5" 175
Trouble Shooter, Charlotte Byj, 1979-90, 5.5" 130
Waiting To Produce, Harry Holt, 1979-90, 6" .... .75
Whose Fish?, Harry Holt, 1972-79, 5.5" 80
Woman Bowler, Skrobek, limited ed of 2500, 1979-90, 7" 100

GOLD

Twenty-four-karat gold is pure gold. Twelve-karat gold is fifty percent gold and fifty percent other elements. Many gold items have more weight value than antique or collectible value. The gold-weight scale is different from our regular English pounds scale. Learn the proper conversion procedure. Review the value of an ounce of gold once a week and practice keeping that figure in your mind.

Take time to research and learn the difference between gold and gold plating. Pieces with gold wash, gold gilding, and gold bands have no weight value. Value rests in other areas. In many cases the gold is applied on the surface. Washing and handling lead to its removal.

Gold coinage is a whole other story. Every coin suspected of being gold should first be checked by a jeweler and then in coin price guides.

GOLF COLLECTIBLES

Golf was first played in Scotland in the fifteenth century. The game achieved popularity in the late 1840s when the "gutty" ball was introduced. Although golf was played in America before the Revolution, it gained a strong foothold in the recreational area only after 1890.

Most golf collectibles are common, so doing your homework pays, especially when trying to determine the value of clubs.

Do not limit yourself to items used on the course. Books about golf, decorative accessories with a golf motif, and clubhouse collectibles are eagerly sought by collectors. This is a great sports collectible to tee off on.

Clubs: Golf Collectors Society, P.O. Box 20546, Dayton OH 45420; World Logo Ball Assoc., P.O. Box 91989, Long Beach, CA 90809, www.hyperhead.com/wlba2.

Ashtray, crystal, silver deposit golfer in bowl, silver rim, 1.25" h, 6" d 90

Book, *Winning Golf,* by Jack Nicklaus, Grow Ahead Press, soft cov, 1969, 32 pgs 25

Booklet, Oak Cliff Country Club Opening, includes photos, drawings, names, and menu, 1954, 32 pgs 25

Cigarette Lighter, figural golf ball with club protruding from top, "Super Match," Japan, 5" h, 3.5" w 30

Golf Balls, box of 3, Titleist DT Distance, Reddy Kilowatt logo, 1980s, MIB 40

Golf Club, iron, wood shaft, head mkd "L Brownlee Special," 33.25" l 125

Golf Club, iron, wood shaft, head mkd "Pro Made, H16, Heather Downs, Mashie Niblick," 33.5" l 145

Golf Club, iron, wood shaft, partially wrapped in black tape, head stamped "Morristown," 33" l 175

Golf Club, iron, wood shaft, unmkd, 33.675" l 95

Golf Club, jigger iron, wood handle, head stamped "Jigger, Handforge," 33.75" l . .95

Golf Club, Schenectady Putter, Mar 24, 1903 patent date, wood shaft, leather grip, 31" l 200

Golf Shoes, saddle shoe style with wing tips, Etonic Engineers, orig box, unused, size 8 1/2 40

Highball glasses, set of 8, "58th Annual Championship of the Professional Golfers' Association of America. Congressional Country Club. Bethesda, Maryland. 12-15 August 1976" etched on front, PGA and CCC logos, etched Bicentennial image on back 130

Magazine,* Sports Illustrated for Kids, *complete with attached trading card insert featuring Tiger Woods' rookie card, Dec 1996, mint condition 325

Planter, golfer figure beside oversized golf ball bowl, mkd "Samson Import Co Chicago 1957 329A," 5.5" h, 4.5" w . . .55

Postcard, Scottish golfer in mid-swing, "The Game Scotsmen Knock 'L' Out Of" caption, 1930s 36

Talcum Powder Tin, Bo-Kay Perfume Co, sports images including gold, baseball, football, diving, polo, and tennis, orange and black 225

Wall Hanging, cotton, 6 multicolor comic golf scenes, British, 30" x 18" 32

GONDER POTTERY

In 1941 Lawton Gonder established Gonder Ceramic Arts, Inc., at Zanesville, Ohio. The company is known for its glazes, such as Chinese crackle, gold crackle, and flambé. Pieces are clearly marked. Gonder manufactured lamp bases at a second plant and marketed them under the trademark "Eglee." Gonder Ceramic Arts, Inc. ceased production in 1957.

Club: Gonder Collectors Club, 917 Hurl Dr., Pittsburgh, PA 15236, www.happysemporium.com/gondermuseum.htm.

Ashtray, #113, fish shape, green and yellow 70

Basket, #H-39, brown and pink, 7" h, 8.25" w 40

Bowl, #H-29, gray ext, pink int, 8" 32

Candleholders, pr, #552, cornucopia shape, light gray and pink, 5" h 32

Candleholders, pr, #561, dolphin, blue with dark blue accents 95
Console Set, #E-29 bowl and pr of #E-14 candleholders, aqua ext with brown specks and drips, pink int, 1940s-50s, 8" bowl, 4.5" candleholders 30
Ewer, #E-65, dark mauve, 6" h 48
Figure, Chinese Water Bearer Woman, silver tag, 1940s-50s 45
Lamp Base, mare and colt heads, brown, 12.25" h, 6.5" w 60
Pitcher, #901, combed design, lavender and aqua on gray ground, 8.5" h 175
Pitcher, #996, miniature, 1.5" h, 3.5" w 12
Planter, #E-3, figural flower and flowerpot, mottled pink and blue, 7" h 35
Planter, #E-44, figural swan, light blue mother-of-pearl glaze, 5.5" h, 5" l, 4" w . .25
Planter, #J-31, figural swan, 9" h, 9" w 85
Salt and Pepper Shakers, figural "S" and "P," matte green glaze, 2.75" h, 1.25" w .25
Vase, #E-12, low, ruffled, mauve and brown mottled glaze, 2.75" h, 7" w 15
Vase, #E-64, twisted form, blue-gray ext, pink-gray int, 6.25" h, 4.5" d 25
Vase, #H-7, double handled, mottled pink .50
Vase, #H-8, double handled, pink, 1940s-50s, 9" h, 6.5" w 30
Vase, #H-14, cornucopia, green, brown, and pink mottled glaze, 9" h 60
Vase, #H-10, double handled, turquoise . .45
Vase, #H-11, tulip shape, pink 40
Vase, #H-34, basket form 45
Vase, #H-47, double swan, turquoise 42
Vase, #H-74, rect block form, gray 35
Vase, #J-57, lyre, gray 85
Vase, #K-15, feathers, pink, 12" 100
Vase, #K-25, swallows, pink 150

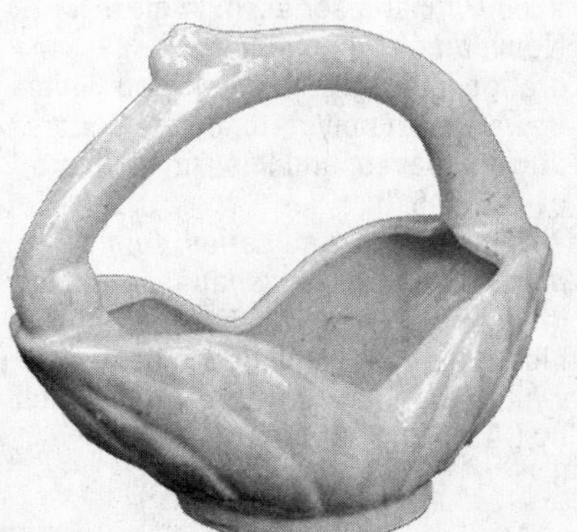

GOOFUS GLASS

Goofus glass is a patterned glass on which the reverse of the principal portion of the pattern is colored in red or green and covered with a metallic gold ground. It was distributed at carnivals between 1890 and 1920. There are no records of it being manufactured after that date. Crescent Glass Company, Imperial Glass Corporation, LaBelle Glass Works, and Northwood Glass Company are some of the companies who made Goofus glass.

Value rests with pieces that have both the main color and ground color still intact. The reverse painting often wore off. It is not uncommon to find the clear pattern glass blank with no painting on it whatsoever.

Goofus glass is also known as Mexican Ware, Hooligan Glass, and Pickle Glass. Says a lot, doesn't it?

Club: The Goofus Glass Information Center, www.goofus.org.

Bowl, paneled, double-handled, flowers at rim, 2.5" h, 5" w 45
Bowl, scalloped lacy edge, red roses, 10" d 35
Child's Plate, "This Little Pig Went To Market" in center, ring of children holding hands on rim, 6.5" d 125
Plate, Double Roses pattern, Northwood, 10.5" d 30
Plate, red roses, blue background, blue border, 9" d 25
Plate, Roses in Snow, 6" d 30

Relish Dish, oval, double-handled, cut glass style pattern, red and silver, 10" x 6.5" 20
Souvenir Plate, 1904 St Louis Expo, Festival Hall and Cascade Gardens 50
Tray, rect, red roses, 11" x 7" 48
Trinket Jar, cabbage 30
Vase, grape cluster, 14" h 12
Vases, pr, corseted cylinder shape with 4 full-length long stemmed pink roses on sides, 12.75" h, 7.5" d 65

GOUDA POTTERY

Gouda and its surrounding area in Holland has been one of the principle Dutch pottery centers for centuries. Gouda art pottery is easlily distinguished by its Art Nouveau and Art Deco designs executed in bright, bold colors.

Bowl, Robur pattern, high glaze, cov flattened ball form, mustard yellow, black, white, and orange abstract florals on black ground, mkd "Regina," c1920, 5" d 165
Candlesticks, pr, semi-matte, partial ovals in gold, orange, black, and blue surrounded by black borders, swirls moving down black column to nearly flat pedestal base, mkd "PZH," 1925, 7" h 450
Chamberstick, Rhodian pattern, semi-matte, mint green, orange, cobalt blue, and white on brown tones, mkd "PZH," 1926, 3" h, 5" d 225

Cigar Ashtray, Victoria pattern, semi-matte, bulbous squatty form, abstract florals in orange, yellow, brown, cobalt blue, lilac, and olive green on white ground, insert on top has yellow, aqua, and olive bands separated by black bands and cigar rest indents, mkd "PZH," c1948, 6.5" d 90
Comport, Syna pattern, semi-matte, goblet form, upper and lower bands with abstract yellow and lilac flower-like shapes outlined in ocher on white ground, contrasting cobalt blue, turquoise, and black bands, mostly black int with one turquoise band and one white band highlighted with ocher dots, two tiny paint skips at base, mkd "PZH," c1923, 6.5" h, 6" d 250
Decanter, Atol pattern, semi-matte, ocher, cobalt blue, lilac, orange, turquoise, and black bands on ribbed neck, bulbous body with abstract design in orange, yellow, cobalt blue, and ocher on white ground, black borders, mkd "PZH," 1930, 9.5" h 325
Inkwell, Dorisa pattern, semi-matte, ribbed sides, ocher-outlined burnt orange and black shapes on turquoise ground, indented brown ribs separate each vertical panel, with glass insert and pen hole, c1925, 2" h, 3" d 140
Tray, Ali pattern, semi-matte, round, symmetrical design of abstract feathery shapes in bold colors of orange, green, blue, and white, outlined in ocher, black and dark brown border, mkd "PZH," c1925, 12" d 275
Urn, cov, Juliana series, high glaze, Art Nouveau design with purple, lilac, orange, blue, green, black, and white flowers with polychrome dot clusters, flowing leaves, and lines, mkd "Ivora," c1915, 12.5" h 325
Vase, Décor Breetvelt series, semi-matte, double-gourd shape, Japanese influence pattern with burnt orange cloud-like forms outlined in ocher, off-white ground, rust borders, decorated by CA Prins, mkd "PZH," c1925, 8.25" h 500

GRANITEWARE

Graniteware, also known as agateware or enamelware, is the name commonly given to iron or steel kitchenware with an enamel coating. American production began in the 1860s and continues today.

White and gray are the most commonly found colors. However, graniteware can be found in shades of blue, brown, cream, green, red, violet, and yellow. Mottled pieces combining swirls of color are especially desirable.

Never lose sight of the fact that graniteware was inexpensive utilitarian kitchen and household ware. Modern prices should reflect this humble origin.

Club: National Graniteware Society, P.O. Box 9248, Cedar Rapids, IA 52409, www.graniteware.org.

Coffeepot, gray, conical, flat bottom, rounded spout, arched handle, hinged rounded tin lid with turned wooden finial painted black, chips and wear, 8.125" h, 5.125" d 10

Coffeepot, light blue and white, conical, flat bottom, curved spout, C-shaped black handle, hinged rounded lid with small ball finial, chips, 9.375" h, 6.5" d .180

Coffeepot, robin's egg blue, 10.25" h 45

Lunch Pail, light blue and white, cylindrical straight sides, arched handle, wire bail with turned wooden grip painted black, chips, 7" h, 6.75" d 110

Miner's Lunch Kettle, blue and white and solid blue, stacked, consists of iron rack with round graniteware handle on top, round dish at bottom with holes around sides, 3 round individual dishes with solid sides stacked on top, and plain blue graniteware rounded lid, minor chipping, 11.125" h 45

Pail, dark blue and white ext, white int, matching lid, round with flat bottom, straight sides with horizontal ribbing, black rim, rounded lid with knob finial, wire bail handle, chips, 6.25" h, 5.5" d ..45

Pail, light blue and white, matching lid, round with flat bottom and straight sides, rounded lid with arched black handle, black rim on pail, wire bail handle with turned wooden grip, chips, 6.5" h, 6.125" d 30

Pan, green and white, round, flat bottom, flared sides, rounded rim, chips, 3.375" h, 10" d 90

Pan, light blue and white, round with slightly flared sides and rounded rim, white int, black rim, wear and chips, 2" h, 5.75" d 5

Percolator, light blue and white, hinged lid, glass dome top, aluminum coffee basket and parts, black handle and rims, flat bottom with rounded base and straight sides, rounded lid, 8.25" h, 5.375" d 45

Pitcher, white, red "Campbell's Tomato Juice" on both sides, 9" h, 10" w 100

Teapot, speckled robin's egg blue, 1904 St Louis Expo, gooseneck spout, 4.75" h 125

GREETING CARDS

Greeting cards still fall largely under the wing of postcard collectors. They deserve a collector group of their own.

At the moment, high-ticket greeting cards are character-related. Someday collectors will discover Hallmark and other greeting cards as social barometers of their era. Meanwhile, enjoy picking them up for 25¢ or less.

Note: See Valentines for additional listings.

Birthday, bi-fold, Raggedy Ann on cov, "Raggedy Ann hopes your birthday will treat you to some fun. She thinks you're extra special and so does everyone. Happy Birthday with lots of Love," 6.5" x 4.5" 15

Birthday, tri-fold, 3 images of black baker with birthday cake, "You're in Receipt of Birthday Wishes," 6" x 5" 20

Birthday, tri-fold, Little Nell, Joan Walsh Anglund, "Dear Granddaughter, A visit from Little Nell the paper doll" and doll on front, 3 pgs of clothing inside, 1975 .25

Christmas, adv, Clinton Furnace, Sheet Metal, black and white photo of storefront window, 1940s 12

Christmas, bi-fold, adv, Strand Baking Co, Marshalltown, IA, holiday scene on front, a wish for "Peace and Victory," Dec 1943 postmark on envelope, 8.25" x 5.25" 5

Christmas, bi-fold, "Merry Christmas Teacher," Santa carrying sack on front, 1970s, 6.5" x 4" 2

Christmas, celluloid, "Remembrance wakes..." and hp violet bouquet on front, 1910s-20s .25

Easter, adv, oversized trade card for Atlantic & Pacific Tea Co, "An Easter Greeting" and child on front, adv text on back 8

Easter, postcard, "Happy Easter," emb vignette of boy and duck, 4" x 4.875" 5

Father's Day, bi-fold, shirt and tie and flowers on front, "There'll always be ties between us, Dad, of affection deep and true; Ties of happy memories that bring proud thoughts of you; So I'm sending you on Father's Day, good wishes by the score; To tie up all your future days with happiness galore," 1940s-50s, 5.25" x 4.25" 5

Greetings, "Happy Memories" by Elizabeth Love, contains poetry about Spring, hope, memories, and faith, bouquet of violets on cov, silk cord with tassles, pub by Artistic Lithographic Co, London, No. 3066, 8 pgs, c1898 26

Halloween, postcard, child with pumpkin, "Hallowe'en Greetings," artist sgd by Ellen Clapsaddle 10

Midsummer, adv, Woolson Spice Co, Toledo OH, distributed in Lion Coffee, mother holding baby and children on swings in park by lake, 6.75" x 5.5" 15

New Year, postcard, emb horseshoe and flowers, "Wishing you a Happy New Year," Good Luck New Year Series No. 1, 1910 postmark 3

GRISWOLD

Matthew Griswold purchased the Selden family interest in Selden & Griswold in 1884. Griswold became a cast iron king in the early 20th century under the leadership of Marvin Griswold, Matthew's son. Roger Griswold, son of Matthew, Jr., became president in 1926. The family's involvement ended in 1944. In 1957 the Griswold trade name was sold to Wagner Manufacturing Company, one of its major competitors. The additional sales eventually resulted in the company being part of the General Housewares Corporation.

Beware of reproductions and fantasy pieces. Many are made in India and imported with easily removable, country of origin paper labels.

Club: Griswold & Cast-Iron Cookware Assoc., P.O. Drawer B, Perrysburg, NY 14129.

Ashtray, #770, red and cream 60
Casserole Dish, #83, black iron with white porcelain int 85
Cornstick Pan, #273, red and cream 100
Cornstick Pan, cast iron, mrkd "No 2700, Griswold, Wheat & Corn Stick Pan Erie, PA, USA Pat No 73,326,632," c1925, 13.5" x 5.75" 325
Dutch Oven, cov, #9, Griswold/Erie 60
French Roll, #17, variation #6 130
French Waffle Iron, #8, mkd "Selden Griswold" 850
Gem Pan, #1 250
Griddle, Aristocraft, aluminum handle 30
Hotel Skillet 625
Lid, #6, high dome, smooth 90
Lid, #7, button logo 85
Lid, #7, high dome, lettered 125
Lid, #8, low dome, lettered 55
Lid, #11, low dome, smooth 750
Muffin Pan, #6, variation #2 85
Popover Pan, #10, aluminum 40
Santa Mold 535
Skillet, #2, smooth bottom 375
Skillet, #3, block with grooved handle 45
Skillet, #3, small bottom, large block, smooth top high lid 155
Skillet, #3, sq, black iron with white porcelain int 225
Skillet, #6, small bottom, large block 50
Skillet, #7, small bottom, small emb, grooved handle 30
Skillet, #8, pattern 777, mkd "OR Chicken Pan" 95
Skillet, #8, sq, pattern 2108 60
Skillet, cov, #8, pattern 2008-2098, hammered hinge 95

Skillet, cov, #9, large emb block letters, with heat ring 90
Skillet Cover, #6, aluminum 55
Skillet Cover, #6, chrome 125
Waffle Iron, #6 575
Waffle Iron, #8, early finger slot hinge, wood handles 165
Wheat Pan, #28, variation #1 235

GUARDIAN SERVICE

In the mid-1930s, stainless-clad carbon steel cookware arrived on the scene. Development was rapid, albeit interrupted by WWII and the Korean War. By the 1960s, several manufacturers offered stainless steel clad aluminum cookware.

Century Metalcraft Corporation's Guardian Service cookware is popular, due largely to demand created by Internet sales. Initially, individuals seeking to complete sets inherited from their parents or to replace damaged pieces caused the price jump. Today, young "retro" collectors are driving the market.

Thus far, Guardian Service stands alone in the collecting realm. Stainless steel and aluminum cookware by companies such as Cory, Ekco, Mirro, and Revere are still garage sale merchandise.

Chicken Fryer, glass top, 12" 100
Cleaner, Guardian Service Cleaner, Century Metalcraft Corp, Los Angeles, CA, paper label over cardboard, unopened, 5.125" h, 2.675" d 25
Coffeepot, drip-o-lator, 5 pcs, metal lid, open Bakelite handle mkd "Guardian" on both sides 125
Cookbook, tested recipes and "how to" instructions for using cookware, 72 pgs, 1930s 25
Double Boiler, 2 qt, 2 pots and glass lid ..100
Griddle, octagonal, tab handles, 13" w 35
Handle, Bakelite, clip-on, 9.5" l 30
Handles, pr, Bakelite, slip-on, Mickey Mouse ear type 20
Ice Bucket and Tongs, glass lid 70
Meat Platter, oval, tab handles, 13" x 10.5" 35
Pot, 7" d 20
Pot, glass lid, 3" h, 9" d 45

Roaster, 3 pcs, deep roaster, shallow roaster/lid/serving tray, and glass lid . . .95
Salt and Pepper Shakers, figural coffee-pots, SP 60
Trio Set, 7 pcs, 3 triangular cov pots and circ tray, 3 qt pots 80

HALL CHINA

In 1903 Robert Hall founded the Hall China Company in East Liverpool, Ohio. Hall produced refrigerator sets and a large selection of kitchenware and dinnerware in a wide variety of patterns. The company was a major supplier of institutional (hotel and restaurant) ware.

Hall also manufactured some patterns on an exclusive basis: Autumn Leaf for Jewel Tea, Blue Bouquet for the Standard Coffee Company of New Orleans, and Red Poppy for the Grand Union Tea Company. Hall teapots are a favorite among teapot collectors.

For the past several years, Hall has been reissuing a number of its solid-color pieces as the "Americana" line. Items featuring a decal or gold decoration have not been reproduced. Because of the difficulty in distinguishing old from new solid-color pieces, prices on many older pieces have dropped.

Club: Hall Collector's Club, P.O. Box 360488, Cleveland, OH 44136.

Note: For additional listings see Autumn Leaf.

Baker, Montgomery Ward, white 45
Butter, Hercules, tilt-top, blue-green 55
Casserole, Beauty .40
Casserole, Rose Parade, tab-handled 30
Casserole, Tritone .70
Cookie Jar, Garden Sundial, blue 275
Cookie Jar, Sundial 275
Irish Coffee Mugs, set of 6, white with black bottom 45
Jug, Riviera, maroon 40
Jug, Silhouette, silver trim 150
Jug, Wildfire, Radiance 25
Leftover, Hercules, tilt-top, blue-green . . .40
Leftover, Hotpoint, dark gray, 4" 35
Leftover, Hotpoint, green, 6" 40
Leftover, Hotpoint, light gray, 4" 35
Leftover, Montgomery Ward, white, large .45
Leftover, Phoenix, delphinium 25
Leftover, Westinghouse, Adonis, small, round 15
Leftover, Westinghouse, Emperor, orange 40
Mixing Bowl, Blue Blossom 40
Mixing Bowl, Radiance, large, ivory, unmkd 25
Mixing Bowl, Radiance, medium, ivory, unmkd 18
Percolator, pink 70
Pitcher, General Electric, Adonis 65
Refrigerator Set, Adonis, water server, large round casserole, 2 small round bowls, 2 leftovers 175
Refrigerator Set, Hotpoint, water server with china stopper, sand rect leftover, green 6" round leftover, maroon 7" round leftover, 4" sq orange leftover, 4" sq gray leftover, green luster 5" sq leftover, yellow 6" sq leftover 340
Refrigerator Set, Montgomery Ward, delphinium water server, small cov bowl, medium cov bowl, and rect leftover, large white rect baker 175
Refrigerator Set, Phoenix, water server and 2 leftovers, delphinium 120
Refrigerator Set, Westinghouse General, delphinium water server, no lid, yellow leftover, orange leftover 120
Salt and Pepper Shakers, Crocus 25
Soup, flat, Wildfire, 8.5" 12
Teapot, Boston, ivory, 1.5 cup 25
Teapot, Donut, gray 45
Water Server, General Electric, Adonis, gray with yellow top, open 35

HALLMARK

Hallmark Cards, Inc., was founded by Joyce C. Hall. Hallmark Keepsakes were first marketed in 1973 and these first-year ornaments are avidly sought by collectors. Handcrafted Keepsakes were added to the line in 1975, followed the next year by Baby's First Christmas and Bicentennial ornaments.

Collecting Hallmark Keepsake Ornaments became a popular hobby in 1987, leading to the creation of The Keepsake Ornament Collector's Club, whose membership roles now exceed 250,000. As with any contemporary collectible, keep in mind that secondary market values can be speculative.

Club: Hallmark Keepsake Ornament Collectors Club, P.O. Box 419034, Kansas City, MO 64141.

Note: Prices listed are for ornaments MIB.

1958 Ford Edsel Citation Convertible, Club ornament, 1995 55
Across the Miles, 1990 4
Angel, Twirl About, 1976 85
Angel, yarn, 1980 12
Angel Bells, Joy, 1995 16
Angel Kitty, 1990 16
Animals' Christmas, 1980 30
Armful of Joy, Club ornament, 1990 22
Baby's First Christmas, bear, 1990 29
Baby's First Christmas, satin ball, 1980 24
Beary Short Nap, 1990 18

Betsey Clark #8, Joy in the Air, 1980 210
Betsey Clark's Christmas, 1980 20
Betsey's Country Christmas, 1993 18
Bugs Bunny, Looney Tunes, 1993 12
Caroling Bear, 1980 55
Carrousel #2, Christmas Carrousel, 1979 .115
Christmas Owl, Little Trimmers, 1980 18
Christmas Treat, 1979 40
Christmas Treat, 1980 40
Christmas Tree, Holiday Highlights, 1979 ..35
Clever Cookie, 1993 15
Coach, 1993 5
Della Robia Wreath, Twirl About, 1977 48
Downhill Run, 1979 70
Elfin Antics, 1980 115
First Christmas Together, glass ball, 1980 .28
Granddaughter, 1980 24
Grandaughter, satin ball, 1979 20
Grandmother, 1980 20
Grandmother, satin ball, 1979 7
Grandparents, 1980 20
Grandson, Snoopy, satin ball, 1979 20
Heavenly Nap, 1980 30
Heavenly Sounds, 1980 40
Here Comes Santa #1, Santa's Motor Car, 1979 425
Here Comes Santa #2, Santa's Express, 1980 145
Holly and Poinsettia Ball, 1978 45
Jolly Santa, 1980 20
Marty Links, 1980 9
Mrs Santa, yarn, 1976 20
Muppets, 1980 20
Nativity, 1980 22
Norman Rockwell Series #1, Santa's Visitors, 1980 125
Outdoor Fun, 1979 55
Partridge, Twirl About, 1976 85
Peanuts, 1980 35
Santa, 1980 45
Santa, Yesteryears, 1976 95
Santa Mobile, Holiday Chimes, 1980 30
Santa's Flight, 1st tin ornament, 1980 68
Santa's Workshop, 1980 18
Skating Raccoon, 1978 45
Snowflake Chimes, Holiday Chimes, 1980 .25
Spot of Christmas Cheer, 1980 48
Star Over Bethlehem, Colors of Christmas, 1979 45
Swingin' On A Star, Little Trimmers, 1980 .35
Teacher, 1980 8
Train, Yesteryears, 1976 125
Wreath, Holiday Highlights, 1980 35

HALLOWEEN

Halloween collectibles deserve a category of their own. There is such a wealth of material out there that it nearly rivals Christmas as the most-decorated holiday season. While you may be spooked by the price listed below, I see Halloween decorations and collectibles traded at these prices all the time.

Note: See costumes for additional listings.

Book, *Dennison's Bogie Book,* 1924 65
Candy Container, glass, goblin head, traces of orig paint 435
Candy Container, witch, hp cardboard, West Germany, 7.125" h 110
Candy Container, witch carrying jack-o'-lantern, Rosbro 22
Candy Container, witch on cycle 300
Costume, Hi-C Spook suit, sewn painted vinyl, orig envelope, unused, 1958 35
Game, Cat and Witch 60
Noisemaker, cat and pumpkin on litho tin rattle, black and orange, wood handle 15
Noisemaker, witch on oblong litho tin ratchet, black plastic handle, US Metal Toy 22
Noisemaker, witch on oblong litho tin ratchet, wooden handle, Kirchof, 4.5" x 2.25" 28
Noisemaker, witch on rect litho tin ratchet, green plastic handle, US Metal Toy, 4.5" x 1.125" 22

Noisemaker, witch on rect litho tin ratchet, wood handle, US Metal Toy . . .24
Noisemaker, wood, ratchet type, jack-o'-lantern candy container head, ruffled crepe paper collar 230
Paper Plates, set of 8, sq, boy holding large pumpkin with owl on top, orange border with black picket fence, black cats and jack-o'-lanterns in corners, Beach Products, MIP 40
Tear Sheet, *Saturday Evening Post,* Ipswich Hosiery, witch graphic, Jun 7, 1919, 14" x 10.5" 8

HANNA-BARBERA

How much is that gorilla in the window? If it's Magilla Gorilla, it could be pricey. Merchandise associated with Hanna-Barbera cartoon characters is becoming increasingly popular as baby boomers rediscover their childhood. Keep in mind that these items were mass-produced. Condition is a key element in determining value.

Flintstones, alarm clock, Fred Flintstone, ceramic body, dial mkd "Sheffield, The Flintstones Alarm, Western Germany," 8.5" h 150
Flintstones, ashtray, ceramic, relief-molded Barney Rubble with bowling ball, Arrow, 1961 75

Flintstones, Big Little Book-type book, *The Flintstones, It's About Time,* ©1977 .6
Flintstones, Hallmark Christmas Keepsake Ornament, Pebbles and Bamm-Bamm building a Dino snowman, 1995 25
Flintstones, hand puppet, Wilma, vinyl head, blue cloth body, flannel hands, mid-1960s, 10.5" l .18
Flintstones, lunch box, litho tin, Aladdin, 1971 95
Flintstones, lunch box and thermos, "A Day At the Zoo," blue plastic, 1989 25
Flintstones, marbles, Bedrock Boulders, 42 marbles, 2 shooters, and pouch, unopened 15
Flintstones, movie, *Golfing's Great,* silent, Super 8mm, orig box, 1963 20
Flintstones, mug, Fred Flintstone vitamins, plastic, 1968, 3.25" h 8
Flintstones, night light, figural Barney Rubble, 1979, 4.5" h, MOC 40
Flintstones, soaky bottle, Barney Rubble, Purex, 7.75" h 28
Flintstones, sticker, 3-D Fred Flintstone with squeaker, 1978, 19.25" x 10", MIP . .35
Flintstones, toy color TV, 4 rolls, 1966 55
Huckleberry Hound, charm bracelet, Pixie, Dixie, Boo Boo, Huck, Yogi, Mr Jinks, and charms, 1959, MOC 80
Huckleberry Hound, flashlight, interchangeable faces of Fred Flintstone, Huckleberry Hound, and Yogi Bear, 1975, 3" l, MOC 15
Huckleberry Hound, lamp, plastic Huck figure on circ metal base, Quick Draw McGraw, Huck, Baba Looey, and Yogi on cardboard shade, 1960s, 20" h 50
Huckleberry Hound, stuffed doll, felt body, tag reads "Huckleberry Hound, 1980, Hanna-Barbera Productions, Inc, Mighty Star," 13" h .10
Huckleberry Hound, wastebasket, litho tin, Huck, Yogi, Quick Draw McGraw, and TV Friends, litho tin, 1960s 35
Jetsons, comic book, Jetsons, #1, Gold Key 60
Jetsons, frame tray puzzle, Whitman 15
Magilla Gorilla, book, *Magilla Gorilla Takes a Banana Holiday,* Whitman Tell-A-Tale, 1965 .10
Magilla Gorilla, Little Golden Book, #547 . .25
Muddlemore and Boo, mug, yellow plastic, dated 1971, 4.25" h 4
Quick Draw McGraw, book, *Quick Draw McGraw Badmen Beware,* Whitman, 1960 12
Quick Draw McGraw, figure, porcelain, 7.5" h, 2.25" w 100
Ruff and Reddy, comic book, *Ruff and Reddy,* Dell Comics, No. 6, Jul/Sep 1960 25
Space Ghost, comic book, deluxe format, Comico, 1987, 48 pgs 10
Yogi Bear, bottle caps, set of 2, 1 Yogi, 1 Boo Boo, flip heads, MIP, 1994 5
Yogi Bear, comic book, Yogi Bear Birthday Party, Dell Comics, #1271, 1961 25
Yogi Bear, cookie jar, American Bisque . .450
Yogi Bear, jigsaw puzzle, Yogi and Boo-Boo on pogo sticks, Whitman, 63 pcs 10
Yogi Bear, pop-up book, *Yogi Bear and the Beaver Dam,* 1974 15
Yogi Bear, spoon, SP, Old Company Plate, Hanna-Barbera copyright, 5.25" l 20

Yogi Bear, stuffed doll, wearing green hat, white collar, and yellow tie 70

Yogi Bear, white paste jar, figural blue plastic Yogi head, 1965, 5" h, MOC 22
Yogi Bear, Yogi magnet, 1988 2

HARKER POTTERY

In 1840 Benjamin Harker of East Liverpool, Ohio, built a kiln and produced yellowware products. During the Civil War, David Boyce managed the firm. Harker and Boyce played important roles in the management of the firm through much of its history. In 1931 the company moved to Chester, West Virginia. Eventually, Jeannette Glass Company purchased Harker, closing the plant in March 1972.

Much of Harker's wares were utilitarian. The company introduced Cameoware in 1945 and a Rockingham ware line in 1960. A wide range of backstamps and names were used.

Amy, Hot Oven, individual bean pot 15
Ashtray, Doral Hotel adv, green on white .10
Bamboo, platter, cocoa 15
Calico Tulip, Skyscraper, range set, salt and pepper shakers and cov drip jar . . .45
Calico Tulip, utility plate 35
Chesterton, bread and butter plate, gray, 6" 7
Chesterton, casserole, cov, gray 25
Chesterton, creamer, gray 8
Chesterton, cup and saucer, gray 4
Chesterton, dessert bowl, gray 3
Chesterton, dinner plate, gray 8
Chesterton, fruit bowl, gray 7
Chesterton, plate, sq, gray 5
Chesterton, platter, gray 20
Chesterton, salad plate, gray, 7.25" 8
Chesterton, saucer 5
Chesterton, soup bowl, gray 9
Chesterton, teapot, gray 26
Chesterton, vegetable bowl, 2-handled, gray 6
Colonial Lady, soup bowl 12
Corinthian, platter, teal, large 9
Corinthian, salt and pepper shakers, teal .10
Dainty Blue, dinner plate, 10" d 8
Dogwood, bread and butter plate 6
Dogwood, cup and saucer 9
Dogwood, dessert bowl 6
Dogwood, dinner plate 12
Dogwood, platter 18
Dogwood, soup bowl 8
Everglades, dinner plate, cocoa 12
Golden Wheat, creamer and sugar, octagonal 22
Heritance Rosebud, butter, cov 25
Heritance Rosebud, creamer and sugar . .36
Heritance Rosebud, cup and saucer 16
Heritance Rosebud, dinner plate 15
Heritance Rosebud, salad plate 15
Intaglio, bread and butter plate, alpine 5
Intaglio, creamer and sugar, alpine 15
Intaglio, cup and saucer, alpine 10
Intaglio, dinner plate, alpine 10
Intaglio, platter, alpine 22
Intaglio, salad plate, alpine 7
Intaglio, saucer, alpine 5
Intaglio, soup bowl, alpine 9
Intaglio, vegetable bowl, divided, alpine . .15
Ivy Wreath, coupe soup, celadon 12

Ivy Wreath, cup and saucer, celadon 12
Lovelace, coupe soup 18
Magnolia, fruit bowl, 6" 5
Magnolia, salad plate, 8.25" 7
Mallow, cake lifter 12
Modern Tulip, pie plate 10
Modern Tulip, rolling pin 125
Modern Tulip, water jug, cov 28
Pate Sur Pate, bread and butter plate, teal 4
Pate Sur Pate, creamer, teal 18
Pate Sur Pate, cup and saucer, teal 5
Pate Sur Pate, dinner plate, teal 10
Pate Sur Pate, fruit bowl, teal 6
Pate Sur Pate, gravy boat, teal 38
Pate Sur Pate, luncheon plate, teal 9
Pate Sur Pate, platter, teal 30
Pate Sur Pate, salad plate, teal 6
Pate Sur Pate, sugar bowl, cov, teal 25
Pate Sur Pate, vegetable bowl, oval, teal .20
Petit Point, serving spoon 15
Pine Cone, bread and butter plate 8
Pine Cone, cereal bowl 7
Pine Cone, cup 10
Pine Cone, dinner plate 4
Pine Cone, soup bowl 8
Pine Cone, vegetable bowl 10
Rolling Pin, blue, white handles 140
Seafare, platter, oval, 11" 40
Seafare, platter, oval, 13" 50
Silhouette, Virginia, fruit bowl, 5" 6
Skyscraper, salt and pepper shakers 45
Tulip, Hot Oven, custard cup 10
Wild Rose, Gadroon, fruit bowl 8
Wild Rose, Gadroon, vegetable bowl 10

HARTLAND PLASTICS, INC.

Although the Hartland trade name survives today, Hartland Plastic collectibles focus on plastic television cowboy and sports figures issued in the 1950s. The baseball figures were reissued in 1989. They have a "25" in a circle on their back just below the belt. Do not confuse them with the earlier figures.

Most figures came with accessories. These need to be present in order for the figure to be considered complete. There are two Lone Ranger figures, the second bearing a much closer resemblance to Clayton Moore.

After a period of rapid rise in the early 1990s, especially for sports figures, prices are now stable. In fact, commonly found figures are a hard sell at full book price.

3-Gaited Saddlebred Horse, woodcut, split seam near rump, 9" scale 40
Arabian Foal, chestnut, light scuffs, 6" h ..25
Chestnut Horse, 11" scale, minor rubs, 9.75" h 50
Chestnut Horse, semi-rearing, light scuff on belly and stockings, 8.5" h 75
Cheyenne Bodie Set, semi-rearing, complete, near mint 50
Cochise and Ring Eye Horse 200
Dale Evans and Buttermilk, with hat, saddle, and reins, no guns, orig box ..325
Dizzy Dean, orig box, excellent condition, 8" h 250
Donkey, unpainted gray, minor scuffs, 1950s-60s, 3.75" h 10
Lone Ranger, on rearing Trigger, complete 225
Lou Gehrig, swinging bat, with box, base, and bat, 8" h 250
Matt Dillon Set, complete, excellent condition 195
Mickey Mantle at bat, Yankees, 6.75" h ..200
Mustang, rearing, woodcut, split seam on back, 9" scale 25
Nolan Ryan, Texas Rangers, #5041, 1990 ..45
Pinto Indian Horse, semi-rearing, slight yellowing, minor scuffs, 8" h 40
Sgt Preston, no horse, some wear on knees and nose 100
Tinymite Brown Thoroughbred, unpainted, 2" h 10

Tinymite Tennessee Walking Horse, MIP, 2" h .24
Tonto and Horse, missing gun, worn paint .70
Whitey Ford, with box and base, 6.5" h .125
Wyatt Earp Set, complete, near mint .125
Yogi Berra, no mask, 1960s .250

HATPINS & HOLDERS

Women used hatpins to keep their hats in place. The ends of the pins were decorated in a wide variety of materials—ranging from gemstones to china—and the pins themselves became a fashion accessory. Since a woman was likely to own many hatpins and they were rather large, special holders were developed for them.

Clubs: American Hatpin Society, 20 Montecillo Dr., Rolling Hills Estate, CA 90274; International Club for Collectors of Hatpins and Hatpin Holders, 1013 Medhurst Rd., Columbus, OH 43220.

HOLDERS

Bavaria, porcelain, hp violets and leaves on white ground, large hole surrounded by 12 smaller holes, 5.5" h, 3" d .150
English, straw-stuffed pincushion on weighted circ SS base, Chester hallmark, 1907-08, 2" d, 4" h .110
Germany, hp porcelain, figural bird on branch, 4 holes in branch, mkd "Germany," 6" h .55

Nippon, porcelain, hp blue daisies on white ground, mkd "E OH China," 4.875" h .185
Noritake, gold dec on white ground, open top, green "Hand Painted (M in wreath) Nippon" mark, 5" l .30
Royal Bayreuth, Bavaria, Sunbonnet Babies sweeping, tan base, c1900, 4" h .475
Royal Doulton, chintz pattern with birds, pink flowers, and green leaves on white ground, 7 holes, 55" h, 4" d .350
RS Prussia, porcelain, hp pink and white roses on white ground, 4.25" h .225

PINS

Amethyst and Rhinestone, large amethyst stone surrounded by rhinestones, c1900, 1.25" d finial, 10.5" l .185
Brass, oval finial with engraved monogram and filigree frame, 8" l pin .35
Cameo, oval carved shell cameo on 14K yg pin, .75" x .625" cameo, 7.5" l pin .185
Carnival Glass, amethyst, oval finial with emb butterfly, 1.375" x 1.25" finial, 10" l pin .160
Cut Glass, pink glass finial on goldtone pin .95
Diamond, 6-point European cut diamond set in center of 14K yg medallion, c1880, .75" d finial, 3.75" l pin .225
Glass Bulb, brass pin, 2.75" d finial, 8" l pin .125
Gold, chased ball finial on hatpin attached by chain to gold hairpin, 3.5" l hatpin, 2.75" l hairpin, 9.375" l chain .125
Gold, enameled gold fleur de lis with seed pearls at center, .75" x .75" finial, 5.25" pin .185
Gold, figural insect finial, 14K yg, wings set with seed pearls, short .110
Ivory Stone, rose gold pin, 11" l pin .65
Jet, figural falcon's claw holding jet black stone, 1" x .25" stone, 6.25" l pin .275
Rhinestone, center rhinestone surrounded by 3 graduated rings of stones, 36 rhinestones, early 1900s, 1.5" d finial, 10" l pin .95
Sterling, faux topaz thistle in large sterling whiplash, hallmarked and monogrammed, Charles Horner, English Arts & Crafts, 2.5" w finial, 9.5" l pin .225

HAVILAND

David and Daniel Haviland, two brothers, were New York china importers. While on a buying trip to France in the early 1840s, David Haviland decided to remain in that country. He brought his family to Limoges where he supervised the purchase, design, and decoration of pieces sent to America. In 1852, Charles Field Haviland, David's nephew, arrived in France to learn the family business. Charles married into the Alluaud family, owner of the Casseaux works in Limoges. Charles Edward and Theodore Haviland, David's sons, entered the firm in 1864. A difference of opinion in 1891 led to the liquidation of the old firm and the establishment of several independent new ones.

Today, Haviland generally means ceramics made at the main Casseaux works in Limoges. Charles Edward produced china under the name Haviland et Cie between 1891 and the early 1920s. Theodore Haviland's La Porcelaine Theodore Haviland was made from 1891 until 1952.

Club: Haviland Collectors International Foundation, P.O.Box 802462, Santa Clarita, CA 91380, www.havilandcollectors.com.

Amstel, fruit bowl, 5.5" d 15
Amstel, soup, flat, 9" d 24
Amstel, vegetable bowl, cov, 7.25" d 45
Aquarius I, vegetable bowl, cov, oval, 2-handled, 12" l .175
Autumn Rose, bread and butter plate 6
Autumn Rose, cup and saucer 10
Autumn Rose, dinner plate 10
Blue Garland, bread and butter plate, 6" d .6
Blue Garland, creamer 25
Blue Garland, cup and saucer 16
Blue Garland, dinner plate 12
Blue Garland, fruit bowl, 6" d 8
Blue Garland, serving bowl 30
Blue Garland, sugar, cov 30
Chanson, bread and butter plate 16
Chanson, creamer .52
Chanson, dinner plate 36
Chanson, fruit bowl, 5" d 19
Chanson, luncheon plate 33
Chanson, salad plate 22
Chanson, saucer 12
Chanson, tray, oval, 8" x 5" 42
Chantilly, meat platter, oval, 16" 275
Delaware, dinner plate 15
Embassy, creamer .30
Forever Spring, bread and butter plate, 6.125" d 9
Forever Spring, creamer 14
Forever Spring, dinner plate, 10.125" d 9
Forever Spring, fruit bowl, 5" d 4
Forever Spring, platter, 12.75" x 9.5" 15
Forever Spring, saucer, 6" d 4
Forget-Me-Not, oyster plate 250
Golden Band, cup .10
Golden Band, saucer 4
Mountain Sky, cup 6
Mountain Sky, saucer 3
Princess, cup and saucer 45
Princess, dinner plate, 9.625" 25
Princess, fruit bowl, 5.5" 18
Princess, gravy and underplate 175
Princess, luncheon plate, 8.5" 35
Princess, platter, oval, 12.5" 125
Princess, sugar bowl, cov, 5" 95
Rosebud, bread and butter plate 10
Rosebud, coaster 5
Rosebud, dinner plate 13
Rosebud, fruit bowl, 4.625" d 10
Rosebud, salad plate 7
Rosebud, saucer 4
Rosebud, soup bowl .8
Scroll, teacup, white 8
Serenade, dinner plate 18
Sweetheart Rose, bread and butter plate . .5
Sweetheart Rose, creamer 16
Sweetheart Rose, cup 10
Sweetheart Rose, dinner plate 16

Sweetheart Rose, fruit bowl 5
Sweetheart Rose, salad plate 7
Sweetheart Rose, saucer 4
Sweetheart Rose, sugar, cov 17
Tawny Willows, butter tray 8
Tawny Willows, creamer 14
Tawny Willows, cup and saucer 8
Tawny Willows, dinner plate 12
Tawny Willows, gravy boat 25
Tawny Willows, salad plate 8
Tawny Willows, salt and pepper shakers .18
Tawny Willows, serving plate 22
Tawny Willows, soup bowl 10
Wave, oyster plate 275

HAZEL ATLAS

Hazel Atlas resulted from the 1902 merger of the Hazel Glass Company and the Atlas Glass and Metal Company, each located in Washington, Pennsylvania. The company's main offices were located in Wheeling, West Virginia.

The company was a pioneer in automated glassware manufacture. A factory in Clarksburg, West Virginia, specialized in pressed glassware and achieved a reputation in the late 1920s as the "World's Largest Tumbler Factory." Two factories in Zanesville, Ohio, made containers, thin-blown tumblers, and other blown ware. Washington and Wheeling plants made containers and tableware, the latter including many of the Depression-era patterns for which the company is best known among collectors.

Continental Can purchased Hazel Atlas in 1956. Brockway Glass Company purchased the company in 1964.

AURORA

Bowl, 5.25" d, cobalt blue 14
Bowl, deep, 4.5" d, cobalt blue 80
Bread and Butter Plate, 6" d, cobalt blue .13
Cereal Bowl, cobalt blue 18
Creamer, cobalt blue 25
Cup and Saucer, cobalt blue 24
Saucer, cobalt blue 7
Tumbler, cobalt blue 28

CLOVERLEAF

Creamer and Sugar, ftd, 3.5" h, black 35
Cup and Saucer, black 25
Cup and Saucer, green 15
Dessert Bowl, 4" d, green 30
Dessert Bowl, 4" d, pink 29
Luncheon Plate, 8" d, black 15
Luncheon Plate, 8" d, green 12
Luncheon Plate, 8" d, pink 9
Salad Bowl, deep, 7" d, green 60
Salt and Pepper Shakers, ftd, black 90
Saucer, pink 4
Sherbet, 6" d, black 39
Sherbet, 6" d, green 5
Sherbet, ftd, 3" h, black 20
Sherbet, ftd, 3" h, green 10
Sherbet, ftd, 3" h, pink 8
Sherbet, ftd, 3" h, yellow 11
Sherbet, ftd, 3.5" h, yellow 16
Sherbet plate, 6" d, yellow 8
Tumbler, flat, flared, 10 oz, 3.75" h, green . .55
Tumbler, ftd, 10 oz, 5.75" h, green 33
Tumbler, ftd, 10 oz, 5.75" h, yellow 35

NEWPORT (HAIRPIN)

Berry Bowl, handled, 4.75" d, amethyst ...17
Berry Bowl, handled, 4.75" d, cobalt 19
Berry Bowl, handled, 4.75" d, pink 7
Cereal Bowl, 5.25" d, amethyst 35
Cereal Bowl, 5.25" d, cobalt 45
Cream Soup Bowl, 4.75" d, amethyst 17
Cream Soup Bowl, 4.75" d, cobalt 19
Cream Soup Bowl, 4.75" d, platonite white 10
Creamer, amethyst 15
Creamer and Sugar, amethyst 31
Creamer and Sugar, cobalt 30

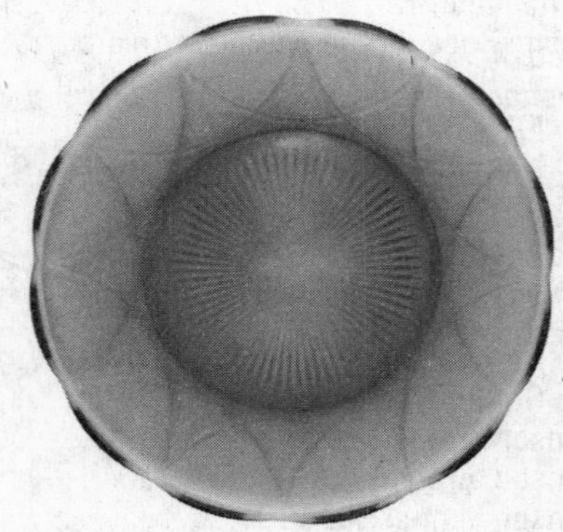

Creamer and Sugar, platonite white 27
Cup, amethyst 10
Cup and Saucer, amethyst 14
Cup and Saucer, cobalt 19
Dinner Plate, 8.75" d, amethyst 30
Luncheon Plate, 8.5" d, amethyst 15
Luncheon Plate, 8.5" d, cobalt 17
Luncheon Plate, 8.5" d, platonite white 5
Salt and Pepper Shakers, amethyst 45
Salt and Pepper Shakers, platonite white .43
Sandwich Plate, 11.75" d, amethyst 42
Sandwich Plate, 11.75" d, cobalt 48
Saucer, amethyst 5
Saucer, cobalt 4
Sherbet, 5.75" d, amethyst 6
Sherbet, 5.75" d, cobalt 8
Sugar, amethyst 13
Tumbler, 9 oz, 4.5" h, amethyst 38
Tumbler, 9 oz, 4.5" h, cobalt 30

HEAD VASES

Heart shaped lips and dark eyelashes mark the charm of the typical lady head vase. Manufactured in the early 1950s, head vases were produced in Japan and the United States. The decoration is thoughtfully done with a flare for the modeled feminine form. Many designs are enhanced with elaborate jewelry, delicate gloves, and a stylized hair-do or decorated hat. The majority of these vases are marked with the manufacturer's or importer's label and a model number.

Club: Head Vase Society, P.O. Box 83H, Scarsdale, NY 10583.

Ardco, hair to bottom of ears, large lashes, earrings and necklace, ruffled collar, 6" h 135
Ardco, hat brim down on one side, hand on hat brim, large lashes, necklace, bow on blue dress, 6.5" h 165
Artmark, large lashes, green hat and dress, earrings and necklace, hand up, 5" h . . .18
Betty Lou Nichols, "Ermyn-Trude," 6" h . .145
Betty Lou Nichols, "Vicky," yellow 700
Brody, N-420, Madonna, all white, folded hands, back planter, 6.25" h 100
Caffco, E3287, blond hair with left side ribbon, earrings, green, 5.5" h 100
Ceramic Arts, Mei Ling, 5" h 55
Dorothy Kendall, black hair, dark skin, green earrings 50
Enesco, E4095, young girl with black bow in brown hair, white ruffled collar 85
Enesco, teenage girl with blonde ponytail, dark pink ribbon and dress 185
Hull, 37, kitten wearing hat and bow, 1955, 6.5" h 25
Inarco, E1904, brown hair, large bow above bangs, large lashes, pink dress with scalloped neckline, hand up 350
Inarco, E1958, Christmas, large lashes, red flower in hair and on front of dress, 1961, 6" h 30
Inarco, E2783, blond hair with blue ribbon on ponytails, sleeveless blue dress, 6" h 450
Kelvin, P-628, eyes closed, large lashes, gray suit with large collar, white scarf tie, hand up, 6" h .154
Kelvin, P-630, blond hair, large lashes, earrings, white dress, ruffle on right, hand up, 5.75" h .225
Lefton, 2097, Christmas, girl with red hat, pigtails, holly 35
Lefton, 2426, pearlized bow on hat and dress shoulder, large lashes, necklace, hand up 100
Lefton, 6525, white ruffled hat with flowers, yellow dress, necklace and earrings, 6" h 65
Lefton, AR5882, Humpty Dumpty, red and black checkered pants 25
Napco, C2706B, ruffled turban, black skin, pearl necklace, 1957 30
Napco, C4556C, girl, maroon and green lines on cuffs, collar, and hat, hands on chin, 1960, 5.5" h 45

Napco, C5036B, collar of coat held in hand, no-brim hat with band, green and white, lashes, 6" h 100
Napco, E1847, German shepherd, mouth open, back planter 125
Norcrest, E-681, Madonna and Child, white and gold, back planter, 7.5" h 18
R, Japan, Lucille Ball, aqua, 11" h 500
Relpo, 2037, blond hair with lavender ribbon, purple dress, necklace, 5.5" h .100
Relpo, 2089, "Marilyn," orig box 1,925
Relpo, 2162, brimmed blue bonnet with bow, black dress with white Peter Pan collar, necklace and earrings, 5.5" h . .175
Relpo, 5598, clown, brown hat with feather, green and white bowtie, 7" h . .45
Relpo, K7664, green and white dress and hat with brim turned up, necklace and earrings, 5.75" h 150
Rubens, 4128, tam type hat, applied lashes, long yellow hair, 5.5" h 175
Rubens, 4135, pigtails with side flower, earrings, high wide white collar, green dress, 5.5" h 225
Sonsco, white hair with gold streaks, green dress with white collar, large lashes, hand up, 5.5" h 55
Trimont, upswept blond hair, eyes closed, large lashes, purple earrings and necklace, hand up, 7" h 175
Ucagco, large brimmed gray hat, black dress with applied flowers, large lashes, gold trim, 5" h 55
Unmarked, cowboy with hat, dark green, 7" h 15
Unmarked, girl with yellow hair in pigtails, ribbons in hair and hat, lavender and white plaid dress, holding umbrella 75
Unmarked, green hat brim tilted forward, green dress, large gold lashes, hand up, 4" h 55
Unmarked, Oriental woman with flowers in headdress and hair, lavender, gold trim, 6.5" h 100
Unmarked, brown-skinned man wearing turban, blue and gold earrings, 3.5" h . .25
Velco, 37472, long blond hair with flower, large lashes, earrings, ring on finger, 7" h 300
Velco, pink and white ruffled hat with band and flowers, hair to side, eyes closed, 6" h 55

HEISEY GLASS

A. H. Heisey Company of Newark, Ohio, began operations in 1896. Its many blown and molded patterns were produced in crystal, colored, milk (opalescent), and Ivorina Verde (custard). Pieces also featured cutting, etching, and silver-deposit decoration. Glass figurines were made between 1933 and 1957.

Not all Heisey glass is marked. Marked pieces have an "H" within a diamond. However, I have seen some non-Heisey pieces with this same marking at several flea markets.

It is important to identify the pattern of Heisey pieces. Neila Bredehoft's *The Collector's Encyclopedia of Heisey Glass, 1925–1938* (Collector Books: 1986) is helpful for early items. The best help for post-World War II patterns is old Heisey catalogs.

Club: Heisey Collectors of America, 169 W. Church St, Newark, OH 43055.

Bookends, pr, fish .145
Basket, gravic cut floral dec, emb diamond mark, first half 20th C, 10" h . .225
Carcassone, soda, 8 oz, alexandrite 130
Console Bowl, ftd, dolphin, 11" d 65
Empress, cup and saucer, alexandrite . . .170
Empress, mayonnaise, dolphin ftd, with spoon, alexandrite 600
Empress, plate, 8" d, alexandrite 87
Empress, plate, 8" sq, alexandrite 95
Figure, elephant, medium 425
Figure, elephant, small 225
Figure, fighting rooster, 8" h 145
Figure, giraffe 275
Figure, goose, half wings 95
Figure, goose, half wings, Carleton roses dec 95
Figure, goose, wings down 375
Figure, goose, wings up 95
Figure, mallard, half wings 125
Figure, mallard, wings up 145
Figure, rearing pony 220
Figure, ringneck pheasant 145
Figure, show horse 95
Figure, sparrow 100

Figure, swan, crystolite 24
Gardenia, torte, waverly blank, 14" d 75
Greek Key, celery, oval, 12" l, crystal 65
Herringbone, flat soup bowl 35
Lariat, berry bowl, 5" d, crystal 20
Lariat, candy dish, cov, crystal 87
Lariat, creamer and sugar, with tray, crystal 60
Lariat, relish dish, 3 sections, crystal, 10" d 45
Martini Server, figural rooster head stopper, ice strainer insert, first half 20th C, 14" h 60
Minuet, fruit bowl, dolphin ftd, 11" d, crystal 165
Minuet, iced tea tumbler, ftd, 12 oz, crystal 65
Minuet, juice tumbler, ftd, 5 oz, crystal . . .46
Minuet, mayonnaise, with liner and spoon, crystal 115
Minuet, water tumbler, 9 oz, crystal 40
Old Colony, creamer and sugar, yellow . . .96
Old Colony, nut dish, yellow 35
Old Dominion, parfait goblet, 5 oz, alexandrite 160
Old Dominion, sherbet, 6 oz, alexandrite .100
Old Dominion, water goblet, 10 oz, alexandrite 200
Orchid, cordial, 1 oz, crystal 145
Orchid, dressing bowl, divided, 8" d 35
Orchid, ice bucket, no handle, crystal . . .240
Orchid, mayonnaise, 3 pcs, crystal 78
Orchid, oil, ftd, 3 oz, with stopper, crystal 195
Orchid, sandwich plate, 14" d 55
Orchid, wine, 3 oz, crystal 75
Plantation, candy dish, cov, ivy etch, 5" d, crystal 180
Plantation, oil, with stopper, crystal 125

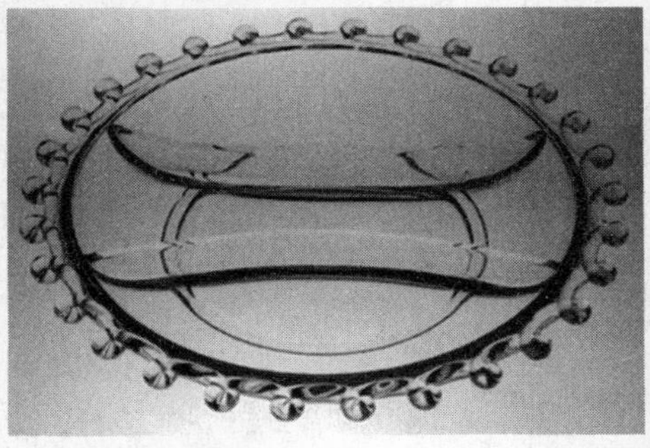

Plantation, relish, 3-part, 11" d, crystal . . .65
Rose, candleholders, pr, 1-lite, crystal 82
Rose, comport, ftd, low, crystal 60
Rose, cordial, #5072, 1 oz, crystal 150
Twist, cheese plate, handled, 6" d, marigold 40
Twist, ice tub, no handle, green 75
Twist, nut cup, green 35

HI-FI EQUIPMENT

1950s and 60s Hi-Fi equipment is now collectible. Vacuum tube-type amplifiers, pre-amplifiers, AM-FM tuners, and receivers are sought. Look for examples from Acrosound, Altec, Eico, Fisher, McIntosh, Marantz, and Western Electric. Some American and English record turntables and speakers are also collectible. Garrard and Thorens are two leading brand names. If a piece of equipment does not work, it has parts value only, usually $25 or less.

Because collectors restore equipment, unused and used working tubes also have value. Tubes listed are in working order.

VACUUM TUBES, FLAT PIN

2A3, generic Russian or Chinese, NOS . . .50
2A3, United Electron matched pr, NOS . .300
5Z3, Coke bottle, NOS 5
6A6, RCA, NOS 10
6C6, used 10
24A, Philco, used .10
24A, RCA, NOS 20
26, used 10
27, used 10
42, Globe, used 50
42, ST style, used .10

43, NOS .15
46, used .15
47, used .10
56, used .10
57, used .10
71A, used .20
77, used .10
80, RCA, NOS .20
80, used .10
82, used .10
83V, used .15
89, used .10
201A, used .25
226, used .10
227, used .10
401, used .25
424, Audion, used .20
8005 RCA NOS Transmitting Tube, orig pkg .150
C281, used .25
C324, Cunningham, used .10
C327, used .15
CX301A, used .15
CX326, used .10
CX327, used .15
CX350, used .50
CX371A, used .20
CX381, used .20
ER58-1, used .10
G27, used .10
UX112A, used .25
UX201A, Radiotron, used .25
UX226, RCA, NOS .20
UX226, RCA/Cunningham, NOS .20

HIGGINS GLASS

Michael Higgins and Frances Stewart Higgins were actively involved in designing and decorating glass in their Chicago studio by the early 1950s. Between 1958 and 1964, the couple worked in a studio provided for them by Dearborn Glass, an industrial company located outside Chicago. Pieces were mass-produced. A gold signature was screened on the front of each piece before the final firing. During the period with Dearborn, the Higginses developed new colors and enamels for their double-layered pieces and experimented with weaving copper wire into glass, fusing glass chips to create crystalline forms, and overlaying colors onto glass panels.

After leaving Dearborn, the Higginses established a studio at Haeger. In 1966 they re-established their own studio. During the late 1960s and early 1970s, the Higginses manufactured large quantities of glass plaques, often framed in wood. In 1972 they purchased the building in Riverside, Illinois, that currently serves as their studio. Pieces made after 1972 have an engraved signature on the back. Unless stated otherwise, all of the listings below have a gold signature.

Ashtray, Balloon, freeform, yellow, green, and orange on colorless ground, gold Dearborn signature, 10.5" l .275
Ashtray, Patchwork, rect, aqua and gold, gold Dearborn signature, 14" x 10" .300
Ashtray, sq, plaid with colorless rim, Dearborn signature, 7.5" sq .250
Ashtray, Stardust, round, ruffled edge, aqua and white, colored signature between layers of glass, 7" d .150
Bookends, pr, marble and glass, multicolor fused glass squares with gold dec set in marble wedges, sgd "Raymor," 1960s .800
Bowl, Apple Arabesque, deep bowl with flattened rim, 1960s, 4" h, 8.5" d .400
Bowl, Carnival Sunburst, square, orange, red, and yellow shades radiating from center, red signature, 2" h, 7" sq .200
Bowl, Carnival, sq, bright orange, red, and gold stripes radiating from center, colored signature between layers, 10" sq .350
Bowl, Classic Lines, round, white and clear, gold Dearborn signature, 12.5" d .225
Bowl, Filigree, sq, aqua and clear, no signature, 10" sq .200
Bowl, intricate scroll and peacock eye design in red, purple, orange, and light aqua, etched studio signature, 8.75" d .300
Bowl, intricate scroll and peacock eye design in red, purple, orange, and light aqua, etched studio signature, 13" d .400
Bowl, Mandarin Orange, round, gold Dearborn signature, 8.25" d .125

Bowl, red, orange, and periwinkle blue flowers, etched signature, 8.25" d 125
Charger, yellow and chartreuse shades radiating from center, 17" d 175
Clock, round, fused glass, orange and yellow triangles on pink ground, gold hands, quartz battery movement 600
Clock, sq, fused glass, black and white triangles on textured colorless ground, gold hands, quartz battery movement 600
Dish, round with ruffled rim, deep orange and yellow stripes, yellow peacock eyes outlined in bright green, etched studio signature, 1960s, 7" d 140
Plate, freeform, chartreuse and white stripes, gold seaweed, 8.5" d 75
Plate, red and white triangular spokes on blue ground, gold Dearborn signature, orig sticker, 12.25" d 375
Tray, Blue Peacock, sq, green-aqua peacock design on blue ground, gold accents, Dearborn signature, 1.5" h, 10" sq 300
Tray, Thistlesdown, round, 3-compartment, green-yellow and brown with gold accents, gold Dearborn signature, 13 .75" w 525
Trays, pr, orange, red, and amber, gold signature, 17" d round tray, 14" l rect tray 200
Vase, dropout form, satin finish, blue with floral design, etched studio signature, 4.5" h 325
Vase, dropout form, satin finish, white and aqua stripes on yellow-green ground, studio etched signature, 3.25" h, 6.5" d 300

HOCKEY COLLECTIBLES

Hockey memorabilia focuses mainly on professional hockey teams. Collecting is highly regionalized. Most collectors focus on local teams. Even with today's National Hockey League, there is a distinct dividing line between collectors of material related to American and Canadian teams.

Superstar collecting is heavily post-1980 focused. Endorsement opportunities for early Hockey Hall of Famers were limited. Collectors want game-related material. Logo-licensed merchandise for sale in sports shops has minimal or no appeal.

Autograph, sgd color photo of Wayne Gretzky, 8" x 10" 70
Book, *The Story of Hockey,* by Frank Orr, Random House, 1971, hard cov, 143 pgs, 8.5" x 5.75" 10
Comic Book, *Gordie Howe,* with 3 trading cards, 1992 10
Comic Book, *Mario Lemieux,* 3 trading cards attached to spine, 1993 15
Magazine, *Time,* Bobby Hull cov, Mar 1, 1968 35
Noisemaker, Detroit Red Wings, red and white flapper clapper inscribed "Back To Back Champs," 1990s, 8.5" l 4
Program, Cleveland Barons, 1940-41 season 60
Program, Dallas Black Hawks vs Fort Worth Wings, 1972-73 season 20
Souvenir Hockey Puck, Speed Stick Deodorant adv, given away at NY Rangers game in late 1980s 16
Tear Sheet, Four Roses Whiskey, 4 red roses and hockey stick in hockey goal on ice, 1957, 11" x 14" 8

Trading Card, Bernie Parent, Philadelphia Flyers goalie, O-Pee-Chee #89, 1968-69, excellent condition 65

Trading Card, Gordie Howe, Parkhurst #20, 1961-62, excellent to mint condition 75

Trading Card, Irvin "Ace" Bailey, Toronto Maple Leafs, Series 1, No. 13, text in English and French, 1930s 70

Trading Cards, 28-card set, Michigan Wolverines, 1993-94 70

HOLIDAY COLLECTIBLES

Holidays play an important part in American life. Besides providing a break from work, they allow time for patriotism, religious renewal, and fun. Because of America's size and ethnic diversity, there are many holiday events of a regional nature. Attend some of them and pick up their collectibles. I have started a Fastnacht Day collection.

This listing is confined to national holidays. If I included special days, from Secretary's Day to Public Speaker's Day, I would fill this book with holiday collectibles alone. Besides, in fifty years is anyone going to care about Public Speaker's Day? No one does now.

Note: See Christmas, Easter, Halloween, and Valentines for additional listings.

Father's Day, greeting card, bi-fold, father in easy chair reading newspaper on front, 1940s-50s, 5.25" x 4.25" 50

Independence Day, candy container, cardboard, emb gold eagle on red and white striped firecracker tube, 2" h 30

Independence Day, postcard, linen, divided back, image of Continental soldiers on shield-shaped flag background, "Ragged Continentals," Raphael Tuck & Sons, No. 109ERA, 1909 postmark 12

Independence Day, thimble, bone china, crossed flags, stars, and "Fourth of July" on front, Liberty Bell and eagle on back, gold trim, Caverswall, England 18

Mother's Day, Avon tin, octagonal, floral dec, bottom mkd "Cannister made in England, Created for Avon, Mother's Day 1982" 15

Mother's Day, collector plate, Wedgwood, 1979, light blue jasperware on white bisque, doe and fawn, 6.5" d, MIB 45

New Year's, postcard, Falstaff Beer, mechanical adv, bottle of beer and "Blow for Falstaff and a Happy New Year," multicolored 600

St Patrick's Day, candy container, Irish top hat, green, shamrock at seam 115

St Patrick's Day, candy container, leprechaun, Germany, 1900s 200

St Patrick's Day, postcard, crossed shillelaghs and shamrocks, "Erin Go Bragh," early 1900s 12

St Patrick's Day, record, *St Patrick's Day,* Bing Crosby, Decca Records ED-579, 45rpm, 2-record set 5

Thanksgiving, bookends, pr, cast metal, rect plaque with emb scene of farming man and woman praying, church in background, 4.5" x 4.75" 40

Thanksgiving, magazine cov, *The Saturday Evening Post,* Dec 2, 1933, JC Leyendecker illus of wigged rotund colonial gentleman holding a tray laden with a roasted turkey over his head as hounds scamper around his feet, 11" x 14" 15

Thanksgiving, pin, figural turkey, mottled plastic, 1930s, 2" h 75

Thanksgiving, planter, figural turkey, Relpo #5293, Japan, gold foil label 15

Thanksgiving, postcard, "Thanksgiving Greetings," pilgrim pulling sleigh carrying large emb metal turkey 25

Thanksgiving, salt and pepper shakers, figural turkeys, Japan 12

Thanksgiving, tip tray, "Thanksgiving Greetings, Compliments of CD Kenny Co," multicolor image of young girl praying at window, 4.375" d 110

HOLT-HOWARD

A. Grant Holt and brothers John and Robert J. Howard formed the Holt-Howard import company in Stamford, Connecticut, in 1948. The firm is best known for its novelty ceramics, including the Cat and Christmas lines and the popular Pixieware line of condiment jars. Designed by Robert J. Howard and produced between 1958 and the early 1960s, these ceramic containers proved to be so successful that knock-offs by Davar, Lefton, Lipper & Mann, M-G, Inc., and Norcrest quickly found their way into the market. Kay Dee Designs purchased Holt-Howard in 1990.

Authentic Pixieware is easily identified by its single-color vertical stripes on a white jar, flat pixie-head stopper (with attached spoon when appropriate), and condiment label with slightly skewed black lettering. An exception is three salad dressing cruets which had round heads. All pieces were marked, either with "HH" or "Holt-Howard," a copyright symbol followed by the year "1958" or "1959," and "Japan." Some pieces may be found with a black and silver label.

Bank, clown, "Coin Clown bobbing bank" on front, 1958, 6.5" h, 4.5" w 225

Bank, Siamese cat head on orange and yellow striped bulbous base, "Coin Kitty bobbing bank" on front, 5.5" h, 4.25" w 300

Beverage Set, Winking Santa, 32oz pitcher and 6 mugs, 1964 45

Candle Climbers, pr, angels 30

Candleholder, 1 wiseman from Wee Three Kings set, 1960, 4.5" h 8

Candleholder, Candle Miss, blue, foil label, 1958, 4.75" h 28

Candleholder, Santa driving car, foil label, 1959, 3.5" h 30

Candleholders, pr, Coq Rouge, figural roosters, 1960, 5" h, 4" w 95

Candleholders, pr, Santa with bag, 3.5" h .40

Candy Jar, Pop Up Santa 285

Coffee Mug, Coq Rouge, 1961, 10 oz 8

Coffee Server, Coq Rouge, 1960, 9.5" h 65

Creamer, Coq Rouge, 1961, 2.5" h 10

Creamer and Sugar, cov, Pixieware, blue stripes, "Lil' Sugar" and "Cream Crock" 290

Jam Jar, cov, jug shape, mkd "Jam & Jelly" on front, base mkd "©1962 Holt Howard," missing spoon, 3.5" h 45

Mayonnaise, cov, Pixieware, blue stripes, 5" h, 4.25" w 325

Mustard Jar, cov, Pixieware, blue stripes, with spoon 90

Napkin Holder, Winking Santa 35

Oil Lamp, white teapot with pink stripes, 7" h, 4" w 125

Olive Jar, Pixieware, 5.25" h, 4.25" w 190

Pansy Ring, pearlized, 1962, 1.25" h, 7" d ..48

Planter, Santa on train, 5.5" h, 7" l 45

Plate, dec with basket of fruits, corn, and nuts on white ground, 7.25" d 7

Punch Set, bowl, 8 cups, and ladle, fluted bowl and cups, red holly berries and green leaves on white ground, paper labels, 5" h, 10" d bowl 125

Salt and Pepper Shakers, candy stripe angels, 3.5" h 60

Salt and Pepper Shakers, Coq Rouge, figural roosters, 4.5" h 0

Salt and Pepper Shakers, Slick Chick, 4.5" h 24

Sponge Holder, Coq Rouge, figural rooster, 1961, 3.75" h, 5.5" w 75

String Holder, Cozy Kitten, Siamese cat head, 4.75" h, 5" w 125

HOMER LAUGHLIN

Homer Laughlin and his brother, Shakespeare, built two pottery kilns in East Liverpool, Ohio, in 1871. In 1896 the firm was sold and new plants were built in Laughlin Station, Ohio, and Newall, West Virginia.

The original trademark used from 1871 to 1890 merely identified the products as "Laughlin Brothers." The next trademark featured the American eagle astride the prostrate British lion. The third mark featured a monogram of "HLC," which has appeared, with slight variations, on all dinnerware produced since about 1900. The 1900 trademark contained a number which identified month, year, and plant at which the product was made. Letter codes were used in later periods.

REPRODUCTION ALERT: Harlequin and Fiesta lines were reissued in 1978 and marked accordingly.

Club: Homer Laughlin China Collectors Assoc., P.O. Box 26021, Arlington, VA 22215.

Note: For additional listings see Fiesta Ware.

Aristocrat, dinner plate 12
Aristocrat, soup plate, flat 12
Century, creamer and cov sugar, Mexican cactus pattern 25
Colonial White, dinner plate, 10" 10
Colonial White, salad plate 4
Countess, Eggshell Georgian, bread and butter plate, 6.25" 7
Countess, Eggshell Georgian, creamer . . .15
Countess, Eggshell Georgian, cup and saucer 10
Countess, Eggshell Georgian, dinner plate, 10" d 14
Countess, Eggshell Georgian, fruit bowl, 5.25" 7
Countess, Eggshell Georgian, platter, oval, tab handles, 13.5" l 45
Countess, Eggshell Georgian, soup bowl, 8" 14
Countess, Eggshell Georgian, sugar, cov .32
Dorothy, casserole, cov, 7.5" 40
Dorothy, creamer 14
Dorothy, dinner plate, 9.875" d 10
Dorothy, fruit bowl, 5.75" 8
Dorothy, gravy boat .20
Dorothy, platter, 13.5" 18
Dorothy, sugar, cov .18
Dorothy, vegetable bowl, oval, 9.5" 9
Dundee Plaid, DuraPrint, bread and butter plate, 6.25" d 8
Dundee Plaid, DuraPrint, fruit bowl, 5.25" d 6
Dundee Plaid, DuraPrint, plate, 9.25" 15
Dundee Plaid, DuraPrint, platter, oval, 11.5" 25
Dundee Plaid, DuraPrint, salad plate, 7.25" 10
Dundee Plaid, DuraPrint , soup bowl 20
Empress, butter dish 60
Empress, jug 55
Epicure, shaker, turquoise 12
Epicure, soup bowl, turquoise 25
Harlequin, bread and butter plate, 6", rose 12
Harlequin, cup, red .10
Harlequin, dinner plate, 9", gray 16
Harlequin, dinner plate, 9", light green 16
Harlequin, dinner plate, 9", rose 16
Harlequin, dinner plate, 9", spruce green .16
Harlequin, dinner plate, 9", yellow 16
Harlequin, eggcup, double, 4", yellow 25
Harlequin, nut dish, basketweave, turquoise 20
Harlequin, pitcher, 22 oz, rose 50
Harlequin, platter, 11", medium green . . .130
Harlequin, salad plate, 7", yellow 12
Harlequin, tumbler, spruce green 55
Hudson, bowl, oval, 9.25" x 7" 12
Hudson, pickle dish, 8" x 6" 12
Jade, dinner plate, 10" 20
Jade, fruit bowl, 5.5" 12
Jean, Republic, bread and butter plate, 6.25" d 7
Jean, Republic, casserole, cov 55
Jean, Republic, fruit bowl, 5" d 6
Jean, Republic, platter, 11" x 8.5" 24
Jean, Republic, soup bowl, 8" d 10
Liberty Historic America, teapot 110
Lotus Hai, Rhythm, bread and butter plate 7
Lotus Hai, Rhythm, creamer 20
Lotus Hai, Rhythm, fruit bowl, 5.5" d 14
Rhythm, bowl, 9", yellow 9
Rhythm, cup, gray 8
Rhythm, fruit bowl, lime green, 5.25" d 6

Riviera, platter, 11.375 x 9.25", yellow 25
Riviera, well platter, red 14
Rose Petit Point, dinner plate, 10" d 18
Rose Petit Point, soup bowl 18
Rose Petit Point, Liberty, bread and butter plate, 6.25" d 9
Rose Petit Point, Liberty, cup and saucer . .8
Rose Petit Point, Liberty, fruit bowl, 5.75" . .8
Rosemary, Eggshell Nautilus, bread and butter plate 4
Rosemary, Eggshell Nautilus, cup and saucer 10
Royal Harvest, bread and butter plate 3
Royal Harvest, dinner plate 10
Royal Harvest, salad plate 4
Vellum Floral, teapot 95
Virginia Rose, vegetable bowl, oval, 9" x 6.25" 12
Yellowstone, butter dish 55
Yellowstone, dinner plate 15

HORSE COLLECTIBLES

This is one of those collectible categories where you can collect the real thing, riding equipment ranging from bridles to wagons, and/or representational items.

The figurine is the most-favored collectible. However, horse-related items can be found in almost every collectible category from Western movie posters to souvenir spoons. As long as there is a horse on it, it is collectible.

A neglected area among collectors is the rodeo. I am amazed at how much rodeo material I find at East Coast flea markets. I never realized how big the eastern rodeo circuit was.

Club: Horse Collectors of America, 4917 Kinsman Rd. NW, Middlefield, OH 44092.

Antimacassar Set, 3 pcs, hand crocheted, horse head surrounded by wreath on center panel, 19" x 15" and 13" x 7" 25
Ashtray, emb polo player on horseback in center, 2 golfers on rim, marigold carnival glass, 5.75" d 65
Ashtray, hp horse head in center, porcelain, Noritake, 4.25" w 150
Bank, figural horse, cast iron, 4.5" h, 4.5" l 300
Bolo Tie, woven leather, horseshoe slide set with rhinestones, 19" l 25
Bookends, pr, grazing horses, cast iron, 3.75" h, 4" w 45
Bowl, Horse Medallion pattern, marigold carnival glass, ruffled rim, 3" h, 7.5" d .375
Bridle Rosette, painted gray horse under glass, 3-ring border, 1.875" d 50
Charm, Indian on horseback, SS, 1960s, .75" h 35
Cigarette Lighter, figural cowboy on horseback, table model, metal, 6" h, 5.5" w 45
Clock, figural horse standing beside clock in upturned horseshoe, electric, cast spelter, Sessions, 1950s 230
Clothing Brush, porcelain horse head handle, Japan 15
Figure, carnival chalkware statue, glitter trim, 8" h, 7.5" l 25
Figure, celluloid, mkd "Made In Occupied Japan," 2.25" h, 3" l 15

Horse Collar, Hames, 29" 30
Movie Poster, *The Horse Soldiers,* John Wayne, William Holden, 1959 250
Paperweight, figural horse, cast iron, Hubley, 2.75" h 80
Pin, horse, SS, Nelson Morgan, sgd, 2.5" h, 2.75" w 60
Pin, horse head with 2 boots and a horseshoe suspended below, orange and red Bakelite, yellow glass eye, c1930, 2.625" h, 2.5" w 350
Planter, 2 fighting horses, pink and white, 1940s-50s, 9" h, 8.5" w 60
Salt and Pepper Shakers, figural horses, 1 rearing, 1 running, 4.5" h 24
Tablecloth, stagecoach motif, oak leaf and acorn border, blue, orange, and black on white ground, cotton, 50" x 48" 58
TV Lamp, mare and foal, ceramic, mkd "Buonamicis," dated 1951 90
Vase, horse head, Ruebens 18
Wall Plaque, horse head, chalkware, bay color, Robia Ware, Roman Art Co, St Louis, MO, 9" h, 7" w 60
Wall Pocket, horse head, 3.5" h, 2.75" w . .55
Windmill Weight, cast iron, Dempster Mill Mfg Co, #58G, 17" h, 17" l 325

HORSE RACING

The history of horse racing dates back to the domestication of the horse itself. Prehistoric cave drawings show horse racing. The Greeks engaged in chariot racing as early as 600 B.C. As civilization spread, so did the racing of horses. Each ethnic group and culture added its own unique slant.

Horse racing reached America during the colonial period. The premier American horse race is the Kentucky Derby. Programs date back to 1924 and glasses, a favorite with collectors, to the late 1930s.

There are so many horse racing collectibles that one needs to specialize. Focuses include a particular horse-racing type or a specific horse race, a breed or specific horse, or racing prints and images. Each year there are a number of specialized auctions devoted to horse racing, ranging from sporting prints sales at the major New York auction houses to benefit auctions for the Thoroughbred Retirement Foundation.

Advertising Trade Card, CT Raynolds & Co Wood Finishes, multicolor horse race image on front, product description on back, c1885, 3.5" x 6.5" 80
Ashtray, figural jumping horse with jockey, chromed brass, 3.5" h, 5.5" w 25
Book, *Ainslie's Complete Guide to Thoroughbred Racing,* 1968 15
Compact, silvertone medallion on lid with emb steeplechase riders, blue enamel ground 85
Drinking Glass, Kentucky Derby, 1948 . . .185
Drinking Glass, Kentucky Derby, 1952 . . .175
Drinking Glass, Kentucky Derby, 1974, 100th Anniversary, error on back misspells 1971 winner as Canonero instead of Candnero II, Federal Glass . .36
Drinking Glass, Kentucky Derby, Churchill Downs, 1979, 5.25" h, 2.75" d . .20
Drinking Glass, Saratoga Sunrise goblet, Saratoga, NY, pyroglazed racehorse and jockey 15
Drinking Glass, "The Meadows, Home of The Adios, 1969," prior years' winners and concessionaire adv text on back, frosted, 5.125" h .10
Necktie, race horse motif, silk, red, blue, and gold 18
Plate, "Dan Patch, Champion Harness Horse of the World, Time 1.56," black and white tinted photo print, East Liverpool Potteries, 8.375" d 60
Program, Greymouth Trotting Club Spring Meeting, 1940, New Zealand 25

Puzzle Key Chain, figural jockey on horseback, plastic, red, yellow, green, and blue, 2.25" l 40

Souvenir Glass, Belmont Stakes Triple Crown Winner, 1978, orange lettering and green horse heads on frosted glass, lists winners from 1867 to 1977, "Seattle Slew 1977" in horseshoe on front, 5.25" h, 2.75" d 75

Toy, horse and jockey, tin, windup, Occupied Japan, 5.25" l 115

Watch Fob, jockey on racehorse surrounded by horseshoe, silver with gold wash, c1910, 1.5" h, 1.25" w 250

HOT WHEELS

In 1968 Mattel introduced a line of two-inch long plastic and diecast metal cars. Dubbed "Hot Wheels," there were originally sixteen cars, eight playsets, and two collector sets.

Hot Wheels are identified by the name of the model and its year, which are cast on the bottom of each vehicle. The most desirable Hot Wheels cars have red striping on the tires. These early vehicles are the toughest to find and were produced from 1968 to 1978. In 1979 black tires became standard on all models. The most valuable Hot Wheel vehicles are usually those with production runs limited to a single year or those in a rare color.

Hop in your own set of wheels and race to your nearest flea market to find your own hot collectibles.

'57 T-Bird, #685 2
'80 Corvette, #503 3
'93 Camaro, #686 4
Armageddon Mission 3 Space Station, Planet Micro, 1997 5
Assault Crawler, #624 3
Big Bertha, #159 3
Bulldozer, #146 2
Camaro Z28, #822 2
Corvette Convertible, #696 3
Corvette Stingray, #688 4
Ferrari, #445 2
Ferrari 308, #816, tan int 2
Ferrari 355, #813 2
Ferrari Testarossa, #834 3
Funny Car, #552 4
Hot Seat, #648 2
Jaguar D Type, #638 3
Jaguar XJ220, #558 .3
Jaguar XK8, #639, black int 2
JPL Sojourner Mars Rover Action Pack, 1996 4
Lamborghini Countach, #768 2
Mercedes 380, #767 .2
Mercedes 540K, #788 2
Mercedes-Benz Unimog, #557, #1 black . . .2
Mini Truck, #697 2
Oscar Mayer Wienermobile, 5-spoke, #204 3
Peterbilt, yellow body, silver tank, 1979 6
Porche 911, #590 3
Power Pipes, #349 2
Proper Chopper, yellow, black blade and base, #185 3
Radar Ranger, #692 2
Radio Flyer Wagon, #827 3
Saltflats Racer, #520 3
Shadow Jet, blue, #691 3
Shadow Jet II, #689 .2
Speed-A-Saurus, #814, large rear wheels 1
Speed Blaster, #576, black base 3
Tractor, #145, green .4
Trailbuster, #525 2

Turbo Flame, #571 3
Van de Kamps Deora, 1997 10
Van de Kamps VW Bus, 1997 15

HOWDY DOODY

The Howdy Doody Show is the most famous of early television's children's programs. Created by "Buffalo" Bob Smith, the show ran for 2,343 performances between December 27, 1947, and September 30, 1960. Among the puppet characters were Howdy Doody, Mr. Bluster, Flub-a-Dub, and Dilly Dally. Clarabell the clown and Princess Summerfall-Winterspring were played by humans.

There is a whole generation out there who knows there is only one answer to the question: "What time is it?"

Club: Howdy Doody Memorabilia Collectors Club, 8 Hunt Ct., Flemington, NJ 08822.

Activity Book, Howdy Doody Fun Book, Whitman #2169, Howdy and Flub-a-Dub on cov 27
Badge, Howdy Doody flip-up, Wonder Bread premium 45
Ballot, Howdy Doody Look-alike, 4.25" x 6" 35
Big Golden Book, *Howdy Doody in the Wild West,* soft cov, 9" x11" 45
Card Game, Howdy Doody Card Game ...35
Catalog/Comic Book, Twin Pop premiums 30
Comic Book, Howdy Doody Comic #24 ...15
Decal, "It's Howdy Doody Time," Howdy's head above "Howdy Doody," 2.5" x 4.25" 10
Doodle Slate 30
Drinking Glass, Welch's, Circus Series, Circus Train, blue, Flub-a-Dub on bottom 8
Drinking Glass, Welch's, Circus Series, Howdy and Mr Bluster shooting Dilly Dally out of a Cannon, blue, Mr Bluster on bottom. 16
Drinking Glass, Welch's, Picnic Series, Howdy, Dilly Dally, Mr Bluster at Picnic, Princess Summerfall-Winterspring on bottom 16
Hand Puppet, Howdy Doody cowboy, terry cloth 38
Hand Puppet, Princess Summerfall-Winterspring, painted eyes, felt hands .40
Ice Cream Wrappers, Howdy Doody Fudge Bar 5
Jigsaw Puzzle, Princess Summerfall-Winterspring 35
Little Golden Book, *Howdy Doody's Animal Friends,* #252, A Edition 20
Little Golden Book, *Howdy Doody's Circus,* #99, 1950, A edition 15
Magic Card, Magic Trick No. 1 32
Magic Card, Mr Bluster, 2.125" x 2.875" ...35
Marionette, Clarabell Clown, cardboard, 12" 75
Marionette, Howdy Doody, Wonder Bread, 7.5" 75
Movie, *A Trip to Fun Land Castle,* 8mm ...42
Movie, *Howdy Doody's Christmas Film,* 16mm 48
Pinback Button, "It's Howdy Doody Time!," 1.75" 15
Placemats, Howdy Doody Circus, paper, Doodyville characters, 10" x 14" 25
Produce Bag, apples 12
Record Set, *Howdy Doody & the Musical Forest,* double 55
Shoe Bag, red plastic, yellow and black dec, 14.5" h 45
Trading Card, Royal Pudding, Mr Bluster .15
TV Guide, Howdy Doody & Rootie Kazootie 45

HULL POTTERY

Hull Pottery traces its beginnings to the 1905 purchase of the Acme Pottery Company of Crooksville, Ohio, by Addis E. Hull. By 1917 a line of art pottery designed specifically for flower and gift shops was added to Hull's standard fare of novelties, kitchenware, and stoneware. A flood and fire destroyed the plant in 1950. When the plant reopened in 1952, the Hull products had a new glossy finish.

Hull is collected by pattern. A favorite with collectors is the Little Red Riding Hood kitchenware line, made between 1943 and 1957. Most Hull pieces are marked. Pre-1950 pieces have a numbering system to identify pattern and height. Post-1950 pieces have "hull" or "Hull" in large script letters.

Club: Hull Pottery Assoc., 15475 Hilltop Rd., Council Bluffs, IA 51503.

Note: See Little Red Riding Hood for additional listings.

Avocado Drip, bowl, 1950s, 5.25" d 4
Avocado Drip, butter dish, cov, 1950s 12
Avocado Drip, cereal bowl, 1950s, 6.75" d . .4
Avocado Drip, coffee cup, 1950s 4
Avocado Drip, creamer, 1950s 4
Avocado Drip, dinner plate, 1950s, 10.5" d . .4
Avocado Drip, onion soup bowl, lug handle, 1950s, 5.25" d 7
Avocado Drip, pitcher, 1950s, 7" h 12
Avocado Drip, salt and pepper shakers, 1950s 12

Avocado Drip, sandwich plate, 1950s, 6.75" d 2
Avocado Drip, sugar bowl, cov, 1950s 8
Avocado Drip, vegetable bowl, oval, divided, 1950s, 11" x 7.5" 12
Bank, Corky Pig, yellow, blue, and maroon, cork stopper nose 200
Basket, Wildflower, #W-16, 10.5" 285
Bud Vase, Iris, #410-7 1/2 155
Candlestick, Iris, #411, 5" 115
Candy Dish, cov, scalloped edge, blue ext, yellow int, #158 40
Cornucopia Vase, Tokay, #10, ftd 60
Cornucopia Vase, Wildflower, #W-10-8 1/2, pink and blue 165
Cornucopia Vase, Woodland, #W5-6 1/2, 1949-50 125
Double Cornucopia Vase, Bow Knot, #B-13-13 235
Flowerpot and Saucer, Water Lily, #L25, 6.75", paper label 165
Head Vase, poodle, wearing bonnet tied with bow at chin, pink, mkd "38" 145
Mirror Brown, bowl, 7" d 12
Mirror Brown, bread and butter plate, 6.5" d 8
Mirror Brown, casserole, cov, 10" x 7.25" .45
Mirror Brown, coffee mug 8
Mirror Brown, coffeepot 45
Mirror Brown, creamer and sugar, cov . . .30
Mirror Brown, cup and saucer 12
Mirror Brown, fruit bowl, 5.25" d 8
Mirror Brown, onion soup bowl, lug handle 4
Mirror Brown, pie plate, #566, 9.375" d 10
Mirror Brown, pitcher, 1 qt, 7" h 20
Mirror Brown, salt and pepper shakers . .25
Mirror Brown, soup bowl, flat 8
Mirror Brown, vegetable bowl, oval, divided, 10.75" x 7.5" 25

Pitcher, Blossom Flite, mkd "Hull T3 USA 55," c1955, 8.5" h 145
Planter, Siamese cat and kitten, 6" h, 11.5" w 145
Tea Bell, Sunglow, #87 90
Teapot, Magnolia, #H-20-6 1/2, gold trim .165
Vase, Dogwood, #502-6 1/2, 1942-43 195
Vase, Magnolia, #2-8 1/2, matte finish, 1946-47 185
Vase, Orchid, #307-6 1/2 175
Vase, Sueno Tulip, #103-33-6 185
Vase, Tulip, #107-33-8 190
Wall Pocket, Rosella, #410-6 1/2 135
Wall Pocket, Sunglow, whisk broom, mkd "USA 82," 8.25" h 125
Wildflower, ewer, 5.5" h 40
Window Box, Woodland, #W14-10, matte finish, 1950 150

HUMMEL LOOK-ALIKES

If imitation is the most sincere form of flattery, Berta Hummel and W. Goebel should feel especially honored. Goebel's Hummel figurines have been stylistically copied by ceramic manufacturers around the world.

A Hummel look-alike is a stylistic copy of a Goebel Hummel figurine or a completely new design done in an artistic style that mimics that of Berta Hummel. It does not require much of an alteration to avoid infringing on a design patent. These copycats come from a host of Japanese firms, Herbert Dubler (House of Ars Sacra), Erich Stauffer (Arnart Imports), Decorative Figures Corporation, Beswick, and Coventry Ware.

Children Under Umbrella, 6.5" h, 4" w 6
Goose Girl, unmkd, 6.25" h, 2.375" w 25
Life on the Farm, boy sitting on fence, holding a cup and spoon, goose begging at his feet, Erich Stauffer, #U8394, 5.5" h 9
Musicians, boy playing mandolin, girl singing, Lipper & Mann label, #15/63, Japan, 6.5" h 10
Pant-ing, dog pulling at pants of boy trying to escape over a fence, Napco, #AHIJ, 5.5" h 9

Picnic, boy eating lunch, sitting beside picnic basket, #2622, Arnart, 5" h 55
Shepherd Girl, with lamb and ewe, mkd "Chase Hand Decorated," 5.5" h, 4.25" w 25
Sore Thumb, U8536, Erich Stauffer, 7.5" h .30
Strummer Girl, girl playing mandolin, #SH1A, 5.375" h 70
The Singer, boy singing, mkd "97" and "07," 5.125" h 68
Umbrella Boy, seated boy wearing red neckerchief, blue jacket, and brown pants and holding closed black umbrella, Enesco, 7" h, 4.5" w 35

HUMMELS

Hummel items are the original creations of Berta Hummel, a German artist. At the age of 18, she enrolled in the Academy of Fine Arts in Munich. In 1934 Berta Hummel entered the Convent of Siessen and became Sister Maria Innocentia. She continued to draw.

In 1935, W. Goebel Co. of Rodental, Germany, used some of her sketches as the basis for three-dimensional figures. American distribution was handled by the Schmid Brothers of Randolph, Massachusetts. In 1967 a controversy developed between the two companies involving the Hummel family and the convent. The German courts decided the Convent had the rights to Berta Hummel's sketches made between 1934 and her death in 1964. Schmid Bros. could deal directly with the family for reproduction rights to any sketches made before 1934.

All authentic Hummels bear both the M. I. Hummel signature and a Goebel trademark. There were various trademarks used to identify the year of production. The Crown Mark (trademark 1) was used from 1935–1949, Full Bee (trademark 2) 1950–1959, Stylized Bee (trademark 3) 1957–1972, Three Line Mark (trademark 4) 1964–1972, Last Bee Mark (trademark 5) 1972–1980, Missing Bee Mark (trademark 6) 1979–1990, and the Current Mark or New Crown Mark (trademark 7) from 1991 to the present.

Hummel material was copied widely. These copycats also are attracting interest among collectors. For more information about them, see Lawrence L. Wonsch's *Hummel Copycats With Values* (Wallace-Homestead: 1987).

Clubs: Hummel Collector's Club, 1261 University Dr., Yardley, PA 19067; M. I. Hummel Club, Goebel Plaza, P.O. Box 11, Pennington, NJ 08534.

A Fair Measure, #345, TM5, 5.5" 140
Apple Tree Boy, #142 3/0, TM3, no paper title, 4" 90
Apple Tree Boy, #142V, TM5, 10" 500
Apple Tree Girl, #141 3/0, TM5, no paper title, 4" 70
Book Worm, #3/1, TM5, 5.5" 135
Brother, #95, TM3, 5.25" 100

Busy Student, #367, TM4, 4.5" 100
Carnival, #328, TM5, 6" 100
Chicken Licken, #385, TM5, 4.75" 125
Cinderella, #337, TM5, 4.5" 90
Good Hunting, #307, TM3, 5" 275
Goodnight, #214/C, TM7, 3.5" 55
Happiness, #86, TM3, no paper title, 4.75" .65
Little Bookkeeper, #306, TM5, 4.75" 100
Little Fiddler, #4, TM3, 4.75" 110
Little Hiker, #16/1, TM3, 6" 125
Little Shopper, #96, TM5, 5" 70
Mischief Maker, #342, TM5, 5" 110
Mother's Darling, #175, TM5, 5.5" 125
School Girls, #177/1, TM4, 7.5" 475
Singing Lesson, #63, TM5, 2.875" h 125
Stitch In Time, #255, TM4, 6.75" 150
Stormy Weather, #71, TM5, 6.25" 265
Street Singer, #131, TM6, 5" 80
Telling Her Secret, #196/0, TM4, no paper title, 5" 135
The Artist, #304, TM5, 5.5" 140
The Builder, #305, TM4, 5.5" 110
The Photographer, #178, TM5, 5" 200
Umbrella Girl, #152/0 B, TM6, 4.75" 225
Wayside Harmony, #111/1, TM6, 5" 110
We Congratulate, #214/E, TM7, 3.25" 85
Worship, #84/0, TM3, no paper title, 4" . . .125

HUNTING COLLECTIBLES

The hunt is on and the only foxes are good flea market shoppers. It is time to take back the fields and exhibit those beautiful trophies and hunting displays. I do not care what the animal activists say. I love it. Old ammunition boxes, clothes, signs, stuffed beasts, photographs of the old hunting cabins or trips, and the great array of animal-calling devices. Oh yeah, this is the stuff that adventures and memories are made from.

Care and condition are the prime considerations when collecting hunting-related items. Weapons should always be securely displayed, insect deterrents and padded hangers are best for clothing or accessories, and humidity-controlled areas are suggested for paper ephemera. Good luck and happy hunting!

Club: Call & Whistle Collectors Assoc., 2839 E. 26th Place, Tulsa, OK 74114.

Ammunition Box, United States Cartridge Co, Climax, 12 gauge shot shells, 2-pc box, empty, 4" x 4" x 2.5" 75
Ammunition Box, Winchester Repeater, 24 gauge, black powder paper shot shells, 2-pc box, empty, 3.5" x 3.5" x 2.5" 275
Calendar, 1928, Remington, artist Henry Watson, image of man sitting in front of fireplace holding rifle and gesturing to dog, 14 calendar pgs, 15" x 27" 650
Catalog, FC Gaylor Fur Co, Book of Traps, Guns and Trappers Supplies, hunting, trapping, and camping supplies, 2-pg full color ad showing Remington Game Load boxes with corresponding animals and birds, 54 pgs, 1923-24 100
Compass, celluloid, compass in center of white celluloid disk with "Dave Cook Sporting Goods..." in red, litho by Parisian Novelty, Chicago, 1.5" d 65
Counter Standup, American Field Hunting Garments, diecut cardboard, jump-out mallard with hunter in background, c1940-50, 14" x 16" 135
Envelope, Hunter Arms Co, Fulton, NY, detailed color graphic of hunting dog with bird in mouth, unused, 6.5" x 3.75" 225
Pinback Button, Peter's Cartridges, celluloid, image of duck flying through letter "P," Bastian Bros, Rochester, NY, .75" d 65
Tin, Dupont Schuetzen Smokeless, paper label with hunter holding rifle on green tin, 1 lb, 4" x 5.75" x 1.25" 70
Trap, Triumph #415X 200
Trap, Newhouse #1, Oneida Community . .35
Trap, Northwood #1.5, coil spring 6
Trap, Northwood #280 Conibear 15
Trap, Oneida #3 . . . . .9 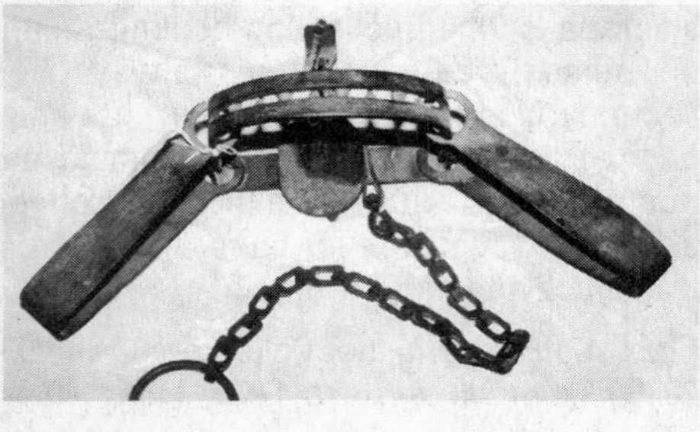
Trap, Triumph #4 DLS, cross pan, orig chain, patented Aug 26, '17 and Jul 9, '18, ...25
Trap, Victor #1.5, stamped jaw 30
Trap, Victor #2, single spring 6
Trap, Victor #3, long spring 8
Trap, Victor #91.5, web jaw jump, orig chain 35

ICE CREAM

The street ice cream vendor dates from the 1820s. In 1846 Nancy Johnson invented the hand-cranked ice cream freezer, a standard household fixture by the mid-1850s. The urban ice cream garden arrived on the scene in the middle of the 19th century.

The ice cream parlor was superseded by the drugstore soda fountain in the 1920s and 30s. Improvements in the freezer portions of refrigerators, the development of efficient grocery store freezers, and the spread of chain drugstores in the 1950s, 60s, and 70s slowly lessened the role of the local drugstore soda fountain.

Beware of reproductions, reputed "warehouse" finds, and fantasy items.

Club: Ice Screamers Collectors Club, P.O. Box 465, Warrington, PA 18976.

Change Tray, Velvet Ice Cream, oval, young woman eating ice cream 275
Clock, "Meadow Gold Ice Cream," neon light up, octagonal, 16.5" w 450
Clock, "Swift's Ice Cream," light up, plastic with metal case, 1960s, 16" sq 75
Display, ice cream cone, papier mache, "Eat-It-All," hanging or stand up, c1950s, 17" h 110
Display, "Safe-T Cup," 2-pc, 24" h 175
Door Push, "5¢ Popsicles Sold Here, a Frozen Drink On a Stick," emb tin, rect, orange, yellow, and black, c1930s-40s, 3" x 9.5" 450
Milkshake Glass, red Elsie image, 1950s . .20
Paper Plate, Borden's Ice Cream, 1930s, 6" x 6" d 20
Serving Tray, Arctic Ice Cream, round, polar bear 975

Serving Tray, Burdan's Ice Cream, round, young woman holding tray with ice cream 725
Serving Tray, Collins Ice Cream, rect, mother serving small children 675
Serving Tray, Cunningham's Ice Cream, oval, factory image, c1910-15, 18" x 15" 350
Serving Tray, Elgin Ice Cream, round, mother and son eating ice cream, 13.5" d 850
Serving Tray, Fairfield Butter Co, round, 2 children at table with lace cloth, 1915 700
Serving Tray, Hoefler Ice Cream, oval, young woman eating ice cream, c1915 425
Serving Tray, Imperial Ice Cream, round, blue sepia, mother and 2 children 500
Serving Tray, Jersey-Creme, round, 12" d 110
Serving Tray, "Pittsburgh Ice Cream Co," rect, woman serving ice cream to children, 1920s-30s 1,200
Serving Tray, Purity Ice Cream, rect, 5 children at table eating ice cream, 1924 700
Serving Tray, Purity Ice Cream, round illus on sq tray, young woman eating ice cream, 1913 425
Serving Tray, Sanitary Ice Cream, round, Haskell Coffin artwork, woman serving ice cream 500
Serving Tray, Velvet Ice Cream, rect, Kinnett's girl with polar bear rug 375
Sign, "Borden's Ice Cream, Sodas – Drugs," 2-sided porcelain, red, white, and black, 1920s-30s, 21" x 19" 1,700
Sign, "Carnation Ice Cream," diecut porcelain shield, multicolored, 1940s-50s, 22" x 23" 1,325

Sign, "Enjoy Ice Cream," Ice Cream Manufacturers, hanging, diamond shaped, red, black, and white, c1940s-50s, 10" x 10" 275
Sign, "Everybody likes Popsicles, Frozen Suckers," emb tin, rect, orange, white, and black, 1930s-40s, 10" x 28" 325
Sign, "Kerr View's, Serving Sweet Cream Ice Cream, Made Fresh Daily," 2-sided porcelain diecut ice cream cone, c1930s-40s, 24" x 54" 3,525
Sign, "Pevely Super Test Ice Cream," 2-sided porcelain, red, white, and black, c1940s, 30" x 36" 165
Sign, "Purity Pasteurized Ice Cream," 2-sided porcelain, 27" w, 27" h 475
Sign, "Sealtest, FrooJoy, Ice Cream," 2-sided diecut porcelain, red, white, and black, 1930s-40s, 17" x 17" 300
Sign, "Serve It And You Please All," porcelain, round, central image of bowl of ice cream, c1910s-20s, 18" d 575
Sign, "Sunfreze Ice Cream by Arden," 2-sided porcelain, red, yellow, and white, c1930s-40s, 28" x 32" 825

ICE SKATING

I hope that I am not skating on thin ice by adding this category to the book, but the staff has found many skating-related items and they were hard to ignore. Since ice skating has been around for centuries and is something I have never gotten the knack of, I can only hope that this is better than letting all these goodies go unnoticed.

Club: Antique Ice Skates Collectors Club, 70-104 Scott St., Meriden, CT 06450.

Calendar Plate, "God Bless Our House Throughout 1981" and children ice skating in center, calendar months and zodiac signs on rim, brown transfer on white ground, Myott Staffordshire, England, 9" d 20
Christmas Ornament, ice skating Garfield the cat, Enesco, orig box, 1983 30
Christmas Ornament, Kristi Yamaguchi, Hallmark Keepsake Ornament, 2000 12

Coca-Cola Tray, rect, female ice skater, 1941, 13.25" h, 10.5" w 375

Compact, sq, enameled skating couple surrounded by stars on lid, goldtone metal, Stratton, 2.25" sq 40

Doll, Ponytail Skipper, Series II, 1963, wearing ice skating outfit 95

Dolls, pr, ice skating couple, Effanbee, Courier and Ives Collection, 1979, 11.5" h 55

Figurine, figure skating man and woman, white, Rosenthal, 11" h, 9.75" w 400

Figurines, pr, ice skating bunnies, Homco, #5305, 4.25" h 18

Magazine, *The Associated Sunday Magazines,* Jan 18, 1914, cov illus of couple out for winter walk, ice skaters in background, 10.5" x 14.5" 90

Music Box, figural ice skating snowman, plays "Winter Wonderland," Williraye Studio #WW2357m 65

Pin, figural female ice skater, enameled goldtone metal, skirt fringe, collar, and hat set with pearls, c1940s-50s, 1.75" h, 1" w 15

Postcard, Century of Progress ice skating show, 1934 postmark, sepiatone 2

Postcard, ice skaters at Grossinger, NY, 1958 postmark, color 2

Skater's Lamp, kerosene, brass with glass globe, mkd "Orion, Made in Germany," 6.5" h .115

Skater's Lamp, kerosene, tin with glass globe, mkd "Jewel," 7" h 85

Snow Globe, ice skating snow baby, hard plastic base, glass dome, c1940-50, 4" h 35

Tear Sheet, woman ice skater, wearing 2-tone green skating outfit, Lucky Strike cigarettes, 1951, 11" x 14" 10

IMPERIAL GLASS

The history of Imperial Glass dates back to 1901. Initially the company produced pattern and carnival glass. In 1916 an art glass line, "Free-Hand," was introduced. However, Imperial's reputation rests on a wide variety of household glassware products, including Depression glass dinnerware patterns.

The company made a practice of acquiring molds from firms that went out of business, e.g., Central, Cambridge, and Heisey. Imperial used a variety of marks over time. Beware of an interlaced "I" and "G" mark on carnival glass. This is an Imperial reproduction.

Club: National Imperial Glass Collectors Society, P.O. Box 534, Bellaire, OH 43906, www.imperialglass.org.

Note: See Candlewick for additional listings.

ANIMAL FIGURINES

Angelfish, 1984, 6.625" h, ruby 325

Baby Rabbit, head down, 1982, sunshine yellow 75

Baby Rabbit, head up, 1982, ultra blue 50

Bulldog, 3", amber 35

Clydesdale, mid-1980s, 5.25" h, amber . . .325

Clydesdale, mid-1980s, antique blue 350

Clydesdale, mid-1980s, rose pink 450

Clydesdale, mid-1980s, ultra blue 100

Clydesdale, mid-1980s, verde green 135

Duckling, floating, 1981, 2" h, sunshine yellow 25

Duckling, floating, 1983, 2" h, ultra blue . . .38

Duckling, standing, 1983, 2.625" h, sunshine yellow 20

Eminent Elephant, early to mid-1980s, 4" h, horizon blue 190

Filly, #1, head forward, 1982, 8.5" h, amber 190

Filly, #1, head forward, 1982, 8.5" h, crystal etched 70

Filly, #1, head forward, 1982, 8.5" h, salmon pink .110
Gazelle, 1982, 11" h, crystal .325
Gazelle, 1982, 11" h, ultra blue clear .110
Giraffe, early to mid-1980s, 11" h, crystal etched .190
Hen, 1983, 4.5" h, sunshine yellow .95
Marmota Sentinel, woodchuck, 4.5" h, amber .55
Mother Pig, mid-1980s, 3.125" h, amber .450
Mother Pig, mid-1980s, 3.125" h, pink .250
Mother Pig, mid-1980s, 3.125" h, ruby .225
Mother Rabbit, 1982, 4.625" h, ultra blue .165
Piglets, pr, 1983, 1" h sitting and .875" h standing, amber .70
Piglets, pr, 1983, 1" h sitting and .875" h standing, pink .40
Piglets, pr, 1983, 1" h sitting and .875" h standing, ruby .90
Regal Ringneck, pheasant, early to mid-1980s, 4.75" h, crystal .110
Rooster, 1984, 5.625" h, amber .450
Scottie, 1982, 3.5" h, amber .250
Scottie, 1982, 3.5" h, nut brown .100
Scottie, 3.5" h, white milk glass .65
Sittin' Duck, 1983, 4.5" h, nut brown .110
Sittin' Duck, 1984, 4.5" h, pink .225
Superb Swan, early to mid-1980s, 7" h, crystal .650
Tiger, early to mid-1980s, 8" l, amber .200
Wild Jack, early to mid-1980s, 6.5" h, ultra blue .70

DINNERWARE

Big Shot, big shot, 14 oz, ruby .35
Big Shot, half shot, 5 oz, green .35
Big Shot, little shot, 2.5 oz, ruby .35
Big Shot, magnum with wooden rod, 40 oz, ruby .125
Big Shot, sure shot, 11 oz, green .30
Cape Cod, 3-pc jam jar set, jam jar, spoon, and underplate .65
Cape Cod, baked apple bowl, 6" .12
Cape Cod, basket, ftd, crystal, 11" .250
Cape Cod, butter, cov .42
Cape Cod, cake plate, 4-toed, 10" sq .150
Cape Cod, candleholders, pr .45
Cape Cod, celery dish, oval, 10.5" .55
Cape Cod, claret, 5 oz .12
Cape Cod, compote, ftd, 6" .48
Cape Cod, creamer and sugar, ftd .30
Cape Cod, egg cup .75
Cape Cod, finger bowl, 5" .12
Cape Cod, float bowl, 9.5" .95
Cape Cod, fruit bowl, ftd, 9" .150
Cape Cod, goblet, 8 oz .5
Cape Cod, heart dish, 5" .25
Cape Cod, luncheon plate, 9" .55
Cape Cod, mayonnaise plate, 7" .15
Cape Cod, mint, handled, 6" .48
Cape Cod, plate, 9" .20
Cape Cod, plate, 14", crystal .50
Cape Cod, plate, handled, 8.5" .35
Cape Cod, relish dish, 4-part .48
Cape Cod, relish dish, oval, 9.5" .30
Cape Cod, salad plate, 8" .12
Cape Cod, salt and pepper shakers, ftd .15
Cape Cod, sherbet, 6 oz .10
Cape Cod, sugar, small .15
Cape Cod, sugar, large .85
Cape Cod, vegetable bowl, 10" .75
Cape Cod, vegetable bowl, oval, 11" .100
Cape Cod, water goblet, 10 oz .18
Cape Cod, wine, 3 oz, 4.5" h .8
Dolphin, candlestick, 10.5", vaseline .125
Grape, biscuit jar, cov, wicker handle, 5.75" h, 3.375" d, white milk glass .60
Grape, bowl, ruffled, 8", green carnival .50
Grape, candy box, cov, hexagonal, white milk glass .35
Grape, water goblet, 10 oz, white milk glass .15
Mayonnaise Set, bowl and ladle, ruby .165
Molly, cup and saucer, ruby .18
Mt Vernon, cup and saucer .18
Reeded, rose bowl, 6", ritz blue .115
Revere, cake stand, 11" .75
Traditional, water goblet, white milk glass 15
Venus Rising, Crown Tuscan .65

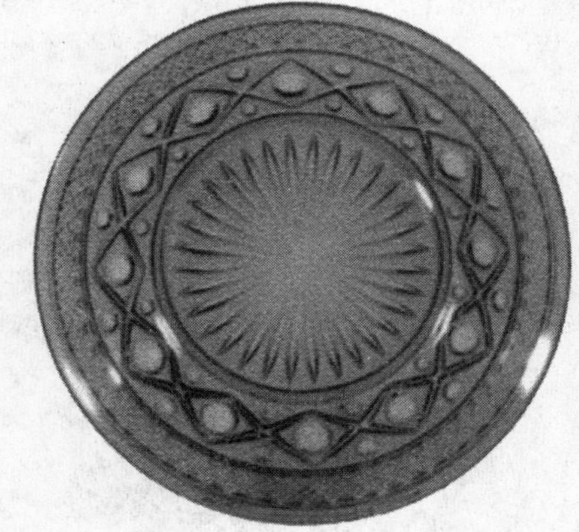

INK BOTTLES

In the eighteenth and early nineteenth centuries, individuals mixed their own ink. The individual ink bottle became prevalent after the untippable bottle was developed in the middle of the nineteenth century.

Ink bottles are found in a variety of shapes ranging from umbrella style to turtles. When the fountain pen arrived on the scene, ink bottles became increasingly plain.

Carter's, 6-sided, emb clover leaf dec, medium cobalt blue, "Carter's" on base, smooth base, c1920-30, 2.875" h .165

Carter's, master cathedral, deep cobalt blue, "CA-RT-ER" around base, "Carter's" on smooth base, c1920-30, 9.75" h 150

Davids', turtle, medium teal, smooth base, tooled lip, c1870-80, 1.75" h 415

Dessauer's Jet Black Ink, turtle, bluish aqua, smooth base, ground lip, c1870-80, 2" h 150

Harrison's Columbian Ink, 12-sided, aqua, "Patent" on shoulder, pontil scarred base, applied mouth, c1845-55 230

Hohenthal Brothers & Co, NY, Indelible Writing Ink, round, deep olive amber, iron pontil, applied sloping collar mouth with pour spout, 1845-55, 7" h 625

SI Comp, cottage, bluish aqua, smooth base, tooled mouth, c1885-95, 2.5" h ..185

Unmarked, 8-sided umbrella, light emerald green, pontil scarred base, rolled lip, c1845-55, 2.5" h 125

Unmarked, 12-sided umbrella, light blue-green, open pontil, rolled lip, c1845-55, 2.125" h 75

WE Bonney, barrel, aqua, smooth base, applied mouth with pour spout, c1855-65, 5.125" h 165

INKWELLS

Inkwells enjoyed a "golden age" between 1870 and 1920. They were a sign of wealth and office. The common man dipped his ink directly from the bottle. The arrival of the fountain pen and ballpoint pen led to their demise.

Collectors seem to have the most fun collecting figural inkwells—but beware, there are some modern reproductions.

Club: The Society of Inkwell Collectors, 5136 Thomas Ave. South, Minneapolis, MN 55410.

CERAMIC

Hexagonal, concave sides, floral dec, cobalt accents, porcelain cup, France, 3.5" h, 5.25" d 85

Round, flared top, beaded dec on rim, landscape on side, gold trim, pen holders encircle well with cup and lid, 3" h, 4.375" d 50

Round, ribbed, scrolled feet, polychrome floral geometric dec, 2.75" h, 4" d 115

Square, concave corners, blue, yellow, and green floral dec, mkd "RC France," 2.875" h, 3.5" w, 3.5" d 60

Urn Shaped, polychrome, stamped designs on brass foot, hinged collar, and hinged inner lid, pen holder inside, France, 7.25" h, 3.75" d 150

GLASS

Amber, cube base cut with raised panel on each side, faceted pyramid-form lid, SP mounts, c1890 275

Amethyst, trapezoidal shape, flat sq swivel glass top, 2" sq at base, 2.25" h 275

Blue and White, Bohemian-type, cased, cube base cut to clear floral motif, mushroom cap top, brass fittings, 2" sq base, 3.25" h 275

Blue Milk Glass, bottle form, smooth base, ground lip, brass neck ring and hinged lid, c1876-90, 1.75" h 90
Clear Crystal, pyramid shape, brass fittings, 1.875" sq at base, 3.125" h 55
Cranberry, cased, cut to clear, globular form with petals radiating from collar to waist, molded sunburst on bottom, bulbous lid with cut 4-petal flower, brass mounted, 4" d, 4" h 500
Deep Amber, flared stepped base with pen holder grooves on all sides, brass fittings, flat rounded and faceted lid, c1880-1900, 3.5" sq at base, 3" h 275
Deep Blue, cylindrical base with rounded shoulder and sunburst cut in bottom, round cut-paneled lid, engraved brass fittings, 2.125" d, 3.25" h 375
Deep Emerald Green, sq, bronze gilt gallery and top, France, 2" sq, 3" h 375
Emerald Green, pyramid form, sq flat set-on lid, c1900, 3" sq at base, 2" h 300
Green, sq arch-molded base with a Gothic panel on each side, bulbous form top with cut panels, brass-mounted, 2" sq at base, 3" h 450
Medium Blue, 4 balls arranged in a pyramid shape, round flattened lid with ball finial, SP fittings, 3.5" w, 4.75" h . . .350
Medium Blue, diamond form with cut panels, round faceted lid, brass mounted, c1860, 2" w, 2" h 200
Pale Blue, hexagonal form with set-on peaked hexagonal top, 2.875" w, 2.5" h 150
Pink, sq base with polished cut edges and rim, conforming swivel top with beveled edge, 2.375" sq, 2" h 225
Vaseline, flared sq base with cut and polished corners, conforming cut and polished top, SP mounts, 3.75" sq at base, 3.25" h .465

METAL

Cold Painted Bronze, mushroom with grasshopper on top ready to pounce on elf squatting underneath, polychrome, 3" h, 4" w, 3.25" d 475
Sterling on Bronze, bulbous, bright green mottled patina with floral SS overlay on lid, stamped Pat 8/27/12, glass insert with lid, Heintz Art Metal Co, 2.25" h, 4.25" d 300

INSULATORS

Insulators were a trendy collectible of the 1960s and prices have been stable since the 1970s.

Insulators are sold by "CD" numbers and color. Check N. R. Woodward's *The Glass Insulator in America* (privately printed, 1973) to determine the correct CD number. Beware of "rare" colors. Unfortunately, some collectors and dealers have altered the color of pieces by using heat and chemicals to increase the rarity value. The National Insulator Association is leading the movement to identify and stop this practice. They are one of the few clubs in the field that take their policing role seriously.

Club: National Insulator Assoc., 1315 Old Mill Path, Broadview Heights, OH 44147, www.nia.org.

CD 12s, Lynchburg #30, green 25
CD 102, CGI Co, purple 17
CD 107, Whitall Tatum #9, olive green 20
CD 108, Whitall Tatum #9, purple 25
CD 112, Lynchburg, 31, straw 15
CD 112, Lynchburg 31, yellow green 20
CD 112, New England Tel, light blue 65
CD 121, Am Tel & Tel Co, purple 35
CD 121, Pleated Skirt, green aqua 80
CD 134, T-HE Co, medium green 40
CD 136, Brookfield B&O, blue 25
CD 138.2, Standard Glass Insulator, light blue with bubbles 125
CD 145, B, gray to light sun-colored amethyst 15
CD 145, B, teal-aqua 10
CD 145, GTP, B, deep turquoise 30
CD 145, HBR, aqua .20

CD 145, HG Co, jade milk 18
CD 145, Star, deep yellow green 12
CD 145, W Brookfield, lime green 125
CD 161, California, deep purple 35
CD 162, Lynchburg 36, yellow green 23
CD 162, NEGM Co, green with bubbles . . .40
CD 164, Lynchburg 38, yellow green 25
CD 166, California, purple 20
CD 166.2, no emb, blue-aqua, twists of amber 15
CD 178, Santa Ana, blue 60
CD 186, Hemingray D510, orange carnival 35
CD 230, Lowex 512, honey amber with bubbles 40
CD 233, Pyrex 661, golden carnival 35
CD 235, Pyrex 662, golden carnival 25
CD 235, Pyrex 662, orange carnival 35
CD 241, Hemingray-23, Hemingray blue . . .30
CD 251, Hemingray #1 Cable, blue 40
CD 257, Hemingray-60, clear 17
CD 257, Hemingray-60, wide ears, Hemingray blue .40
CD 281, Hemingray #1 High Voltage, Hemingray blue .18
CD 297, Fred M Locke, narrow neck, light blue aqua 25
CD 302, Hemingray Muncie Type, blue aqua 35
CD 1070, Hemingray 109, aqua 10
CD 1070, Hemingray 109, ice blue 10

IRONS

Country and kitchen collectors have kept non-electric iron collecting alive. The form changed little for centuries. Some types were produced for decades. Age is not as important as appearance—the more unusual or decorative the iron, the more likely its value will be high. There are still bargains to be found, but cast iron and brass irons are becoming expensive. Electric irons are the iron collectible of the future.

Club: Midwest Sad Iron Collectors Club, 24 Nob Hill Dr., St. Louis, MO 63138.

Aladdin, Australian, kerosene, enameled cream, c1950 150
Albee DRGM, German, press, 2 handles, c1930, 7.75" l 300
Aqua Steam, Strobel, Munchen, German, electric, steam, c1950. 7.75" l 70
Billiard Table, English, electric, c1935, 6.25" l 300
Bugel Fix, German, electric puffer iron, c1950, 2.75" d top .70
Challenge Electric, English, electric, glass-cov dial, c1930, 6.75" l 150
Chicago Electric Mfg Co, Chicago, IL, electric, green marbleized enamel, c1920, 7" l 300
Coleman Lamp & Stove Co Limited, Toronto, Canada, gasoline, Model 4A Instant Lite, streamlined design on sides, c1940, 10.5" l 300
Crown, American Machine Co, Phila, PA, fluter machine, Nov 2 1875 patent date, yellow and red pinstriping on black, crown decal, 5.75" roll 175
Czechoslovakian, flat, cold handle, c1930, 6.75" l 300
Czechoslovakian, flat, cold handle, enameled green, c1930, 7" l 100
Diskus, German, travel, c1950, 5.25" l 70
DRP, German, electric, c1930, 10" l 100
Etna, European, gas jet, black enamel surface, black plastic handle, c1930, 6" l 200
Foster Equipment, Billiard Table, English, electric, c1935, 6.25" l 300
Graetzor, German, electric, switch on handle, c1940, 7.25" l 150
Grossag, German, electric, 1929, 9.75" l . .200
High Steam Corp, NY, electric, steam, chrome, c1950, 7.5" l 150
Hotpoint, electric, white enamel, c1940, 8.25" l 300

Imperial Self Heating Iron, LG Dyson Co, Brisbane, Australia, gasoline, c1940, 7" l 300
Impuls, German, steam, big sole, c1940, 8.25"l 70
Neumarker, German, electric, c1940, 5.5" l 70
Nu-Pantz Creaser, pant presser, heated with meta fuel, squeeze to open, orig box, c1920, 6.75" l .300
Ostarica, Austrian, natural gas, plastic handle, c1930, 7.25" l 150
Pluto, Austrian, natural gas, plastic handle, c1930, 7.75" l 150
R & R Electric Corp, Mt Joy, PA, Greyhound, air cooled model, c1950, 7.75" l 100
Radiant, Toronto, electric, radiating lines dec, c1920, 6.25" l .200
Royal Self Heating Co, Big Prairie, OH, gasoline, Model D, orig box, c1930, 7.25" l 300
Sensat, German, electric, steam, c1950, 9" l 50
Stotz, German, china body, c1935, 8" l . . .200
Stotz, German, electric, iron rest on back, plastic handle, c1950, 7.25" l 150
Sunflame, Pyrex, glass, electric, c1930, 7.75" l 500
Tilley, English, natural gas, post 1940, 7.5" l 200
Vulkan Dampf Bugler, German, electric, steam, aluminum, c1935, 7.5" l 50
Westinghouse, electric, detachable handle, c1920, 5.5" l 100

IRONSTONE POTTERY

This was the common household china of the last half of the nineteenth century and first two decades of the twentieth century. This ceramic ware was supposed to wear like iron—hence the name "ironstone." Many different manufacturers used the term ironstone when marking their pieces. However, the vast majority of pieces do not bear the ironstone mark.

Pieces that are all white, including the pattern, are known as White Patterned Ironstone. A more decorative appearance was achieved by using the transfer process.

Club: White Ironstone China Assoc., Inc., P.O. Box 536, Redding Ridge, CT 06876.

Cake Plate, square, handled, Madrigal pattern, Mason's Ironstone, 10.375" w . .45
Chamber Pot, flower transfer on front, mkd "John Maddock & Sons, England Royal Vitreous" and "WC Hendrickson Decorated Pottery," 8.25" d 40
Egg Cup, ftd, emb grape design, unmkd, 3.75" h, 2.5" d 32
Egg Cup, Regency pattern, mkd "Mason's Patent Ironstone China Regency England," small rim chip, 1930s, 2" h . . .20
Food Mold, oval with geometric design, c1900, 5.5" h, 7.5" x 6" 95
Gravy Boat, Pankhurst shape, floral dec on thumb rest, 5.5" h, 9" l 55
Pie Plate, fluted rim, Hanley, England, rim chip, 3.25" h, 10.25" d 18
Pitcher, English, unmkd, 10" h 80
Plate, Moss Rose pattern, mkd "Burgess and Campbell Warranted Superior Ironstone China," 8.875" d 70
Plate, Regency pattern, mkd "Mason's Patent Ironstone China Regency England," 1930s, 10.5" d 55
Platter, beige and gold floral pattern, Brockman Pottery, Cincinnati, OH, c1888-1912, 15.5" x 10.25" 25
Platter, Harvest pattern, scalloped edge, John Edwards, imp "Imperial, Rd. 153150," c1890, 16.5" l 125
Platter, purple flowers and green leaves on emb scroll rim, gold trim, mkd "Excelsior Porcelain, TSC Co," Salem China, 17.75" l 25
Platter, scalloped edge, mkd "OP Co China," Onondaga Pottery Co, Syracuse, NY, 1871, 20" x 12.75" 100

Platter, Tea Leaf pattern, rect, mkd "Royal Ironstone China (crown and shield, lion and unicorn) WH Grindley & Co England," 1891-1914 70

Platter, Wheat pattern, Ceres shape, mkd "Ceres, W&E Corn, Burslem," rim flake, c1864-91, 14.5" l 110

Platter, Wheat pattern, mkd "Ironstone China, JF Jacob Furnival," c1860, 17.75" x 12.5" 135

Relish Dish, mkd "Royal Patent Ironstone, George Jones & Sons, England," 10" x 5" 45

Relish Dish, oval, mkd "J&G Meakin," 8.75" x 6" 40

Sauce Boat, matching underplate, Strathmore pattern, mkd "Mason's Patent Ironstone China Strathmore England," 1930s, 4" l 120

Soap Dish, rect, red floral dec, mkd "Porcelain Royale, Pitcairns Limited, Tunstall, England, Pandora (shield and plume)," 4.25" x 3.25" 25

Soup Bowl and Underplate, Mandalay pattern, mkd "Mason's Patent Ironstone Mandalay Made in England," 6.5" d 50

Teacup, Strathmore pattern, mkd "Mason's Patent Ironstone China Strathmore England," 2" h 45

Teapot, Blue Willow pattern, Sadler, England, 10 oz 125

Teapot, Vista pattern, mkd "Mason's Patent Ironstone China, Vista, England, Guaranteed Permanent & Acid Resisting Colours," incised "24," blue transfer dec, 6.75" h, 9.5" w 150

Tureen, cov, Chetwynd, England, c1880s, 6" h, 13" l 90

Vegetable Bowl, cov, Moss Rose pattern, gold trim, .25" chip on inner rim 85

Vegetable Bowl, oval, Grosvenor pattern, blue and white rim dec, mkd "Imported Community China, Grosvenor Design, Bavaria Germany," 10" l 48

Wash Basin, mkd "West End Pottery Co, East Liverpool, Ohio," 1919-26, 4.25" h, 14.5" d 95

ITALIAN GLASS

Italian glass, also known as Venetian glass, is glassware made in Italy from the 1920s into the early 1960s and heavily exported to the United States. Pieces range from vases with multicolored internal thick and thin filigree threads to figural clowns and fish.

The glass was made in Murano, the center of Italy's glass blowing industry. Beginning in the 1920s many firms hired art directors and engaged the services of internationally known artists and designers. The 1950s was a second golden age following the flurry of high-style pieces made from the mid-1920s through the mid-1930s.

Club: Murano Glass Society, 32040 Mt. Hermon Rd., Salisbury, MD 21804.

Alfredo Barbini, vase, amber glass with applied clear glass around closed-in rim, unmkd, 9.5" x 4.5" 385

Aureliano Toso, pitcher with exaggerated spout, mezza-filigrana in black, white, and gold, Dino Martens, 11" h 1,375

Avem, figurine, rooster, blown glass, acid-etched "Murano/AVEM/Oro/24k/ Fatto Interamente Amano," 8.25" x 9" . .275

Barovier E Toso, bowl, Cordonato d'Oro, floriform, designed by Ercole Barovier, gold and opalescent glass with controlled bubbles, unmkd, 3.5" x 7.5" 225

Barovier E Toso, bowl, hemispherical, designed by Ercole Barovier, unmkd, 3" x 5.75" 165

Cenedese, bowl, low, tear-shaped, light green glass with dark band, unmkd, 10" x 6" .225

Cenedese, figure, yak, Antonio Da Ros, orange and vaseline sommerso with orange swirled horns, 9" x 9" 700

Cenedese, urn, Scavo, possibly designed by Alfredo Barbini, bright green glass with applied swirl, unmkd, 13" x 4" 775

Murano, bowl, elliptical, green and orange glass with controlled bubbles throughout, unmkd, 3 x 8" 275

Murano, vase, attributed to Seguso, bulbous, lattimo glass with fine dusting of black gold, unmkd, 7.25" x 7" 825

Salviati, compote, blue and white zamfirico and latticino glass, ruffled rim, unmkd, 9" x 8.5" 450

Seguso, vase, designed by Flavio Poli, orange sommerso, tear-shaped form, unmkd, 12" x 7.5" 715

Sommerso, vase, possibly by AVEM, organically shaped, clear, green, and lattimo glass, unmkd, 13" x 6.5" . . .825

Venini, bowl, white and smokey topaz swirled glass canes, etched "Venini/Italia," 4.25" x 9" 165

Venini, decanter, 3-sided, dark blue inciso glass, etched "Venini/Murano/Italia," 8" x 4.25" 275

Venini, paperweight, figural egg, purple and gold swirls, etched "Venini/Murano/Italia," 6.25" x 3" 150

Venini, vase, Fazzoletto, Fulvio Bianconi, turquoise opaque glass, unmkd, 6" x 7" 300

Vico Magistreti for Artemide, table lamp, free standing, scrolled translucent white body, lamp on tripod white painted metal base, makers mark on base, 30.25" h, 8.75" w 550

Vistosi, paperweight, sommerso with concentric rings of white, olive, and black glass, etched signature, 2" x 4" 150

IVORY

Ivory is a yellowish-white organic material that comes from the teeth and tusks of animals. In many cases, it is protected under the Endangered Species Act of 1973, amended in 1978, which limited the importation and sale of antique ivory and tortoise shell items. Make certain that any ivory you buy is being sold within the provisions of this law.

Vegetable ivory, bone, stag horn, and plastic are ivory substitutes. Do not be fooled. Most plastic substitutes do not approach the density of ivory nor do they have crosshatched patterns. Once you learn the grain patterns of ivory, tusk, teeth, and bone, a good magnifying glass will quickly tell you if you have the real thing.

Club: International Ivory Society, 11109 Nicholas Dr., Silver Spring, MD 20902.

Back Scratcher, open hand on long handle, 8" l 60

Brush Holder, carved, reticulated roses, Chinese, c1920, 3" h 175

Cane Handle 125

Card Case, book form, cartouche on front, gilded edges, c1880 250

Card Case, book form, silver trim 175

Figure, owl, glass eyes, round base, c1900, 2.5" h 75

Netsuke, bug on a leaf, walrus ivory, 1868-1912, 2.5" x 1.25" 225

Page Turner, carved stag's head crest with "Spes Anchor Vitae" on banner below, c1900-20s, 10.75" l, 1" w 55

Pen Holder/Letter Opener, 7" l 50

Picture Frame, pierced and carved floral design, 1.25" x 2.25" 75

Snuff Bottle, relief carved, flute player and calligraphy on front, scrimshaw dec on back, Chinese, 2" h 200

Toothpick Box, rect, citrine set in hinged lid, green velvet lining, 3.25" l, .75" w . .425

JEANNETTE GLASS

The Jeannette Glass Company, Jeannette, Pennsylvania, was founded in 1898. Its first products were glass jars, headlight lenses, and glass brick.

During the 1920s, the company supplied glass candy containers to other firms and introduced its own lines of pressed table and kitchenwares.

In 1952 Jeannette purchased the McKee Glass Corporation, enabling the company to expand into the production of heat-resistant and industrial glass. Jeannette ceased oeprations in the mid-1980s.

ADAM

Ashtray, 4.5" d, green 22
Ashtray, 4.5" d, pink .30
Berry Bowl, 4.75" d, green 22
Berry Bowl, 4.75" d, pink 22
Bowl, cov, 9" d, pink 75
Bowl, oval, 10" d, pink 32
Butter, cov, pink 105
Cake Plate, ftd, 10" d, green 25
Cake Plate, ftd, 10" d, pink 25
Candy Jar, cov, 2.5" h, pink 120
Cereal Bowl, 5.75" d, pink 62
Creamer, green 30
Creamer and Sugar, cov, pink 72
Cup and Saucer, green 32
Cup and Saucer, pink 32
Dinner Plate, 9" sq, green 28
Dinner Plate, 9" sq, pink 34
Grill Plate, 9" d, green 26
Pitcher, square base, 32 oz, 8" h, pink 45
Platter, oval, 11.75" d, green 34
Platter, oval, 11.75" d, pink 20
Relish Dish, divided, 8" d, green 22
Salad Plate, 7.75" sq, green 16
Salad Plate, 7.75" sq, pink 18
Salt and Pepper Shakers, 4" h, pink 100
Saucer, sq, green 6
Sherbet, 3" d, pink .30
Sherbet, 6" d, green 39
Sugar, cov, green 75
Tumbler, 4.5" d, green 30
Tumbler, 4.5" d, pink 35
Vase, 7.5" h, green .85
Vase, 7.5" h, pink .450

CHERRY BLOSSOM

Berry Bowl, 4.75" d, green 22
Berry Bowl, 4.75" d, pink 24
Berry Bowl, 8.75" d, green 55
Berry Bowl, 8.75" d, pink 50
Bowl, 2-handled, 9" d, pink 50
Butter, cov, pink .125
Cake Plate, 3 ftd, 10.75" d, pink 40
Cereal Bowl, 5.75" d, green 45
Child's Junior Dinnerware Set, 14 pcs, delphite 450
Child's Junior Dinnerware Set, 14 pcs, pink 435
Coaster, green 13
Creamer, delphite .35
Creamer, pink 20
Cup and Saucer, delphite 50
Cup and Saucer, green 28
Cup and Saucer, pink 26
Dinner Plate, 9" d, green 28
Dinner Plate, 9" d, pink 25
Flat Soup Bowl, 7.75" d, green 100
Fruit Bowl, 3-ftd, 10.75" d, green 100
Fruit Bowl, 3-ftd, 10.75" d, pink 110
Grill Plate, 9" d, pink 35
Mug, 7 oz, green .350
Pitcher, flat, 42 oz, 8" h, green 60
Platter, 11" d, green 50
Platter, 11" d, pink .49
Platter, 13" d, pink 125
Platter, 13" d, divided, pink 85
Salad Plate, 7" d, pink 26
Salad Plate, 7" d, pink 26
Sandwich Tray, 2-handled, 10.5" d, green .35
Sandwich Tray, 2-handled, 10.5" d, pink . . .30
Saucer, delphite 8
Saucer, green 9
Saucer, pink 6
Sherbet, green 22
Sherbet, pink 22
Sugar, cov, green 45
Sugar, cov, pink 30
Tumbler, ftd, 4 oz, 3.75" h, green 20

DORIC

Berry Bowl, 8.5" d, green .30
Bowl, 4.5" d, pink .14
Butter, cov, green .90
Cake Plate, ftd, pink .27
Candy Dish, pink .70
Cereal Bowl, 5.5" d, pink .90
Creamer and Sugar, pink .18
Cup and Saucer, pink .15
Dinner Plate, green .18
Dinner Plate, pink .40
Platter, pink .30
Relish Dish, 8" x 4", pink .38
Sherbet, green .12
Sherbet, pink .15
Sugar, cov, pink .35
Tray, 4" x 4", pink .18
Tumbler, 10 oz, pink .75
Tumbler, 12 oz, pink .14

WINDSOR

Candlesticks, pr, pink .210
Chop Plate, 13.5" d, pink .48
Pitcher, green .50
Pitcher, 5 oz, 6.75" h, pink .35
Plate, 9" d, green .28
Platter, green .22
Platter, pink .15
Salad Plate, 7" d, green .30
Sherbet, pink .7
Sugar, cov, pink .40
Tray, divided, no handle, 8.75" sq, pink .210
Tumbler, 4" h, green .28
Tumbler, 4" h, pink .15

JEWELRY

In the current market, "antique" jewelry refers to pieces that are one hundred years old or older, although much of the jewelry from the 1920s and 1930s is passed as "antique." "Heirloom/estate" jewelry normally refers to pieces between twenty-five and one hundred years old.

Diamonds might be a girl's best friend, but costume jewelry is what most women own. "Costume" refers to quality and type, not age. Costume jewelry exists for every historical period and there is a piece for everyone's taste—good, bad, or indifferent.

Collect it by period or design—high-brow or lowbrow. Remember that it is mass-produced. If you do not like the price the first time you see a piece, shop around. Most sellers put a high price on the pieces that appeal to them and a lower price on those that do not. Since people's tastes differ, so do the prices on identical pieces.

Clubs: Assoc. for Collectors of Mourning Jewelry, P.O. Box 641, Burlington, WI 53104; Vintage Fashion & Costume Jewelry Club, P.O. Box 265, Glen Oaks, NY 11004.

Bow Pin, Bjarne, sterling silver with chrysoprase rect central stone, fine detail work, stamped "Sterling Handwrought by BJARNE," 1.75" w .170
Bracelet, Benedikt of NY, faux topaz oval and faceted rhinestones, antiqued gold-tone metal setting 7.5" l .120
Bracelet, Eisenberg, rhinestones, 1947, 7.5" l .395
Bracelet, filligree oval medallions each set with a diamond-shaped amber crystal, c1920s, 7" l .70
Bracelet, gold colored metal expandable band set with clear rhinestones, early 1940s .75
Bracelet, large diamond shaped blue crystal stones alternating with smaller sq blue crystals, c1920s, 7" l .80
Bracelet, Weiss, aurora borealis stones, sgd, 7.25" l .85
Bracelet and Earrings, Miriam Haskell, summer white beads and crystal clear rhinestones, 8" long bracelet, 1" x .75" clip earrings .325

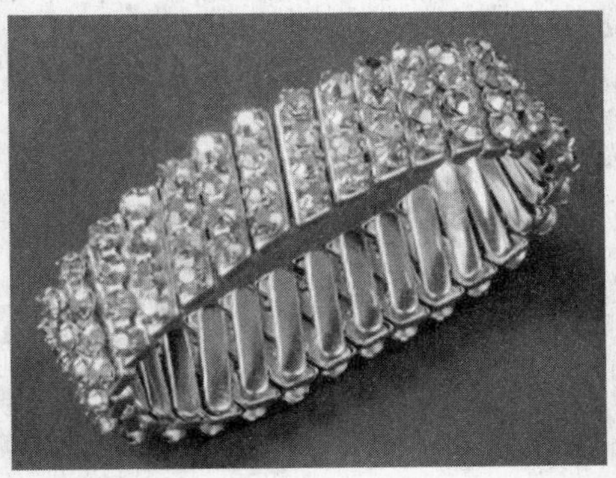

Brooch, Bogoff, 5-point star shape with pear, emerald, and chaton crystal rhinestones, silvertone metal with hallmark stamped on back, 2" d 30
Brooch, Coro, SS with vermeil wash, amber and topaz colored prong-set rhinestones, sgd "Coro" and "Sterling," 4.5" h 45
Brooch, Eisenberg, flower, smoke and clear prong-set rhinestones, sgd, 2" x 1.75" 210
Brooch, Eisenberg, gold leaves with rows of pavé clear stones, sgd, 3.5" w 225
Brooch, Juliana, teal rhinestones on outside, royal blue centers with pink aurora borealis stones, 2.25" 58
Brooch, Miriam Haskell, red glass beads and gray metal leaves wire-strung on gray filigree metal, 3" l 225
Brooch, Regency, faceted rhinestones in shades of rose, pink, and blue-green aurora borealis tones, 2 layers, 2.5" sq .75
Brooch, Trifari, flower basket, painted yellow with red and blue flowers, rhinestone accents, sgd, 1950s 200
Brooch, Weiss, flower, purple and yellow aurora borealis cushion stones topped with purple chatons, 1" w 35
Brooch/Pendant, Florenza, Maltese cross, ornate Russian gold metal with huge dark blue rhinestone center, baby blue rhinestones, and emerald green cabochons, 2.25" sq 145
Brooch/Pendant, Sarah Coventry, center amethyst cabochon surrounded in an ornate metalwork design incorporated with amethyst chatons, 1.75" h, 1.5" w ..30
Clip, Trifari, dragon fish, gilt and enameled metal with pearl belly, pavé accents, and orig clip back, stamped, 2" h 560

Cuff Bracelet, Miraglia, SS, modernist design with geometric cross-hatched etching, stamped "Miraglia sterling modern," 2.25" w 70
Cuff Bracelet, Rebajes, patinated copper, modernist design with pointed table and many individual slit cut-outs, stamped "REBAJES," 2.25" w cuff 225
Cufflinks, pr, David Andersen, SS and enamel with brilliant geometric orange and yellow hue, stamped, 1" w 250
Earrings, dark glass oval plaques flanked by colorless rhinestones, unmkd, screw-on backs, c1940s, 1" h 15
Earrings, delicate wirework pendants each suspending a sq faceted blue stone, clip-on, mkd "Napier," c1920s, 2" l 30
Earrings, Florenza, cabochon blue and green navettes accentuated with aurora borealis chatons, silvertone metal with hallmark on back, clip-on, 1.5" x 1" 25
Earrings, Hector Aguilar, SS, bead-worked domed and dangles, stamped, 1" h 395
Earrings, Juliana, watermelon rhinestone center with clears, grays, and fiery iridescents, clip-on, 1.5" x 1" 49
Earrings, pop-art, metal and plastic, round disk suspending 2 rectangular pendants, mkd "Western Germany," clip-on, c1960s, 3" l 30
Earrings, Weiss, flower, turquoise opaque marquis-shaped stones surround rhinestones of same color, silvertone setting, clip-on, 2" d 42
Earrings, Weiss, "Whirly Gig," light blue topaz stones, 1" sq 25
Fur Clip, Coro Craft, SS, lady's face, blue eyes, clear rhinestone earrings with band of clears on top, pink rhinestone crown, 1.5" 250
Link Bracelet, Greta, SS, waffle-like modernist design, sgd "GRETA," 1.25" w 280
Link Bracelet, Los Castillos, SS, modernist studded and frame design, stamped and hallmarked, 1" w 300
Necklace, copper, flattened figure-8 shaped links, mkd "Renoir," c1950s, 1" w link, 29" l 100

Necklace, copper and brass, large medallion with Aztec design and wire scroll border on figure-8 link chain, mkd "Mexico," c1950s .20

Necklace, Hobé, black glass faceted beads, strung on very fine linked chain with black spacers, sgd, 17" adjustable length 16

Necklace, large oblong 8-sided amber crystal suspended from a beaded chain with faceted diamond-shaped amber crystal beads alternating with filigree spheres, 1920s, 18" l 70

Necklace, Leo Glass, fiery yellow faux moonstones and yellow, citrine, and amber rhinestones, 16" adjustable 145

Necklace, Miriam Haskell, 2 strands of yellow glass beads with 1.5" drops of yellow and white beads, ornate Russian gold filigree closure with floral design, sgd, graduated to 17" 185

Necklace, Miriam Haskell, 6-strand, baroque pearls with purple glass accents and hook closure, 18" l 200

Necklace, Miriam Haskell, glass beads, faux coral, and ornate Russian gold filigree balls, sgd, 54" l 165

Necklace, Miriam Haskell, lucite center flower and surrounding leaves and bellflowers, 16" l .295

Necklace, Miriam Haskell, white milk glass, irregularly shaped beads with goldtone spacers, sgd, 22" l 165

Necklace and Earrings Suite, Miriam Haskell, 5-strand, red and orange glass seed beads, hook closure, 16" l, matching earrings, .75" w, both mkd . .225

Necklace and Earrings, Weiss, various shaped citron, peridot, rose, tangerine, and lemon rhinestones, 16" l necklace, 1.25" x 1" earrings 125

Parure, Guillermo Cini, SS, rose, 7" x 1.5" bracelet, 16" l necklace, 1" earrings, presentation box 375

Parure, Trifari, textured goldtone metal with clear rhinestones, sgd, 16" adjustable length necklace, matching 1" clip earrings .125

Parure, Weiss, olivine, citron, rose, peridot, and aurora borealis prong-set stones, 7" bracelet with push-in clasp and safety chain, 2" brooch, 1" clip earrings, sgd 325

Pendant, Hollycraft, faux moonstone, 3" . .45

Pendant Necklace, Bjorn Weckstrom for Lapponia, Barbarella, SS, long chain, 3.75" h 845

Pendant Necklace, Leo Glass, pendant has pearls, clear baguettes and rounds, and green rhinestones, 15.5" l with 1.75" drop 125

Pendant Necklace and Earrings, copper, triple-leaf pendant, matching single-leaf clip-on earrings, c1950s, 24" l chain, 1.5" l earrings 30

Pin, Coro, toucan, gilt and enameled SS, pavé rhinestone detailing, mkd "CORO sterling," 3.5" h 45

Pin, Guillermo Cini, cabbage rose, SS 76

Pin, Levin, SS and anodized detail and elegant pearl accents, modernist space-age design, stamped "LEVIN sterling," 2.5" w .300

Pin, pop-art, plastic triangle shape with contrasting center set with 3 "diamonds," c1960s, 3" l 30

Pin, Trifari, mushrooms, goldtone, 2 mushrooms with multicolor jeweled caps, sgd, 1.5" x 1.375" 235

Tiara, Weiss, "The Countess," clear rhinestones in a silvertone setting, metal side combs, sgd, c1950s, 2.25" h 110

JOHNSON BROTHERS

The Johnson Brothers, Alfred, Frederick, and Henry, acquired the J. W. Pankhurst pottery located in the Staffordshire district of England in 1882 and began manufacturing dinnerware the following year. Another brother, Robert, joined the company in 1896 and took charge of American distribution.

Over the years the company produced hundreds of variations of patterns, shapes, and colors. One of the most popular and readily found patterns is blue and white Coaching Scenes, first introduced in 1963. Although it was also made in green and white, pink and white, and brown multicolored, only blue and white was shipped to the United States. Other popular patterns include Old Britain Castles and Friendly Village.

Barnyard King, dinner plate, 10.75" 40
Barnyard King, turkey platter, 20.5" x 16" .150
Castle on the Lake, dinner plate, 10.5" 6
English Chippendale, berry bowl, 5.25" 8
English Chippendale, bread and butter plate, 6.25" 5
English Chippendale, cereal bowl, 6" 10
English Chippendale, chop plate, 12.25" . . .55
English Chippendale, cup and saucer 18
English Chippendale, dinner plate, 10" 12
English Chippendale, platter, 12" x 10" 16
English Chippendale, platter, 15.75" x 13" . .55
English Chippendale, relish tray, 8" x 5.25" 30
English Chippendale, salad plate, 8" 14
English Chippendale, soup bowl, 8" 30
Eternal Beau, cereal bowl, 7" 5
Eternal Beau, dinner plate, 10" 6
Eternal Beau, gravy boat 7
Eternal Beau, platter, 13.5" x 10" 15
Eternal Beau, salad plate, 7.5" 6
Friendly Village, creamer, "Old Mill" 12
Friendly Village, cup and saucer, "Ice House" 3
Friendly Village, dinner plate, "Old Mill" . . .8
Fruit Sampler, creamer 8
Fruit Sampler, gravy boat, 7" x 2" 13
Fruit Sampler, salt and pepper shakers, 4" 20
Fruit Sampler, teapot, pear finial 40
Ironstone, white, octagonal, creamer and cov sugar 12
Ironstone, white, octagonal, platter, 11.875" x 9.125" 12
Ironstone, white, octagonal, soup tureen, cov, 10.5" w handle to handle, 6" h 28
Old Britain Castles, bouillon cups, 5" 8

Old Britain Castles, bread and butter plate, 6.5" 3
Old Britain Castles, dessert plates, 6.5" 4
Old Britain Castles, salad plate, 7.5" 10
Old Britain Castles, sugar bowl, cov 20

JOSEF ORIGINALS

Josef Originals were designed and produced by Muriel Joseph George. She began sculpting ceramics in California during World War II. In 1959, in order to compete with cheap Japanese imitations, she formed a partnership with George Good's "George Imports" and began their own production in Japan. Muriel Joseph continued designing until 1984–85. George Good sold the company to Applause Co in 1985. While some lines continued to be made, no new designs have been produced under the Josef Originals name. Muriel passed away in 1995.

California Josef figurines are marked with a black oval paper label that reads "Josef Original California." In addition, the pieces may have an incised Josef Original marking on the bottom or sometimes merely an incised "X." The Japan pieces usually have two paper labels, an oval black label that reads "Josef Original," and a separate small oval sticker that reads "Japan." Some pieces were also ink stamped, and large pieces almost always have an incised Josef Original signature on the bottom.

Bell, angel, white, 3.875" h 20
Card Holder, blue bird, 2.25" h 45
Cone Doll, Doll of the Month, September .60
Figurine, Birthday Angel, #5 35
Figurine, Birthday Angel, #7 35
Figurine, Birthstone Doll, October 36
Figurine, Colonial Days, Caroline 190
Figurine, Doll of the Month, July 65
Figurine, Doll of the Month, May 60
Figurine, Favorite Sayings, Hearts and Flowers, 4" h 48
Figurine, Favorite Sayings, Mighty Like A Rose 55
Figurine, Favorite Sayings, Peaches and Cream 55
Figurine, Greetings Series, Bon Voyage . .60
Figurine, Little Internationals, England 50
Figurine, Little Internationals, Germany . . .65
Figurine, Little Internationals, Russia 70
Figurine, mama hippo 22
Figurine, Mary Ann, yellow dress, green stones, 3.5" h 18
Figurine, miniature bull, 2.5" h 20
Figurine, nurse with pills, Mouse Village, 3" h 35
Figurine, Papa Elephant, 4.5" h 45
Figurine, Pekingese, pink ribbon, 3" h 35
Figurine, Persian Cat, white, 4.25" h 25
Figurine, Siamese Cat, arched back, 4" h .28
Figurine, Wee Ling, 5" h 30
Figurines, Renee and Jacques 100
Half Doll, Nanette, 5.375" h 75
Music Box, girl playing piano, 6" h 65
Music Box, girl playing violin, plays "Fascination," 6.5" .75
Music Box, Love Theme Music Boxes, plays "Impossible Dream" 80
Pie Bird, yellow chick, 3.25" h 55
Planter, owl on log, "Bless Our Nest," 5" x 6.25" 40
Soap Dish, pink dress, gold trim, 3" h 35
Toothpick Holder, hippo, light blue with dark blue accents, Korea, 2.5" h 10

JUGTOWN

Jugtown is the pottery that refused to die. Founded in 1920 in Moore County, North Carolina, by Jacques and Julianna Busbee, the pottery continued under Julianna and Ben Owens when Jacques died in 1947. It closed in 1958 only to reopen in 1960. It is now run by Country Roads, Inc., a nonprofit organization.

The principal difficulty in identifying Jugtown pottery is that the same glazes are used on modern pieces as were used decades ago. Even the mark is the same. Since it takes an expert to distinguish between the new and old, this is certainly one category which novices should avoid until they have done a fair amount of study.

Carolina pottery is developing a dedicated core group of collectors. For more information read Charles G. Zug III's *Turners and Burners: The Folk Potters of North Carolina* (University of North Carolina Press: 1986).

Bean Pot, orange tobacco spit glaze, 1930-40, 5.5" h, 6.5" d 50
Bowl, 1.75" h, 5" d 100
Bowl, cov, orange-brown flecked glaze, 5.5" d 125
Candlesticks, pr, sewer type clay, 11.75" h, 5.5" d 125

Creamer and Sugar, cov, red clay body, tobacco spit glaze, c1940 150
Cup and Saucer, tobacco spit brown glaze, c1940, 3" h cup, 6.25" d saucer . . .70
Dish, tobacco spit brown glaze with green spots, imp mark, c1940, 2" h, 9.75" d 75
Pitcher, chrome red-orange, c1940, 3.5" h 75
Saucer, salt glaze with cobalt dec and orange peel effect, small chip on rim, 2 flakes on ft, c1940, 6.25" d 50
Sugar Bowl, cov, lug handles, buff-colored glaze with running blue highlights throughout, sgd in script "Sid Luck 1988," 4" h, 4" d 25
Tumbler, cobalt flower on white ground, 2 incised lines below rim, 1982, 4.25" h, 3.25" d 7
Vase, bulbous form, 3 incised lines at shoulder, applied medallions, frogskin green glaze, 1989, 6.75" h, 6" d 90
Vase, egg-shaped, red clay, brushed-on running frothy Chinese white glaze, 1.5" tight hairline on rim, c1940, 6.75" h, 5" d 175

JUKEBOXES

A jukebox is an amplified coin-operated phonograph. The 1940s and early 1950s were its golden age, a period when bubble machines ruled every teenage hangout from dance hall to drugstore. Portable radios, television's growth, and "Top 40" radio were responsible for the jukebox's decline in the 1960s.

Pre-1938 jukeboxes were made primarily of wood and resemble a phonograph or radio cabinet. Wurlitzer and Rock-Ola, whose jukeboxes often featured brightly colored plastic and animation units, made the best of the 78 rpm jukeboxes of the 1938-1948 period. The 45 rpm jukebox, popularized by the television show Happy Days, arrived on the scene in 1940 and survived until 1960. Seeburg was the principal manufacturer of these machines. Beginning in 1961, manufacturers often hid the record mechanism. These machines lack the collector appeal of their earlier counterparts.

AMI, A 1,500
CTI-1 300
Evans 2045 Century 1,100
Festival 300
JBM 300
JAN 250
JAO 300
Jupiter, 160L Astral 250
MM3 300
MM5 300
Mills, Do-Re-Me 500
NSM, Consul 120 .200
Prestige, E160 300
Rock-ola, 446 300
Rock-ola, 468 275
Rock-ola, 470, restored 750
Rock-ola, 474 300
Rock-ola, 488, restored 550
Rock-ola, 496, restored 650
Rock-ola, 1422 2,000
Rowe, JAO 275
Seeburg, 100R, restored 2,300
Seeburg, 222, restored 3,995
Seeburg, AY160 600
Seeburg, BL, restored 3,795
Seeburg, HF100R, restored 4,495
Seeburg, LPC 480 275
Seeburg, LS1 300
Seeburg, SPS160 .325
Seeburg, SS160 300
Seeburg, USC2 350
Seeburg, VL2000 5,000
Wurlitzer, 1015, restored 8,500
Wurlitzer, HF 1700, restored 3,300

KAY FINCH

After over a decade of ceramic studies, Kay Finch, assisted by her husband, Braden, opened her commercial studio in 1939. A whimsical series of pig figurines and hand-decorated banks were the company's first successful products.

An expanded studio and showroom located on the Pacific Coast Highway in Corona del Mar opened on December 7, 1941. The business soon had forty employees as it produced a wide variety of novelty items. A line of dog figurines and themed items were introduced in the 1940s. Christmas plates were made from 1950 until 1962.

When Braden died in 1963, Kay Finch ceased operations. Freeman McFarlin Potteries purchased the molds in the mid-1970s and commissioned Finch to model a new series of dog figurines. Production of these continued throught the late 1970s.

Ambrosia, Persian Cat, .125" flake on ear, 10.75" h 600
Baby Cottontail, rabbit, pink, blue eyes and ears, tiny flake on nose 110
Biddy Hen, 7" h 70
Cat, Muff, blue 3.5" 75
Godey Lady, crazing and glaze chips, 8.875" h 45
Hoot Owl, brown and gold, flake on tail feather, 8.75" 100
Moon Vase, turquoise, 19" h, 15" w 250
Mug, Santa, iridescent finish with gold highlights, 4.5" h, 4.5" w 50

Peasant Boy, 6.5" h, .125" chip on base edge 35
Peasant Girl, 7" h 50
Pee Wee Penguin, crazing, 3.25" h 145
Planter, Jezzy Kitten, 6" h, 7" l 185
Planter, teddy bear, 8" h, 7.5" x 5" 225
Rearing Lamb, pink, hp features, rough spot on ear, 5.75" h, 3.5" w 225
Smiley Pig, tiny rough spot on ear, 6.75" h, 8" 350
Swans, pr, pink, 3.5" h, 3.5" l 180
Toot Owl, pink and green, 5.75" h 110
Western Burro, #4769 125

KEWPIES

Kewpies are the creation of Rose Cecil O'Neill (1876–1944), artist, novelist, illustrator, poet, and sculptor. The Kewpie first appeared in the December 1909 issue of *Ladies' Home Journal.* The first Kewpie doll followed in 1913.

Many early Kewpie items were made in Germany. An attached label enhances value. Kewpie items also were made in the United States and Japan. The generations that grew up with Kewpie dolls are dying off. O'Neill's memory and products are being kept alive by a small but dedicated group of collectors.

Club: International Rose O'Neill Club, P.O. Box 668, Branson, MO 65616.

Bank, carnival chalkware, glitter trim, 1930s, 12" h 150
Biscuit Tin, kewpies walking a tightrope, 1920s, 3.5" h, 6" d 175
Doll, Cameo, black, wearing pink floral dress and lace apron, mkd "Jesco," orig box, 12" h 85
Doll, Cameo, Kewpie Goes To School doll, orig label and box, mkd "Jesco Cameo 7" on back of head, 11" h 150
Doll, Cameo, mkd "JCKC 23 Cameo 74" on back of head, 10" h 60
Doll, Cameo, vinyl, pink and white dotted Swiss pinafore, 1950s, 11" h 325
Doll, red vinyl, 10" h .75
Napkin Ring, figural Kewpie standing beside ring, pewter, 2.5" h 115
Paper Doll Book, *Kewpies in Kewpieville,* 1966, uncut 15

Paperweight, kewpie on rect slab with emb "Purdue Foundry," 2.75" x 1.5" 45
Piano Babies, pr, bisque, blue wings, Lefton, mkd "KW228," Made In Japan sticker, 4.625" h seated kewpie, 4.5" l reclining kewpie 50
Pin, figural, 3 kewpies sitting on leaf, silver, 2" l 40
Postcard, Kewpieville "Dressing a Frog," from the art of Rose O'Neill by Florence Baker 8
Shaker, bisque, 4 holes in head, white rubber stopper, mkd "61," 5.5" h 45

KEY CHAINS

Talk about an inexpensive collecting category. Most examples sell under $10. If you are really cheap, you can pick up plenty of modern examples for free. Why not? They are going to be collectible in thirty years and antiques in a hundred. Who knows, maybe you will live that long!

One of the favorite charity fundraising gimmicks in the 1940s and 1950s was the license plate key chain tag. There is a collectors' club devoted to this single topic.

Club: License Plate Key Chain & Mini License Plate Collectors, 888 Eighth Ave., New York, NY 10019.

Advertising, Duquesne Brewing Co, Pittsburgh, PA, aluminum token with 1948 D penny 12
Advertising, Esso, plastic, diecut Esso "Happy" oil drop character, late 1960s, 2.75" h 12
Advertising, "Larimer's Barber Shop, 108 S Center, Marshalltown, Iowa," flashlight, 1960s, 2.75" l 7
Advertising, Old Crow Distillery, plastic, figural crow, 1.75" h 12

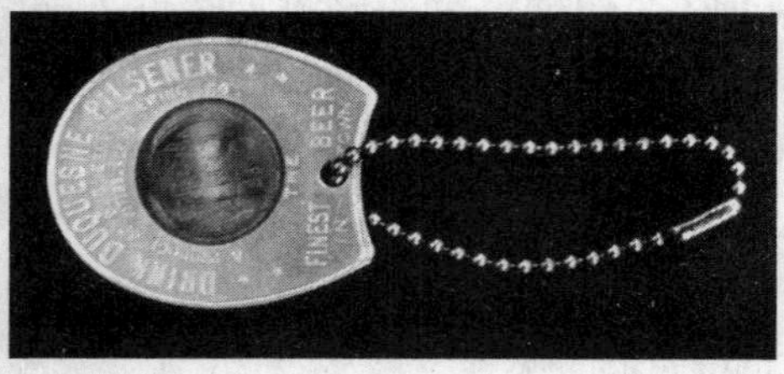

Advertising, "Payday Salted Nut Roll," white rect plastic tag with red and blue lettering 6
Advertising, Sally Shops of California, emb stylish woman walking a dog, "The most walked about clothes in town" on 1 side of rect metal tag, "Sally's Silver Anniversary Celebration 1963" on other side, 1.625" x 1" 16
Advertising, "VanDenberg Supply Co, Plumbing & Heating Supplies, Rockford, Ill" on 1 side of oval tag, "Owner identified by No. 221 for return of keys. 50 cent reward" on other side, 1.75" 18
Change Purse, goldtone mesh purse with filigree sides, 2.75" w 15
Fraternal, Eastern Star, enameled star emblem 18
License Plate, New York, Disabled American Veterans, 1955 8
Political, Carter, figural brass donkey emb with "Carter" 25
Political, JFK, emb profile on silver medallion, "John Fitzgerald Kennedy 1917-1963" on 1 side, "Ask Not" quote on other side 15
Puzzle, plastic, circ, 2-sided, 2 steel balls . .6
Railroad, ST, Santa Fe Railroad, circ fob with 4 screwdriver bits, "Get the Santa Fe Safety Habit" and "Fight Axy Dent" on 1 side, clover and "Pocket Screwdriver Fits Most Screws" on other side 20
Souvenir, Disneyland Haunted Mansion, 3 ghosts hitching a ride 5
Souvenir, Golden Nugget Casino, pewter, 2-tone gold- and silver-plated, spinning center disk 18

KEYS

There are millions of keys. Focus on a special type of key, e.g., automobile, railroad switch, etc. Few keys are rare. Prices above $10 are unusual.

Collect keys with a strong decorative motif. Examples include keys with advertising logos to cast keys with animal or interlocking scroll decorations. Be suspicious if someone offers you a key to King Tut's Tomb, Newgate Prison, or the Tower of London.

Cabinet, brass, 2.875" 12
Cabinet, bronze, 3.25" 25
Cabinet, iron, 1890s-1920s, 1.75" 4
Car, Cadillac, SP 35
Car, Esso, gold plated 10
Car, Pontiac, gold plated, Indian head 35
Chest, iron, 2.875" 18
Clock, brass, jewelers, 3" 32
Clock, steel, iron, Waterbury Clock Co, 2.25" 16
Door, bronze, 4.25" 12
Door, iron, Lockwood Mfg, 2.75" 3
Door, steel, Norwalk, 3.25" 4
Door, steel, Reading Hardware, 4" 4
Gate, iron, 6" 7
Handcuff, iron, Taylor, 1.75" 2
Pocket Door, bronze, Sargent, 1.625" 14
Railroad, CS-63 signal lock key, steel, "PU RR Signal" stamped on hilt 40
Railroad, switch key, Atlantic & Pacific Railroad, "A&PRR" serif letters single ring, reverse "S," W Bohannan 235
Railroad, switch key, brass, "B&O" small serif letters stamped on hilt, "B3635" on reverse, Fraim keystone hallmark 15
Railroad, switch key, brass, "CCC&STLRR" stamped on hilt, "S 13812" on reverse, A&W oval hallmark 32
Railroad, switch key, brass, tapered barrel, "DUSY CO" stamped on hilt, "7" on reverse .140
Railroad, switch key, steel, "C&SRY" stamped on hilt, "S 99" on reverse, A&W oval hallmark 525
Ship, bronze, bit type, foreign ship tags 6

KITCHEN COLLECTIBLES

Kitchen collectibles are closely linked to Country, where the concentration is on the 1860–1900 period. This approach is far too narrow. There are a lot of great kitchen utensils and gadgets from the 1900 to 1940 period. Do not overlook them.

Kitchen collectibles were used. While collectors appreciate the used look, they also want an item in very good or better condition. It is a difficult balancing act in many cases. The field is broad, so it pays to specialize. Tomato slicers are not for me; I am more of a chopping knife person.

Clubs: International Society of Apple Parer Enthusiasts, 735 Cedarwood Terrace, Apt. 735B, Rochester, NY 14609; Kollectors of Old Kitchen Stuff, 354 Rte. 206 North, Chester, NJ 07930.

Advertising Paperweight, None Such Mince Meat, glass, rect, black and white image of housewife in apron carving pie, 1" x 2.5" x 4" 65
Beverage Set, Color Craft, anodized aluminum, pitcher, 8 tumblers, and round tray, pink-red pitcher, tray, and 2 tumblers, 2 tumblers each in yellow, blue, and green, 1950s 100
Cake Tester/Pie Bird, Benny the Baker pie bird holding cake tester in left hand, missing pastry cutter from right hand, 1940s-50s 65
Coffee Urn, Chase Chrome and Brass Co, Coronet, chrome, orig tag and cord, crack in Bakelite base 500
Cookie Cutter, heart and cupid, hard plastic, red, Hallmark, 1974 50
Cookie Cutter, turkey, hard plastic, orange, tan or brown, Hallmark, 1976, 2.75" h 4
Eggbeater, A&J, rotary, wood handle, Oct 9, 1923 patent date 25
Eggbeater, Androck, green Bakelite handle, c1940s 40
Eggbeater, Ekco A&J, red wood handle, glass jar 45
Eggbeater, Maynard, off-white gear housing, handle, and knob 18
Eggbeater, slanted black and white "D" handle 20

Eggbeater, Taplin Mfg, New Britain, CT, green wood handle and knob 15
Egg Separator, figural turtle, yellow and green, mkd "Josef Originals," 2.5" h . . .25
Egg Timer, Dutch girl figurine holding glass egg timer, mkd "Germany" 75
Kitchen Accessory Set, retro, consisting of two 11" h canisters, two 9.5" h canisters, 12" h coffeepot, creamer, sugar, and salt and pepper shakers, high gloss yellow glaze, mkd "USA," 1950s . .85
Measuring Spoon Holder, figural ceramic sailboat and lighthouse, 4 slots in lighthouse hold plastic spoons, souvenir of Florida, 5" h 50
Pot Scraper, adv, Babbitt's, 2-sided, blue, yellow, and white with product image and text for cleanser on front, red, yellow, and black with 2 product images and text for soap powder and bar soap on back, 3.125" x 3.625" 350
Pot Scraper, adv, Henkel's Flour, red, white, and blue, "Pot and Pan Scraper, Don't Take Untried Brands, Henkel's Flour Makes Best Bread and Pastry Sure To Satisfy, Economical Too" on front, blank back, 2.875" x 3.375" 240
Pot Scraper, adv, Nye's Bread, black and white, "'Nye's' Pot and Pan Scraper Fits Any Corner Of Pot Or Pan, For Goodness Sake Eat Wholesome Bread, Better Than Mother Ever Baked, Get It At Your Grocers, 5 & 8 Cent Loaves," 2.875" x 3.375" 275
Scoop, litho tin, Golden Sun Coffee adv, green lettering on white ground "Golden Sun Coffee, The Daily Choice Of Countless Thousands," 4" x 1.75" . . .175

Scoop, litho tin, King Midas Flour adv, red, white, and black, 4" x 1.75" 300

KNOWLES DINNERWARE

In 1900 Edwin M. Knowles established the Edwin M. Knowles China Company in Chester, West Virginia. The company made semi-porcelain dinnerware, kitchenware, specialties, and toilet wares.

In 1913 a second plant in Newell, West Virginia, was opened. The company operated its Chester, West Virginia, pottery until 1931, at which time the plant was sold to the Harker Pottery Company. Production continued at the Newell pottery. Edwin M. Knowles China Company ceased operations in 1963.

In the 1970s the Edwin M. Knowles Company entered into a relationship with the Bradford Exchange to produce limited edition collector plates, with titles such as *Gone With the Wind* and *The Wizard of Oz* in addition to Norman Rockwell subjects.

Accent Solid Colors, bread and butter plate, dark brown, 6.25" d 7
Accent Solid Colors, cup and saucer, chartreuse 12
Accent Solid Colors, fruit bowl, gray, 5.625" d 12
Chalet, bread and butter plate, 6.25" d 3
Chalet, creamer 11
Chalet, cup and saucer 9
Chalet, dinner plate, 10.25" d 7
Chalet, fruit bowl, 5.625" d 4
Chalet, soup bowl, 7.625" d 7
Chalet, sugar, cov .14
Chalet, vegetable bowl, 8.875" d 14
Deanna, pink band, gold trim, bread and butter plate, 6.25" d 7
Deanna, pink band, gold trim, cup and saucer 5
Deanna, pink band, gold trim, dinner plate, 9.25" d 10
Deanna, pink band, gold trim, fruit bowl, 5.25" d 7
Deanna, pink band, gold trim, plate, 7" sq . .7
Deanna, pink band, gold trim, platter, 13.25" l 15
Deanna, pink band, gold trim, soup bowl, 7.75" d 10

Deanna, pink band, gold trim, vegetable bowl, oval, 9.5" l 20
Forsythia, bread and butter plate, 6.5" 10
Forsythia, creamer, 3" h, 7" w 16
Forsythia, cup 6
Forsythia, dessert bowl, 5.5" 10
Forsythia, dinner plate, 10" 12
Forsythia, saucer, 6.5" 6
Forsythia, sugar, cov 22
Forsythia, vegetable bowl, 8.5" 20
Golden Wheat, bread and butter plate, 6" d 3
Golden Wheat, dinner plate, 9" d 5
Golden Wheat, salad plate, 7" d 4
Golden Wheat, saucer 2
Golden Wheat, soup bowl, 7.5" d 4
Grapevine, saucer 5
Orange Poppy, bread and butter plate, 6.5" d 5
Orange Poppy, creamer 14
Orange Poppy, cup and saucer 25
Orange Poppy, dinner plate, 10" d 18
Orange Poppy, fruit bowl, 5.375" d 9
Orange Poppy, platter, 13.5" x 10.25" 45
Orange Poppy, soup bowl, 8" d 16
Orange Poppy, sugar bowl 14
Petit Point Pastel Bouquet, bread and butter plate, 6.5" d .5
Petit Point Pastel Bouquet, chop plate, 10.75" d 28
Petit Point Pastel Bouquet, creamer 13
Petit Point Pastel Bouquet, cup and saucer 12
Petit Point Pastel Bouquet, dinner plate, 9.5" d 12
Petit Point Pastel Bouquet, fruit bowl, 5.5" d 8
Petit Point Pastel Bouquet, sugar bowl . . .13
Petit Point Pastel Bouquet, vegetable bowl, 8.5" d 26
Rhondo, bread and butter plate, 6.5" d 6
Rhondo, cup and saucer, ...14
Rhondo, dinner plate, 10" d 10
Rhondo, fruit bowl, 5.25" d 8
Rhondo, platter, 12.75" x 10" 16
Rhondo, vegetable bowl, 8.5" d 15
Yellow Trim Poppy, chop plate, 12.5" d . . .15

KREISS CERAMICS

In 1946 Murray Kreiss founded Murray Kreiss and Company as an importer and distributor of Japanese-made ceramic figurines to the five-and-dime store and souvenir trade. Products covered a wide range from Santas and animals to Disney-like characters. As the 1960s ended, the company's focus shifted to fine furniture. Look for ashtrays, mugs, napkin ladies, and planters as well as figurines.

Animal Figure, black panther, gold collar with red and turquoise rhinestones, 5.5" h, 9" l 35
Animal Figure, brown dog with yellow bow on head, 4.375" h 10
Animal Figure, cocker spaniel, jeweled collar, 5.75" h 30
Animal Figure, elephant Santa, 3.875" h . . .14
Animal Figure, gray bunny, 3.5" h 16
Animal Figure, monkey, 2.75" h 25
Animal Figure, sitting donkey, 5.25" h 40
Bell, Christmas angel 20
Figure, Elegant Heir, rhinestones for eyes and on shoes, 6.25" h 95

Military Figures, set of 5, orig tags 150
Psycho Figure, blue, 5.5" h 65
Psycho Figure, pink with rabbit ears, 5.125" h 65
Psycho Figure, with hair and red rhinestone eyes, "Only my modesty prevents me from mentioning my other virtues," 5.5" h 70
Queen of Spades and King of Clubs, 6.5" and 7" h 60
Salt and Pepper Shakers, cuckoo clocks, 2.75" h 15

LABELS

Labels advertising anything from cigars and citrus fruits to soaps and tobacco make great decorative accents. Properly framed and displayed, they become attractive works of art.

The first fruit crate art was created by California fruit growers about 1880. The labels became very colorful and covered many subjects. Most depict the type of fruit held in the box. The advent of cardboard boxes in the 1940s marked the end of fruit crate art and the beginning of a new collecting category. When collecting paper labels, condition is extremely important. Damaged, trimmed, or torn labels are significantly less valuable than labels in mint condition.

Clubs: American Antique Graphics Society, 5185 Windfall Rd., Medina, OH 44256; Cigar Label Collectors International, P.O. Box 66, Sharon Center, OH 44274; Florida Citrus Labels Collectors Assoc., P.O. Box 547636, Orlando, FL 32854; Society of Antique Label Collectors, P.O. Box 24811, Tampa, FL 33623; The Citrus Label Society, 131 Miramonte Dr., Fullerton, CA 92635.

Can, Boiled Mutton, sheep, cowboy on range chasing cow 8
Can, Buster Boy, farmer boy riding horse through tomato 18
Can, Butterfly Brand, butterfly, wax beans .7
Can, Campfire Coffee, coffeepot on campfire 8
Can, Cherry Hill, Indian holding arrows, teepees 7
Can, Cobcut, hand cutting corn from ear on plate, 1930 10
Can, Commercial Floor Paint, view of int of house, 4.5 x 6" .6
Can, Dana's Jardiniere, plant in ornate plant stand 1
Can, Defender Brand Tomatoes, sailing ship on ocean, white 5
Can, Dellford White Potatoes, young boy with basket of food 1
Can, Dinette Pork & Beans, 2 fancy bowls of beans 2
Can, Edmondson's Favorite Blackberries, boy picking berries, owls on branch . . .20
Can, Elkay Baking Powder, cake, factory, blue and white 1
Can, Ethiopan Black Enamel, black children holding sign 12
Can, Forest City Lima Beans, beans in pod, bright leaves 2
Can, Gold Bond, peas in pods 1
Can, Holly Pineapple, bunch of holly, large pineapple 7
Can, Ibex, ibex on summit, mountains, pear 40
Can, Iona, Indian head, peas in pod 15
Can, Jack Sprat Chili Con Carne, man dressed in green, bowl of chili 25
Can, La Perla, olives on branch, boy's face 2
Can, Monarch Chicken Soup, lion head, 1922 25
Can, Old East Maine Clams, three clams, red, blue, and yellow, 1929 12
Can, Osseo Early Peas, two prospectors, knight on horse 25
Can, Penn-Harris, bowls of fruit, map of Pennsylvania 20
Can, Purity, embossed cupid in red heart . .4

Can, Rose Bowl Apricots, football players .35
Can, St George Jam, St George slaying dragon, fruit .6
Can, Supreme Court Carrots, judicial building, carrots .1
Can, Vadco Talcum Powder, city skyscraper, 1923 .30
Can, Wel-Don, baby in diapers, yellow stringless beans .1
Can, Yankee Brand, smiling Uncle Sam sitting on stool .30
Fruit Crate, Athlete, Olympic runners in stadium, lemons, 1930 .8
Fruit Crate, Belt, belt around large orange, 1930 .10
Fruit Crate, Blue Goose, large blue goose, 1940 .5
Fruit Crate, Boyhood, smiling boy driving mule cart, grapefruit, 1920 .95
Fruit Crate, California Beauty, bouquet of roses, pear, 1930 .10
Fruit Crate, Camel, Arab in desert next to camel, 1930 .75
Fruit Crate, Golden Rod, bunch of gold flowers, 1930 .5
Fruit Crate, Green Mill, green windmill, 1920 .8
Fruit Crate, Kiltie, large grapefruit, purple plaid, 1930 .4
Fruit Crate, King David, bust of bearded king, 1930 .15
Fruit Crate, Majorette, pretty girl holding baton, 1930 .6
Fruit Crate, Marc Antony, bust of Roman, 1930 .15
Fruit Crate, Master Brand, view of El Capitan, 1930 .35
Fruit Crate, National Brand, Capitol building, orange, 1930 .50

Fruit Crate, Orange Queen, beautiful woman holding oranges, 1920 .250
Fruit Crate, Placer, view of gold mining camp, 1930 .15
Fruit Crate, Rainbow Brand, rainbow over orchard, 1920 .200
Fruit Crate, Tick-Tock, large grandfather clock face, 12:55, 1930 .75
Fruit Crate, Tree Top, majestic twin sequoia trees, blue, 1940 .15
Fruit Crate, Vandalia, peacock, earlier art deco version, 1930 .175

LACE

While there are collectors of lace, most old lace is still bought for use. Those buying lace for reuse are not willing to pay high prices. A general rule is the larger the amount or piece in a single pattern, the higher the price is likely to be. In this instance, the price is directly related to supply and demand.

Items decorated with lace that can be used in their existing forms, e.g., costumes and tablecloths, have value that transcends the lace itself. Value for these pieces rests on the item as a whole, not the lace. Learn to differentiate between handmade and machine-made lace.

Club: International Old Lacers, Inc., P.O. Box 554, Flanders, NJ 07836.

LAMPS

Collecting lamps can be considered an illuminating hobby. Not only is the collection practical, versatile, and decorative, but it keeps you out of the dark. Whether you prefer a particular lamp style, color, or theme, you will find a wonderful and enlightening assortment at any flea market.

Clubs: Fairy Lamp Club, 6422 Haystack Rd., Alexandria, VA 22310; Night Light Miniature Lamp Club, 38619 Wakefield Ct., Northville, MI 48167.

Note: For additional listings see Aladdin, Motion Lamps, and TV Lamps.

Bedroom, genie lamp shape base with chimney top, floral dec on white milk glass, 6.75" h 10
Bedroom, white milk glass, Hobnail pattern 30
Candlestick, brass, Baldwin 20
Child's, ceramic, figural Billy the Kid, 10.5" h 35
Child's, cylindrical slag glass base, heavy glass shade dec with decals of cartoon cats and dogs, 9.5" h 95
Figural, blue glass, lady with harp, blue glass parasol shade, 12" h, price for pr 135
Figural, ceramic, steam locomotive, black and red drip glaze, 1973, 18.5" h . .40
Figural, metal elephant balanced on ball, green clambroth pedestal base, 1930s, 8.25" h 175
Figural, plaster, Charlie Tuna, Star-Kist Foods adv, stiff paper shade, c1970, 9" h 50
Hanging, figural bunch of grapes, 1970s . .35
Table, ceramic, crock shape with green pineapple dec on white ground, 10" h . .15
Table, Eames style, inverted fiberglass cone on chartreuse chalkware base modeled in the shape of a sofa, 10.5" h, 10" w 40
Table, figural black and gold ceramic stylized rooster, 1950s, 14" h 45
Table, metal base with figural pineapple, fabric shade with fringe, 9.25" h 125
Vanity, wire tripod base, conical silk shade with alternating vertical green and gold stripes, black and gold braid trim at top and bottom, 13" h 28

Wall Sconces, pr, Art Deco, curved frosted glass panels shading from white to amber, 1930s, 8" h, 5" w 225

LAW ENFORCEMENT

Do not sell this category short. Collecting is largely confined to the law enforcement community, but within that group, collecting badges, patches, and other police paraphernalia is big. Most collections are based upon items from a specific locality. As a result, prices are regionalized.

There are some crooks afoot. Reproduction and fake badges, especially railroad police badges, are prevalent. Blow the whistle on them when you see them.

Badge, "Allegheny County Constable Snowden Twp Pa," center eagle flanked by 2 horses, eagle perched at lop looking right, c1940s, 2.5" h 15
Badge, "AS & W Co Police," sunrise scene with hills and valleys and river in foreground, eagle crest, 3.125" h 15
Badge, "Captain Salem Police," eagle on top looking right, rising sun with mountains, boat, and river scene, blue lettering, 2.75" h 25
Badge, "Coal & Iron Police," round with star in center, overall fading, c1880-1900, 2.25" d 30
Badge, "Patrol Inspector Border Patrol US Immigration Service," eagle looking right, Patrol Inspector, Department of Labor, USA, 2.25" h 25
Badge, "Patrolman Munhall Boro State of Pennsylvania 6," 6-color cloisonne center with PA state logo, 2.75" h 25

Badge, "Pittsburgh Police 357," raised castle on top with raised belt buckle at bottom, raised copper numbers in center, 3.125" h 15

Badge, "Police," eagle looking right, 2 figures on either side of shield, 2.375" h 15

Badge, "Railway Police PRR Co Patrolman," raised "1518" at bottom, eagle and horse in center, 2.5" h 35

Badge, "USS Sappho Police 5," eagle sitting on anchor in high relief at center, debossed "5" at bottom, 2.75" h 20

Handcuffs, mkd "Harvard Lock Co, New York" on each cuff .95

Key Chain, Royal Canadian Mounted Police, plastic 28

Manual, *Manual of Police Revolver Instruction,* National Rifle Assoc, Washington, DC, 1934, 3rd printing, illus, soft cov, 55 pgs, 4.5" x 6" 25

Movie Poster, *Police Car 17,* image of policeman with drawn revolver on orange ground, "He never knew when the voice from headquarters would send him to fame and glory or to his doom," Tim McCoy 400

Tear Sheet, 2-pg adv for 1952 Ford Police Car, 10.25" d x 14" .12

Toy, police car, Auburn Rubber, blue with silver trim, mkd "Auburn Police" on trunk and "576" on doors, 1.25" h, 4.5" l .65

Toy, Rookie Cop, Police Tipover Motorcycle, Marx, litho tin, windup, orig box, 5.75" h, 8" l 1,200

Toy Badge, "Special Police," tin, 1.25" x 1.125", MOC 12

Uniform Button, Hartford, CT police, emb brass, made by Smith Gray Co, NY, 1920s, 1" d 7

LEFTON CHINA

Lefton China was founded by George Zoltan Lefton in Chicago, Illinois, in 1941. The company markets porcelain giftware from suppliers in Japan, Taiwan, Malaysia, and China, with the bulk imported from Japan.

Club: National Society of Lefton Collectors, 1101 Polk St., Bedford, IA 50833.

Ashtray, figural hat with pipe resting on brim, 3" h, 6" w 55

Bank, #07176, black and white sitting pig, 1989, 6" h 145

Bells, pr, Christmas snowball man and woman, foil labels, 5" h 25

Bookends, pr, figural owls, #H4837 18

Candy Dish, divided, 3-part, pink and blue flower dec on white ground, gold trim, 3-part handle, #7056, 8.5" w 25

Candy Dish, figural sleigh, Green Holly pattern, #1346, 8" l 55

Candy Jar, gift box shape, holly dec, red bow finial, white ground, paper label, #6073, 6" h, 4" sq .18

Decanter, figural monk, #166, 8.5" h 85

Dish, Green Holly pattern, holly leaf shape, #00351 12

Figurine, August Angel of the Month, pink flower, green rhinestone, 4" h 22

Figurine, cat, pearl lustre, blue rhinestone eyes, 6.25" h 35

Figurine, choir boy, #K8266, 5.25" h 15

Figurine, dachshund, #H03103, 4" h, 7.5" l .35

Figurine, pink poodle, wearing a hat with flowers, spaghetti trim, 7" h 85

Figurine, swan, white with gold dec, 5.5" h, 6.5" l 45

Figurines, pr of kissing angels, 1 dec with blue stars, the other with pink stars, 1990, 4" h 10

Music Box, February Birthday Girl, plays "Happy Birthday," dated 1983, 6.5" h . . .30

Piano Babies, pr, kewpies with blue wings, bisque, 1 sitting, 1 lying on tummy, KW228, 4.625" h seated 45

Pitcher, modeled as a tree trunk with mushrooms and leaves at bottom, #6466, dated 1970, 7" h 40
Planter, donkey and cart, 5" h, 6" l 15
Planter, man wearing tailcoat, striped trousers, bow tie, and top hat, riding high wheeler bicycle, gold trim, foil sticker, #996 20
Salt and Pepper Shakers, Santa and Mrs Claus 10
Teapot, rose chintz, gold trim, 6.5" h 75
Tidbit Tray, 2-tier, poinsettia design, goldtone handle, #4391, 6.75" d and 8.75" d plates 65
Vase, egg shape, ftd, floral dec with large yellow rose, gold trim, #183, 5" h . .45
Vase, Green Heritage, Rose, ewer shape, gold trim, #748, 5.5" h 18
Wall Plaque, mermaids, 3-pc set, #3107, 8.75" h, 5.5" h, and 4.25" h 150
Wall Plaque, railroad man's head, smoking a pipe, bisque, matte finish, #4713, 5" h .25
Wall Pocket, bluebird, #283, 6" h, 6.5" w . .125

LENOX

Jonathan Cox and Walter Scott Lenox founded the Ceramic Art Company, Trenton, New Jersey, in 1889. In 1906 Lenox established his own company. Much of Lenox's products resemble Belleek, not unexpectedly since Lenox lured several Belleek potters to New Jersey.

Lenox has an upscale reputation. China service sets sell, but within a narrow price range, e.g., $600 to $1,200 for an ordinary service of eight. The key is Lenox gift and accessory items. Prices are still reasonable. The category has not yet been truly "discovered." Lenox also produces limited edition items whose potential for long-term value is limited.

Ashtray, circ with match holder, pink rose dec on white ground, #2030/K341, 5" d 45
Basket Plate, "5th Anniversary," gold on white, #6673, metal handle, 10.5" d 10
Candleholder, pink rose dec on white ground, gold trim, 3" h, 3.5" d base 10
Cigarette Lighter, table model, goblet shape, white, Ronson insert, 4.75" h 20
Compote, Pineapple pattern, ivory with gold trim, 7" h, 10.5" d 150
Compote, Summer Terrace pattern, green, emb flowers and leaves, 6.25" h, 13" d . .65
Dinnerware, Fairfield pattern, cup and saucer 35
Dinnerware, Fairfield pattern, platter, 16" l 120
Figurine, basset hound wearing Santa hat and holding candy cane in his mouth, #XH7069, 4.25" h 10
Figurine, cat with butterfly, white, 4.25" h .55
Mint Dish, double leaf shape, center handle, 3" h, 10.5" w 30
Salt and Pepper Shakers, figural owls, 3" h 8
Salt and Pepper Shakers, Fruits of Italy, #1207, 3.25" h 8
Tea Set, cov teapot, cov sugar, and creamer, white with gold trim, 1963 . . .130
Toby Pitcher, white, 6.75" h 95
Vase, ewer shape, pink flowers and green leaves on white ground, blue mark, 8" h 85

L. E. SMITH

L. E. Smith Glass Company was founded in 1907 in Mount Pleasant, Pennsylvania, by Lewis E. Smith. Although Smith left the company shortly after its establishment, it still bears his name. Early products included cooking articles and utilitarian wares such as glass percolator tops, fruit jars, sanitary sugar bowls, and reamers.

In the 1920s, green, amber, canary, amethyst, and blue colors were introduced along with an extensive line of soda fountain wares. The company also made milk glass, console and dresser sets, and the always popular fish-shaped aquariums. During the 1930s, Smith became the largest producer of black glass. Popular dinnerware lines were Homestead, Melba, Do-Si-Do, By Cracky, Romanesque, and Mount Pleasant. Today, L. E. Smith manufactures colored reproduction glass and decorative objects.

Ashtray, Moon and Star, amber, 8" w 35
Basket, Moon and Stars, green basket, clear handle, 8" h, 9.125" w 70
Bonbon, Mt Pleasant, ftd, black amethyst, #525 20
Bowl, Mt Pleasant, cobalt, ftd, 4.75" sq ...30
Bowl, Mt Pleasant, pink, 5.5" 22
Candleholder, Moon and Star, amber, 4.5" h, 4" d 30
Candlesticks, Mt Pleasant, double, cobalt 35
Compote, Moon and Star, flared, #4201, white, 6.75" h, 8" w 35
Console Bowl, Melba, green, 12" l 40
Covered Dish, turkey, amethyst carnival glass 55
Cup and Saucer, Mt Pleasant, cobalt 25
Fern Bowl, black amethyst, 5" h 18
Figurine, Scottie dog, amethyst, 5" h, 6" w .45
Grill Plate, Mt Pleasant, green, 9" 12
Juice Glass, Crackle, flat, clear, 3.75" h, 2.125" d 3
Leaf Plate, Mt Pleasant, cobalt with silver band, 8" 25
Party Plate, Cloverleaf, green, 10.125" w ..16
Plate, Crackle, amber, 8" d 7
Plate, Mt Pleasant, black amethyst, 7.75" .14
Salt and Pepper Shakers, Mt Pleasant, black amethyst 60
Salt and Pepper Shakers, Mt Pleasant, cobalt 54
Server, Mt Pleasant, black amethyst, center handle, 9" d 40
Sherbet, Crackle, star-shaped foot, clear, 4.75" h, 3.5" d 5
Sugar, Melba, pink 16
Toothpick Holder, Moon and Star, amber, 2.5" h, 2" d 25
Tray, Mt Pleasant, 2-handled, amethyst, 10" w 38
Tumbler, Melba, amethyst, 7 oz, 4.25" 18
Tumbler, Moon and Star, flat, red, 4.5" h ..35
Tumbler, Mt Pleasant, ftd, cobalt with silver band 32
Vase, #102, black amethyst, silver trim, 6.5" h, 3" d 30
Vase, #432, crimped rim, ftd, black amethyst, 1930s 25

LETTER OPENERS

Isn't it amazing what can be done to a basic form? I have seen letter openers that are so large that one does not have a ghost's chance in hell of slipping them under the flap of a No. 10 envelope. As they say in eastern Pennsylvania, these letter openers are "just for nice."

Advertising letter openers are the crowd pleaser in this category. However, you can build an equally great collection based on material (brass, plastic, wood, etc.) or theme (animals, swords, etc.).

Advertising, "Aetna Life Companies, Hartford, Connecticut, Milton Insurance Agency, WE Milton, Bristol, Vermont," blue plastic 5
Advertising, Fuller Brush, clear plastic, figural salesman handle, 7.5" l 6
Advertising, Fuller Brush, ivory plastic, emb salesman on 1 side of handle, emb saleswoman on other side, 8" l 10
Advertising, Fuller Brush, pink plastic, figural salesman handle, 7.5" l 20
Advertising, "Meyers Engel Co, Insurance, Harrison, 7-4002," copper, 6" ruler, 8" l ...6

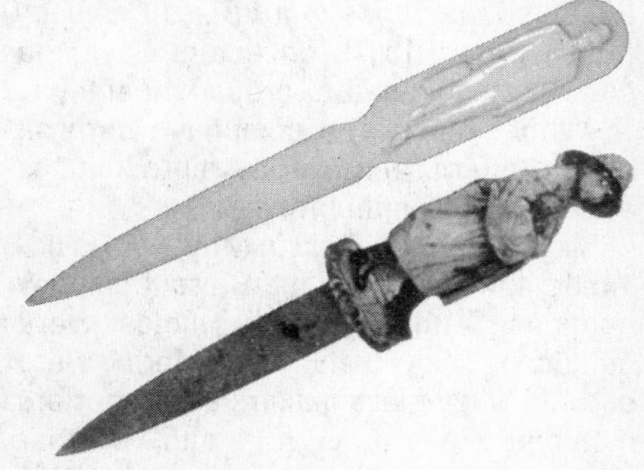

Advertising, Neighborhood News, Nordmann Printing Co, 9.75" l 10
Advertising, Pen 'N Sword Restaurant, E Stroudsburg, PA, sword shape, hp wooden sheath and handle, red nylon tassel, 8" l 15
Advertising, "Powci Manufacturers Insurance Company Waterloo, Iowa" on handle and "Greetings 1909-10" on blade of 1 side, other side has buildings and a bridge on handle and "Capital $100,000.00 Fully Paid" on blade, goldtone handle, silvertone blade, 9" l 50
Advertising, Southwestern Life Insurance, Dallas, leather handle, plastic blade ...12
Advertising, Uneeda Biscuit Co, metal, litho trademark boy wearing slicker on handle, 8.25" l 75
Figural, alligator head, wood, 9.125" l 20
Figural, fish handle, brass, 7" l 8
Figural, horse head, SP, Reed & Barton ...95
Figural, Pan and small bird on handle, floral emb blade, brass, c1900, 8" l 110
Figural, seated black boy handle, celluloid, Germany, 7" l 125
Figural, sword, mkd "Chenonceaux," 6" l .32
Jeweled, green, red, and clear stones on handle, prism ball end, pewter blade ...18
Masonic, Grand Lodge, NM, brass blade .20
Southwestern Motif, turquoise plastic, molded Native American birds and geometric designs 8
Souvenir, celluloid, figural alligator opener with a figural wooden black boy pencil in its mouth, mkd "Greetings from Hot Springs, Ark," 1930s-40s, 6.25" l 145

L. G. WRIGHT

Thanks to James Measell and W. C. Roetteis' *The L. G. Wright Glass Company* (Glass Press, 1997), collectors have the checklist they need to properly identify L. G. Wright Glass. The company's carnival glass, pattern, and overlay reproductions are collectible in their own right.

An auction was held in May 2000, to liquidate the L. G. Wright Glass Company holdings. Although some molds were bought by individuals, the majority were purchased by glass makers and importers including Fenton, L. E. Smith, Mosser Glass, Weishar Enterprises, and an unidentifed importer planning Chinese production. Watch for reproductions in the near future.

Ashtray, Daisy and Button, ftd, crystal, 2.125" h, 3.75" d 15
Basket, Daisy and Button, vaseline, 7.5" h, 2.75" w 100
Candy Dish, cov, Daisy and Button, vaseline 125
Candy Dish, cov, Moon and Star, vaseline 200
Compote, grapes and a plum, vaseline, opalescent beaded and ruffled rim 85
Creamer, Beaded Curtain, blue satin over opal, 4" h 95
Creamer, Honeycomb, blue, opalescent ruffled rim, 5.25" h 55
Creamer, windows pattern, cranberry, ruffled rim, clear ribbed applied handle, 5.25" h, 5" w 150
Dish, Daisy and Button, vaseline, 5" sq ..160
Shaker, Daisy and Fern, blue opalescent, 4.5" h 75
Tumbler, Dot, green opalescent, 3.5" h 30
Tumbler, Maize, honey amber overlay, 4" h 70
Tumbler, Stars and Stripes, cranberry opalescent 50
Vase, Wreathed Cherry, vaseline, opalescent ruffled rim 85

LIBERTY BLUE

In 1973 the Grand Union Company commissioned Liberty Blue dinnerware to be offered as a premium in grocery stores throughout the eastern United States. Ironically, though intended to celebrate America's Independence, the dinnerware was produced in Staffordshire, England.

Liberty Blue dinnerware, introduced in 1975, portrayed patriotic scenes in blue on a white background. Original engravings depicted historic buildings and events from the American Revolutionary period. The Wild Rose border was reproduced from a design dating back to 1784.

Liberty Blue is easy to identify. Most pieces contain the words "Liberty Blue" on the back and all are marked "Made in

England." The back of each dish also contains information about the scene illustrated on it.

Baker, oval 50
Bread and Butter Plate, 6" d 9
Cereal Bowl, 6.5" d 22
Creamer 35
Cup and Saucer 15
Dinner Plate, 10" d 17
Fruit Bowl, 5.5" d 10
Platter, 12" 65
Platter, 14" 85
Salad Plate, 7" d 20
Soup Bowl, flat, 8.5" d 30
Sugar Bowl, cov 40
Teapot, 6.5" h 170
Vegetable Bowl 50

LICENSE PLATES

License plates appeal to collectors because they are colorful, diverse, and can be found virtually anywhere, usually for minimal cost. Modern silkscreened graphics are now the rule rather than the exception on America's highways. These colorful specialty plates have transformed the lowly "number plate" into a 6" x 12" artist's palette.

Quality older issues continue to rise in value, but prices are often arbitrary, regional, and hard for the novice to accurately determine. Condition is primary; badly chipped porcelains or rusty metal plates with only traces of original paint remaining are usually of little value.

Plates from the industrialized North and East are most easily found; pre-war southern and western issues are much less common. Rare early issues still turn up on a regular basis, often from the unlikeliest of locations. Wartime scrap drives did not get them all—a good old "tag" can still be found by the treasure hunter or flea market frequenter, and the reward for a choice plate can be substantial.

Club: Automobile License Plate Collectors Assoc. (ALPCA), P.O. Box 7, Horner, WV 26372.

Arkansas, 1959 National Guard, black on white 33
Colorado, 1958, skier graphic, glass-beaded reflective numbers 145
Dayton, Ohio, 1953 bicycle plate, maroon on silver 12
District of Columbia, 1937, error plate with inverted numbers, yellow on black 375
Illinois, 1955 Antique Car, navy and red on white 26
Illinois, State Police, black on white 55
Iowa, graphic motorcycle 6
Kansas, 1924, passenger, white on green .23
Kansas, Pickup Coach, white on black 10
Maine, 1940 Coach, green on silver 45
Maryland, House of Delegates, white on blue 32
Massachusetts, 1936 Tow Truck, white on brown 32
Massachusetts, 1953 P series, white on black 12
Michigan, 1960/61 Truck, white on red, price for matched pr 28
Michigan, 1964 Farm, yellow on mud brown 10
Michigan, Historic Vehicle, yellow on dark blue 24
Minnesota, 1954 Ham Operator, blue on cream 28
Mississippi, 1979 Dealer, red on reflective white 7
New Hampshire, 1953 pasenger, black on white 12
North Dakota, 1979, green on white 7
Ohio, error plate with inverted numbers, blue on white 38
Ohio, House Vehicle, blue on white 7
Oklahoma, 1957 Semi-Centennial, red on white 28
Oklahoma, Motorcycle, red on cream 42
Pennsylvania, 1938 Motorbike, blue and yellow 100

Pennsylvania, 1950 Motorboat Dealer, red on white, price for pr 110
South Dakota, 1952 passenger, Rushmore logo 75
South Dakota, 1977 National Guard, red on white 9
South Dakota, 1987 Disabled Veteran, red and blue on white 16
Vermont, 1952 passenger, #777, black on white 30
Wisconsin, 1964, passenger, blue on white 12
Wisconsin, 1998 School Bus, red on white 12
Wyoming, 1968 passenger, yellow on brown 10

LILLIPUT LANE

Collectible cottages, also known as architectural collectibles, are the 1980/90s version of commemorative plates and whiskey bottles. The secondary market is highly speculative; and, there are more than ample signs that the bubble is bursting. Limited Edition and Collector Club models are among the most speculative.

In 1982 David Tate of Skirsgill, near Penrith, Cumbria, England, issued the first series of fourteen Lilliput Lane cottages, inspired by buildings in England's Lake District.

The company has used over a dozen different backstamps on its buildings, making them easy to date. Before buying on the secondary market, always check to see if the building is still in production and what its current suggested retail price is. A cottage needs to have its period box and certificate to be considered complete.

Clubs: Enesco Lilliput Lane Collectors' Club, 225 Windsor Dr., Itasca, IL 60143; Lilliput Lane Collectors' Club, P.O. Box 498, Itasca, IL 60143; Lilliput Lane Collectors Club, Brunthill Rd., Kingstown, Carlisle, Cumbria, England, CA3 0EN, www.lilliputlane.co.uk.

Belle Isle, L2417 25
Bobby Blue, L2176 120
Bwthyn Bach Swyn (Little White Cottage), L2160 35
Christmas Cake, L2397 150
Cockington Forge, L2355 65
Coke Country Five & Dime 95
Cowslip Cottage, L2126 120
Edinburgh Castle, L2247 110
Fragrant Haven, L2197 90
Frost Bite, L2366 30
Fruits Of Eden, L2250 80
Golden Years, L2048 .25
Granny's Bonnet, L2080 25
Green Gables, L2100 225
Haberdashery, L2053 .90
I'll Be Home For Christmas, L2165 95
Independence Hall, #723150 55
Katie's Kite, L2428 25
Kensington Gardens, L2456 95
Lilac Lodge, L2090 60
Loch Ness Lodge, L2175 170
Milk For Mom And Cake For Me, L2166 . . .95
Morning Has Broken, L2150 85
Mother's Garden, L2323 30
Mount Rushmore, #723193 50
Nature's Bounty, L2263 140
Nothing Runs Like A Deere, L2216 38
Picnic Paradise, L2195 80
Queen Of Winderemere, L2458 250
Safe Harbor, L2154 75
Scotch Mist, L2159 70
Seek And Find, L2121 90
Sore Paws, L2022 70
Stars And Stripes Forever, L2164 75
Statue Of Liberty, #723185 55
Strawberry Teas, L2158 100
Sweets And Treats, L2315 160
The China Shop, #740 85
The Drayman, L2362 100

The Honesty Box, L2454 .75
The Lunch Line, L2069 .42
The Nineteenth Hole, L2409 .120
The Old Mill At Dunster, L2396 .150
The Planetarium, L2246 .210
The Poppies, L2058 .50
To The Rescue, L2408 .95
Tower Bank Arms, L2270 .65
Tranquil Treasure, L2196 .80
Tuppenny Bun, L2131 .35
Ullswater Boat House, L2254 .32
Water's Edge, L2173 .170
Watson's Collectibles, L2267 .110
White House, #723169 .45

LIMITED EDITION COLLECTIBLES

Collect limited edition collectibles because you love them, not because you want to invest in them. While a few items sell well above their initial retail price, the vast majority sell between twenty-five and fifty cents on the original retail dollar. The one consistent winner is the first issue in any series.

Whenever possible, buy items with their original box and inserts. The box adds another ten to twenty percent to the value of the item. Also, buy only items in excellent or better condition. Very good is not good enough. So many of each issue survive that market price holds only for the top condition grades.

Clubs: Collectors' Society of America, 32725 McConnell Court, Warren, MI 48092, www.collectors-society.org; International Plate Collectors Guild, P.O. Box 487, Artesia, CA 90702; National Assoc. of Limited Edition Dealers, 5235 Monticello Ave., Dallas, TX.

In addition, many companies that issue limited edition collectibles have company-sponsored clubs. Contact the company for further information.

Architecture, David Winter, Castle Gate, 1984 .185
Architecture, David Winter, Cornish Tin Mine, 1983 .112
Architecture, David Winter, Little Market, 1980 .65
Architecture, David Winter, Rose Cottage, 1980 .70
Architecture, David Winter, Spinners Cottage, 1985 .40
Architecture, David Winter, Willow Wisp Cottage, 1991 .120
Architecture, Dept 56, Apotek and Tabak, Alpine Village, 1986 .45
Architecture, Dept 56, Fezziwig's Warehouse, 1986 .40
Architecture, Dept 56, Fire House #3, Snow Village .50
Architecture, Dept 56, Kukuck Uhren, Alpine Village, 1992 .25
Architecture, Dept 56, Otis Hayes Butcher, 1988 .75
Architecture, Dept 56, Season's Bay Chapel on the Hill, 1988 .75
Architecture, Dept 56, Small Chalet Gingerbread, 1976 .275
Architecture, Dept 56, Wayside Chapel, 1976 .240
Architecture, Dept 56, White Horse Bakery, 1988 .55
Architecture, Harbor Lights, Alcatraz .15
Architecture, Palm Lounge Supper Club, #55046 .80
Architecture, T Kinkade, Swanbrooke Cottage, 1993 .95
Bell, Anri, Ferrandiz, O Come All Ye Faithful, 1978 .55
Bell, Bing & Grondahl, Cathedral of Trier, 1984 .90
Bell, Bing & Grondahl, Christmas, 1980 .32
Bell, Bing & Grondahl, Christmas, 1982 .40
Bell, Bing & Grondahl, Christmas, 1983 .35
Bell, Fenton, Bleeding Heart, Burmese, 1998 .80

Bell, Fenton, Magical Meadow .... .75
Bell, Goebel, Praying Boy, 1978 .... .35
Bell, Hummelwerk, Noel 1978 .... .95
Bell, Hutschenreuther, Baltic Sea Islands, 1994 .... .32
Bell, Hutschenreuther, Bell of the Year, 1981 .... .70
Bell, Jan Hagara, Lydia, 1986-87 .... .50
Bell, Kaiser, Christmas Angel, 1977 .... .30
Bell, Kaiser, Christmas Annual, The Nativity, 1978 .... .18
Bell, Norman Rockwell Museum, For A Good Boy, 1982 .... .45
Bell, Norman Rockwell Museum, The Toymaker, 1985 .... .12
Bell, River Shore, Allison, World of Children, 1979 .... .35
Bell, River Shore, Kuluk, World of Children, 1980 .... .75
Bell, Royal Doulton, Cherub, 1991 .... .60
Bell, Sandstone, DeGrazia Little Prayer Bell 400
Bell, Schmid, Disney Characters, 1979 .... .39
Bell, Schmid, Disney Christmas, 1978 .... .50
Bell, Schmid, Hummel, Christmas, 1973 .... .90
Bell, Schmid, Hummel, Christmas, 1979 .... .25
Doll, American Dreams, Erin, #3102 .... .20
Doll, Ashton Drake, Buckwheat, Little Rascals, 1994 160
Doll, Ashton-Drake, Edwin M Knowles, Mary Had A Little Lamb, Children from Mother Goose, 1987 100
Doll, Ashton Drake, Lucy, *I Love Lucy*, blue polka-dot dress, 1990 300

Doll, Ashton Drake, Meredith, Jane Zidjunas Party Doll, 1993 135
Doll, Ashton Drake, Rosalee #4, Helen Carr, 1996 195
Doll, C Byj Praying Dolls, Mark and Mary, 1996 175
Doll, Danbury Mint, Mei-Hui, Chinese Bride 215
Doll, Danbury Mint, Rachel 175
Doll, Franklin Heirloom, Jumeau 245
Doll, Franklin Heirloom, Victorian Bride 300
Doll, Hamilton Collection, Katherine, Connie Walser Derek 165
Doll, Hamilton Collection, Mallory, Recital Dolls, 1997 265
Doll, Hamilton Collection, Swan Princess, 1993 150
Doll, Hamilton Collection, Winter Angel, D Zolan 100
Doll, Laura Cobabe Dolls, Amber, 1992 250
Doll, Maud Humphrey Bogart Doll Collection, Playing Bride, 1989 250
Doll, Mavis Snyder Angel Dolls, I Pray The Lord My Soul To Keep .... .95
Doll, Morgan Brittany, Angel, 1993 .... .45
Doll, Proud Indian Nation, Dressed Up For The Pow Wow, Swanson, 1996 150
Doll, Sandra Kuck Dolls, A Kiss Goodnight, 1993 125
Doll, World Gallery of Dolls, Amy, 1995 345
Figurine, Anri, Butterfly Boy 150
Figurine, Anri, Circus Serenade 115
Figurine, Anri, Freedom Bound .... .35
Figurine, Anri, Girl With Dove .... .70
Figurine, Anri, Golden Sheaves 100
Figurine, Anri, Leading The Way .... .65
Figurine, Anri, Small Talk .... .75
Figurine, Armani, Kelly 190

Figurine, Armani, Lady with Book, #384C, 1988 475
Figurine, Calico Kittens, My Love Blossoms For You 5
Figurine, Franklin Mint, John Wayne 500
Figurine, Lenox, Ivory Debutante Ball . . .110
Figurine, Maud Humphrey, The Bride, H1313 60
Figurine, Memories of Yesterday, We Belong Together 7
Figurine, Museum Collections, Christmas Prayers, 1985, 5" h 65
Figurine, Possible Dreams, Merry Heart . .25
Figurine, Precious Moments, You Have Touched So Many Hearts 40
Ornament, Calico Kittens, 1997 10
Ornament, Christopher Radko, Billy Bunny Goes Shopping 38
Ornament, Christopher Radko, Flower Power 47
Ornament, Christopher Radko, Greenhouse Greetings 42
Ornament, Christopher Radko, Skiin' Steve 32
Ornament, David Winter, What Cottage . . .20
Ornament, Goebel, West Germany, MI Hummel Annual, Flying High, 1988 . .75
Ornament, Lladro, Christmas Bell, 1988 . . .85
Plate, Beauties of the Red Mansion, set of 12 425
Plate, Bing & Grondahl, Christmas, 1962 . .55
Plate, Bing & Grondahl, Moments of Truth, set of 6 115
Plate, Boca Raton Museum of Art, Anne Herbst 45
Plate, Boehm Studios, Ring-Necked Pheasant, Gamebirds of North America 38
Plate, Bradford Exchange, Purr-Fect Packages, set of 4 200
Plate, Bradford Exchange, The Koala, Natures Lovables 25
Plate, Bradford Exchange, The People's Princess 38
Plate, Danbury Mint, Heavenly Angels, set of 5 75
Plate, Davenport Pottery Co, Toby Fillpot, #1 30
Plate, Delphi, For Our Boys In Korea, The Magic of Marilyn 30
Plate, Dresden, Mother's Day, 1975 25
Plate, Franklin Mint, Three Little Kittens, 1991 23
Plate, Hamilton Collection, In Disgrace, Bessie Pease Gutmann 38
Plate, Hamilton Collection, Precious Moments, Nativity 15
Plate, Hamilton Collection,* The Honeymooners, *1987 20
Plate, John McClelland, Tommy the Clown, McClelland Children's Circus 30
Plate, Knowles, Rockwell, Valentine 1981 .26
Plate, Norman Rockwell, Flirting In The Parlor, Rediscovered Women 30
Plate, Norman Rockwell, Grandma's Love, Golden Moments 25
Plate, Pemberton & Oakes, Curious Kitten 25
Plate, Rockwell Society of America, Making Believe At The Mirror, Rediscovered Women, 1982 45
Plate, Royal Copenhagen, Annual, 1975 . .24
Plate, Royal Copenhagen, Annual, 1976 . .36
Plate, Royal Copenhagen, Christmas, 1975 25

Plate, Sandra Kuck, A Cherished Time, Mother's Day, 1987 35
Plate, Sandra Kuck, Cat's in the Cradle, #764F 15
Plate, Sandra Kuck, Sunday Best, Days Gone By series 75
Plate, William Chambers, *The King And I,* set of 4 75

LITTLE GOLDEN BOOKS

Read me a story! For millions of children that story came from a Little Golden Book. Colorful, inexpensive, and readily available, these wonderful books are a hot collectible. You see them everywhere.

Be careful, you may be subject to a nostalgia attack because sooner or later you are going to spot your favorite. Relive your childhood. Buy the book. You won't be sorry.

LITTLE GOLDEN BOOKS

Baby Dear, #306-42, 1962 5
Cheyenne, *#318, 1958* *20*
Chipmunks' Merry Christmas, The, *#375, 1959* *9*
Christmas Carols, #26, 1946, 1st edition ...14
Fix It, Please, #32, 1947, "E" edition 16
Friendly Book, The, #199, 1954, "A" edition 6
Grover's Own Alphabet, #109-51, 1978 6
Howdy Doody and the Princess, #135, 1952 5
Howdy Doody's Lucky Trip, #171, 1953 5
Life and Legend of Wyatt Earp, The, #315, 1958 14
Little Gray Donkey, #206, 1954, "A" edition .9
Peter Pan and Wendy, D24, 1952, "A" edition 6
Roy Rogers and Cowboy Toby, #195, 1954 7
Sailor Dog, The, #156, 1953, "A" edition 3
Snow White and the Seven Dwarfs, D4, 1949 6
Tiger's Adventure, #208, 1954, "A" edition .5
Uncle Mistletoe, #175, 1953, "A" edition ..12
Uncle Remus, *#D6, 1947* *10*
Wiggles, #166, 1953, "A" edition 20
Wizard of Oz, The, #107-69, 1975 2
Yogi Bear, #395, 1960, "C" edition 4

LITTLE GOLDEN BOOK TYPES

Golden Press Ding Dong School Book, *Here Comes the Band,* DIN5, 1956 11
Golden Press Ding Dong School Book, *Lucky Rabbit,* DIN7, 1955 10
Golden Press Ding Dong School Book, *Magic Wagon, The,* DIN6, 1955 1
Golden Tell-A-Tale Book, *Animal Train,* #2556, 1969 1
Golden Tell-A-Tale Book, *Yogi Bear and the Super Scooper,* #2642, 1961 1
Rand McNally Ding Dong Book, *The Baby Chipmunk,* #208, 1953 4
Rand McNally Ding Dong Book, *Daddy's Birthday Cakes,* #207, 1953 10
Rand McNally Ding Dong Book, *Grandmother Is Coming,* #216, 1954 12
Rand McNally Ding Dong Book, *I Decided,* #204, 1953 3
Rand McNally Ding Dong Book, *Jingle Bell Jack,* #219, 1955 6
Rand McNally Ding Dong Book, *My Goldfish,* #211, 1954 4

Rand McNally Ding Dong Book, *Your Friend, the Policeman,* #200, 1953 2

Rand McNally Elf Book,* Adventures of Robin Hood and His Merry Men, The, *#532, 1955* *12

Rand McNally Elf Book, *Bugle, a Puppy in Old Yorktown,* #1027, 1958 2

Rand McNally Elf Book, *Four Little Puppies,* #578, 1957 17

Rand McNally Elf Book, *Little Horseman,* #8649, 1961 2

Rand McNally Elf Book, *So Long,* #1036, 1958 6

Rand McNally Elf Book, *Zippy the Chimp,* #487, 1953 7

Treasure Book, *Cinderella,* #879, 1954 10

Treasure Book, *Little Engine That Laughed, The,* #857, 1950 2

Treasure Book, *Little Red Caboose That Ran Away, The,* #852, 1952 4

Treasure Book, *Mighty Mouse and the Scared Scarecrow,* #884, 1954 4

Treasure Book, *Terry Bears Win the Cub Scout Badge, The,* #903, 1955 4

Treasure Book, *Tubby the Tuba,* #873, 1954 16

Wonder Book, *Let's Play Indian,* #538, 1950 3

Wonder Book, *Little Cowboy's Christmas, A,* #570, 1951, 1st cov 7

Wonder Book, *Make-Believe Parade, The,* #520, 1949 13

Wonder Book, *Mighty Mouse–Santa's Helper,* #662, 1955 8

Wonder Book, *My Book About God,* #644, 1956 5

Wonder Book, *My Poetry Book,* #621, 1954 2

Wonder Book, *Peter Goes To School,* #600, 1953, 2nd cov 5

Wonder Book, *Playful Little Dog, The,* #562, 1951 7

Wonder Book, *Popeye Goes on a Picnic,* #697, 1958 1

Wonder Book, *Sonny the Bunny,* #591, 1952 3

Wonder Book, *Three Mice and a Cat,* #533, 1950 ....8l

LITTLE ORPHAN ANNIE

Little Orphan Annie is one of those characters that pops up everywhere—radio, newspapers, movies, etc. In the early 1930s "Radio Orphan Annie" was syndicated regionally. It went network in 1933. The show's only sponsor was Ovaltine. Many Little Orphan Annie collectibles were Ovaltine premiums.

Radio and cartoon strip Little Orphan Annie material is becoming expensive. Try the more recent movie- and stage-related items if you are looking for something a bit more affordable.

Book, *Little Orphan Annie and the Lucky Knife,* Wee Little Book, 40 pgs, 1934, 3" x 3.5" 35

Book, *The Pop-Up Little Orphan Annie and Jumbo, the Circus Elephant,* hard cov, Blue Ribbon Press, 1935 190

Christmas Card, bi-fold, Harold Gray, 1939 125

Coloring Book, Saalfield Pub, 1974-75, 8.25" x 10.75" 8

Decoder, Mysto-Matic, brass, 1939, 1.75" .30

Decoder, Speed-O-Matic, brass, 1940, 1.25" 35

Doll, Annie and Her Dog Sandy, rag doll wearing red, white, and blue dress with her name on pocket, yarn hair, small plush Sandy in her pocket, orig box, ©1977 25

ID Bracelet, brass plate and chain, emb American flag tied into shape of a bow on plate, Ovaltine Premium, 1939 60

Map, "Radio's Little Orphan Annie," textured paper with full color aerial view of Tucker County community, Ovaltine premium, 1936, 19" x 24" 75

Pinback Button, color portrait of Annie in red dress, black text "Some Swell Sweater," c1928, 1.25" d 45

Ring, raised name and portrait on top, metal with goldtone luster, adjustable band, Ovaltine premium, 1934 45

Ring, Secret Society Silver Star Member, star design, crossed keys, and "ROA," metal with silver luster, Ovaltine premium, 1936 150

Shake-up Mug, Ovaltine, white beetleware cup with image of Annie and Sandy, red top, 1931, 4.75" h 80

LITTLE RED RIDING HOOD

On June 29, 1943, the United States Patent Office issued design patent #135,889 to Louise Elizabeth Bauer, Zanesville, Ohio, assignor to the A. E. Hull Pottery Company, for a "Design for a Cookie Jar." Thus was born Hull's Little Red Riding Hood line. It was produced and distributed between 1943 and 1957.

Early cookie jars and the dresser jars with a large bow in the front can be identified by their creamy off-white color. The majority of the later pieces have very white pottery, a body attributed to The Royal China and Novelty Company, a division of Regal China. Given the similarity in form to items in Royal China and Novelty Company's "Old McDonald's Farm" line, Hull possibly contracted with Royal China and Novelty for production as well as decoration.

Variations exist in many pieces, e.g., the wolf jar is found with bases in black, brown, red, or yellow. Prices for many pieces are in the hundreds of dollars. Prices for the advertising plaque and baby dish are in the thousands.

Undecorated blanks are commonly found. Value them between 25 and 50 percent less than decorated examples.

Club: Red Riding Hood!, P.O. Box 105, Amherst, NH 03031.

REPRODUCTION ALERT: Be alert for a Mexican-produced cookie jar that closely resembles Hull's Little Red Riding Hood piece. The Mexican example is slightly shorter. Hull's examples measure 13" high.

Batter Pitcher, mkd "Pat. Des. 135889," Regal, 8" h 425

Butter Dish, cov, mkd "Pat. Des. 135889," 5.5" h, 6.75" w 490

Cookie Jar, floral skirt, closed basket, mkd "Pat. Des. 135889" 550

Cookie Jar, gold stars on apron, open basket, 13" h 400

Cookie Jar, No. 967, small chip on bottom, 13.25" h 600

Cookie Jar, poinsettia design, green basket, ruffled skirt, emb "79," 13" h . .850

Cookie Jar, poppies, gold trim 400

Creamer and Sugar, mkd "Pat. Des. 135889," 5.25" h creamer, 5.125" h sugar 450

Salt and Pepper Shakers, orange-red flowers, 3" h 125
Sugar Shaker, cold painted, 5.25" h 100
Teapot, mkd "Pat. Des. 135889" 425
Wall Pocket, gold collar, 8.625" x 5.25" . . .350

LITTLE TIKES

Thanks to Beanie Babies, collector interest in infant and juvenile toys is growing. Rubbermaid's Little Tikes' toys and playtime equipment are one of the beneficiaries.

Little Tikes sturdy products are made of heavy-gauge plastic. They have proven virtually indestructible, one of the reasons they frequently appear in the garage sale, recyclable market. In fact, most are bought to be reused rather than collected.

While you should not expect to find examples that look factory new, do not buy pieces that are deeply scratched or incomplete.

LLADRÓ PORCELAINS

Lladró porcelains are Spain's contribution to the world of collectible figures. Some figures are released on a limited edition basis; others remain in production for an extended period of time. Learn what kinds of production numbers are involved.

Lladró porcelains are sold through jewelry and "upscale" gift shops. However, they are the type of item you either love or hate. As a result, Lladró porcelains from estates or from individuals tired of dusting that thing that Aunt Millie gave for Christmas in 1985 do show up at flea markets.

Club: Lladró Collectors Society, 43 W 57th St., New York, NY 10019.

#1454, Flowers of the Season, wooden base, orig box and paperwork, 12" x 10.75" 1,565
#4510, Girl with Umbrella, 1969-1993, 11" h 170
#4542, Angels Group, bisque, 6" h 175
#4808, Wedding, 7.75" h 150

#4824, Golfer, orig box and paperwork, 10.5" h 140
#4838, Clean Up Time, 7.5" h 100
#4849, Feeding the Ducks, 6.5" h 125
#4854, Quixote Standing Up, orig box, 1973, 12" h 175
#4894, Tennis Player Boy, 10.5" h 125
#6016, Wednesday's Child Girl, 7.75" h . . .175
#7036, Girl with Umbrella, 10" h 315
#7603, Spring Bouquets, retired in 1988, no box, 8" h 300
#7604, School Days, retired in 1988, 8.5" h 165
#7610, Can I Play?, boy with bat, orig box, 1990, 8.25" h 150
#7611, Summer Stroll, 9" h 220
#7612, Picture Perfect, 8" h 290
#7619, All Aboard, orig box, 1992 250
#7620, Best Friend, orig box, 1993 125
#7635, Ten and Growing, 1985-1995 210
#7642, Now and Forever, no box, 1995, 10" h 255

LOCKS & PADLOCKS

Padlocks are the most desirable lock collectible. While examples date back to the 1600s, the mass-production of identifiable padlocks was pioneered in America in the mid-1800s.

Padlocks are categorized primarily according to tradition or use: Combination, Pin Tumbler, Scandinavian, etc. Fakes and reproductions are a big problem. Among the trouble spots are screw key, trick, iron lever, and brass lever locks from the Middle East, railroad switch locks from

Taiwan, and switch lock keys from the U.S. Midwest. All components of an old lock must have exactly the same color and finish. Authentic railroad, express, and logo locks will have only one user name or set of initials.

Club: American Lock Collectors Assoc., 8576 Barbara Dr., Mentor, OH 44060, http://alca-online.org/.

Brass Lever, Yale, 4 patent dates 30
Combination, Master Champ 35
Combination, Seargent and Greenleaf, model 8077 75
Eight-Lever, Samson, brass 45
Four-Lever, Bingham's Best, brass 125
Logo, AC Spark Plugs, Best 40
Pancake Style, Yale, warded, #215 40
Pin Tumbler, Yale 25
Push Key, Yale, brass schackle 60
Push Key, Yale, US military 50
Railroad, "C&EIRR" stamped on brass Corbin-style special purpose lock with steel shackle, mkd key 15
Railroad, "CI&LRR" cast down panel of brass heart-shaped lock, "WS" on shackle, mfg by A&W, brass Fraim key mkd "CI&L" with "WS" on reverse 380
Railroad, "CM&STPRR" cast down panel of brass heart-shaped lock with steel chain, "FREIGHT" cast on key cov, mkd "CM&STPRR RC" key 450
Railroad, "GNRY SIGNAL" cast down panel of small brass heart-shaped signal lock mfg by Slaymaker, key cov cast "Remove Key When Locking" 75
Railroad, "MCRR" stamped on shackle of brass heart-shaped Slaymaker switch lock with chain 60
Railroad, "NYCRR" stamped on shackle of steel Miller Co special purpose lock 15
Railroad, "OREGON SHORT LINE" cast stairstepped from bottom up in panel of brass heart-shaped switch lock, mkd brass "A&W OSL" switch key ...425
Railroad, "SOUTHERN PACIFIC" sunset logo cast on brass heart-shaped special purpose lock 95
Railroad, "UNION PACIFIC" cast stair-

stepped down panel of brass switch lock with chain, cast "SWITCH CS 1" on body mfg by Adlake 64
Railroad, "V&CRR" stamped in panel of brass heart-shaped switch lock with 1854 patent date on key cov, unmkd steel key, cast iron clevis 132
Railroad, "WSTL&PRR" stamped on shackle of brass heart-shaped switch lock mfg by Bohannan, mkd brass single ring "WSTL&PRR S" key, no spring in key cov 275
Six-Lever, Slaymaker 5
Two-Lever, DM & Co, wrought iron with brass trim 25
Two-Lever, Miller Lock Co, buffalo 25

LONGABERGER BASKETS

Collectors of antique and vintage baskets will tell you that Longaberger baskets are vastly overrated. While not something a Longaberger basket collector wants to hear, they may regret not paying attention when the current speculative bubble bursts.

Dave Longaberger founded The Longaberger Company, based in Newark, Ohio, in 1973. While the company stresses a handmade, craft ancestry for its baskets, the fact is they are mass-produced. The company sold 7.7 million baskets in 1997, an indication that scarcity is a word that will not be used to describe a Longaberger basket, even fifty years from now.

Acorn Basket, Shades of Autumn, 1991, 4.5" x 3.5" 150
Bread Basket, 1993, 14.5" x 8" 75
Cranberry Basket, Christmas Collection, red weavers, woodcrafts lid with red handle, 1995 120
Darning Basket, 1991 40
Doll Cradle, 1991, 18.25" x 12.25" x 6" 175
Easter Basket, medium, oval, 1997, 10.25" x 6.5" x 3.75" 55
Holiday Cheer, Christmas Collection, red weavers, red and green liner, with protector and product card, 1996 145
Memory Basket, Christmas Collection, 1989, 8.75" x 4.75" x 6.5" 135
Pansy Basket, May Basket series, with liner, 1992 250
Picnic Basket, medium, with pie shelf, 12" x 12.5" 250
Poinsettia Basket, Christmas Collection, red weavers, 1988 175
Pumpkin Basket, terra cotta pumpkin tie-on, plastic liner, fabric liner, orig tags, 1995, 7.125" h, 10.125" d 150
Purse, with liner, 1991 50
Remembrance Hostess Basket, 1991 160
Serving Tray, small, Collector Club, 1996, 11.5" x 15.5" x 3.75" 225
Sweetheart Sentiments, #995, red trim strip, red shoestring weave, 1995, 3" h, 4" sq 85
Tissue Basket, tall, 6.25" h, 6.25" w 20
Umbrella Basket, 1994, 17.75" h, 10.25" d .200

LUGGAGE

Until recently luggage collectors focused primarily on old steamship and railroad trunks. Unrestored, they sell in the $50 to $150 range. Dealers have the exterior refinished and the interior relined with new paper and then promptly sell them to decorators who charge up to $400. A restored trunk works well in both a Country or Victorian bedroom. This is why decorators love them so much.

Collector interest is growing in old leather luggage. It is not uncommon to find early twentieth century leather overnight bags priced at $150 to $300 in good condition. Leather suitcases sell in the $75 to $150 range.

LUNCH BOXES

Lunch kits, consisting of a lunch box and matching thermos, were the most price-manipulated collectibles category of the 1980s. Prices in excess of $2,500 were achieved for some of the early Disney examples. What everyone seemed to forget is that lunch boxes were mass-produced.

The lunch kit bubble has burst. Prices dropped for commonly found examples. A few dealers and collectors attempted to prop up the market, but their efforts failed. If you are buying, it will pay to shop around for the best price.

Buy lunch kits. Resist the temptation to buy the lunch box and thermos separately. I know this is a flea market price guide, but lunch kits can get pricy by the time they arrive at a flea market. The best buys remain at garage sales where the kits first hit the market and sellers are glad to get rid of them at any price.

METAL

Beatles, Aladdin, 1965 250
Bedknobs and Broomsticks, no handle . . .40
Dick Tracy, with thermos, Aladdin, 1967 300
Flinstones and Dino, Aladdin, 1962 100
Heathcliff, Aladdin, 1982 45
Holly Hobbie, Aladdin, with thermos, 1979 45
Masters of the Universe, Aladdin, with thermos, 1983 50

Munsters, with thermos, Kayro Vue, 1965 .165

Plaid, red and green, American Thermos Bottle Co .95

Six Million Dollar Man, with thermos, 1974 .35

Strawberry Shortcake, Aladdin, 1980 .40

Transportation Theme, trains, planes, etc., 1940s .250

VINYL

Barbie and Midge, Thermos, black, Barbie and Midge faces and full-figure poses, with thermos, 1963 .100

Beany and Cecil Lunch Kit, Thermos, Beany, Cecil, and man with treasure map on island, with thermos, 1961 .175

Bobby Soxer, Aladdin, boy and girl talking on telephone, with Poodle thermos .125

Fess Parker Kaboodle Kit, American Tradition, brown, Fess Parker and long rifle above white lettering "Fess Parker Kaboodle Kit From The Daniel Boone TV Show," 1964 .160

Junior Nurse Lunch Kit, Thermos, black, nurse and medical emblems, with thermos, 1963 .115

Peanuts, Thermos, green, Linus, Schroeder, Lucy, Charlie Brown, and Snoopy at pitcher's mound, with thermos, 1965 .225

Roy Rogers, Thermos, brown, saddlebag with vignette of Roy with Trigger against blue background, lacking latch, 1960 .115

Sabrina, Aladdin, Sabrina and 2 witches stirring cauldron, 1972 .115

Smokey Bear, Thermos, black, Smokey and forest animals by sign pointing the way to Happy Valley and Frog Lake, with thermos .225

The Flying Nun, Aladdin, Flying Nun amidst clouds, with thermos, 1968 .100

The Monkees, Thermos, white, band members' faces and names with "Monkees" written in shape of guitar, with thermos, 1967 .225

The Pussycats, Aladdin, girls dancing, with thermos, 1968 .80

The World of Dr Seuss, Aladdin, blue, Cat in the Hat juggling while Thing One and Thing Two try to trip him with wire, with thermos, 1970 .350

Twiggy, Aladdin, lavender, Twiggy's face above 3 full size Twiggy images, with thermos, 1967 .175

Wonder Woman, Aladdin, yellow, Wonder Woman in action, with thermos, 1977 .115

MADE IN JAPAN

Prior to 1921, objects made in Japan were marked NIPPON or MADE IN NIPPON. After that date, objects were marked JAPAN or MADE IN JAPAN.

Although MADE IN OCCUPIED JAPAN was the primary mark used between August 1945 and April 28, 1952, some objects from this period were marked JAPAN or MADE IN JAPAN.

Bowl, 8-sided, beaded rim, hp house on wooded riverbank, yellow sky, lavender horizon, blue and green river, 7" w .15

Cigarette Box, scrolled ft, hp flowers, gold trim, lid serves as ashtray, 2" h, 4" w .32

Condiment Set, salt and pepper shakers and cov jar on oblong tray, peach luster, gold trim .50

Cornucopia Vase, hp flowers .25

Creamer, blue luster ext, peach luster int, 3.5" h .20

Creamer, hp fruit, green leaves, and green bands on white ground .20

Creamer, hp rose, blue and yellow Art Deco band, gold trim, white ground .12

Creamer and Sugar, cov, hp floral dec, gold trim, mkd "Gold Castle Made In Japan," 4" h sugar, 3.5" h creamer .30

Creamer and Sugar, cov, tomato-shaped, red .50

Demitasse Saucer, floral bouquet on white and peach luster ground, 4.25" d .5

Dish, cov, basket-weave body with rope twist edges, rose finial, Nanri Boeki & Co, 4.5" h, 6" d .45

Dolls, set of 5, 3 girls, 2 boys, hinged arms and legs, 2.5" h .150

Double Vase, floral dec on white ground, gold trim, 4" h, 7" w .15

Jug, narrow mouth, bulbous body, large abstract floral dec in bright glazes, 3.75" h, 3" w .12

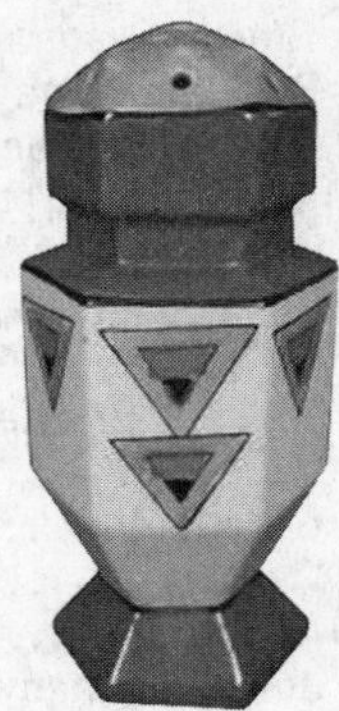

Muffineer, Art Deco design, 6-sided, white body with orange, green, and black inverted triangles on white ground, peach luster top, orange band at neck and base, 6" h, 2.5" w 50

Nappy, heart-shaped, Geisha Girl dec with trellis, 3 geishas in a garden, flowers, lantern, and teahouse and river in background, 4.5" w 25

Nut Cups, set of 9, tulip-shaped, peach luster int, blue luster ext, 1.5" h, 2.4" w . .50

Plate, hp rose, Art Deco rim band, and gold trim on white ground, 6.5" d 10

Relish Tray, 4 sections, floral dec, pear finial 40

Relish Tray, 5 sections, hp green and yellow flowers on white ground, gold trim, 10" d 15

Salt and Pepper Shakers, bulbous bodies with molded swirls, hp roses on white ground, top painted silver to resemble screw-on lids, silver band at top and bottom, 3" h 18

Salt and Pepper Shakers, tapered cylindrical form with windmill dec, gold tops, cork stoppers, Japan, 2.75" h 20

Teacup and Saucer, hp purple pansies, gold highlights 8

Teapot, hp floral band, luster ware 35

Teapot, hp flowers and blue bands, 5.25" h, 10" w 40

Tea Set, miniature, gold fish dec, includes teapot, fondue pot and sticks, and 4 each cups, saucers, and tumblers . . .12

Vase, 2-handled, black-outlined flowers on luster ground, 2.75" h 5

Vase, 2-handled, hp flowers on gray center band, peach luster ground, 2.75" h 5

Vase, bright blue with oriental flower dec, 4.5" h 25

Vase, ewer shape, hp flowers, scrolling gold handle, 7" h 30

Vase, hp flower cart on shaded celery-green ground, gold trim, 3.75" h 8

Vase, hp pagoda and peonies on rust-red ground, gold highlights 8

Vases, pr, 2-handled, waffle-textured body, emb Wedgwood blue roses, 8" h, 4" d 30

MAGAZINES

Most magazines, especially those less than forty years old, are worth between 10 cents and 25 cents. A fair number of pre-1960 magazines fall within this price range as well. There are three ways in which a magazine can have value: the cover artist, the cover personality, and framable interior advertising. In these instances, value rests not with the magazine collector, but with the speciality collectors.

At almost any flea market, you will find a seller of matted magazine advertisements. Remember that the value being asked almost always rests in the matting and not the individual magazine page.

16 Magazine, 1975, Feb, Chico 7

American Rifleman, 1943, Dec 15

Arthur Murray's Popularity, 1950s 12

Boys' Life, 1934, May, Reusswig cov 30

California Review, 1903, Jan, Vol 1, No 1 . .65

Coronet, 1961, Apr, Leslie Caron 5

Crazy, 1982, Dec, #92 15

Drag Racing USA, 1971, Mar 20

Family Circle, 1939, Jan 20 2

Good Housekeeping, 1949, May, Alex Ross illus cov 8

Good Housekeeping, 1959, Jun 6

Harper's New Monthly Magazine, 1880, Mar 30

Humble Way, The, 1958, Jul/Aug 12

Jewel, 1988, Winter, premiere issue 25

John Wayne & The Great Cowboy Heroes, *1979* *25*

Life, 1936, Dec 7, skiing 48

Life, 1937, Dec 20, chorus girl 12

Life, 1938, Feb 7, Gary Cooper, NY World's Fair 35

Life, 1939, Jan 23, Bette Davis 25
Life, 1940, Jan 29, Lana Turner 22
Life, 1941, Jul 7, Gen George S Patton 14
Life, 1942. Mar 30, Shirley Temple 22
Life, 1943, Feb 15, Princess Elizabeth 14
Life, 1944, Jun 26, Statue of Liberty 12
Life, 1945, Apr 9, WWII bomb blast 12
Life, 1946, Dec 2, Ingrid Bergman 15
Life, 1947, Mar 24, Arctic Circle 12
Life, 1948, Jun 21, Cape Cod 10
Life, 1949, Oct 3, football 15
Life, 1950, Oct 23, Ed Wynn 10
Life, 1951, Nov 5, Ginger Rogers 20
Life, 1952, Sep 1, Ernest Hemingway 15
Life, 1953, Sep 14, Casey Stengel 35
Life, 1954, Mar 29, Pat Crowley 15
Life, 1955, Feb 21, Princess Margaret 10
Life, 1956, Jun 25, Mickey Mantle 15
Life, 1957, Jul 1, Billy Graham 10
Life, 1958, May 19, Margaret O'Brien 14
Life, 1959, Apr 13, aerospace testing 15
Life, 1960, Oct 10, Doris Day 10
Life, 1961, Aug 11, Sophia Loren 14
Life, 1962, Sep 28, Don Drysdale 25
Life, 1963, Apr 26, Jackie Kennedy 10
Life, 1964, Dec 11, Rockettes 7
Life, 1965, Apr 9, Robert Kennedy 10
Life, 1966, Mar 11, Batman 25
Life, 1967, Dec 15, heart transplant 5
Life, 1968, Apr 12, Martin Luther King 15
Life, 1969, Mar 21, Woody Allen 10
Life, 1970, Jul 17, Rose Kennedy 4
Life, 1971, Mar 26, Walter Cronkite 4
Life, 1972, Jun 9, Bella Abzug 4
Life, 1978, Dec, Prince Charles 4
Life, 1979, May, Three Mile Island 3
Life, 1980, Jun, folk art 3
Life, 1981, May, Ronald Reagan 7
Life, 1982, Dec, Princess Diana 15
Life, 1983, Dec, Barbra Streisand 5
Life, 1984, Apr, penguins in Arctic 3
Life, 1985, Jun, Bill Cosby 3
Life, 1986, Mar, Molly Ringwald and Teens 3
Life, 1987, Feb, Christine Brinkley and Baby 4
Life, 1988, Mar, Gilda Radner 2
Life, 1989, Aug, Woodstock 4
Life, 1990, Nov, Al Pacino 2
Life, 1991, Dec, John F Kennedy 2
Life, 1992, May, Johnny Carson 1
Life, 1993, Jun, Michael Jackson 4
Literary Digest, The, 1921, Oct 1 18
Magazine Antiques, The, 1973, Sep 5
National Geographic, 1957, Jun 30
Nature Magazine, 1944, Apr 5
Photoplay, 1965, Jackie Kennedy 10
Popular Home Craft, 1935, Nov 4
Popular Mechanics, 1942, Aug 10
Popular Mechanics, 1943, Feb 8
Rolling Stone, 1980, Apr, 314, Linda Ronstadt 2
Rolling Stone, 1980, Sep, 326, Rodney Dangerfield 5
Rolling Stone, 1980, Nov, 330, Mary Tyler Moore 5
Rolling Stone, 1981, Mar, 339, Warren Zevon 5
Rolling Stone, 1981, Oct, 354, Meryl Streep .5
Rolling Stone, 1985, Dec, 463/464, year-book, 25 pictures on cov 2
Rolling Stone, 1986, Jan, 465, Michael Douglas 5
Saturday Evening Post, 1950, Jul 22, beach scene cov by Donahos 10
Saturday Evening Post, 1956, Jan 7, Hughes illus cov .8
Saturday Evening Post, 1985, Dec 8
Southern Methodist University Mustang, 1957, Mar 12
Sports Illustrated, 1976, Jul 28, Paul Warfield, Larry Czonka, and Jim Kiick cov 10
Successful Farming, 1924, Nov 10
Super Stock and Drag Illustrated, 1980, Mar 20
Time, 1944, Jun 19, pony ed, General Eisenhower 24
Time, 1969, Jul 18, To The Moon 24
TV Guide, 1997, May 3-9, Xena 4

MAGIC COLLECTIBLES

Presto, chango—the world of magic has fascinated collectors for centuries. The category is broad; it pays to specialize. Possible approaches include children's magic sets, posters about magicians, or sleight-of-hand tricks.

When buying a trick, make certain to get instructions—if possible, the original. Without them, you need to be a mystic rather than a magician to figure out how the trick works.

Club: Magic Collectors Assoc., P.O. Box 511, Glenwood, IL 60425; New England Magic Collectors Assoc., 3 Chandler St., N. Providence, RI 02911, www.nemca.com.

Book, *84 Card Tricks,* by Hugh Morris, 1936, 57 pgs, soft cov 25
Book, *Magic Tricks,* 1934, Oakite adv, includes Mandarin hide-away ring, Satan's matchbox, jumping joker, magic television, mysterious initial, leaping rainbow colors, ghostly message, bewitched thimbles, witch's cauldron rubber bands, etc, soft cov, 5" x 6.75" 25
Booklet, Doug Henning "World of Magic," contains biography and questions and answers, 8.5" x 11" 25
Business Card, Carter the Great, "Charles J Carter, LLB, San Francisco" on front, "Egyptian Hall Museum" on back, 1.5" x 3" 85
Catalog, Heaney's Professional Catalog of Wonders, 1920 .20
Manual, "Manual of Instructions for Gilbert Mysto Magic. Fun for Boys and Their Friends," 36 pgs, 1917 40
Poster, Dayton The Great, stock poster, "Don't Worry See The Great Dayton Show And Forget Your Troubles," large dragon 550
Poster, "Triumphant American Tour, George The Supreme Master of Magic, 18 People, Carload of Scenic Effects," half sheet, Otis Litho 325
Stereoview Card, "Magician," #703b, by Herman Knutzen, caption reads "And place zem all upon my nose, like zis," 1906 10
Trick, Adams Ball and Vase, with box and instruction sheet, 1960s 12

MAGNIFYING GLASSES

The majority of magnifying glasses offered for sale at flea markets are made-up examples. Their handles come from old umbrellas, dresser sets, and even knives. They look old and are highly decorative—a deadly combination for someone who thinks he is getting an authentic antique. There are few collectors of magnifying glasses. Therefore, prices are low, often a few dollars or less, even for unusual examples. The most collectible magnifying glasses are the Sherlock Holmes type and examples from upscale desk accessory sets. These often exceed $25.

MARBLES

Marbles divide into handmade glass marbles and machine-made glass, clay, and mineral marbles. Marble identification is serious business. Read and re-read these books before buying your first marble: Paul Baumann, *Collecting Antique Marbles, Second Edition* (Wallace-Homestead, 1991) and Mark E. Randall and Dennis Webb, *Greenberg's Guide to Marbles* (Greenberg Publishing, 1988).

Children played with marbles. A large number are found in a damaged state. Avoid these. There are plenty of examples in excellent condition. Beware of reproductions and modern copycats and fakes. Comic marbles are just one of the types being reproduced.

Clubs: Marble Collectors' Society of America, P.O. Box 222, Trumbull, CT 06611, www.marblecollecting.com; Marble Collectors' Unlimited, P.O. Box 206, Northborough, MA 01532; National Marble Club of America, 440 Eaton Rd., Drexel Hill, PA 19026.

Advertising, mother-of-pearl with green "Freshen Up With 7-Up, 5 cents," 3/4" . . .2
Champion, blue swirl metallic 10

Champion, white whirlwind 3
Champion Agate, fluorescent brown swirl, 1940s 3
Champion Agate, fluorescent yellow swirl, 1940s 4
Champion Agate, purple whirlwind 6
Champion Agate, yellow cat's-eye, shooter 2
Champion Agate Shooters, bag of 6, MIP .16
Christensen Agate Turkey Swirl, purple, white, and green, 1/2" 7
Hybrid Popeye, red, yellow, and white, 23/32" 20
Jackson, translucent yellow, #00 15
Lone Ranger Silver Bullets, steel, set of 6, MIP 8
Peltier, National Line Rainbow Graycoat, red, blue, and gray, 5/8" 25
Popeye, green and yellow, 21/32" 20
Popeye, purple and yellow, 5/8" 85
Purple Slag, transitional type, 6-pattern, 5/8" 13
Ribbon Swirl, red, white, and blue ribbon, yellow swirl ext, 2 1/2" 150
Scottie Dog, black with white dog 9
Sulphide, white bird, 1 1/2" 150
Swirl, clear with red and white swirl, shooter 10
Swirl, transparent with pink and white swirl core, 1 1/8" 150
Vitro Agate, parrot, oxblood and blue, 11/16" 14
Vitro Agate, parrot, peach, cream, blue, 5/8" 24

MARILYN MONROE

In the 1940s a blonde bombshell exploded across the American movie screen. Born Norma Jean Mortonson in 1926, she made her debut in several magazines in the 1940s and in the movie *Scudda Hoo! Scudda Hey!* in 1948.

Now known as Marilyn Monroe, she captured the public eye with her flamboyant style and hourglass figure. Her roles in such films as *Bus Stop* and *Some Like It Hot* brought much attention to this glamour queen.

Marilyn's marriages to baseball hero Joe DiMaggio and famous playright Arthur Miller, not to mention her assorted illicit affairs with other famous gentlemen, served to keep her personal life on the front burner. It is commonly believed that the pressures of her personal life contributed to her untimely death on August 5, 1962.

Club: Eternally Marilyn, 3248 G South Holden Rd., Greensboro, NC 27407.

Collector Plate, Sweet Sizzle, Marilyn: The Gold Collection, Bradford Exchange, 1996 45
Cookie Jar, bust of Marilyn, Clay Art, 1996, 14" h 50
Hallmark Keepsake Ornament, figural Marilyn with swirling skirt, 1998 15
Head Vase, Marilyn wearing black hat and dress, mkd "Made by Rosalie," 6" h 40
Magazine,* Life, *Aug 17, 1962, 10.5" x 13.5" .35
Magazine, *Photoplay,* Marilyn on cov, Sep 1975 13
Magazine, *Playboy,* Marilyn cov and centerfold, Jan 1997 50
Magazine, *Video Review,* Marilyn on cov, Feb 1982 10
Necktie, red and maroon diagonal stripes, lining has picture of Marilyn in a bikini, 1950s 80
Paper Doll, Marilyn wearing blue dress, crease on neck, no other clothes, 12" h .3
Poster, The Last Sitting, 28.25" x 22.25" . . .140
Salt and Pepper Shakers, figural gold shoes, mkd "200 The Estate of Marilyn Monroe" on back 15
Trading Card, Series L, 20th Century Fox 26, Dutch language bio on back, 2.75" x 1.75" 25
Velvet Picture, nude Marilyn, 28.5" x 19" . .30

MARX TOYS

The Marx Toy Company was founded after World War I when Louis and David Marx purchased a series of dies and molds from the bankrupt Strauss Toy Company. In the following years the Marx Toy Company produced a huge assortment of tin and plastic toys, including 60 to 80 playsets with hundreds of variations. These playsets, some with lithographed tin structures, are very collectible if complete. Marx also manufactured a number of windup and action toys like Rock-em Sock-em Robots and the very popular Big Wheel tricycle.

The company was bought and sold a number of times before filing for bankruptcy in 1980. The Quaker Oats Company owned Marx from the late 1950s until 1978, at which time it was sold to its final owner, the British toy company, Dunbee-Combex.

Astronaut, white plastic, 5.5" h 10
Balky Mule, litho tin, windup, 1950s, 8" l .125
Bop-A-Bear, battery operated, complete with bear, rifle, and darts, 1 dart tip missing, orig box 250
Busy Bridge, litho tin, windup, 5 cars, 8" h, 23.75" l, 3.5" w 400
Circus Figures, light yellow plastic, includes sword swallower, lion tamer with whip and pistol, juggler, clown cop, and strong man lifting weights, some cracks, c1955 25
Dan Dipsy Car, litho tin, windup, orig box, 1950 400

Dick Tracy Squad Car, litho tin, battery operated, 20" l, MIB 1,500
Dora Dipsey Car, litho tin, windup, 1950 . .350
El Capitan Train, 3 cars, #3197 and two #3152 225
Fred Flintstone and Dino, litho tin, windup, 1962, 5.5" h, 8.375" l 50
Funny Flivver, litho tin, windup, 1926 550
Hi-Bouncer Moon Scout, robot, litho tin torso, plastic arms, battery operated, 1960s, 11.5" h 900
Honeymoon Express, litho tin, windup, orig box, 2.5" h, 9" d 350
Jumpin Jeep, litho tin, windup, worn paint 225
Locomotive, diecast metal, #999, minor rust 100
Mechanical Delivery Motorcycle, litho tin, 1938, 10" l, MIB 1,350
Midget Racer #5, litho tin, windup, 2.25" h, 5.25" l 175
Moon Creature, litho tin, windup, c1968, 5.5" h 200
Planet Patrol, litho tin, windup, 5" h, 10" l 350
Race Time, 5-horse race game, battery operated, 26" l 225
Ramp Walker, bull, c1950s-60s 12
Sky Cruiser Transport Plane, litho tin, friction drive, 2-motor, orig box, c1948, 18" wingspan 675
Sparkling Tank, litho tin, orig box, 1951, 10" l 700
Tank, tin and plastic, windup, olive drab, 6" l 50
Watch Me Roll Over Pluto, litho tin, windup, 1939 300
Xylophone Mickey Mouse, litho tin, windup, 11.375" h, 6.125" w 625

MATCHBOOKS

Don't play with matches. Save their covers instead. A great collection can be built for a relatively small sum of money. Matchcover collectors gain a fair amount of their new material through swapping. A few collectors specialize in covers that include figural shaped or decorated matches. If you get into this, make certain you keep them stored in a covered tin container and in a cool location. If you don't, your collection may go up in smoke.

Clubs: Casino Matchcover Collectors Club, 5001 Albridge Way, Mount Laurel, NJ 08054; Rathkamp Matchcover Society, 432 N. Main St., Urbana, OH 43078, www.matchcover.org; The American Matchcover Collecting Club, P.O. Box 18481, Asheville, NC 28814.

Note: There are over thirty regional clubs throughout the United States and Canada.

Feature, 20 strike, Eleanor Shop, Portsmouth, VA, garment and word "Blouses, Slips, Robes, Skirts," or "Sweaters" on each stick, pink, purples, blue, and white, Lion Match 12

Feature, 20 strike, Trainer's Seafood, hearth and "Trainer's" on front, lobster, fish, crab, and "Trainer's Seafood at its best" on back, seafood illus on sticks, mfg by Harry R Dubbs, Allentown, PA ..12

Midget, "Doc's" front, blank saddle, "Doc's Cocktail Lounge 1817 N Charles St Baltimore" and drawing of 2 men leaning against lamppost on back, name and address on inside, white on blue, Lion Match 6

Midget Type, "The Brass Rail Bar & Cocktail Lounge Cor. 3rd at Central Great Falls, Mont" on front, "Great Falls' finest" on saddle, "Brass Rail, The Best at Popular Prices" and int restaurant scene on back, blank int, white on green, Diamond Match 7

Military, Air Force, "Officers' Club, Victorville, Calif" around winged star on front, blank saddle, bomber action scene on back, blank inside, silver on dark blue, Lion Match 6

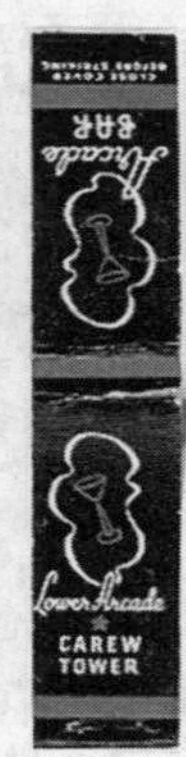

Patriotic, Bond Bread Navy Plane Set, Wildcat Fighter, Lion Match, 1942 10

Patriotic, For Safety, Buy Defense Bonds, Stamps and minuteman on front, "Own a Share in America" on saddle, "A Safe Investment for a Safe America, Buy Defense Bonds, Stamps," and eagle and shield on back, blank inside, Universal Match 8

Patriotic, Letter "V" above Morse Code symbol front, "Keep 'em Flying America!" saddle, "Buy War Bonds" and 3 planes in formation on back, Lion Match 8

Printed Sticks, Downingtown Inn Resort and Golf Club, aerial view of grounds on front, list of club features on back, printed sticks with black "Gateway To The Pennsylvania Dutch Amish Land," Amish man's head, and horse and buggy, Universal Match 10

Ten Strike, "Arcade Bar" and cocktail glass on front, "Lower Arcade, Carew Tower" and cocktail glass on back, blank saddle, "In Cincinnati it's the Arcade Bar, Lower Arcade, Carew Tower" inside, Universal Match 5

Transportation, Railroad, "Broadway Limited" on front, "Pennsylvania Railroad" on bottom flap, "Safety-Speed-Comfort" on saddle, 4-color photo of streamlined locomotive on back, striker located on flat bottom edge, blank inside, Diamond Match 8

21-Feature, 30 stick, "The Sands, Las Vegas, Nevada" on front, hotel on back, penguin on each stick, "Why be formal? ...Come as you Are!" across sticks, Lion Match 12

MATCHBOX TOYS

Leslie Smith and Rodney Smith founded Lesney Products, an English company, in 1947. They produced the first Matchbox toys. In 1953 the trade name "Matchbox" was registered and the first diecast cars were made on a 1:75 scale. In 1979 Lesney produced over 5.5 million cars per week. In 1982 Universal International bought Lesney.

Clubs: American-International Matchbox Collectors & Exchange Club, 532 Chestnut St., Lynn, MA 01904; Matchbox Collectors Club, P.O. Box 977, Newfield, NJ 08344; Matchbox U.S.A., 62 Saw Mill Rd., Durham, CT 06422; The Matchbox International Collectors Assoc., P.O. Box 28072, Waterloo, Ontario N2L 6S8 Canada.

A Nightmare On Elm Street, Character Car Collection, 1999 5
Beach Hopper, #47, 1972, MIB 35
Brady Bunch Station Wagon, Series 1 Star Car Collection, 1997 4
Citroen SM, #51, 1971 18
CJB Jeep, #53, 1977 8
Claas Combine Harvest, 1960s 15
Coca-Cola Dad's 1955 Chevy Bel Air and Son's 1998 Camaro Convertible, 1999 6
Commer Ice Cream Canteen truck 10
Corvette "T" Roof, #40, MOC 8
Crane Truck, #49, 1981, MOC 18
Disney Series 7, Pinocchio 25
E Type Jaguar, 1960s 15
Excavator, red, #32, MOC 18
Foamite Crash Tender, #63 10
Ford Zodiac MK IV 15
Freeman Inner City Commuter, #22 28
Friday The 13th, Character Car Collection, 1999 5
GMC Tipper Truck 10
Happy Days '56 Ford Pick-Up, Series 1 Star Car Collection, 1997 4
Horse Van, #40, 1980s, MOC 15
I Dream Of Jeannie, Character Car Collection, 1999 5
Jaguar NRFP, #47 10
Jaws and Amity Police Boat, Series 2 Star Car Collection, 1998 4
K17 Scammell Container Truck 5
Kennel Truck, #50, 1960s 20
Knightrider Car 12
Lamborghini Countach, #27 5
Land Rover Fire Truck, 1960s 10
Lesney, fire truck, 1975 20
Leyland Royal Tiger Coach, #40 55
Lincoln Continental, #28, MOC 15
Lotus Europa, electric, #5 20
M*A*S*H 4077 Jeep, Series 1 Star Car Collection, 1997 4
MB40 Horse Box 5
MB46 Blue Tractor 5
MB58 Dump Truck 5
MB72 Yellow Jeep 10
Mercedes Container Truck, #42 18
Mercedes Truck 20
Mission Impossible Surveillance Van, Series 1 Star Car Collection, 1997 4
Model A Ford, white, #73 15
Model T, truck, Kellogg's 10
Montiverdi 450SS, #3, MOC 12
Office Site Hut Truck, #60 60
Peterbuilt Cement Mixer 8
Porsche 928, #59, 1980, MOC 15
Porsche Turbo, #3, 1981, MOC 16
Rallye Royale, #14, 1980, MOC 12
Refuse Truck, Mag wheels, #7 35
Renault 17 TL, #62, MOC 15
Series Unimog, 1960s 15
Soopa Coopa, #37, 1971 25
Stake Truck, #4 5
Sunshine Taxi Cab, Series 1 Star Car Collection, 1997 4
Superfast BMC 1800 .50
Swamp Rats Airboat, 30-F, 1976 6
The Londoner, #17, 1972 10
The Mask, Character Car Collection, 1999 5
Untouchables Car 15
Wild Life Truck, #57, 1973 10

MCCOY POTTERY

The Nelson McCoy Sanitary Stoneware Company was founded in 1910. Early production consisted of crocks, churns, and jugs. Pieces were marked with an "M" above a stenciled clover within a shield.

Molded artware was introduced in the mid-1920s; cookware, dinnerware, floral industry ware, gardenware, kitchenware, and tableware followed a decade later.

McCoy pottery is attractive and sought after by collectors unwilling to pay the prices commanded by Roseville and Weller pottery.

Console Bowl, Garden Club, peach, 1940s 45
Cookie Jar, bamboo 75
Cookie Jar, Bobby Baker 50
Cookie Jar, Chilly Willie 70
Cookie Jar, green pepper 50
Cookie Jar, Little Red Riding Hood 275
Cookie Jar, Mother Goose 250
Cookie Jar, owl 125
Cookie Jar, panda bear 300
Cookie Jar, windmill 85
Jardiniere, Springwood Line, mint green, 10" 75
Lamp, cowboy boots, 1956 90
Mug, mottled brown, #1412 12
Pitcher Vase, Rustic Line, brown-green, 9" 45
Planter, double, flying bird 100
Planter, Dutch shoe, dark blue with pink flower, 1947, 7.5" 35
Planter, Dutch shoe, yellow, 1940s, 5" 25

Planter, Mary Ann shoe, light blue, 1940s, 5" 25
Planting Dish, Springwood Line, mint green, 8" 45
Teapot, Sandstone 30
Vase, Arcature, yellow-green, 1951, 8" x 6" 50
Vase, pitcher shape, emb daisy panels, red ext, white int, 1972, 9" h 20
Vase, Rustic Line, brown-green, 5" 40

MEDICAL ITEMS

Anything medical is collectible. Doctors often discard instruments, never realizing that the minute an object becomes obsolete, it also becomes collectible. Many a flea market treasure began life in a garbage can. Stress condition and completeness. Specialize in one area. Remember some instruments do not display well.

Club: Medical Collectors Assoc., Montefiore Medical Park, 1695A Eastchester Rd., Bronx, NY 10461.

Almanac, *Dr Jayne's Medical Almanac,* catalog of diseases and corresponding treatments, 1870, 49 pgs 35
Bookmark, Standardized Capes, image of nurse wearing cape, red, white, and blue 80
Doctor's Bag, leather, black pebble ext, 2 upper compartments, lower compartment with adjustable bottle loops, brass lock, double leather handles, mkd "Emdee by Schell, Patent No 2293363" on brass plate, 11" h, 15" l . . .125
Door Push, Foley Kidney Pills, emb porcelain, oval, black lettering on yellow ground, 6.625" s 3.125" 375
Ledger Marker, Vaseline Petroleum Jelly, Chesebrough Mfg Co, litho tin, black lettering on red ground, adv text on back, 3" x 12.5" 225
Medicine Bottle, "Warner's Safe Cure (motif of safe), Frankfurt A/M," German, bright amber, smooth base, applied mouth, c1890-1900, 9" h 200
Otoscope, chrome and plastic attachments, brown Bakelite case, mkd "Welch Allyn, 147475," c1940-45 90

Paperweight, glass, rect, "PP Van Vleet, President, Van Vleet Mansfield Drug Co, Memphis, Tenn," black and white photo portrait, 1" x 2.5" x 4" 30
Pot Scraper, Ward's Remedies, red, white, gold, and black, 2.875" x 3.375" .235
Ribbon Retractors, silver, 12" l, 1" w 50
Tray, Hick's Capudine Medicine, litho tin, images of cherubs holding up giant medicine box, 9.75" d 850
Vapo-Cresolene Lamp, orig box, 6.5" h . . .150

MELMAC

Durable Melmac dinnerware was all the rage in the late 1960s and early 1970s. Children could finally be assigned the chore of washing the dishes without fear of loss and breakage. Despite its claims of being indestructable, continued dishwasher washing takes its toll. If you plan to use the Melmac you collect you'll have to revert to hand washing.

Ashtray, Futura, sq, tangerine orange 10
Child's Dish, Boonton, #6209-12, Pebbles Flintstone and Bamm-Bamm Rubble in center, white ground 12
Coasters, Imperial Ware, speckled, 2 pink, 1 each yellow, aqua, and white, 3.25" d, set of 5 25
Creamer, Royalon, #311, yellow 10
Creamer and Sugar, cov, Home Decorators, Daileyware, pink marbleized, gray lid . .12
Cup, Northern, Residential Line, designed by Russel Wright, salmon color 6
Cup and Saucer, Oneida Deluxe, peach-colored cup, white saucer with autumn foliage dec, mkd "OD" 5
Dinner Plates, Harmony House, Bouquet, set of 8 22
Dinner Service, Oneida, consisting of 6 patterned 9.75" dinner plates, 6 blue 7" bread plates, 8 blue cups, 8 patterned saucers, blue creamer, and blue cov sugar, 1950s-60s .35
Dinnerware Setting, Boonton Molding Co, Normandy Rose, 1 patterned 10" dinner plate, 1 brown 6" bread and butter plate, 1 patterned 6" saucer, and 1 brown cup, orig box 22
Gravy Boat, Branchell, Royale, gray, 3.5" h, 7" l 28
Luncheon Plates, green and white gingham, mkd "Genuine Melamine, Made in USA, GG," 9.25" d, set of 4 15
Meat Platter, #418, oblong, turquoise, 11.5" x 8" 9
Mixing Bowl, Dallas Ware, multicolor speckles on brown, 4.5" h, 9.75" w 20
Platter, Boonton, #606, pink, wing handles, 14.5" l 18
Platter, Branchell, Color Flyte, gray speckled, 14" x 10" 20
Salad Bowl, Boonton, #604-10, turquoise, wing handles, 2.5" h, 9.75" d 16
Salt and Pepper Shakers, Royalon, cone-shaped, lavender, 4" h 15
Soup Bowl, Florence, Prolon, Chinese red 8
Sugar Bowl, PR Mallory Plastics, Mallo-ware, #40, orange 6
Tray, Byrd's Plastics, Tranquil Ware, rect, yellow, 14" x 9" 12
Turkey Platter, Brookpark, Americana, Bicentennial theme, 21" x 15" 28
Turkey Platter, Brookpark, Wheat, 21" x 15" 26
Turkey Platter, Brookpark, wine, fruit, and cheese design, 21" x 15" 25
Vegetable Bowl, Branchell, charcoal gray 10
Vegetable Bowl, Brookpark Modern Design, orange 8
Vegetable Bowl, Carleton, oval, divided, turquoise, 2" h, 11.25" x 8" 15
Vegetable Bowl, divided, turquoise, mkd "Table to Terrace Melmac Dinnerware, Chicago," 3" h, 9" d 12

METLOX

In 1921 T. C. Prouty and Willis, his son, founded Proutyline Products, a company designed to develop Prouty's various inventions. Metlox (a contraction of metallic oxide) was established in 1927. The company began producing a line of solid color dinnerware similar to that produced by Bauer. In 1934 the line was fully developed and sold under the Poppytrail trademark. New patterns were regularly introduced.

When Vernon Kilns ceased operations in 1958, Metlox bought the trade name and select dinnerware molds, establishing a separate Vernon Ware branch. This line rivaled the Poppytrail patterns.

Between 1946 and 1956 Metlox made a series of ceramic cartoon characters under license from Walt Disney. A line of planters and Poppets were marketed in the 1960s and 1970s. Recent production includes novelty cookie jars and Colorstax, a revival solid color dinnerware pattern. The company ceased operations in 1989.

Aztec, coffee server, stoppered 225
Aztec Poppytrail, platter, mkd "Aztec Poppytrail," 13" x 10" 45
California Aztec, tray, jawbone, white, 16" l 300
California Aztec, vegetable bowl, cov, jawbone 250
California Provincial, bowl, 6" 15
California Provincial, bowl, 10" 50
California Provincial, chop plate, 12" 65
California Provincial, cup 12
California Provincial, plate, 6" 10
California Provincial, plate, 7.5" 15
California Provincial, saucer 8
California Provincial, shaker 8
California Strawberry, bowl, 5.5" 15
California Strawberry, creamer 20
California Strawberry, cup 10
California Strawberry, mug 18
California Strawberry, plate, 6" 8
California Strawberry, salt shaker 12
California Strawberry, saucer 5
California Strawberry, soup bowl 15
California Strawberry, sugar, cov 25

Freeform, water pitcher 300
Homestead Provincial, dinner plate, blue, 10" d 20
Homestead Provincial, turkey platter 225
Homestead Provincial, vegetable bowl, basket style, green tab handles, 8.5" . . .55
Homestead Provincial, vegetable bowl, divided, rect 55
Mobile, water carafe and matching tumbler 395
Provincial Blue, bread container 65
Provincial Blue, chop plate, 12" 60
Provincial Blue, creamer, cov 35
Provincial Blue, cruet set, 5-pc 180
Provincial Blue, cup and saucer 18
Provincial Blue, cup 15
Provincial Blue, dinner plate 18
Provincial Blue, flat soup bowl 25
Provincial Blue, fruit bowl, small 15
Provincial Blue, gravy boat 35
Provincial Blue, hen on nest, 6.5" 100
Provincial Blue, plate, 6" 10
Provincial Blue, plate, 7.5" 15
Provincial Blue, plate, 9" 20
Provincial Blue, salad bowl, 11.5" 80
Provincial Blue, shaker 15
Provincial Blue, sugar, cov 35
Provincial Blue, tea canister 55
Red Rooster, bowl, 6" 12
Red Rooster, butter dish 70
Red Rooster, coaster 18
Red Rooster, coffee mug, 8 oz 25
Red Rooster, cookie jar, cylindrical 200
Red Rooster, creamer 18
Red Rooster, cruet set, vinegar, oil, and holder 80
Red Rooster, cup 10
Red Rooster, dinner plate 15

Red Rooster, fork and spoon 65
Red Rooster, mug, 1 pt 35
Red Rooster, pepper mill 50
Red Rooster, plate, 6" 8
Red Rooster, plate, 7.5" 12
Red Rooster, platter, 13.5" 40
Red Rooster, saucer .5
Red Rooster, soup bowl, 8.5" 25
Sculptured Daisy, creamer 18
Sculptured Daisy, cup 10
Sculptured Daisy, dinner plate 15
Sculptured Daisy, platter, 14.5" 45
Sculptured Daisy, teapot 80

MEXICAN COLLECTIBLES

Within the past year there has been a growing interest in Mexican jewelry. In fact, several new books have been published about the subject. Mexican pottery and textiles are also attracting collector attention. At the moment, buy only high-quality, handmade products. Because of their brilliant colors, Mexican collectibles accent almost any room setting. This is an area to watch.

MILITARIA

Soldiers have returned home with the spoils of war as long as there have been soldiers and wars. Many collectors tend to collect material relating to wars taking place in their young adulthood or related to re-enactment groups to which they belong.

It pays to specialize. The two obvious choices are a specific war or piece of equipment. Never underestimate the enemy. Nazi material remains the strongest segment of the market.

Reproductions abound. Be especially careful of any Civil War and Nazi material.

Clubs: American Society of Military Insignia Collectors, 526 Lafayette Ave., Palmerton, PA 18071; Assoc. of American Military Uniform Collectors, P.O. Box 1876, Elyria, OH 44036, www.naples.net/clubs/aamuc/info.html; Company of Military Historians, North Main St., Westbrook, CT 06498; Order & Medals Society of America, P.O. Box 484, Glassboro, NJ 08028.

Ashtray, brass, made from 105 mm shell, bullet cigarette rests, dated 1943, 4.5" d 25
Book, *Military Panorama Journal,* Issue #1, modern military weaponry, 68 pgs, 1969 8
Certificate, ROTC, Senior Division, College of the City of New York, basic infantry course, issued 1929 30
Cleaning Kit, 44 pistol, metal box with fitted wood block interior holding a brass oil container, rod, brushes, metal tin, and cleaning patches, 1911 100
Comic Book, "Funland," 1-line comic on each page, printed by Bulco, WWII 12
Commemorative Plate, General MacArthur, brown transfer, Vernon Kilns, 10.5" d 35
Handkerchief, 5th Army Air Force insignia on white silk, sgd "Fuji Yama, To My Darling Sister," 10" sq 20
License Plate, Vietnam Veterans of America, Chapter 154, Mt Clemens, MI .12
Matchbook, Marines, USMC crest on front, "Camp Lejune, North Carolina" on back, blank saddle, blank inside, orange on olive drab, Diamond Match . .7
Pin, Army Air Force AWS Observer 10
Plate, blue Air Force insignia on white china, Hazel Atlas, 7" d 12

Postcard, photo of RCAF dining hall, St Thomas, Canada, black and white, dated Oct 26, 1943, 3.5" x 5.625" 6
Recruiting Poster, US Naval Aviation, 1974, 11" x 14" 55
Trading Cards, Desert Storm, Series 1, aircraft, MIP 1
Window Flag, silk, blue star on white field, red border, 8" x 11.5" 60

MILK BOTTLES

There is an entire generation of young adults to whom the concept of milk in a bottle is a foreign idea. In another ten years we will need to include a chapter on plastic milk cartons. I hope you are saving some.

When buying a bottle, make certain the glass is clear of defects and the label and wording in fine or better condition. Buy odd-sized bottles and those with special features. Don't forget the caps. They are collectible too.

Club: National Assoc. of Milk Bottle Collectors, Inc., 4 Ox Bow Rd., Westport, CT 06880, www.collectoronline.com/club-NAMBC-wp.html.

Adams Milk, Rawlins, WY, red pyro, bucking bronco on back, qt 75
Blais Dairy, Lewiston, ME, red pyro, "A Child's Vitality..." on back, babytop qt 250
Burroughs Brothers Walnut Grove Farm, creamtop, red pyro, boy wearing diaper and "I'm demanding 1 of the best so you might as well make it Burroughs Brothers milk" on back, qt 65
Dan-Maid, Batavia Dairy Co, black and orange pyro, baseball and football players, "Milk Builds Great Champions," qt 40
Dyke's Dairy, Warren, PA, red pyro, war slogan on back, qt 100
Farley's Dairy, Thatcher and Safford, AZ, red pyro, map of AZ on front, woman holding glass of milk and "Beauty begins at breakfast when breakfast begins with Milk" on back, qt 180
Indian Hill Farm Dairy, Greenville, ME, red pyro, Indian head, qt 55
Ledge Ever Farms Dairy, Ticonderoga, NY, yellow pyro, barn, qt 70
Lexington Dairy, Lexington, KY, red pyro, cow's head on front, hand holding glass of milk and "Here's to You! for Health Happiness Vitality" on back, qt 45
Model Dairy, Waukon, IA, red pyro, "Try Our Creamed Cottage Cheese" on back, qt 45
Modern Dairy, Idaho Falls, red pyro, war slogan, qt 325
Molen's Dairy Farm, Dayton, OH, blue pyro, "There's Cream in Every Drop...," qt 95
Nelson's Cloverland Creamery, Manistique, MI, black pyro, ice cream sundae on back, qt 75
Nevada Creamery & Dairy, Colorado Springs, CO, blue pyro, silhouette of family at table and "Milk for All the Family" on back, qt 75
Norris Bros Dairy, New Windsor, IL, black pyro, war slogan, "Food Fights Too, Use It Wisely, Plan All Meals For Victory," qt 100
Old Tavern Farm Inc, Portland, MI, red and black pyro, "Old Tavern Farm Inc" in shield on front, waving man and "Here's your daily sunshine, Old tavern Irradiated Vitamin D Milk" on back, qt 75
Pettibon Dairy Co, Rochester, PA, green pyro, man in robe with milk and "Before Retiring" on back, qt 75
Price's Sunset Creamery, Roswell, NM, orange pyro, setting sun, qt 65

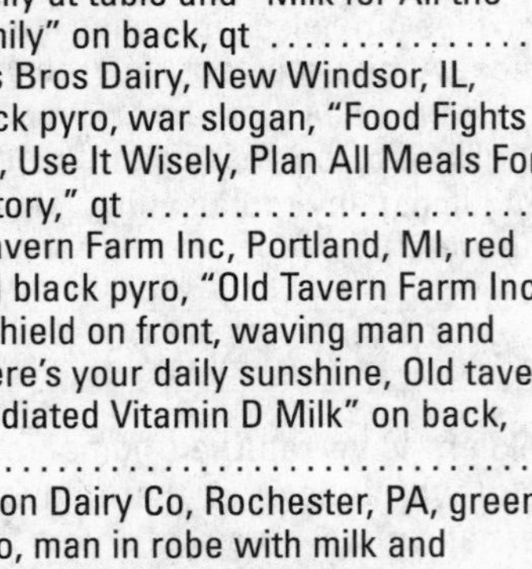

Westover Dairy, Inc, Lynchburg, VA, black pyro, "3¢ Westover Dairy Inc 'Taste Tested' Ice Cream," qt 70

MILK GLASS

Milk glass is an opaque white glass that became popular during the Victorian era. A scientist will tell you that it is made by adding oxide of tin to a batch of clear glass.

Companies like Atterbury, McKee, and Westmoreland have all produced fine examples in novelties, often of the souvenir variety, as well as household items. Old timers focus heavily on milk glass made before 1920. However, there are some great pieces from the post-1920 period that you would be wise not to overlook.

Milk glass has remained in continuous production since it was first invented. Many firms reproduce old patterns. Be careful. Watch out for a "K" in a diamond. This is the mark on milk glass reproductions from the 1960s made by the Kemple Glass Company.

Club: National Milk Glass Collectors Society, 46 Almond Dr., Hershey, PA 17033.

Note: Items listed are white unless otherwise noted.

Animal Dish, duck cov, grass base, 5.5" l 100

Bowl, Vallerysthal, Ribs & Scallops, oval, turquoise, 8.5" x 4.75" 65

Box, cov, Westmoreland, Beaded Grape, sqe, 4" h 40

Candlesticks, pr, Tiffin, twisted openwork stem, 8" h 95

Candy Dish, cov, Anchor Hocking, ribbed body, 1950s, 5" h, 6.5" d 10

Candy Dish, cov, Westmoreland, Sawtooth, 5" h, 6.5" d 45

Cologne Bottle, Fenton, Hobnail, with stopper, 5.25" h 50

Condiment Tray, Fostoria, Berry 15

Creamer, Westmoreland, Paneled Grape .15

Cruet, Fenton, Hobnail, with stopper, 4.75" h 20

Dinner Plate, scalloped edge, 10.5" d 20

Goblet, Imperial, Tradition, ftd 15

Hatchet, Cambridge, hp cherries, 6" l 50

Jar, cov, Imperial, Grape, wicker bail handle, 5.75" h, 3.375" d 60

Orange Bowl, McKee, Innovation Line 412 75

Pitcher, Anchor Hocking, Hobnail, 64 oz ..20

Plate, Imperial, Rose, 10.5" d 28

Plate, Westmoreland, Forget Me Not, lacy rim, 8.5" d 20

Rose Bowl, Westmoreland, Doric 45

Salt Shaker and Pepper Mill, Fenton, Arlington, vertical ribs, lacy base, 5" h .75

Sherbet, Westmoreland, Della Robbia ...10

Top Hat Vase, Daisy and Button, 1940s, 3" h 20

Vase, Westmoreland, Old Quilt, pedestal ft, 9" h 75

MODEL KITS

Manufacturers such as Aurora, Horizon, and Revell/Monogram produce detailed model kits that let the builder's imagination run wild.

Most model kits are packed in a cardboard box with an image of the model on the surface. Pieces are snapped or glued together. Painting and decoration is up to the assembler. Model kits are produced from plastic, resin, or vinyl, often requiring a bit of dexterity and patience to assemble.

Buying model kits at flea markets should be done with a degree of caution. An open box spells trouble. Look for missing pieces or lost instructions. Sealed boxes are your best bet, but even these should be questioned because of the availability of home shrink wrap kits. Don't be afraid—inquire about a model's completeness before purchasing it.

Clubs: Kit Collectors International, P.O. Box 38, Stanton, CA 90680; Society for the Preservation and Encouragement of Scale Model Kit Collecting, 3213 Hardy Dr., Edmond, OK 73013.

2 in 1 Dragster Exterminator, motorized, 1/8 scale, Lindberg, 1964 250
Bionic Woman Bionic Repair, MPC, MISB 25
Black Falcon Pirate Ship, Aurora, MISB . .50
Bride of Frankenstein, Horizon, MIB 75
Captain Kidd, Aurora, MIB 100
Castle Creature the Vampire, Aurora, partial assembly, with box and instructions 225
Comic Scenes Batman, Aurora, MIB 60
Comic Scenes Lone Ranger, Aurora, MISB 60
D'Artagnan the Musketeer, Aurora, partial assembly, no paint, complete, with box and instructions 225
Dracula, Aurora, MIB 275
Flying Reptile, Aurora, complete with instructions, no box 35
Forgotten Prisoner, Aurora, complete 65
Frankenstein, Aurora, MIB 275
Frightening Lightning Dracula, Aurora, MIB 375
George Washington, Aurora, MISB 135
Glow Mummy, Aurora, MISB 125
Green Beret, Aurora, MISB 250
John F Kennedy, Aurora, MIB 110
Luminators King Kong, Monogram, MIB . .35
Man From U.N.C.L.E., Napoleon Solo, Aurora, complete with box and instructions 225
Monsters of the Movies Frankenstein, Aurora, MIB 195

Predator, Billiken, MIB 60
Prehistoric Scenes Cave, Aurora, second edition, MISB 65
Prehistoric Scenes Cro-Magnon Man, Aurora, MISB 150
Prehistoric Scenes Giant Wooly Mammoth, Aurora, built-up, complete 65
Prehistoric Scenes Sail-Back Reptile, Aurora, MISB 150
Roman Bireme Warship, Aurora, MIB 50
Spider-Man, Aurora, loose, unassembled, with box and instructions 250
Sweathogs Dream Machine, MPC, MISB 45
The Mummy, Aurora, MIB 275
The Visible Woman 25
The Witch, Aurora, MIB 375
Vegas '57 T-Bird, AMT, MIB 40
Weirdohs Davey the Way-Out Cyclist, Hawk, 1963, MIB 65
Wolfman, Horizon, MIB 60

MONSTERS

Collecting monster related material began in the late 1980s as a generation looked back nostalgically on the monster television shows of the 1960s and horror movies of the 1960s and 1970s. Fueling the fire was a group of Japanese collectors who were raiding the American market for material relating to Japanese monster epics featuring reptile monsters such as Godzilla, Rodan, and Mothra. This spurred a collecting revival for Frankenstein, King Kong, and the Mummy.

While an excellent collection of two-dimensional material, e.g., comic books, magazines, posters, etc., can be assembled, stress three-dimensional material. Several other crazes, e.g., model kit collecting, cross over into monster collecting, thus adding to price confusion.

Club: Munsters & The Addams Family Fan Club, P.O. Box 69A04, Dept. MalWest Hollywood, CA 90069, http://www.geocities.com/tmafc/.

Dracula, action figure, Playmates, 1994 . .12
Frankenstein, shopping bag, AM PM Mini Market 1

Godzilla, automobile cup holder, Taco Bell premium, 1998 4
Godzilla, key chain, Taco Bell premium, Godzilla Hatchling, 1998 3
Godzilla, Magic Rocks, with clear tank, foil insert, magic solution, one bag Magic Rocks, paint, brush, and Godzilla figure, 1995, MIB 12
Hunchback Of Notre Dame, action figure, Uncle Milton Ind, glow-in-the-dark, 1990, MOC 7
Invisible Man, doll, Kenner, 1998, 12" 25
Mummy, action figure, Uncle Milton Ind, glow-in-the-dark, 1990 5
Phantom of the Opera, doll, Hasbro, 1998, 12" 20
Universal Monsters, gift wrap set, includes two 30" x 20" sheets of gift wrap, bow, and gift card, Unique, 1991 3
Werewolf, action figure, McFarlane, 1997 12
Wolfman, doll, Kenner, 1998, 12" 30
Wolfman, key chain, light-up figure, 1995, 4" 6

MOSSER GLASS

The glassmaking art has been passed down through three generations of the Mosser family. Mosser Glass, Cambridge, Ohio, makes reproductions and copycats of late 19th- and early 20th-century glassware as well as figurines and decorative accessories.

Animal Dish, hen on nest, amethyst, split tail, sgd, 6.25" h, 7.5" l 36
Beverage Set, paneled pitcher and 4 tumblers, jadeite, 8.5" h pitcher, 4" h tumblers 70
Bonbon, Shell, amethyst, 2.75" h 30
Butter Dish, dome cov, Inverted Thistle, pink, 6" h, 7.25" d 25
Cake Plate, jadeite pedestal base, clear dome cov, 9.5" h, 12.25" d 85
Cake Plate, Queens, vaseline, pedestal base, 9" d 14
Christmas Tree, hp crystal satin, 2.75" h . .15
Cookie Jar, Cherry Thumbprint, ruby, 10" h 125
Creamer and Sugar, jadeite, matching tray 30

Figure, collie, vaseline opalescent, 3" h . . .15
Figure, flying bird, pink, 5" h 25
Figure, rabbit, crystal, 5.25" h 20
Figure, standing colt, blue willow, sgd, 6" h 20
Figure, "Uwe," clown sitting on a barrel, light green slag, 3.25" h 24
Paperweight, figural pheasant, light blue carnival, 4" h, 4.5" l 25
Punch Set, miniature, Inverted Strawberry, bowl and 6 cups, cobalt, 3.5" h bowl . . .32
Shoe, rose slipper, cobalt, 3" h, 6" l 15
Sleigh, cobalt, 2" h, 3.5" l 20

MOTION LAMPS

Motion lamps feature a scene that lights and gives the illusion of motion. They first appeared in the 1920s and are still produced today, but their popularity peaked in the 1950s. Early lamps were constructed of metal and glass, while later lamps were primarily plastic. All feature some type of rotating cylinder that spins from the power of the heat produced by the bulb.

Early lamps used a complex system of animation sleeves to produce sophisticated motions like water running, wheels turning, or fire blazing. Today's motion lamps use simple colorful cylinders whose moving images project onto the surface of an outer shade. Besides scenic lamps, psychedelic, advertising, and figural lamps are among others that are collectible.

Note: Values listed below are for complete lamps in very good condition that are free of cracks, dents, and scratches, and have good color. Perfect or restored examples will be more valuable.

Buddha, Scene-in-Action, 1931 300
Budweiser Beer, adv, Visual Effects Co, 1970s 75
Butterflies and Flowers, LA Goodman, 1956 175
Campfire and Waterfall 135
Chicago World's Fair, Scene-in-Action, 1933 350
Cook's Goldblum Beer, adv, Hal Mfg Co, 1950s 75
Fireside Roasted Peanuts, adv, 1930s 350
Fountain of Youth, Roto Vue Junior, 1950s 175
Niagara Falls, Econolite, 1955, 11" h 145
Phillips 66 Trop-Arctic Motor Oil, adv, 1960s 100
Railroad, The John Bull and The General, Econolite, 1956 115
The Bar Is Open, Visual Effects Co, 1970s 50
Waterfall, 7.5" h 45

MOTORCYCLE COLLECTIBLES

Motorcycles are generational. My father would identify with an Indian, my son with the Japanese imports, and I with a Harley.

Some of these beauties are as expensive as classic and antique cars. If you see a 1916 Indian Power Plus with sidecar for a thousand or less, pick it up. It books at around $15,000.

Do not overlook motorcycle-related items.

Clubs: American Motorcyclist Assoc., 13515 Yarmouth Dr., Pickerington, OH 43147; Antique Motorcycle Club of America, P.O. Box 300, Sweetser, IN 46987.

Booklet, "Jobbers Price List, Goodrich Motorcycle and Bicycle Accessories," Mar 18, 1920, 6.25" x 3.25" 12
Camera, Harley-Davidson 20
Helmet, British Army dispatcher, orig ETO paint, leather padding, straps, and laces, pad dated 1942 with ordnance marks 95
Key Chain, 1960 Tour award, 1.125" d 25

Miniature Building, Harley-Davidson Showroom, Department 56, #54886 65
Movie Poster, *The Savage 7*, motorcycle gang helps Indians fight town despot, 1968 65
Pocket Mirror, Emblem Motorcycle Co, Angola, NY, celluloid, rect, early 2-seat motorbike, 1.75" x 2.75" 685
Telephone, Harley-Davidson Heritage Softail, plastic, red flame design, studded detail on saddlebags and seat, engine revs and lights flash when phone rings, MISP 70
Toy, Curvo 1000, litho tin, key-wind, Schuco, US Zone, Germany, c1946-49 .285
Toy, General Motor-Cycle, litho tin, friction, Masudaya, Japan, c1948, 6" h, 8.25" l 1,500
Toy, Harley-Davidson motorcycle, Hubley, cast iron, blue, metal wheels, 7" l 650
Toy, motorcycle with sidecar, Dinky, 1.75" l 45
Toy, Police No. 51, litho tin, friction, Japan, 8.75" l 65
Toy, motorcycle, rubber, red with yellow wheels, Auburn Rubber 30

MOVIE MEMORABILIA

The stars of the silent screen have fascinated audiences for over three-quarters of a century. In many cases, this fascination had as much to do with their private lives as their on-screen performances.

This is a category where individuals focus on their favorites. There are superstars in the collectibles area. Two examples are Charlie Chaplin and Marilyn Monroe.

Posters are expensive. However, there are plenty of other categories where a major collection can be built for under $25 per object. Also, do not overlook present-day material. If it's cheap, pick it up. Movie material will always be collectible.

Club: The Manuscript Society, 350 N. Niagara St., Burbank, CA 91505, www.manuscript.org.

Children of the Corn, inflatable ear of corn, 3' l 35
Cleopatra, movie program, 1963 10
Great Muppet Caper, drinking glass, McDonalds premium, 1981 5
Independence Day, action figure and CD, Alien Attacker Pilot, Trendmasters, 1996 15
Jaws, board game, Jaws Action Game, Just Toys, 1989 15
Laurel and Hardy, chalk figures, repair to Laurel's hat, mkd "Esco Prod 1971" . . .145
Lost In Space, action figure set, Dr Smith, Major Don West, Professor John Robinson, Will Robinson, Dr Judy Robinson, and Sabotage Action Dr Smith, Trendmasters, 1997, 5" h 45
Lost In Space, Electronic Talking Robot Bank, Toy Island, 1998, MIB 20
Lost In Space, Robot B9, electronic light and sounds, Trendmasters 32
My Fair Lady, souvenir book, Warner Bros, 44 pgs, 1964, 8.5" x 11.5" 15
Nightmare Before Christmas, key chain, Lock, Shock & Barrel, Applause 3
Terminator 2, Endoskeleton, Toy Island, 1995, 15" h 50
The Harvey Girls, sheet music, *On the Atchison, Topeka and the Santa Fe,* Judy Garland cov, 1945 10
The Sky's the Limit, sheet music, *My Shining Hour,* Fred Astaire, 1943 10
Tomorrow Never Dies, boxed action figure, Wan Lin, Exclusive Premiere, 1997, 7" h 10
Wizard of Oz, Dixie cup dispenser, 1989 . .35
Wizard of Oz, Scarecrow doll, plush, Applause, 1989, 15" h 15
Wizard of Oz, Scarecrow figure, Block Buster premium, 1998, MIP 3

MUSICAL INSTRUMENTS

Didn't you just love music lessons? Still play your clarinet or trumpet? Probably not! Yet, I bet you still have the instrument. Why is it that you can never seem to throw it out?

The number of antique and classic musical instrument collectors is small, but growing. Actually, most instruments are sold for reuse. As a result, the key is playability. Check out the cost of renting an instrument or purchasing one new. Now you know why prices on "used" instruments are so high. Fifty dollars for a playable instrument of any quality is a bargain price. Of course, it's a bargain only if someone needs and wants to play it. Otherwise, it is fifty dollars ill-spent.

Clubs: American Musical Instrument Society, RD 3 Box 205-B, Franklin, PA 16323; Automatic Musical Instrument Collectors Assoc., 2150 Hastings Ct., Santa Rosa, CA 95405; Miniature Piano Enthusiast Club, 633 Pennsylvania Ave., Hagerstown, MD 21740.

Clarinet, bass, French, stamped "P Gerard Paris" at bell and on body, ebony body, nickel plated bell, neck, and keys, with case 800
Clarinet, English, boxwood, stamped "H Wrede, 15, St Johns – Square, Clerkenwell, London, C" at bell and "H-Wrede, London" throughout, 5 brass keys with sq covers, ivory fittings, 19th C, 29.25" l 525
Clarinet, French, boxwood, stamped at bell "J Grandjon Boulevard de Sebastopol 105, Rue Réamur, 48 Paris," nickel plated keys, 27" l 375
Clarinet, multiple stamps "Chibonville Freres, B" with brass keys and ivory fittings, 26.25" l 575
Flute, English, illegibly mkd, boxwood body with ivory fittings, 4 brass keys with round covers, later cap, 24.25" l . .500
Guitar, Martin D-18, #144000, spruce top, mahogany body, old finish, replaced bridge and nut, stabilized stress crack in center, 1955 2,250

Harmonica, All American, Harmonic Reed Corp, Phila, resembles streamlined railroad car, red, white, and blue dec on harmonica and box 35

Recorder, tenor, stamped "Moeck" on maple body, 1 brass key, modern, 25.5" l 175

Saxophone, alto, French, stamped "A Lecompte, 8, Cie, Paris" and "11371" at bell, nickel plated body with double octave key, with mouthpiece and case, c1920 1,500

Saxophone, baritone, stamped "The Buescher, Elkhart, Ind. USA" on bell, with case and music stand 925

Transversed Flute, English, bearing multiple stamps "GX Astor & Co London," boxwood, single brass key with sq cover, ivory fittings, 19th C, 24" l 575

NAPCO

David Rein, Irwin Garber, and a Mr. Payner established the National Potteries Corporation (NAPCO) in 1939. Initially, it was an importer and manufacturer of floral containers. NAPCO ended its manufacturing operations after World War II.

NAPCO imported products include decorative accessories, kitchenware, and other ceramic items. The company moved its operations from Cleveland, Ohio, to Jacksonville, Florida, in 1984.

Beware of NAPCO look-alikes. Few early designs were copyrighted. A NAPCO label or solid reference book documentation are keys to identification.

Bank, money bag, 1962, 5" h, 4.75" w 28

Bank, piano baby, 1960, 5.5" h 30

Condiment Set, jam jar, creamer and sugar 45

Cup and Saucer, gold trim with green branch on background 20

Egg Cup, double, salt shaker head 28

Egg Cups, male and female, salt shaker hats, 5.25" 185

Figurine, angel boy playing a banjo, 3.75" h 25

Figurine, angel girl playing a violin, 3.75" h 25

Figurine, basset hound, 3.5" h, 5" l 20

Figurine, Calendar Cuties October 1962, 5.25" h 30

Figurine, cat and mouse sleeping in basket 15

Figurine, cymbal player, 6.5" h 30

Figurine, dog, 5.5" h 25

Figurine, Feeding Time, 5.75" h 24

Figurine, lady in pink gown and bonnet, 6" h 20

Figurine, Madonna, matte white, 12" h 20

Figurine, Mary with Holy Child 30

Figurine, November harvest angel, 4.5" h . 35

Figurine, palomino, 7.75" h 20

Figurine, rooster, 7" 42

Figurine, spaghetti Santa, 6.75" 50

Figurine, washday girl, 5.25" h, 3.25" w 32

Figurines, elephants, pink, set of 3 70

Head Vase, pearl earrings, 6" 125

Head Vase, pearl earrings and necklace, 3.5" 75

Planter, Baby, 6.5" h, 4.5" w 20

Planter, Davy Crockett, 4.25" h, 4.75" w ... 45

Relish Dish, rooster 10.5" x 10.5" 30

Vase, oriental girl, 5" h 24

Wall Plaque, rabbit 30

NAPKIN DOLLS

Figural napkin dolls, clothes sprinklers, and salt and pepper shakers spruced up many a post-World War II kitchen. While ceramic holders are the most plentiful and desirable, do not overlook wood and wire examples.

Brockmann, lady wearing pink dress, holding heart-shaped candy box, 6.5" h 70

California Originals, woman wearing red hat and white dress with red trim, hands clasped behind her back, candle socket in hat, 13" h .85

Holland Mold, girl wearing white dress with laced bodice and flowers on skirt, napkin slits in back, 8.5" h 85

House of Ceramics, southern belle wearing flounced dress and holding sun hat with large ribbon and brim, 9.75" h 175

Japan, angel, folded napkins in back form wings, 5.375" h 110

Japan, dark-haired woman wearing pink hat and dress, carrying a flower basket that holds toothpicks, 10.5" h . .125

Japan, oriental woman, carrying salt and pepper shaker buckets suspended from a yoke on her shoulders, holes around waist for toothpicks, candleholder in hat, 10.25" h 135

Kreiss, lady wearing green dress and hat, 10.375" h, 5.5" d 115

Mallory Ceramics, red-haired girl wearing yellow and white peasant dress, 9.5" h 80

NAPKIN RINGS

If you really get lucky, you may find a great Victorian silver-plated figural napkin ring at a flea market. Chances are that you are going to find napkin rings used by the common man. But do not look down your nose at them. Some are pretty spectacular. If you do not specialize from the beginning, you are going to find yourself going around in circles. Animal-shaped rings are a favorite.

CERAMIC

Franciscan, Fresh Fruit pattern 28

Japan, figural Mickey Mouse wearing Santa suit standing beside ring with a green bow base, 1970s, 2.75" h, 3" w . . .25

Japan, figural pink bird perched atop a small ring, 3.5" h 10

Japan, porcelain, figural cupid beside wreath "ring" with bow base, 2.5" h, 2.75" w 10

Noritake, hp Art Deco design with gentleman wearing a top hat and checkered cape, peach luster ground, white int, 2.25" d, 1.375" w 130

Noritake, hp bird in wreath design, gold trim, white ground, flattened bottom, 1.625" h, 2.25" w 80

Sanford, England, bone china, set of 4, each with a different flower repeated 8 times around the octagonal ring, 1.5" d 25

Tivoli Toscany, orange flower, green leaves and stem, white ground, boxed set of 6 15

Wade, Chintz Thistle pattern inside and outside, ftd, 2.25" h, 2.75" w 18

METAL

Brass, engraved lattice design, 1" w 6

Pewter, figural kewpie, 2.5" h, 1.75" d 115

Silver Plated, Billy Goat nursery rhyme motif, 1.625" d, 1" w 85

Silver Plated, figural parrot, 3.5" h 150

Silver Plated, figural swans 175

Silver Plated, Meriden, ring flanked by 2 figural eagles, 2" h 125

Silver Plated, ring mounted on pedestal base, engraved "Jack," 2.5" h, 1.5" w .100

Silver Plated, souvenir of Washington, DC, emb Capitol 18

Silver Plated, Victorian, ring mounted on pyramid base, leaf garland pattern, 3" h, 2.25" d 70
Silvertone, engraved fern design, 1.125" w 6
Sterling Silver, child's, flattened oval band with cutout and emb hen and 3 chicks, 2.25" l, .5" w 95
Sterling Silver, engine-turned design, Birmingham (England) hallmark, 1930, 1.75" d, .75" h 60
Sterling Silver, Gorham, beaded rims, 1.625" d, 1.125" w 110

PLASTIC

Bird, head, tail, and feet on round "ring" body, yellow Bakelite, 2.5" h 135
Chili Pepper, red pepper with hollow center, 4.75" l 2
Elephant, head and feet on round "ring" body, blue marbleized Bakelite, 2.5" h, 2" d 125
Monogrammed, ornate silver "B" on celluloid ring 10
Striped, 3 dark blue stripes on white ground 2

NAUTICAL

There is magic in the sea, whether one is reading the novels of Melville, watching Popeye cartoons, or standing on a beach staring at the vast expanse of ocean. Anyone who loves water has something nautical around the house. This is one case where the weathered look is a plus. No one wants a piece of nautical material that appears to have never left the dock.

Club: National Maritime Historical Society, 5 John Walsh Blvd., Peekskill, NY 10566, www.seahistory.org/.

Boat Model, wooden, Langcraft battery operated outboard motor, 12" l 200
Book, *The Big Book of Sailing: The Sailors, the Ships, & the Sea,* New York, Barron's, 1979, 309 pgs, 10" x 14" 25
Charm Bracelet, metal nautical charms including a fish, sailfish, shell, and seahorse, 7" l 22
Clock, wall mount, battery-operated, anchor shape, brass with bronze finish, 10" h 25
Coasters, each with a different lighthouse picture, boxed set of 4 20
Compass, Polaris, 6" x 6" x 4.25" dovetailed wooden box 100
Diorama, ship in a bottle, green-hulled liner with cotton wool smoke rising from 3 stacks, lighthouse, houses, and palm trees in background, 8" l bottle ... 55
Drinking Glasses, Libby, nautical flags on clear glass, 1950s-60s, 5.25" h, boxed set of 6 65
Instrument, steam anchor winch gauge, brass, pewter-colored metal dial with single hand, 0-300 increments, mkd "Steam to Kedge Anchor Winch, Single Spring, The Jas Morrison Brass Mfg Co Ltd, Toronto," 6.25" d 60
Porthole Window, green, rubber seal 50
Postcard, black and white photo of the *Intrepid* and the *Iphigenia,* sunk to blockade the harbor in Zeebrugge, Holland, printed in Brussels 18
Print, sailboat with red, white, and blue diagonally-striped sail, sgd and dated "Kipp Soldwelel 66," wooden frame, 18" x 24" 50
Ship Ladder, teak, 11' h, 18" w 350
Sugar Shaker, Ships pattern, red on white, McKee 20
Tablecloth, printed nautical theme with red tall ships and lighthouses on blue ground, 1940s, 34" x 36" 30
Telescope, silver-plated brass, single draw, brown leather covering, No. 869, 6.25" d 235

NEMADJI POTTERY

The Nemadji Pottery was located in Moose Lake, Minnesota. Founded by C. J. Dodge in 1923, it made swirl-decorated earthenware pottery similar in appearance to Niloak. In addition to vases and other decorative accessories, the company also made tiles. Nemadji Pottery ceased operations in 1973.

Club: Nemadji Collectors, P.O. Box 95, Moose Lake, MN55767, www.cpinternet.com/~nemadji/.

Bud Vase, orange, green, black, brown, and cream, 6" h, 4.25" d 8
Planters Pot, 3" h, 5.5" d 30
Pot, brown rust tones, 7" h 15
Pueblo Oven Incense Burner, 4.5" l, 3" w .. 12
Vase, brown, blue and orange, 6" h, 3.5" w 20
Vase, brown tones, 12.25" h 20
Vase, decorated with earthy, southwestern hand painting 35
Vase, miniature blue-green, 3.25" h 12
Vase, red and orange, 2.75" h, 4.75" w 15

NEWSPAPERS

"Extry – Extry, Read All About It" is the cry of corner newspaper vendors across the country. Maybe these vendors should be collected. They appear to be a vanishing breed. Some newspapers are collected for their headlines, others because they represent a special day, birthday, or anniversary. Everybody saved the newspaper announcing that JFK was shot. Did you save a paper from the day war was declared against Iraq? I did.

Club: Newspaper Collectors Society of America, Box 19134, S. Lansing, MI 48901.

1843, *Albany Weekly Patriot*, Albany, NY, Jun 22, front page story of "Kissame: A Tale of American Slavery," other stories about slavery, taken from bound version 50
1843, *Emancipator and Free American*, Boston, MA, May 25, front page coverage of "Omens of Democracy," "Proclaim Liberty Throughout All the Land, Unto all the Inhabitants Thereof" on masthead 35
1868, *New-Orleans Commercial Bulletin*, New Orleans, LA, Nov 2, front page endorsement for "National Democratic Ticket, For President, Horatio Seymour of New York, For Vice President, Frank P Blair of Missouri" 38
1926, *The Havana Post*, Havana, Cuba, Jul 4, printed in English, message by Republic of Cuba President Gerardo Machado congratulating US on sesquicentennial anniversary of independence on front page 45
1932, *New York Daily Mirror*, May 14, "Avenge Baby! Lindy Demands," full front page of photos relating to Lindbergh baby kidnapping, "Lindy Collapses at Baby's Bier" and photos on back page . 50
1936, *Rockford Register-Republic*, Rockford, IL, Dec 10, "King Edward Abdicates; Duke of York to Reign," front page photos of King Edward VIII and Duke of York 40
1952, *The Baltimore Evening Sun*, Feb 6, Baltimore, MD, "King George is Dead, Elizabeth is Queen," with photos of King George VI and Princess Elizabeth on front page, 8 pgs 20
1964, *The Baltimore Evening Sun*, Baltimore, MD, Apr 6, "US Pays Homage To MacArthur, His Body Will Lie in Capitol Rotunda, Burial in Norfolk; Khrushchev Blasts War Talk by Chinese Leaders" 12
1977, *Hagerstown Daily Mail*, Hagerstown, MD, Jan 17, "Gilmore Executed" headline with sketch of Gary Gilmore on front page 15
1981, *The Washington Star*, Aug 7, "Final Edition" banner, "128 Years of Service Ending" 16
1982, *The Washington Times*, May 17, first edition, "Falklands invasion near, British blast two vessels," front page photo of editors and publisher and story of historic first edition of this paper 50
1993, *New York Daily News*, Feb 27, "New York's Day of TERROR," Trade Center bombing 40

1995, *USA Today,* Sep 7, "Cal Stands Alone at 2,131," coverage of Baltimore Oriole shortstop Cal Ripken, Jr breaking Lou Gehrig's record 20
1998, *Apple Valley News,* CA, Jul 10, "King of the Cowboys Rides Into Eternity. EXTRA," full color picture of Roy Rogers and Dale Evans Rogers on front page, Roy Rogers' hometown newspaper 35

NILOAK POTTERY

When you mention Niloak, most people immediately think of swirled brown, red, and tan pottery, formally known as Mission Ware. However, Niloak also made items in a host of other designs through 1946. These included utilitarian wares and ceramics used by florists that can be bought for a reasonable price. If Niloak prices follow the trend established by Roseville prices, now is the time to stash some of these later pieces away.

Club: National Society of Arkansas Pottery Collectors, 2006 Beckenham Cove, Little Rock, AR 72212.

Basket, ivory, mkd on bottom, 3.5" h, 3" d . .8
Bowl, Hywood, melon form, mkd "Hywood By Niloak Benton Ark," c1932, 1.5" h, 2.75" d 85
Candlesticks, pr, Mission Ware, 8" h 375
Cornucopia Vase, matte tan with green Lewis glaze, mkd "Niloak," 7" h, 7" w . . .50
Creamer, Hywood, mottle blue semi-matte glaze, mkd "Niloak," c1930s, 4.25" h, 4" w 60
Ewer, dark blue, mkd, 6.5" h 35
Planter, figural Art Deco elephant, blue, mkd "Niloak," 5.5" h, 7.25" l 70
Planter, figural circus elephant, ivory, 5.75" h 25
Planter, figural deer, dark blue, 7" h, 6.75" l 65
Planter, figural deer and fawn, pale blue, mkd "Niloak," 7.5" h, 7" l 45
Planter, figural frog, chocolate brown, mkd "Niloak," 4.5" h 55
Planter, figural swan, Ozark Dawn II glaze, 5" h, 7" l 38
Planter, figural swan, pink and blue glaze, mkd, 8" h 65

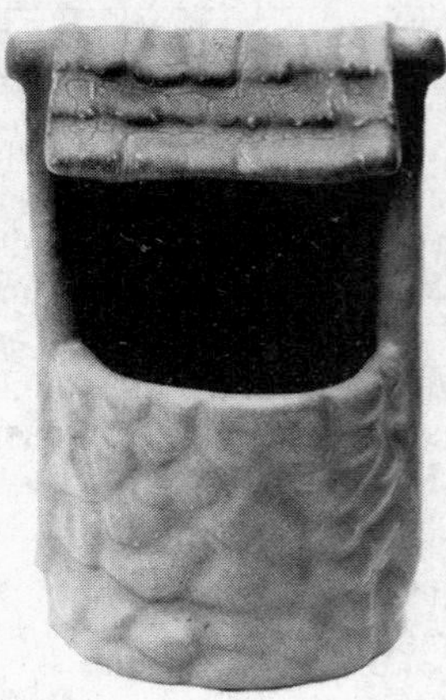

Planter, figural wishing well, Ozark Dawn II glaze, 8" h .35

Vase, double-handled, lavender, 6.5" h . . .36
Vase, Mission Ware, baluster form with flat flaring rim, second art mark, 4" h 110
Vase, Mission Ware, corseted, mkd "Niloak," 5.5" h 175
Vase, Mission Ware, ovoid, partial Niloak Pottery sticker on bottom covering imp mark, 5.375" h 100
Vase, Mission Ware, spherical, red, blue, and cream, 6.25" h, 6.375" d 300
Vase, twisted form, glossy pink glaze, partial Niloak sticker, 6.5" h 22

NIPPON

Nippon is hand-painted Japanese porcelain made between 1891 and 1921. The McKinley tariff of 1891 required goods imported into the United States to be marked with their country of origin. Until 1921, goods from Japan were marked "Made in Nippon."

Over two hundred different manufacturer's marks have been discovered for Nippon. The three most popular are the wreath, maple leaf, and rising sun. While marks are important, the key is the theme and quality of the decoration.

Nippon has become quite expensive. Rumors in the field indicate that Japanese buyers are now actively competing with American buyers.

Club: International Nippon Collectors' Club, 9101 Sulkirk Dr., Raleigh, NC 27613.

Bowl, shallow, 3-handled, hp sailing ship with palm tree and ruins in background, gold rim and handles, green wreath mark, 8.5" d 145

Chocolate Pot, cylindrical form, gold handle, hp cottage and lake, green wreath mark, 7.5" h 260

Chocolate Pot, etched panels dec with landscape, flowers, and wreath, gold and jeweled dec, green wreath mark, 9.5" h 175

Ewer, 3 hp floral medallions outlined in gold, unmkd, 13.5" h 375

Tankard, slender tapering form, gold-dec rim and base, applied gold scroll handle, gold-trimmed green arches and pink flowers on blue base, blue maple leaf mark, 13" h 350

Tray, oblong with outset corners and handles, hp center scene flanked by rose medallions, green wreath mark, 8" l, 6.25" w 150

Urn, bolted, gold handles, square foot, hp landscape, 12" h 425

Urn, bolted, paneled body with hp scenic vignettes, gold and cobalt dec with Greek key design, multicolored flowers on white band at neck and foot, gold trim, green wreath mark, 17" h 1,000

Vase, cup-form mouth, tapering body, 2-handled, hp pink and yellow flowers on white ground, gold ferns, jeweled designs, and handles, magenta maple leaf mark, 12" h 400

Vase, cup-form mouth with wavy rim, spherical body, ftd base, 2-handled, all-over Moriage dec with 4 hp floral panels, 7" h 430

Vase, cylindrical, 2-handled, hp roses, gold handles, rim, and base, 11" h 315

Vase, cylindrical body, narrow neck with flared mouth, coralene dec, Art Deco lotus leaves and pink flowers on cream body, mkd "KinRan U.S. patent, Feb. 9, 1909" in magenta, 9" h 650

Vase, cylindrical with gold scroll-form handles, gold dec at rim and ft, black and gold silhouette trees, green maple leaf mark, 11" h 425

Vase, narrow neck, ovoid body, ftd base, 2-handled, all-over Moriage dec, large flowers on magenta ground, unmkd, 8.5" h 750

Vase, narrow neck, tapering body, 2-handled, hp flowers and grapes, gold handles and trim, patented "sharkskin" glaze, mkd "Patent No 1705, Feb. 26, 1910 Royal Kinjo Japan," 11" h 500

Vase, ovoid form with 3 gold handles with rings, hp yellow and gold roses, green "M" in wreath mark, 11.5" h 315

Vase, slightly tapering body with flaring rim and foot, 2-handled, hp landscape of trees and a lake, gold rim, handles, and foot, 9.5" h 300

Vase, tall cylindrical neck, bulbous body, 2-handled, heavy etched gold dec of flowers and striped band around neck and lower half of body, hp landscape around upper half of body, green "M" in wreath mark, 13" h, 7" d 500

NON-SPORT TRADING CARDS

Based on the publicity received by baseball cards, you would think that they were the only bubble gum cards sold. Wrong, wrong, wrong! There is a wealth of non-sport trading cards.

Prices for many of these card sets are rather modest. Individual cards often sell for less than $1. Classic cards were issued in the 1950s. More recently released sets are also collectible, as witnessed by prices realized for Beatles and television-related cards from the 1960s.

Club: United States Cartophilic Society, P.O. Box 4020, St. Augustine, FL 32085.

Note: Prices listed are for sets in excellent condition.

Alfred Hitchcock, Famous Film Directors, Cecil Court, London, 1992 5
Batman Movie, Topps, 2nd series, 143 cards, 22 stickers, 1989, MISB 20
Batman Saga of the Dark Knight, Skybox, set of 100, 1994 10
Cops & Robbers, Fleer, set of 35 cards and 6 detached "Evidence" tabs, pastel-tinted cards, 1930s 1,000
Dallas, TV series, imcomplete set of 19, puzzle piece backs, 1981 30
Defenders and Offenders Tobacco Album, Buchner, cloth bound with full-color pictures of 10 Defenders (police chiefs) and 200 Offenders (criminals), detailed biography of each, 1888 600
Elvis, #51, Boxcar Enterprises, 1978 3
Elvis Presley, Topps, complete set of 66 cards, color photos of Elvis in early concerts and Hollywood films on fronts, detailed text on reverse, 1956 700

Frank Sinatra, Series F, No. 23, Dandy Bubble Gum, printed in Holland, 1960s . .9
Heinz Famous Aviators, #2 Amelia Earhart variation card, 1930s 240
I Love Lucy, Pacific Trading Card Co, complete box with 36 packs, 10 cards per pack, 1991 20
John Glenn, #32 30
Mars Attacks, #25, Topps, 1962 20
Rails & Sails, Topps, complete set of 200 cards, 1955 735
Roy Rogers Pop Out Card, Post Cereal, #5, "Roy Sees Signs of Trouble," 1950s .10
Speed Buggy, #17, series of 25, Wonder Bread, Wacky Arithmetic trick on back .5
Star Trek, Primrose Confectionery Co Ltd, set of 12, 1971 30
The Tick, set of 72, comic images, 1997 . . .12
Wonders of the World, Sweet Cigarettes, England, set of 25, 1956 15

NORITAKE AZALEA

Noritake china in the Azalea pattern was first produced in the early 1900s. Several backstamps were used. They will help date your piece.

Azalea pattern wares were distributed as a premium by the Larkin Company of Buffalo and sold by Sears, Roebuck and Company. As a result, it is the most commonly found pattern of Noritake china. Each piece is hand-painted, adding individuality to the piece. Hard-to-find examples include children's tea sets and salesmen's samples. Do not ignore the hand-painted glassware in the Azalea pattern that was manufactured to accompany the china service.

Bread and Butter Plate, 6.5" d 9
Butter Tub, with insert, 5.5" d 100
Cake Plate, handled, 9.5" d 40
Candy Dish 35
Celery Dish, open handles, 12.5" l 30
Cranberry Bowl, 5" d 90
Creamer 20
Creamer and Sugar, gold finials, 3.625" h creamer, 4.375" h sugar 190
Cup and Saucer 8
Dinner Plate, 10" d 15
Egg Cup, 3" h 50

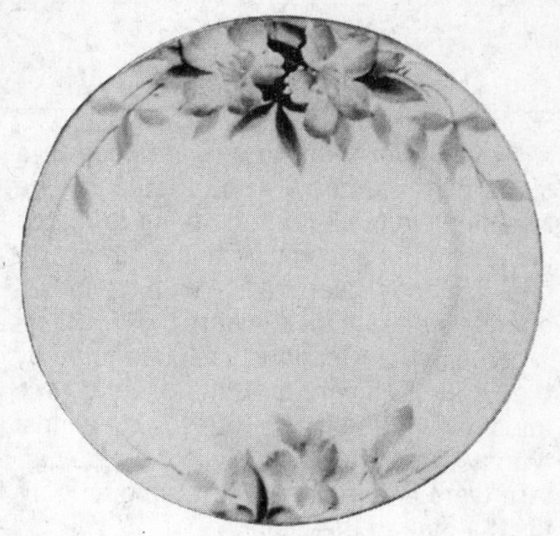

Fruit Bowl, 5.5" d 9
Lemon Dish, 5.5" d 12
Olive Dish, oval, 8.25" l 40
Platter, 11.5" l 40
Platter, 13.5" l 45
Relish Dish, divided, 8.25" l 40
Salad Plate, 7.625" d .12
Salt Shaker, bulbous, 3" h 10
Serving Bowl, handled, 9" w 50
Shell Bowl, ftd, 3.625" h, 7.125" w 430
Sugar, cov 30
Vegetable Bowl, cov, handled, 10" w 50

NORITAKE CHINA

Noritake is quality Japanese china imported to the United States by the Noritake China company. The company, founded by the Morimura brothers in Nagoya in 1904, is best known for its dinnerware lines. Over one hundred different marks were used, which are helpful in dating pieces. The Larkin Company of Buffalo, New York, issued several patterns as premiums, including the Azalea, Briarcliff, Linden, Savory, Sheridan, and Tree in the Meadow patterns, which are readily found.

Be careful. Not all Noritake china is what it seems. The company also sold blanks to home decorators. Check the artwork before deciding that a piece is genuine.

Club: Noritake Collectors' Society, 145 Andover Pl., West Hempstead, NY 11552.

Asparagus Dish, oblong, 2-handled, blue luster flowers on peach luster rim band, white ground, 12" l, 5.5" w 50
Bowl, flower shaped, violet, blue, and gold flowers, heavy gold trim, 4" h, 8" d 175
Bowl, peach and white luster, Art Nouveau design with orange, black, and white geometric band on flared rim, black edge stripe, "M" in wreath mark, 3" h, 5" d 20
Butter Dish, Art Deco design, yellow and black, 4" h, 7.875" l 150
Cake Set, handled tray and 6 plates, gold dec, red "M" mark 125
Celery Set, rect tray and 4 octagonal plates, gondola scene, green tree crest mark, c1925, 11" l tray 115
Coffee Server, Irene, white raised floral on ivory body, silver scrolls and trim . .130
Creamer and Sugar, cov, hp country scene, gold trim, magenta "M" in wreath mark, 4" h sugar, 3" h creamer . .45
Creamer and Sugar, cov, hp floral dec, white ground, gold trim, 3" h sugar 65
Dessert Set, Burma pattern with peacocks, 3 each cup, saucers, and plates 62
Gravy Boat, oval, Carolyn pattern 68
Jam Jar, cov, with ladle, hp band with landscape, white ground, gold trim, 5" h, 3.375" w 70

Match Holder, hp cottage scene, 3.75" h, 2.625" w 120

Mayonnaise Set, bowl, ladle, and underplate, multicolor flowers, yellow trim, white ground 70

Nappy, hp with yellow cartouches and multicolored flowers, black and gold trim, 7.25" w 56

Nut Bowl, handled, moriage dec chestnuts, green "M" in wreath mark, c1891-1919, 10" l 35

Oil and Vinegar, 1-pc with 2 spouts, cottage and lake scene, gold handle, 3.5" h, 6.5" w 225

Pancake Serving Dish, cov, #16034, gold trim, 3.625" h, 8.75" d 130

Plate, hp landscape, mkd "Noritake, Hand Painted, Made in Japan," "M" in green, 7.25" d 35

Relish Dish, with 4 salts, pond scene with swan, cottage, and foliage, purple rim with gold trim, "M" in wreath mark, 5.5" x 12" relish, 3.5" l salts 85

Sandwich Server, center handle, hp landscape, 3.875" h, 9.75" d 70

Saucer, Howo pattern, flying phoenix birds and roses, geometric border, blue on white, mkd "Noritake, Made in Japan," c1908, 5.375" h 10

Starter Set, Rosemary, 20 pcs including 4 each dinner plates, berry bowls, bread and butter plates, cups, and saucers 160

Sugar Shaker, Art Deco design with exotic birds, 6.5" h 130

Vegetable Bowl, cov, Jasmine, #585 160

NORITAKE TREE IN THE MEADOW

If you ever want to see variation in a dinnerware pattern, collect Tree in the Meadow. You will go nuts trying to match pieces. In the end you will do what everyone else does. Learn to live with the differences. Is there a lesson here?

Tree in the Meadow was distributed by the Larkin Company of Buffalo, New York. Importation began in the 1920s, almost twenty years after the arrival of azalea pattern wares. Check the backstamp to identify the date of the piece.

Berry Bowl, red mark, 5.125" d 10

Bowl, handled, 6.5" x 5.5" 45

Bowl, oval, handled, 2.75" h, 10.5" w 50

Bread and Butter Plate, gold trim, red mark, 6.5 d 6

Cup and Saucer, gold trim, red mark 15

Dolly Varden Basket, gold trim, red "M" in wreath mark, 4.5" l 125

Luncheon Plate, gold trim, red mark, 8.5" d 14

Oatmeal Bowl, gold trim, red mark, 6" d, 1.5" h 12

Pancake Set, gold trim, 5.625" h syrup pitcher and 6.375" h powdered sugar shaker 100

Platter, oval, red mark, 11.625" l 40

Salad Plate, gold trim, red mark, 7.5" d 10

Salt and Pepper Shakers 45

Soup Bowl, gold trim, 7.5" d 20

Vase, baluster form, 8.125" h, 5.125" d 150

Wall Pocket, blue luster ground, red "M" in wreath mark, 8" h, 4.75" w 100

NUTCRACKERS

Lever-action cast-iron nutcrackers, often in the shape of animals, appeared in the mid-19th century. Designs mirrored the popular design styles of each era. Art Deco and 1950s-era nutcrackers and sets are eagerly sought by collectors. Beginning in the 1960s, wooden nutcrackers from Germany's Erzgebirger region began flooding the American market. These Erzebirger-style figures are now being made around the world, especially in the Far East, and from a wide variety of materials.

Club: Nutcracker Collectors' Club, 12204 Fox Run Dr., Chesterland, OH 44026.

Bavarian Santa, wooden gift box 60
Bavarian Wanderer 250
Boy Scout 210
Captain Smith of the *Titanic* 255
Chubby Soldier 260
Cowardly Lion 275
Crossover Plier, nickel-plated, 1899, 6" l . .22
Dentist 210
Dorothy 15
Fireman 25
Fisherman 20
Folk Art Head, wooden 35
Humpty Dumpty, wooden 22
Irishman, wooden 25
Irish Setter, bronze, 13.5" l 300
Juggling Frosty the Snowman 20
King 120
King Henry VIII 265
Maid Marion 265
Man's Head, aluminum, A B Hagen, patented Oct 17, 1950 50
Marionette Maker 24
Mouse King with Sword, wooden 50
Nativity Windmill 25

Nude Female, brass, English, 8.5" l 150
Pere Noel 270
Peter Pan with Tinker Bell 275
Pharaoh 245
Pliers, cast iron, 1930-40 20
Rabbit, cast iron 15
Robin Hood, wooden gift box 72
Sailing Ship, brass, English, 1939 75
Scrooge, miniature, wooden gift box 70
Shepherd 215
Sherlock Holmes, wooden 65
Skiing Snowman 15
Soldier, Christmas ornament, 3.25" h 35
Soldier, wooden 105
Soldier Bear 15
Standing Dog, cast iron, late 19th C, 6" h, 5.5" l 125
Sugar Plum Chef 20

OCCUPIED JAPAN

America occupied Japan from 1945 to 1952. Not all objects made during this period are marked "Occupied Japan." Some were simply marked "Japan" or "Made in Japan." Occupied Japan collectors ignore these two groups. They want to see their favorite words.

Beware of falsely labeled pieces. Rubber-stamp marked pieces have appeared on the market. Apply a little fingernail polish remover. Fake marks will disappear. True marks are under glaze. Of course, if the piece is unglazed to begin with, ignore this test.

Club: The Occupied Japan Club, 29 Freeborn St., Newport, RI 02840.

Ashtray, wide-eyed frog, open mouth, 3.25" h 12
Bookends, pr, colonial ladies 30
Bookends, pr, polar bears, bisque, Ucagco 55
Bowl, cov, Acanthus pattern, mkd "Aladdin Made in Occupied Japan Acanthus," 8.5" d 15
Bowl, fish design, blue reticulated rim, 5" d 10
Bud Vase, tulip, hen and chick at bottom, 2.5" h 4
Candleholders, pr, tulip, pink, gold highlights, 7" h 100

Child's Saucer, lavender and rust flowers on bright yellow ground, Gold China, 4.5" d 8
Coaster Set, Lacquerware, pink and yellow flowers on brown ground, price for 8 15
Creamer, elephant, trunk up, Ucagco, 5" h 25
Creamer, Old King Cole, 3.25" h 10
Cup and Saucer, dragon pattern, blue and white 20
Cup and Saucer, Geisha Girl motif, gold highlights 30
Cup and Saucer, multicolored floral dec, white center, pale yellow ground, gold trim, mkd "Noritake, Made in Occupied Japan," 1949 25
Cup and Saucer, pink poppies on blue ground 15
Demitasse Tea Set, service for 6, teapot, creamer and sugar, cup and saucer, pink and purple floral motif, Chugai China 150
Dish, double lotus leaf, pink flower, green leaves, 3.5" w 15
Dish, leaf shape, hp violets, mkd "Spring Violets, Hand Painted/Made in Occupied Japan," crown emblem with "Rossetti Chicago, U.S.A.," 4" d 7
Dish, shell shaped, birds and dragons, black, white, and gold, Hokutosha, 9.5" x 8.75" 45
Dollhouse Furniture, ceramic, in box 25
Figure, angel in row boat, bisque, 4.5" h, 6" l 65
Figure, boy holding bouquet, porcelain, yellow shirt, pale blue overalls with dark blue stars, 5" h 18
Figure, boy playing flute, lamb behind, 4.25" h 4

Figure, boy with bee on head, 3.5" h 25
Figure, cherub on pedestal, bisque, 7" h . . .45
Figure, colonial man carrying flowers, bisque, 7.25" h 25
Figure, dancing colonial couple, lace trim, gold highlights, 10" h 75
Figure, elf on caterpillar 20
Figure, fish, pink, blue fins and tail 10
Figure, lady carrying baskets, 6" h 18
Figure, man and woman with lamb, Maruyama, 6" h 70
Figure, mother cow nursing calf, 4" h, 6" l 40
Figure, stork, white, orange, and black, gold trim, 3.75" h 15
Figure, terrier, 5" h 15
Figure, woman holding pocketbook, pink and yellow dress with blue apron, red slippers, gold trim, 6.25" h 12
Figures, pr, oriental man and woman, porcelain, mkd "Moriyama, Made in Occupied Japan, 1017" 7.5" h 50
Fish Bowl Ornament, tropical fish amid seaweed and coral, 2.5" h, 3" l 10
Game, Checkers, Elgee, 2.5" x 4.75" box . . .20
Lamp, flamenco dancer, 12.75" h 60
Lamps, pr, Wedgwood style 125
Lighter, camera on tripod, mkd "KL Camera Lighter" around lens 15
Mug, Old King Cole, 3.5" h 50
Needle Book, Full Speed, men riding motorcycles, 3.5" x 6.5" 8
Pin, 2 Scottie dogs, celluloid 10
Planter, baby bootie 5
Planter, dancing lady, 4.5" h 20
Planter, duck, 4" h, 6" l 5
Planter, Dutch clog shoe 10
Plate, floral motif, sgd "T Kita," 10" d 35

Plate, pink roses motif, Gold Castle, 10" d 5

Salt and Pepper Shakers, Humpty Dumpty, mkd "Ardalt, Occupied Japan" 35

Salt and Pepper Shakers, Indian and squaw in canoe, 3" h, 6.25" w 15

Salt and Pepper Shakers, windmill, cobalt blue and white, 2" h 5

Shelf Sitter, girl playing mandolin, 3" h 8

Smoking Set, 2 ashtrays and cigarette box mkd "Rosetti, Chicago USA, Hand Painted, Made in Occupied Japan" 25

Sugar and Creamer, figural tomatoes, black "Made in Occupied Japan," 3.25" h 25

Teacup and Saucer, floral motif, Shata China 8

Teapot, cov, Orchid pattern on yellow ground, gold trim, 4" h 20

Toby Mug, MacArthur, mkd "Merit, Made in Occupied Japan," 4.25" h 50

Toby Mug, man, wearing granny glasses, 3.5" h 30

Toy, crawling baby, celluloid, windup, orig box, Asahi 60

Toy, ostrich, plush body, windup, orig box, 5.5" x 4.75" 150

Toy, trapeze acrobat, celluloid figure, wire frame, windup, mkd "My Friend" in globe on acrobat's back, inspection sticker on leg, 1930s, 8.25" h 85

Toy, trumpet, tin, 7.25" l 20

Vase, dancing girl 18

Vase, girl with raised arm, bisque, mkd "Paulux, Made in Occupied Japan," 7.5" h 25

Vase, ladies wearing ball gowns, 6.5" h . . .55

Vases, dragon dec, mirrored pr 175

OCEAN LINER COLLECTIBLES

Although the age of the clipper ships technically fits into this category, the period that you are most likely to uncover at flea markets is that of the ocean liner. Don't focus solely on American ships. England, Germany, France, and many other countries had transoceanic liners that competed with and bested American vessels. Today is the age of the cruise ship. This aspect of the category is being largely ignored. Climb aboard and sail into the sunset.

Clubs: Steamship Historical Society of America, Inc., 300 Ray Dr., Suite #4, Providence, RI 02906, www.sshsa.net; Titanic Historical Society, P.O. Box 51053, Indian Orchard, MA 01151; Titanic International Society, P.O. Box 7007, Freehold, NJ 07728.

Ashtray, Holland American Lines, white ceramic with picture of ship at center, mkd "Zenith," 4" d 28

Ashtray, *Normandie,* Opalex glass, made in France, 1945, 3.375" x 2.75" 55

Ashtray, *SS France,* French Line, cobalt blue glass, picture of ship in gold at center, topmarked "France," 4.25" d . . .25

Brochure, French Line, includes ships *Washington, Wisconsin, Wyoming,* and *Oregon,* "The Sunshine Trail" to Europe, 12 double-fold pgs with maps, cabin photos, deck plans, sample menus, and ship photos, 1930s 55

Brochure, *Normandie,* foldout illus of ship entering harbor, 1930s, 17" x 30.5" unfolded size 145

Brochure, *Queen Elizabeth,* Cunard Line, plan of first class accommodations, with deck plan and color photos, 3 double-sided pgs, opens to 9" x 45" . . .50

Butter Pat, Clipper Line of Sweden, Stella Polaris pattern of gold crowned lion and star on a blue shield with trident above and "Clipper Line" below, gold trim, white ground, 1952-69, 3.5" d 18

Demitasse Cup and Saucer, *Andrea Doria,* oriental scenes, Genova shape, mkd "Richard Ginori DO Italy" 75

Drinking Glass, Celebrity Lines, peach-striped Phalaenopsis Hennessy orchid on frosted ground, back lists recipes for 3 cocktails (Bon Voyage, Zodiac, and Blue Moon), 7" h 15

Hand Fan, French Line, Spanish woman holding fan watching ship sail past, chromolithograph paper on wood sticks, tassel, blank back, c1910s, 16" x 9" 85

Matchbook, "French Line, *Normandie*, The World's Largest Ship" and drawing of ship on outside, lists 4 ships and their tonnage on inside, full length, Lion Match 12

Menu, *RMS Carinthia*, Cunard Line, luncheon menu for May 23, 1937, cov illus of Westminster Abbey by Walter Thomas, 9.75" x 7" .15

Menu, *SS Uruguay*, Moore-McCormack Lines, en route from Rio de Janeiro to Trinidad, printed in English, Spanish, and Portuguese, "Bahia – Brasil – Food Vendor" cov art by Ada Peacock, serial #19, 9" x 12" .25

Paperweight, *SS Homeric* and *SS Oceanic*, Home Lines, bronze, 2 ships pictured on front, Home Lines insignia on back, 3" d 65

Passenger List,* RMS Aquitania, *Cunard Line, sailing from Southampton to New York via Cherbourg, Saturday June 20, 1925, 32 pgs, 7.5" x 5" 30

Passenger List, *SS Algonquin*, Mallory Line, 8 pg onboard newspaper, includes articles on "The Treaty of Paris" and "Musical Strike in New Orleans," 1928 20

Peanut Holder, Cunard Line, cobalt blue glass, topmark of lion holding a globe over "Cunard," 5.5" h 15

Pennant, *Queen Mary*, multicolor image of ship, 8.5" x 26" 110

Track Chart, *SS Anchoria*, Anchor Line, voyage from NY to Glasgow, ship transported Irish and Scottish immigrants to US in 1870s-90s, 6" x 10.5" 75

OLYMPIC COLLECTIBLES

Why has the collecting of Olympic memorabilia lagged behind other sports collectibles?

There are several reasons: the infrequency of the Olympics; the international flavor of the event; the "baggage" of social, political, and economic factors: and the failure, with few exceptions, to develop and market the super athletes that have participated.

Since the 1984 Los Angeles Olympics, pin collecting has been the driving force bringing the Olympics to public attention. In most cases the initial expense is small and the pin collectors trade frequently, putting the emphasis on pin collecting as a hobby, rather than an investment.

Olympic items can be found at garage sales, flea markets, auctions, and antique shows. Beginners should focus on a specific collecting category.

Club: Olympic Pin Collector's Club, 1386 Fifth St., Schenectady, NY 12303.

Book, *Creating an Olympic Champion* by Mary Lou Retton and Bela Karolyi 10

Book, *The Russian Rose* by Randall Wallace 8

Cigarette Holder, Royal Canadian Air Force, 1948 Olympics 220
Collector Plate, McDonalds, 1996 Olympics, 9.5" d 5
Creamer, cow, 1976 Olympics 40
Flag, tobacco felt, Haiti Olympics, 8.25" w, 5.5" h 5
Flag, tobacco felt, Norway Olympics, 8.25" w, 5.5" h 5
Game Pin, 1996 Olympics 10
Patch, 1980 Olympic Committee, 5" x 3" 6
Patch, arrowhead, 3" x 3" 8
Patch, Coca-Cola, 3" x 4" 12
Pen and Pencil, 1984 Olympics 10
NOC Team Pin, 1976 Montreal, XXI Summer Games Yugoslavia, rect, Olympic rings, red star on Yugoslav flag, and "JUGOSLAVIJA/ MONTREAL" 160
NOC Team Pin, 1988 Calgary, XV Winter Games Jamaican Bobsleigh, enamel, shield shape, 2-man bobsled over stylized mountain with palm trees at base, "JAMAICA/Calgary 1988" above and "BOBSLEIGH/TEAM" below 46
TV Guide, Feb 7-15, 1998, set of 4, each with different cover 30
Wallet, 1996 Olympics, 3.5" x 5" 15

OPALESCENT GLASS

Victorian opalescent glass is transparent with a milky white decoration which looks fiery (or opalescent) when held to light. The effect was achieved by applying bone ash chemicals to designated areas while a piece was still hot and then refiring it at tremendous heat.

Bonbon, Button Panels, blue, Dugan, c1899 55
Bowl, Abalone, blue, Jefferson, c1903 65
Bowl, Astro, blue, Jefferson, c1906 75
Bowl, Button Panels, white, ftd, Dugan, c1902 50
Bowl, Many Loops, green, Jefferson, c1906 55
Card Receiver, Opal Open, blue, ftd, Dugan, c1901 60
Card Receiver, Pressed Coinspot, vaseline, Dugan, c1901 100
Card Receiver, Pressed Coinspot, white, Dugan, c1902 60

Compote, Pearls & Scales, vaseline, ftd, Jefferson, c1906 85
Compote, Spools, blue, Northwood, c1902 55
Cruet, Daisy and Fern, parian swirl mold, blue, applied blue handle, clear faceted stopper, 6.25" h .200
Jelly, Pressed Coinspot, blue, ftd, Northwood, c1901 75
Olive Dish, Blooms & Blossoms, white, handled, Northwood, c1905 50
Toothpick Holder, Beatty Honeycomb, blue, AJ Beatty & Sons, small flake on side, c1888 50
Toothpick Holder, Iris with Meander, blue, Jefferson, c1903 250
Vase, Boggy Bayou, green, Fenton, c1907 55
Vase, Ocean Shell, blue, Northwood, c1903 95
Vase, Ribbed Spiral, white, Model Flint Glass Co, c1902 60
Water Pitcher, Coinspot, blue, Northwood, c1896 275

OWL COLLECTIBLES

Most people do not give a hoot about this category, but those who do are serious birds. Like all animal collectors, the only thing owl collectors care about is that their bird is represented.

Club: International Owl Collectors Club, 54 Triverton Rd., Edgware, Middlesex HA8 6BE, U.K.

Candy Mold, metal 5

Coffee Canister, with spoon, 6" h 8
Cookie Cutters, 1973 Hallmark Halloween Set 25
Cookie Jar, 10" h 20
Cookie Jar, green owl with hat 55
Cookie Jar, ivory, 11" h 15
Cookie Jar, McCoy, green, 10.5" h 125
Cookie Jar, winking owl, 11.5" h 125
Creamer, 4.25" h 55
Creamer, gold and brown, 4" h 5
Creamer, white with blue flowers, 4.75" h .30
Lamp, 23" h 65
Measuring Spoon Holder, holds 4 spoons .12
Mug, Atlantic City souvenir 5
Pie Bird, 6" h 75
Pin, red-breasted owl 75
Salt and Pepper Shakers, owl and elephant, 3" h 45
Salt and Pepper Shakers, owl chefs, 3.5" h 10
Serving Tray, 12.5" x 18" 45
Toothpick Holder, 2.25" h 5
Toothpick Holder, brown with wiggly eyes, 2.25" h 5
Trivets, black iron, set of 5 15
Tumbler, ceramic, 16 oz 5
Vase, porcelain, 15" h 50

PACIFIC CLAY PRODUCTS

Pacific Clay Products, located in Los Angeles, California, operated from 1881 until the late 1940s. The company first produced utilitarian stoneware and yellowware pieces, then introduced its art ware line starting in the 1930s.

Coffee Carafe, cov, Apache Red glaze, mkd "Pacific," 9.5" h, 7.5" w 100
Coffee Carafe, cov, yellow, mkd "Pacific," 9.5" h, 7.5" w 100
Coffee Set, carafe and 4 cups, wooden handles, Apache Red carafe, cobalt blue, peach, turquoise green, and Apache Red tumblers, 9.5" h carafe, price for set 175
Fan Vase, light blue, mkd "Pacific," 7.5" h, 6.5" w 65
Figure, swan, pink, mkd "Pacific," 6" h . . .25
Plate, orange, 9" d .15
Vase, Art Deco design, lime green, 2-handled, mkd "Pacific USA," 8" h, 5" w 130
Vase, light pink, mkd "Pacific," 8" h, 5.5" w 55
Vase, rect, antelope design, pink, 10" h, 7.5" w 225

PADEN CITY GLASS

The Paden City Glass Manufacturing Company, Paden City, West Virginia, was founded in 1916. The plant closed in 1951, two years after acquiring the American Glass Company. Paden City glass was handmade in molds. There are no known free-blown examples. Most pieces were unmarked. The key is color. Among the most popular are opal (opaque white), dark green (forest), and red. The company did not produce opalescent glass.

Club: Paden City Glass Society, Inc., P.O. Box 139, Paden City, WV 26159.

Bowl, Crowsfoot, green, 10" d 35
Bowl, Crowsfoot, oval, red, 10.75" d 50
Bowl, Party Line, pink 35
Cake Plate, Peacock and Rose, 10.25" d .130
Candleholder, Party Line, pink 30
Candleholders, Crowsfoot, mushroom, black 80
Candleholders, Crowsfoot, mushroom, blue 90
Candlesticks, Crowsfoot, red, 5.25" h 80
Candlesticks, Orchid, orchid etching, crystal 125
Candy Container, military hat 50
Center Handle Plate, 11.5" d 65
Cheese and Cracker Plate, Spire 65
Comport, Crowsfoot and Rose etching . . .55
Console Bowl, 3.25" h, 13" d 55
Console Set, silver overlay 165
Cotton Holder, bunny, 5" h 170
Creamer and Sugar, Black Forest, crystal .75
Creamer and Sugar, crystal 30
Creamer and Sugar, Cupid, light green . .295
Creamer and Sugar, Vermillion 28
Cup, Gadroon, royal blue 16
Cup and Saucer, Penny Line, amethyst . . .15
Dinner Plate, Black Forest, 10.25" d 230
Double Candleholder 36
Lamp, figural rooster, 11" h 230
Figurine, pheasant, blue, 6.5" h, 13" l 125
Ice Bucket, black, 6.75" h, 7" w 290
Ice Tub, Glades, red 60

Mayonnaise, 3.5" h, 5.75" w 90
Mayonnaise and Underplate, mint green 125
Plate, Crowsfoot, black, 8.5" w 15
Plate, Gazebo, crystal, 11" d 50
Relish Tray, Spring Orchard, 7" x 7" 28
Salad Bowl, Gazebo, 12" d 40
Serving Dish, green, 6" h, 7.5" w 30
Serving Plate, Crowsfoot, silver overlay . .68
Sugar Bowl, open, Gazebo 10
Tray, center handle, crystal, 11" d 75
Tumbler, Crowsfoot, flat, blue 100
Tureen, 5.5" h, 7.5" w 65
Underplate, Nerva Cut, 11.5" d 30
Vase, Black Forest, Regina, black, 10" h .185
Vase, Crowfoot, ruby, 9.75" h 150
Vase, Peacock and Rose, 10" h 290
Vase, Utopia, 10" h .75

PAINT-BY-NUMBER

Paint-by-number pictures are most frequently collected according to subject matter. Crossover collectors are the biggest customers. A modest interest is building for paint-by-number metal crafts such as kitchen trays and other accessories.

Kit, Popeye Oil Painting By Numbers TV Edition, Hasbro, 5 pictures, 12 paints, MIB 75
Kit, Raggedy Ann and Andy, 2 pictures, 1 partially painted, orig box dated 1988 .15
Letter Basket, metal, oval, flowers and ribbons on black ground, gold trim, 5" h, 7.125" l, 4.75" w 25
Picture, autumn mill scene, pine frame, 1950s, 23" x 19" 16
Picture, Barbie and the Rockers, NRFB . . .15

Picture, blonde boy kneeling in prayer, beagle puppy beside him, Simpson's order label on back, 12.5" x 6.5" 9
Picture, collie head, white wood frame, 1950s, 13.5" x 10.5" 30
Picture, desert scene, arched rocks in background, prospector, donkey, pick, and cholla cactus in foreground, wood frame, 1950s-60s, 18" x 14" 28
Picture, English setter, framed, 1950s-60s, 16.5" x 12.75" 25
Picture, geisha girl holding fan, painted on velvet, black and gold frame with glass, 12" x 16" 22
Picture, sailing ship, oak frame, 1950s, 19.5" x 23.5" 14
Picture, winter landscape, wood frame, c1950, 13" x 17" 15
Tray, Metal Artcraft Co, floral design on black, orig box, 16.25" x 11" 35
Tray, Tole Craft, metal, PA Dutch floral design and gold trim on black, unused but paint is dried out, orig box, 12" x 18" 48

PAPERBACK BOOKS

This is a category with millions of titles and billions of copies. Keep this in mind before paying a high price for anything.

A great deal of the value of paperbacks rests in the cover art. A risqué lady can raise prices as well as blood pressure. Great art can make up for a lousy story by an insignificant author. However, nothing can make up for a book's being in poor condition, a fate which has befallen a large number of paperbacks.

For a detailed listing, I recommend consulting Kevin Hancer's *Hancer's Price Guide to Paperback Books, Third Edition* (Wallace-Homestead, 1990, out-of-print) and Jon Warren's *The Official Price Guide to Paperbacks* (House of Collectibles, 1991). Both are organized by company first and then issue number. Hence, when trying to locate a book, publisher and code number are more important than author and title.

The vast majority of paperbacks sell in the 50¢ to $2.50 range.

PAPER CLIPS

Oversized paper clips were once popular advertising giveaways. Early examples consisted of a celluloid button, similar to a pinback button, with advertising on the front attached to a large metal spring clip. These are the most desirable and highly sought after by collectors.

Advertising, LF Grammes & Sons, Allentown, PA, brass, bell-shaped, inscribed design with colonial woman's portrait, 3.125" x 2.125" 25

Advertising, RC Cola, brass, emb "Drink Royal Crown, Reg US Pat Off, RC Cola, Because It's Good, Good Luck," debossed horseshoe on thumb lift, 2" x 1.5" 10

Advertising, Rexall Drugs, red plastic, nose-shaped, giveaway from Hendon Drug Co, St Paul, MN, 2.5" h 5

Advertising, Starr Egg Carriers and Trays, celluloid button with multicolor product image, 1.75" d 125

Advertising, "Steckley's Lincoln, Nebr - DeWitt IA.," celluloid button with large ear of corn with "Genetic Giant" superimposed over silhouette map of the Americas, yellow ground, 1.75" d . .125

Automatic Safety File, silvertone metal with foliate design, mkd "Automatic Safety File Ptd Apr 1915 USA," 4.25" l . .25

Figural, bug, goldtone metal, green enameled body with flat stones on back, red cabochon eyes, 1.75" x 1.5" . .25

PAPER DOLLS

Paper dolls have already been through one craze cycle and appear to be in the midst of another. The publication of Mary Young's *A Collector's Guide To Magazine Paper Dolls: An Identification & Value Guide* (Collector Books, 1990) is one indication of the craze. It also introduces a slightly different approach to the subject than the traditional paper doll book.

The best way to collect paper dolls is in uncut books, sheets, and boxed sets. Dolls that have been cut out, but still have all their clothing and accessories, sell for fifty percent or less of their uncut value.

Paper doll collectors have no desire to play with their dolls. They just want to admire them and enjoy the satisfaction of owning them.

Club: The Original Paper Doll Artists Guild, P.O. Box 14, Kingfield, ME 04947, www.opdag.com.

Amanda Goes West, Texas Tech Press, 1983 10

Annie Oakley Cut-Out Dolls, Whitman, 10.25" x 12" 20

Baby Tender Love, Whitman, 1971 10

Barbie Boutique, Whitman, 1973 30

Barbie Design a Fashion Paper Doll, 1979 10

Beverly Hillbillies, Whitman, 1964 40

Boots and Her Buddies, Saalfield, #2460, 1943 25

Bride Originals, 1991 5
Colonial Williamsburg, Williamsburg Restoration, 1967, set of 8 .... .38
Daisy and Donald, Whitman, 1978 .... .20
Debbie Reynolds, Whitman, 1955 .... .65
Denim Deb, Whitman, 1977 8
Dodie, Artcraft, 1971 .... .30
Doll Wedding, Athena Publishing, 1976 ... .10
Dream Girl, Merrill, 1947 .... .15
Elly May, Watkins Strathmore, 1963 ...... .60
Family Affair, 1968 .... .65
Fashion Photo Barbie and PJ, Whitman, 1978 .... .25
First Date Paper Dolls, Merrill, 1944 ..... .170
First Family, Dell, 1981 .... .12
Flying Nun, Artcraft, 1972 .... .30
Four Playmates, Lowe, 1944 .... .30
Girl Friends, Whitman, 1944 .... .150
Good Neighbor, Saalfield, 1944 .... .110
Hopi Indian and Clothes .... .22
Janet Lennon, Whitman, 1959 .... .45
Julia, Whitman, 1971 .... .30
June Allyson, Whitman, 1955 .... .125
Lennon Sisters, Whitman, 1958 .... .70
Malibu Skipper, Whitman, 1973 .... .16
Marge's Little Lulu Doll Book, Whitman, #1970, ©1971, 6 pgs, 7.25" x 15.5", unused .... .40
Merry Mermaids, Reuben H Lilja .... .44
Mickey and Minnie, Whitman, 1977 ...... .18
Molly Dolly, Lowe, 1965 .... .24
Mother Goose Characters, Merrimack Publishing, 1960s-70s, set of 4 .... .40
My Little Margie, Saalfield .... .50
Nanny and the Professors, Artcraft, 1970 .... .35
Nixon Ladies, Saalfield, 1969 .... .24

Oklahoma Paper Dolls, Whitman, 1956 ... .65
Partridge Family, Artcraft, 1971 .... .45
Pat Boone, Whitman, 1959 .... .45
Patti Page, Lowe, 1958 .... .140
Pebbles & Bamm Bamm, Hanna Barbera, 1964 .... .45
Princess Caroline of Monaco, Sandy Williams, 1979 6
Queen Elizabeth II, Sandy Williams, 1978 6
Raggedy Ann, Whitman, 1970 .... .24
Simply Sam, Whitman, 1980 4
Snow White, Peck-Gandre, 1987 8
Susan Dey, Laurie of The Partridge Family, Artcraft, 1971 .... .90
Teddy Bear, Crystal Collins, 1983 .... .10
Teen Town Paper Dolls, Merrill, 1946 .... .165
That Girl, Saalfield, 1967 .... .40
The Munsters, Whitman, 1966 .... .50
The Victorian Parlor, Dover, 1975 .... .10
The Waltons, Whitman, 1975 .... .20
Welcome Back Kotter, Toy Factory, 1970s .... .25
White House Party Dresses, Merrill, #1550, ©1961 .... .35

PAPERWEIGHTS

This is a tough category. Learning to tell the difference between modern and antique paperweights takes years. Your best approach at a flea market is to treat each weight as modern. If you get lucky and pay modern paperweight prices for an antique weight, you are ahead. If you pay antique prices for a modern paperweight, you lose and lose big.

Paperweights divide into antique (prior to 1945) and modern. Modern breaks down into early modern (1945 to 1980) and contemporary (1980 and later). There is a great deal of speculation going on in the area of contemporary paperweights. It is not a place for amateurs or those with money they can ill afford to lose. If you are not certain, do not buy.

Clubs: International Paperweight Society, 761 Chestnut St., Santa Cruz, CA 95060, www.paperweight.com/; Paperweight Collectors Assoc., Inc., P.O. Box 40, Barker, TX 77413.

ADVERTISING

"Aikin, Lambert & Co, New York City," glass, rect, black and white, fountain pen point, 1" x 2.5" x 4" 100

"Babcock Printing Press Mfg Co, New London, Conn," glass, rect, black and white engraving style illus of printing press titled "The Optimus," 1" x 2.5" x 4" 65

"Boston Safe Deposit and Trust Company, Boston, Mass," glass, oval, red and black lettering listing bank services, 1" x 2.5" x 4.25" 45

"Burdett-Rowntree Mfg Co, Dumbwaiter Guides," steel with chrome-like luster, U-shaped, incised black lettering, 1" h, 2.25" w, 1" d .18

"Burlington Venetian Blind Co, Burlington, VT," glass, rect, black and white image of Venetian blind, .75" x 2.5" x 4" 70

"Consolidated Ice Co," hollowed white metal, figural polar bear reclining on ice formation, c1930s, 3.5" h 50

"Dayton Ball & Co, Albany, NY, Manufacturers of Lasts," glass, rect, black and white image of shoe last, .75" x 2.5" x 4" 60

"Geo W Fulton & Co, Paterson, NJ, Tapestries, Interior Decorations, Etc," glass, rect, black and white inscriptions and art, .75" x 2.5" x 4" 50

"Groton Bridge And M'F'G Co," Groton, NY, glass, rect, black and white image of factory and listing of products, .75 x 2.5" x 4" 55

"Hartley Grain Co, October 14, 1901," glass, rect, black and white photo of farm grain service structure and office building, 1" x 2.5" x 4" 40

"John A Griffith & Co, Inc, Tailors' Trimmings," glass, round, flattened base, 1933 Century of Progress World's Fair souvenir, 3" d 50

"John W Pechin & Bro, Philadelphia, PA, Oak Belting," glass, round, black and white logo, 3" d, .75" h 30

"Jones, McDuffee & Stratton," Boston & Chicago, glass, rect, black and white engraving style illus of tall office building rising from busy street corner, 1" x 2.5" x 4" 35

"MM Rhodes & Sons Co, Taunton, Mass, Shoe Buttons," glass, rect, black and white logo of shoe button hanging from cross, 1" x 2.5" x 4" 75

"PP Van Vleet, President, Van Vleet Mansfield Drug Co, Memphis, Tenn," glass, rect, black and white photo portrait, 1" x 2.5" x 4" 30

"Shackamaxon Worsted Co," glass, rect, domed, black and white engraving style illus of factory building, 3.5" d, 2" h 45

"Thomas Potter, Sons & Co, Philadelphia-New York-Boston, Oil Cloth, Linoleum & Rubber," glass, oval, black and white logo, maroon and black lettering, 1" x 2.5" x 4.25" 60

"Union Trust Company, Springfield, Mass, Springfield's Leading Commercial Bank," glass, rect, arcade style int partially tinted in subtle colors, 1" x 3" x 4.25" . . .30

"Vulcan Rail & Construction Company," hollowed brass, figural aproned worker holding hammer resting on anvil, 1920-30s, 3" h, 2" x 2.5" contoured base .48

"Waite, Thresher Company, Providence, RI," glass, rect, black and white image of display trunk mkd "The Celebrated Case" with gold and silver jewelry and thimbles, 1" x 2.5" x 4" 70

"Walter J Moses & Co, Beauty Rice," New York City, glass, rect, image of white rice grains on blue ground, gold lettering, 1" x 2.5" x 4" 20

"William E Bixby & Co, Haverhill, Mass, Dealers in Cut Straw and Leather Board," glass, rect, black and white portraits of William E and George M Bixby, .75" x 2.5" x 4" 55

OTHER

American, magnum patriotic with a pr of US flags over an upright red and green lily, surrounded by 4 speckled lilies, unfinished pontil, 4.5" d 325

American, turtle whimsy with a brown turtle with articulated legs inside a hollow molded glass dome, green felt base, late 19th/early 20th C, 3" d 165

Bohemian, butterfly composed of blue and pink millefiori wings within a low dome on clear ground, 3.25" d 120

Bohemian-Czechoslovakian, 3D sulphide of a male lion resting on speckled green ground next to a green palm tree and encircled by a border of looped orange ribbons, high dome with allover geometric facets, 3.25" dia 500

John Ford and Company, Duke of Wellington ftd sulphide with the cameo centered over clear ground, 3.5" d 450

Nailsea-Stourbridge, green bottle glass with a column of 3 petunias, 1 atop the other, growing from a pot, 4" h, 3" d . . .415

New England Glass Co, red double poinsettia with a flower with 2 tiers of pointed petals around a complex cane center, growing on a stem with 5 green leaves, in a double-swirl white latticinio basket, 3" d 1,000

St Clair, pink flowers with air pocket centers on green and white ground 60

Whitefriars, concentric millefiori pied-ouche composed of a blue and white floret cane center encircled by canes in aqua, ruby, blue, and white in a basket of white staves, clear ftd base, 2.5" h, 3" d 500

PARKING METERS

I have seen them for sale. I have even been tempted to buy one. The meter was a lamp base, complete with new lamp wiring and an attractive shade. To make the light work, you put a coin in the meter. I'm not sure why, but they are rather pricey, usually in the $50 to $100 range. Maybe it has something to do with the fine that you will pay if you obtain one illegally. Might be a good idea to stash a few coin-operated meters away.

PATRIOTIC COLLECTIBLES

Americans love symbols. We express our patriotism through eagles, flags and shields, the Liberty Bell, Statue of Liberty, and Uncle Sam. We even throw in a few patriots, such as Benjamin Franklin.

Club: Statue of Liberty Collectors' Club, 26601 Bernwood Rd., Cleveland, OH 44122, www.statueoflibertyclub.com/.

Note: For addition listings see Flags and Flag Collectibles.

Candy Container, drum, litho tin, red, white, and blue, print by John Kranz, Chicago, mkd "Made in Germany," 3.5" h, 13" d 65

Catalog, Detra Flag Company, #24, New York and Los Angeles, 1941, 6.5" x 9" . .100

Child's Book, *The Notable History of Abraham Lincoln,* Lincoln on cov speaking to Union troops, printed by Donohue – Henneberry – Chicago 65

Clock, Uncle Sam, pot metal, United Clock Co, commemorates Roosevelt's involvement in NATO, c1944, 11.5" h, 13" w, ...315

Comic Book, *Captain America's Bicentennial Battles,* Vol 1, #1, Marvel Comics Group, 1976 20

Cookie Cutter, eagle, tin, 6.5" l 85

Creamer, Uncle Sam, Royal Winton, c1920 75

Doll, Uncle Sam, composition, cloth body with silk pin-striped pants and cummerbund, felt tail coat, orig tag reads "Kimcraft American Type Dolls, Independence, MO," 10" h 225

Dresser Scarf, embroidered Uncle Sam's top hat, c1940 18

Figure, Uncle Sam, celluloid, mkd "Made in USA" on back, 7" h 250

Game, Heroes of America, Games of the Nations Series, Paul Educational Games, box with flag illus, 1920s 30

Jigsaw Puzzle, hound dog dressed as Uncle Sam, Wolverine World-Wide, 19" x 12.75" 12

Magazine Tear Sheet, "Greyhound Presents A Great New Super-Coach," Uncle Sam waving at bus, 1939 15

Pillow Cover, silk, 48-star flag, "Tennessee Maneuvers – 1944" and poem to Mother and Dad in shield, red and blue flocking, white ground, red fringed border, 17.5" sq 35

Pitcher, Uncle Sam, ceramic, polychromed dec, mkd on base "Uncle Sam Genuine Staffordshire…, Shorter & (?), England," c1900-20s, 5.75" h 10

Planter, figural top ht, molded polyceramic, red, white, and blue, Ruben's Originals, 1974 15

Postcard, bust of Uncle Sam front, story of Samuel Wilson on back, Yankee Colour Corp, 1966 .10

Postcard, Independence Hall, Philadelphia, sepiatone 5

Statue, Statue of Liberty, goldtone metal, 4.5" h 10

Still Bank, Uncle Sam, ceramic, white base, brown-painted rim around hat . . .55

PEANUTS

Peanuts is a newspaper cartoon strip written and illustrated by Charles M. Schulz. The strip started about 1950 and starred a boy named Charlie Brown and his dog, Snoopy. Its popularity grew slowly. In 1955, merchandising was begun with the hope of expanding the strip's popularity. By the 1970s Charlie Brown and the gang were more than just cartoon strip characters. They greeted every holiday with TV specials; their images adorned lunch boxes, pencils, pins, T-shirts, and stuffed toys.

While Peanuts collectibles have been gaining momentum over the years, Charles Schulz's recent death has triggered a temporary increase in values.

Club: Peanuts Collector Club, Inc., 539 Sudden Valley, Bellingham, WA 98226, http://www.peanutscollectorclub.com/.

Banner, felt, Snoopy lying on doghouse, "The Secret To Life Is To Reduce Your Worries To A Minimum," red and black, 34" l 38
Book, *A Charlie Brown Thanksgiving,* Charles Schulz, 1975 4
Book, *Charlie Brown Dictionary,* Scholastic Book Services, 400 pgs, 1975 14
Book, *Charlie Brown's All Stars,* Charles Schulz, 1966 10
Book, *Charlie Brown's Super Book of Things To Do,* Charles Schulz 10
Book, *Good Grief Charlie Brown,* Charles Schulz, 1967 5
Book, *Good Ol' Charlie Brown,* Rinehart Co, 128 pgs, 1957, 5" x 8" 25
Book, *Here Comes Snoopy,* Charles M Schulz, Fawcett, c1958 18
Book, *Peanuts Jubilee, My Life and Art with Charlie Brown and Others,* Charles M Schulz, 1976 10
Book, *Peanuts Revisited,* Charles M Schulz, Rinehart & Co, 1959 5
Book, *Think About It Tomorrow, Snoopy,* Fawcett Crest Books, 1st printing, 1980 3
Bracelet, enameled figures of Snoopy . . .32
Comic Book, *Peanuts,* Charlie Brown reading upside down book seated next to Snoopy with nose in air, Dell, 1958 20
Comic Book, *Peanuts,* Charlie Brown rollerskating beside Snoopy on skateboard, Dell, 1962 25
Cookie Jar, 12" h 45
Doll, Charlie Brown, stuffed, 1963, 18" h . .28
Doll, Charlie Brown Pocket Doll, 6.75" h, 1966 55
Doll, Snoopy, stuffed, plush, wearing color fabric Santa outfit, Determined Products, 1968, 15" h 20
Doll, Snoopy astronaut, vinyl, fabric uniform, plastic helmet, ©1969, 7.5" h . .50
Figure, Batter Up Charlie Brown, 1972 50
Figure, Charlie Brown, wearing baseball cap, vinyl, Pocket Pal 55
Figure, Charlie Brown golfing with Snoopy, 4.5" h 25
Figure, Fun in the Sun, 7.5" h 22
Figure, Lucy, molded plastic, painted, United Features, Hungerford, 1950s, 9" h 115
Figure, Snoopy, camping out, musical 25
Figure, Snoopy, on skateboard, plastic, Aviva, 1966 30
Figure, Snoopy, wearing tuxedo, vinyl 50
Figure, Snoopy, WWI Flying Ace, molded plastic, brown helmet, blue scarf, 1966, 7.25" h 70
Keychain, Charlie Brown at stone wall 5
Keychain, Charlie Brown kicking a football 10
Light Switch Plate, "Snoopy's Disappearing Light Trick" 15
Limited Edition Plate, Christmas Eve at the Doghouse, Peanuts Christmas Series, Schmid, 1973 95
Limited Edition Plate, Home Is Where The Heart Is, Peanuts Valentine's Day Series, Schmid, 1977 35
Lunch Box, metal 45
Movie Poster, *A Boy Named Charlie Brown,* 1969 125
Movie Poster, *Bon Voyage Charlie Brown,* 1980 85
Movie Poster, *Race for Your Life Charlie Brown,* 1977 150
Mug, ceramic, Lucy being crowned Miss New Jersey while Sally and Peppermint Patti look on, smiling Snoopy announcer, unused, c1965, 3.5" h 20

Ornament, Charlie Brown, Going Up?, Hallmark, 1998 10
Ornament, Charlie Brown and snowman, Hallmark, 1993 28
Pennant, felt, Snoopy, "I Think I'm Allergic To Morning," 1968, 15" x 33" ...40
Pez Dispenser, Charlie Brown 4
Play Set, Good Ol' Charlie Brown, Memory Lane 30
Snow Globe, Charlie Brown and his girlfriend in globe, Snoopy outside on dock 38
Snow Globe, miniature, Charlie Brown playing soccer 12
Snow Globe, "The Doctor Is In" scene ...40

PEDAL CARS

Pedal car is a generic term used to describe any pedal-driven toy. Automobiles were only one form. There are also pedal airplanes, fire engines, motorcycles, and tractors.

By the mid-1910s pedal cars resembling their full-sized counterparts were being made. Buick, Dodge, Overland, and Packard are just a few examples. American National, Garton, Gendron, Steelcraft, and Toledo Wheel were the five principal pedal car manufacturers in the 1920s and 30s. Ertl, Garton, and Murray made pedal cars in the post-1945 period. Many mail-order catalogs, e.g., Sears, Roebuck, sold pedal cars. Several television shows issued pedal car licenses during the mid-1950s and 60s.

Pedal car collecting is serious business in the 1990s. The $10,000 barrier has been broken. Many pedal cars are being stripped down and completely restored to look as though they just came off the assembly line. Some feel this emphasis, especially when it destroys surviving paint, goes too far.

American National, Auburn Roadster, 1935, 66" l 5,500
American National, Chrysler Air Flow, c1935, 51" l 12,500
American National, Fire Ladder #2, full spring rear suspension, ladders restored, 1920s, 72" l 5,500
American National, Fire Truck, with hose reel, 2 passenger, fire boots and helmet, restored, c1935, 70" l ...4,400
American National, Lincoln Tandem, "Skippy Line," 1935, 66" l 5,500
American National, Shark Nose Graham, "Skippy Line," c1938, 48" l 5,000
American National, Spirit of St Louis, tri-motor bi-wing, restored, c1932, 63" l, 36" wingspan 5,000
Garton, Lincoln Zephyr, restored, 1937, 45" l 4,500
Garton, Stutz, c1934, 47" l 4,200
Gendron, Fire Chief, restored, c1927, 50" l 5,200
Gendron, Race Car #6, c1924, 53" l 4,000
Gendron, Packard Rumble Seat Roadster, c1928, 68" l 6,270
Gendron, Pontiac Sedan, "Skippy Line," c1935, 45" l 4,000
Gendron, Sunbeam No. 8, c1932, 70" l 4,000
Marmon, Wasp #32 1,500
Murray, Champion Straight Side, hard rubber wheels and pedals, professionally restored, 22" h, 15" w, 34" 1,325
Steelcraft, American Express Delivery Truck, screened back panels, restored, 64" l 6,000
Steelcraft, dump truck, "High Speed Oil Co. No. 40, Mark 5," restored, c1929, 62" l 3,200
Steelcraft, dump truck, Mack 2.5 ton, pneumatic tires, restored, 1930s, 50" l 4,000
Toledo Wheel Goods, locomotive, "Fast Mail," orig paint and stenciling, 1920s, 41.5" l 3,500

PENCIL CLIPS

A pencil clip has a celluloid button with a metal pencil holder and was used to hold a pencil in one's pocket. They were a popular advertising premium in the first half of the twentieth century. Unfortunately, the form is seldom used today. After seeing several hundred examples, I think they should be missed.

7-Up, orange, black, and white logo, green rim 10
Carey's Salt, white lettering on red ground, .75" d 12
Carstairs Whiskey, logo with white seal balancing a red ball against dark blue ground, c1940s, 1.5" h 15
District 751 Machinists & Aerospace Workers, rocket and jet images, red, white, and blue 14
Fleer's Candy Coated Gum, "Remember!," light blue and white lettering on yellow ground, 1950s, 1.5" h 30
Morton Salt, "It Pours!," blue and white, 1.5" l 12
Reddy Kilowatt, Reddy and electric socket 10
Reddy Kilowatt, Reddy wearing a military hat and running through a Victory "V," 1942, .875" d 10
Sterling Oils, logo at center, orange and yellow 10
Vote UAW, black lettering on white ground, .875" d 5

PENCIL SHARPENERS

Pencil sharpeners divide into two distinct groups: (1) mechanical counter, desk, and wall models and (2) miniature hand-held novelty sharpeners. The first group is expensive, the second still affordable.

When buying a mechanical sharpener, make certain it is complete. The period box and instruction sheet add value.

Novelty sharpeners were produced in vast quantities. Comparison shopping keeps the cost low. Do not buy any example that is not in fine or better condition.

16mm Film Projector, zinc-alloy bronzed . . .5
1917, Auto Convertible, red bronze, 1.75" x 2.75" x 2", ...25
1917, Model A, bronzed metal 15
1919, Dandy Pencil Sharpener, Automatic Pencil Sharpener Company, 4.25" h, 8" l 150
Aircraft Carrier, bronzed metal, 5" l 8
Antique General Store Balance Sheets, bronzed metal, 2" h 6
Antique Table Fan, bronzed metal, 2.75" h . .6
Bi-Plane, cast bronze, 1920s, 3" x 3.5" 50
Coffee Grinder, metal, 3" h 8
Conestoga Wagon, bronzed metal with plastic top, 2.5" l 6
Dinosaur, bronzed metal 10
Early Explorer's Sailing Vessel, diecast metal, 3.5" h, 3.5" l 5
Elderly Chinese Man, metal 15
Fire Fighter, metal, 3.5" 6
German Cuckoo Clock, metal with copper finish, 1940s-50s, 2.25" h, 1.25" w 50
Globe, in traditional holder with tripod legs, diecast metal, 3" h 6
Grandfather Clock, diecast metal 6
Grand Piano, with music sheet, metal, 2" x 2" 8
Gun, metal, Japan, pre-1950, 1.75" 10
Horse and Covered Wagon, metal, 3.75" . . .6
Human Skull, hinged jawbone, diecast metal, 2" h 6
Lantern, metal, 3" h 10
Motorcycle, bronzed metal, 3.75" l 6
Parrot, plastic, 1.75" l, 1960s 6
Record Player, diecast metal 6
Remington Typewriter, diecast metal 10
Steamboat, diecast metal 6

Student Lamp, bronzed metal, removable shade, 3" h 6
Train, diecast metal 6
US *Columbia* Spacecraft, metal, 3.25" l 8
Volkswagen Bug, bronzed metal, 3.5" l 8

PENNANTS

Pennants were produced in large enough quantities for collectors to be picky. Buy pennants only if they are in good condition. Images and lettering should be crisp and the pennant should show no signs of moth or insect damage.

When storing pennants, keep them flat or roll them on a cylinder. Do not fold! Creases left from years of folding can be very difficult to remove.

American Freedom Train, Bicentennial Celebration, 29.5" l 12
Anti-Axis, Australian soldier and sailor riding a kangaroo, spearing a running enemy soldier, "Target For 1943, AUS-USA, from The Boys Down Under," made in Australia 100
Beatles, yellow felt, John, Paul, George and Ringo with copies of their signatures, 18" l 100
Boston Celtics, 1983-84 World Basketball Champions, 30" l, 12" h 20
Buffalo, New York, 8.5" x 26" 10
California, synthetic blend material, mid-1970s, 29.5" l .10
Columbia University, tobacco felt, 1908, 5" x 8" 8
Corpus Christi, Texas, 15" l, 1970s 10
Daytona, "Pedro's South of the Border," 26.5" l, 12" h 30
Disneyland, Cinderella's Castle, cotton felt, 24" l, mid-1970s 20
Los Angeles Olympic Stadium, dark blue felt, white spine, color image of stadium with football game in progress, "Los Angeles Calif.," 1930s, 23" l 125
New York City, China Town, red, yellow and green, dragon, China house, and Chinese writing 25
Oakland Athletics, 1988, celebrates the American League Western Division Champions, lists manager and players, 30" l, 12" h 20
Pittsburgh Pirates Championship, black felt, gold spine and streamers, color team photo framed within a gold pirate's hat and neckerchief, gold lettering "Pittsburgh Pirates," 1960, 29" l 335
St Louis Cardinals, mkd "Official License Major League Baseball," 30" l, 12" h . . .20
Super Bowl XVII, Rose Bowl 1983, celebrates 17th Super Bowl held at the Rose Bowl, Pasadena, CA, 30" l, 12" h 20
Toronto Blue Jays, blue jay with maple leaf, "Toronto Blue Jays," 30" l, 12" h . . .20
Universal Studios, Hollywood, 1970s, 24" l 15
Universal Studios, Hollywood, in the shape of Frankenstein, 1970s, 20" h 15
Venice, Italy, Ponte Di Rialto, pre-WWII, cotton, waterway and bridge of Venice with a gondola, 11" l, 6" h 10
World Series, Cleveland Indians, red felt, gold spine and streamers, color image of Indian chief, white scroll with players' names in black, white lettering "Cleveland Indians World Series 1948," few minor glue spots on reverse, 29.5" l .550

PENNSBURY POTTERY

Henry and Lee Below established Pennsbury Pottery, named for its close proximity to William Penn's estate, in 1950. The Belows had previously worked for Stangl Pottery, thus the similarity in styles.

Pennsbury motifs are heavily nostalgic, farm and Pennsylvania German oriented. The pottery made a large number of commemorative, novelty, and special-order pieces. Many of these relate to businesses and events in the Middle Atlantic States, thus commanding their highest price within that region.

Pennsbury Pottery was sold at auction in December, 1970.

Look-Alike Alert: The Lewis Brothers Pottery, Trenton, New Jersey, purchased fifty of the lesser Pennsbury molds. Although they were supposed to remove the Pennsbury name from the molds, some molds were overlooked. Further, two Pennsbury employees moved to Lewis Brothers when Pennsbury closed. Many pieces similar in feel and design to Pennsbury were produced. Many of Pennsbury's major lines, including the Harvest and Rooster patterns, plaques, birds, and highly unusual molds, were not reproduced.

Ashtray, Amish, "Don't Be So Doppich," 5" d 8
Ashtray, Amish, "Dutch Haven Pretzel & Root Beer," 5" d .20
Ashtray, Amish, "What Giffs? What Ouches You?," 5" d .8

Ashtray, commemorative, Fairless Iron Works 8
Beer Mug, Barbershop Quartet, 5" h 10
Bird, Audubon Warbler, #122 175
Bowl, Red Rooster, 6.5" d 10
Candy Dish, Hex, 6" x 6" 15
Chip and Dip Set, Tree Tops, holly motif, 11" d 60
Christmas Plate, Angel, 1970, 8" d 15
Cookie Jar, Red Rooster, 8" h 95
Creamer, Amish, 4" h 18
Eggcup, Red Rooster, 4" h 20
Figure, chick sitting on a gourd 25
Ladle, Black Rooster, 11" l 20
Oil and Vinegar, Amish, "Vee get too soon old...Vinegar," "...undt too late schmart...Oil" 30
Pie Plate, boy and girl, "Whispered Words beneath the Bower, holding hands at some late hour, usually lead as you well know, to raising young one's crops and dough," 9" d 45
Pitcher, Amish, 2.5" h 12
Pitcher, Amish, 6" h .18
Pitcher, Eagle and Shield, 7" h 75
Plate, Courting Buggy, 8" d 35
Plate, Hex, 8" d 5
Pretzel Bowl, family of farmers, 11.5" x 8.5" 65
Pretzel Bowl, Gay Nineties 45
Pretzel Bowl, Red Barn, 12" x 8" 25
Pretzel Plate, "Here's Looking at You," 11.5" x 8.5" 65
Salt and Pepper Shakers, Red Rooster, with tray, 2.5" h shakers, 5" x 4" tray 20
Serving Dish, Rooster, divided, 9.5" l, 6" w, 2.5" h 35
Snack Set, Black Rooster 25
Teapot, Black Rooster, 8" h 35
Tray, commemorative, National Newark and Essex Banking Co 1804–1954, ship motif, 7.5" x 5.5" 15

Tray, commemorative, Pennsylvania RR 1856, "Tiger" below train motif, 7.75" x 5.5" 5
Wall Plaque, commemorative, Centennial Anniversary of the National Education Association, 1957 .15

PENS & PENCILS

Forget the ordinary and look for the unusual. The more unique the object or set is, the more likely it is that it will have a high value. Defects of any kind drop value dramatically. When buying a set, try to get the original box along with any instruction sheets and guarantee cards (you will be amazed at how many people actually save them).

Clubs: American Pencil Collectors Society, 640 Evergreen Dr., Mountain View, WY 82939; Pen Collectors of America, P.O. Box 821449, Houston, TX 77282.

PENS

Barrington, malacite colors with black, gold-filled trim, heavy build, original wood box 15
Carters, #1125, solid orange, gold-filled trim, lever filler 132
Century, red and white marbled, gold-filled trim, lever filler, black caps 85
Conklin, chased black hard rubber, gold-filled trim, Crescent filler 77
Conklin, red and black marbled, self-filling 205
Eclipse, orange chased hard rubber, gold-filled trim, lever filler 22
Moore, #72, green marbled, gold-filled trim, lever filler 25
Parker, Deluxe Challenger, yellow pearl marbled, nickel plated trim, button filler 35
Parker, Duofold, jade green, gold-filled trim, button filler .40
Parker, green, cream, and gold stone marbled, gold-plated trim, button filler 275
Parker, Lucky Curve, Jack Knife Safety pen, black hard rubber, eye dropper filled, 1912 patent date 198
Parker, Parkette, green and black marbled, gold-plated trim, lever filler . . .10
Pick Pen Co, purple and black marbled, gold-filled trim, lever filler 8
Sheaffer, #875, golden brown Radite, gold-filled trim, vacuum filler 15
Swan, MT & Co, "Eternal," blue lapis, lever filler 110
Wahl, Eversharp, black hard rubber, Greek key design, gold-filled trim 14
Wahl, gold-filled mounted, lever filler 88
Wahl, Tempoint, black chased hard rubber, gold-filled trim, lever filler, 1904 44
Wasp, Vacuum Fill, green and maroon swirl, gold-plated trim, lever filler 10
Waterman, green and yellow ripple 120
Weidlich, black and blue marbled, gold-plated trim, lever filler 28

PENCILS

Century Pen Co, black and cream marbled, gold-filled trim 50
Century Pen Co, green marbled, gold-filled trim, 1926 .33
Century Pen Co, silver-plated metal, herringbone design 40
Conklin, silver-plated metal, 1920 6
Eagle Pencil Co, #1025, mechanical, 1939 New York World's Fair souvenir, wood, orig box 40
Moore, red hard rubber, gold-filled trim, 1925 14
Parker, green pearl 15
Parker, Parkette, burgundy marbled, gold-plated trim, Kantor Bottling Company adv 10
Parker, red plastic on metal, gold-filled trim, worn 15
Ronson, Penciliter, dark blue and chrome 40
Salz, black and cream marbled, gold-filled trim 5
Sheaffer, Lifetime Demonstrator, nickel-plated metal, cut-outs in body show mechanics of pencil 40
Sheaffer, pearl and black 8
Wahl, Eversharp, gold-filled mounted 10

PEN/PENCIL COMBINATION

Century, black and cream marbled, gold-filled trim, lever filler 132

Newbanker, brown and cream swirl, red trim, gold metal mounted, lever filler . . .40

Sheaffer, #5-30, black, gold-filled trim, lever filler 35

PEPSI-COLA

Caleb D. Bradham, a pharmacist and drugstore owner in New Bern, North Carolina, developed "Brad's Drink," a soda mix, in the mid-1890s. By 1898, Brad's Drink had become Pepsi-Cola. Six years later he sold his first franchise.

Pepsi-Cola's fortunes soared in 1933 when the company doubled its bottle size and held its price to a nickel. Pepsi challenged Coca-Cola for the number one spot in the soda market. One of the most popular advertising jingles of the 1950s was "Pepsi-Cola Hits The Spot, Twelve Full Ounces That's A Lot."

Beware of a wide range of Pepsi-Cola reproductions, copycats, fantasy items, and fakes. A Pepsi and Pete pillow issued in the 1970s, a Pepsi glass-front clock, and a 12" high ceramic statue of a woman holding a glass of Pepsi are a few examples.

Club: Pepsi-Cola Collectors Club, P.O. Box 817, Claremont, CA 91711, www.pepsigifts.com/pcccinfo.html.

Bottle Rack and Display, metal, 3-tier, blue rack, sign panels with red "Pepsi-Cola" on blue and white ground on sides at each tier, blue metal parts and hardware restored, 1940s, 42" h, 18" w, 12" d 358

Carton, 6-pack, 1960s, 8" x 9" x 5" 25

Cash Register Topper, "Purity...Pepsi-Cola...In The Big, Big Bottle," red, white, and blue, emb diecut cardboard with orig wooden base and counterfeit bill information on back, c1940 468

Clock, "say Pepsi, please" and bottle cap on yellow and white ground, double bubble light-up clock, 1954, 15" d 578

Door Handle, "Drink Pepsi-Cola, Bigger - Better" on rect back plate, red, white, and blue, Bakelite handle, narrow version, 1940s, 12" h 145

Fan Pull, cop carrying 6-pack of bottles, diecut, 2-sided, c1941, 7" h 825

Matchbook, Disney/Pepsi-Cola Set, Type I (10 lines of inside type), gray, National Match Co, 1942, 2nd Signal Armored Battalion, No. 23, Indian playing with tank 12

Mirror, "Pepsi-Cola" bottle cap with "Bigger..." above and "...Better" below, lower half is mirror, rect, modern frame, 1930s-40s, 12" h, 4" w, 8.5" 330

Scorekeeper, football and baseball, heavy cardboard, 2-sided, 1940, 13" x 29" 550

Serving Tray, bottle cap, red, white, and blue, 1940s, 13" d 230

Sign, "Big, Big Glass" in black, glass of soda, bottle cap, and "5¢" in red circle on blue-gray and white ground, celluloid over tin over cardboard, 9" d .440

Sign, "Drink Pepsi-Cola Bigger-Better," red and blue lettering on blue and white ground, oval, heavy cardboard, 1-sided string hanger, 1938, 5" h, 8" w .165

Sign, "Ice Cold" and "Sold Here" in white on black ground, "Pepsi-Cola" in red on white ground in center, celluloid over tin over cardboard, 1940s, 9" d 255

Sign, "Pepsi-Cola," neon, red lettering in blue oval ring, orig rusty metal frame, 1930s-40s, 19" h, 28" w 880

Sign, "Pepsi-Cola," red, white, and blue bottle cap, celluloid over tin over cardboard, 9" d 160

Sign, "Pepsi taste beats the others cold!" in white, smiling black woman wearing pink sweater and hoop earrings and holding soda bottle, red ground, gold rim, oval, celluloid over tin over cardboard, 1970s, 10" h, 8" w . . .88

Thermometer, soda bottle with "Bigger" above and "Better" below, thermometer at left, white lettering, dark blue ground, rect, litho tin, c1940s, 16" h, 6" w 440

Trolley Sign, 2 cops, 1 holding oversized bottle and saying "I make sure you get a big, big bottle – 12 full ounces," other holding glass and soda bottle and saying "I make sure it's wholesome and grand tasting," "5¢, Worth A Dime" below, yellow ground, 1941, 11" h, 21" w 775

PERFUME BOTTLES

Perfume bottles come in all shapes and sizes. In addition to perfume bottles, there are atomizers (a bottle with a spray mechanism), colognes (large bottles whose stoppers often have an application device), scents (small bottles used to hold a scent or smelling salts), and vinaigrettes (ornamental boxes or bottles with a perforated top). The stopper of a perfume is used for application and is very elongated.

Today's collectors are also interested in commercial bottles. They enjoy the pretty shapes and colors as well as the sexy names.

Clubs: International Perfume Bottle Assoc., 3314 Shamrock Rd., Tampa, FL 33629, www.perfumebottles.org; Miniature Perfume Bottle Collectors, 28227 Paseo El Siena, Laguna Niguel, CA 92677.

Art Glass, clear, curlicue top, 6.75" h 35

Art Glass, violet blue shading to clear, Quintessence Glass Studios, 1996, 4.5" h 80

Baccarat, atomizer, amethyst panels, clear cut daisies, acid-etched mark, 5.875" h 125

Balbani, "Chypre Egyptian," bottle by Dépinoix, gold colored, Egyptian bird motif, 3.75" h 800

Bavarian, porcelain, floral design with gold trim 15

Bichara "Myrbaha," designed c1913, bottle by Baccarat, 4" h 635

British Depression, blue 45

Bryenne, "Chu Chin Chow," designed by GK Benda, c1918, in the form of a seated Chinese man, 1.5" h 460

Byblas Italian Perfume, cobalt blue with brown plastic flower disk top, 1.5" x 1.75" 15

Caron Bellodgia, mkd "Bellodgia Caron 1 fl oz Paris France" 25

Ciro, "Le Chevalier de la Nuit," designed by Julien Viard, 1923, frosted glass, in the form of a knight's armored torso, stopper is a plumed helmet, 7.75" h . . .345

Fenton, glass, Dusty Rose color, 1994, 8.5" h 20

Fete, Molyneux, emb bouquet on both sides 35

France Limoges, porcelain, floral design, 4.75" h 75

Germany, hp, brass caps, 4" h 95
Glass, Hobnail pattern, pink, 6.5" h 40
Gold-tone, stamped and cut metal-clad clear glass, ball feet, glass dauber, floral and leaf motif adorned with stones and pearls 45
Guerlain, "Bouquet de Faunes," designed by Rene Lalique, 1925, clear and frosted colorless glass, in the form of an urn, gray stain, 3.75" h 490
Guerlain, Rosebud, 4.5" h 20
Italian, glass, multicolored, 4" h 25
Italian Style, porcelain, pink roses over cobalt blue and white ground, 6" h 40
Lalique, glass, gold colored top 15
Ota, "Lilas," in the form of 3 pearl-shaped flasks, orig fitted box, 3.5" l 920
Pelissier Aragon, "Les Fontaines Parfumes Grasse," designed in 1924, bottle by Dépinoix, in the form of a fountain, bottle used for various scents, 5.5" h 460
Veolay, "Pourpre d'Automne," designed by Lucien Guillard, c1922, molded, enameled flowers, orig box, 3.5" h 460
Weil, "Noir," black rect bottle, flattened circ stopper, orig black, gray, and white striped box, 3.75" h 345
Wrisley, Wisteria, pink bottle 12

PETER MAX COLLECTIBLES

Peter Max has been creating collectibles since 1967. He's the quintessential pop icon whose works symbolized the colorful 1960s hippie era. Interest in Peter Max collectibles has escalated since the first Psychedelic Show in New York City in 1995.

Collectors should note that items dated pre-1973 are most in demand. Unsigned Peter Max look-alike items should be avoided. Find the Peter Max signature on the item before purchase. Since Peter Max owns the copyrights to all his designs, he has not authorized any reproductions or reprints to his works. Prices continue to rise in this area, as well as the entire psychedelic era field.

Bedsheet, black, yellow, blue, orange, and purple on white, pr of heads positioned at top and bottom surrounded by flowers and other abstract designs, c1970, 66" x 104" 45
Blouse, multicolored, 1970s 45
Book, *God Book,* by Swami Sivananda, illus by Peter Max, 1970 50
Book, *Thought Book,* by Swami Sivananda, illus by Peter Max, 1970 50
Cookbook, *Well Dressed Dessert,* first printing, stand-up, spiral flip page, 1969 15
Cooler, Borden Yogurt adv, round, vinyl, white plastic bucket insert, hinged lid with zipper and carrying handle, Borden logo and Max artwork including profile portrait, pr of walking figures, butterfly, planets, and flowers on front, checkerboard design with pr of repeated flower designs on back, Elsie portrait on lid, ©Peter Max, c1970, 10" h, 10.5" d 250
Curtain Panel, bird motif, 44" x 66", 1971 . .26
Curtain Panels, multicolored printed cotton, French pleats, stamped "Peter Max," 1960s, 26" x 28" panels, price for 16 panels 375
Dress, psychedelic 1960s print 44
Fabric, mushroom print, 1970s 20
Flag with Heart, sgd by Peter Max 500
Gown, Japanese scenery and figurals . . .10
Ice Bucket, face with plastic purple sunglasses as handle 90
Jumpsuit, 1960s 40
Magazine, *Arts and Crafts: Pop Art,* 1st issue of Peter Max Magazine, 1970, 74 pgs 195
Necklace, enamel on copper, silver beads, strung on leather, 1960s-70s 55

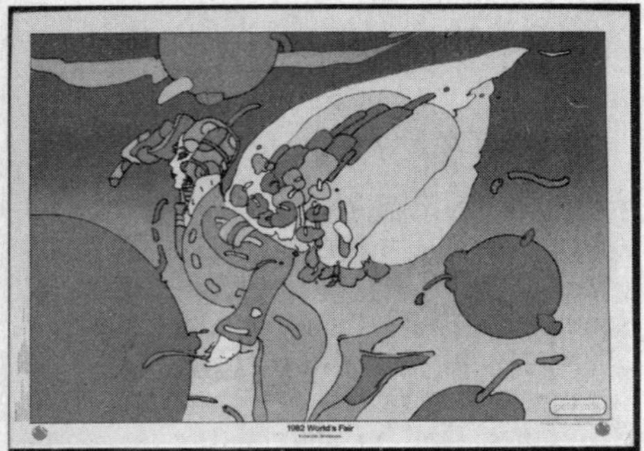

Pinback Button, 4H Theme, 1960s-70s, 1.5" .3
Pinback Button, Max portrait, dark blue on white, 1" d 45
Pinback Button, "Peter Max Clan Fub," brightly colored smiling mouth on white ground, 2.5" d 150
Plate, "Love," Iroquois China Company, 1960s 32
Poster, 1982 Knoxville World's Fair 75
Poster, "Graham Nash's Children Of The Americas Radiothon," held Nov 12, 1988, girl riding on back of winged woman who holds a flower in 1 hand and a wand in the other, 24" x 36" 45
Poster, "Toulouse-Lautrec," portrait of the artist wearing a psychedelic-patterned bowler hat, 36" h, 24" w 350
Puzzle, "Love," from *Life* magazine, 1970, 6.75" x 11" 5
Teapot, enameled metal, gooseneck spout, strap handle, lid missing, multicolored fan-shaped design marquee with star at center, green ground, 7.5" h 75
TV Guide, Super Bowl XXVI, Peter Max cov, 1992 8

PEZ DISPENSERS

The Pez dispenser originated in Germany and was invented by Edvard Haas in 1927. The name "Pez" is an abbreviation of the German word for peppermint—pfefferminz. The peppermint candy was touted as an alternative to smoking.

The first Pez container was shaped like a disposable cigarette lighter and is referred to by collectors as the non-headed or regular dispenser.

By 1952 Pez arrived in the United States. New fruit flavored candy and novelty dispensers were introduced. Early containers were designed to commemorate holidays or favorite children's characters including Bozo the Clown, Mickey Mouse, and other popular Disney, Warner Brothers, and Universal personalities.

Collecting Pez containers at flea markets must be done with care. Inspect each dispenser to guarantee it is intact and free from cracks and chips. Also, familiarize yourself with proper color and marking characteristics.

Club: The Fliptop PEZervation Society, 1368 Dearing Downs Circle, Birmingham, AL 35080.

Baloo, blue-gray head, with feet 20
Bugs Bunny, black stem, no feet, late 1970s 15
Chick in Egg, with hat, no feet 18
Cockatoo, with feet, mid-1970s 45
Cow B, no feet, mid-1970s 85
Crocodile, green, no feet, mid-1970s 100
Donald Duck, no feet, early 1960s 15
Donatello (Teenage Mutant Ninja Turtles), smiling, with feet 3
Duck, with flower, yellow head, no feet, early 1970s 125
Dumbo, blue trunk and mouth, yellow base and hat, turquoise head and ears, no feet 62
Foghorn Leghorn, with feet, early 1980s ..60
Football Player, red, tape strip on helmet, no feet 150
Goofy, green hat, with feet, late 1980s 3
Icee Bear, big eyes, with feet, 1990s 2
Jerry (Tom & Jerry), no feet, early 1980s ..30
Kermit the Frog, with feet, early 1990s 2
Lamb, with feet, 1970s 25
Lil Lion, no feet, late 1960s 70
Merlin Mouse, with feet, early 1980s 12
Miss Piggy, with eyelashes, early 1990s ..10
Monkey Sailor, no feet, late 1960s 60
Mr Ugly, olive green face, no feet, early 1970s 60
Panda, Pony Go Round sticker, Austria, MIP 150
Pebbles Flintstone, with feet, mid-1990s ...2
Peter Pez, dark green stem, no feet, late 1970s 75

Peter Pez, red stem, with feet, 1990s 3
Pink Panther, red stem, with feet, late 1990s 3
Pluto, flat head, moveable ears 10
Popeye, molded hat, no feet, late 1950s .150
Practical Pig, lion sticker, MIP 150
Princess Leia, Star Wars, MIP 5
Pumpkin, green stem, mkd "1980" 3
Puzzy Cat, black head, no feet 85
Roman Soldier, green, with feet 4
Rooster, white, no feet, mid-1970s 40
Santa, white face and beard, no feet, late 1950s 135
Skeleton, Halloween, Slovenia 5
Skull, Halloween, MIP 12
Space Gun, red 80
Spider-Man, with feet 5
Tom (Tom & Jerry), no feet, early 1980s . .25
Tweety Bird, blue base 10
Woodstock, with feather markings, 1990s . .4
Yoshi (Nintendo), with feet, late 1990s 2

PFALTZGRAFF

The name Pfaltzgraff is derived from a famous Rhine River castle, still standing today, in the Pfalz region of Germany. In 1811, George Pfaltzgraff began producing salt-glazed stoneware in York, Pennsylvania.

Initial production consisted of stoneware storage crocks and jugs. When the demand for stoneware diminished, the company shifted to animal and poultry feeders and red clay flowerpots. The production focus changed again in the late 1940s and early 1950s as the company produced more and more household products, including its first dinnerware line, and giftwares.

Club: Pfaltzgraff America Collectors Club, 2536 Quint Ln., Columbia, IL 62236.

Aura, casserole, cov 25
Aura, platter, oval .25
Aura, salad bowl 30
Blue Tulip, vegetable bowl, cov 35
Folk Art, pitcher and bowl 110
Gourmet, bean pot, cov, 8.5" h 100
Gourmet, coffeepot, metal and wooden stand 125
Gourmet, salt and pepper shakers 30
Gourmet, snuffer and coaster 65
Gourmet, teapot 40
Heirloom, canister set of 4 85
Heirloom, mixing bowls, cov, set of 3 40
Heirloom, platter, 14.5" 38
Heirloom, vegetable bowl 24
Heritage, soup tureen 50
Heritage, teapot 38
Meadow Lane, casserole, cov 48
Meadow Lane, gravy boat and underplate 60
Norman Rockwell Jester Mug 100
Northwinds, canister set, 3-pc set 85
Oatmeal, casserole, 3 qt 40
Royale, coffeepot .125
Secret Rose, sugar bowl 34
Sleepy Sam Mug 45
Spring Song, platter, 14" l 30
Village, dinner plate 8
Village, platter, oval 30
Village, soup mugs, set of 4 25
Village, soup tureen 65

Wyndham, candlesticks, 3.75" h 25
Wyndham, canister, 6" h 25
Wyndham, canister, 6.5" h 35
Wyndham, canister, 7.25" h 45
Wyndham, canister, 8" h 55
Wyndham, casserole, cov, 9" 75
Wyndham, gravy with underplate 35
Wyndham, platter, oval 50
Wyndham, salt and pepper shakers 24
Wyndham, soup tureen, cov, with ladle 120
Wyndham, vegetable bowl, 8.25" d 34
Yorktowne, accessories set 85
Yorktowne, canister, set of 4 40
Yorktowne, coffeepot 38
Yorktowne, dinner plate, 10.25" d 4
Yorktowne, kitty bowl 25
Yorktowne, pitcher 25
Yorktowne, pitcher and basin set 70
Yorktowne, teapot 50
Yorktowne, tureen, cov, with ladle 60

PHOENIX GLASS

In 1880 Andrew Howard founded the Phoenix Glass Company in Phillipsburg (later Monaca), Pennsylvania, to manufacture glass tubes for the new electrical wires in houses. Phoenix bought J. A. Bergun, Charles Challinor's decorating business, in 1882. A year later Phoenix signed a contract with Joseph Webb to produce Victorian art glass. Phoenix began producing light bulbs in the early 1890s. In 1893 Phoenix and General Electric collaborated on an exhibit at the Columbian Exposition.

In 1933 the company introduced its Reuben and Sculptured lines. Phoenix acquired the Co-Operative Flint molds in 1937. Using these molds, Phoenix began manufacturing Early American, a pressed milk glass line, in 1938.

In 1970 Anchor Hocking acquired Phoenix Glass. The construction of Phoenix's new plant coincided with the company's 100th anniversary in 1980. In 1987 Newell Corporation acquired Anchor Hocking.

Club: Phoenix & Consolidated Glass Collectors' Club, 41 River View Dr., Essex Junction, VT 05452.

Banana Boat, Diving Girl pattern, frosted crystal, 14" w 230
Banana Boat, Diving Girl pattern, green and yellow highlights on satin finish, 14" h 175
Candlestick, purple wash, 6.75" h, 5.5" w .170
Candy Dish, cov, Phlox, tan shadow 175
Cigarette Box, Phlox, light blue over milk glass 150
Cookie Jar, Con-Cora, violets on white ground, 6.5" h 170
Goblet, Lacy Dewdrop, Beaded Jewel, milk glass, 6" h 40
Lamp, lilac and blue, dogwood blossoms in relief, 21" h .100
Lampshade, globe, Art Nouveau, nude figures in relief, 8" d 300
Lampshade, opalescent, 7" h, 5.5" w 145
Pillow Vase, flying geese, white on brown, 9.5" h, 12" w 180

Salt and Pepper Shakers, Flying, blue and white, 3" h 32
Sugar Dish, cov, Lace and Dewdrop, 6.25" x 4" 45
Vase, Blackberry, baluster form, purple wash, 18" h 425
Vase, Blackberry, baluster form, white wash, 18.5" h 500
Vase, Jewel, brown over milk glass, 4.75" h 195
Vase, Wild Rose, baluster form, blue wash on French crystal, 10.5" h 175
Vase, Zodiac, 4-paneled sides with Zodiac symbol medallion on each side, white, 10" h 230

PHOTOGRAPHS

Cartes de visite (calling card) photographs flourished from 1857 to 1910 and survived into the 1920s. The cabinet card was the preferred form of photograph by the 1890s.

The family photo album was second only to the Bible in importance to late 19th- and early 20th-century families. The principal downfall of family albums is that the vast majority of their photographs are unidentified. Professional photographers produced and sold "art" folios.

Before discarding family photos, check them carefully. A photograph showing a child playing with a toy or dressed in a costume or an adult at work, in military garb, or shopping in a store has modest value. Collectors prefer black and white over color prints, as the latter deteriorate over time.

Clubs: American Photographic Historical Society, 1150 Avenue of the Americas, New York, NY 10036, www.superexpo.com/aphs.htm; The Photographic Historical Society, P.O. Box 39563, Rochester, NY 14604, www.rit.edu/~andpph/tphs.html.

CARTE DE VISITE

Abraham Lincoln, name printed below ..100
Andrew Johnson, signature printed below 80
Austrian Hunter, hand-colored mountain scenery in background, 1906 18
Bearded Man, seated, JH Beeson's Excelsior Gallery, Muncie, IN, 2-cent Washington stamp on back 35
Elderly Woman, wearing wire frame glasses, Chicago Photo Gallery, Princeton, IL 10
Family, mother, father, and baby, GW Barnes, Rockford, IL 8
Girl, standing with hands folded on top of a chair 6
Grant and Daughter, "Grant in Peace" printed at bottom 40
Grant Family, shows 6 family members ...55
High School Building, teenagers standing outside 10
Man, with long muttonchop sideburns, sgd on back "Your friend, JH Goodison," Beer & Co, Trenton, NJ 12
Mrs Stephen Douglas, her name and "Charles Taber & Co, New Bedford, Mass" on back 50
Policeman, in uniform, decorative back ..25
Woman, wearing long dark dress, seated by small table, Tintype & Gem Gallery, Polo, IL 12

CABINET CARD

Actresses, Sarah Jewett and Bijou Heron 45
Aerial View, unidentified town, Ed Mehner, Dorchester, WI, 4.25" x 6.5" ...15
Baby Boy, wearing dress, seated in chair, 4" x 2.5" 3
Black Baby, wearing white dress 20
Boxers, 3 boxers and 6 other men, seated and standing by flag-draped table with trophies, 7.5" x 9.5" 35
Boy, wearing suit, ring, and watch chain, standing beside table, Nye's Studio, Duluth, MN, 6.5" 4.25" 12
Five Children, 3" x 6" 16
Flowers, 7 funeral arrangements on a gallery prop log, JO Hole, Novelty Gallery, Mulberry St, Muscatine, IA, 6.5" x 4.25" 6
Three Brothers, 1 sitting in wooden "Express" wagon, Savannah, IL 50
Two Boys, wearing patched pants and socks, Parsons POP Ainsworth, NB, 6.5" x 4.25" 10

Woman on Horseback, plain back, 4.25" x 6.5" 6

Young Girl, wearing first holy communion dress, Sol Young, NY, 1909, 5" x 8" 12

PHOTOGRAPH, BLACK AND WHITE

Barbershop, int view, 8" x 10" 30

Christmas Tree, dec, toys and dolls underneath, 10" x 12" 40

Circus Wagon, pulled by ponies 8

Hunters, 2 men and 2 dogs, "Compliments of AL Guthrie, Manchester, Ind – The Gang," 8" x 10" 25

Logging Camp Cooks, 1 holding large horn 8

Man and Motorcycle, 1943 8

Seed Store, int view, shows Ferry Seed Co display racks and salespeople, 1920, 5" x 7" 10

Supermarket, int view, 1950s, 8" x 10" 15

Two Black Men, holding liquor bottles, 1920s 8

PICTURE FRAMES

We have reached the point where the frame is often worth more than the picture in it. Decorators have fallen in love with old frames. If you find one with character and pizazz at a flea market for a few dollars, pick it up. It will not be hard to resell. Who said picture frames have to be used for pictures? They make great frames for mirrors. Use your imagination.

Club: International Institute for Frame Study, 443 I St. NW, P.O. Box 50156, Washington, DC 20091.

Black wood, brass corner pcs, 8" x 10" 25

Brass, oval center surrounded by leaves and scrollwork, 9.5" x 12.5" 100

Brass, rope and flower designs at corners, Denmark 20

Brass, Victorian, oval frame with chain, 7" x 12" 185

Bronze, small oval frame with beaded edge beside bronzed baby shoe, both mounted on oval base, c1885, 7.25" l, 3" x 3.75" frame 25

Celluloid, bi-fold, rect with 2 oval openings, stamped "French Ivory" 25

Leather, ivory and red, with Eleanor Parker store picture, 8" x 10" 25

Lucite, faux tortoise shell, lime green and brown, rect with wavy sides, linen backing, holds 3" x 5" picture 25

Mosaic, green leaves, white, yellow, and aqua flowers, Italy, 2" x 2.5" 30

Oak, swivels on turned posts, 5" x 7" 55

Plastic, molded, wood-grained mahogany, mkd "No. 9800, Nu-Dell Plastics Corp, Chicago," 10.5" x 13" 15

Rosewood, oval, convex glass, 8" x 10" ..200

Silver Plate, filigree dec, velvet backing, 9.5" x 12" 175

Snake Skin, shades of brown, 6" x 7.75" 35

Sterling Silver, oval, ftd stand, 3" x 4" 75

Wood, painted ivory-colored thin frame with floral dec at corners, 8" x 10" 18

Wood and Gesso, gilded, some damage, 25" x 27.5" 60

PIE BIRDS

Pie birds and pie funnels continue to be a hot collectible and functional kitchen novelty. The basic criteria for pie birds are: ceramic pottery (e.g. stoneware, porcelain), glazed inside and outside, 3 to 5 inches tall, arches (cutouts) at the base to allow steam to enter and exit through a top vent hole. There are Pyrex and aluminum (non-US) pie funnels.

Many novelty pie vents have found their way into the market in the last 25 years. Beware of figural pie vents from England that are stained with brown gook that allude to age and usage. Note: age crazing is a process that can be applied to new pie vents.

Club: Pie Bird Collectors Club, 158 Bagsby Hill Ln., Dover, TN 37058.

Bird, green eyes and wings, white body, pink beak and base, made by Shawnee for Pillsbury, 5.5" h 85
Bird, pink eyes and wings, light blue base, Shawnee, 5.5" h 70
Black Bird, c1960, 4" h 15
Black Chef, blue clothing, 4.375" h 160
Blushing Bride, carrying bouquet of flowers, 4.5" h 65
Brown English, 4.5" h 90
Bull, light brown face and patches, 3.75" h 65
Cat, red and white checked dress, 4" h . . .60
Dalmatian, Bud Higby, 1950s 90
Dragon, green, 4.25" h 60
Duck, red, Boyd Glass Co, mkd "B" in diamond 25
Elephant, Nutbrown Pie Funnel Company, 1940s, 3.5" h 185
Funnel, clear glass, mkd "Phoenix," 2.75" h, 2.125" d 50
Funnel, white, 2.875" h, 2.125" d 60
Goose, white body, blue luster back, orange beak and feet, orange and blue wings, Japan, 5.25" h 95
Groom, smiling, striped suit, 4.5" h 65
Humpty Dumpty, 4" h 50
Indian, 4.5" h 65
Kitty Cat, green striped dress, 4" h 60
Lady Badger, green striped dress, white bonnet and apron, 3.5" h 65
Little Red Riding Hood, 4.5" h 65
Long Neck Duck, blue, 1940s-50s, 5" h . . .105
Long Neck Duck, maroon, 1940s-50s, 5" h 115
Long Neck Duck, yellow, 1940s-50s, 5" h .110
Mammy, holds 3 measuring spoons 100
Patch, Morton Pottery, 1950s, 5" h 85
Percy Penguin, black pants, gray vest and baker's hat, 3.75" h 65
Pig, bridegroom, striped pants, black coat and top hat, 4.5" 65
Piggy Bride, 4" h 65
Pillsbury, Shawnee Pottery, 1940s-50s, 5.5" h 90
Rooster, Cleminson of California, brown, blue, and lavender, 1940s-50s, 4.5" h . . .95
Rooster, Cleminson of California, pink, lavender, and yellow, 1940s-50s, 4.5" h .95
Rooster, Marion Drake, 5" h 125

Rosie Bunny, blue and white skirt, yellow with blue polka dot top, 4" h 65
Sammy Snowman, 4" h 50
Songbird, American Pottery Co, 1940s-50s, 4.5" h .100
Squirrel, holding nut, brown and white, 3.75" h 60
Teddy Bear, blue and white overalls, 4" h 65
Tommy Toad, black and white striped pants, white coat, yellow vest 65
Wizard, commercial size, black hat and gown with white stars, long white beard, mkd "England," 7.5" h 75

PIERCE, HOWARD

Howard Pierce established his pottery studio in LaVerne, California, in 1941. Initially he produced small pewter animal figurines. A lack of metal supplies during World War II forced him to close. He reopened in 1945 and produced a line of contemporary ceramic figurines.

Pierce's work was sold in high-end gift shops and department stores. A satin-matte brown on white combination glaze was his favorite. In 1956 he introduced a line of Jasperware products.

Pierce entered semi-retirement in 1968 when he moved to Joshua Tree, a desert community near Palm Springs. He still produces a small range of limited production pieces that are sold through select outlets.

Figurine, bird, textured .80
Figurine, coyote, brown, 6" h .90
Figurine, dolphin riding a wave .125
Figurine, girl holding bowl, 9.25" h .75
Figurine, girl with goose .80
Figurine, goose .40
Figurine, Madonna and Child, 13.5" h .85
Figurine, native girl, 7.25" h .90
Figurine, owl, 8.25" h .95
Figurine, owl, white, 5" h .60
Figurine, quail in tree .100
Figurine, raccoon, 8.5" l .115
Figurine, resting deer, 5.5" h .70
Figurine, roadrunner, female, 9" l .95
Figurine, roadrunner, male, 12" .125
Figurine, rooster, 9.25" h .80
Figurine, sparrows on log .75
Figurines, pr, brown birds .100
Figurines, pr, chipmunks .90
Figurines, pr, ducklings .25
Figurines, pr, owls .90
Flower Holder, owls in tree .95
Planter, shadow box, 7" x 9.25" x 3" .145
Teapot, 7" h .65

PIG COLLECTIBLES

This is one animal that does better as a collectible than in real life. Pig collectibles have never been oinkers.

Established pig collectors focus on the bisque and porcelain pigs of the late 19th and early 20th centuries. This is a limited view. Try banks in the shape of a pig as a specialized collecting area. If not appealing, look at the use of pigs in advertising. If neither pleases you, there is always Porky. "That's All, Folks!"

Club: The Happy Pig Collectors Club, P.O. Box 17, Oneida, IL 61467.

Note: Items either feature the image of a pig or are pig-shaped.

Advertising Plaque, Royal Doulton, 4" h .30
Bacon Press, 7.25" x 4" .10
Basket, 9" h, 11" l, .15
Bottle, 6.25" h .105
Bud Vase, Norcrest .10
Cookie Jar, Carlton of Cleveland Ohio, 12" h .45
Cookie Jar, Farmer Pig, 12.5" h .26

Cookie Jar, Happy Pig, 10" h .22
Cookie Jar, Pig Chef holding cooking utensils .20
Cookie Jar, Poppies on Blue, Barnyard Collection, 10" h .55
Cookie Jar, Porky Pig emerging from TV, 10.5" h .90
Cookie Jar, Shawnee .175
Cookie Jar, Sheriff Pig, Robinson-Ransbottom, 12.5" h .165
Cookie Jar, Smiley, Terrance Ceramics, 11.75" h .95
Creamer, 1940s, 3" h, 5.5" l .48
Creamer, 1950s, 3.25" h, 5.5" l .38
Creamer, mkd "Made In Japan," 4" h .20
Figure, clown sitting on pig, mkd "Ardalt, Occupied Japan," 5" h, 4.25" w .100
Figure, Royal Doulton, 4.5" l, 3" h .30
Footscraper, cast iron, 6" h, 11.5" l .15
Hand Puppet, 1950s .20
Jam Jar, pink with lid and plastic spoon, 4" l, 3" h .8
Measuring Spoon Holder, blue, holds 4 spoons .5
Planter, mkd "SS, Made in Occupied Japan," 3.25" h .15
Salt and Pepper Shakers, bride and groom nodders, 1940s-50s .345
Salt and Pepper Shakers, jeweled, 2.25" h .18
Salt and Pepper Shakers, Pig Chef, ceramic, 3" h .10
Salt and Pepper Shakers, Shawnee, dressed in tuxedos and bow ties .18
Salt and Pepper Shakers, Silly Symphony Pig, 1930s, 4" h .60
Salt and Pepper Shakers, pink pigs, Occupied Japan .15

Soap Dish, cast iron 12
Sugar Bowl, black character pig, 3.5" h ...42
Tape Measure, figural pig, blue celluloid, Occupied Japan 45
Tea Kettle, black pig, 5.5" h 65
Teapot, Hampshire Pig, 8.75" h, 1992 115

PINBACK BUTTONS

Around 1893 the Whitehead & Hoag Company filed the first patents for celluloid pinback buttons. By the turn of the century, the celluloid pinback button was used as a promotional tool covering a wide spectrum, ranging from presidential candidates to amusement parks.

This category covers advertising pinback buttons. To discover the full range of non-political pinbacks consult Ted Hake and Russ King's *Price Guide To Collectible Pin-back Buttons 1896–1986* (Hake's Americana & Collectibles Press: 1986).

"Archway Cookies," blue on white, image of spokesman Archie the Baker, 1.5" d 12
Baltimore Orioles, World Series, Memorial Stadium, orange and black button and ribbon, 1.754" d button, 4.5" l ribbon 15
"Borden's, Uncle Don's Ice Cream Club," red, white, and black 15
Bush, "Stop The Monster! Frankenbush Son of Reaganstein!," red and white with blue image of Frankenstein, 1992, 2.25" d 12

"Buster Brown Blue Ribbon Shoes," brown images on lighter brown ground, company back paper with 5-star logo, early 1900s, 1" d 20
Cameo Gum, 5 young children with wings among clouds, c1898, 1.25" d 20
Carter, "The South Has Risen," green on white with cartoon image of Carter as a running peanut holding a Confederate flag, 2.125" d 15
"Ceresota," trademark young boy seated on stool slicing giant bread loaf, 1900-12, 1.25" d 20
Convention, New York Retail Bakers, pretzel surrounded by white lettering, dark blue ground, 1937, 1.5" d 20
Convention, "The Associated Bill Posters of the United States and Canada," white on blue, torch design above union logo, "We Enlighten the World 1891," .875" d 20
Dewey, "For President Thomas E Dewey," black on cream, elephants on edges, 1.25" d 12
"Don't Eat Grapes," green on black with bunch of grapes forming a skull image, 1.5" d 10
"Drink Peacock It Makes You Proud," blue, white, and gold bird, red lettering, St Louis Button Co back paper, front pushed in, 1908-25, 1" d 35
Eisenhower, "For President Eisenhower," red, white, and blue litho with bluetone photo and draped flags, 1" d 12
Election Official, black on orange, "Supt Of Elections – Deputy – General Election – Nov 7, 1972 – Hudson County, NJ," 2.125" d 12

"Electrical League of Niagara Frontier," red seal and multicolor image of falls surrounded by blue "For Service and Satisfaction Buy Where You See This Sign" on cream ground, c1920, .875" d .15
"Foley Sportsmen Club," brown on white, pheasant image, c1940s, 1.5" d 15
Goldwater, alternating lettering and background colors, "Vote Republican Row A," 1.25" d 12
"Hat's Off To the New Frigidaire," red, white, and blue litho, Uncle Sam image, late 1930s, .75" d 15
Lindbergh, image of Charles Lindbergh above US shield, red, white, and blue, off-center, 1.25" d 20
"Minnesota House Paints," red, white, black, yellow, and green, product can on cream ground, W&H back paper, 1900-12, 1.25" d 35
"Mrs Wagner's Pie Champeen," chubby young boy wearing first prize badge and holding a pie in 1 hand and a trophy in his other arm, 1930s, 1.25" d ..25
"NAACP Democracy For All," litho, red and cream logo on dark blue ground, c1930s, .75" d 40
"Nixon For Peace," black, white, and dark blue litho, 2.25" d 15
Nixon/Lodge, "Our Nation Needs Nixon & Lodge," oval, multicolor litho, 3.25" l .25
"Pfeiffer's" Beer, red, white, and blue on yellow ground, waiter in formal dress carrying tray with bottles and glasses, 1930s, 1" d 20
Reagan, "I Love Ronnie Reagan '80," red border text on white, black illus, blue text and red heart accent at center, 2.125" sq 12
"The Constitutionalists, No Third Term," red, white, and blue, .875" d 15
"The Girl of the Pingree Shoe," multicolor portrait of girl on dark green ground, company copyright and 1910 date on curl, 1.25" d 65
Truman Memorial, "The Uncommon Common Man," black and white, 1972, 2.25" d 12
Vietnam, "Stop the War Against Vietnam," black on orange, "Youth Against War & Facism" on bottom edge, 1.75" d 25
"Wilkie Club Of Marion Co," litho, red, white, and blue, .875" d 10

PINBALL MACHINES

The introduction of Gottlieb's "Baffle Ball" in 1931 marked the beginning of the modern pinball machine era. Pre-1940 pinball machines typically had production runs of 25,000 to 50,000 machines. After 1945 production runs fell within the 500 to 2,000 range with an occasional machine reaching 10,000. Some scholars suggest that over 200 manufacturers made over 10,000 models, a result of a machine's high attrition rate. Several companies released a new model every three weeks during the 1950s.

The first electric machine appeared in 1933. Bumpers were added in 1936. Flippers arrived in 1947, kicking rubbers in 1950, score totalizers in 1950, multiple player machines in 1954, and solid state electronics in 1977. Machines by D. Gottlieb are considered the best of the pinballs, primarily because of their superior play and graphics.

The entire pinball machine was collected through the mid-1980s. More recently, collecting back glasses has become popular. Manufacturers were not concerned with longevity when making these glasses. Flaking paint is a restoration nightmare.

Aces of the Sky, Marx, bagatelle, vintage military airplanes on playing field, 1974, 40" h, 30" l, 15" w 75
Addams Family, Bally 3,300
Attack from Mars, Bally 4,375

Bullseye, Marx, bagatelle, litho tin, wood grain finish playing field, target marble cups, factory sample, 1953, 23" h, 11" w, NRFB 125
Cactus Canyon, Williams/Bally, 76" h, 29" w, 55" d 4,500
Casanova, Williams, 1957 2,000
Daisy May, Gottlieb, 1954 3,550
Disney Mickey Mouse, Wolverine, bagatelle, tin bottom, plastic top, 5" crack at center, 1970s-80s, 15.5" h, 10" w 50
Indiana Jones, 1990s 4,500
Kiss, Bally, 1978 .1,800
Lite A Card, Gottlieb, not working, 1960 1,600
Medieval Madness 5,000
MidWay, Marx, battery-operated, litho-styrene cov playing field, litho tin backboard with automatic score counter, circus theme, 1952, 27" h, 14.5" w, NRFB 500
Pachinko, Niskiyin, Japan, 32" h, 20.5" w, 9.5" d 280
Pink Panther, Gottlieb, not working 3,000
Playboy, Bally, 1978 1,900
Push M Up Jr, Northwestern Products Co, St Louis, MO, 4 in 1 game with Baseball, Bagatelle, Put-N-Take, and Colors, metal frame, glass top, No. 1925018 30

Scared Stiff, Bally, 1996 3,650
Stage Coach, Gottlieb, late 1940s-early 1950s 2,400
Star Trek The Next Generation, Williams 3,700
Tales of the Arabian Nights, Williams, 1996 5,100
Twilight Zone, Bally, 1993 2,500

PINUP ART

The stuff looks so innocent, one has to wonder what all the fuss was about when it first arrived upon the scene. Personally, I like it when a little is left to the imagination.

George Petty and Alberto Vargas (the "s" was dropped at Esquire's request) have received far more attention than they deserve. You would be smart to focus on artwork by Gillete Elvgren, Billy DeVorss, Joyce Ballantyne, and Earl Moran. While Charles Dana Gibson's girls are also pin-ups, they are far too respectable to be included here.

Arcade Cards, WWII, set of 5, 3.25" x 5.25", 1944-45 50
Ashtray, Elvgren, metal, "Help Wanted," 4" x 4" 80
Blotter Card, Earl Moran, Sep 1952, 9" x 4" 30
Book, hard cov, "Le Rire," 1961, 6" x 9" 65
Calendar, Devorss, "Liberty Belle," 16" x 33.5" 275

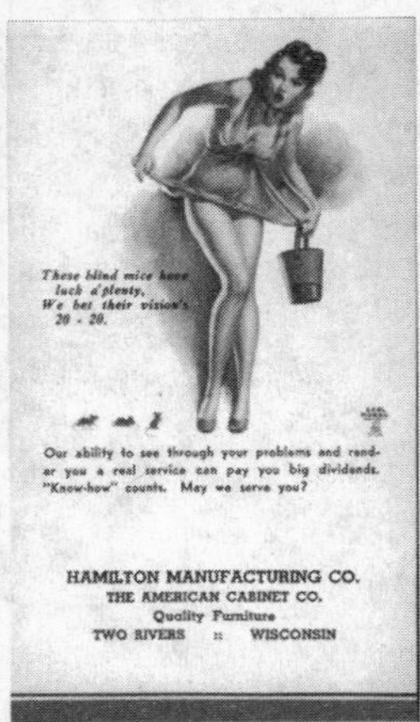

Calendar, Erbit, "Beauty on Telephone," 1951 75
Calendar, Irene Patten, Budweiser, "Captivating," 1939, 5" x 11" 115
Calendar, Jayne Mansfield, 1954, 10.5" x 12" 80
Calendar, Moran, "...Three Blind Mice," 3.25" x 6" 60
Calendar, Playboy, Jan 1977 65
Calling Card, prepaid, Playboy Home Video Limited Edition, 1995 65
Drawing, Munson, wood frame, 10" x 12" .95
Key Ring, color photo, 1.25" x 2.25" 28
Lighter, Manor by Windsor, 1.5" x 32" 95
Matchbook, Elvgren pin-up girl on back, Faiman's Café adv on front, radio "Station WOW" and "We Never Sleep" on saddle 8
Matchbook, Petty pinup girl on front 25
Notepad, Elvgren, 1966, "Taken to Heart," 3.25" x 6" 28
Pencil, plastic, nudie girl, 1.5" x 4.75" 70
Pendant, 3D, girl covering herself with feathers, feathers move when you move the pendant, 2" x 2.75" 85
Pendant, heart-shaped, girl on phone, 1" x 1.75" 38
Pendant, nudie girl, oval, .75" x 1" 75
Photo Box, glass, includes black and white photos, 2" x 2" x 3.5" 65
Photograph, Betty Page, color, 8" x 10" . . .35
Picture, Earl Moran, "Bet you are thinking I'm dressed for a tan. Well, this suit's my bait for trapping a man!" .55
Pill Box, girl in black negligee, 1.75" d 42
Playing Cards, Al Moore, double deck . . .125
Playing Cards, Elvgren, double deck 95
Postcard, French pinup in matte frame, 5" x 7" 28
Print, litho, Earl MacPherson, unframed, 12" x 18" 100
Print, sailing lady, Jules Erbit, 15" x 20" . .150
Print, Vargas, "Summertime," lady in pastel gown, 16" x 20" 145
Shot Glass, Playboy femlin, 2" x 3" 28

PLANTERS

A planter is any container suitable for growing vegetation. It may be constructed of any number of materials ranging from wooden fruit crates and painted tires found on suburban front lawns to ceramic panthers stalking 1950s television sets. If you thought all those planters you got from the florist were junk, read on. Too bad you threw them out or sold them for a dime each at your last garage sale. This category deals with the figural ceramic variety found in abundance at all flea markets.

African elephant, pearly gray body with pink at ears, mkd "Japan," 5" h, 5.5" l . .55
Art Deco Egyptian Princess, pale green glaze, drilled as lamp base, 10" h, 8.25" w, 4.5" d 125
Baby, sitting on large shoe planter, pink and white, Relpo Ceramics, Japan, 1950s, 3" h, 4" w .25
Bass, ceramic, opalescent, curved tail, 7.5" h, 4" d 20

Boy and Basket, boy is kneeling beside basket, Japan, 3.25" h, 4.25" w 12
Bunny Rabbit, Relpo, T969, 4" h, 6.75" l 18
Cat and Kittens, Siamese Cat and 3 kittens, Napco, 4.75" h, 5" w 25
Cherubs, 2 cherubs carrying large basket, gold highlights, Japan, 4" h, 5" w 15
Child with Lantern, pr, wearing huge hats and pale yellow coats, 7" h, 5" w 25
Cocker Spaniel, black and white, 8" l, 6" h .30
Cowboy Western Boot, 9" x 9" 22
Cupid Child, with horn, gold tone scrolls, applied flowers, 7" l, 5.5" h 22
Dutch Boy, pink, 9" h 35
Elephant, brown, mkd "Made In Occupied Japan," 1945-52, 4.5" l 35
Elephant, dec with multicolor flowers on white body, Japan 12
Elf on Shoe, 7" h, 8" l 25
Frog, Norcrest, 4.5" h 35
Gilner Hat, elf sitting on either side of the front edge of the turned up brim, glossy dark green glaze, 4.25" h 70
Kitten and Basket, white, red ribbon collar on kitten and trim on basket, Lefton, #04947, 1985, 3.75" h 10
Old African Lady, sitting next to a basket, 6.25" h 50
Puppy, winking, wearing a polka dot bowtie and beanie, 6" h, 7" l 30
Puppy and Shoe, burgundy, Shawnee 12
Ram, pr, 4" h, 6" l 50
Roman Chariot, Hickok, white with gold trim, 8" l, 5" h 20
Rooster, 6.5" h, 7.25" w 20
Stork and Baby Bassinette, white, 7" x 7" x 3.75" 30
Swan, head tucked down on wing, Japan, 4" w 10
Swan, Royal Copley, blue, gold accents on eyes, bill, feet, wings and neck, 9" l .55
Teddy Bear, sitting, pastel colors, mkd "7970 Japan," 8" h .6
Toucan, bright mix of colors, 6" x 9" 25
Whale, glossy brown, gold trim around tail, 2.5" x 7" x 4" 15
Whimsical Girl, wearing long dress with green and yellow flowers, apron, and green scarf, carrying basket, 6" h . .40

PLANTERS PEANUTS

Amedeo Obici and Mario Peruzzi organized the Planters Nut and Chocolate Company in Wilkes-Barre, Pennsylvania, in 1906. The monocled Mr. Peanut resulted from a trademark contest in 1916. Standard Brands bought Planters only to be bought themselves by Nabisco. Planters developed a wide range of premiums and promotional items. Beware of reproductions.

Club: Peanut Pals, P.O. Box 652, St. Clairsville, OH 43950.

Advertisement, Mr Peanut Premiums, full color, 1954, 11" x 14" 10
Advertisement, Planters Peanuts Fall Fiesta, full color, 1954, 9" x 13" 12
AM Radio, plastic, yellow, Mr Peanut shape, 10" h 35
Ashtray, ceramic, 4.25" h 110
Belt Buckle, peanut-shaped 15
Blotter, "The Nickel Lunch," 6.25" x 3.25" . .60
Bookmark, diecut cardboard, 1939 New York World's Fair souvenir, yellow, black, and white, 6.5" h 25
Bowl Set, Mr Peanut, 5-pc set, tin,

4 small bowls and 1 large bowl, all with image of Mr Peanut in center 25
Box, Planters Roasted Peanuts, image of Mr Peanut and a large peanut labeled "The Peanut Store," cardboard, 3 lb, 10" x 6.25" x 6.25" 55
Coaster, tin, Mr Peanut in center, 3.5" d . . .10
Figurine, Mr Peanut, bendable, 5.75" h 5
Jar, 75th Anniversary commemorative, 1981, 8" h 15
Jar, "Lady" Jar, clear glass, orig lid and paper labels (unattached), c1937, 9.25" x 5" x 7.75" 550
Jar, Mr Peanut Store, clear glass, sq, 1930s 50
Jar, Mr Peanut Store, pink glass, 12" h, 8" w 95
Mug, Mr Peanut head, blue, 3.75" h 6
Peanut Dispenser, wood base, glass globe, 13.5" h 25
Presidential Coloring Book, filled with illus and information about US presidents 8
Salt and Pepper Shakers, Mr Peanut, plastic, red, 3" h 15
Serving Spoon, SP, Mr Peanut at top and peanuts leading down to the bowl of the spoon, 5.25" l 22
Tin, girl sitting in front of fireplace reading a book to Mr Peanut, 1997 15
Tin, Planters Cocktail Peanuts, 3" h, 3.25" .45
Tin, Planters Salted Peanuts, 5.25" x 6.25" . .6
Tin with Chopper, 1938, 4.25" h 20
Toy Tractor Trailer, plastic, 2-pc, red cab, yellow and blue trailer, Pyro, 1950s, 1.75" h, 5.5" l 250
Whistle, Mr Peanut, plastic, orange, 2.5" h 15

PLAYBOY COLLECTIBLES

Playboy memorabilia, from magazines to calendars to Playboy Club items is a popular collecting category, especially now since all the clubs have closed. Hugh M. Hefner began his empire in 1953 with the debut of the first issue of *Playboy Magazine.* Marilyn Monroe graced its cover and centerfold. Many Playboy collectibles can be found at yard sales, swap meets, flea markets, collectible shows, and antique malls. Value on items listed are in good condition, but will be higher if they are in excellent condition and/or unopened or unused such as sealed puzzles and playing cards.

Club: Playboy Collectors Assoc., P.O. Box 653, Phillipsburg, MO 65722.

Ashtray, glass, 3.5" sq 15
Bar Set, 4-pc, SS 65
Calendar, Miss March, Stella Stevens, 1961 68
Calling Card, prepaid, limited edition 65
Cocktail Shaker, plastic, 4" x 9" 48
Earrings, bunny, goldtone with rhinestone eyes 65
Egg Cup, "Good Morning," ceramic 48
Invitation, "Cocktails never looked so good," 4" x 6" 5
Key Charm, enameled goldtone metal . . .45
Money Clip, club casino, 1.5" 75
Mug, 1976 "Playmate of the Year" 20
Mug, black, bunny head on front 12
Mug, white frosted glass with bunny logo, 4" x 6" 32

Necklace, rhinestone charm 36
Patch, bunny logo, 2.75" x 3" 15
Pin, bunny head logo, goldtone metal 32
Pin, bunny head logo with rhinestone eye, .75" x 1.25" 85
Pinback Button, zodiac sign, nude woman holding bow and arrow 32
Plaque, wooden, 5.25" x 7.5" 125
Playboy Magazine, Oct 1982 45
Playboy Magazine, Dec 1982 60
Playboy Magazine, Jan 30, 1984, 30th Anniversary Collector's Edition, features last nude picture taken of Marilyn Monroe .175
Playboy Magazine, Sep 1985, "Unlike a Virgin...for the Very First Time," featuring Madonna 150
Playboy Magazine, Nov 1985 55
Playing Cards, nude playmates, 1968 48
Poster, Miss January 65
Ring, 14k gold, bunny logo 85
Ring, pink rhinestones, adjustable 32
Shot glass, 2" x 3" 15
Stirrers, Playboy bunny heads, plastic, set of 3 12
Tumbler, glass, 3.25" h 14

PLAYING CARDS

The key is not the deck, but the design on the deck surface. Souvenir decks are especially desirable. Look for special decks such as Tarot and other fortune-telling items.

Always buy complete decks. There are individuals who just collect Jokers and have a bad habit of removing them from a deck and then reselling it. Prices listed are for complete decks.

Clubs: 52 Plus Joker, 204 Gorham Ave., Hamden, CT 06514, www.52PlusJoker.org; American Game Collectors Assoc., P.O.Box 44, Dresher, PA 19025, www.chaichart.com; Chicago Playing Card Collectors, Inc., 1826 Mallard Lake Dr., Marietta, GA 30068; International Playing Card Society, 3570 Delaware Common, Indianapolis, IN 46220.

Amalgamated Meat Cutters/Butcher Workmen of America, mid-1950s 10
American Airlines, astrojets, orig box 25
Avon, bridge, blue and white playing card design, US Playing Card Co, Cincinnati, OH, plastic coated 6
Card Box, Bakelite, Art Deco design, divided, KEM, c1935, 3.75" x 1.625" x 2.75" 25
Card Box, wood with emb copper plate image of the Metropolitan Life Insurance Co building in New York City on lid, bottom mkd "Chamberlain, SC," wooden divider for 2 decks, 6.5" x 4.5" . .50
Card Shuffler, Nestor Johnson Mfg Co, shuffles 1, 2, or 3 decks 25
Cats, Gladys Emerson Cook illus, US Playing Card Co, double deck in box 40
Coca-Cola, button sign on yellow ground, 1994, NRFB 5
Delta Airlines Miami, sailboats, orig box, sealed in plastic 14
Flying Geese, Hallmark, bridge decks, double deck boxed set 8
Geishas, St Regis, plastic coated, double deck boxed set 16
Gucci, travel set, red leather case with gold monogram in corner, contains score pad and 2 unopened decks mkd "Gucci" 55
Horse Playing Cards, wearing leather jacket, double deck boxed set 38
Moller Steamship Co, 1 blue set, 1 red, Moller logo on each, double deck, boxed set 22
Pinup, different girl on each card, Art Studio Cards 30
Polynesian Dancer and Drummer, Cel-U-Tone, Congress, double deck boxed set 28
Redislip, 2 bridge decks in red plastic box mkd "Jiffy Manufacturing Company" 18
Royal Canadian Mounted Police, 2-deck set in blue flocked box, MIB 25

Royale Playing Cards, US Playing Card Co, double deck boxed set 42
Souvenir of California, Glendale, boxed set 45
Spaniel Puppies, Canasta, Congress, double deck sealed boxed set 20
Sunbeam, appliances on back, 1950s, unopened in orig box 12
Tom Thumb Jr, ARRCO, orig box 32
Toy Story, US Playing Card Co 15

POCKETKNIVES

American manufacturers such as Samuel Mason and C. W. Platts of the Northfield Knife Company began making pocketknives in the 1840s. Collectors consider the period between the 1880s and 1940 as the pocketknife's golden age.

The period between 1945 and the early 1960s is considered a dark age. Many prewar manufacturers went out of business. A renaissance occurred in the 1970s as individual knife craftsmen began making pocketknives geared more for collecting and display than use. Recently, collector and limited edition knives have flooded the market.

Case, Tested XX, 2-blade, stag handle, blade stamped "Case Tested XX," sharpened, 1932-40 200
Case, XX, #6445R, 4-blade, red bone handle 55
Case, XX 1 Dot, #A62351/2, 2-blade, bone handle 25
Case, XX 2 Dot, #31043, 1-blade, yellow composition handle 45
Case, XX 2 Dot, #6347HP, 3-blade, bone stag handle 35
Case, XX 3 Dot, #61111/2, 3-blade, bone stag handle, sharpened 30
Case, XX 6 Dot, #640045 R, 4-blade, bone stag handle 30
Case, XX 7 Dot, #3318HE, 3-blade, yellow composition handle 35
Case, XX 8 Dot, #3318 SH SP, 3-blade, yellow composition handle, red lettering and logo "United Steelworkers of America" on handle 20
Case, XX 9 Dot, #6292, 2-blade, bone stag handle 25
Case, XX Tested Bulldog, #51072, 1-blade, stag handle, "Case XX Bulldog" etched on blade, stamped "Case XX Bradford, PA," hinged wood box 88
Cattaraugus Cutlery Co, Little Valley, NY, 3-blade, stag handle 75
Collins Brothers, 3-blade, wood handle ... 25
Friedr Olbertz, 3-blade, wood handle, "Premium Stock Knife" engraved on handle, Eurocut Solingen, Germany 20
Gerber, 2-blade, wood and SS handle 38
Henry Boker, 2-blade, smooth black handle, stamped "Henry Boker, Germany" 20
JA Henkels, hunting knife, 4-blade, stag handle, guard stamped with numbers "16" and "12," locking mechanism for large blade, stamped "JA Henkels," sharpened 260
Parker Edwards, 2-blade, wood handle, "Etched Eagle Brand Knives" etched on blade, stamped "Parker Edwards, Alabama, USA," orig box 30
Parker Edwards, 2-blade, wood handle, stamped "Parker Edwards, Jacksonville, AL," eagle etched on blade, orig box .. 20
Remington, Bullet Lockback, #R1306, 1-blade, stag handle, etched "Remington" on blade, stamped "Remington UMC, Made in USA," orig box 110
Remington, UMC, 3-blade, smooth black handle, made in USA 35
S & W, 1-blade, laminated wood-like handle, locking blade stamped "Made in USA," orig blue box 74
Sam McDowell, 2-blade, bone handle with etched duck, floral pattern bolster, etched duck on blade 25

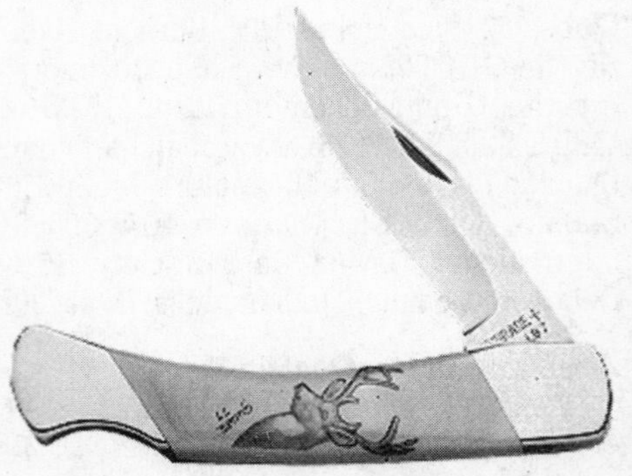

Schrade, LB-7, folding hunting knife, custom scrimshaw deer head by Jim Gulette, Greer, SC, 1979 65

Schrade, switch blade, 2-blade, yellow composition handle, 1 locking blade at each end 55

Syracuse Knife Company, 2-blade, yellow composition handle, 2 cracks in handle 5

Ulster, bone stag handle, "Ulster Mark 40" faintly engraved on blade, stamped "Ulster Knife USA" 15

Winchester, Cattle, #3009, 3-blade, celluloid handle, worn "Winchester Cattle Knife" inscription on handle, sharpened 265

Winchester, Daddy Barlow, #1701, 1-blade, bone handle, stamped "Winchester Trademark Made in USA" 605

Winchester, Easy Open Jack, #2959, 2-blade, bone handle, stamped "Winchester Trademark" 115

POLITICAL ITEMS

Collect the winners—time does not treat losers well. Do not pay much for items less than thirty years old. Also concentrate on the non-traditional categories. Everyone collects pinbacks and posters. Try something unusual. How about political ties, mugs, or license plates?

Clubs: American Political Items Collectors, P.O. Box 340339, San Antonio, TX 78234; Third Party & Hopefuls, 1901 Ridgeway, Apt. #8, De Pere, WI 54115.

Note: See Pinback Buttons for additional listings.

Agnew, drinking glass, red, white, and blue painted side panels with satirical graphics and text on sides, c1970s, 4" h, 3" d 8

Agnew, patch, oval, white cloth, red, white, and blue Agnew figure giving victory sign, yellow edge trim, 3.5" d 14

Agnew, pendant, brass luster white metal with high relief portrait, c1970 8

Browder/Ford, pinback button, "For A Free, Happy, Prosperous America Vote Communist," center photos, "Browder For President/Ford For Vice-Pres.," 1936 35

Bush, pinback button, "Re-Elect President Bush," red, white, and blue eagle and gold sparkle design 5

Carter, key chain, goldtone with color image of Carter, "Jimmy Carter 39th President," 1.5" l 18

Carter, pin, metal cov lifts to reveal Carter portrait, black and gray 8

Dewey, pinback button, "God Bless America/Dewey 1944-1948," red, white, and blue, bluetone photo on light blue ground 5

Eisenhower, bank, bust, cast white metal, KLT, Banthrico, c1940s, 5.5" h 50

Eisenhower, necktie, purple fabric, white "Stick With Ike," 1956, 51" l 35

Eisenhower, poster, "Vote Republican/ Re-Elect Ike," red, white, and blue with center bluetone photo, 1956, 11" x 14" 15

Goldwater, cufflinks, pr, white metal with brass luster, image of elephant wearing black metal eyeglasses, .75" x .75", on white glossy card 35

Goldwater, license plate, metal, dark blue "Goldwater" with "AuH20" at bottom and eagle at top left and right corners, red and blue accent border, 1964, 6" x 12" 14

Goldwater, pinback button, "Welcome The Bomb," black and white exploding bomb 15

Political Items

Harriman, bracelet, enamel on brass, "Win With Harriman," blue enamel lettering with red and green enamel rose dec, 7" l brass link chain with snap ring, c1952 18

Humphrey, pinback button, "Little People For Humphrey," yellow on black 8

Humphrey/Muskie, license plate, plastic, yellow and blue shape of Pennsylvania, 6" x 12" 15

Kennedy, John F, Christmas card, from Senator and Mrs John F Kennedy, sgd "Best—Jack," dated Dec 21, 1959, front shows poinsettias on left with photo of family on right, seal above inside message and greeting, addressed to Mr Carter O Lowance, Governors office, Richmond, VA, 5" x 6" 500

Kennedy, John F, paper cup, bright red inscription "Coffee With Kennedy" on sides, unused, 3.25" h 30

Kennedy, John F, pinback button, black and white portrait, white lettering, red, white, and blue ground 10

Kennedy, John F, sash, felt, red, white, and blue, "Vote John F. Kennedy for President," 70" l, 5" w 75

Kennedy, Robert, primary campaign folder, 4 pgs, blue text with photos of Kennedy campaigning with his family, inside notes Kennedy's views on various issues, 1969, 8.5" x 10.75" 8

Kennedy/Johnson, drinking glass, "Vote To Win In 1960 With Jack Kennedy/Lyndon Johnson," 4.5" d 50

McGovern, tie tack, silver luster metal, initial "M" with inscription "FMBM" 5

Nixon, cap, cardboard and paper, red, white, and blue, camp-style, "Nixon's The One," cardboard sides, crepe paper top, 3.5" x 11.5" 14

Nixon, clicker, "'Click with Dick' Nixon for President," blue on silver, 2" h 5

Nixon, flicker, "Win With Nixon," clear plastic case, blue and white flicker alternates between slogan and portrait 38

Nixon, sheet music, *Richard Nixon Is The One,* 4 pgs, red, white, and blue image of Nixon looking at viewer against stars and stripes shield on purple ground, ©1968 Raymond J Meurer Sr & Jr, 9" x 12" 4

Nixon, smock, white cotton mini-dress with self-tie neckline, blue trim, "Nixon" printed in bold block letters slightly off-centered down the front, c1968 87

Reagan, inauguration invitation, paper, gold emb Reagan/Bush inaugural seal at top, 1981, 8.5" x 11.5" 8

Roosevelt, Franklin D, dinner menu, from Willard Hotel, stiff paper cov with red, white, and blue flag design, black and white FDR and Garner jugate photos, 4 pp insert with welcome message and menu, bound by red, white, and blue fabric sash, 1937 .35

Shriver, pinback button, "Sargent & Eunice 1972 Democratic Candidates," browntone photos on white ground 15

Truman/Barkley, membership card, "Truman—Barkley Club," red, white, blue, and gold, reverse Truman/ Barkley jugate photos with white Capitol building illus in center, unused, 2.25" x 3.5" 35

POODLE COLLECTIBLES

People who collect dog and cat memorabilia are a breed apart. While most cat collectors collect items with any cat image (except Siamese collectors), dog collectors tend to specialize. Poodle collectors are more fortunate than most because the poodle was a popular decorating motif during the 1950s and 1960s. Poodles were featured on everything from clothing to lamps.

Bank, Barkie the Poodle, 7" h 22
Coasters, set of 4 20
Cookie Jar, black, 8.5" h, 1950s 25
Cookie Jar, poodle at cookie counter, 13.5" h 250
Cookie Jar, Zolton Lefton Co 300
Decanter Cup Set, ceramic, 6.25" h 35
Doll, Raggimals Patti Poodle, cloth, 16" h .45
Figurine, 2 poodles frolic on green grass base, Shafford, 5" h, 7" l 35
Figurine, Christmas girl carrying presents and walking poodle, dark green dress, mkd "AX2749A," "Napco Ceramic Japan" foil label, 5.25" h 12
Figurine, old woman and poodle, 7" h 35
Figurine, poodle, Boehm, 5" 100

Figurine, young girl and poodle, 5.5" h 30
Oil and Vinegar Cruets, made by Royal China Co for Jim Beam, 5.5" h 25
Planter, black poodle pulling cart, Shafford, 5" h, 8" l 45
Playing Cards, black poodle with blue bows 16
Playing Cards, white poodle, Arrco, 2.5" x 1.5" 8
Poster, cardboard, girl wearing poodle skirt and boy dancing in front of sign reading "At the Hop" 15
Radio, zippered inside a plush poodle, 9" h, 9" l 50
Salt and Pepper Shakers, black French poodles, ceramic, 3.75" h 15
Salt and Pepper Shakers, poodle head, 3" h 18
Salt and Pepper Shakers, yellow, brown and orange poodles 25
Sprinkler Bottle, figural poodle, 8.25" h, 3.25" w 350
Teapot, figural poodle, shades of gray on black, 10" h 135
Toy, Butterfly the Flying Poodle, battery operated 40
Toy, turquoise plush poodle, 5" h, 9" l 15
Toy, wind-up, pink French poodle talking on the phone 50
TV Lamp, figural poodle, 1950s, 13" h 160
Wine Decanter, poodle image on white and blue tinted glass, 7" h 30

POP-UP BOOKS

Ask any child to describe his favorite book and the answer may well include a special pop-up book. More is better in this collecting category; the more pop-ups and the more elaborate the details, the more desirable the book.

Action Pop-Up Alphabet Book, The, Modern Promotions, 1985, 20 pgs 6
Fenway Park, A Stadium Pop-Up Book, Little Brown, 1992, 14 pgs 50
Happy Pixies' Cookbook, The, Hallmark, 22 pgs 25
How Many Bugs In A Box?, Simon and Schuster, 18 pgs .18
Lion Cubs and Their World, National Geographic Society, 1992, 5 double-pg pop-ups, 10 pgs .30

Lion King, The, Disney Press, 1995, 6 double-pg pop-ups, 12 pgs 15
Little Polar Bear, North-South Books, 1993, 14 pgs 35
Maxfield Parrish Pop-Up Book, The, Pomegranate Artbooks, 1994, 12 pgs . . .75
Night Before Christmas, The, mini pop-up, Landoll's, 1997, 5 double-pg pop-ups, 10 pgs 10
Number Of Bears, A, Troll/Hallmark Cards, 1987, 12 pgs 15
Nutcracker Pop-Up, The, Stoneway Books, 1989, 3 double-pg pop-ups, 12 pgs 5
"Pop-Up" Goldilocks and the Three Bears, The, Blue Ribbon Press, 1934, 3 pop-ups, 22 pgs .175
Pop-Up Merry Christmas, Grosset & Dunlap, 1992, 10 pgs 3
Red Riding Hood Pop-Up Book, Grandreams Limited, 1993, 6 double-pg pop-ups, 12 pgs 10
Santa's Toyshop, mini pop-up, Landoll's, 1997, 5 double-pg pop-ups, 10 pgs 10
Santa Visits Mother Goose, White Plains Greeting Cards, 1953, 22 pgs 50
Sesame Street Riddle Book, The, Random House, 1977, 12 pgs 25
Shining Time Station, Yes Entertainment, 1993, a 2-pg pop-up of train station and arcade, 2 pgs 40
Six Brave Explorers, Price Stern and Sloan, 1988, triangle-shaped book, 12 pgs 12
Sleeping Beauty, Giant Pop-Up Book, Modern Publishing, 1990, 4 double-pg pop-ups, 8 pgs 8
Snow White Pop-Up Book, Grandreams Limited, 1993, 6 double-pg pop-ups, 12 pgs 10
Story of Small Pine, The, mini pop-up, Landoll's, 1997, 5 double-pg pop-ups, 10 pgs 10
Universe, The, Random House, 1985, 6 double-pg pop-ups, 12 pgs 45
Victorian Farmhouse, A, St Martin's Press, 1993, opens to a free-standing 4-room scene, 4 pgs 25
Wizard of Oz, The, Random House, 1972, 4 double-pg pop-ups, 2-page pop-up of Emerald City, 24 pgs 75
World Without Elephants?, A, Dial Books, 1993, 5 double-pg pop-ups of elephants, 10 pgs 8

PORCELIER

The Porcelier Manufacturing Company was incorporated on October 14, 1926, with business offices in Pittsburgh, Pennsylvania, and a manufacturing plant in East Liverpool, Ohio. In 1930 Porcelier purchased the vacant plant of the American China Company in South Greensburg, Westmoreland County, Pennsylvania.

Initially, Porcelier produced light fixtures. Electrical kitchen appliances were added by the mid-1930s. Some credit Porcelier with making the first all-ceramic electrical appliances. In the course of its history, Porcelier made over 100 patterns of kitchenware and over 100 different light fixtures.

Sears, Roebuck and Company and Montgomery Ward were among Porcelier's biggest customers. Many products appear with brand names such as Heatmaster and Harmony House.

In March 1954 Pittsburgh Plate Glass Industries bought the Porcelier plant and adjacent land. The company was dissolved in the summer of 1954.

Club: Porcelier Collectors Club, 21 Tamarac Swamp Rd., Wallingford, CT 06492.

Coffeepot, basketweave pattern, wildflower decal, #5007, 13" h 75

Coffeepot, Dutch couple on front, 12.75" h 85
Coffee Server, Mexican scene, 8" h, 9.25" w 90
Creamer, Hostess Field Flowers, platinum trim 16
Creamer and Sugar, cov, floral design 75
Double Boiler, pink, orange and blue flowers 35
Light, ceiling fixture, log, 2-light, 4.5" x 10.5" 85
Light, ceiling fixture, oval, 2-light 50
Light, ceiling fixture, round, 2-light, 11.25" d 85
Light, ceiling fixture, triangular, 3 light 80
Salt and Pepper Shakers, floral design, 3.5" h 12
Sconces, pr, with hardware, black 75
Teapot, Chevron, orange, 3-cup 60
Teapot, cov, yellow and white, 3-cup 75
Teapot, flamingo on front, cream colored, 6.5" h 50
Tea Set, teapot, creamer, and sugar, Cobblestone, emb figure of a girl in dark brown 95
Tea Set, teapot, creamer, and sugar, geese and ducks 120
Wall Sconce, emb flowers and leaves on basketweave ground, 6" x 4.5" 35

POSTCARDS

This is a category where the average golden age card has gone from 50¢ to several dollars in the last decade. Postcards' golden age is between 1898 and 1918. As the cards have become expensive, new collectors are discovering the white border cards of the 1920s and 30s, the linens of the 1940s, and the early glossy photograph cards of the 1950s and 1960s.

It pays to specialize. This is the only way that you can build a meaningful collection. The literature is extensive and can be very helpful.

Clubs: Deltiologists of America, P.O. Box 8, Norwood, PA 19074; Gateway Postcard Club, P.O. Box 28941, Saint Louis, MO 63132; International Federation of Postcard Dealers, Inc., P.O. Box 1765, Manassas, VA 20108, www.playle.com/IFPD/.

Note: *Barr's Post Card News* (70 S. 6th St., Lansing, IA 52151) and *Postcard Collector* (P.O. Box 1050, Dubuque, IA 52004) are two periodicals that list over fifty regional clubs scattered across the United States.

Advertising, Gold (Red) Cross Shoes, CT Art-Colortone, 1947 postmark 30
Advertising, Munich Traffic Exhibition, comical graphic of man riding bicycle, 1st day cancellation, 1953 80
Art Deco, lady with cigarette, hand-colored, unused 32
Black, caricature black couple, "Aint I yo' Honey?," 1907 postmark 38
Circus, lady with tiger on her shoulders, "Cilly" below, German Circus Krone, unused 28
Gibson Girl, unused, 1912 55
Harrison Fisher, parents and new baby, "Their New Love," illus sgd, Charles Scribners Sons, NY, Reinthal and Newman, Pubs, NY, glued to backing paper and framed, 7.5" x 9.5" 50
Holiday, pictures Washington's farewell to his officers, emb, Raphael Tuck & Sons, George Washington's Birthday Series No. 124 25
Leather, "Look before you leap...," 1908 postmark, 5.375" x 3.25" 50
Lindbergh, "I Helped to Welcome Lindbergh at Milwaukee Aug 20-21, 1927," "Lindbergh Souvenir Air Mail Card" on back, unused 28
Photographic, circus freaks, black and white real photo, undivided back, 1900s, 3.5" x 5.5" 30

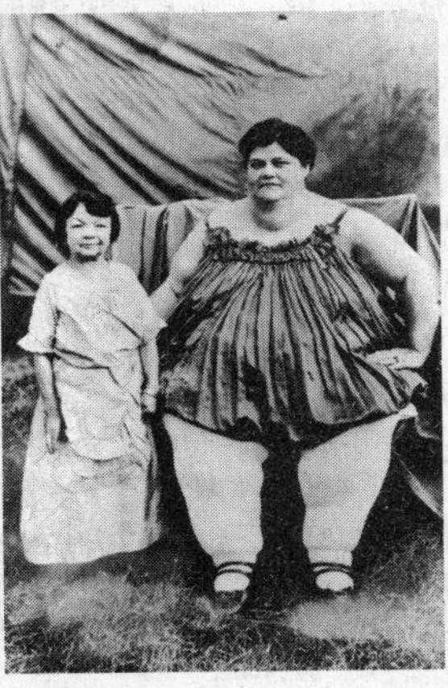

Photographic, girl holding bisque doll, unused, c1910 20
Photographic, men digging for gold, printed in Germany, undivided back, 1910 postmark 36
Photographic, sepiatone photo insert of 2 ladies on emb floral theme card, glitter highlights, unused 30
Photographic, Zeynard's Lilliputian Troupe, European circus act 26
Raphael Kirchner, Japanese man and pretty girls in kimonos, illus sgd, 1901 Austrian postmark 40
Shirley Temple, hand-colored portrait, 1938 postmark 16
Silk, "Token of Love," girl and floral heart, 1911 16
Silk, WWI, "From Your Soldier Boy," butterfly design formed from allies' flags, 3.5" x 5.5" .125
Souvenir, Atlantic City, NJ, color image of 2 women in vintage bathing costumes holding a large life preserver between them, "Greetings From Atlantic City" inside preserver, 1908 postmark 30
Transportation, black and white photo of dirigible, "Captive Balloon and Rigging Crew," divided back, 1940s, 5.5" x 3.5" . .35
Transportation, black and white photo of ship "Her Majesty's Konigin Wilhelmina," Netherlands, c1915 18
Transportation, litho of lady and bicycle, Lithographie Anstalt, Muenchen, Serie VII No. 15978, undivided back 28
WWI, litho of a pilot soliciting donations for war victims, "And You? Sign in for War Bonds," unused 32
WWII, anti-Japanese theme showing crashing and burning Japanese war plane, MWM, Aurora, MO, #AV210, unused 25

POSTERS

Want a great way to decorate? Use posters. Buy ones you like. Concentrate on one subject, manufacturer, illustrator, or period. Remember that print runs of two million copies and more are not unheard of. Many collectors have struck deals with their local video store and movie theater to get their posters when they are ready to throw them out. Not a bad idea. But why not carry it a step further? Talk with your local merchants about their advertising posters. These are going to be far harder to find in the future than movie posters.

Because so many people save modern posters, never pay more than a few dollars for any copy below fine condition. A modern poster in very good condition is unlikely to have long-term value. Its condition will simply not be acceptable to the serious collector of the future.

Circus, Bill Lynch Shows Ltd, colorful midway scene, Globe Poster Corp, USA, 42" x 14" 125
Circus, Carson and Barnes Circus, America's Largest "5–Rings–5" Under A Gigantic Big Top, laughing clown, red, yellow, and blue on white paper, 42" x 28" 65
Circus, Cole Brothers Circus, Big Railroad Show, Kay Hanneford, Greatest Bareback Rider of All Time, full color litho, Erie Litho & Ptg, Erie, PA, 18" x 26" 125
Circus, Dailey Brothers, Big Railroad Circus Presents, Pina Medel, World's Most Beautiful and Graceful Circus Star, color photo portrait, 42" x 14" 165

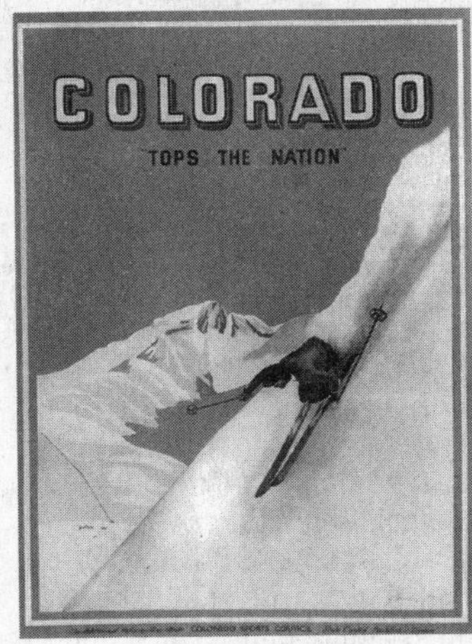

Concert, Big Brother, Rick Griffin poster for Sep 12, 1968 Bill Graham Presents concert at Fillmore West in San Francisco, CA, featuring Big Brother & the Holding Company, Santana, and The Chicago Transit Authority, 14" x 22" 310

Concert, Muddy Waters, Wes Wilson poster for Nov 4, 1966 Bill Graham Presents concert at Fillmore West in San Francisco, CA, featuring Muddy Waters and Quick Silver Messenger Service, red and green, 14" x 22" 300

Concert, The Great Society, Wes Wilson poster for Feb 26, 1966 "Family Dog" concert at Fillmore West in San Francisco, CA, featuring The Great Society, Grass Roots, Big Brother, and Quick Silver Messenger Service, 2nd printing, FD2, 14" x 20" 200

Concert, The Mothers, John H Myers poster for Sep 9, 1966 Bill Graham Presents concert at Fillmore West in San Francisco, CA, featuring The Mothers and Oxford Circle, purple, orange, and white, 14" x 20" 275

Magic, "Kar-Mi Swallows a Loaded Gun Barrel," color litho by Joseph B Hallworth, Kar-Mi in yellow, green, and red robe, with gun barrel protruding from his mouth, shooting a cracker off the head of a blind-folded assistant, while crowd of scantily-clad turbaned Indians watches, 28.25" x 41.5" 450

Magic, "The Floyds/Unique Entertainers," color litho, oval portraits of Walter and Mary Floyd imposed on red ground, Boston, Libbie Show Print, c1915, 15" x 19.75" 200

Travel, "American Airlines, Arizona," towering green cactus in foreground with horseback riders in blue and purple on orange mounts, purple hills and white hacienda in background, yellow sky, orange lettering, 40" x 30" .460

Travel, "Aspen, Ski Capitol of the Americas," skier with mountain and chairlift in background, turquoise on black, white lettering, c1950, 39.75" x 25.25" 1,375

Travel, "Go Union Pacific Railroad, Hoover Dam and Lake Mead," family motorboating in shadow of dam, brown cliffs strung with power cables, orange sky, green and red lettering, 1950s, 32.5" x 24.5" 525

Travel, "Yeoward Line, Sunshine Cruises, To Lisbon, Madeira, Canary Islands," blue harbor and yellow crescent coastline dotted with houses, ship framed between brown palm trees forming green leafy canopy, yellow lettering, Cawthorne, 34.625" x 25" 575

PRAYER LADIES

Prayer Ladies were manufactured by Enesco in the mid 1960s. Originally marketed under the name Mother-in-the-Kitchen, the figurines were made of highly glazed porcelain and modeled with reddish brown hair swept up into a bun, bowed head, closed eyes, hands folded or holding a household object, and wearing a high-necked dress. A prayer is inscribed on the white apron.

Dress colors include pink, blue, yellow, and white with blue trim. Forms range from common napkin holders, toothpick holders, and salt and pepper shakers to elusive sprinkler bottles and canister sets.

Cup, white, girl in purple dress and hat, green apron 10

Napkin Holder, blue 16

Napkin Holder, pink 25

Napkin Holder, yellow .45
Salt and Pepper Shakers, pink .34
Salt Shaker, pink .18
Scouring Pad Holder, pink .100
Teapot, pink .325
Toothpick Holder, blue .16
Toothpick Holder, pink .38
Wall Plaque, pink .160

PRECIOUS MOMENTS

During a visit to the Los Angeles Gift Show in 1978, Eugene Freeman, president of Enesco, saw some cards and posters featuring the drawings of Samuel J. Butcher. At first, Butcher and Bill Biel, his partner in Jonathan & David, were not thrilled with the idea of having Butcher's art transformed into three-dimensional form. However, after seeing a prototype sculpted by Yashei Fojioka of Japan, Butcher and Biel agreed.

Initially twenty-one pieces were made. Early figures are darker in color than those made today. Pieces produced between 1978 and 1984 and licensed by Jonathan & David Company have smaller heads than pieces relicensed by the Samuel J. Butcher Company and Precious Moments. Jonathan & David closed in 1988.

The Enesco Precious Moments Club was established in 1981. In 1989, Butcher opened the Precious Moments Chapel in Carthage, Missouri. In 1995 Goebel introduced hand-painted bronze miniatures. The year 1995 also saw Enesco launch its Century Circle Retailers, a group of 35 retailers selling a limited edition line of Precious Moments material.

Bell, Christmas, 1985, 2.5" h .10
Bell, Christmas, 1994, 4.5" h .10
Bell, girl holding gingerbread boy cookie, 1993, 5" h .10
Doll, boy, vinyl head and arms, cloth body, 8" h .10
Doll, Graduation Edition, 10.5" h .20
Doll, Tell Me the Story of Jesus, 14" h .45
Figurine, angel blowing trumpet, 6" h .30
Figurine, baby, Jesus Loves Me .30
Figurine, boy in overalls with candy canes in a flowerpot .35
Figurine, bride .20
Figurine, elephant and mouse, Blessing of Showers .25
Figurine, family, Mother Sew Dear .35
Figurine, Friendship Grows When You Plant a Seed .25
Figurine, Healing Begins With Forgiveness .45
Figurine, Jesus Is the Answer .150
Figurine, Jesus Loves Me, 5" h .60
Figurine, Jonathan and David, 25th Wedding Anniversary Couple, 5.5" h .30
Figurine, Jonathan and David, It's What's Inside that Counts .110
Figurine, Jonathan and David, Love Cannot Break a True Friendship .135
Figurine, Jonathan and David, Thou Art Mine, 5.25" h .95
Figurine, Lord Help Me to Stay On Course, 5.25" h .35
Figurine, Lord Let Our Friendship Bloom .40
Figurine, Love Lifted Me .60
Figurine, Loving is Sharing .35
Figurine, nativity, donkey .15
Figurine, Sharing Sweet Moments Together .42
Figurine, The Lord Bless You and Keep You .40
Figurine, We All Have Our Bad Hair Days .34
Figurine, wedding couple, Bless You Two, 5.5" h .25
Figurine, You Are My Once in a Lifetime .40
Figurine, You Are The Type I Love, 5.5" h .45
Figurine, You Can't Take It With You .25
Figurine, You Complete My Heart .40
Mug, Precious Moments, 1992 .5

Music Box, bride and groom, plays "Wedding March," 18" h 175
Ornament, elephant, May Your Christmas Be Gigantic 15
Ornament, giraffe, Christmas Keeps Looking Up 15
Ornament, Holiday Expressions, 1995 12
Ornament, lamb, Merry Christmas Little Lamb 15
Ornament, lion, Christmas is Something to Roar About 15
Ornament, pig, Heaven Bless Your Special Christmas 15
Ornament, satin, Holiday Fun Times Make Memories to Treasure, 1979 12
Ornament, seal, God Bless You This Christmas 15
Plate, Christmas Love Series, "My Peace I Give Unto Thee," 1987 20
Plate, Meowie Christmas, 6.5" d 15
Plate, Winters Song, 1995, 6.5" d 15
Wristwatch, angel, precision quartz, blue leather band, 1994 15

PRINCESS HOUSE

Princess House, Inc., is a direct seller of household and tabletop wares headquartered in Taunton, Massachusetts. Charles Collis founded the company in 1963. The company's state-of-the-art distribution center is located in Rural Hall, North Carolina.

Princess House sells its wares primarily through mail-order catalogs and a network of 15,000 independent consultants known as Lifestyle Consultants, who demonstrate Princess House products in approximately 500,000 homes each year.

In 1993, Princess House, Inc., was a division of the Colgate-Palmolive Company, with affiliates in Australia, Canada, England, and Mexico. Today, the company is privately owned.

Ashtray, bone china 5
Bar Set, pitcher and 4 glasses, crystal . . .35
Basket, lead crystal, 10.5" h 36
Bell, Heritage, crystal, 6" h 20
Bowl, copper bottom, 6.25" x 3" 30
Bowl, Highlights, divided 25
Brooch, swan, 14 clear rhinestones on body, 1 in eye 16
Bud Vase, Diamond, 7.5" h 10
Carafe, copper and crystal 30
Charger, Veranda Gold 10
Coffeepot, Windsor Rose 80
Condiment Bowl and Plate, Heritage 20
Creamer, Windsor Rose 25
Creamer and Suger, Heritage, 3.25" d, 2.5" h 12
Cup, Fantasia 5
Cup and Saucer, Fantasia 8
Cup and Saucer, Windsor Rose 25
Decanter, hand-blown, green glass with red stopper, 12" x 6.5" 20
Decanter, Heritage .25
Drinking Glass, Heritage, crystal, hand-blown, 9" h, 3.5" d 25
Drinking Glass, Heritage, etched flowers, 6" h 6
Goblets, long stem, set of 6 65
Ice Bucket, Heritage, 6" d, 5.5" h 15
Luncheon Plates, 8.25" d, set of 4 32
Margarita Glasses, Heritage, 7" h, 4.75" d, set of 4 20
Mug, crystal, tavern scene and humorous poem, 4.5" x 5" 25
Mug, Fantasia 5
Ornament, clear glass, mkd "Princess House Exclusive Made in USA," etched horn and bow design 8
Pitcher, Heritage, crystal, hand-blown, fluted spout, 10" h, 4.5" d 6
Punch Set, bowl and 7 cups, crystal 45
Salad Bowl, Heritage, 9.5" d, 6" h 25
Salt and Pepper Shakers, crystal, etched flowers and leaves, 3.5" h 14
Snifter, etched design, set of 4 15
Snifter, Heritage, 4.5" h 6

Spoon/Fork Holders, 3" h, 5" w 30
Sugar Bowl, cov, Fantasia 10
Vase, Highlights, 6.5" h 25
Wine Glasses, lead crystal, set of 4 30

PRINTS

There are many types of prints. Artist prints are original works of art. Mass-produced prints can be a reproduction of an artist's paintings, drawings, or designs or feature illustration art developed for mass appeal as opposed to an aesthetic statement.

When evaluating a framed print, think of two values: (1) the print outside the frame and (2) the matting and framing. All too often, there is more value in the matting and framing than the print itself.

Clubs: American Antique Graphics Society, 5185 Windfall Rd., Medina, OH 44256; American Historical Print Collectors Society, P.O. Box 201, Fairfield, CT 06430; Arthur Szyk Society, Inc., 1200 Edgehill Dr., Burlingame, CA 90410; Gutmann Collectors Club, 24A E. Roseville Rd., Lancaster, PA 17601; Hy Hintermeister Collectors Group, 5 Pasture Rd., Whitehouse Station, NJ 08889; Kate Greenaway Society, P.O. Box 8, Norwood, PA 19074; Philip Boileau Collector's Society, 1025 Redwood Blvd., Redding, CA 96003; R. Atkinson Fox Society, 8141 Main, Kansas City, MO 64114; Rockwell Society of America, P.O. Box 705, Ardsley, NY 10502; The Harrison Fisher Society, 123 N. Glassell, Orange, CA 92666.

"Fawn," Waldo Chase, doe and fawn in forest glen, matted and framed in Arts & Crafts oak frame, pencil sgd and titled, c1930, 8.5" x 4.75" image 750
"Haymakers," Hall Thorpe, farmers and a hay wagon against a sky with puffy white clouds, matted and framed in Arts & Crafts oak frame, pencil sgd, c1920, 13" x 10.5" image 975
"La Serenade," litho printed in color on wove paper, with blindstamp of publisher, margins, framed, 1979, 19.75" x 15.5" sheet 575
"Lovers and Idol," silkscreen printed in colors on wove paper, sgd and numbered 163/300, with blindstamp of publisher, margins, framed, 1980, 18.5" x 13" sheet .350
"Puget Sound, Washington," Lewis Carleton Ryan, shades of blue, green, and ocher, matted and framed in Arts & Crafts molding, pencil sgd lower right, 30/60 (Oriental Method, 15 blocks), 8" x 12" image 800
"Toward Evening," Leo Blake, 3 sailboats in a harbor on calm waters, pencil sgd lower right, matted and framed, 9.25" x 9.5" image 450
"Venus," silkscreen with foil stamping printed in colors on wove paper, sgd in pencil and numbered 165/300, with blindstamps of publisher and printer, full margins, 1982, 32.5" x 24" sheet 800

PSYCHEDELIC

Psychedelic collectibles describes a group of objects made during the 1960s and 70s that are highly innovative in their use of colors and design. American Indian tribal art, the artworks of Toulouse Lautrec and Alphonse Mucha, the color reversal approach of Joseph Albers, dancer Loie Fuller's diaphanous material, late 19th-century graphics, paisley fabrics, and quilts are just a few of the objects and techniques that are the roots of psychedelic design.

The period is marked by eclecticism, not unity—there were no limits on design. Psychedelic artists and manufacturers drew heavily on new technologies, e.g., inflatable plastic furniture. Coverings such as polyester and vinyl were heavily used.

Peter Max is the most famous designer associated with the psychedelic era. His artwork graced hundreds of objects. Although mass-produced, some items are hard to find.

Blouse, long tunic, swirl pattern on black ground, Lady Blair 20
Dress, fitted, high collar, side slits, dark blue, red, white, purple, gold, and black, size 6 44

Dress, peasant style with empire waist, gold buttons, puffy sleeves, full pleated skirt, fuchsia, orange, lemon, emerald, maroon, and white 45
Dress, swirl print, bateau neckline, slightly lower in back, half sleeves, green, gold, orange, and purple, size 20 42
Handbill, Creedence Clearwater Revival, Steppenwolf, Butterfield Blues Band, 10 Years After the Truth, Bill Graham Production, 1968 .125
Handbill, Disney's *Fantasia,* The Pasadena Hastings Theatre, 9" x 6" 35
Handbill, Jeff Beck Group, Spirit, Sweet Linda Divine, Sweetwater at the Filmore West, Bill Graham Production, 1968 100
Music Box, "Piano Man," 6" x 9.5" x 4.5" . . .45
Piggy Bank, pink and purple, Arthur Wood, 9" l 30
Poster, Allman Brothers, green tones, reprint 20
Poster, Jimi Hendrix, Rick Griffin psychedelic poster for the Feb 10, 1968 "Experience" concert at the LA Shrine Auditorium, Los Angeles, CA, red, white, and black on purple ground, 14" x 22" .550
Tea Plates, mkd "Czechoslovakia," price for 2 10
Waste Basket, plastic, folding 15

PUNCHBOARDS

Punchboards are self-contained games of chance that are made of pressed paper and contain holes with a coded ticket inside each hole. After paying an agreed upon amount, the player uses a "punch" to extract the ticket of his choice. Cost to play ranged from 1¢ to $1.00.

Animal and fruit symbols, cards, dominos, and words were used as well as numbers to indicate prizes. While some punchboards had no printing, most contained elaborate letters and/or pictures.

Punchboards initially paid the winner in cash. In an effort to appease the anti-gambling crowd, some punchboards paid off in cameras, candy, cigar, cigarettes, clocks, jewelry, radios, sporting goods, toys, etc.

The 1920s through the 1950s was the golden age of the punchboard. An endless variety were made. Many had catchy names or featured pin-up girls. Negative publicity resulting from the movie *The Flim Flam Man* hurt the punchboard industry.

Value rests with unpunched boards. Most boards sell for $15 to $30, although some have broken the $100 barrier.

Note: All boards are old and unused.

Ace High, deck of cards for jackpot, 13" x 17" 90
Baker's Dozen, baker wearing chef's hat watches 13 $20 winners, 10" x 14" 45
Barrel Of Cigarettes, Lucky Strike Green and others, 10" x 10" 44
Bars and Bells, fruit symbols and deck of cards, 13" x 18.5" 135
Beat the Seven, card tickets determine winners, 10" x 10" .35
Bell of Victory, picture of bell for jackpot, 5" x 7" 35
Best Hand, poker hand tickets, 6.5" x 11" . .35
Big Battle, "WH Brady & Co, Eau Claire, Wis" 25
Big Game, 8" x 10.5" .30
Candy Bars Put & Take, trade stimulator to sell candy bars, 7" x 7" 32
Candy Special, penny candy, 4.5" x 7.5" . . .24

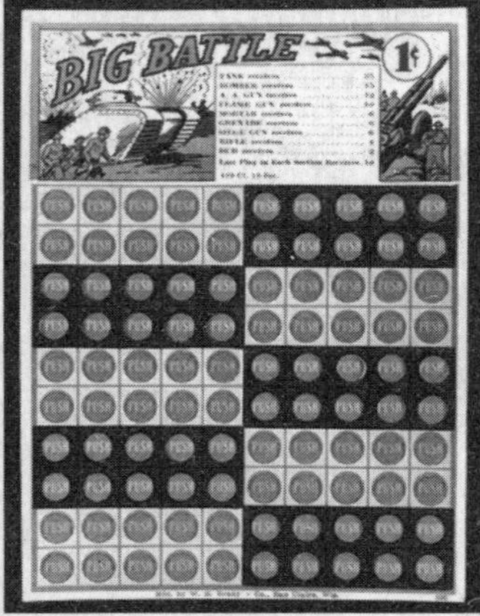

Cash In, sack of money, 8.5" x 9" 18
Cigar Game, small board to sell cigars, 4" x 3.5" 15
Double or Nothing, trade stimulator with 60% double and 40% nothing, 9" x 10" ..36
Extra Bonus, unusual dice tickets, 13" x 12" 40
Five on One, 11" x 11" 18
Five Tens, 10" x 13" 18
Football, 1¢, 1930s, 7.25" x 10" 20
Giant Win, $1 board, lots of foil, slot symbols, factory wrapped, 14" x 16" ...100
Girlie Board, prize space to be filled in by operator, 9" x 13" 32
Glade's Chocolates, set of three boards, factory wrapped, 7" x 9" 85
Good As Gold, gold foil, cash board, 12" x 15" 35
Good Punching, cowboy theme, 9.5" x 10" .36
Hit the Barrel, old wooden barrel as jackpot, 9" x 11" 35
Home Run Derby, baseball theme with ball park, 10" x 12" 75
Huff & Puff, 2¢, big bad wolf puffs at old cigarette packs including Lucky Strike Greens, 9" x 9" 60
Joe's Special Prize, 11" x 14" 20
Johnson's Chocolates, Elvgren girl, 9" x 11" 35
Little Sawbuck, cash jackpot board, 7.5" x 8.5" 28
Lu Lu Board, colored tickets, 10" x 11" 28
More Smokes, red, white, and blue tickets, 10.5" x 10.5" 24
Musical Money, thick, 12" x 14" 45
Nestle's Chocolate Bars, 2¢ board, 9" x 8.5" 45
Nickel Charley, 10" x 9" 18
Nickel Fin, cash board with colorful jackpot, 12" x 15" 40
Nickel Play, cash board, 5" x 7" 28
Odd Pennies, 2¢ and 3¢, 6.75" x 11" 45
Odd Pennies, 3¢, glamour girl looks at old cigarette packs including Lucky Strike Greens, 6.5" x 8.5" 65
Open Field Board, diecut opening for operator's prizes, 11" x 16.5" 12
Perry's Prizes, assorted girls and silver coins, 9.5" x 13" 60
Pocket Board, cartoon graphics, 2" x 2.75" 8
Positive Prizes, diecut field for operator's prizes, 12" x 17" 25
Pots-A-Plenty, 11" x 17.5" 26
Premium Prizes, 10" x 12" 20
Professor Charlie, comical professor overlooking board, 10" x 12" 18
Real Sport, $1 punch, $500 possible win, riveted, 11" x 13" 55
Section Play, 8.5" x 10" 18
So Sweet, pin-up girl, 13.5" x 13" 40
Speedy Tens, 10" x 13" 18
Sunshine Special, bathing beauty, boat with water skiers, divers, and palm trees, cash board, 12" x 12" 55
Take It Or Leave It, for the gambler who wants to push his risk, 12" x 14" 85
Tavern Maid, win cans of beer, 9.5" x 13.5" 55
Three Sure Hits, 10" x 14" 24
Tu Pots, 12" x 18" 44
Valuable Prizes, diecut field for operator's prizes, 12" x 16" 14
Win a Buck, 4.5" x 7.5" 12
Win a Seal, 3 colors of foil, wooden board, factory wrapped, 13.5" x 16" 50

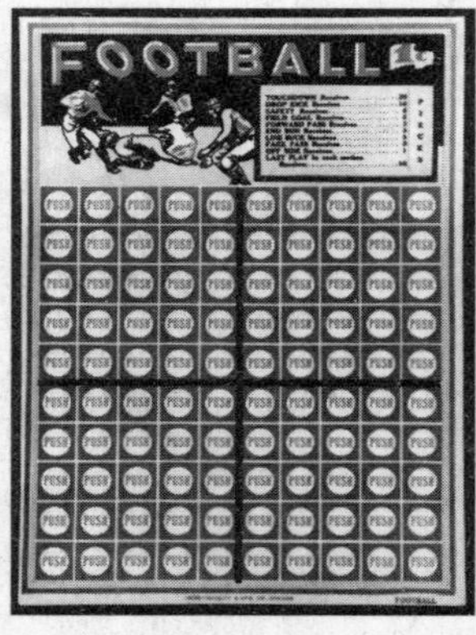

Yankee Trader, sailing ship, surprise gifts, 11" x 13" 35

PUPPETS

No, somebody is not pulling your strings, there really is a category on puppets. This category covers marionettes and related jointed play toys, as well as finger and hand puppets and ventriloquist dummies. You are bound to see a few of your favorite character collectibles hanging around.

FINGER PUPPET

Buster Brown, die cut mask, 8.5" h 12
Quasimodo, Hunchback of Notre Dame, cloth body, plastic feet, arms and head, Burger King Corp, 9" h 6

HAND PUPPET

Angel, felt 25
Black Female, cloth, black yarn hair, maid's uniform, 1945 15
Bug, green, 9" l 10
Country Boy, wooden hands, feet and head, cloth outfit, 12" h 60
French Girl, wooden hands, feet, and head, cloth outfit, 9" h 60
Knucklehead Smiff, plastic head, vinyl body, by Paul Winchell, 1966 125
Mickey Mouse, vinyl head, printed cloth body, mkd "Walt Disney Productions, Made in Korea," 10.5" h 20
Policeman, black, Childcraft, 1968, 10.25" h 38
Popeye, vinyl head, corncob pipe in mouth, 10.5" h 40
Raggedy Andy, Knickerbocker, 10" h 30
Raggedy Ann, Knickerbocker 30
Santa, felt 20
Smurf, Peycor, 1981 10
Snowman, felt 20

MARIONETTE

Bandit, papier-mâché face, wood body, plastic hands and gun 20
Elephant, Ringling Brothers and Barnum & Bailey on headpiece, 11" h, 12" w 12
Giraffe, plush soft fleece, Dakin, 1978, 12" h 8

Mexican Bandit, composition face, hands, and guns, wood body, 15" h 25
Mexican Clown, composition head, straw hat, plastic hands and feet, cloth body, 15" h 40
Pelham, wooden, felt clothing, 1960s 100
Pinocchio, soft plastic head, cloth body, Gund 50
Pluto, Gabriel Ind, 1977, 3.25" h 16
Smokey Bear, mkd "1965 Ideal Toy Corp, SB-M-266," 9" h 195
Tribal Princess, cloth with buttons and beads for joints 40

PUSH PUPPET

Atom Ant 25
Candy the Cat, Kohner, plastic, orange, 3" h 12
Crackle, Kellogg's Rice Krispies, Talbot Toys, 1984 65
Howdy Doody, Kohner Products #180 25
Snoopy, Peanuts, wearing top hat and tails with arms outstretched, standing on red base, mkd "Snoopy Corp ©1958, 1965 United Feature Syndicate, Inc" 75

VENTRILOQUIST DUMMY

Charlie McCarthy, Juro 75
Daniel Boon Dummy Dan, moving eyes ..300
Danny O'Day, composition, wearing Texaco uniform, Brooklyn Mass Co ...800
Howdy Doody, Ideal 350
Humphrey Higsby, composition, Brooklyn Mass Co 800
Jerry Mahoney, moving eyes, Juro, c1955 950

Jerry Mahoney, Paul Winchell Co, ©1966, 24" h 575
Knucklehead Smiff, Paul Winchell Co, ©1966, 24" h 575
Mortimer Snerd, Juro 75

PURINTON POTTERY

Bernard Purinton founded Purinton Pottery in 1936 in Wellsville, Ohio. In 1941 the pottery relocated to Shippenville, Pennsylvania. Dorothy Purinton and William H. Blair, her brother, were the chief designers for the company. Maywood, Plaid, and several Pennsylvania German designs were among the patterns attributed to Dorothy Purinton. William Blair designed the Apple and Intaglio patterns.

Purinton did not use decals, as did many of its competitors. Greenware was hand painted and then dipped into glaze. A complete dinnerware line and many accessory pieces were produced for each pattern.

The plant closed in 1958, reopened briefly, and then closed for good in 1959.

Apple, chop plate, 11.75" d 70
Apple, jug, 4.5" h, 5.5" w 35
Apple, salad plate, 6.875" w 12
Apple, salt and pepper shakers, 2.5" h 15
Apple, teapot 125
Cookie Jar, Pennsylvania Dutch 125
Fruit, apple and grapes, oil and vinegar cruets, small hairline on 1, 5" h 35
Fruit, apple and pear, coffee canister, 8.5" h 60
Fruit, apple and pear, creamer and cov sugar, tiny chip on bottom of creamer . .20
Fruit, apple and pear, grease jar, 5.75" h . .40
Fruit, apple and pear, night set, bottle and tumbler 75
Fruit, apple and pear, pitcher, ice lip 35
Fruit, apple and pear, sugar canister, 8.5" h 60
Intaglio, baker 20
Intaglio, bread and butter plate, 6.75" d 6
Intaglio, casserole, cov 55
Intaglio, cup and saucer 10
Intaglio, custard cup, 4" h 6
Intaglio, dinner plate, 9.75" d 12
Intaglio, mug 18

Intaglio, platter, 12.75" l 25
Intaglio, salad plate, 8.5" d 10
Intaglio, saucer 4
Intaglio, serving bowl 18
Ivy, creamer, 4.5" h 30
Ivy, teapot, 2-cup, 4.5" h 40
Ivy and Red Blossom, honey jug 30
Morning Glory, honey jug, 6.5" h 45
Plaid, cup and saucer 15
Plaid, dinner plate, 9.75" d 8
Plaid, sugar, cov 18
Plaid, teapot 50
Shooting Star, honey jug 35

PURSES

It is amazing what people will carry draped over their shoulders! Remember those alligator purses, complete with head and tail? Or how about those little metal mesh bags that held a lady's hankie and a book of matches, at most? As impractical as they were, these are some of the most collectible purses on the market, as witnessed by the prices listed below.

Club: California Purse Collector's Club, P.O. Box 572, Campbell, CA 95009.

Mesh, allover diamond pattern, multicolor, zigzag bottom edge, Whiting and Davis 85
Mesh, Art Deco allover swirl design, blue, pink, yellow, and brown, zigzag bottom edge, Whiting and Davis 100
Mesh, Art Deco design, multicolor, zigzag bottom edge, Whiting and Davis 145

Mesh, Art Deco geometric design, red, greens, brown, yellow, and white, scalloped bottom edge, Whiting and Davis 165

Mesh, Art Deco stepped geometric design, greens, brown, cream, and blue, zigzag bottom edge, Whiting and Davis 110

Mesh, Art Nouveau design, black, yellow, and pale green, zigzag bottom edge, Whiting and Davis 95

Mesh, central cartouche with single line border, black on pink ground, zigzag bottom edge, unmkd Whiting and Davis 100

Mesh, central floral medallion, black, white, and yellow, zigzag bottom edge, sgd "El–Sah" 75

Mesh, diamond grid pattern, cream and browns, zigzag bottom edge, Whiting and Davis 85

Mesh, diamond inside sq above repeating overlapping arches, blue, green, and pink, scalloped bottom edge, Whiting and Davis 140

Mesh, fancy floral spray design, yellow, orange, black, and gray, zigzag bottom edge, Whiting and Davis 110

Mesh, floral design, blue and black on cream ground, V-shaped fringed bottom edge, Mandalian 150

Mesh, floral design, pink and black on cream ground, V-shaped fringed bottom edge, Mandalian 165

Mesh, floral design, white silver metal frame, chain link fringe 75

Mesh, geometric design, red and black dominant on yellow and blue ground, scalloped bottom edge, Whiting and Davis 145

Mesh, geometric diamond bands, blue, white, and gold, zigzag and fringed bottom edge, Mandalian 145

Mesh, gold tone, Whiting and Davis, 7" w 65

Mesh, repeating geometric design, pink, brown, and greens, zigzag bottom edge, Whiting and Davis 100

Mesh, snakeskin pattern, green and yellow, straight bottom edge with band of crested waves, Whiting and Davis, replaced chain 65

Mesh, stepped geometric design, greens, brown, cream, and blue, zigzag bottom edge, Whiting and Davis 110

PUZZLES

The keys to jigsaw puzzle value in order of importance are: (1) completeness (once three or more pieces are missing, forget value); (2) picture (no one is turned on by old mills and mountain scenery); (3) surface condition (missing tabs or paper or silver fish damage causes value to drop dramatically); (4) age (1940 is a major cutting off point); (5) number of pieces (the more the better for wood); and (6) original box and label (especially important for wooden puzzles). Because of the limitless number of themes, jigsaw puzzle collectors find themselves competing with collectors from virtually every other category.

Puzzle collectors want an assurance of completeness, either a photograph or a statement by the seller that he actually put the puzzle together. Unassembled cardboard puzzles with no guarantees sell for $1 or less, wooden puzzles for $3 or less. One missing piece lowers price by 20 percent, two missing pieces by 35 percent, and three missing pieces by 50 percent or more. Missing packaging (a box or envelope) deducts 25 percent from the price.

Club: Assoc. of Game & Puzzle Collectors, PMB 321 197 M Boston Post Rd. West, Marlborough, MA 01752.

Note: Unless noted otherwise, prices are for puzzles that are complete, in very good condition, with their original box.

Against the Purple Cliffs the Breakers Roar, Tuck's Crazy Cut Puzzle, Raphael Tuck & Sons, Ltd, Raphael House, London, stormy ocean and rocky shore at sunset, 3-ply, .25" hardwood, interlocking cut, 499 pcs, 2 knobs replaced, orig box, c1930s, 15" h, 21" w 125

Anne Hathaway's Cottage, Bradley's Picture Puzzles: The Latest Novelty, .25" hardwood, non-interlocking wavy cut, sawed by #357, 106 pcs, 1 replaced, orig box with picture of women doing puzzle, c1910s, 6" h, 8" w 15

Decoys, Woodcraft Jig Saw Puzzle, Woodcraft Manufacturing Co, Berlin, NH, hunter in boat amid marsh reeds aiming rifle at ducks, 3-ply, .25" hardwood, interlocking with some color-line cutting, tight cut, 150 pcs, orig box, c1930s, 10" h, 8" w 20

Dignity & Impudence, Put Me Together Picture Puzzle, WS Herendeen, Woburn, MA, amusing picture juxtaposing gentry in Stanley Steamer with boys in wooden cart, 3-ply, .25" mixed wood, non-interlocking, 101 pcs, 9 missing throughout (all faces intact), orig box, c1910, 8" h, 6" w 5

Ford, The, Academy Jig-Saw Puzzle, J Salmon, Seven Oaks, England, horses and haywagon crossing a stream, .25" mahogany, interlocking, repetitive, loose-fitting cut, 500 pcs, orig box, c1930s, 12" h, 18" w 100

Good Dog, untitled, Hy Hintermeister scene of boy with fishing pole pausing to remove a splinter from his dog's paw, 3-ply, .25" hardwood, interlocking with very good color-line cutting, 139 pcs, 1 replaced, box may be orig, c1930s, 10" h, 9" w 45

Indian Maiden, untitled, young native American woman standing by canoe in moonlight, 3-ply, .25" hardwood, interlocking cut, 153 pcs, 1 missing (part of arm and background), 1 paper tip off, Christmas box may be orig, c1930s, 10" h, 8" w 25

Landing Pier, The, Pastime Picture Puzzle, Parker Bros, Salem, MA, Claude Monet impressionist painting of 2 women, 1 bathing her feet, 3-ply, .25" hardwood, interlocking with color-line cutting and 106 figurals, 761 pcs, 1 replaced, orig box, c1930s, 25" h, 23" w 375

Moonlight Beams, William H Hayes, Augusta, ME, sunset on the Grand Canal, 3-ply, .125" hardwood, interlocking cut, 540 pcs, 2 missing (pink sky and dark green lower edge), orig box, c1930s, 14" h, 18" w 40

Mother's World, Premier Jig Saw Puzzles, Milton Bradley Co, Springfield, MA, artist possibly Arthur J Elsley, 3-ply, .25" hardwood, sawed by #186, interlocking with color-line cutting and 10 figurals, 153 pcs, orig gray and gold box, c1930s, 12" h, 10" w 65

Norway, Pastime Picture Puzzle, Parker Bros, Salem, MA, Nordic house in summer, artist Ivan Dmitry, 3-ply, .25" hardwood, sawed by #753, interlocking with color-line cutting and 25 figurals including a pair of chicks, a giraffe, and a woman at a piano, 202 pcs, orig box, c1930s, 10" h, 15" w .100

Shepherd Comes Home From the Hills, The, pastoral scene by Scottish loch, 3-ply, .25" hardwood, interlocking and push-fit with good color-line cutting, minor warping, 505 pcs, 6 replaced (including shepherd) and 3 to 4 with minor chewings, no box, c1920-30, 17" h, 25" w 50

Ship & Gulls, Kathleen M Putney, sq rigger in full sail, artist Anton Otto Fischer, 3-ply, .25" hardwood, non-interlocking and push-fit, small pcs, irregular top edge, 286 pcs, 1 missing (small lower left edge in dark sea), orig candy box with hand-written label, c1930s, 10" h, 10" w 50

State Fair, Movie Cut-Up Co, Inc, No.10, Janet Gaynor, Will Rogers, Lew Ayres, and Sally Eilers, 13.5" x 10" orig box 25

Tallyho, Joseph K Straus, Brooklyn, NY, mounted huntsman hailing hunt party to follow the hounds, 3-ply, .25" softwood, interlocking, hand-cut, 197 pcs, orig box, c1930s, 12" h, 9" w ...45

When the Evening Sun Is Low, winter landscape with house and barn, artist SP Drake, 3-ply, .25" birch, interlocking and push-fit with color-line cutting and 28 figurals, 196 pieces, 1 replaced, orig Fanny Farmer candy box with penciled label (name of probable cutter not decipherable), c1930s, 10" h, 12" w 40

PYREX

I'll bet everyone has at least one piece of Pyrex glassware in his/her house. This heat resistant glass can be found in many forms, including casserole dishes, mixing bowls, sauce pans, and measuring cups. Pyrex was manufactured by Corning Glass Works.

Baking Dish, oval, 10oz 8

Baking Dishes, 2-pc set, pink and yellow, 10" x 8.5" 40

Bowl, cov, oval, divided 40

Bowl, green with flowers, 9" x 5" 32

Bowl, red, 10" 40

Bowl, tan with flowers, 2.5 qt 32

Bowl, white with black leaves, 2.5 qt 36

Bowls, #404 yellow, #403 green, #402 red, and #401 blue, set of 4 40

Bowls, Autumn Harvest, set of 4 55

Bowls, brown, set of 4 50

Bowls, Butterfly Gold, set of 4 55

Bowls, Butterprint, set of 4 70

Bowls, Colonial Mist, clear, set of 4 45

Bowls, Deco Blues, set of 3 44

Bowls, Homestead, set of 4 55

Bowls, Mushroom, set of 4 45

Casserole Dish, cov, Butterfly Gold, 2.25 qt 48

Casserole Dish, cov, red, 1.5 qt 50

Casserole Dish, etched lid, 9" w, 7.5" h 45

Casserole Dish and Rack, cov, 1.5 qt 35

Casserole Dish and Rack, Golden Leaf ...48

Casserole Dish and Rack, Old Orchard, 2.5 qt 50

Casserole Set, Green Butterfly, 6 pcs 42

Chip and Dip Set, Blue Bell 50

Coffeepot, clear 50

Oven Tray, 10" x 16" 35

Percolator, clear, 4-cup 60

Percolator, clear, 9-cup 65

Percolator, Flameware, 6-cup 40

Pie Plate, clear, orig label 12

Plates, 12.5" d, set of 6 90

Refrigerator Dishes, set of 8 80

Refrigerator Dishes, sq, set of 4 44

Roaster, clear, 3 qt 35

Serving Bowl and Matching Bowls, sq, set of 5 70

Snack Set, 4 pcs 55

Teapot, clear 55

Teapot, etched glass 55

Teapot, Flameware, 6-cup 45

RADIOS

If a radio does not work, do not buy it unless you need it for parts. If you do, do not pay more than $10. A radio that does not work and is expensive to repair is a useless radio.

The radio market went through a number of collecting crazes in the 1980s and 1990s. It began with Bakelite radios, moved on to figural and novelty radios, and now is centered on early transistors and 1940s plastic case radios. These crazes are often created by manipulative dealers. Be suspicious of the prices in any specialized price guide focusing on these limited topics. There are several general guides that do a good job of keeping prices in perspective.

Clubs: Antique Radio Club of America, 81 Steeple Chase Rd., Devon, PA 19333; Antique Wireless Assoc., Box E, Breesport, NY 14816.

Admiral, #5Y22AN, radio/phonograph, 1952 40
Airline-Belmont, #14BR-514 125
Arvin, #440T, red metal case, 1950 45
Atwater Kent, #60, floor model 95
Atwater Kent, #206 (center) 350
Atwater Kent, #4560-10A, breadboard .1,000
Coronado, #438190, table set 95
Crosley, #68TA, Bakelite 65
Emerson, #520, Catalin 165
Emerson, #888, transistor gift set 65
Emerson, #BJ200, Bakelite 65
Fada, #106, Super-Fadalette 55
General Electric, #114, table model, 1946 .45
Globe, transistor 90
Gloriton, #27-A, 5-tube, 1931 110
Grunow, #5E 75
Grunow, #8A, console 160
Guild, #556, Country Belle 65
Hallicrafters, #SX-62A 230
Magnavox, type M-4, horn speaker 240
Majestic, #91, console, 7-tube 55
Midland, #M6B-M6C, 6-tube 75
Motorola, #10-Y 275
Motorola, #60-X-2, 1941 65
Musicaire, #576, table model, wood, 1948 60
Neutrowound, 6-tube, 1926 450
Philco, #20, cathedral 200
Philco, #37-600 75
Philco, #37-623, tombstone (left) 80
RCA, #82, Radiola 130
RCA, #87X, wood, 1938 65
RCA, #121, refinished 325
RCA, #R28-P, 5-tube, 1933 165
Silvertone, #1660, cathedral, wood, 1935 .150
Silvertone, #7057, radio/phonograph, wood 45
Stewart Warner (right) 250
Wards Airline, #62-406 150
Westinghouse, #H126, ivory 120
Westinghouse, Aeriola Sr. 170
Zenith, #245, console, c1933 140
Zenith, #6S27, tombstone, black 300
Zenith, #5S249, chairside 500
Zenith, #5S327 250
Zenith, #6S238, half-round chairside 415
Zenith, #9S307, radio/phonograph, console 145
Zenith, Long Distance, tombstone 185

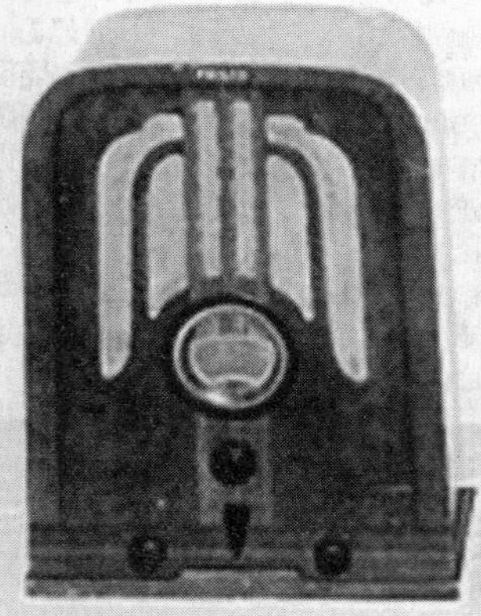

RADIOS, TRANSISTOR

In the early 1960s transistor radios were the rage. Music was now both portable and convenient. Today, the transistor has gone the way of the early hand held calculator—both are clumsy and obsolete.

Admiral, model PR290, AM, white with red, white, and blue stripe, missing ear plugs, orig box and papers 20
Aera 7 Transistor Pocket Radio, solid state, model 5019, ear phones, orig box, German instructions, 3.75" x 2.5" . . .25
Emerson, Vanguard 888, pocket size, black case, 1958, 6.5" h, 4" w 125
General Electric, model P1871A, 8-transistor, AM, gray case, audio jack, folding handle, 9-volt battery 20
Novelty, 1931 Rolls Royce, AM, 9-volt battery, 10" l 50
Novelty, Avon toilet water bottle, 2 AA batteries, 5.5" h 30
Novelty, Barbie, AM, image of Barbie above her name on front, carrying strap, 9-volt battery, 1980, 7" h 30
Novelty, Bozo the clown, 9-volt battery, missing ear plug, orig box, 1973 80
Novelty, Coca-Cola bottle, plastic, base is channel changer, turn neck for on/off and volume, 2 AA batteries, mkd "Made under authorization of the Coca-Cola Company," 8" h, 2.25" d 45
Novelty, Grand Old Parr Scotch Whiskey bottle, plastic case, cap adjusts volume and on/off, dial under lid changes channels, 9-volt battery, 6" h 35
Novelty, harp-shaped, on/off and station dial, 9-volt battery, Franklin 75
Novelty, Heinz ketchup bottle, 2 AA batteries, orig box, 1980s 75
Novelty, Jimmy Carter peanut, mkd "Copyright 1977 Kong Wah Industrial Co," plastic case and carrying strap, 9-volt battery, 7.5" h, 3.5" w 50
Novelty, smiley face, yellow plastic, missing strap, AA battery, 3" w 20
Novelty, Snoopy Joe Cool shower radio with TV, white plastic case with Snoopy on front, AM/FM, 2 TV stations (radio), WB (weather), Salton/Maxim Housewares, c1965 50

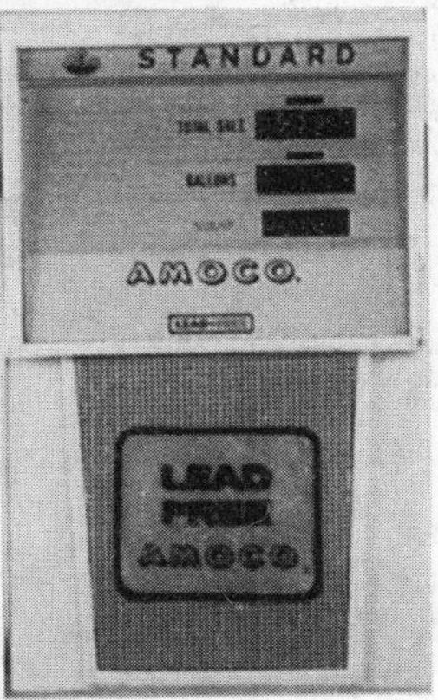

Novelty, Standard Amoco gas pump, 4.25" h, 2.5" w, 1.5" d 30

Novelty, wristwatch, metal case, wood back, knob adjusts volume and on/off, turn hands to change channels, mkd "517 Japan" 45
RCA Victor, 3RH22G, 4-volt battery, orig holder and paper inserts 25
Sanyo, Transistor 6, 4.5" x 2.75" x 1.25" 48

RAGGEDY ANN

Johnny Gruelle registered the trademark and patented a Raggedy Ann doll pattern in 1915. Three years later, he published *The Raggedy Ann Stories,* the first of twenty-five books about Raggedy Ann that Gruelle wrote before his death in 1938. Andy first appeared in 1920.

The first Raggedy Ann dolls were produced by Volland in 1915. When Volland went bankrupt in 1934, the Exposition Doll Company took over production for a year. Molly-'es, owned by Mollye Goldman, produced an unlicensed Raggedy Ann doll between 1935 and 1938. Gruelle sued for trademark and patent infringement and won. Gruelle contracted with Georgene Novelties Company to resume production. Knickerbocker Toy Company became the licensee in late 1962. In 1982, Warner Communications, owner of Knickerbocker, sold the company to Hasbro. In 1993, Applause issued a Raggedy Ann, Andy, and Baby Ann doll based on the unauthorized Molly-'es.

Bedspread, 81" x 95" 95
Book, *Raggedy Ann,* Johnny Gruelle Co, 1944, 6 animated pgs, full color 50
Book, *Raggedy Ann and the Golden Butterfly,* Johnny Gruelle, 1940 135
Book, *Raggedy Ann in Cookie Land,* Bob Merrill, 1960 45
Book, *Raggedy Ann's Magical Wishes,* Donohue, 1930 75
Book, *Raggedy Ann's Wishing Pebble,* Donohue, 1930 75
Bowl, china, Crooksville 55
Coloring Book, Hallmark, 1974, 48 pgs, 5" x 6" 30
Contact Paper, 9' l, 18" w 55
Cookie Jar, mkd "A Price Import, Japan," 11" h 95
Cookie Jar, mkd "Maurice of California USA," 12" x 10" 145
Cookie Tin, 1987, 9.75" d, 3.25" h 45
Doll, Raggedy Ann, Georgene Novelties Co, 15" h 300
Doll, Raggedy Ann, Hasbro, 18" h 45
Doll, Raggedy Ann, Knickerbocker, 31" h .110
Doll, Raggedy Ann, Knickerbocker, wide face, 36" h 145
Doll, Raggedy Ann, stitched nose and "I Love You" heart, yarn hair 85
Doll, Winter Raggedy Ann, 15.5" h 30
Drapes, 21.5" w, 61" h 65
Figurine, Purinton Pottery, 4.25" h 45
Figurine, watering flowers, Flambe, 4.25" h 55
Gift Set, Raggedy Ann Fashion, Applause, includes traditional dress, pinafore and bloomers ensemble, tea time dress, red flannel nightie, and heart-shaped travel case 45
Hand Puppets, pr 95
Lamp, 4.75" h, 3.5" w 30
Lunch Box, metal, with thermos 85
Lunch Box, plastic, with thermos, 8.5" x 7" 75
Nodder, huge head, 5.5" h, 5" d 175
Puzzle, Playskool, 9 pcs 35
Radio, Bobbs-Merrill, 1978, 6" x 6" 45
Sheet, white with Raggedy Ann and Andy on top edge, twin size 45
Tablecloth, cotton, 36" d 55
Toy, Colorforms, Tea Party, includes, Raggedy Ann and Andy, Uncle Clem, Belindy, French Doll, and a frog 75
Tray, Chein, 1972, 7.5" x 5.5" 25
Wall Plaque, plastic, with hangers, 1977, 12" l 22

RAILROADIANA

Most individuals collect by railroad, either one near where they live or grew up or one for which they worked.

Railroad collectors have been conducting their own specialized shows and swap meets for decades. Railroad material that does show up at flea markets is quickly bought and sent into that market. Collectors use flea markets primarily to make dealer contacts, not for purchasing.

Railroad paper from timetables to menus is gaining in popularity as railroad china, silver-plated flat and hollow wares, and lanterns rise to higher and higher price levels. The key to paper ephemera is that it bear the company logo and have a nice displayable presence.

Clubs: Key, Lock and Lantern, Inc., P.O. Box 66, Penfield, NY 14526; Railroadiana Collectors Assoc., Inc., P.O. Box 4894, Diamond Bar, CA 91765; Railway & Locomotive Historical Society, P.O. Box 193552, San Francisco, CA 94119.

Advertising Trade Card, Great Western & Michigan Central RW Line, color image of Niagara Falls and suspension bridge, adv text on back 20
Bread Plate, Chicago Milwaukee & Puget Sound, Puget, Warwick, top mkd with intertwined logo, 7" d 72

Bread Plate, Denver & Rio Grande Western, Prospector, Syracuse, 1948, 5.5" d 85

Coffee Cup and Saucer, Atchison Topeka & Santa Fe, California Poppy, Syracuse 45

Coffee Cup and Saucer, Great Northern, Empire, Syracuse, 1950s 20

Condiment Bowl, Canadian Pacific, white with blue floral design and crude bird, blue band along top edge, vine band along bottom, Spode, 3" d 95

Creamer, Pullman, Indian Tree, Lamberton 100

Demitasse Cup and Saucer, Baltimore & Ohio, Centenary, Scammel's Lamberton Design Patented backstamp 55

Double Egg Cup, Missouri Kansas & Texas, Blue Bonnet, Buffalo 210

Fruit Bowl, Great Northern, Glacier, OP Co Syracuse, 1930, 5.25" d 100

Lantern, short globe, Burlington Route, "BR" on shoulder of flat top Handlan frame, 3.25" red unmkd globe, bottom wire guard slightly bent 50

Lantern, short globe, Delaware Lackawanna & Western, "DL&WRR" on shoulder of Dietz Vesta frame, clear unmkd Dietz Vesta globe 35

Lantern, short globe, Denver & Rio Grande Western, "D&RGW" on shoulder of flat top Handlan frame, clear unmkd 3.25" Kopp glass globe 85

Lantern, tall globe, Colorado & Southern, "C&SRY" on shoulder of 1895 Adams & Westlake bell bottom frame with double wire guards and fixed bell, clear Corning-style globe etched "C&SRY" 550

Lantern, tall globe, Delaware Lackawanna & Western, "DL&WRR" on shoulder of 1913 Reliable frame with single wire guard and drop-in pot, 5.5" red-flashed extended base globe with cast "DL&WRR" 250

Lantern, tall globe, Kansas City Terminal, "KCTRY" on shoulder of 1913 Reliable frame with fixed bell bottom and drop-in pot, clear 5" globe with cast "UD CO" and extended base 185

Lantern, tall globe, Southern Pacific, "SPCO" on shoulder of Adlake Kero 3-52 frame, clear unmkd 3.25" globe, frozen pot with small hole 40

Letter Opener, "1852-1952 A Century of Service, Rock Island Lines," red plastic, locomotive handle, 9" l 6

Lock, C&EIRR stamped on body of brass Corbin-style special purpose lock with steel shackle and mkd working key 15

Lock, CM&STPRR cast down panel of brass heart-shaped lock with steel chain, reverse key cov cast "REPAIR TRACK," mkd working key 400

Lock, GNRY SIGNAL cast down panel of small brass heart-shaped signal lock mfg by Slaymaker, key cov cast "Remove Key When Locking" 75

Lock, MCRR stamped on shackle of brass heart-shaped Slaymaker switch lock with chain 60

Lock, NYCRR stamped on shackle of steel Miller Co special purpose lock 15

Lock, RUTLAND stamped on body of steel Adlake switch lock 35

Lock, SOUTHERN PACIFIC sunset logo cast on body of brass heart-shaped special purpose lock 95

Lock, WAB RR stamped on shackle of brass heart-shaped switch lock mfg by MM Buck, St Louis, iron forged chain 110

Luncheon Plate, Great Northern, Glacier, OP Co Syracuse, 1925 110
Matchbook, New Jersey Central Railroad, Terminal Restaurant adv on front, "New Jersey Central Railroad" on saddle, "Ride the 'Crusader' Between New York and Phila, The Blue Comet Between New York and Atlantic City" and drawings of trains on back, "Choice Beer, Wines, Liquors, Excellent Food, Prompt-Courteous Service" inside, Diamond Match 7
Presentation Lantern, Adams & Westlake, nickel-plated bell bottom frame with 1864 patent date, clear globe with wheel-cut "JR JONES" between 2 floral bands 525
Presentation Lantern, Pullman, "3" on bottom of nickel-plated frame with single wire guard, clear globe etched "PULLMAN" 275
Service Plate, Illinois Central, Panama Limited, red diamond logo and Syracuse backstamps, 1923, 10.25" d . .750

RAMP WALKERS

These comical toys have waddled their way into many toy collections. While you may find some ramp walkers made from metal, wood, or celluloid, the majority of those available are plastic. Subjects vary from advertising figures to generic animals to popular television cartoon characters.

Circus Elephant, 2.25" h 70
Cow, 2.25" h 45
Donald Duck, Marx, 1950s, 3.25" h 75
Elephant, 2.25" h 65
Farmer, 2.5" h 60
Hap and Hop, Marx 48
Horse, yellow and red 15
Little Girl 115
Mickey Mouse, 3" h .30
Penguin, 2.5" h 60
Penguin, 3" h 5
Popeye, 1960s, 3" h .20
Primitive Soldier, wood and cloth, 1920s, 4.75" h 75
Snoopy, 1958 15
Soldiers, 2.5" h 65
Toucan, 3" h 5
Walking Milking Cow, 1950s 125

RANSBURG

Harper J. Ransburg founded a glass cutting firm in Indianapolis, Indiana, in 1911. Following World War I, he introduced two decorated candles and hand-decorated glassware to his product line. Hand-decorated stoneware followed in 1931, then hand-decorated metalware in 1933.

The period from 1945 to the end of the 1960s was the Golden Age of Ransburg kitchen and bathroom hand-decorated metal and stoneware products. Designs are very period driven from the Fab Fifties to the Psychedelic Sixties.

PLASTIC

Canisters, Mexican on yellow ground, sq, set of 4 20

STONEWARE

Bowl, asters on orange ground, model 205, label on bottom, 4.5" h, 11.25" d 24
Bowl, Mexican on blue ground, model 205, 11.25" d 36
Cookie Jar, asters on blue ground, model 207, missing lid 15
Cookie Jar, asters on green ground, model 207, missing lid 45
Cookie Jar, asters on orange ground, model 700, round, 10" h, 8.5" d 20
Cookie Jar, asters on yellow ground, model 207, 9" h, 6" d 55

Cookie Jar, water lilies on blue ground, model 207, 11" h 65
Creamer, asters on orange ground, 3.25" h, 4.5" w 14
Donut Jar, hollyhocks on orange ground, 5.5" h 20
Munch Jar, asters on black ground, #528, 5" h, 8.75" d 75
Range Set, salt and pepper shakers and cov grease jar, asters on orange ground 36
Salt and Pepper Shakers, asters on orange ground, pear-shaped 25
Salt and Pepper Shakers, asters on yellow ground, pear-shaped, 5" h 25
Salt and Pepper Shakers, Mexican on yellow ground, round, ftd 18

TIN

Canister Set, 4 pcs, Meissen pattern on yellow ground, plastic lids 10
Cookie Tin, clown face on yellow ground, "I Have Cookies," wooden lid, 8.5" h 45
Tissue Holder, gold design on pink ground, 2.5" h, 10.75" l 18
Tissue Holder, jewel stars on metallic gold ground, 2.5" h, 11.5" l 12
Tray, pink flamingo and multicolor flowers on black ground, 14" x 10.5" 25
Wastebasket, multicolor boy and flowers on blue ground, wooden ball feet, 14" h, 7.5" w 25
Wastebasket, white daisies and green leaves on yellow ground, 11.5" h, 8.75" w 15
Wastebasket, white poodle and parasol in textured paint on black ground, rhinestone trim, 13" h 30

REAMERS

Finding reamers in mint condition is next to impossible. The variety of materials from which they were made is staggering, ranging from wood to sterling silver. As in many other categories, the fun examples are figural.

Reamers are identified by a number system developed by Ken and Linda Ricketts in 1974. This cataloging system was continued by Mary Walker in her two books on reamers. Edna Barnes has reproduced a number of reamers in limited editions. These are marked with a "B" in a circle.

Club: National Reamer Collectors Assoc., 47 Midline Court, Gaithersburg, MD 20878.

Barnes, forest green glass, 3.5" h 35
Child's Face, ceramic, 3" h 235
Citrus, face, orange, ceramic, 5.25" h 210
Citrus, fruit, ceramic, 1940s, 3.5" h 185
Citrus, open, ceramic, 1960s-70s, 6.5" l, 4" w 100
Citrus, orange, ceramic, 6" h 285
Clown, ceramic, 1940s, 4.75" h 285
Clown, ceramic, 1940s, 7.25" h 295
Depression Glass, green 25
Depression Glass, pink 45
Duck, ceramic, 2.5" h 185
England, lemon, amber glass 25
Federal, clear glass 15
Floral, ceramic, 1940s, 4" h 130
Floral, open, ceramic, 1940s, 2.5" h 115
Fry, green glass 45
Fry, opalescent glass 65
Grapefruit, crystal 10

Grapefruit, pressed glass, clear 15
Hazel Atlas, Crisscross, clear glass 18
Hazel Atlas, Crisscross, green glass 22
Hocking, green glass 20
Japan, ceramic, 2 pcs 45
Japan, floral, ceramic, 4.75" d 40
Japan, lotus flower, ceramic 85
Jeannette, jadeite glass 120
Jeannette, pink glass 35
Lusterware, duck, 1940s, 3.5" h 195
Lusterware, fruit, 1940s, 5" h 175
Stoneware, 4.5" h 40
Sunkist, pink glass 30
Sunkist, white glass 45
Vaseline, green 25

RECORDS

Most records are worth between 25¢ and $1. A good rule to follow is the more popular the record, the less likely it is to have value. Who does not have a copy of Bing Crosby singing *White Christmas*? Until the mid-1980s the principal emphasis was on 78 rpm records. As the decade ended 45 rpm records became increasingly collectible. By 1990 33⅓ rpm albums, especially Broadway show-related, were gaining in favor.

By the way, maybe you had better buy a few old record players. You could still play the 78s and 45s on a 33⅓ machine. You cannot play any of them on a compact disc player.

Clubs: Assoc. of Independent Record Collectors, P.O. Box 222, Northford, CT 06472; International Assoc. of Jazz Collectors, P.O. Box 518, Wingate, NC 28174.

45 RPM

Annette, Buena Vista Records BVF-414, *Teenage Wedding,* wedding dress sleeve 375
Beatles, MGM Records K-13227, *Why,* paper sleeve 201
Bryan Brent and The Cut Outs, Penny Records 2201, *Vacation Time/For Eternity* 195
Buddy Holly, Coral Records 9-61885, *Peggy Sue* 315
Carl Perkins, Columbia Records 4-41131, *Pink Pedal Pushers,* picture sleeve 45
Eddie Cochran, Liberty Records F-55112, *Twenty Flight Rock,* paper sleeve 185
Elvis Presley, RCA Victor 61-7777, *It's Now Or Never,* paper sleeve 315
Johnny Powers and His Rockets, Fortune Records 199, *Honey, Let's Go (To a Rock and Roll Show)* 90
Martha and the Vandellas, Gordy Records 7033, *Dancing in the Street,* picture sleeve 125
Paul McCartney, Apple Records 1851, *Mary Had a Little Lamb/Little Woman Love,* illus sleeve 160
Shelly Fabares, Colpix Records CP 621, *Johnny Angel,* picture sleeve 125
Smokey Robinson and The Miracles, Standard Groove 13090, *I Care About Detroit,* promotional 1-sided label, paper sleeve 60
The Arc-Angels, Lancer Records, *Goddess/Little Wheel* 90
The Chartbusters, Mutual Records 508, *Why (Doncha Be My Girl),* label sleeve 90
The Four Gents, Oncore Records ON-83, *Young Girls Beware* 225
The Miracles, Tamla Records T-54028, *Way Over There,* paper sleeve 60
The Rolling Stones, London Records 45-9725, *Heart of Stone,* picture sleeve 345
The Ronettes, Philles Records 123, *Walking in the Rain,* picture sleeve 80

LP

Bob-B-Soxx and the Blue Jeans, Philles Records PHLP-4002, includes *Zip-A-Dee Doo Dah* 185
Eddie Holland, Motown Records 604, includes *Eddie Holland* 200
Hot Rod Rumble Soundtrack, Liberty LRP-304B, 1957 100
Martha and the Vandellas, Gordy Records 902, includes *Come and Get These Memories,* autographed on back cov 200
Ronnie Hawkins and the Hawks, Roulette Records SR 25102, includes *Mr Dynamo* 125
The Belmonts, Sabina Records SALP-5001, includes *Carnival of Hits* 70

The Contours, Gordy Records 901, includes *Do You Love Me (Now That I Can Dance),* autographed on back cov 275
The Crystals, Philles Records PHLP-4001, includes *He's a Rebel* 275
The Dells, Vee Jay Records LP 1010, includes *Oh, What a Nite* 225
The Duke of Earl, Vee Jay Records LP-1040, includes *The Duke of Earl* 45
The Marvelettes, Tamla Records 228, includes *Please Mr Postman* 300
The Miracles, Tamla Records 220, includes *Hi We're The Miracles* 375
The Skyliners, Calico Records LP-3000, includes *The Skyliners* 220

RED WING

Red Wing, Minnesota, was home to several potteries. Among them were Red Wing Stoneware Company, Minnesota Stoneware Company, and the North Star Stoneware Company. All are equally collectible. Red Wing has a strong regional base. The best buys are generally found at flea markets far removed from Minnesota. Look for pieces with advertising. Red Wing pottery was a popular giveaway product.

Club: Red Wing Collectors Society, Inc., 2000 W. Main St., Ste. 300, Red Wing, MN 55066; The Rumrill Society, P.O. Box 2161, Hudson, OH 44236.

Ashtray, Minnesota Twins 1965 World Series 150
Ashtray, Red Wing Potteries 75th Anniversary, wing-shaped 150
Butter Churn, commemorative, 20#, 1994 .85
Casserole Dish and Stand, Bob White, 2 qt 65
Chicken Feeder, commemorative, 1993 . . .80
Clock, Mammy, with label 450
Cookie Jar, cov, Cabbage, orange, bottom mkd 950
Cookie Jar, cov, RoundUp 425
Figurine, princess, #1308, chartreuse 55
Hors d'Oeuvres Holder, Bob White 45
Jug, commemorative, 1990 130
Jug, commemorative, North Star, 1992 . .110
Lamp Base, cattail with flowers 250
Lobby Jar, stag scene, tan 500
Pantry Jar, commemorative, 1991 125
Pitcher, commemorative, 1989 225
Pitcher, RumRill, blue 80
Planter, lamb, blue, Red Wing sticker . . .125
Salad Bowl, Montmartre, large 70
Salad Bowl, Random Harvest, large 55
Side Salad Plate, Northern Lights 12
Teapot, Fondoso, Gypsy Trail line, pastel green, 7.5" h 65
Vase, #1183, eggshell ivory antiqued with brown, bottom mkd, 6" h 70
Vase, Georgia Rose Line, #174, ivory with pink int, 5" h .110
Vase, Indian and deer, #1151, white 75
Vase, nudes, #20, glossy green glaze, bottom mkd 230
Vase, rooster, M-1436, ivory with mint green int, bottom mkd 225
Vase, ship, #1140, shell pink 100
Vase, urn, #778 70
Wall Planter, black violin, M-1484, with sticker and sealed instruction packet of strings 50
Water Pitcher, Golden Viking, large 70
Water Pitcher, Tampico, Village Green shape 85

RITTGERS SPORTS FIGURES

Remember those caricature sports figures with the hilarious antics and expressions? Well, search your attic because Rittgers figures are now highly collectible.

Baseball Duo, batter standing with weight shifted to back foot, waiting for pitch, catcher in squatting position, both dated "1946" and sgd 825

Baseball Trio, with variation umpire, batter and pitcher with menacing expressions looming over indignant umpire, paint flecks and cracks, 1940s 845

Baseball Wall Plaque, 3-D baseball scene of a batter who has just cracked a bat over the head of an opponent, a fellow teammate consoles the forlorn-looking batter as the umpire banishes him from the game, dated "1947," sgd on base, 12" l, 9" h 1,425

Basketball Set, 2 basketball players and basket, 1 player just made rebound and came down with his opponent's head, headless player standing and pointing, 1949 4,850

Bowling Duo, buxom female "clocks" her boyfriend with her bowling ball as she approaches the foul line 400

Boxing Trio, larger boxer is blinded with "black eyes" and inadvertently slugs the referee as the other boxer ducks, 1942, minor paint flecks 515

Exercise Girl, posed in a "bicycle" position, figure and looks resemble Rita Hayworth, dated "1944" and sgd "L Rittgers," scattered paint loss ... 1,000

Football Duo, tackler who has pulled the pants off the ball carrier, very minor paint flecks, 1941 275

Gorgeous George Wrestling Set, consisting of a frightened trainer, a monstrous gorilla-like wrestler, and a self-promoting "George" wrestler, 1952 . . 1,500

ROAD MAPS

The majority of collectible road maps were issued after 1910. Previously, maps were issued by railroads, and from the turn of the century to 1920, guide books were issued for bicycle routes and brave early automobile owners.

In the mid-1920s a uniform national highway marking system was adopted, roads got better and America became mobile. Maps were published and given free to motorists by oil companies and state governments. Although other private interests published atlases and special maps, the oil company and state issues have the largest following among collectors.

Scarce maps issued by obscure or regional oil companies and those with interesting graphics command the highest prices. Maps published by major oil companies after World War II are plentiful and their value has remained modest.

As in all collectibles, especially paper items, condition is all important. Prices listed are for road maps in excellent condition.

Club: Road Map Collectors of America, 5832 NW 62nd Terrace, Oklahoma City, OK 73122.

American Oil, Ohio, 1973 3

Ashland Flying Octanes, Kentucky and Tennessee, 1950s 15

Chevron, California, 1973 3

Conoco, Illinois, 1970 3

Esso, Delaware, Maryland, Virginia, and West Virginia, 1961 8

Esso, New England, 1936 15

Esso, New York World's Fair, 1963-64 12

Esso, War Map II (Europe), 1942-43 15

Standard Oil Co of California, 1930 12

Standard Oil Co of California, Seattle/ Tacoma and Vicinity, Gousha "CC" code, 1955 6
Tydol, Trails Through New Hampshire and Vermont, 1930s 12
Tydol, Trails Through New Jersey, 1930s .12

ROBOTS

This category covers the friction, windup, and battery-operated robots made after World War II. The grandfather of all modern robot toys is Atomic Robot Man, made in Japan between 1948 and 1949.

Robots became battery operated by the 1950s. Movies of that era fueled interest in robots. R2D2 and C3PO from Star Wars are the modern contemporaries of Robbie and his cousins.

When buying at a flea market, take time to make certain the robot is complete, operational, and has its original box. The box is critical.

Cragstan Astronaut, Yonezawa, Japan, litho tin, windup crank handle, advances with moving arms, 10" h 600
Golden Gear Robot, SH, Japan, battery-operated, tin, advances with moving legs and arms, flashing light on head, bullet-shaped plastic eyes, orig box, 9" h 600
Magic Mike II, battery-operated, 1984, 11.5" h 100
Shogun Warrior, Y&K, Japan, rocket launchers in legs, 1970s, 23" h 125
Son of Garloo, Marx, windup, metal and plastic, missing name sign, 5.5" h 160

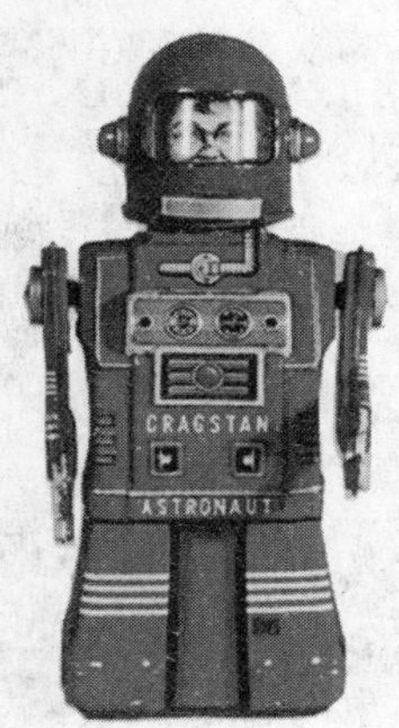

Space Fighter, Horikawa, brown with multicolored details, doors in chest for twin lasers, walking movement, 16" h 230
Sparking Ratchet Robot, Nomura, Japan, windup, metallic blue body with black and chrome accents, ratchet tool in right hand, light-up red plastic eyes and mouth, coiled silver antenna across head from ear to ear, adjustable wire antenna in pack on back, sparking action viewed through window in chest, 1955, 8" h .635
Sparky Planet Robot, KO, Japan, windup, orig box, 8.75" h 475
Star Strider, tin, 12" h 175
Strobot Laser Moving Robot, 19.5" h 200
Television Spaceman, Alps, metallic gray with TV screen in chest with lunar images, clear plastic head, radar, walking action, in box, 14" h 920

ROCK 'N' ROLL

Most collectors focus on individual singers and groups. The two largest sources of collectibles are items associated with Elvis and the Beatles. As revivals occur new interest is drawn to older collectibles. The market has gotten so big that Sotheby's and Christie's hold Rock 'n' Roll sales annually.

Club: Kissaholics, P.O. Box 22334, Nashville, TN 37202.

Note: See Beatles and Elvis for additional listings.

Beach Boys, record album, *Surfin' Safari* 25
Brothers Four, black and white promotional photo from *Top 40 Hits* magazine, 1964, 8.5" x 11" 6
Grateful Dead, poster, Sep 22, 1967 "Family Dog" concert, Denver, CO, gray and white skull with "Pig Pen" image in nose cavity, text information in blue and yellow banners, green and red ground, 14" x 20" 300
Grateful Dead, poster, silk screened on satin, Skeleton and Roses theme, 1983, 45" x 54" 250
Hot Tuna/John Mayall, Rick Griffin poster, Jun 13, 1975 "Orange County Jam" concert at Anaheim Convention Center, special guest stars Honk, Sons of Champlin, and Les Moore, orange, yellow, black, and white, 15" x 23" 150
Iron Butterfly, record album, ATCO, In-A-Gadda-Da-Vida 18
Kiss, action figure, Paul Stanley/The Jester, Psycho Circus 12
Michael Jackson, comic book, *Moonwalker* #1, 3-D, 1989 50
Monkees, Mike, finger puppet, Remco, vinyl head and arms, stretchy suit with red vinyl vest, mkd "MONKEES ©1970 & ™ of Columbia Pictures Industries, Inc Remco Ind, Inc.," 5" h 45
Pink Floyd, comic book, The Wall 25
Rolling Stones, concert ticket, 1981, unused 40
Rolling Stones, poster, "Sucking In Seventies," tongue sticking out through lips, 37" x 22" 25

ROCKWELL, NORMAN

The prices in this listing are retail prices from a dealer specializing in Rockwell and/or limited edition collectibles. Rockwell items are one of those categories for which it really pays to shop around at a flea market. Finding an example in a general booth at ten cents on the dollar is not impossible or uncommon.

When buying any Rockwell item, keep asking yourself how many examples were manufactured. In many cases, the answer is tens to hundreds of thousands. Because of this, never settle for any item in less than fine condition.

Club: Rockwell Society of America, P.O. Box 705, Ardsley, NY 10502.

Bell, Christmas, Santa holding a drum with the name "Tommy" on gift card . . .18
Bells, porcelain, set of 4 on wooden stand, 7" h, 3.25" w 95
Book, *Saturday Evening Post Norman Rockwell Memory Album,* 1979 10
Cookbook, illus by Norman Rockwell 20
Doll, bisque, Bess, jointed arms and legs 125
Drinking Glasses, different print on each, 4.25" h, set of 8 20
Figurine, Artist's Daughter, 6.5" h 100
Figurine, Fisherman's Paradise, Goebel, 2 young boys napping under umbrella with black and white dog by their side, 4.5" h 225

Figurine, ill man being cared for by his wife, Goebel 150
Limited Edition Plate, Freedom from Want, Gorham, 1976, 10.5" d 125
Limited Edition Plate, Looking Out to Sea, River Shore Ltd, 10.25" d 170
Limited Edition Plate, Triple Self-Portrait, copper, 7.75" d 150
Limited Edition Plate, Under the Mistletoe, etched silver, 1971, 8" d 125
Magazine, *Saturday Evening Post,* July 1942 20
Magazine, *Saturday Evening Post,* Sep 1949 15
Magazine,* Saturday Evening Post, *Aug 16, 1958 6
Mug, boy surrounded by his dog and her puppies, cream ground 8
Mug, Looking Out to the Sea, 1985, 4.5" h .12
Ornament, "Gramps at the Reins," 1997 . . .5
Ornament, "Santa at the Map," 1998, 3" d . .5
Pillow, Christmas, Santa sleeping among working elves, 15.5" x 15.5" 25
Planter, earthenware, Two's Company, 1983 30
Print, litho, *Saturday Evening Post* cov, 1972 7
Print, The Shoemaker, 1987, 8" x 10" 10
Print, The Street was Never the Same, 17.25" x 18" 40
Tray, tin, "Who's having more fun?," 2 children eating corn on the cob, 17.5" x 12.75" 70
Tumbler, The Rocking Horse, 1933, 16 oz . . .6

ROOKWOOD

In 1880 Cincinnatian Maria Longworth Nichols established Rookwood, a pottery named after her father's estate. She and a number of other Cincinnati society women designed and produced the first forms and decorative motifs.

Financial difficulties resulted in the company changing hands several times before its closing in 1967.

Basket, gondola shape, standard glaze, K Shirayamadani, yellow slip-painted daisies on shaded green ground, imp flame mark and artist cipher, 1888, 8" x 15.5" 650

Bowl, low, Z Line, imp geometric pattern, matte green glaze, flame mark, 1904, 2.25" x 6" 413
Cornucopia Vase, #27645, 3-ftd, satin blue, 7.5" 300
Ewer, Sallie Toohey, standard glaze, oak leaves on shaded brown and umber ground, flame mark, 1899, 11" x 8" 413
Humidor, Constance A Baker, standard glaze, pipes, matches, and cigars on shaded ocher, orange, and green ground, flame mark, 1896, 5.5" x 6" 650
Jardiniere, faience, emb steer skulls and garlands, matte green glaze, imp flame mark, 11.5" x 14" 715
Lamp Base, #6775, celadon green, 1945, 9.5" h 225
Vase, #2312, pink and green, 1920 240
Vase, #2413, matte pink, 1925, 8" h 350
Vase, #6314, lily-shaped, turquoise, sgd "65," 1945, 7.25" h 200
Vase, bulbous, incised chevron lines under matte caramel glaze, imp flame mark and artist's cipher "AM," 7" x 5.75" 600

ROOSTER COLLECTIBLES

Country has always had a barnyard favorite. Pigs were popular in the late 1980s and early 1990s. Cows commanded Country stylists' loyalties in the mid-1990s.

The rooster reigned supreme from 1946 through the end of the 1950s. Rooster images flooded the kitchen on everything from metal bread boxes and canister sets to dish towels and trays. Several American pottery manufacturers made dinnerware featuring a rooster motif, e.g., Metlox's California Provincial and Red Rooster patterns. Japanese manufacturers followed suit with inexpensive imports. Several of the Japanese patterns featured rose motifs surrounding the rooster.

Note: Items listed are either decorated with an image of a rooster or are in the shape of a rooster.

Batter Pitcher, 7.25" h 40
Bowl and Saucer, Rooster and Roses, Early Provincial Ucago 14
Bread Mold, West Germany, 13" x 8.5" 65
Burlap Bag, 7.5" x 4" 5
Candy Dish, brightly colored 30
Coasters, 4 different designs, set of 4 20
Coffee Canister, wooden lid, 6" h, 4" w 15
Condiment Set, Rooster Head pattern, pressed glass, consisting of shakers, mustard, and holder 175
Cookbook Stand, cast iron, 10.5" w, 9.5" h .30
Creamer, 1940s, 5" h 75
Creamer, Cleminson, 5.5" h 65
Creamer, Germany, 4.75" h, 8" l 125
Decanter Set, pitcher and 4 juice glasses 90
Double Egg Cup 20
Drippings Jar, wooden lid, 3" h, 4" w 15
Egg Cup, pink int, 3.5" h 15
Figurine, porcelain, pink, 3.5" h 10
Figurine, rooster standing on log, 10" h . . .10
Flat Iron, cast iron, 7" h, 7.5" l 15
Hamburger Press, wooden, 5" d 15
Hand Towel, linen-cotton blend, 15" x 26" .10
Ice Bucket, Watt 325

Juice Glass, enamel-painted, 2.5" h 10
Lazy Susan, wooden 16
Letter Holder, cast iron 15
Nutcracker, cast iron, wooden base 10
Oil and Vinegar Set, 5" h 15
Pepper Mill, 4" h 16
Pitcher, metal, ivory crackle finish, 9.25" h 20
Plate Set, pr of dec plates on stands, 10" d 45
Pot Rack, hanging 55
Salt and Pepper Shakers, yellow 24
String Holder, chalk, 8.5" h 225
Supper Trays, large serving tray and 10 individual servers 35
Tablecloth, linen 32
Teapot, 9" h 55
Tiles, framed, 9.5" h, 9.5" w 20
Wall Clock, battery-operated, pendulum . .25
Wall Plaques, pr, chalkware, 9" l, 6.5" w . .10

ROSEMEADE

If you live in the Dakotas, you probably know about Rosemeade. If you live in California, Georgia, or Maine, I am not so sure. Rosemeade is one of the many regional pottery manufacturers that American collectors rediscovered in the past decade.

Rosemeade is actually a trade name for ceramic pieces made by the Wahpeton Pottery Company between 1940 and 1953 and Rosemeade Potteries between 1953 and 1961. Production included commemorative and souvenir pieces and household and kitchen wares.

Rosemeade prices are stronger in the Midwest and Plains states than elsewhere across the country. Figurines and figural pieces command top dollar.

Club: North Dakota Pottery Collectors Society, P.O. Box 14, Beach, ND 58621.

Candlestick Ring Vase, cream, 4" d 30
Console Set, flower dish and pr of matching candleholders, black gloss, price for 3-pc set 85
Creamer and Sugar, Blue Tulip, 2" h 85
Creamer and Sugar, miniature, light blue 100

Figurine, pheasant, 3" h, 3.5" w 50
Figurines, Fox Trio 95
Flower Frog, deer, 6" h 85
Luncheon Plates, Prairie Rose, 6.75" d 25
Miniature Shoe, Indian moccasin 65
Pitcher, miniature, 3.5" h 34
Planter, deer, 3.25" h 35
Salt and Pepper Shakers, bear, 3" h 80
Salt and Pepper Shakers, fox terrier, 2" h .56
Salt and Pepper Shakers, mice, 1.75" h, 2" l 95
Salt and Pepper Shakers, pheasant, 3" h 75
Salt and Pepper Shakers, quail 75
Salt and Pepper Shakers, Siamese cat, 2.75" h 32
Salt and Pepper Shakers, skunk, 3" h 70
Salt and Pepper Shakers, terrier, 3" h 80
Shaker, single duck, 2.5" h 26
Spoon Rest, pheasant, 3.25" x 5.5" 75
Television Lamp, palomino horse 900
Tidbit Tray, pheasant, 4 sections, 5" h, 9" w 225

ROSEVILLE

Roseville rose from the ashes of the J. B. Owen Company when a group of investors bought Owen's pottery in the late 1880s. In 1892 George F. Young became the first of four succeeding generations of Youngs to manage the plant.

Roseville grew through acquisitions of another Roseville firm and two in Zanesville. By 1898 the company's offices were located in Zanesville. Roseville art pottery was first produced in 1900. The trade name Rozane was applied to many lines. During the 1930s Roseville looked for new product lines. Utilizing several high gloss glazes in the 1940s, Roseville revived its art pottery line. Success was limited. In 1954 the Mosaic Tile Company bought Roseville.

Pieces are identified as early, middle (Depression era), and late. Because of limited production, middle period pieces are the hardest to find. They also were marked with paper labels that have been lost over time. Some key patterns to watch for are Blackberry, Cherry Blossom, Faline, Ferella, Futura, Jonquil, Morning Glory, Sunflower, and Windsor.

Clubs: American Art Pottery Assoc., P.O. Box 834, Westport, MA 02790; Roseville's of the Past Pottery Club, P.O. Box 656, Clarcona, FL 32710.

Apple Blossom, hanging planter 250
Bittersweet, vase, #881-6, gray 100
Bleeding Heart, vase, #961-4 125
Bushberry, basket, #370-8, orange 250
Bushberry, basket, blue, 12" 450
Bushberry, jardiniere, #657-3, brown 110
Bushberry, jardiniere and pedestal, rust, 8" d 800
Bushberry, planter, #411-6, green 250
Bushberry, vase, #24-4, brown, 1948 110
Carnelian I, candlesticks, pr, blue-green, 1910, 2.5" h 150
Carnelian I, vase, bowed handles, blue, 1910, 8.5" h 270
Carnelian I, vase, green-gold, 7" h 150
Carnelian II, flower frog, ink stamp, 1921 50
Carnelian II, urn, handled, mauve and purple, 5" h, 7" w .230
Cherry Blossom, bowl, 4" d 350
Clematis, vase, #102-6, green 115
Clematis, vase, #110-9, green 200
Clematis, vase, #188-6, green 115
Columbine, bowl, #655-3, blue 100
Dogwood, bowl, green 100
Freesia, candlesticks, pr, #1160-2, brown 100
Freesia, candlesticks, pr, #1160-2, green 100
Freesia, console bowl, #469-14, brown . .230

Freesia, vase, #119-7, green 115
Freesia, vase, #120-7, green 115
Gardenia, planter, #658-8, green 100
Imperial II, wall pocket 500
Iris, vase, #917-6, pink 115
Magnolia, bowl, 2-handled, #447-6, green 120
Magnolia, candlesticks, pr, #1157-11½, brown 100
Magnolia, vase, #89-7, brown 115
Magnolia, vase, #91-8, blue 230
Magnolia, vase, #94-9, blue 250
Magnolia, vase, #179-7, brown 100
Ming Tree, basket, white, 14" d 300
Panel, wall pocket, green, 7" h 350
Peony, vase, #6308, yellow 150
Pinecone, vase, #745-7, green 325
Raymor, coffeepot, terra cotta 500
Raymor, cup and saucer, autumn brown 30
Raymor, plate, #152, mottled, terra cotta 40
Raymor, plate, #154, autumn brown 20
Raymor, vegetable bowl, #160, gray 40
Rosecraft, console bowl and flower frog, #15-3½, blue, 1916, 13" x 8" bowl 150
Silhouette Nude, vase, #783-7, beige 500
Snowberry, candlesticks, pr, #1CS2, brown 100
Snowberry, cornucopia vases, pr, #100-8, blue 200
Snowberry, ewer, #1TK-6, blue 100
Tourmaline, cornucopia vases, pr, white, 7" 160
Tourmaline, vase, 2-handled, 1933, 5.5" h 160
Water Lily, bowl, #663, blue 100
Water Lily, vase, #79-9, blue 225

White Rose, candlesticks, pr, #114-1, pink 100
Wisteria, vase, #636-8, blue, orig sticker 1,000
Zephyr Lily, cornucopia vases, pr, #203-6, green 175

ROYAL CHINA

Royal China began operations in 1934. The company produced an enormous number of dinnerware patterns. The backs of pieces usually contain the names of the shape, line, and decoration. In addition to many variations of company backstamps, Royal China also produced objects with private backstamps. All records of these markings were lost in a fire in 1970.

In 1964 Royal China purchased the French-Saxon China Company, Sebring, Ohio, which it operated as a wholly-owned subsidiary. On December 31, 1969, Royal China was acquired by the Jeannette Corporation. When fire struck the Royal China Sebring plant in 1970, Royal moved its operations to the French-Saxon plant. The company changed hands several times, until operations ceased in August 1986.

Collectors concentrate on specific patterns. The two most favored are Currier and Ives (introduced 1949–50) and Willow Ware (1940s). Because of easy availability, only purchase pieces in fine to excellent condition.

Club: The Currier & Ives Dinnerware Collectors Club, RD 2, Box 394, Hollidaysburg, PA 16648.

Ashtray, Clinchfield Railroad 25
Blue Heaven, platter, oval 15
Blue Willow, bread plate, 6.25" d 15
Blue Willow, cake plate, tab handled, 10.5" d 40
Blue Willow, cup and saucer 15
Blue Willow, serving bowl, 8.5" d 20
Blue Willow, serving bowl, 10" d 18
Blue Willow, soup bowl 25
Blue Willow, vegetable bowl, 10" d 18
Cattail, soup bowl, 7.75" d 5
Celeste, soup bowl .8

Coasters, orange, set of 5 24
Colonial Heritage, pie plate, blue, 10" d . . .18
Colonial Homestead, cream pitcher 14
Colonial Homestead, cup and saucer 15
Colonial Homestead, serving platter, 12" x 11" 10
Creamer, National Brotherhood of Operative Potters .5
Currier & Ives, ashtray 15
Currier & Ives, cake plate, tab handled, 10.75" d 20
Currier & Ives, calendar plate, 1969 36
Currier & Ives, chop platter, 11.75" d 20
Currier & Ives, coffee mug 15
Currier & Ives, creamer 5
Currier & Ives, cup and saucer 5
Currier & Ives, gravy and underplate 35
Currier & Ives, cup and saucer, Old Grist Mill 10
Currier & Ives, pie plate 35
Currier & Ives, plate, 9" d 20
Currier & Ives, plate, tab handles 20
Currier & Ives, platter, 12" l 30
Currier & Ives, rimmed bowl, maple sugaring 15
Currier & Ives, salt and pepper shakers . . .30
Currier & Ives, serving bowl, 10" d 25
Currier & Ives, teapot 125
Early Morn, bowl, rooster, 5.75" w 24
Early Morn, creamer, rooster 10
Early Morn, gravy boat, rooster 30
Jeanette Hampshire, dinner plate 8
Memory Lane, ashtray, red transfer, 5.5" d 15
Old Curiosity, bowl, 8" d 10
Salad Plate, floral design, 7.25" d 5
Starglow, bowls, 5.5" d, set of 4 10
Starglow, bread and butter plate, 6.5" 8
Starglow, creamer and cov sugar, mustard gold and white 25
Starglow, cup 8
Starglow, dessert bowl, 6" d 10
Starglow, dinner plate, 10" d 14
Starglow, platter, oval, 13" l 20
Starglow, salt and pepper shakers, rocket-shaped, 5" h 18
Starglow, saucer, 6.5" d 8
Starglow, soup bowl, 8" d 12
Starglow, vegetable bowl, 9" d 18
Sussex Brown, dinner plates, 10.5" d 16

ROYAL COPLEY

Royal Copley ceramics were produced by the Spaulding China Company located in Sebring, Ohio. These attractive giftware items were most often marked with a paper label only, making identification a challenge. For hints on identifying unmarked Royal Copley, refer to Leslie C. and Marjorie A. Wolfe's *Royal Copley (plus Royal Windsor and Spaulding)* published by Collector Books, 1992.

Newsletter: The Copley Courier, 1639 N. Catalina St., Burbank, CA 91505.

Ashtray, pink and black, 5.25" l, 2" h 10
Bank, "For My Cadillac" 55
Bank, pig, 5.5" h 25
Bowl, dark pink 20
Bowl, sky blue and pink 12
Candleholder, star behind angel 40

Figurine, Airedale dog, 6" h 22
Figurine, Cocker Spaniel, 6.5" h 24
Figurine, parrot, 8" h 55
Figurine, Schnauzer dog, 6.25" h 30
Figurine, wren, 3.5" h 30
Figurines, mallard ducks, pr 60
Figurines, rooster and hen, 8" h 75
Pillow Vase, gray, pink, and black, 5.5" h ..18
Pin Dish, leaf with flower 12
Pitcher, roses on cream ground, 6" h 15
Pitcher, floral design, 6.25" h 12
Pitcher, pink and blue, 7.25" h 45
Planter, black and white, 4" h 32
Planter, box with bucket, 6.25" h 25
Planter, deer and fawn head vase, 9" h ...40
Planter, duck, 8" h 38
Planter, duckling, 5.5" h 30
Planter, elephant, 7.5" h 28
Planter, elephant with ball, pink, 7.5" h ...25
Planter, horse with mane, 8" h 40
Planter, kitten in basket, pastel colors, glossy finish, 1950s, 8" h, 8.5" l 35
Planter, oriental figure leaning on basket, 6.5" h 22
Planter, oriental figures 75
Planter, Peter Rabbit, 6.25" h 25
Planter, puppy dog with mailbox, 8.25" h ..40
Planter, rooster, 7" h 38
Planter, Teddy Bear, 6.75" h 24
Planter, woodland creature, 4.75" h 20
Table Lamp, draped handles and flowers .30
Vase, black floral leaf and stem, 7.75" h ..18
Vase, cobalt floral relief, 7.75" h 35
Vase, fish design, cylindrical, green and brown with gold highlights, 8" h 35
Vase, floral, pink and blue, 3" h 30
Vase, floral, yellow and green, 3" h 30
Vase, floral design, 4.25" h 20

Vase, pink and blue fish, 5.25" h 20
Vase, purple and brown, 5" h 40
Wall Pocket, angel, 6" h 80
Wall Pocket, bird, 5" h 32
Wall Pocket, hat 48
Wall Pocket, Lady Head Vase, with gloves 60
Wall Pocket, red apple 85
Wall Pocket, rooster, 7" h 35
Wall Pockets, pr, angels, 6.25" h 50

ROYAL DOULTON

The chance of finding a piece of Royal Doulton at a flea market is better than you think. Often given as a gift, the recipient seldom realizes its initial value. As a result, it is sold for a fraction of its value at garage sales and to dealers.

Check out any piece of Royal Doulton that you find. There are specialized price guides for character jugs, figures, and toby jugs. A great introduction to Royal Doulton is the two-volume video-cassette entitled *The Magic of a Name,* produced by Quill Productions, Birmingham, England.

Clubs: Royal Doulton International Collectors Club, 700 Cottontail Ln., Somerset, NJ 08873; Royal Doulton International Collectors Club (Canadian Branch), 850 Progress Ave., Scarborough, Ontario M1H 3C4 Canada.

HN 1298, Sweet and Twenty 200
HN 1315, Old Balloon Seller 145
HN 1368, Rose 145
HN 1517, Veronica 295
HN 1537, Janet 80
HN 1607, Cerise 95
HN 1626, Bonnie Lassie 350
HN 1679, Babie 40
HN 1731, Daydreams 95
HN 1890, Lambing Time 145
HN 1926, Roseanna 300
HN 1934, Autumn Breezes 100
HN 1949, Lady Charmian 125
HN 1953, Orange Lady 130
HN 1975, The Shepherd 160
HN 1977, Her Ladyship 225
HN 1978, Bedtime 35
HN 1982, Sabbath Morn 100
HN 1985, Darling 30

HN 1992, Christmas Morn 165
HN 2020, Deidre 375
HN 2038, Peggy 50
HN 2041, The Broken Lance 390
HN 2062, Little Boy Blue 125
HN 2078, Elfreda 765
HN 2100, Sairey Gamp 300
HN 2107, Valerie 65
HN 2110, Christmas Time 300
HN 2136, Delphine .170
HN 2165, Janice 200
HN 2178, Enchantment 95
HN 2184, Sunday Morning 225
HN 2221, Nanny 150
HN 2222, Camellia .100
HN 2227, Gentleman from Williamsburg .125
HN 2233, Royal Governor's Cook 200
HN 2236, Affection 70
HN 2267, Rhapsody 135
HN 2278, Judith 190
HN 2307, Coralie 85
HN 2318, Grace 100
HN 2330, Meditation 200
HN 2335, Hilary 150
HN 2337, Loretta 145
HN 2339, My Love .175
HN 2341, Cherie 50
HN 2359, The Detective 190
HN 2396, Wistful 75
HN 2399, Buttercup .80
HN 2441, Pauline 145
HN 2446, Thanksgiving 145
HN 2479, Pamela 80
HN 2487, Beachcomber 100
HN 2712, Mantilla .295
HN 2716, Cavalier .145
HN 2718, Lady Pamela 140

HN 2719, Laurianne 125
HN 2790, June 60
HN 2804, Nicola 35
HN 2806, Jane 100
HN 2865, Tess 80
HN 2892, The Chief 135
HN 2913, Gollum 100
HN 2914, Bilbo 85
HN 2916, Aragorn 90
HN 2917, Legolas 85
HN 2926, Tom Sawyer 75
HN 3033, Springtime 130
HN 3042, Gillian 75
HN 3137, Summertime 100
HN 3219, Sara 70
HN 3248, Ninette 175
HN 3305, Kathy 80
HN 3350, Henry VIII 715
HN 3440, HM Queen Elizabeth II 175
HN 3802, Daisy 90
HN 3891, Sir Henry Doulton 75

ROYAL HAEGER

David H. Haeger founded Haeger Potteries in Dundee, Illinois, in 1871. The company produced its first art pottery in 1914. The Royal Haeger line was introduced in 1938. Haeger Potteries began production for the florist trade and organized the Royal Haeger Lamp Company in 1939.

Many Haeger pieces can be identified by molded model numbers. The first Royal Haeger mold was assigned the number "R-1," with subsequent numbers assigned in chronological order. Giftware in the Studio Haeger line, designed by Helen Conover, have an "S" number. Royal Garden Flower wares, produced between 1954 and 1963, have an "RG" number.

The initial collecting craze that established Royal Haeger as an independent collecting category is over. Prices have stabilized for commonly found pieces. Speculative price prevails for high-end pieces.

Club: Haeger Pottery Collectors Club of America, 5021 Toyon Way, Antioch, CA 94509.

Ashtray, 9.75" x 8.5" .20
Ashtray, Briar Agate, 3-ftd, 13" l .40
Ashtray, green frogskin, 5-ftd .32
Ashtray, guest design color band .35
Ashtray, marbled, 12.5" w .34
Bowl, brown, 14" l .28
Bowl, flower petal, sky blue, 8" x 3.25" .20
Candleholder, 13" h, 7.75" w .28
Candlelight Lamp, 13.5" h .20
Candlestand, white with blue trim, 9.25" h .25
Coffeepot, 10.5" h .55
Compote, gold tweed .18
Console Bowl, green agate, 13" l, 6" w .22
Console Bowl, gray, 4.75" h, 14.75" w .45
Dish, ash gray, 7" x 14" .15
Fan Vase, 9" h, 13" w .75
Figurine, Egyptian black cat, 20.5" .130
Figurine, gazelle, black, 18" .50
Figurine, panther, ebony, 24" .95
Figurine, pheasant, 10.5" .30
Figurine, rearing ram, 19" h, 16" w .75
Figurine, Sea Shell Crane .45
Figurine, seated gazelle, glazed ebony, 14" .35
Horse Head, gold tweed, 11" .62
Lighter, 10" .45
Lily Vase, 14" .85
Pitcher, pink, 6" h, 6.75" w .55
Planter, monkey .75
Three Lily Vase, 16" .85
Vanity Tissue and Powder Holder .30
Vase, emb leaf, 15.5" .65
Vase, flow blue, 9" h .20
Vase, gazelle, #3386, 12.125" h .45
Vase, jade crackle, 12.25" .55
Vase, Peacock glaze, 12" .95
Vase, Pegasus, turquoise agate .85
Vase, praying Madonna .55
Vase, shell shaped, 7" h, 11" w .45
Vase, sunflower, 8" h .20

ROYAL WINTON

Royal Winton is more than chintz, a fact appreciated by collectors familiar with Eileen Busby's *Royal Winton Porcelain: Ceramics Fit for a King* (Glass Press, 1998). Royal Winton production includes commemorative and patriotic ware, handpainted ware, an assortment of luster wares, mottled ware, mugs and jugs, pastel ware, souvenir ware, and transfer ware.

In 1885 Sidney and Leonard Grimwade founded the Grimwade Brothers Pottery in Stoke-on-Trent. The firm became Grimwades, Ltd., when it acquired the Winton Pottery Company and Stoke Pottery in 1900. Atlas China, Rubin Art Pottery, Heron Cross Pottery, and Upper Hanley Pottery were added in 1906–07. The "Royal" attribution grew out of the company's promotion of a visit to the plant in April 1913 by King George V and Queen Mary.

Royal Winton's first chintz patterns were introduced in the late 1920s and flourished in the 1930s. In 1997 the company began making limited reproductions of some of its most popular 1930s chintz pieces.

Club: Royal Winton International Collectors' Club, Dancer's End, Northall, Bedfordshire LU6 2EU U.K.

Ashtray, Summertime, 4.25" w .65
Basket, Royalty, Hampton shape, 4" h, 4.25" w .500
Biscuit Jar, Marguerite, chrome lid and handle, Bakelite finial, c1930, 6" h .325
Bowl, Queen Anne, 8-sided, 9" w .100
Breakfast Set, Royalty, 7 pcs including 10" tray, cup, toast rack, cov teapot, sugar, and creamer, 1934 .2,250
Butter Dish, cov, Gera, 1934, 6" sq .175
Butter Dish, cov, Summertime pattern .200
Condiment Jar, cov, Old Cottage, 4.25" h .125
Creamer, Cromer, Norman shape .100
Creamer and Sugar, Majestic, Stuart shape, c1936 .225

Creamer and Sugar, Poppy pattern 90
Creamer and Sugar, Tapestry pattern . . .175
Cup and Saucer, Marguerite pattern 35
Cup and Saucer, Old Cottage pattern 120
Dish, Pekin, handled, 9.25" x 6.5" 65
Gravy and Underplate, Old Cottage, 5.5" l 100
Jug, Old Cottage, 4" h 215
Milk Jug, Grimwades, Tiger Lily, yellow with pink Tiger Lily, 4.75" h 375
Pin Dish, Rose, 4.25" x 3.5" 80
Place Setting, Summertime, 10.5" d plate, 8" d plate, 6" d plate, and teacup 175
Plate, Garden Wall, 6.125" sq 55
Plate, Hazel, 7" sq 140
Plate, Marguerite, 8" d 70
Plate, Old Cottage, 8" d 120
Plate, Royalty, 8" sq 150
Platter, Hazel, 2-handed, 1934, 11" w 500
Platter, Tea Rose, oval, 11.25" l, 7.25" w . .260
Sandwich Plate, Sweetpea, 10" x 6" 200
Snack Set, Kew pattern 95
Sugar Bowl, pink and yellow swirl, with tongs, 4" h, ...68
Sugar Bowl, Royalty, Hector shape, c1936 100
Sugar Bowl, Summertime, 2" h, 2.75" d 70
Teapot, Chanticleer .350
Teapot, Mayfair, Grimwades, 4.5" h 285
Teapot, Queen Anne, 6 cup 260
Teapot, Royalty, 9" w 800
Teapot, Tiger Lily, yellow, 5.75" h 350
Teapot and Trivet, Clyde, 10.25" w teapot, 5.75" sq trivet 525
Tea Set, Summertime, cov teapot, sugar, and creamer 900
Tray, Hazel, Grimwades, 8" l 125

R.S. PRUSSIA

R.S. Prussia is a term used to identify porcelain made at several factories in the Thuringia region of Germany beginning in the second half of the eighteenth century. "R.S." stands for Reinhold Schlegelmilch, who founded a factory in Suhl, Germany in 1869. Production consisted primarily of tablewares exported to Australia, the Balkans, England, Holland, Indonesia, Scandinavia, Switzerland, and the United States.

Berry Bowl Set, RS Germany, master bowl and 6 individual bowls, floral dec, gold trim, blue RSG star and wreath mark, 9.25" d master bowl, 2.25" d individual bowls 75
Bowl, ES Germany, scenic with bird dec, Prov Saxe ES mark, early 20th C, 5.75" l 35
Bowl, RS Germany, hexagonal relief petal border, gray tones in border, 4 red roses and buds, gold edge, light green mark, 10" d 100
Bowl, RS Prussia, cranberry colored florals on cranberry ground in mold 25 "Iris," red RSP mark, late 19th C, 9.25" d 175
Bowl, RS Prussia, floral dec, red RSP mark, some professional repair, late 19th C, 10" d .85
Bowl, RS Prussia, multicolored florals in mold 20, tiny flecks on underside of the bowl on the petals 275

Bowl, RS Prussia, multicolored florals in mold 86, unmkd, late 19th C, 10" d 345

Bowl, RS Prussia, red and pink roses, gold highlights, red RSP mark, 10.75" d 150

Bowl, RS Prussia, red poppies on blue ground in mold 90, red RSP mark, late 19th C, 10" d .175

Bowl, RS Prussia, satin finish, mold 128 with red roses, red RSP mark, late 19th C, 10" d .260

Cake Plate, RS Germany, open handles, floral dec of roses and cosmos with shadow gray leafing motif, heavily scalloped edge, mold 205, green RSG mark, 10.75" w 40

Card Receiver, RS Germany, hp lily mold form, blue RSG mark, early 20th C, 5.5" l 35

Card Receiver, RS Germany, red and yellow roses, green RSG mark, early 20th C, 7" l 35

Celery, RS Germany, double-handled, multicolored florals, gold trim, RSG steeple mark, 12.25" l 80

Celery, RS Germany, multicolored florals, gold trim, RSG steeple mark, 12.25" l . . .80

Creamer and Sugar, RS Poland, white roses in a fitted silver-plated caddy, red RSP mark, early 20th C, 8" l 60

Creamer and Sugar, RS Prussia, floral spray dec and blue arched panels, unmkd, late 19th C, 5" h 100

Egg Box, cov, RS Prussia, rose band dec, red RSP mark, late 19th C, 4.75" l 115

Flower Vases, pr, ES Germany, dec with purple violets, Prov Saxe ES mark, early 20th C, 4.5" h 80

Muffineer, RS Germany, floral dec, gold RSG steeple mark, early 20th C, 4" h . . .70

Nappy, ES Germany, stage coach scene, Prov Saxe ES mark, early 20th C, 8" l . . .70

Nappy, RS Germany, heart shaped dish with parrot in cut-out handle, hp vine roses, black RSG star and wreath mark, 6.5" l, 6.5" w 40

Pitcher, RS Prussia, dec with 4 fruits, mold #584, unmkd, c1900, 9.75" h 375

Powder Box, RS Germany, Art Deco mold with white roses, blue RSG mark, early 20th C, 4" l 35

Shaving Mug, RS Prussia, floral dec in mold 609 "Fleur-de-lis," red RSP mark, late 19th C, 3.5" h 115

Tea Set, RS Prussia, 3 pcs, floral dec in mold 664, unmkd, professional repair to teapot lid, late 19th C, 8" l 200

Vase, RS Prussia, poppies and snowball dec, red RSP mark, late 19th C, 6" h . . .265

RUSSEL WRIGHT

Russel Wright was an American industrial engineer with a design passion for domestic efficiency through simple lines. Wright and his wife, Mary Small Einstein, wrote *A Guide to Easier Living* to explain the concepts.

Some of his earliest designs were executed in polished spun aluminum. These pieces, designed in the mid-1930s, included trays, vases, and teapots.

Russel Wright worked for many different companies in addition to creating material under his own label, American Way. Wright's contracts with firms often called for the redesign of pieces which did not produce or sell well. As a result, several lines have the same item in more than one shape. Among the companies for which Wright did design work are Chase Brass & Copper, General Electric, Imperial Glass, National Silver Company, and the Shenango and Steubenville Pottery Companies.

Though most collectors focus on Wright's dinnerware, he also designed glassware, plastic items, textiles, furniture, and metal objects. His early work in spun aluminum often is overlooked, as is his later work in plastic for the Northern Industrial Chemical Company.

DINNERWARE

American Modern, after dinner coffeepot, chartreuse 90
American Modern, after dinner cup and saucer, chutney .25
American Modern, after dinner cup and saucer, gray 25
American Modern, bread and butter plate, coral 6
American Modern, casserole, cov, bean brown 75
American Modern, casserole, cov, gray . .45
American Modern, celery, gray 25
American Modern, child's bowl, chartreuse 50
American Modern, child's gravy boat, coral 50
American Modern, child's sugar, coral . . .50
American Modern, chop plate, gray 30
American Modern, coaster, dec, coral . . .22
American Modern, coffee cup cov, coral 120
American Modern, creamer, bean brown 18
American Modern, creamer, coral 12
American Modern, creamer, white 18
American Modern, cup, chartreuse 5
American Modern, dinner plate, Spencerian white 25
American Modern, gravy boat, coral 20
American Modern, hostess set, plate and cup, chartreuse 80
American Modern, hostess set, plate and cup, coral 85
American Modern, pickle dish, coral 15
American Modern, pitcher, coral 90
American Modern, platter, chartreuse, 12.75" l 12
American Modern, platter, coral 25
American Modern, ramekin, cov, gray . . .175
American Modern, relish, divided, no handle, coral 80
American Modern, salad bowl, coral 80
American Modern, salad fork and spoon, gray 125
American Modern, salad plate, bean brown 15
American Modern, soup dish, coral 15
American Modern, sugar, bean brown . . .18
American Modern, sugar, white 18
American Modern, teapot, coral 100
American Modern, vegetable bowl, cov, seafoam 70
American Modern, vegetable bowl, cov, coral 60
American Modern, vegetable bowl, divided, coral 85
American Modern, vegetable bowl, divided, white 100
American Modern, vegetable bowl, open, coral 20
American Modern, vegetable bowl, open, seafoam 20
American Modern, water pitcher, chartreuse 90
American Modern, water pitcher, cov, chartreuse 150
Iroquois Casual, after dinner coffeepot, ice blue 85
Iroquois Casual, bowl, 5" d, nutmeg 13
Iroquois Casual, bread and butter plate, 6.5" d, pink 4
Iroquois Casual, carafe, apricot 150
Iroquois Casual, carafe, charcoal 265
Iroquois Casual, carafe, lemon 140
Iroquois Casual, carafe, pink 135
Iroquois Casual, casserole, charcoal 60
Iroquois Casual, coffeepot, white 185
Iroquois Casual, creamer, pink 18
Iroquois Casual, cup and saucer, ice blue 12
Iroquois Casual, cup and saucer, nutmeg .15
Iroquois Casual, dinner plate, 10" d, ice blue 8
Iroquois Casual, dinner plate, 10" d, white 10
Iroquois Casual, gumbo bowl, ice blue . . .50
Iroquois Casual, mug, avocado 80
Iroquois Casual, place setting, 5-pc, charcoal 35
Iroquois Casual, platter, 14.5" l, parsley . . .12
Iroquois Casual, salad plate, 7.5" d, lemon 15
Iroquois Casual, salt and pepper, stacking, apricot 15
Iroquois Casual, sherbet, pink 6
Iroquois Casual, soup dish, deep, white . .50
Iroquois Casual, vegetable bowl, open, avocado 10

METAL

Corn/Pancake Set, complete with spherical syrup pitcher, salt and pepper globes, and round cobalt blue glass tray, Chase Chrome and Brass Co 300

Punch Set, aluminum, includes punch bowl, undertray, ladle, and 12 cups, imp marks 550

PLASTIC

Child's Teacup, gray, Ideal 10

Child's Tea Set, consisting of teapot, creamer, and sugar, coral, Ideal 60

SALEM CHINA

Biddam Smith, John McNichol, and Dan Cronin, formerly with Standard Pottery in East Liverpool, Ohio, founded the Salem China Company in Salem, Ohio, in 1898. Due to financial problems, it was sold to F. A. Sebring in 1918. Under the management of Frank McKee and Sebring's son, Frank Jr., the company became very successful through the sale of fine dinnerware, much of which was trimmed with 22K gold.

Viktor Schenckengost created many of Salem's shapes and designs during the 1930s and 40s. Salem China continued to manufacture dinnerware until 1967. Beginning in 1968, Salem was exclusively a distribution and sales business.

Bowl, red and white, 8.5" d 8

Bowl, tan, gold trim around edge, 8" d 45

Casserole, cov, Petit Point Basket, 9" d . . .80

Child's Plate, "My Own Plate," 9" d 75

Commemorative Plate, General Arnold, 11" d 40

Creamer, Parsley, 6.75" w 10

Creamer and Sugar, Biscayne, blue and green leaves and white flowers 18

Creamer and Sugar, cov, Southwind 70

Creamer and Sugar, English Village, 3.5" h, 5" w 45

Cup and Saucer, Aristocrat, red border with gold and floral decal 12

Cup and Saucer, Dominion, floral pattern, orange, blue, and pink foliage with golden wheat 20

Cup and Saucer, English Village 16

Dinner Plate, English Village, 9.75" d 28

Dinner Plate, Maple Leaf, 9.75" d 18

Dinner Plate, Minuet, 10" d 15

Fruit Bowl, Century, gold trim 8

Place Setting, 5-pc set, English Village 30

Platter, Briar Rose, 11.5" d 25

Platter, Jubilee Peach 10

Platter, Maple Leaf, 13" d 30

Platter, North Star, oval, 11.75" l 20

Platter, Rust Tulip, Victory, oval, 1940s-50s, 11.5" x 8.75" 12

Platter, Sheffield, oval, 11.75" l, 9.25" w . . .25

Platter, tab handles, purple grapes and leaves in center, 1962, 13.25" d 30

Platter, triangular, Petit Point, Dutch Couple, 11.5" l 20

Salt and Pepper Shakers, Petit Point, cork stoppers 30

Saucer, English Village, 5.5" d 10

Service Plate, cobalt edge, 1940, 10" d . . .45

Soup Plate, Chantung, 8.5" d 10

Sugar Bowl, cov, Dominion, floral pattern .18

Sugar Bowl, cov, Sheffield 25

Teacup, Streamline, mandarin orange 8

Teapot, Petit Point Basket, 9.5" h 135
Vegetable Bowl, Dominion, round, 2.5" h, 8.75" d 20
Vegetable Bowl, oval, forest green, 10.5" x 9" 10
Vegetable Bowl, Sheffield, round 25

SALT & PEPPER SHAKERS

Hang on to your hats. Those great figural salt and pepper shaker sets from the 1920s through the 1960s have been discovered by the New York art and decorator crowd. Prices have started to jump. What does this say about taste in America?

When buying a set, make certain it is a set. Check motif, base, and quality of workmanship. China shakers should have no cracks or signs of cracking. Original paint and decoration should be present on china and metal figures. Make certain each shaker has the right closure.

Salt and pepper shaker collectors must compete with specialized collectors from other fields, e.g., advertising and black memorabilia. I have been searching for a pair shaped like jigsaw puzzle pieces. So far I have neither seen a pair nor found a dealer who has seen one, but I will not give up.

Club: Novelty Salt & Pepper Shakers Club, P.O. Box 677388, Orlando, FL 32867.

Note: Shakers are ceramic unless noted otherwise.

American Indians, Japan, 3" h 60
Apple, 2" h 10
Aunt Jemima and Chef, souvenir label from 1,000 Islands, NY, Occupied Japan 45
Baseball Bat and Ball, Vandor 14
Baseball Player Mice, 3.25" h 60
Bellboy, Occupied Japan, 4" h 45
Boy Blue and Bo Peep, Shawnee 50
Bride and Groom, Goebel, 1951, 3.25" h . . . 55
Bulls, mkd "Victoria Ceramics Japan," 4" l, 3.25" h 15
Cat and Dog, Goebel 75
Comical Dogs, green and red spots on pink ground, 1 winking, 1 laughing, Japan, 2.25" h 15
Dobbin Horses, Japan, 3.75" h 20
Dressed-Up Wolves, 3.5" h 75
Dumbo, 3.25" h 65
Dutch Boat, nesters 50
Dutch Boy and Girl in Shoes 20
Exxon Tiger, plastic 15
Flowers with Butterflies, Occupied Japan 3.25" h 20
Fork and Spoon People, Japan, 5" h 25
Frogs, Fitz & Floyd, 2.75" h, 2.5" d 14
Granny in Rocking Chair, Norcrest, Japan, 4" h 22
Greek Female Statues, plastic, 1 black, 1 white, 4" h 40
Hillbillies, Twin Winton 25
Horse Heads, Rosemeade 85
Idaho Spuds, Japan 85
Indian in Canoe, Japan, 3.25" l 15
Inverted Light Bulbs, glass, 6" h 40
Mammy and Butler, plastic, F&F Mold & Die Works, 3.5" h 45
Martians, green, Japan, 4.5" h 35
Moon Walkers 55
Mr & Mrs Pig, wearing colorful outfits with plastic buttons, Enesco, 3.5" h 20
Ocean Liner, plastic and glass, 3-pc set, 4.5" l, 2" h 20
Parrots, Fitz & Floyd 35
Poodles, Goebel 35
Prayer Ladies, pink 15
Puss 'n Boots, Shawnee 50
Roses, hp, mkd "RS Germany," 2.75" h 55
Sailboats, 3 pcs, 1 pink ship, 1 brown ship, blue ocean base with emb waves, Japan, 3" h 20
Sailor Boy and Dutch Girl, huggies, 3.5" h . 45
Siamese Cats, blue glass eyes, cork stoppers, Japan, 1950s 25
Squirrels, Japan, 3.75" h 4
Teapot and Coffeepot, brown, Japan 12
Venus de Milo Statues, plastic, white salt, black pepper 20

SAND PAILS

The illustrations found on litho tin sand pails are truly works of art. Innumerable child's themes from animals to cartoon characters have graced the sides of these seashore toys. Despite the fact that sand and salt water are natural enemies of tin toys, concentrate on pails in very good condition with little surface damage. Pails were mass-produced in large quantities, making condition an important part of value.

Club: Ohio Art Collectors Club, 18203 Kristi Rd. West, Liberty, MO 64068.

Bear driving a motorcycle, boy in sailor suit, boy on hobby horse and dog biting a man's pants, 3" h 55
Big Bad Wolf, rabbits, brown bear, gnome, and a squirrel against red background, 3" h .65
Boy, fishing, red with blue handle, Ohio Art, 1950s-60s, 7.75" h 90
Children at Beach, blue, Ohio Art, 1950s-60s, 7.75" h 90
Children at Beach, building a sand castle, Chad Valley, 4.25" h 100
Cowboys and Horses, Ohio Art, 3.5" h 85
Cowboy Theme, J Chein, 4.25" h 100
Disney, various characters from the time, red wooden carrying handle, Chein, 8" h 150
Flowers, red and yellow, metal, 6" h 50
Patriotic Theme, litho tin, spread-wing eagle and shield with stars and stripes, "SEA SIDE" around bottom 325

Turtles and Other Sea Creatures, Ohio Art, iridescent, 1960s, 6" h, 5.5" w 60
Yogi Bear, with gang from Yellowstone Park, Ohio Art, 1950s, 8" h 75

SCANDINAVIAN GLASS

Scandinavian Glass is a generic term for glassware made in Denmark, Finland, and Sweden from the 1920s through the 1960s and heavily exported to the United States. Collectors assign a high aesthetic value to Scandinavian glass. Focus at the moment is on key companies, e.g., Kosta Glasbruk and Orrefors, and designers such as Edward Held, Nils Landberg, Vicke Lindstrand, Tyra Lundgren, Ingeborg Lundin, Sven Palmqvist, and Sven Erik Skawonius.

Interest in Scandinavian glass is strongest in metropolitan regions in the Middle Atlantic States and West Coast. It is now regularly featured in 20th-Century Modern auction catalog sales across the United States.

Ekends, vase, vasiform vessel, bubbled glass, int green powder dec in lower portion, mkd "Ekends, Sweden L1331/KC-KO-T-0 Lare," 6" h 115
Flygsfors, vase, designed by Berndt, freeform, cobalt blue at base cased to clear and red at pulled and pierced rim, base mkd "Flygsfors 58 Berndt," 1958, 5.5" h 200
Gunel Nyman, vase, ovoid, pink sommerso glass int, controlled submerged bubbles, acid-etched signature and "Nuutajarvi Notsjo," 8.5" x 3.5" . . .225
Hadeland, vase, designed by Severin Brorby, flaring form, transparent olive glass with 6 applied freeform medallions, etched "Hadeland 7020 SB," 11" x 7.5" 350
Holmegaard, bowl, designed by Per Lutken, emerald green, closed-in rim, domed bottom, etched signature and number, 4.5" x 12.5" 200
Kosta, vase, designed by Vicktor Lindstrand, gourd-shaped, black and white lines, etched "LH1257,"

10.5" x 2.5" 125

Kosta Boda, bowl, flaring form, mottled speckled violet, blue, and green ext, etched artist signature and number with foil label, 6.5" x 9.5" 110

L Fraucek, goblet, clear glass, int diagonal lines, acid-etched "L Fraucek" and number, 3" x 3.5" 150

Orrefors, Graal fish vase, heavy-walled ovoid clear glass internally dec with fish among seaweed, base inscribed "Orrefors Graal No. 558N Edvard Hald," c1940, 4.75" h 750

Orrefors, vase, 4-sided, green sommerso glass int, acid etched "Orrefors NU 3538-2," 10" x 5" 225

Orrefors, vase, rect, heavy walled, deep blue-green glass, serpentine faceted panels, base inscribed "Orrefors 1930/G.A. 276," 1930, 3.75" h 145

SCHOOL MEMORABILIA

"School Days, School Days, good old golden rule days." I've been singing this refrain ever since I moved into the former Vera Cruz elementary school in Pennsylvania.

Atlas, *Goode's School Atlas,* 1946, 286 pgs 15

Autograph Book, green-gray, 1926, 4.5" x 6.25" 8

Bell, brass, wooden handle, 6" x 2.25" 18

Bell, wooden handle, black painted steel with brass clapper, 6.5" h, 4" w 45

Book, *Bob and Judy,* Educational Reader, 1936 25

Book, *Eclectic English Classics,* Lincoln Addresses and Letters, 1914 25

Book, *Graphic Speller,* 1884 95

Chairs, wooden, painted red and green over black undercoating, 10" h 20

Clay, Permoplast, silhouettes of children and nursery rhyme characters dance around box 22

Desk, student's, wood, cast iron base, 21.75" l, 13.5" d 70

Graduation Program, Victorian, NY area school, Jun 22, 1904 8

Lunch Check Coin, aluminum, Wright and Sons, 1" d 38

Lunch Pail, tin, c1850 50

Pencil Box, lid image of girl, boy, and dog on their way to school, 1950s 25

Pencil Case, wooden, King Edward VII and Queen Alexandra on lid, 1902 45

Pencil Sharpener, Boston Model, 4" x 4.5" x 3" 36

Pinback Button, "Penny's 'Back to School Days' with Popeye," 1930s 18

Postcard, High School, Sylacauga, AL, 1941 5

Poster, school bus drivers, cardboard, 20" x 9", 1950s 10

Ring, high school, red glass stone, 1935 . .35

Ruler, 6" 10

Slate, 7.5" x 10.75" 10

Tassel, graduate's, royal blue, 1960, 8.5" l . .8

SCHOOP, HEDI

Hedi Schoop, born in Switzerland in 1906, was educated at Vienna's Kunstgewerbeschule and Berlin's Reimann Institute. In the early 1930s she and her husband, Frederick Hollander, a well-known composer, emigrated to America.

After arriving in Los Angeles, Schoop began making and marketing a line of plaster of Paris dolls dressed in contemporary fashions. Discovered by a representative of Barker Brothers, she was advised to scrap the textile clothing and do figures that were entirely ceramic.

Hedi's mother financed a plant in North Hollywood. Schoop employed many displaced European actors, dancers, and musicians as decorators. In 1942 the company became Hedi Schoop Art Creations. Business was strong in the late 1940s and early 1950s. The company introduced a line of TV lamps in the mid-1950s. A fire ended production in 1958. Schoop did not rebuild. Instead, she worked as a free-lance designer for several Los Angeles area firms. She retired permanently from the ceramics business in the 1960s, devoting her time after that to painting.

Bowl, shell-shaped, pink with gold glaze, marked "Hedi Schoop Hollywood," 2.5" x 7" 50
Candleholder, twisted branches, 2 cups, polychrome glaze, mkd "Hedi Schoop Hollywood," 8" h 65
Candy Dish, blue-green 35
Figurine, Asian girl, 8" h 36
Figurine, oriental man, 12.5" h 60
Figurine, oriental man, ivory jacket and pink pants, 12" h 20
Figurine, owl, 6" l, 6" h 65
Figurine, peasant woman in red scarf with basket, stamped "Hedi Schoop Hollywood CA," 13" h 165
Figurine, rooster, green and brown, 13" h 125
Figurine, young girl with bowl, white dress, light blue bowl, scarf, apron, and shoes, polychrome glaze, mkd "Hedi Schoop," 13.5" h 225

Figurines, pr, Dutch couple 95
Figurines, pr, male and female peasants, 13" h 180
Figurines, pr, man and woman, 12" h 105
Figurines, pr, Spanish dancers, aqua and cream dresses, 10" h 325
Planter, Book Lady, 9" h 60
Planter, duck, turquoise and gold, 5.5" h, 8" l 40
Planter, girl in front of book, 8" h 105
Planter, horse, pink and white, 10.5" h 85
Planter, Marguerita, 12.5" h 95
Planter, Tyrolean girl holding out skirt to hold flowers, 11" h 90
Salad Bowl, with matching fork and spoon, Metlox, 12" d 165
Soap Dish, lady holding dish on shoulder, 10.5" h 75
Tray, butterfly shaped, orange 40
Vase, Dutch boy, cream and green, 11" h 45
Vase, girl, green dress with white flowers and darker green leaves, holding bowl on her head, polychrome glaze, mkd "Hedi Schoop," 13" h 225
Vase, girl holding bouquet of flowers, 9.25"h, 6.75" w 85

SECONDHAND ROSES

This is a catchall category—designed specifically for those items which are bought solely for their utilitarian use. Anyone who regularly attends country auctions, flea markets, or garage sales has undoubtedly seen his fair share of "recycled" household goods. Ranging from wringer washers to electronic video games, these products and appliances are neither decorative nor financially lucrative. They are strictly secondhand merchandise.

There is not much reason to focus on brand names, with two exceptions—Maytag and Craftsman. First, Maytag, widely regarded as the Cadillac of washers and dryers, consistently realizes higher prices than any other brand. Second, Craftsman hand tools, distributed by Sears, generally bring higher prices due to the company's generous replacement policy.

As a result of advances in technology and space constraints in modern homes, several larger sized appliances have little or no value on today's market. For example, console stereos and large chest freezers can often be had free for the hauling.

All items listed below are in good, clean condition. All parts are intact and appliances are in working order. The prices are designed to get you in the ballpark. Good luck in getting a hit.

Air Conditioner, purchased in fall or winter 65
Air Conditioner, purchased in spring 85
Air Conditioner, purchased in summer...150
Air Mattress, double 8
Attaché Case, leather, fitted int, locking ..10
Answering Machine 15
Barbecue Grill, charcoal 10
Barbecue Grill, propane gas 65
Bedroom Suite, French Provincial, white, single bed, nightstand, chest of drawers, and dresser with mirror 175
Bicycle, 16", coaster brakes 15
Big Wheel, plastic, 3 wheels 5
Bird Bath, concrete, bowl and pedestal ..15
Booster Seat 5
Camp Stove, Coleman, 2-burner 25
Can Opener, electric 2
Car Seat 15
CD Player, multiple disc 40
Coffee Table, wood, modern 20
Computer, with monitor, 2-5 years old ...150
Computer, with monitor, 5+ years old 20
Dehumidifier, 15 pt 20
Diaper Bag 2
Dishwasher, portable, 5 years old 40
Dutch Oven 5
Exercise Bicycle, stationary 12
DVD Player 40
Extension Ladder, aluminum, 40' 60
Fan, battery-operated, hand-held 1
Fan, window, puchased in spring, fall, or winter 12
Fan, window, purchased in summer 20
Filing Cabinet, metal, 4 drawers 40
Freezer, upright, full size, 5 years old 125
Garden Tools, hoe, rake, shovel, etc. 5
Grill Cover 4
Grill Utensils, fork, spatula, and brush 8
Hair Dryer, hand held, full size, multiple settings 3
Highchair, metal, plastic, and vinyl 15
Kerosene Heater, purchased in spring, summer, or fall 35
Kerosene Heater, purchased in winter ...60
Lawn Mower, electric, purchased in fall or winter 20
Lawn Mower, electric, purchased in spring or summer 30
Lawn Mower, gas, purchased in fall or winter 30
Lawn Mower, gas, purchased in spring or summer 45
Microwave Oven, large, 1-5 years old 30
Mixer, counter top, 2 bowls 15
Movie Projector, 8mm or Super 8 1
Playpen 10
Pots and Pans, 8 pc set, ST 40
Refrigerator, bar size 50
Refrigerator, full size 125
Rug Shampooer 15
Snow Shovel, purchased in spring, summer or fall 4
Snow Shovel, purchased in winter 10
Stemware, 3 sizes, 24 pcs 50
Step Ladder, wooden, 5' 20
Stereo, turntable/cassette, receiver and 2 speakers 20
Stroller 12
Television, color, console 60
Television, color, portable, 19" 40
Television Stand, casters 10
Toaster Oven 8
Trailer Hitch 15
Traveling Liquor Cabinet, complete 30
Typewriter, electric 2
Vacuum Cleaner, canister or upright 20
VCR, 5 years old 25
Wardrobe, metal 20
Weight Lifting Bench 15

SEWING ITEMS

This is a wide open area. While many favor sterling silver items, only fools overlook objects made of celluloid, ivory, other metals, plastic, and wood. An ideal specialty collection would be sewing items that contain advertising.

Collecting sewing items received a big boost as a result of the Victorian craze. During the Victorian era a vast assortment of practical and whimsical sewing devices were marketed. Look for items such as tape measures, pincushions, stilettos for punchwork, crochet hooks, and sewing birds (beware of reproductions).

Modern sewing collectors are focusing on needle threaders, needle books, and sewing kits from hotels and motels. The general term for this material is "20-Pocket" because pieces fit neatly into 20 pocket plastic notebook sleeves.

Clubs: International Sewing Machine Collectors Society, 551 Kelmore St., Moss Beach, CA 94038; National Button Society, 2733 Juno Pl., Apt. 4, Akron, OH 44313; The Thimble Guild, P.O. Box 381807, Duncanville, TX 75138; Thimble Collectors International, 2594 E. Upper Hayden Lake Rd., Hayden, ID 83835; Toy Stitchers, 623 Santa Florita Ave., Millbrae, CA 94030.

ACCESSORIES

Needle Book, Pocket-Rocket, litho paper, Hartford Federal Savings and Loan 12

Pincushion, celluloid half doll wearing provincial German costume, Germany .75

Pincushion, figural crouching dog, porcelain, green and white, mkd "Made In Japan," 2" h, 3" w 20

Pincushion, figural elephant, porcelain, blue and peach luster, howdah holds red velvet pincushion, mkd "Made In Japan," 3.75" h, 5" l 35

Pincushion, figural girl standing beside large rose pincushion, hp porcelain, mkd "Made In Japan," 2.75" h 12

Pincushion, figural girl wearing bonnet, tape measure in base, Erphila, Czechoslovakia, 4" h 75

Pincushion, heart-shaped, blue silk, Occupied Japan 5

Embroidery Scissors, stork-shaped, steel, Germany, c1890-1920 25

Tape Measure, figural Mammy, mkd "Japan," 2" h, 1.75" w 265

Tape Measure, figural pig, pink, mkd "Japan," 1.25" h .65

SEWING MACHINES

Davis, electric 25

Domestic B, wooden base, c1900 95

Eldredge, electric 45

Elsa, cast base, Lehmann Brunswick, 1895 100

Gold Medal, chain stitch, c1870 595

Grant Brothers, chain stitch, c1870 264

Greyhound Electric .45

Grover & Baker, 2-spool, chain stitch, 1861 295

Grover & Baker, plain treadle base, c1869 365

Howe, treadle, cast iron base, drop-leaf work surface, AB Howe, NY, c1880 . . .100

New Home, "Little Worker," c1915 290

Raymond, "New England," chain stitch, c1872 290

Rowley Electric Automatic, c1935 200

Running Stitch, Durbrow & Hearne, NY, c1890 365

Singer, Featherweight, electric, portable, original case, c1940 150

Singer, "New Family," treadle, c1872 100
Singer Sewhandy Model No. 20, orig box, c1960 100
Weed, "Family Favorite," treadle base with 2 drawers, 1873 175
Wheeler & Wilson, No. 1, c1868 200
White, American, c1895 15
White, treadle, decorative wooden cabinet, c1885 245
White Number 2, electric 10
Willcox & Gibbs, electric, c1930 200
Willcox & Gibbs, ornate treadle base with 3 drawers, c1895 230

SHAWNEE POTTERY

The Shawnee Pottery company was founded in Zanesville, Ohio, in 1937. The plant, formerly home to the American Encaustic Tiling Company, produced approximately 100,000 pieces of pottery per working day. Shawnee produced a large selection of kitchenware, dinnerware, and decorative art pottery. The company ceased operations in 1961.

Club: Shawnee Pottery Collectors Club, P.O. Box 713, New Smyrna Beach, FL 32170.

Bowl, King Corn, #5 .40
Casserole, King Corn, 11" x 5.25" 75
Circus Light, elephant, 10.5" h 65
Coasters, pastel colors, set of 4 55
Cookie Jar, green, 8" x 7" 45
Cookie Jar, Smiley Pig, chrysanthemum .200
Corn Holders, 1" h, 8.25" w 80
Creamer, elephant, 1940s 65
Creamer, King Corn, 1940s 45
Creamer, Puss n Boots, 4.75" h 90
Figurine, miniature turtle, 3.75" l, 1.5" h 30
Figurine, raccoon, 1950s, 3.5" h 65
Lamp, clown with umbrella, 7" h 42
Measuring Spoon Holder, flowerpot 28
Mug, man's face with hat, 5.25" h 55
Pie Bird, Pillsbury Company, 5.5" h 85
Pitcher, Fern, 2 qt 65
Pitcher, Smiley Pig, clover blossom, red bandanna 165
Planter, covered wagon, 9.5" l, 4.5" w 35
Planter, deer, green and yellow 50
Planter, elf on shoe, 5.5" h 45
Planter, fish, 7.25" h 70
Planter, flying goose, 6" h 35
Planter, globe, 7" h, 5" d 38
Planter, pony, red, 7.75" h 48
Planter, round, ivy design, 9" d 42
Planter, shoe and dog, red 35
Planter, swan, pink and gold, 8" h 22
Plate, King Corn, oval 40
Salt and Pepper Shakers, Boy Blue and Bo Peep 22
Salt and Pepper Shakers, Chanticleer, 3.25" h 50
Salt and Pepper Shakers, chef, gold trim, 3.25" h 60
Salt and Pepper Shakers, duck, 3.25" h . . .45
Salt and Pepper Shakers, Dutch couple, 5" h 70
Salt and Pepper Shakers, King Corn, 3.25" h 40
Salt and Pepper Shakers, sprinklers, 2" h 30
Salt and Pepper Shakers, Swiss kids, 5" h 40
Salt and Pepper Shakers, winking owl with gold trim 75
Spoon Rest, red int, white ext 15
Teapot, floral design, 5.5" h 45
Teapot, floral, gold dec, 6.5" h 90
Vase, aqua gloss, 7" h 32
Vase, cornucopia, blue, 1940s 30
Vase, fawn, 7" h 80
Vase, white, 10" l, 4" w 35
Wall Pocket, birdhouse, 6" x 5" 38
Wall Pocket, wheat, 4.75" h 32

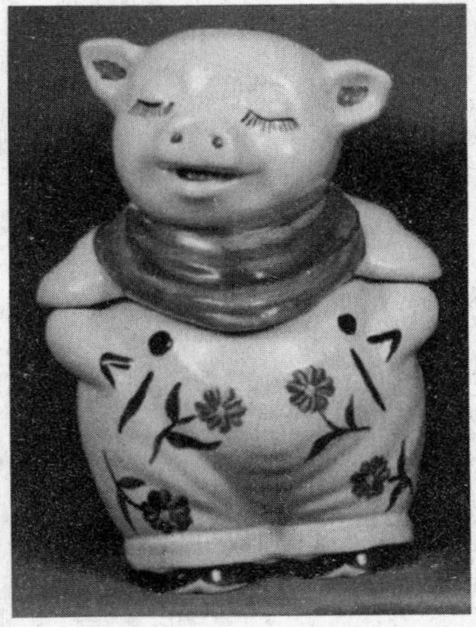

SHEET MUSIC

Sheet music is collected primarily for its cover art. The late 1880s through the early 1950s is considered the golden age of sheet music cover art. Every conceivable theme was illustrated. Leading illustrators lent their talents to sheet music covers.

Covers frequently featured a picture of the singer, group, or orchestra responsible for introducing the song to the public. Photographic covers followed the times. Radio stars, movie stars, and television stars appeared on sheet music covers to promote their show or latest screen epic.

Most sheet music is worth between $3.00 and $5.00, provided it is in near mint condition. In spite of this, many dealers ask an average $8.00 to $12.00 per sheet for mundane titles. Part of the reason for this discrepancy in pricing is the crossover influence of subject collectors. These collectors have little patience with the hunt. Not realizing how easy it is to find copies, they pay high prices and fuel the unrealistic expectations of the general dealer.

Further complicating the picture is the inaccurate, highly manipulative values in the Pafik and Guiheen price guide (Collector Books, 1995). The book has been roundly criticized, and rightly so, within the sheet music collecting community.

Clubs: National Sheet Music Society, 1597 Fair Park Ave., Los Angeles, CA 90041; New York Sheet Music Society, P.O. Box 354, Hewlett, NY 11557; Remember That Song, 5623 N. 64th Ave., Glendale, AZ 85301.

"Beauty Must Be Loved," *Happiness Ahead,* Fain/Kahal, photo of Dick Powell, Josephine Hutchinson in triangle, 1934 18

"High Noon," *High Noon,* Tiomkin/ Washington, Gary Cooper, Grace Kelly, Katy Jurado, 1952 8

"How Do I Rate With You," *Coronado,* Coslow/Whiting, E Duchin, J Haley, J Downs, 1935 6

"Icky," *The Great Gabbo,* McNamee/ Zany, Erich Von Stroheim, Betty Compson, Babe Kane, 1929 10

"I Leave for Dixie to Day," Swift, drawing of black woman in cotton field, music, staff, and head photos of The Four Harmony Chaps as notes, green background, 1918 5

"It's the Same Old Dream," *It Happened in Brooklyn,* Styne/Cahn, Sinatra, Lawford, Durante, Grayson, 1947 6

"I've Got My Eye On You," *Show Girl In Hollywood,* Stept/Green, Alice White, concentric circles behind, 1930 10

"June In January," *Here Is My Heart,* Robin/Rainger, Bing Crosby and Kitty Carlisle, 1934 3

"Life Begins When You're in Love," *The Music Goes Round,* Schertzinger/ Brown, Harry Richman, Rochelle Hudson, 1936 12

"Love Theme," *Superman III,* Moroder, full color Christopher Reeve flying with Richard Pryor over Grand Canyon, 1983 10

"Marines' Hymn, The," Twentieth Century Fox, John Payne, Maureen O'Hara, and Randolph Scott on cov 5

"Mellow Mountain Moon," Howard/ Vincent, Calumet pub, moon rising over mountain peaks, left inset of Herbie Kay, 1935 4

"Milkman Keep Those Bottles Quiet," *Broadway Rhythm,* DePaul/Raye, Ginny Simms, Tommy Dorsey, 1944 5

"Must Be Love," *Sunny Skies,* Jason/ Burton, Benny Rubin, Marceline Day and others, 1930 12

"My Hat's on the Side of My Head," *Jack Ahoy,* Woods/Hulbert, man with hat and bird, large inset of Mary Small, 1933 4

"My Pal Harry," Francis, Day & Hunter Ltd, black and white photo, 1926 4

"Shadow of Your Smile," *The Sandpiper,* Mandel/Webster, Elizabeth Taylor picture, Richard Burton, Academy Award credit, 1965 3

"Sitting on the Moon," *Sitting On The Moon,* Stept/Mitchell, Roger Pryor, Grace Bradley, crescent moon, 1936 . . . 12

"So Good Night," *Hi Ya Sailor,* Rosen/ Carter, D Woods, E Knox, E Quilan, Ray Eberle orchestra, 1943 10

"Spellbound," Greer/Adams, bamboo trees on shore, moon, inset of Estelle Taylor, 1934 3

"Spring Came Back to Vienna," *Luxury Liner,* Rotter/Torre/Spielman, George Brent, Jane Powell, Melchior, Cugat, 1948 8

"Too Beautiful for Words," *Wake Up and Dream,* Columbo/Grossman/Stern, Russ Columbo, June Knight, Wini Shaw, chorus women, 1934 12

"When My Prince Charming Comes Along," *All the King's Horses,* Coslow, drawing of man on rearing horse, inset of Brisson, Ellis, 1935 10

"Zorba the Greek," *Zorba the Greek,* Theodorakis, Anthony Quinn, man dancing 3

SHMOOS

Al Capp (Alfred Gerald Caplin) introduced the world to Li'l Abner and the residents of Dogpatch on August 20, 1934. The comic strip ran until 1977. The enormous popularity of the strip led to an amusement theme park, a Broadway musical, several Fleischer cartoons, a wealth of comic books and softcover paperbacks, two movies, and Kickapoo Joy Juice (a short-lived soft drink). The March 1952 Sunday strip in which Li'l Abner married Daisy Mae holds the record for the most widely read comic strip of all time.

Capp's fertile imagination created Fearless Fosdick, a strip within a strip, and a host of classic comic characters from the Bald Eagle to the ham-shaped Schmoo. The Schmoo lived in a Garden of Paradise. Capp had no qualms about licensing the images of his characters. Look for Schmoo banks, drinking glasses, paperbacks, salt and pepper shakers, sheet music, and more.

Clock, Lux Clock Mfg Co, 1948 200

Coupon, offering 6 comic books for 15¢ and box top from Oxydol or Dreft or 2 wrappers from Ivory Soap, offer expired Aug 31, 1950, 3.25" x 6.5" 8

Drinking Glass, green Pappy Yokum and Shmoo around sides, Federal Glass Co, 1949, 5" h 35

Figure, plaster, boy and girl Schmoo, 4.75" boy, 4.25" girl 175

Magnet, plastic figural, c1948, 1.5" h 40

Nesting Figures, set of 6, plastic, white, black inked smiling face on front, removable bottom, 1.75" to 5.25" h 175

Pin, goldtone metal, 1.5" h 30

Pin, plaster, unmkd, 1" x 2" x .5" 75

Tattoo Transfers, Orange Crush premium, includes Lena the Hyena, Moonbeam McSwine, Lil Abner, Pappy Yokum, William Shmoo, Daisy Mae, Big Barnsmell, and Sadie Hawkins, 1950, 1.5" h 25

Tumbler, set of 8, different images on each tumbler, UFS, 1949, 5.25" x 10.75" x 5.25" box 175

SHOE RELATED COLLECTIBLES

This is a category with sole. Nothing more needs to be said.

Bill Hook, Busch Shoe Repair Co, celluloid button on wire hook, image of shoe-shaped automobile, 7.75" h, 2" w 185

Clicker, "Poll-Parrot Shoes" and green and red parrot on yellow ground 15

Clicker, "Sundial Shoes Are All Leather" and airplane, multicolor, 2.5" 30

Clicker, Weather Bird Shoes, red and black, 4.25" 25

Paperweight, glass, rect, "MM Rhodes & Sons Co, Taunton, Mass, Shoe Buttons," black and white logo of shoe button hanging from cross, 1" x 2.5" x 4" 75

Tip Tray, litho tin, "Clover Brand Shoes Are Always Just Correct," multicolor image of 2 puppies, 2.625" d 45

SILHOUETTE PICTURES

Marlys Sellers' *Encyclopedia of Silhouette Collectibles on Glass* (Shadow Enterprises, 1992) introduced collectors to colored pictures in a silhouette style that were painted on the back of a piece of flat or convex glass and were popular from the 1920s through the early 1950s. They are usually found with a paper scenic or tinted background or a background of textured foil. A popular promotional giveaway, examples are found with an imprinted advertising message. Forms range from a simple two-dimensional picture to a jewelry box.

Boy Fishing at Pond, rect, black plastic, "Best Wishes, The Vernon Company, Newton, Iowa, 8V-242," calendar top, 6" x 8" 15

Colonial Couple, curved glass, copper frames, probably Benton Glass Co, c1940s, 3.5" x 4.5", price for pr 40

Couple, leaning against porch railing, rect black and silver frame, 8.75" x 10.75" 32

Ducks, taking flight from pond, ducks and autumn woodland setting in background, rect, adv for "Dick's Café Manchester, Maryland," with thermometer, gold metal frame, 4" h, 5" w 15

Family, camping and fishing, trees in background, rect, adv for Sam Amendola, Massena, NY, gold metal frame 20

Mother and Daughter, Mother sitting on bench, girl playing with cat, drapes, fireplace, and table with potted plant in background, rect, curved glass, 6" h, 8" w 35

Southern Belles, one holding parasol and sniffing flower, other bending and picking flower, rect, curved glass, 5.125" h, 4.125" w, price for pr 35

Standing Deer and Dog Sled Team, curved glass, full color snowy mountain landscape background, rect, 4" x 5" 50

Two Women, sitting before hearth flanked by portraits, 1 woman in rocking chair knitting, other seated at spinning wheel, thermometer at right, 1941 slide-out calendar at bottom 40

Woman Feeding Parrot, curved glass, white background, rect, 4" x 5.125" 45

SILVER PLATED

G. R. and H. Ekington of England are credited with inventing the electrolytic method of plating silver in 1838. In late nineteenth-century pieces, the base metal was often Britannia, an alloy of tin, copper, and antimony. Copper and brass also were used as bases. Today the base is usually nickel silver.

Rogers Bros., Hartford, Connecticut, introduced the silver-plating process to the United States in 1847. By 1855 a large number of silver-plating firms were established.

Extensive polishing will eventually remove silver plating. However, today's replating process is so well developed that you can have a piece replated in such a manner that the full detail of the original is preserved.

Identifying companies and company marks is difficult. Fortunately there is Dorothy Rainwater's *Encyclopedia of American Silver Manufacturers, 4th Edition* (Schiffer Publishing, 1998).

Baby Rattle, bells inside, rocking horse design on 1 side, bricks on other side, 4.5" l, 2" w 25
Bank, figural rocking horse, English, 4" h .45
Butter Dish, cov, glass tray, mkd "Sheridan, Silver Plated," 3.5" h, 8.75" l, 5" w 45
Candelabra, 3-cup, 7" h 30
Child's Tumbler, emb rabbit, Napier Co, 3.25" h, 2.5" d 45
Cigarette Case, SP brass, emb scrolls, flowers, and strapwork, 1920s-30s, 4.25" x 3" 60
Comb Holder, emb floral design, with faux tortoise shell comb, 4.875" l, 1.25" w 30
Creamer and Sugar, cov, rope design around center, tray with scroll design, scalloped edge, and floral design on center handle, mkd "Cromwell Mfg Co, Silver Plated" 80
Crumb Set, matching brush and tray, mkd "quadruple Plate, Crescent Silver Co, 94," 7" w 25
Finger Bowl, 2.25" h, 4" d 8

Fruit Dish, Victorian, in the shape of 3 shells with center handle, 10" l 65
Hair Brush, oval shape with engraved initials, c1920, 8.75" l, 2.75" w 45
Meat Dish, well and tree, Rogers Bros, 18" l 150
Napkin Ring, engraved floral design 15
Pickle Fork, Simeon L & George H Rogers Co 10
Rocker Blotter, engraved Baroque Baronial style design, 3" h, 5.625" l, 3" w 125
Rose Bowl, sectioned lid, pedestal ft, 1930s, 6" d 75
Salt and Pepper Shakers, weighted bases, Oneida, 4.75" h 20
Trinket Box, round, pressed glass bottom with starburst design, dark blue velvet lining, 1.75" h, 3.75" d 25
Trinket Dish, Victorian, mkd "W&S," English 24

SLEDS

Sleds divide into two basic groups: (1) clippers with pointed runners and (2) cutters with runners that curl upward in a bow-like fashion.

By the mid-1930s, Flexible Flyer, headquartered in Philadelphia, dominated the sled market. Its lines include the Airline Series, Flexy Racer, Ski Racer, and the Yankee Clipper. Other sled manufacturers included: American Toy and Novelty Works/American Acme (Emigsville, PA); Buffalo Sled Company/Auto Wheel Coaster (North Tonawanda, NY); Ellington Turing Co. (South Paris, ME); Garton Toy Company (Sheboygan, WI); Kalamazoo

Sled Company (Kalamazoo, MI); and, Standard Novelty Works (Duncannon, PA).

Sledding lost its popularity in the late 1960s. Balzon-Flexible Flyer filed for Chapter 11 bankruptcy in 1975. The Roadmaster Corporation revived the company in 1993 and continues to manufacture sleds.

Classic Comet, Christmas dec, 1940s, 58" x 25" 300
Dutch, oak, woven fabric seat, 1960s, 48" x 14" 160
Flexible Flyer, Yankee Clipper #10, 37" l . . .75
Oak, painted red, oak runners capped with iron, 36" x 13" x 6" 140
Victorian, painted flowers on red ground, 33" x 8.5" 200

SLOT CARS

Aurora, the premier name in slot car racing, marketed its first electric slot car play set in the fall of 1960. Since then, slot cars have successfully competed with electric trains for their share of the model hobbyist's dollars.

Clubs: National Slot Car Racing Club, 1903 Middlefield Rd. #3, Redwood City, CA 94063; United Federation of H.O. Racers Assoc., 6800 W. Kilgore Ave., Yorktown, IN 47396.

AFX, Mustang, dark green, aluminum rims 40
AMT, Ford Ranchero, 1961, 1:24 scale 50
Aurora, 1961 Thunderbird, gray 46
Aurora, Dodge Fever Dragster 44
Aurora, Ford Thunderjet GT40 8
Aurora, Thunderjet Thunderbird Convertible, yellow 45
Aurora, Thunderjet Tow Truck, white 50
Aurora AFX, Ford Van, black 55
Aurora AFX, Roadrunner #43, red 50
Corgi, Police Wagon, repainted 16
MPC, Mako Shark, 1:24 scale 55
Ninco, AC Cobra LeMans, 1:32 scale 55
Polistil, Alfa Romeo Formula 1 Race Car, 1:55 scale, late 1970s, MIP 12
Polistil, Braham Parmalat BT 46 F1, 1978, MIB 40
Polistil, McLaren Texaco F1, 1976, MIB . . .42

Strombecker, McLaren Convertible, white 45
Tyco, Curve Hugger Porsche, yellow, MOC 45
Tyco, Turbo Train, MIB 16

SMOKEY BEAR

It is hard to believe that Smokey Bear has been around for more than fifty years. The popularity of Smokey started during the Second World War, as part of a national awareness campaign for the prevention of forest fires. The National Forest Service ran slogans like "Keep 'Em Green; Forests Are Vital to National Defense" in an attempt to keep the public's attention on the war effort.

From then to now Smokey has been more than just a crusader for fire awareness and prevention; he has been a collectible character and a source of enjoyment to many admirers. There was a wide variety of Smokey collectibles produced: watches, radios, toys, posters, and many games and books. Most had short production runs and were used as Forest Service giveaways or were sold by a select number of department store chains.

Good luck in your collecting and remember, "Only you can prevent forest fires."

Activity Book, 1971, 126 pgs 8
Ashtray, bucket, tin, 4" h 55
Ashtrays, aluminum, 4" d, 4-pc set 20
Badge, 3" d 10
Bobber, Wacky Wobbler, 7" h 15
Book,* The Smokey Bear Book, *Golden Shape Book, Mel Crawford, Western Pub Co, 24 pgs, 1970, 8" x 8" 10
Comic Book, "The True Story of Smokey Bear," 1969 10
Comic Book, "The True Story of Smokey Bear," full color reprint of 1969 edition . .5

Doll, plastic body, rubber head, 8" h 45
Doll, plush, 15" h 8
Doll, plush, 22" h 75
Film, Forest Fire Prevention Campaign, Series XXI, color, orig box 12
Hat, adjustable 35
Key Chain, plastic, 2" x .5" 4
Little Golden Book, *Smokey the Bear,* 1955 20
Mug, yellow, 3.75" h .5
Patch, "Prevent Forest Fires," 2" d 15
Pinback Button, "I'm Smokey's Helper" 2.75" d 5
Plate, Melmac, 7" d .15
Ring, soft metal 25
Ruler, 1962, 8" h 18
Salt and Pepper Shakers, Japan, 1960s, 3.75" h 95
Scarf, cotton/rayon blend, Japan, 22" sq . .65
Sign, tin, "Only You," 11.5" x 16" 10
Sign, tin, "Shameful Waste," 11.5" x 16" . . .10
Soaky Bottle, 8.75" h 24
Song Book, paperback, 32 pgs 45
Sugar Shaker, Smokey at Mailbox, 4.75" h 55
Tie Tac, brass-colored metal, .75" h 8
Toy, Talking Smokey Bear, Knickerbocker 145
Trading Card, Smokey Bear with Mike Krukow 5
Trading Card, Smokey Bear with Ozzie Smith 5
Trading Cards, "Smokey Bear's Fire Prevention Team," 1987, 4" x 6", set of 3 18

SMURFS

Pierro "Peyo" Culliford, a Belgian cartoonist, created the Smurfs. The name is a shortened version of "Schtroumpf," a French colloquialism meaning "whatchamacallit." Over 100 characters are known.

The Smurfs first appeared as a comic strip. Soon the strips were collected into books and a line of licensed toys. In 1965 Schleich, a German firm, began marketing a line of two-inch high, PVC Smurf figures. A full collection numbers in the hundreds, the result of numerous decorating variations and discontinued markings. The first Smurf figures arrived in the United States in 1979.

After appearing in the movie *Smurfs and the Magic Flute* in 1975, Smurfs secured a permanent place in the collecting field when Hanna-Barbera launched its Smurf Saturday morning cartoon show in 1981.

Club: Smurf Collectors Club International, 24 Cabot Rd. W., Massapequa, NY 11758.

Bicycle License Plate, "Smurfs Ride Free," 1983 4
Book, *Smurfing in the Air* 4
Comic Book, "Smurfs," #1, 1982 8
Cup and Bowl Set, plastic, Deka, 1980 5
Dish Set, 4 pcs, plastic, plate, 2 bowls, and cup 6
Doll, Baseball Player Smurf, 14" h 8
Doll, plush, Smurf with nut shell filling, 1980, 7.5" h 5
Figurine, Smurf Drummer, plastic, 1966 5
Figurine, Smurfette on skate board, plastic, 2.5" h 8
Figurine, Smurfette tennis player, plastic, 1981 4
Figurine, Smurf Pirate, with eye patch and sword, plastic, 1978, 2.5" h 8
Figurine, Smurf with mirror, plastic, 1972, 1" h 8
Hat, pointing Smurf on front, red, white, and blue 3
Mug, Smurf surrounded by hearts, 3.25" w, 3.5" h 8
Playset, Smurf Village 7
Promotional Glass, Brainy and Jokey,

1982 6
Promotional Glass, Brainy lecturing 2 other Smurfs, 1982, 6" h 5
Promotional Glass, Clumsy and Handy, 1983 6
Promotional Glass, Grouchy carrying sign that reads "I Hate Music" while other Smurfs play instruments, 6" h, 1982 5
Puzzle, girl Smurf shooting Pez into Papa Smurf's mouth, 3" x 3.5" 10
Record Player, 1982, 11" x 14" 65
Toy, Smurf, wind-up, 3" h 12
Toy, Smurfette in red VW with butterfly on hood, Ertl, 1982 8
Toy, Smurf in red fire truck, Ertl, 1982 5
Toy Telephone, plastic and vinyl, 1982, 9" h 20
Transistor Radio, blue plastic case with blue and white Smurf on front, AM, 9-volt battery, 1982, 5" h, 3" w 45

SNACK SETS

The earliest snack sets (originally called tea and toast sets) were porcelain and earthenware examples manufactured overseas. Glass sets produced in the United States were a popular hostess accessory during the boom years following World War II. American dinnerware manufacturers of the time, such as Purinton and Stangl, also produced sets to match their most popular dinnerware patterns.

Anchor Hocking, Classic 10
Anchor Hocking, Fancy Glass 35
Anchor Hocking, Wheat pattern, set of 4 .65

Crown Staffordshire, Daisy 20
Federal, black, blue, pink, and yellow flowers on white, set of 4 16
Federal, Blossom 15
Federal, floral pattern 10
Federal, Hawaiian Leaf 30
Federal, Homestead Wheat 15
Federal, milk glass 17
Federal, red rose pattern 5
Federal, Thumbprint 25
Federal, Yorktown, crystal 5
Fire-King, Azurite, set of 4 20
Fire King, Fleurette 25
Fire King, Primrose .6
Fire King, Rachael .10
Floral Design, blue and purple 8
Georges Briard, Wildlife 45
Hazel Atlas, Apple Waffle Block 10
Hazel Atlas, Colony Square 20
Hazel Atlas, Sea Shell, blue, set of 4 75
Indiana, Harvest Grape, milk glass 8
Indiana, Kings Crown, amber 12
Indiana, Snowflake, set of 4 20
Indiana, Sunburst 24
Japan, blue floral design 15
Japan, Fred Roberts 12
Japan, Moss Rose .12
Japan, Pine 12
Jeanette, Dewdrop .10
Lancaster, Daisy and Button, amber 15
Lancaster, Daisy and Button, clear 10
Lancaster, Daisy and Button, olive 30
Lefton, Feather 12
Lefton, Golden Wheat 25
Lefton, Poinsettia 20
Lefton, Summertime 30
Lefton, Violets, gold trim 5
Lustreware, set of 4 70
Milk Glass, Grape 8
Noritake, red rose dec, gold trim 18
Royal Winton, Kew Chintz 95
Sandwich Glass, amber, set of 4 50
Seymour Mann, Flower Garden, 1976, set of 4 20

SNOW GLOBES

The majority of plastic and glass snow globes found at flea markets are imported from the Orient. A few are produced in France, Germany, and Italy. There are no American manufacturers, but rather dozens of large gift companies who design and import an array of styles, shapes, and themes. Enesco Corporation of Elk Grove Village, Illinois, is one of the largest.

Club: Snowdome Collectors Club, P.O. Box 53262, Washington, DC 20009.

Beatles, Beatles in Pepperland, musical, *Yellow Submarine,* 6.5" h 65
Beatles, Tour Bus moves around base, musical, *Magical Mystery Tour,* 8" h . . .80
Beetlejuice sitting on roof of house, 7.5" h 50
Betty Boop, skating with friends, musical, *California Girls,* 7" h 60
Betty Boop, standing on top of yellow radio, musical, *Blue Suede Shoes,* 5.25" h 35
Charlie Brown, Charlie and girl friend inside globe playing pattie cake, Snoopy lying on dock outside globe, musical, *You Are My Sunshine,* 5.5" h 38
Dove, musical 15
Dr Seuss, *Cat in the Hat,* cats inside globe with A, B, C and Whozits outside of globe, musical, *That's What Friends Are For* 35
Dr Seuss, Horton with a bird sitting on his back, 2.5" h 12
Elvis, standing on record player and holding guitar, musical, *All Shook Up,* 6" h 48

Frog Prince, plastic, hp panel, white oval ftd base, mkd "3/1072/Ges. GESCH 1675631," 2.5" h 15
Grateful Dead, 3 bears playing in a band, musical, *Uncle John's Band,* 5.5" h 45
Halloween, pumpkins and Strawman, when shaken, bats fly around, when switched on, Strawman says, "Happy Halloween," 4" h 10
Horton and Morton, musical, *Fly Me to the Moon,* 7" h 35
I Love Lucy, conveyer belt with chocolates, musical, I Love Lucy theme song, 7" h 55
Lighted Cottage, wood base, 5" x 3.75" 25
Little Miss Muffet, musical, *Toyland,* 6.5" h 20
Peanuts, Back to School, Snoopy at desk, musical, Peanuts theme song, 6" h 40
Peanuts, Woodstock and friends in Happi-nest, 5.5" h 18
Rocky and Bullwinkle, Rocky J Squirrel, 2.5" h 12
Rugrats, Angelica standing on color tv box, holding wand and wearing cape, 2.5" h 15
Rugrats, Tommy sitting in big baseball glove, 2.5" h 15
Snowman, jar topper, 4.5" h 15
Speed Racer, Speed with gang sitting on mag racing tire with checkered flags, 5" h 48

SOAKIES

Soakies, plastic figural character bubble bath bottles, were developed to entice children into the bathtub. Soakies, now a generic term for all plastic bubble bath bottles, originates from "Soaky," a product of the Colgate Palmolive Company.

Colgate Palmolive licensed numerous popular characters, e.g., Rocky and Bullwinkle, Felix the Cat, and Universal Monsters. Colgate Palmolive's success was soon copied, e.g., Purex's Bubble Club. Purex licensed the popular Hanna-Barbera characters. Avon, DuCair Bioessence, Koscot, Lander Company, and Stephen Reiley are other companies who have produced Soakies.

Soakies arrived on the scene in the early 1960s and have remained in production since. Most are 10" high. Over a hundred different Soakies have been produced. Many are found in two or more variations, e.g., there are five versions of Bullwinkle.

Atom Ant, Purex, 1965 40
Bambi and Thumper, matching pr, 1960s, 10" h 30
Barney Rubble, Flintstones, Purex, 1960s 28
Bozo, holding unicycle in right hand, Colgate-Palmolive, Capitol Records copyright, mid-1960s, 9.75" h 25
Casper the Friendly Ghost, Colgate-Palmolive 28
Dopey, Snow White and the Seven Dwarfs, standing on wooden fence, purple and yellow body, 1960s, 10" h . . .25
El Kabong, Purex, 1964 45
Goofy, 1960s, 8.5" h 10
Mickey Mouse, Band Leader, 10" h 45
Muskie, Terrytoons, Colgate-Palmolive, 1965, 9.75" h 25
Pinocchio, 10" h 35
Pluto, Palmolive, 8.5" h 15
Porky Pig, 9.5" h 30
Santa, Colgate-Palmolive, 7" h 10
Smokey Bear, Colgate-Palmolive, 8.75" h .50
Snow White, 10" h 30
Top Cat, 10" h 45
Top Cat, standing in trash can, Hanna-Barbera copyright, mid-1960s, 9.75" h 35

SOAP COLLECTIBLES

At first you would not think that a lot of soap collectibles would survive. However, once you start to look around you'll see no end to the survivors. Many Americans are not as clean as we think.

There is no hotel soap listed. Most survivors sell for 50¢ to $2 per bar. Think of all the hotels and motels that you have stayed at that have gone out of business. Don't you wish you would have saved one of the soap packets?

Advertising Trade Card, Good Will Soap Alphabet Card 10
Advertising Trade Card, Pearline Washing Compound, cute and clean girl in white dress on hammock, 1885 6
Chauvinist Pig Soap, Avon, orig box, yellow, 1960s 20
Geppetto Soap, Geppetto standing with hands behind back, orig box, 1939, 3.75" h 45
Hansel and Gretel Soap, Avon, box shaped like a candy house 15
Label, Queen Beauty, lady in purple surrounded by an emb gold frame 10
Laundry Soap, White King, unopened, 1933 75
Magazine Tear Sheet, All Detergent, Christmas 1952, "All – The Wonderful Washing Powder" 10
Magazine Tear Sheet, *Companion Magazine,* Woodbury's Facial Soap, 1900s, 6" x 8" 8
Magazine Tear Sheet, *Ladies Home Journal,* 1953, LUX Toilet Soap, features Janet Leigh 10
Magazine Tear Sheet, *The Delineator,* 1890, Pear's Soap, black and brown . . .12
Magazine Tear Sheet, *The Graphic,* 1894, Lifebuoy Royal Disinfectant Soap, 9.5" x 6.25" 15
Magazine Tear Sheet, *Women's World Magazine,* Proctor and Gamble Soap, 10" x 13" 8
New Huck & Yogi Bubbles, box has image of Yogi scrubbing Huck's back in bathtub on front, yellow ground, Yogi, Mr Jinks, and Pixie & Dixie on side panels, 1961, 2.25" x 6" x 8.5" h, unopened 45

Soap Bottle, Larkin Soap 8
Soap Box, Goblin Soap, Cudahy Soap Works, cardboard 10
Soap Box, La France Bluing, 2 oz box, 5" x 3.25" x 1.25" 15
Soap Dish, Avon, white milk glass hands, 5.5" x 7" 15
Soap Dish, brass, hanging, 3" x 5" 60
Soap Dish, graniteware, 5.5" l 22
Soap Dish, majolica, emb green flowers and leaves, mkd, "Portugal," 6" x 4" 25
Soap Dish, porcelain, 2 bear figures standing upright and arm in arm on dish, blue and white, 5" x 4" 10
Soap Dishes, pr, Avon, "Butterfly Fantasy," round, 4" d 10
Soap Saver, 11" l 20

SODA FOUNTAIN

The local soda fountain and/or ice cream parlor was the social center of small town America between the late 1880s and the 1960s. Ice cream items appeared as early as the 1870s.

This is a category filled with nostalgia—banana splits and dates with friends. Some concentrate on the advertising, some on the implements. It is all terrific.

Club: National Assoc. of Soda Jerks, P.O. Box 115, Omaha, NE 68101

Cookie Jar, Coca-Cola, in the shape of a soda fountain dispenser, 10" h, 5.2" w . .50
Float Glass, 1940, 7" h, 3" w 25
Ice Cream Scoop, Indestructo No. 4, 1.5" d scoop, 9.5" l 50

Ice Cream Scoop, tin, conical, 3" d scoop, 8.5" l 60
Magazine Tear Sheet, *National Geographic*, 1941, Coca-Cola Coke, newspaper reporter at soda fountain . .10
Menu, Riani's of Springfield, burgundy with gold lettering 40
Menu Board, framed glass, "Real 7-Up Sold Here," 1930s-40s, 17" h, 10" w 132
Milkshake Machine Glasses, hard plastic, 6.75" h, 4" w, set of 4 15
Mug, A&W Root Beer, clear with orange logo, 3.25" h 10
Parfait Tumblers, white plastic with lacy design, 5" h, set of 8 30
Soda Fountain Mixer Cup, aluminum with glass insert 5
Spoon, Wm A Rogers, 1900s, 5" l 15
Sundae Glass, clear, tulip-shaped, 5.75" h .15
Sundae Glasses, Anchor Hocking, scalloped rims, 4 oz, set of 4 15
Textile, soda fountain scene, 1920, 6" x 6" .30
Vee Cup, Chicago Vortex, black amethyst, 2.75" d, 4.25" h 28
Whipped Cream Dispenser, mkd "Kidde MFG Com," 10" h .35

SOFT DRINK COLLECTIBLES

National brands such as Coca-Cola, Canada Dry, Dr Pepper, and Pepsi-Cola dominate the field. However, there were thousands of regional and local soda bottling plants. Their advertising, bottles, and giveaways are every bit as exciting as those of the national companies. Do not ignore them.

Clubs: Crown Collectors Society International, 4300 San Juan Dr., Fairfax, VA 22030; Dr Pepper 10-2-4 Collector's Club, 3100 Monticello, Ste. 890, Dallas, TX 75205; Grapette Collectors Club, 2240 Hwy. 27N, Nashville, AR 71852; National Pop Can Collectors, 19201 Sherwood Green Way, Gaithersburg, MD 20879; New England Moxie Congress, 445 Wyoming Ave., Millburn, NJ 07041; Painted Soda Bottle Collectors Assoc., 9418 Hilmer Dr., La Mesa, CA 91942; The Cola Club, P.O. Box 392, York, PA 17405.

Note: For additional listings see Coca-Cola and Pepsi-Cola.

Door Push, aluminum, "Come in, 7-Up likes You," 1940s, 9" h, 3.5" w 165

Drinking Glass, 7-up, Anchor Hocking, 10 oz, 1950s, 5.25" h 22

Drinking Glass, Nesbitt, clear with white lettering, 4" h, 2.5" d 22

Kick Plate, heavily emb, hand holding bottle of soda with "Your 'Fresh Up' 7-Up," 1947, 11" h, 31" w 358

Sign, 7-Up, diecut bottle, "7-Up, You Like It, It Likes You," on label, 1962, 45" h, 13" w 100

Sign, 7-Up, emb, "'Fresh Up' with 7-Up" in oval with fan detail at bottom, 1963, 41" h, 41" w 385

Sign, 7-Up, flange, "7-Up" logo, sq, 1965, 16" sq 176

Sign, 7-Up, neon, 3 colors, 28" h, 13" w . .220

Sign, Bubble Up, "...just pure pleasure!" in white above red "Bubble Up" in large white bubbles, dark ground with fizzing bubbles background, celluloid over tin over cardboard, 9" d 85

Sign, Cherry Smash, "Cherry Smash" in white on red banner with "Drink" above and "A True Fruit Blend" below, white ground, black rim, celluloid over tin over cardboard, 9" d 88

Sign, Coleman's, "Ask For Coleman's Ginger Ale," red and blue lettering on white ground, celluloid over tin over cardboard, 9" d 138

Sign, Double Cola, "Drink Double Cola," yellow and red lettering on black ground, gold rim, oval, celluloid over tin over cardboard, 1940s-50s, 8" h, 12" w .185

Sign, Eight Ball, "Here's Your Cue! Drink" Eight 8 Ball The Big Favorite," billiard ball, and soda bottle on green ground, celluloid over tin over cardboard, 9" d .145

Sign, Hires, "Drink Hires Root Beer," blue and yellow lettering on light blue and white vertically striped ground, gold rim, tin face, 9" d .85

Sign, M&S, red-orange "Enjoy M&S Orange" on gold ground, black rim with transparent "Mellow And Smooth Fresh Fruit Flavor," with envelope, celluloid over tin over cardboard, 9" d . .94

Sign, Mason's Root Beer, "Enjoy Mason's Root Beer ice cold," large brown "M," and soda bottle on yellow and white ground, celluloid over tin over cardboard, 1940s, 9" d 145

Sign, Mission Orange, "Ice Cold Mission Orange Makes Thirst A Pleasure," black and orange lettering on yellow ground, gold rim, tin face, 9" d 105

Sign, Nesbitt's, "Don't Say Orange, Say Nesbitt's (on bottle), A Delicious Drink," large soda bottle, and professor on blackboard background, gold rim, celluloid over tin over cardboard, 9" d .198

SOUVENIRS

This category demonstrates that, given time, even the tacky can become collectible. Many tourist souvenirs offer a challenge to one's aesthetics. But they are bought anyway.

Tourist china plates and glass novelties from the 1900 to 1940 period are one of the true remaining bargains left. Most of the items sell for under $25. If you really want to have some fun, pick one form and see how many different places you can find from which it was sold.

Clubs: Souvenir Building Collectors Society, P.O. Box 70, Nellysford,VA 22958; Statue of Liberty Collectors' Club, 26601 Bernwood Rd., Cleveland, OH 44122.

Building, Empire State Building, New York City, embellished with paint, rhinestones and blue glass seed beads, 12.5" h 75
Cup and Saucer, Montana, "Treasure State," State Capitol Building on both pcs 8
Cup and Saucer, "Washington DC" hp on white china with gold trim 20
Figurine, Dallas, Texas, cowboy on horse, bronze 35
Lamp, figural Leaning Tower of Pisa 100
Hankerchief, US Capitol Building 10
Inkwell, metal, Le Sacre Coeur, Paris, France 110
Matchbook, 1939 New York World's Fair, depicts the Railroad Building, Hall of Pharmacy Building, Electrical Products Building, and the Glass Center Building, 4" x 4" 85
Matchbook, New Zealand Crest and House of Representatives on 1 side, Parliament Buildings on other, 4.75" x 2.5" 25
Paperweight, Buffalo Nickel, Washington DC, Capitol and "Souvenir of Washington DC The Capitol" on front, buffalo and "Lucky Nickel 1926" on back, 3" d 30
Plate, Empire State Building, Rockefeller Center, and Statue of Liberty, brown ...18
Plate, Mammoth Cave entrance, Staffordshire, c1950 20
Plate, Monon Township School Building in center, off-white with emb fruit and leaves around rim, 10" d 30
Plate, Yellowstone National Park, Old Faithful Geyser in center, blue and white, 7" d 30
Postcard, Station and Park, Ashbury Park, NY 6
Postcard, The Statler Center, Los Angeles, California 5
Salt and Pepper Shakers, figural binoculars, salt has view of Washington Monument, pepper has US Capitol, 3.5" h, 4" w 35
Salt and Pepper Shakers, figural German steins picturing a Bavarian town by a mountain, 2.5" h, 1.25" d 28
Salt and Pepper Shakers, figural Washington Monument and Capitol, white porcelain 25
Scarf, "Aloha Hawaii," hula girl, 29" x 29" .28
Serving Tray, Silver Springs, FL, picture of grounds and springs at Silver Springs and famous Glass Bottom Boats, 17.5" x 11.5" 25
Snow Globe, Paris Buildings, plastic, mkd, "Made in France," 2.25" h, 3" w ...20
Stein, Boston, MA, Old State House and Old South Church, German Stoneware, 4.5" h, 2" w 85
Thermometer, Washington, DC, cast metal key with Capitol and thermometer on 1 side, Seal of USA on other side, orig tassel, 7" l 15
Tray, Abraham Lincoln Hotel, Reading, PA, curved glass, 4.5" x 3.25" 5
Tray, Eifel Tower, Paris, France, metal, 4.24" w, 3" h 15
Vase, Niagara Falls, Occupied Japan 6

SOUVENIR SPOONS

Collecting commemorative spoons was extremely popular from the last decade of the 19th century through 1940. Actually, it has never gone completely out of fashion. You can still buy commemorative spoons at many historical and city tourist sites. The first thing to check for is metal content. Sterling silver has always been the most popular medium. Fine enamel work adds to value.

Clubs: American Spoon Collectors, 7408 Englewood Ln., Raytown, MO 54133; The Scoop Club, 84 Oak Ave., Shelton, CT 06484.

Apollo 11, "One small step...," July 1969, 4.5" l 10
Canada, abbreviations of 10 provinces on handle, "Vancouver BC" in bowl, mkd "Sterling BMCo," 3.75" l 15
Canal Street, New Orleans, LA, SS, 5.375" l 15
Colorado, mule, prospector, and state flower on handle, "Fishers Peak" in bowl, SS, 5.5" l 70
Firenze, Italy, figural nude handle, cherub head, "1900" in bowl, 5.125" l 45
Ft Worth, TX, monogrammed on handle, "Ft Worth, Texas" in bowl, mkd "925/1000, Sterling, JE Mitchell," 5.5" l 40
Kansas, map in bowl mkd "Topeka, Kansas City, Wichita," Kansas seal on handle, mkd "TH Marthinsen, EPNS, Norway" 10
Lansing, MI, bird, flower, and pine tree surrounded by "Robin, Apple Blossom, and White Pine" on handle top, "Capitol Lansing" down stem, "Mackinac City Soo Locks, Sleeping Bear Dune, Grand Rapids, Detroit" in bowl, mkd "Gish," 3.5" l 8
London, enameled red, white, and blue crest and "London" on handle, mkd "BII Chrome Sheffield England," 4.5" l . .12
Maine, blue and copper medallion finial with a lobster and "Maine Pine Tree State," mkd "USA," 3.5" l 7
Montreal, yellow enameled finial with "I (heart) Montreal," mkd "Taiwan," 4.5" l 5

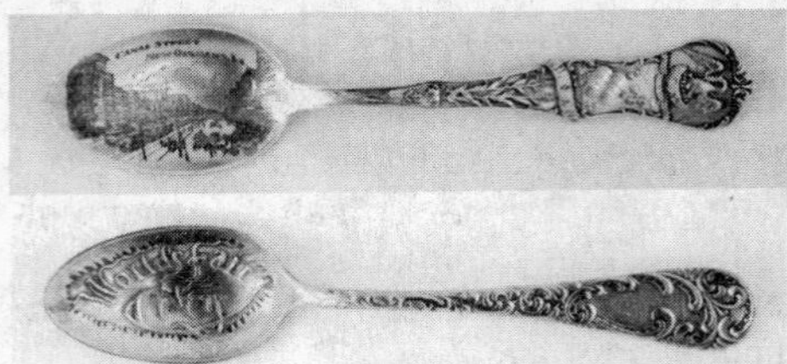

New Jersey, state symbols engraved on handle, mkd "W Rogers & Son AA Silverplate" 10
New York World's Fair, 1939, Oneida Community Silver Plate, 1939, 4.375" l . .20
Niagara Falls, twisted handle with fleur-de-lis top, emb view of Niagara Falls in bowl, SS, 4.5" l 20
Oslo, "Stavkirke Oslo" beneath tall roof at handle top, back mkd "B, Made In Holland," 4.5" l 12
RA Long Building, Kansas City, MO 45
San Francisco Exposition, gold, 1915 30
Seattle, WA, Indian and corn stalks on handle, "Seattle, WA" on bowl, mkd "SMB Sterling" 30
St Roch's Chapel, New Orleans, Mardi gras jester and horn on handle, chapel in bowl, gold-washed, 3.5" l 48
United Nations, blue enameled UN building on handle top, mkd "TH Martninsen Sterling Norway" 10
Washington, twisted handle with lacy design at top, bowl engraved "Washington," 4" l 20

SPACE COLLECTIBLES

This category deals only with fictional space hero toys. My father followed Buck Rogers in the Sunday funnies. I saw Buster Crabbe as Flash Gordon in the movies and cut my teeth on early television with Captain Video. My son belongs to the Star Trek generation. Whichever generation you choose, there is plenty to collect.

Club: Galaxy Patrol, 144 Russell St., Worcester, MA 01610.

Battlestar Galactica, action figure, Cylon Centurian 50
Battlestar Galactica, poster, space fleet in a battle against the Cylons, attempting to reach Earth, 1978 45

Buck Rogers, Big Little Book, *Buck Rogers in the City of Floating Globes,* 1933 .70
Buck Rogers, movie poster, 1979 .65
Buck Rogers, mug, ftd, spaceship scene .20
Buck Rogers, pinback button, promotes Saturday's comic section of *Chicago American* .165
Buck Rogers, thermos, Aladdin, 6.5" h, 1979 .35
Captain Laser, action figure, 12" h .40
Flash Gordon, Big Little Book, *Flash Gordon in the Water World of Mongo,* 1937 .65
Flash Gordon, Halloween mask, plastic, 1960s .8
Mug, space shuttle, 5.5" h .10
Lost in Space, print, 13" x 18" .85
Lost in Space, sgd photo, Jonathan Harris, 8" x 10" .30
Planet of the Apes, autograph, Charlton Heston, 1985 .40
Planet of the Apes, coloring book .10
Planet of the Apes, Halloween mask, gorilla or neanderthal man .20
Planet of the Apes, puzzle, Galen, 1974, 44" x 30" .25
Salt and Pepper Shakers, boys in space suits, 3.75" h, 1950s .40
Space Shuttle, cookie jar, Enesco, 17" l, 8" h, 11" wingspan .60
Space Shuttle, salt and pepper shakers, 5.5" h .95
Tom Corbett, Space Cadet Rocket ring, Kellogg's Cereal, hard plastic, 1952 .15
Tom Corbett, Wonder Book, *A Trip to the Moon,* 1953 .12
Toy, Mystery Action Satellite, litho tin, battery operated, 3 actions, includes styro saucer, Cragstan, 1960s .160
Toy, squirt gun, soft plastic, 1960s, 4" l .8
Toy, troll, spaceman with magenta hair, silver space suit .6

SPACE EXPLORATION

Collector interest in artifacts relating to the manned space program began in the early 1980s. After a brief fascination with autographed material, collectors moved to three-dimensional objects.

The collapse of the Soviet Union coupled with Russia's and several cosmonauts' need for capital has resulted in the sale of space memorabilia by several leading auction houses around the world. Everything from capsules to space suits are available for purchase.

This category focuses primarily on material associated with manned space flight. Collector interest in material from unmanned flights is extremely limited.

Carafe, clear glass with white plastic lid, space capsule-shaped with red, white, and blue depictions of Apollo Missions 11, 12, and 13 around sides, "Three Giant Leaps for Mankind," 9" h .40
Drinking Glass, clear with red, white, and blue painted label, "USA Apollo 13, Safe Return, A Triumph of Courage, Ingenuity, Teamwork. James A Lovell Jr, Fred W Haise Jr, John L Swigert Jr," illus of spacecraft and route .15
Flight Patch, NASA .6
Map, solar system and outer space, Book Enterprises, full color, 1960, 36" x 48" .10
Pennant, felt, commemorates moon landing, images of Armstrong, Aldrin, and Collins, spacecraft, and planted US flag on moon's surface, "One small step..." in white lettering, Apollo 11 logo, blue ground, 26.75" l plus tails .35
Photo, official NASA photo of crew of 11th space shuttle orbital flight (41-C) plus schedule and patch .15
Plate, John Glenn commemorative, black and white sketch of smiling astronaut and orbiting space capsule in center, "John H Glenn Jr Feb 20, 1962. First American to Orbit the World," black lettering, gold scrollwork border, 9.25" d .35
Postcard, Neil Armstrong portrait, color, 4" x 5.5" .4

Tray, Western Union Presentation commemorative, smoky gray glass, rect with rounded corners, concave center with replica of plaque placed on moon featuring 2 hemispheres and "Here men from the planet Earth first set foot upon the moon July 1969, AD. We came in peace for all mankind," astronaut signatures below, 7.5" x 5.75" 75

SPARK PLUGS

Over 4,000 different plug names have been identified by collectors, the most common of which are Champion, AC, and Autolite. Spark plugs are classified into six types: name plugs, gadget plugs, primer plugs, visible plugs, coil plugs, and quick detachable (QD) plugs.

There is no right or wrong way to collect spark plugs. Some people collect a certain style of plug, while others grab any plug they can find.

Use care when examining old spark plugs. Many have fragile labels which can be destroyed through improper handling.

Club: Spark Plug Collectors of America, 9 Heritage Ln., Simsbury, CT 06070.

PLUGS

AC 75th Anniversary 12
AC IHC 8
AC Titan 2
Aldor ThermoReactor, intensified 4
Allstate, USA outline .4
Auburn 78A, NOS 5
Auto-Fire, NOS 10
Bethlehem, aviation, extra brass clip on top terminal 15
Blue Crown Husky, NOS 8
Brighton, NOS 6
Champion 6 Com, NOS 3
Champion 13, NOS 5
Champion 15A, NOS .3
Champion 45, odd electrode, NOS 18
Champion A-25, Canada, NOS 12
Defiance 5
Edison Albanite 39-T, NOS 5
Energex P 5
Firestone Polonium SH-60, NOS 5
Flash, Ring Mfg Co, Kalamazoo, MI, NOS 275
Iskra Super, 14 mm, Poland 5
J-M, NOS 30
Leonard High Compression 5
Liberty, hand holding torch, Casey-Hudson Co, NOS 145
Myles Standish Oil Proof, NOS 35
National, NOS 3
Rentz, NOS 12
S&K Spark Govenor, with literature, NOS . .5
Super Power 18
Wizard Standard 3

ADVERTISING

Box, Bethlehem 5-Point Spark Plug, yellow, black, and red, empty 12
Bulletin, Champion Spark Plug Co, Sep/Oct 1961, 8 pgs, color illus 15
Conversion Chart, Defiance Spark Plugs, 1955, 4 pgs 15
Poster, Blue Crown Spark Plugs, cardboard, full color, cut-away and complete views of spark plugs, power line towers in background, 17" x 22" 38

STAMPS, MISCELLANEOUS

A secondary market is being established for trading stamps such as S&H Green Stamps and Gold Bond Stamps; look for listings under "Trading Stamps & Related."

Other nonpostage stamps of interest to collectors include revenue stamps (often collected by philatelists), savings bond stamps, and war ration stamps.

Clubs: American Revenue Assoc., P.O. Box 56, Rockford, IL 50468; State Revenue Society, 27 Pine St., Lincroft, NJ 07738.

STAMPS, POSTAGE

When I was a boy, everybody and his brother had a stamp collection. In today's high tech world that is not often the case. Most stamps found at flea markets will be cancelled and their value is negligible. They can usually be bought in batches for a few dollars. However, there are rare exceptions. Who knows? If you look long and hard enough you may find an "Inverted Jenny."

Club: American Philatelic Society, P.O. Box 8000, State College, PA 16803.

STANGL POTTERY

Stangl manufactured dinnerware between 1930 and 1978 in Trenton, New Jersey. The dinnerware featured bold floral and fruit designs on a brilliant white or off-white ground.

The company also produced a series of three-dimensional bird figurines that are eagerly sought by collectors. The bird figurines were cast in Trenton and finished at a second company plant in Flemington. During World War II the demand for the birds was so great that over 60 decorators were employed to paint them. Some of the birds were reissued between 1972 and 1977. They are dated on the bottom.

Club: Stangl/Fulper Collectors Club, P.O. Box 538, Flemington, NJ 08822.

BIRD FIGURES

Bluebird, #3815, stamp mark, 6.5" h 300
Blue Jay, #3715, stamp mark, paper label, 10" h, 10" w 550
Blue Jay with Maple Leaf, #3716, stamp mark,10.5" h, 7" w 500
Chickadee-3-on-a-Branch, #3561, stamp mark, nick to 1 tail, 6" h, 8" w 90
Cockatoo, #3584, stamp mark, 12.5" h 150
Della Ware Pheasant, #3586, 9" h, 15.5" l .450
Flying Duck, #3443, imp mark, 9" h, 13" w .180
Flying Duck, #3443, stamp mark, 10" h, 13" w 190
Gray Rooster and Hen, #3446, stamp mark, 9.75" h and 7" h, price for pr 225
Key West Dove, #3454, stamp mark, paper label, 9.25" h, 10.5" w 160
Magpie Jay Bird, #3358, stamp mark, 10.5" h 775
Owl, #3407, stamp mark, 4.5" h 350
Pheasant, #3491, stamp mark, 6" h, 8.5" w 225
Pheasant, #3492, stamp mark, 6.5" h, 10" w 110

Pheasants, #3498 male and #3491 female, stamp mark, 6" h, price for pr 250
Scissor-tailed Flycatcher, #3757, stamp mark, foil label, 11" h 550
Shoveler Duck, stamp mark, 12" h, 15" w 1,125
Western Tanningers, double, #3350, incised mark, 8" h, 7" w 275
White Cockatoo, #3580, stamp mark, 9" h 400
Yellow Rooster and Hen, mkd, 9.75" h and 7" h 250

DINNERWARE & ACCESSORIES

Bittersweet, vegetable bowl, divided, 10" x 8" 25
Blueberry, platter, 14" d 40
Burlap, dinner plate .15
Carnival, celery dish 20
Child's Dish, Kitten Kapers, 3-part 160
Child's Set, ABCs, 3-part plate and mug .190
Country Garden, coffee cup 10
Country Garden, salt and pepper shakers 25
Country Garden, snack set, plate and cup 20
Country Garden, teacup 9
Dahlia, tidbit, 2-tier 25
First Love, cup and saucer 8
First Love, dinner plate, 10" d 10
First Love, fruit bowl, 5.5" d 8
Florette, cup and saucer 14
Fruit, bread and butter plate 12
Fruit, cup and saucer 18
Fruit, dinner plate, 10" d 40
Fruit, luncheon plate 20
Fruit, salt and pepper shakers 35
Fruit, vegetable bowl, 13" d 38
Fruit, vegetable bowl, divided, oval, 10" x 8" 48

Fruit, vegetable bowl, divided, round, 10" d 35
Garland, cup and saucer 12
Golden Blossom, cup and saucer 12
Golden Blossom, dinner plate, 10" d 12
Golden Blossom, mug 15
Golden Blossom, tidbit, 1-tier, center handle, 10" d 12
Magnolia, cereal bowl 25
Magnolia, chop plate, 14.5" d 38
Magnolia, dinner plate 25
Magnolia, fruit dish 22
Magnolia, platter, 10" d 10
Magnolia, salad plate 22
Magnolia, soup bowl 25
Orchard Song, cup and saucer 12
Orchard Song, dinner plate, 10" d 10
Provincial, cup and saucer 12
Thistle, bread and butter plate, 6" d 5
Thistle, cup and saucer 14
Thistle, plate, 8" d .12
Thistle, platter, 12" d 25
Thistle, teacup 8
Town & Country, bowl, green, 3.625" h, 8.25" d 25
Town & Country, coffeepot, blue, 6.5" h 38
Town & Country, creamer, blue 35
Town & Country, dinner plate, blue, 10.625" d 40
Town & Country, platter, blue, 14.75" x 10.125" 145
Vase, Aztec, rainbow colors, 8" h 35
Vase, freeform, blue and purple, 5.5" h, 3.875" w 125
White Dogwood, lug soup bowl 15

STANLEY TOOLS

Mention the name Stanley to a carpenter and the first tool that comes to mind is a plane. While Stanley planes are the best documented and most widely collected planes on the market, Stanley also produced many other tools, many of which are becoming desirable to tool collectors.

Bevel Gauge, rosewood and brass, 8" l . . .20
Block Plane, #9½ 60
Block Plane, #65 .150
Brace and Eclipse Bit, 14" brace, .5" bit . . .20
Bull Nose Plane, #75 40
Butt Chisel, #1252, set of 4 50
Butt Gauge, #95 50
Caliper Rule, #136 .30
Carpenter's Balance 25
Carpenter's Bevel, #42 55
Chamfer Shave, #65 85
Folding Ruler, hinged, 24" l 35
Folding Ruler, sweetheart wood and brass, #53, 24" l 35
Hammer, straight claw, 32 oz 35
Hand Crank Drill, #624 45
Hand Drill, Handyman 15
Hand Drill and Bit Set, pr of hand drills and an 18-bit set 45
Level, #0, 28" l 50
Level, #260, 1939 .20
Level, adjustable, #30 50
Level, metal, miniature, 3" l, .5" h 40
Mallet, #1 30
Mortise Guide with heart 45
Plane, Bailey, #6, 18" l 45
Plane, Defiance, #1204 50
Plane, Iron Jack 85
Plane Cutter, #55 12
Punch Drill, #41, chrome 15
Ratchet Screwdriver 15
Ruler, #70 40
Scraper, #82 50
Scraper Plane, #112 215
Scraping Tool, adjustable 65
Screwdriver, #64 45
Socket Chisels, beveled 45
Spoke Shave, #151 30
Try Square, #12 25
Upholstery Tack Hammer, #601 30
Wood Caliper, 3" l .40

STAR TREK

In 1966, a new science fiction television show aired that introduced America to a galaxy of strange new worlds filled with new life forms. The voyages of author Gene Roddenberry's starship *Enterprise* enabled the viewing audience to boldly go where no man had gone before. These adventures created a new generation of collectors: "Trekkies." From posters, costumes, and props to pins, comic books, and model kits, there is no limit to the number of Star Trek collectibles that can be found.

With the release of Paramount's *Star Trek: The Motion Picture* in 1979, the Star Trek cult grew. The *Enterprise*'s new devotees inspired the inevitable new sequels: *Star Trek II: The Wrath of Khan, Star Trek III: The Search for Spock, Star Trek IV: The Voyage Home, Star Trek V: The Final Frontier, Star Trek VI: The Undiscovered Country, Star Trek: Generations,* and *Star Trek: First Contact.*

In 1988, Trekkies demanded the return of the *Enterprise* to television and were rewarded with *Star Trek: The Next Generation.* A new starship, manned by a new crew, continued the quest for the unknown. More recent spinoffs include *Star Trek: Deep Space 9* and *Star Trek: Voyager.* Whether you are an old Trekkie or a Next Generation Trekkie, keep seeking out those collectibles. May your collection live long and prosper.

Clubs: International Federation of Trekkers, P.O. Box 242, Lorain, OH 44052; Starfleet, 200 Hiawatha Blvd., Oakland, NJ 07436; Star Trek: The Official Fan Club, P.O. Box 111000, Aurora, CO 80042.

Action Figure, 1st Borg, black skull cap, Next Generation, Playmates, 1990s, 5" . . 15
Action Figure, 1st Data, Next Generation, Playmates, 1990s, 5" 10
Action Figure, 1st Ferengi, regular version, Next Generation, Playmates, 1990s, 5" . . 12
Action Figure, 1st Gowron, no gold trim, Next Generation, Playmates, 1990s, 5" . . 12
Action Figure, Antican, Galoob, 1988-89, NMOC 35
Action Figure, Data, 2nd version with darker skin and freckles, Galoob, 1988-89, NMOC 16
Action Figure, Dr Crusher, 3rd version with space cap pog, Next Generation, Playmates, 1990s, 5" 9
Action Figure, Esogg, Next Generation, Playmates, 1990s, 5", NMOC 40
Action Figure, Ferengi, Galoob, 1988-89, NMOC 40
Card Game, Star Trek Next Generation Alternate Universe, limited edition booster pack box, 15 cards/pack, 36 packs/box, black border, unopened . 50
Collector Plate, Hamilton Mint, Mr Spock, 25th Anniversary Series, 1991 40
Collector Plate, Mr Spock, 1984 85
Doll, Playmates Collectors Series, Captain James T Kirk, 9.5" 50
Doll, Playmates Collectors Series, Lt Montgomery Scott, 9.5" 30
Doll, Playmates Collectors Series, Lt Uhura, 9.5" 30
Enterprise, Smithsonian Version, MOC . . . 15
Hallmark Ornament, 1997 Deep Space Nine DS9 Defiant Ship 25
Klingon Bird of Prey, NMOC 10
Phaser, Next Generation, MOC 25
Trading Cards, 1991 Star Trek 25th Anniversary, complete 320-card set with 4 holograms and 2 exclusive cards in tin, Impel 35
Walkie Talkies, pr, Crest Toothpaste premium, PJ McNerney, Inc, Taiwan, orig mailer, MIP 85

STAR WARS

It was in a galaxy not so long ago that author/director George Lucas put into motion events that would change the way we think of space. In 1977 a movie was produced that told the story of an evil Empire's tyrannical rule over the galaxy and of the attempts of a young man from a distant world to end this tyranny. Luke Skywalker's adventures became the Star Wars saga and spanned six years and three separate movies: *Star Wars, The Empire Strikes Back,* and *Return of the Jedi.*

The enormous success of the *Star Wars* movies inspired the release of a wide range of movie-related products including toys, games, costumes, records, and comic books. "May the Force Be With You"as you travel through the flea market aisles in search of Star Wars treasure.

Club: Official Star Wars Fan Club, P.O. Box 111000, Aurora, CO 80042.

Action Figure, *Return of the Jedi,* Admiral Ackbar, Tri Logo series 15
Action Figure, *Return of the Jedi,* Ben Obi-Wan Kenobi, gray hair, Tri-Logo series 50
Action Figure, *Return of the Jedi,* Bespin, yellow hair, Tri-Logo series 125
Action Figure, *Return of the Jedi,* Biker Scout, 6th series 35
Action Figure, *Return of the Jedi,* Darth Vader, Tri-Logo series 40
Action Figure, *Return of the Jedi,* Emperor's Royal Guard, 6th series 40
Action Figure, *Return of the Jedi,* Greedo, Tri-Logo series 60
Action Figure, *Return of the Jedi,* Klaatu, 6th series 30
Action Figure, *Return of the Jedi,* Yoda, with brown snake, Tri-Logo series 50
Action Figure, *Star Wars,* Ben Obi-Wan Kenobi, gray hair, 1st series 225
Action Figure, *Star Wars,* Chewbacca, green blaster rifle, 1st series 225
Action Figure, *Star Wars,* Death Star Droid, 2nd series .150
Action Figure, *Star Wars,* Greedo, 2nd series 150
Action Figure, *Star Wars,* Han Solo, brown hair, 1st series 500
Action Figure, *Star Wars,* Luke Skywalker, blonde hair, 1st series 325
Action Figure, *Star Wars,* Power Droid, 2nd series 135
Action Figure, *Star Wars,* Snaggletooth, red, 2nd series 125
Action Figure, *Star Wars,* Stormtrooper, 1st series 225
Action Figure, *Star Wars,* Walrus Man, 2d series 135
Action Figure, *The Empire Strikes Back,* Dengar, 4th series .50
Action Figure, *The Empire Strikes Back,* Han Solo, Bespin outfit, 4th series 125
Action Figure, *The Empire Strikes Back,* Imperial Stormtrooper, Hoth Battle gear, 3rd series 60
Action Figure, *The Empire Strikes Back,* Lobot, 4th series 45
Action Figure, *The Power of the Force,* Amanaman, 8th series 200
Action Figure, *The Power of the Force,* EV-9D9, 8th series 150
Action Figure, *The Power of the Force,* Luke Skywalker, battle poncho, 8th series 100
Activity Book, *Return of the Jedi,* contains 8" x 10" panel, 7 acrylic paints, glow-in-the-dark paint, brush, and instructions, Craft Master 25
Autograph, movie still, black and white, ink sgd by Mark Hamill, Carrie Fisher, and Harrison Ford, 10" x 8" 100

Cereal Box, Kellogg's C-3PO's, "a new force at breakfast," empty 40

Cookie Jar, R2-D2, hp blue and red details, removable dome, Handcrafted Cumberland Ware by Roman Ceramics Corp, orig box, 12.5" h 275

Costume, Luke Skywalker, *Return of the Jedi,* size large, orig box, Ben Cooper, 1983 50

Dinnerware Set, child's, Wicket the Ewok, 3 pc, china, 8" d plate, cereal, and coffee mug, litho Ewok and pals, orig box 35

Dixie Cups, box of 100 five oz cups with 40 different scenes 15

Hand Puppet, Yoda, rubber, 1980, 8.5" h, MIB 50

Kite, Wicket the Ewok, MIP 35

Mask, Admiral Ackbar, *Return of the Jedi,* Don Post Studios, 1983 85

Mask, Yoda, rubber, Ben Cooper 25

Model Kit, Star Wars, Imperial Speeder Bike Kit, orig box, MPC, 1983 45

Model Kit, *The Empire Strikes Back,* Snowspeeder, orig box, MPC, 1980 35

Paperweight, plastic, Darth Vader hologram, Third Dimension Arts 25

Party Hats, *Return of the Jedi,* set of 8, MIP 25

Play-Doh, *The Empire Strikes Back,* contains 3 hinged molds, plastic vehicle, playmat, trim knife, and can of dough, orig box 35

Playset, Droid Factory, orig box, 1977 ...135

Playset, Hoth Turret Defense Playset, *The Empire Strikes Back,* micro collection, orig box, 1982 30

Playset, Imperial Attack Base, *The Empire Strikes Back,* orig box, 1980 ...125

Race Set, Star Wars, Duel at Death Star Racing Set, orig box, Lionel, 1978 85

Wristwatch, R2D2 and C3PO, Bradley Time, 1977 80

STEIFF

Giengen on the Brenz, Bad Wurtemburg, Germany, is the birthplace and home of Steiff. In the 1880s, Margarette Steiff, a clothing manufacturer, made animal-theme pincushions for her nephews and their friends. Fritz, Margarette's brother, took some to a county fair and sold them all. In 1893 an agent representing Steiff appeared at the Leipzig Toy Fair.

Margarette's nephew, Richard, suggested making a small bear with movable head and joints. It appeared for the first time in Steiff's 1903 catalog. The bear was an instant success. An American buyer placed an order for 3,000. It was first called the "teddy" bear in the 1908 catalog.

In 1905 the famous "button in the ear" was added to Steiff toys. The first buttons were small tin circles with the name in raised block letters. The familiar script logo was introduced in 1932, about the same time a shiny, possibly chrome, button was first used. Brass ear buttons date after 1980.

Steiff's popularity increased tremendously following World War II. After a period of uncertainty in the 1970s Steiff enjoyed a renaissance when it introduced its 1980 Limited Edition "Papa" Centennial Bear. A series of other limited edition pieces followed. Many credit the sale of the "Papa" Bear with creating the teddy bear craze that swept America in the 1980s.

Clubs: Steiff Club, 425 Paramont Dr., Raynham, MA 02767; Steiff Collectors Club, P.O. Box 798, Holland, OH 43528.

Arco German Shepherd, mohair, straw stuffed, orange glass eyes, open mouth with felt tongue, script button, 1950-60, 12" h 70

Brontosaurus, gray, yellow, and pale green on beige mohair, glass eyes, with button, 11" h, 29" l 1,900

Cockie Cocker Spaniel, black and white mohair, straw stuffed, swivel head with glass eyes, squeaker, red collar, script button, 1950-60, 6.5" h, 9.5" l 90

Coco Monkey, silver-gray mohair, full collar mane, felt face and hands, glass eyes, with chest tag, 12" h 400
Dally Dalmatian, white mohair with black spots, straw stuffed, swivel head with open felt lined mouth, glass eyes, red collar with paper tag, 1950s, 4" h 100
Elephant on Cast Iron Wheels, shoe button eyes, 11" h, 14" l 300
English Sheep Dog, long pile white mohair, straw stuffed, swivel head with brown glass eyes, 1950s, 11.5" h 38
Fawn, straw stuffed, glass eyes, felt lined ears, metal nose, ribbon collar with bell, 6" h, 4.5" l 27
Grissy Donkey, gray Dralon, soft stuffed, black plastic eyes, open felt lined mouth, felt lined ears, 10" h 28
Kangaroo, red and beige mohair, glass eyes, jointed head and arms, no joey, with button, 20" h .700
Lamby, white wool, straw stuffed, green and black glass eyes, pink neck ribbon with bell, felt lined ears, 1950s, 8" h 38
Leo Lion, mohair, straw stuffed, orange glass eyes, 1950-60, 4.5" h 60
Lion, standing, glass eyes, wooden teeth, stitched muzzle, flowing mane, pull-ring roaring mechanism, button and cloth tag in ear, 39" h, 69" l 2,175
Molly Dog, white and brown mohair, straw stuffed, swivel head with glass eyes, 1950-60, 6.5" h 110
Nelly Snail, velvet, plastic shell, with chest tag 350
Peggy Penguin, mohair, straw stuffed, paper chest tag, script button and yellow flag, 1950s, 4" h 60
Pony, brown and white mohair, straw stuffed, red leather saddle, felt ears, bristle mane and tail, glass eyes, script button, paper chest tag, 1960s, 5" h 60
Rocking Horse, plush, red saddle and reins, pull-ring whinny mechanism, mounted on glider platform, 36" h, 48" l 1,600
Seal, tan mohair with gray shading and spots, straw stuffed, black eyes, 1950-60, 4.25" h, 4.5" l 27

Seated Rabbit, tan, black tipped ears and upper tail, glass eyes, 1950-60, 4" h 50
St Bernard, white mohair with inset brown, straw stuffed, swivel head with clear and black glass eyes, 1950-60, 9.5" h 100
Stegosaurus, green, turquoise, burgundy on yellow mohair, glass eyes, felt ear fins, no button, 9" h, 31" l 1,500
Teddy Bear, tan mohair, straw stuffed, fully jointed, swivel head, script button, 6" h 150
T-Rex, blue, orange and yellow on beige mohair, glass eyes, 18" h 1,900

STEINS

Steins are mugs made especially to hold beer or ale. Their graduated sizes range from ¼-liter to 5 (and sometimes even 8) liters. Most are fitted with a metal hinged lid with a thumblift. Earthenware character-type steins are usually German in origin.

Club: Stein Collectors International, Inc., http://steincollectors.org.

Anheuser-Busch, Animals of the Prairie, Wild Mustang, GL-15, NIB 35
Anheuser-Busch, Bevo Fox, CS-160, NIB 125
Anheuser-Busch, Cherub, CS-182, NIB . . .45
Anheuser-Busch, Christmas Collection, #3, GM-13, NIB 70
Anheuser-Busch, Civil War Commemorative, Abraham Lincoln, CS-189, NIB 95
Anheuser-Busch, Coca-Cola, Candy Cane, CS-391, NIB 30

Anheuser-Busch, First Hunt, Labrador, GM-17, NIB 100

Anheuser-Busch, Founders Series, Adolphus Busch, CS-216, NIB 95

Anheuser-Busch, Gerz Meisterwerke, Panda, GM-3, NIB 80

Anheuser-Busch, Great Cities of Germany, Berlin, CS-328, NIB 30

Anheuser-Busch, *Saturday Evening Post,* Do Unto Others, GM-21, NIB 35

Anheuser-Busch, Winchester Rodeo Series, Saddle Bronc, GM-25, NIB 30

Budweiser, American Original, Faust, CS-330, NIB 90

Budweiser, Birds of Prey, Peregrine Falcon, CS-183, NIB 65

Budweiser, Character Stein, Penguin, CS-315, NIB 100

Budweiser, Endangered Species, Bald Eagle, CS-106, NIB 240

Budweiser, Holiday, #2, C2-50 165

Budweiser, NASCAR, Bill Elliot, CS-182, NIB 55

Budweiser, Opera Card Series, #1, Martha, CS-300, NIB 70

Budweiser, Sports Legends, Joe Louis, CS-206, NIB 125

Character, monk, pottery, Goebel full bee mark, .5L 28

Character, Munich maid, inlaid lid, glaze chips on hood, J Reinemann, .3L 75

Glass, musician's, etched and cut, zipper notched panels, etched medallion with "Die Sauger Ibrem Chormeister 1887" in lyre, etched verse on base, etched motif under base, relief pewter lid with lyre, lyre thumblift, .5L 130

Hamm's Beer, figural bear on top, Gerz, West Germany 100

Marriott's Great American Beer, porcelain, Japan, 7" h 10

Mettlach, 2 hp vignettes of castle and knight, Gruk aus Binger, #1526, pewter lid, .5L 110

Mettlach, 3 panels of drinkers in relief, #1266, inlaid lid, .5L 110

Mettlach, 5 relief figures, #171, inlaid lid, .5L 110

Mettlach, plain, #1526, pewter lid, stain on edge of handle, .5L 10

Mettlach, PUG, gnomes drinking from horn, #1032/2333, pewter lid, pewter dent, .3L 185

Porcelain, skull and crossed bones over student shield "EN," enameled, named to "George Weinicke," pewter lid, lithophane of boy and goat, .5L 300

Pottery, 3 panels of Vikings in relief, pierced top border, .5L 25

Pottery, etched color tavern scene with relief stag's head, #1434, inlaid lid, .3L ..75

Pottery, full color outdoor drinking scene in relief, pewter lid, crazing, 1.5L 35

Pottery, "Heiden Roslein," relief, #1097, green and brown on cream, pewter lid, 2.0L 35

Pottery, knight and shield with stein, transfer, pewter lid, .5L 35

Pottery, knights drinking, relief, #1031, green and brown on cream, pewter lid, 1.5L 45

Pressed Glass, pewter lid, .4L 10

Regimental, porcelain, "1 Train Batt. 3 Co 1901/02 München," to "Franz Huber," with mounted soldier charging, 4 side scenes, roster, lithophane portrait of soldier, pewter lid, .5L 650

Regimental, porcelain, "5 Batt 2 Wurth Feld Art Rg N 29 Prinzer, Lui v Bayern Ludwigsburg (18)94-96" with shield flanked by roster, to "Gefr Lamprecht," 2 side scenes, lithophane, pewter lid, .5L 275

Silverplate and Wood, oak body with plated rims, handle, lid, and liner, engraved "William Kronenberg," St Louis Silver Co, .3L 25

Souvenir, Niagara Falls, miniature, 3" h 5

Sprenger Brewing Co, Lancaster, PA, pottery, transfer, made by Thuemeer Mfg Co, .5L 10

Stoneware, cobalt foliage and "Franz," blue salt glaze, etched, #KK206, pewter lid, .5L 55

Stoneware, cobalt panel with etched colorful horse-drawn coach, Art Nouveau, blue salt glaze, Rein Merkelbach, #426/1, pewter lid, .5L ...145

Stoneware, cobalt panel with etched colorful trumpeter, Art Nouveau, blue salt glaze, Rein Merkelbach, #427/16, pewter lid, .5L 120

Stoneware, cobalt panel with etched horse-drawn coach (not colored), Art Nouveau, blue salt glaze, Rein Merkelbach, #426/1, pewter lid, .5L 35

Stoneware, Falstaff centered among hops vines, blue salt glaze, relief, inlaid lid with transfer of weightlifter, 1.5L 65

Stoneware, Klapperstorch's Musterlager, babies hanging from hooks, mkd "1276/Germany" (right) 325

Stoneware, lady cleaning clothes with early washing machine, E Goldman & Co, 7.5" h (left) 120

Stoneware, miniature, etched "HB," tin lid emb "SS11," 2.25" h 35

STEMWARE

There are two basic types of stemware: (1) soda-based glass and (2) lead- or flint-based glass, often referred to as crystal. Today crystal is also a term synonymous with fine glassware and used to describe glass that is clear. Lead crystal, which must contain a minimum of 24% lead oxide, has a brilliant clarity, durability, and a bell-like tone that emanates when the glass is struck.

Free blown, mold blown, and pressed are the three basic methods used to make stemware. Decorating techniques include cutting and etching. Color also is used to create variety.

There are thousands of stemware patterns. If you do not know your pattern, consider sending a drawing of the stem and a rubbing of its decoration to Replacements, Ltd. (P.O. Box 26029, Greensboro, NC 27420). Replacements has an excellent research staff. Also check Harry L. Rinker's *Stemware of the 20th Century: The Top 200 Patterns* (House of Collectibles, 1997) and/or Bob Page and Dale Frederiksen's *Crystal Stemware Identification Guide* (Collector Books, 1998). If you do not find your specific pattern, you will find ample comparables.

The following is a simple approach to determining a quick price per stem for your stemware: (1) soda glass stem, plain, $2 to $4; (2) soda glass stem, pressed, $5 to $8; (3) soda glass stem, elaborately decorated, $12 to $15; (4) lead glass stem, plain, $15 to $18; (5) lead glass stem, simple decoration, $20 to $25; (6) lead glass stem, elaborate decoration, $25 to $30; and (7) lead glass stem, streamline modern or post-war modern design style, $15 to $20. Add a 20% premium for patterns from Baccarat, Gorham, Lenox, Waterford, and Wedgwood.

Bryce, cobalt, 9.25" h, set of 6 8

Cambridge, Rock Crystal, Minuet cutting, 6" h 18

Colony, Danube, champagne, 6" h 10

Colony, Park Lane, juice goblet, blue, 4.5" h 7

Cristal d'Arques, Chantelle, cocktail, 5.5" h 40

Duncan & Miller, Teardrop, goblet, 7"h . . .15

Fostoria, Jamestown, crystal, 5.75" h 10

Fostoria, Jamestown, ruby red, 5.75" h . . .12

Fostoria, Meadow Rose, champagne, 5.75" h 32

Fostoria, Meadow Rose, cocktail, 5.25" h .25

Fostoria, Mesa, goblet, olive green, 5" h . . .8

Fostoria, Navarre etching, champagne/ low dessert (left) .25

Fostoria, Royal, champagne, green, 5" h . .20
Fostoria, Wavecrest, set of 6 75
Fostoria, wine, 7.5" h, set of 6 80
Hawkes, crystal with green stem and base, goblet, 6.5" h 45
Hawkes, Diana, goblet, 6.5" h 35
Heisey, Fairacre, sherbet, 4.25" h, set of 6 60
Heisey, Low Orchid, sherbet, 4"h 30
Lenox, Silver Mist, goblet, 7" h 8
Lenox, Silver Mist, wine, 5" h 8
Libby, Case style, goblet, cobalt, 8.75" h, set of 4 32
Libby, Stardust, cocktail, 6" h, set of 6 35
Mikasa, Tea Rose, water goblet, 9.25" h . .15
Romania, lead crystal with love birds on a heart-fluted glass, 11.5" h, pr 25
Romania, Queen's Lace, wine, 5.75" h 25
Royal Leerdam, Netherlands, champagne, 4.75" h 60
Royal Ruby, crystal, water goblet with bubble stem, 8" h 10
Tiffin, Apollo Diana, sherbet, 4.75" h 22
Tiffin, Classic, champagne, crystal, platinum band (right) 25
Tiffin, Dolores, sherbet, pr 35
Tiffin, Fuchsia, cocktail, 4.25" h 25
Tiffin, Fuchsia, saucer champagne, 5.25" h 32
Tiffin, King's Crown, cranberry and crystal, set of 6 80
Tiffin, Rambler Rose, cordial, gold 45
Tiffin, Thistle, sherbet, 3.5" h 10
Weston, Optic Louie, tumbler, amber, 4.75" h 16

STEREO CARDS & VIEWERS

Stereo cards (also known as stereographs and stereo views) and viewers were introduced in the United States in 1854. Popular subjects included famous people, natural wonders, and major news events.

Club: National Stereoscopic Assoc., P.O. Box 14801, Columbus, OH 43214, www.stereoview.org.

CARD

Bear, facing 2 hunters and dog in icy cavern 25

Bell on Iowa Wesleyan College Campus, Mt Pleasant, IA .25
Big Tree Logging, Converse Basin, CA . . .15
Cat, "Princess Gray Paws" 10
Cuban Farmhouse, Havana Province, 1899 20
Ed Hissong and Elliot Chandley, on back porch, Winfield, IA 25
Giant Tree, with sign reading "Rhode Island," 1867 35
Grown Men Fighting, 1906, set of 3 scenes 20
Iowa State Capitol, From the South, Des Moines, IA, 1882 12
Laplander Family, with sledge-dog outside their summer home in Norway 10
Mauch Chunk and Vicinity, Lehigh Valley Views No. 175, coal pockets, loading canal boats 12
Niagara, Horseshoe Falls, taken from Goat Island 15
Petrified Water, Pulpit Terraci, and Mammoth Springs Hotel, Yellowstone Park 8
Railroad New York, elevated rairoad tracks and sign reading "For Sale" 10
Regalia of Scotland, crown, jewels, sword 25
Royal School Honolulu, Hawaiian Islands .12
Street Scene, Mukden Manchuria 45
Twelve monks, in front of hospice on Mountain of Grande St Bernard, Switzerland 18
Woman's Liberation, Atlanta Exposition, 1896 35

VIEWER

StereoGraphoscope, wooden, 1896 60
Stereopticon, wooden, with emb metal eyepiece, early 1900s, 13" l 95
Stereo Realist Viewer, 3D, leather case and handle, 1950s 225
Unmarked, wood and metal, 1900 75

STRADIVARIUS VIOLINS

In the late 19th century inexpensive violins were made for sale to students, amateur musicians, and others who could not afford older, quality instruments. Numerous models, many named after famous makers, were sold by department stores, music shops, and by mail. Sears, Roebuck sold "Stradivarius" models. Other famous violin makers whose names appear on paper labels inside these instruments include Amati, Caspar DaSolo, Guarnerius, Maggini, and Stainer. Lowendall of Germany made a Paganini model.

All these violins were sold through advertisements that claimed that the owner could have a violin nearly equal to that of an antique instrument for a modest cost; one "Stradivarius" sold for $2.45. The most expensive model cost less than $15. The violins were handmade, but by a factory assembly line process.

If well cared for, these pseudo antique violins often develop a nice tone. The average price for an instrument in playable condition is between $100 and $200.

STRING HOLDERS

I have fond memories of the plaster face of a Dutch girl with a piece of string coming out of her mouth that hung in my mother's kitchen. I also remember saving string, attaching accumulated pieces and wrapping them into a ball.

Few save string any longer. It is a lost art. Fortunately, plenty of collectors are saving the string holders that were found in virtually every kitchen from the 1920s through the 1950s.

Beware of fake string holders made by hollowing out the back of a figural head wall plaque and drilling a hole in the mouth, e.g., a Chinese or Siamese man or woman, or altering a figural wall lamp, e.g., a pineapple or apple face.

Apple, chalkware, 7.75" h 95
Apple House with Worm, chalkware, 6.5" h 65
Aunt Jemima, chalkware, 7.75" h 300
Bird, pottery, 7" h 85
Bird on Branch, ceramic, Royal Copley . . .75
Black Cat, ceramic, yellow bow 35
Bride, ceramic, mkd "Made in Japan," 6.25" h 145
Bunch of Balloons, ceramic, Fitz & Floyd, 1983 50
Cat, on ball of string, Miller Studio, 1948 45
Cat, on a ball of yarn, chalkware 65
Cat Face, chalkware, black and white . . .100
Chipmunk, ceramic, wearing black bow tie and top hat, 5" h 135
Collie, ceramic, mkd "Royal Trico," Japan 125
Dutch Girl, chalkware, green hat 45
Elephant, ceramic, yellow, Hoffritz Co, 5" h, 4.25" w 38
Gourd, chalkware, green, 7.5" h 135
Grapes, chalkware, 5.5" h 100
Heart, ceramic, silver, "You'll Always Have a 'Pull' with Me," Cleminson Art Studios, 5" h 110
Hippo, ceramic, counter-top, 6" h 75
Kozy Kat, ceramic, Holt Howard 65
Lady with Bonnet, cloth 75
Mammy, ceramic, plaid and polka dot dress, Japan 125
Mammy, ceramic, wearing red bandana, hands folded across white dress, McCoy, 7" h 45
Mexican Man, wearing sombrero, chalkware, 8.25" h 95
Monkey, sitting on ball of string, chalkware 225

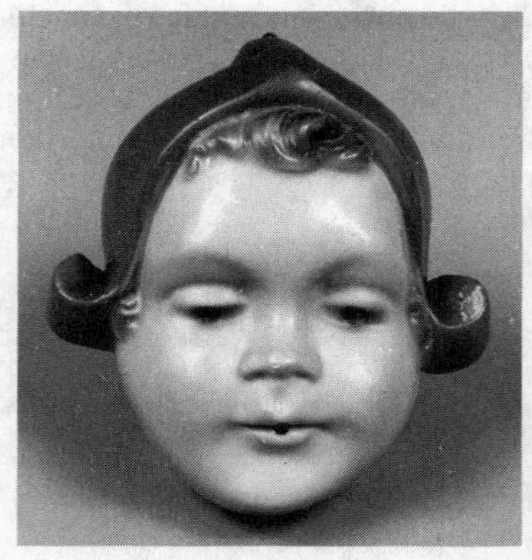

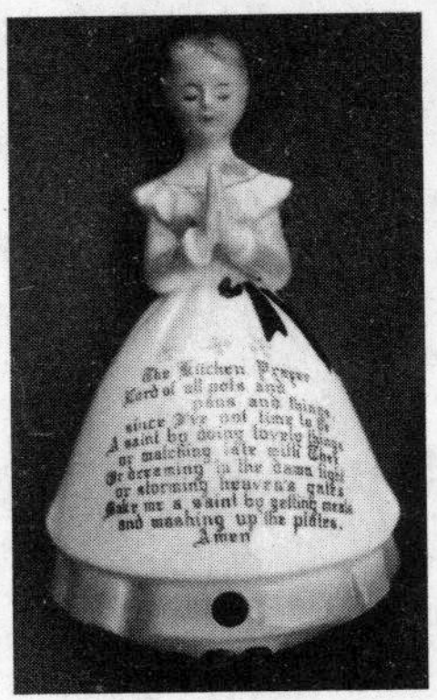

Mouse, ceramic, Josef Originals 55
Mrs Mouse, composition, counter-top, 7" h 90
Oriental Lady, white, counter-top, mkd "Made in Japan," 7" h 15
Owl, ceramic, Josef Originals 35
Pear, chalkware 70
Prayer Lady, pink, 6.5" h 150
Red Bird in Birdhouse, chalkware 125
Scottie Dog, chalkware, white, studded collar 125
Strawberry Face, chalkware, red, 6.5" h ..75
Susie Sunfish, chalkware, Miller Studio, 1948 225
Teapot, ceramic, parakeet motif, Japan ..85
Teapot, floral design, mkd "Made in Japan by Fred Roberts Co," 6.25" h, 5.25" w 155
Two Birds in Cage, chalkware 100
White Dove, ceramic 50
Witch, sitting on a pumpkin, broom and potion book in hand, cat on lap, Corl Pottery Co, 9.5" h, 7" w 60

STUDIO SZEILER

Joseph Szeiler was born in Hungary in 1924. He moved to England in search of work in 1947. After working at various potteries and attending the Burslem School of Art, Szeiler began modeling his own designs in 1951 in a one-room studio in Hanley. In 1955 he relocated to larger accomodations in Burslem.

Cruet Bottles, pr, brown leaves on tan ground, 4" h 25
Cruet Bottles, pr, dark brown stripes and white bands on chocolate brown ground, 4" h 25
Dish, cow's head, 3" h 35
Figurine, bloodhound, 2.5" h 65
Figurine, bloodhound, 4.5" h 125
Figurine, bulldog, 2.5" h 65
Figurine, cat, 1" h, 1.5" l 25
Figurine, comic cow, 2" h, 2.25" l 40
Figurine, cow, 2" h, 2" l 50
Figurine, cow, 3.5" h, 5" l 75
Figurine, dachshund, 3.5" h, 8.5" l 110
Figurine, dog, 3.5" h 60
Figurine, dog, 5" h 75
Figurine, donkey, blue, 2.5" h 80
Figurine, donkey, brown, 2.75" h 65
Figurine, duck with bonnet, 2.5" h 60
Figurine, fawn, 1.25" h, 1.5" l 25
Figurine, fawn, 1.75" h 60
Figurine, fawn, 3" h 65
Figurine, fawn, white, 1.5" h, 2" l 40
Figurine, giraffe, 3" h 75
Figurine, horse, lying down, 5.5" h, 7.5" l .125
Figurine, puppy and kitten in basket, 2" h 30
Figurine, puppy in basket, .5" h, 1.5" l 40
Figurine, puppy on back, 2" l 25
Figurine, seal, 1.5" h, 4" l 60
Figurine, seated Corgi, 3.5" h 65
Figurine, sleeping cat, 1.5" l, ...25
Figurine, swan, 1.5" l 20
Flask, dancing bear, 4.75" h 65
Money Box, pig, 3" h, 6" l 75
Money Box, rugby ball and boots, 4" h 45
Money Box, telephone, 4" h 50
Money Box, tortoise, 4" h, 7" l 60
Posy Pocket, bird, 3.5" l 30
Posy Pocket, bird, 4" h 16
Posy Pocket, chamois, 4" h 30
Posy Pocket, flowers, 4" h 30
Posy Pocket, hummingbirds, 3.5" l 30

STUFFED TOYS

Stuffed toys is a generic term for plush toys. Normally one thinks first of the teddy bear when considering stuffed toys. Yet, virtually every animal and a fair number of characters and personalities have appeared as stuffed toys. Margarette Steiff's first stuffed toy was not a bear but an elephant.

By the early 1920s, many companies, e.g., Gund, Ideal, and Knickerbocker, were competing with Steiff for their share of the stuffed toy market. Collectors pay a premium for examples from these companies. The 1970s stuffed toys of R. Dakin Company, San Francisco, are a modern favorite.

Following World War II, stuffed toys became a favorite prize of carnival games of chance. Most are inexpensive Asian imports and hold only modest interest for collectors. Do not pay more than a few dollars for these poor quality examples.

Note: See Steiff and Teddy Bears for additional listings.

Abominable Snowman, Rudolph the Red-nosed Reindeer Series, 16" h 85
Alf, talking, 18" h 75
Bear, Ashton Drake, corduroy overalls, holding a puppy, 1996 50
Bunny Rabbit, seated, patchwork dress and kerchief, 18" h 45
Bunny Rabbit, silky mohair, flexible ears, Chad Valley, 10.5" h 80
Champ the Bulldog, mkd "Rushton," 14" h 25
Cookie Monster, when squeezed he laughs, vibrates, and says "Oh boy oh boy," 11" h 25
Elephant, mohair, wooden tusks 45
Fox, vinyl head, red, 10.5" h 30
Goosey Gander, velveteen and brocade vest and top hat, 24" h 30
Grandmother Wolf, plush, 1 side is grandmother, other is wolf, 15" h 25
Little Quincy Koala, pillow pet, Dakin, 1981, 11" h 30
Michigan J Frog, Warner Brothers, bendable arms and legs, 20" h 25
Mickey Mouse, Knickerbocker, 1960s, 21" h 65
Millennium Mickey Mouse, with pocketwatch counting down minutes, 20" h 50
Moe, Three Stooges, black and white striped jailbird suit, hard plastic head, 15" h 24
Monkey, puppet, Wynn Millers Mopkins .75
Phillies Phanatic, Harrison/Erickson, mkd "Made in Korea," 1976, 19" h 35
Puppy Dog, floppy, Gund, 7" h 30

Rabbit, pink, Doll Craft Industries, 1960s ..45
Rabbit, white and yellow, plays a lullaby ..45
Scottie Dog, black, 9" l, 8" h 60
Slumber Zipper Cat, zipper on back to store pajamas, Gund, 1950s 50
Sock Monkey, corduroy pants and red-checked shirt, hat, 16" h 35
Spaniel, real dog fur, black and white, 12" h 35
Tickle Me Elmo, giggles and talks, 11" h ..25
Toys R Us Rabbit, velveteen, Rabbit Ear Productions, Inc, 15" h 28
Woody Woodpecker, talking, vinyl head, stuffed corduroy body, felt hands and feet, orig box, Mattel, 1960s, 18" h 200

SUGAR PACKETS

Do not judge sugar packets of the 1940s and 1950s by those you encounter today. There is no comparison. Early sugar packets were colorful and often contained full color scenic views. Many of the packets were issued as sets, with a variety of scenic views. They were gathered as souvenirs during vacation travels.

There is a large number of closet sugar packet collectors. They do not write much about their hobby because they are afraid that the minute they draw attention to it, prices will rise. Most sugar packets sell for less than $1. It's time to let the sugar out of the bag. Get them cheap while you can.

Club: Sugar Packet Clubs International, 15601 Burkhart Rd., Orrville, OH 44667.

SUPER HERO COLLECTIBLES

Super heroes and comic books go hand in hand. Superman first appeared in Action Comics in 1939. He was followed by Batman, Captain Marvel, Captain Midnight, the Green Hornet, the Green Lantern, the Shadow, Wonder Woman, and a host of others.

The traditional Super Hero was transformed with the appearance of the Fantastic Four—Mr. Fantastic, the Human Torch, the Invisible Girl, and the Thing.

It pays to focus on one hero or a related family of heroes. Go after the three-dimensional material. This is the hardest to find.

Clubs: Air Heroes Fan Club (Captain Midnight), 19205 Seneca Ridge Ct., Gaithersburg, MD 20879.

Aquaman, action figure, 12" 9
Fantastic Four, action figure, Attuma, Series 3, Toy Biz, 1995, 5" 8
Fantastic Four, action figure, Black Bolt, Series 1, Toy Biz, 1995, 5" 10
Fantastic Four, action figure, Blastaar, Series 2, Toy Biz, 1995, 5" 10
Fantastic Four, action figure, Gorgon, Series 2, Toy Biz, 1995, 5" 15
Fantastic Four, action figure, Human Torch/Johnny Storm, Series 4, Toy Biz, 1996, 5" 12
Fantastic Four, action figure, Medusa, Series 4, Toy Biz, 1996, 5" 8
Fantastic Four, action figure, Mr Fantastic, Series 1, Toy Biz, 1995, 5" 18
Fantastic Four, action figure, Terrax, Series 1, Toy Biz, 1995, 5" 12
Fantastic Four, Fantasticar, Toy Biz 50
Fantastic Four, Thing Cycle, Toy Biz 12
Fantastic Four, tin pencil box 5
Green Hornet, pinback button, Green Hornet Adventure Club, litho tin, green and yellow, 1941, 1.25" d 18
Green Lantern, action figure, Green Lantern vs Dr Polaris, 5" 12
Hulk, action figure, Incredible Hulk with breakout containment unit, Toy Biz, 1997 15
Hulk, action figure, She Hulk, Toy Biz, 1996, 6" 10

Hulk, action figure, Zzzax with electric trap, Toy Biz, 1997 12
Hulk, playset, Rage Cage, electronic sound and action, Toy Biz, 1996 20
Hulk, soaky bottle, Benjamin Ansehl Co, 1990 15
Justice League Of America, action figure with display stand, Atom, Hasbro, 5" . . .50
Justice League Of America, action figure with display stand, Green Arrow, Hasbro, 5" 20
Justice League Of America, action figure with display stand, Huntress, Hasbro, 5" 25
Justice League Of America, action figure with display stand, Impulse, Hasbro, 5" 12
Justice League Of America, action figure with display stand, Plastic Man, Hasbro, 5" 10
Justice League Of America, action figure with display stand, Steel, Hasbro, 5" . . .15
Justice League Of America, action figure with display stand, Zauriel, Hasbro, 5" 10
Marvel Super Heroes, action figure, Daredevil, red body, Toy Biz, 1990, Series 1, 5" 24
Marvel Super Heroes, action figure, Deathlock, Toy Biz, 1992, Series 3, 5" 6
Marvel Super Heroes, action figure, Invisible Woman, Toy Biz, 1992, Series 3, 5" 45
Marvel Super Heroes, action figure, Magneto, Toy Biz, 1992, Talking Heroes 6

Marvel Super Heroes, action figure, Punisher, trench coat, Toy Biz, 1994, Series 5, 5" 10
Marvel Super Heroes, action figure, Venom, living slime pores, Toy Biz, 1990, Series 1, 5" 10
Marvel Super Heroes, action figure, Venom, squirting alien liquid, Toy Biz, 1993, Series 4, 5" 8
Mighty Morphin Power Rangers, Saba the Talking Tiger Saber, 1994, MIB 20
Mighty Morphin Power Rangers, Tyrannosaurus Battle Bike with Red Ranger, 1993 15
Shazam, action figure, Hasbro, 1999, 7" 20
Shazam, die-cast figure, Ertl, 1989, with mini comic 7
Supergirl, die-cast figure, Ertl, 1989, with mini comic 7
Superman, action figure, Lex Luthor, Toy Biz, 1989-90, 5" 5
Superman, action figure, Superboy vs King Shark, 5" 12
Wonder Woman, figural scissors, Syno Corp, 1978 8
Wonder Woman, Hallmark Keepsake Ornament 15

SWANKYSWIGS

Swankyswigs are decorated glass containers that were filled with Kraft Cheese Spreads. They date from the early 1930s. See D. M. Fountain's *Swankyswig Price Guide* (published by author in 1979) to identify pieces by pattern.

Most Swankyswigs still sell for under $5. If a glass still has its original label, add $5.

Club: Swankyswigs Unlimited, 201 Alvena, Wichita, KS 67203.

Anchor Hocking, New Year's, 3.25" h 20
Animals and Birds, red, 3.75" h 25
Antique, pink and blue 6
Aqua, sailboat, 3.5" h 16
Archie Comic, 4.25" h 12
Bear and Pig, blue, 3.75" h 5
Bunnies and Kittens, green, 3.75" h 7
Bustling Betsy, brown, 3.75" h 7
Bustling Betsy, green, 3.75" h 7
Bustling Betsy, orange, 3.75" h 8
Bustling Betsy, yellow, 3.75" h 20
Churn and Cradle, orange, 3.75" h 20
Cornflower, #2, light blue, 3.5" h 10
Cornflower, #2, yellow, 3.5" h 5
Daisy, aqua, ecru, orange and yellow, 4.5" h 25
Daisy, red, white and green, 3.75" h 10
Deer and Squirrels, brown, 3.75" h 8
Diamond, white 18
Father Knows Best, blue 5
Flowers, blue, 3.5" h 6
Flowers, green and white, 4.75" h 6
Flowers, red and white, 3.75" h 6
Forget-Me-Not, red, 3.5" h 4
Hazel Atlas, instruments, red and black 3
Hazel Atlas, red and white flowers, 4" h 8
Kiddie Cup, black duck and horse, 3.25" h 15
Lamp and Kettle, blue, 3.75" h 7
Medieval Jousting, 3.75" h 10
Merry Christmas, poinsettia, wreath and bell 10
Oranges, Continental Can Company, 4 oz 8
Rooster and Puppy, orange, 3.75" h 7
Spinning Wheel and Bellows, red, 3.75" h 8
Tomato, red and green, 3.5" h 5
Tulips, #1, blue, 3.5" h 6
Tulips, #3, light blue, 3.75" h 4
Tulips, #3, red, 3.75" h 4
Tulips, #3, yellow, 3.75" h 4
Tulips, white 5
Umbrella, 4.5" 20

SWAROVSKI CRYSTAL

Swarovski introduced its crystal decorative accessories and jewelry in the 1970s. They were an immediate success. High lead content, stringent quality control and remarkable design sophistication are hallmarks of Swarovski crystal pieces which set them apart from crystal bibelots produced by other manufacturers.

Most pieces are marked with a variation of the Swarovski logo. Occasionally you will find a piece bearing the artist's signature in script. Some collectors are willing to pay an additional 10% for this feature, but it is subjective and somewhat controversial among Swarovski enthusiasts. Collectors of Swarovski crystal are very keen on obtaining complete original packaging, without which prices are compromised 10–25%. Only the annual and numbered limited editions came with certificates of authenticity.

Clubs: Swan Seekers Network, 9740 Campo Road, Ste. 134, Spring Valley, CA 91977, Swarovski Collectors Society (company-sponsored), 1 Kenney Dr., Cranston, RI 02920.

Bangle, stretch, lavendar, 7.75" l 12
Bracelet, cuff, crystal and ruby enamel, 1" w 275
Bracelet, gold tone, 7.5" l 60
Brooch, butterfly, blue rhinestone, 3" w ...75
Brooch, golf bag, 2-bar, gold plated 15
Brooch, parrot head, clear and citrone crystals, gold tone, 4" h 65
Candleholder, brass and crystal, 4.25" h ..24
Crystal Tattoo, American Star, red, white, and blue aurora borealis crystal, 1.5" h .18
Earrings, Austrian blue crystal, heart-shaped, silver plate 15
Earrings, Borealis Heart, silver plate 18
Earrings, crystal drop, .75" l 8
Figurine, bird, 1" h 8
Figurine, butterfly on leaf, 2" x 2.25" x 1.25" 85
Figurine, dragon, colored wings, 4" h 38
Figurine, Kris Bear, .75" h 75
Figurine, owl, 1.75" h 75
Figurine, rowboat, gold trim, .25" l, .5" h ...60
Figurine, Silver Crystal City Series, cathedral 215
Figurine, Silver Crystal City Series, poplar trees 175
Figurine, Silver Crystal City Series, tower 130
Figurine, swan, 1.25" h 55
Figurine, teddy bear tennis player, gold plated and crystal pave 50
Figurine, two baby snails, resting on a frosted vine leaf 50
Necklace, aurora borealis, silver plate, 31.5" l 75
Necklace, choker, 14.5" l, .75" w 150
Necklace, oval beads, gold tone, adjustable, 21"-23" l 25
Ornament, angel, 3" l 90
Ornament, snowflake 145
Pendant, American flag, clear and blue crystal mounted on red enamel 50
Perfume Bottle, heart shaped, stopper depicts hat of Napoleon 145
Picture Frame, silver crystal, with butterfly 85
Pin, cat, 1" h 20
Pin, Chanukah Candles, 3" x 3" 45
Pin, gold, triple layer with brown and topaz rhinestones and aurora borealis rhinestones 25
Pin, gold tone, crystals and an amethyst, .5" x 2" 18
Windchime, teapot, silver plated 120

SWIZZLE STICKS

There is no end to the number of ways to collect swizzle sticks—advertising, color, motif, region, time period, and so on.

You can usually find them for less than $1. In fact, you can often buy a box or glass full of them for just a few dollars. Sets bring more, but they must be unusual.

Club: International Swizzle Stick Collectors Assoc., P.O. Box 1117, Bellingham, WA 98227.

Adirondack Lounge, amber glass, set of 4 20
American Airlines, eagle and double "A" logo on end, plastic, gold lettering on blue 8
Ballerina Dancer, on toes, right arm above head, yellow plastic 65
Champagne glass, Hotel Statler, white lettering on red plastic 10
Corby's Liquor, parrot, red, yellow, blue, green, set of 24 24
Duck, 1950s, set of 4 20
Fish, glass, red, green, white, orange, blue, 7.5" h, set of 3 25
Glass, hollow with amethyst ball on bottom 15
Leprechaun, dressed in green with shamrock on hat, green plastic 3
Millennium, plastic, 8.25" l, set of 8 12
Palm Tree, olive green 35
Pineapple, plastic, gold lettering on black, "Hospitality House" 5
Playboy, rabbit head, bright green, 8" l ...10
Santa Claus, metallic plastic 5
Seagram's, "Seagram's Gin Cooler" in rope lettering, yellow plastic 4
Seagram's Seven, crown on top, set of 3 .10
Seagull, glass, highball stirrer, 4.5" h 12

Spike-Stirs, plastic, nail-shaped, Dorcy Mfg Co, boxed set of 8 15

SYLVAC POTTERY

Although most commonly recognized by its whimsical animal figures, Sylvac pottery also produced realistic animal models and a vast array of advertising and table wares. The pottery ceased production in 1982.

Ashtray, green with fawn-colored dog, 5" d 50
Basket, duck scene, 8.75" l, 5" h 50
Bookends, pr, light brown bunnies on green ground 225
Figurine, Corgi, sitting, 4" h 100
Figurine, dog, light brown, 5.5" h, 6" l 110
Figurine, elephant, beige, 4" h, 6" l 65
Figurine, frog, green, 2.5" h, 3.5" l 140
Figurine, kittens in green boot, 5" h 80
Figurine, kittens in light brown basket, 4.5" l, 4" h 85
Figurine, man's shoe, shiny black, 1930s . .15
Figurine, rabbit, light brown, 5.5" h 75
Figurine, Scottie dog, brown, 11" h 260
Figurine, spaniel, brown and white, 6" l, 4" h 85
Figurine, spaniel, sitting, green, 5" h 100
Figurine, squirrel, green, 6.75" h, 3.75" w .160
Figurine, squirrel, light brown, peering into green acorn .35
Figurine, terrier, sitting, green, 8" h 100
Flower Bowl, 3 rabbits around edge, 8" d, 3.75" h 75
Flower Bowl, lavendar and yellow, 10.5" d 65
Jug, blue splatter pattern, 6" h, 5.25" w . . .50
Jug, stork handle, fawn color, 10" h, 1960 100
Pitcher, green with white swan floating along base, 4" h, 2.5" w 35
Planter, kitten and top hat, green, 4" h 65
Vase, dog, lying down, green, 7" l, 2 h 85
Vase, Falcon ware, gray with blue budgie, 5" h, 9.5" l, 7" w .120
Vase, green and pink swirl, 5" h 45
Vase, mushroom, lop-eared rabbit, green and brown, 5.5" h .70
Vase, mythical scenes, tan, 8.25" h, 5" w .135
Wall Pocket, budgie, blue, 8.5" l, 7.75" w .120
Wall Pocket, budgie, white and green, 8.5" h, 7.75" w 160
Wall Pocket, rabbit in front of tree trunk, 5.5" h, 5.5" w 100

SYROCO

In the 1890s, Adolph Hostein, owner of the Syracuse Ornamental Company, developed a formula of wood compound and casting liquids that could be poured into molds. The resulting casting appeared to be hand-carved. The company manufactured a wide range of decorative accessories ranging from ashtrays to wall sconces. The Syracuse Ornamental Company became Syroco, Inc., in the 1930s.

In 1943 Walt Disney licensed Multi-Products of Chicago to produce a set of comic figures from Pinocchio. Multi-Products did them in Syroco wood. Collectors insert a second "c," Syrocco, to indicate a figure or object made by the parent company, Syroco, Inc. In addition to the Disney figures, Multi-Products did a series of twenty-four figures based on comic characters from the King Features Syndicate which were distributed as premiums by Pillsbury.

Bookends, pr, bowling pins and ball, partial Syroco label on back, 6.5" h, 4.5" w 25
Bookends, pr, cowboy on bronco, ranch in background, OrnaWood sticker on back, 6.5" h, 4.5" w 28
Bookends, pr, elephant, front legs on tree stump, Syroco Wood labels 16

Bookends, pr, flower basket, mkd "Syroco Wood, Made in USA, Syracuse, NY," 6.5" h 20
Bookends, pr, fruits and flowers, 1 Syroco sticker intact 16
Bookends, pr, Indian Chief, Syroco, Syracuse, NY 35
Bookends, pr, office clerk, wearing frock coat and sitting at high desk, bookcases in background, 7.25" h 16
Bookends, pr, white pinecones, green pine needles, rust colored maple leaves, 7.5" h, 5" w 20
Bookends, pr, Scottie dog, label reads "Made in USA Syroco Wood, Syracuse, NY," some chips and scuffs, 7" h, 5" w . .40
Bookends, pr, squirrel, eating nut, 1 ear damaged, 5.5" h, 4" w 16
Bowl, flower shaped, 12" d, 3" deep 25
Cigarette Box, small bear finial on rect box in the shape of half a log, "Orna-Wood USA" foil sticker, 2" h, 4.5" sq 14
Corkscrew, butler, 8.5" h 96
Corkscrew, codger, 8.5" h 105
Corkscrew, drunk butler, ivory finish, marked "Syroco," 4.5" h 55
Corkscrew, monk, Syracuse Ornamental Company, "King" sticker on bottom, 1940s, 8.5" h 395
Corkscrew, waiter, natural finish, mkd "Syroco," 4.5" h .75
Dresser Tray, shallow glass bowl rests on horse head plaque in center, horseshoe with recessed centers on either end, 10.5" l 15
Figure, Dagwood Bumstead, mkd "©1944 KFS," 5" h 62
Figure, Pinocchio, mkd "©Walt Disney Prod Multi Products Chicago," 5.5" h . . .15
Pipe Holder, figural hobo standing on log base, holds 2 pipes, 7.25" h, 4" x 6" base 16

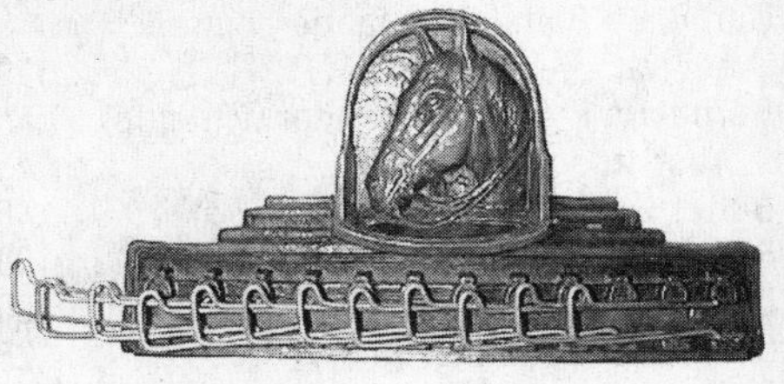

Thermometer, hobo, standing beside round thermometer mounted on base, 5.75" h, 4.5" w 16
Tie Rack, Boy Scouts, emblem above "Boy Scouts of America" banner and "Be Prepared, Do A Good Turn Daily" slogan, holds 8 ties, orig box 35
Tie Rack, horse head, covered bridge and cabin in background, partial Syroco label on back, holds 12 ties, 7.5" h, 13" w 30
Tie Rack, Irish setter head, rifle, hunting cap, and bag in background, holds 12 ties, 12.5" l, 5.25" h 16
Tie Rack, Revolutionary War drummer, black, gold, and white uniform, holds 8 ties, "Syroco Wood Made in USA Syracuse, NY" label on back, 9" h, 9" w .14
Tie Rack, sailing ship with white sails above 5 pairs of crossed oars resting on wooden dock, ties rest on ends of oars protruding from dock, "Syroco Wood" label on back, 10.25" h, 6.75" w .20
Tie Rack, Scottie dog head, green collar with gold buckle and studs, black nose and eye, holds 8 ties, 9" w, 7.25" h .25
Tie Rack, spaniel head, holds 8 ties, 6" h, 8" w 18
Wall Plaques, pr, fighting roosters, gold, red, and green, Syroco, 1965, 14" x 11" and 13" x 11" 2

TAMAC POTTERY

Tamac Pottery was founded in Perry, Oklahoma, in 1946 by Leonard and Marjorie Tate (TA-) and Allen and Betty Macauley (-MAC). The company produced kitchenwares, decorative accessories, and advertising pieces until its closing in 1972.

Ashtray, state of Texas, avocado 80
Barbecue Cup, frosty fudge . . . .

Barbecue Plate, one-hander, butterscotch 120
Barbecue Plate, one-hander with cup, frosty fudge 45
Butter Dish, frosty fudge 45
Butter Dish, ivory .100
Candleholder, double, raspberry 150
Cocktail Stem, frosty fudge 25
Coffee Cup and Saucer, frosty fudge 25
Coffee Cup Saucer, frosty pine 10
Creamer, frosty pine 20
Creamer and Sugar, cov, frosty pine 45
Dish Garden, frosty pine 45
Dish Garden, raspberry 200
Flowerpot, freeform, frosty pine, 6" 45
Fruit Bowl, frosty fudge 18
Juice Set, ice lip pitcher and 4 ftd tumblers, avocado 150
Mantel Planter, raspberry 300
Pitcher, frosty fudge 90
Pitcher, frosty pine .90
Planter, frosty pine .45
Plate, 7" d, frosty fudge 15
Plate, 7" d, frosty pine 15
Plate, 10" d, frosty fudge 25
Salt and Pepper Shakers, frosty fudge . . .25
Salt and pepper Shakers, frosty pine 25
Saucer, frosty fudge 10
Soup Bowl, frosty fudge 20
Spoon Rest, "For My Stirring Spoon," avocado 25
Tumbler, frosty fudge 30
Tumbler, frosty pine 25

TAYLOR, SMITH & TAYLOR

W. L. Smith, John N. Taylor, W. L. Taylor, Homer J. Taylor, and Joseph G. Lee founded Taylor, Smith, and Taylor in Chester, West Virginia. In 1903 the firm reorganized and the Taylors bought Lee's interest. In 1906 Smith bought out the Taylors. The firm remained in the Smith family's control until it was purchased by Anchor Hocking in 1973. The tableware division closed in 1981.

One of Taylor, Smith, and Taylor's most popular lines was Lu-Ray, produced from the 1930s through the early 1950s. Designed to compete with Russel Wright's American Modern, it was produced in Windsor Blue, Persian Cream, Sharon Pink, Surf Green, and Chatham Gray. Coordinating colors encouraged collectors to mix and match sets. Taylor, Smith, and Taylor used several different backstamps and marks. Many contain the company name as well as the pattern and shape names.

A dating system was used on some dinnerware lines. The three number code included month, year, and crew number. This system was discontinued in the 1950s.

Lu-Ray, coupe soup, 7.75", cream 20
Lu-Ray, coupe soup, 7.75", green 20
Lu-Ray, creamer, pink 15
Lu-Ray, cream soup and saucer, yellow 85
Lu-Ray, eggcup, double, yellow 30
Lu-Ray, fruit dish, blue 10
Lu-Ray, fruit dish, green 10
Lu-Ray, fruit dish, pink 10
Lu-Ray, fruit dish, yellow 10
Lu-Ray, plate, 6" d, blue 8
Lu-Ray, plate, 6" d, green 8
Lu-Ray, plate, 6" d, pink 8
Lu-Ray, plate, 6" d, yellow 8
Lu-Ray, plate, 7" d, pink 15
Lu-Ray, plate, 9" d, blue 15
Lu-Ray, plate, 9" d, green 15
Lu-Ray, plate, 9" d, pink 15
Lu-Ray, plate, 9" d, yellow 15
Lu-Ray, salad bowl, yellow 60
Lu-Ray, sauceboat, attached stand, yellow 40
Lu-Ray, saucer, 6" d, blue 8
Lu-Ray, saucer, 6" d, green 8
Lu-Ray, sugar, cov, pink 18

Lu-Ray, teacup, green 15
Lu-Ray, teacup, pink .15
Lu-Ray, teacup and saucer, blue 16
Lu-Ray, teacup and saucer, green 16
Lu-Ray, teacup and saucer, pink 16
Lu-Ray, teacup and saucer, yellow 16
Lu-Ray, vegetable bowl, 9" d, yellow 55
Versatile, Coffee Server, Pebbleford pattern, turquoise, 7.875" h 30
Versatile, dinner plate, surf green 8
Vistosa, cup, green .20
Vistosa, cup, yellow .18

TEAPOTS

Tea drinking was firmly established in England and its American colonies by the middle of the 18th century. The earliest teapots were modeled after their Far Eastern ancestors. Teapot shapes and decorative motifs kept pace with the ceramic and new design styles of the 19th century. The whimsical, figural teapot was around from the start.

Teapots were a common product of American ceramic, glass, and metal manufacturers. The "Rebekah at the Well" teapot appeared in the mid-1850s. Hall China of East Liverpool, Ohio, was one of the leading teapot manufacturers of the 1920s and 1930s. Figural teapots were extremely popular in the 1930s. The first etched Pyrex teapot was made in the late 1930s.

Cardew, ivory with gold accents, 9.75" h . .75
Cardew, Mickey Sorcerer, *Fantasia*, musical notes around teapot, 7" h 55
Cardew, Popeye blowing smoke from his pipe, 7" h 100
Cardew, Winnie the Pooh, 7.5" h 100
England, Art Deco style, petit-point pattern, mkd "Old English Sampler," H&K, c1920 120
England, Gone Shopping, chair with Gucci shoes, handbag, and hat 110
England, Jolly Policeman, British bobby, 5" h 35
Gibson's of England, Georgian design, silver lustre, 1920, 10" w, 5.5" h 95
Hall, black with gold foliage design 55
Hall, Boston, metal clad, 6-cup 110
Hall, McCormick, maroon with white infuser 55
Hong Kong, plastic, figural elephant, painted dec, mkd "Made in Hong Kong," 1960s 12
Japan, Art Deco style, house on river-bank scene, lustre glazes, mkd "Made in Japan," 1940s 50
Japan, Dragon Ware, air-brushed blue, gold dec, mkd "H Katu, Pearl China," Nagoya, Japan, c1940–60s 75
Japan, enameled flowers and scrolls on dark brown ground, 5.5" h 20
Japan, hp windmill scene, mkd "Made in Japan" 20
Japan, relief design of fruit, flower, and leaf on 1 side, apple, grapes, and leaf on other side, 7" h 45
Lomonosov, porcelain, cobalt net design .85
Occupied Japan, white flowers on turquoise ground, 4.125" h, 7.75" w 30
Sadler, Golden Wedding, flower decal with gold trim, 6.25" h, 9.25" w 70
Souvenir, chicken motif, mkd "Chowning's Tavern, Williamsburg, Virginia" 28
Souvenir, mammy baking cookies, lobster, woman, and boat, "Souvenir of Beloxi, Ocean Springs, Bay St Louis, Pass Crestian, and Golf Port," 6" h 85
Staffordshire, Autumn, floral and leaf design with gold accents on rim, spout, and handle, 6" h, 10" w 40
Staffordshire, Price Bros, emb windmill, door, windows, and climbing flowering vine, green, trimmed in gold, 6" h, 8" l . .50
Teleflora, raised pink rose, creamy white ground, brown handle, 5.25" h, 9" w 40
Tony Carter, dining table with nice tablecloth, candle, and 2 place settings, 7" h, 10.25" l 100

TEDDY BEARS

The name "Teddy" Bear originated with Theodore Roosevelt. The accepted date of their birth is 1902–1903. Early bears had humped backs, elongated muzzles, and jointed limbs. The fabric was usually mohair; the eyes were either glass with pin backs or black shoe buttons.

The contemporary Teddy Bear market is as big or bigger than the market for antique and collectible bears. Many of these bears are quite expensive. Collectors speculating in them will find that recouping their investment in ten to fifteen years will be a bearish proposition.

Club: Good Bears of the World, P.O. Box 13097, Toledo, OH 43613

Boyds, beige, velvet paws, handstiched mouth, jointed, 8.5" h 15
Boyds, Panda, black and white, fully jointed, 10" h 15
Care Bear, Grumpy, blue, cloud on stomach, 14" h 35
Dakin, red velvet heart, red bow, 1983, 7" h 20
Dakin, sailor, plush, plastic eyes, embroidered nose, 18" h 35
Dean, Ernest, black mohair, glass eyes, orange ribbon around neck, fully jointed, 8.5" h 60
Dean, Snowball, white mohair, slate gray paw pads, green ribbon around neck, fully jointed, 8" h 75
Dean, wool mix, brown, fully jointed, growler, 16" h 110

Fisher-Pirce, light brown, gingham dress with apron, velcro-tipped paws, plastic eyes, suede nose, 15" h 25
Ganz, brown, long haired plush, gingham heart patch, ears, and footpads, 12.5" h 10
Gund, nutmeg, green ribbon around neck, plastic eyes, red felt tongue, white ears, 14" h 45
Gund, Theo, light brown, 17" h 20
Hermann, black mohair with green glass eyes, fully jointed, 11.5" h 140
Hermann, Cinnamon Hip Hop Hop, light brown mohair, 11" h 100
Hermann, light brown mohair, wearing Bavarian vest and hat, designed for the 1995 Munich Oktoberfest in Germany, fully jointed, growler, 17" h . .140
Hermann, plush, beige, red bow around neck, 16" h 50
Hermann, Unification Bear, commemorates reunification of Germany, light brown mohair, growler 150
Robert Raikes, Winter Fairy, wooden face, gossamer wings, 9" h 60
Steiff, cream, jointed, 5.5" h 195
Steiff, rose mohair, jointed, squeaker 200
Timid Timmy #13, dark brown, fully jointed, glass eyes, brown leather back paws with fur front paws and fabric nose, 17" h 120
Ty, Beanie Baby, Peace the Bear, plush, tie-dyed 15
Unknown Maker, plush body with soft knit velour pads, embroidered nose and mouth, 16" h .195
Vermont, yellow, with red dress, black velvet nose, soft suede leather paws, jointed, 16" h 25

TELEPHONE CARDS

Telephone cards, commonly known as telecards, have been big in Europe for years. Telecards are credit cards issued by major telephone companies and many private companies. You purchase a card and then use up the credit each time you place a call. Once the credit value of the card is exhausted, you have an instant collectible.

Some telecards are produced as part of a series, some are limited editions. Most stand alone. The cards are issued in quantities that start in the hundreds and continue into the tens of thousands. Collector value rests in a card's graphics, issuing telephone company, and the number issued. Prices are highly speculative. Only time will tell how this collectible will "reach out and touch" collectors.

Prices listed here are from current sales lists issued by several individuals selling directly to collectors. The market has yet to determine if a premium is to be paid for cards with unexpended credit balances.

Access Telecom Inc (ACT), Earthline/US ACMI, Cheetah 6
ACMI, Zerynthia butterfly, black and yellow 5
Amerivox, American Cancer Society 20
Amerivox, Cats the Musical 20
Amerivox, soaring bald eagle on blue 15
Amerivox, Walt Disney World, Disney Dolphin Hotel 20
AT&T, cat peeking from flowers 5
AT&T, Coca-Cola, Santa Claus holding bottle 10
AT&T, Rock & Roll Hall of Fame, Cleveland 12
B&J, Off Hook Comm., Northport Centennial Specimen, 1994 4
BCC, Grateful Dead, skull 30
BT, 40 units, green, drum major logo 10
Cable & Wireless, Kentucky Fried Chicken, Colonel logo 5
Cable & Wireless, Telecard Times, STS Roundup, 1997 4
DC Enterprises, Eagles Aerobatic Flight Team, 1995 Final Performance Tour 4
Express Communications, flag and eagle .15
GAF, "Sultan," white tiger, 1996 4
GTE, Aloha Fest, 1993, Maui girl on horseback 30
GTI, Budweiser, Bud One airship 10
IDC Communications, Disneyland 40th Anniversary, Indiana Jones Attraction opening 8
IDC Communications, Disneyland 40th Anniversary, Mickey in front of Castle . .12
Interactive Telecard Service, Kentucky Derby, Run for the Roses 10
MCI, Independence Day, the Movie, spaceship over White House 6
MCI, Statue of Liberty with US flag 5

Multi-Media Publishing, TeleCard World, 1996 New York 4
Networks Around The World, Seasons Greetings from Networks Around the World, 1995 4
Phone Line, bighorn sheep 10
Phone Line USA, Save the Whales, green strip 10
Sprint, Free Willie 2/Arm & Hammer 15
Sprint, Vista Hotel at World Trade Center 16
USACard, Marilyn Monroe at Cardex, in front of castle, 1995 50
WorldLink, Exxon Tiger, Superflo Motor Oil 8

TELEPHONES & RELATED

Although Alexander Graham Bell filed his telephone patent in 1876, rude telegraph and sound-operated devices existed prior to that date.

Beware of reproduction phones or phones made from married parts. Buy only telephones that have the proper period parts, a minimum of restoration, and are in working order. No mass-produced telephone in the United States made prior to 1950 was manufactured with a shiny brass finish.

Concentrating on telephones is only half the story. Telephone companies generated a wealth of secondary material from books to giveaway premiums.

Clubs: Antique Telephone Collectors Assoc., P.O. Box 94, Abilene, KS 67410; Telephone Collectors International, Inc., 3207 E. Bend Dr., Algonquin, IL 60102.

Address Book/Telephone Note Pad, blue and white, picture of Charles Lindbergh and the *Spirit of St Louis,* "New York/Paris," Peoples National Bank, Delta, PA adv, 3.25" x 4.25" 200
Advertising Plate, Bell Pay Telephone, celluloid-type plastic, reads, "Speak Close to Mouthpiece," 2" x 1.5" 30
Advertising Sign, Bell Telephone, blue enamel, flange, 11" x 10.5" 90
Advertising Sign, "Public Telephone," porcelain, round 16
Advertising Telephone, Coca-Cola, 12" d .170
Almanac, Bell System, 1941, 32 pgs 12
Bottle, Ford Model T Telephone Truck, 8" h, 11.5" l, 6.5" w 90
Brooch, celluloid telephone, 1.5" h, 2.5" lh .32
Charm, telephone, enamel dial, gold, .5" l 150
Cookie Jar, telephone, black and silver, 9" x 8" 28
Cufflinks, goldtone, 1" d 14
Figurine, telephone girl with phone book, 1950s, 3.25" h, 2.75" w 28
Key Chain, telephone dial 10
Mug, Telephone Pioneers of America, mkd "1875-1911" 20
Music Box, vintage telephone, plays, "Edelweiss," 4" h, 3.5" x 3.5" 22
Paperweight, glass, Bell Telephone Logo, 3.25" h, 3.25" d 55
Pay Telephone, reconditioned and rewired, 23" h to top of marquee 400
Pencil Sharpener, hard plastic, 1.75" l 5
Phone Booth, Superman, Hallmark, switch on booth and Clark Kent changes into Superman, 1995 32

Planter, Lefton, old-fashioned telephone, roses and leaves on white porcelain, gold trim, 1950s, 3.5" x 4.5" 10
Purse, telephone cord, white and black, round, 7" d, 1950s 75
Salt and Pepper Shakers, receiver is pepper, bottom of phone is salt, red 28
Squeeze Toy, girl with telephone wearing a towel, squeaker, Alan Jay, 1957 48
Teapot, Lucy telephone, 7" h 40
Telephone, figural mallard duck decoy, 12.5" l 50
Telephone, rotary, 1920s 100
Telephone, Gumby, table top, touchtone, 1985, 11" l 100
Telephone, Mickey Mouse, touchtone, mkd "Made in China for AT&T Co," 14.5" h, 10" w 60
Telephone Clock/Cigar Lighter, Timelite, silver finish 275
Telephone Directory, 1937, Plainview, TX .70
Telephone Directory, 1950, Cadiz, OH and vicinity, 64 pgs 25
Tray, Telephone Pioneers of America, metal, 5" d 10

TELEVISION CHARACTERS & PERSONALITIES

The golden age of television varies depending on the period in which you grew up. Each generation thinks the television of its childhood is the best there ever was. TV collectibles are one category in which new products quickly establish themselves as collectible. The minute a show is cancelled, anything associated with it is viewed as collectible.

The golden age of TV star endorsements was the 1950s through the 1960s. For whatever reason, toy, game, and other manufacturers of today are not convinced that TV stars sell products. As a result, many shows have no licensed products associated with them.

Note: Consult the most recent edition of *Maloney's Antiques & Collectibles Resource Directory,* by David J. Maloney, Jr., for information about fan clubs for specific television shows.

A-Team, board game, 1984 26

Baywatch, doll, Toy Island, CJ Parker Ocean Lifeguard, 1997, 12" h 15

Baywatch, Lifeguard Training Set, Toy Island, 1997, includes CJ Parker, jet ski, and beach accessories 25

Ben Casey, sweater guard, 1962, MOC . . .30

Captain Kangaroo, Golden Record, Captain Kangaroo and Mr Greenjeans Sleigh Ride, #560, 45 rpm 12

Captain Kangaroo, lunch box, Thermos, red, Captain Kangaroo, Dancing Bear, and Mr Greenjeans walking arm in arm, Grandfather Clock nearby, with thermos and packaging, 1964 200

Casper the Friendly Ghost, lunch box, Thermos, dark blue, Casper and Wendy Witch waving and pointing at 3 ghosts flying out of haunted house, with thermos 375

Charlie's Angels, doll, Kate Jackson, Mattel, 1978, 12" .45

Daniel Boone, board game, Fess Parker Wilderness Trail Card Game, "As Seen on the Daniel Boone Show," Transogram, 1964 .40

Daniel Boone, Fess Parker Inflatable Indian Canoe, #7103, Multiple Toy Makers, 1965, MIP 50

Dennis the Menace, paper cocktail napkins, orig box, 1954 40

Family Affair, Colorforms, #515, 1970 20

Family Affair, coloring book, Whitman, 1968 40

Family Affair, doll, Talking Mrs Beasley, wearing glasses, Mattel, 1967 250

Family Ties, board game, unopened, 1987 25

Flintstones, salt and pepper shakers, figural Pebbles and Bamm Bamm, 4" h .50

Flying Nun, board game, Milton Bradley, 1968 45

Gentle Ben, comic book, #3, 1968 9

Gilligan's Island, figure, Skipper, 1977 15

Gumby, jigsaw puzzle, Gumby and Pokey, Springbok/Hallmark, 1984 15

Honeymooners, napkins, caricature images, box of 38 55

Land of the Giants, model, spaceship, Aurora, unassembled, 1968 600

Laverne & Shirley, doll, Laverne Defazio, Mego, 1977, 12" 45

Mork & Mindy, action figure, Mork From Ork, talking back pack 45

Mork & Mindy, board game, Parker Bros, 1979 28

Mork & Mindy, card game, 1978 18

Patty Duke, board game, Milton Bradley, 1963 30

Pee Wee's Playhouse, action figure, Ricardo, MOC 30

Rocky & Bullwinkle, lunch kit, Thermos, blue vinyl, Bullwinkle in spacesuit on moon, holding USA banner while standing with foot on Boris' back, aliens nearby, with thermos, 1962 285

Rocky & Bullwinkle, Musical Band, 3 plastic instruments, 1969, MOC 50

Sonny & Cher, doll, Growing Hair Cher . . .45

Soupy Sales, lunch box, Thermos, blue, Soupy Sales image, with thermos, 1965 316

Space Cadet, Golden Record, Tom Corbett's Space Cadet Song and March, 1951 25

Starsky & Hutch, paperback book,* Starsky & Hutch, *by Max Franklin, Ballantine Books, #2, #25124, New York, NY, 153 pages, ©1976 5

Tarzan, comic book, 1967 12
The Munsters, board game, Milton Bradley, 1964 65
The Waltons, doll, John Boy, 1974 35
Travolta, John, postcard book, 1978, 23 full color postcards, 8.5" x 11" 25
Underdog, lunch box, Ardee, Underdog rescuing Sweet Polly from crocodiles, with thermos, 1972 575
Wally Walrus, wall plaque, ©Walter Lantz, Napco, 1958, 7" h 75
Yogi Bear, lunch box, Aladdin, yellow, Yogi taking picture of Boo Boo, Cindy, and other cubs, Ranger peeking out from behind tree, with thermos, 1961 .. 345
Yogi Bear, paste jar, blue plastic, in the shape of Yogi's head, 1965, NOS, MOC . 25

TELEVISIONS

Old television sets are becoming highly collectible. It is not unusual to see a dozen or more at a flea market. Do not believe a tag that says "I Work." Insist that the seller find a place to plug it in and show you. A good general rule is the smaller the picture tube, the earlier the set. Pre-1946 televisions usually have a maximum of five stations, 1 through 5. Channels 7 through 13 were added in 1947. In 1949 Channel 1 was dropped. UHF appeared in 1953.

In order to determine the value of a television, you need to identify the brand and model number. See *The Official Rinker Price Guide to Collectibles* (House of Collectibles, 2000) for a more detailed list.

Club: Antique Wireless Assoc., Box E, Breesport, NY 14816

Admiral, P17E31, painted metal top, top handle, 1959 35
Air King, A-1016, console, sq lines, drop-down door at center, 16" screen .. 50
Ansley, 701, Beacon, wooden tabletop, 13-channel tuner, grill cloth and mesh panels, 4 knobs at bottom, 1948, 10" screen 75
Crosley, 9-4-7, wooden tabletop, metal mesh around screen, continuous tuner control and window to the right, 1949, 12" screen 35
DeWald, ET-171, console, pull-out phono, 1951, 17" screen 45
Emerson, 614, Bakelite tabletop, porthole-style screen, ribs across front and sides, 1950, 10" screen 75
Fada, S20C10, console, screen on left, 4 knobs behind door, 1951, 20" screen .. 20
General Electric, 835, tabletop, metal mesh grill, 10" screen 50
Hallicrafters, T-506, wooden tabletop, 12-channel push-button tuner, 1949, 7" screen 150
Motorola, 17T5, Bakelite tabletop, 2 knobs under screen, 1952, 17" screen 35
Panasonic, TR 542c, rounded space age design, 1970s 150
RCA, 8T-241, tabletop, blonde, 1940s 50
RCA, 9T246, metal tabletop, grill around screen, imitation mahogany finish, 1949, 10" screen 25
Sentinel, 402, console, 4 knobs below screen, 10" screen 50
Silvertone, 112, wooden tabletop, 1950, 12" screen 35
UHF Box, Bakelite, blue, 1950s 250
Westinghouse, H-661C12, console, double doors, 1949, 12" screen 55
Zenith, portable, AC/DC, yellow, 1974 60

TENNIS COLLECTIBLES

Tennis came to America in the mid-1870s. After a tennis craze in the 1880s, the sport went into a decline. International play led to a revival in the early 1900s. The period from 1919 to 1940 is viewed by many tennis scholars as the sport's golden age.

Tennis collectibles are divided into two periods: (1) pre-1945 and (2) post-1945. There is little collector interest in post-1945 material. There are three basic groups of collectibles: (1) items associated with play such as tennis balls, ball cans, rackets, and fashions, (2) paper ephemera ranging from books to photographs, and (3) objects decorated with a tennis image or in a tennis shape. Because tennis collecting is in its infancy, some areas remain highly affordable (rackets) while others (tennis ball cans) already are in the middle of a price run.

Advertisement, *Newsweek Magazine,* "1936 Brooks Brothers & Tennis-Men's Fashion," 4" x 10.25" 10
Advertisement, *The Century Illustrated Monthly Magazine,* "1886 Lawn Tennis 15 Specialties," 6" x 4" 10
Ashtray, porcelain, Spalding Inn & Tennis Club, 4" d 10
Autograph, Anna Kournikova, 8" x 10" 70
Autograph, Venus and Serena Williams, Dec 2002, 8" x 10" 100
Book, *Wimbledon Centre Court of the Game,* by Max Robertson, BBC 30
Drinking Glass, tennis players dec, 1950s, 5.5" h 5
Figure, carved wood, male tennis player, 11" h 365
Figure, lead, lady tennis player, 2.25" h . . .20
Ice Bucket, tennis players dec, 1950s, 4.75" h, 6" w 10
Medal, 1" d 10
Mug, glass, "World's Worst Tennis Player" 15
Mug, Royal Bradwell, Sports Series, 1920, 4.5" h 75
Pin, gilded silver, 1930s lady tennis player 185
Pin, Victorian 14K yg, tennis racket 125
Racket, mkd "Chemold, Margaret Court, Tournament. Reg. No. 411733" 20
Racket, wooden, Spalding case, 14 oz 25
Racket, wooden, Wilson, sgd, "Tony Trabert" 25
Racket, wooden, Wilson Court Star, 1950s 30
Salt and Pepper Shakers, tennis-playing dogs, 2.5" h 20
Spoons, pr, crossed tennis rackets and tennis ball handles, SS, England, 4.25" l 60
Stick Pin, Krementz, tennis racket with faux pearl ball 12
Tray, SS, inscribed "Presented to Malcolm R Munroe by the Fine Paper Industry in affectionate memory of J Pierre Rolland for Low Net at the Mills Merchants Tournament," mkd "Birks Sterling," 1956, 7" d 125
Tray, wood with brass inlay, "Winner Hilton Head Island Tennis Professional's Association, Bank of Beaufort," 8.5" x 8.5" 20

THERMOMETERS

The thermometer was a popular advertising giveaway and promotional item. Buy only thermometers in very good or better condition that have a minimum of wear on the visible surface. Remember, thermometers had large production runs. If the first example you see does not please you, shop around.

Club: Thermometer Collectors Club of America, 6130 Rampart Dr., Carmichael, CA 95608.

Calumet Baking Powder, wood, "Call For Calumet Baking Powder, Best By Test, Trade Here and Save," product image above thermometer tube, trademark boy next to tube, 1920s-30s, 22" h, 6" w 300
Coca-Cola, emb tin, "Drink Coca-Cola In Bottles" button above thermometer tube, "Quality Refreshment" at bottom, 1950s, 9" h 415
Coca-Cola, pam thermometer, "Drink Coca-Cola, Be Really Refreshed!," 1960s, 12" d 935
Coca-Cola, pam thermometer, "Drink Coca-Cola In Bottles," white lettering on red ground, 1950s, 12" d 275
Coca-Cola, pam thermometer, "Things go better with Coke" above "Drink Coca-Cola" button, 1960s, 12" d 275
Dr Pepper, pam thermometer, "Hot or Cold, Drink Dr Pepper," 1960s, 12" d . . .225
Dr Pepper, tin, "Hot or Cold Enjoy the friendly 'Pepper-Upper' Dr Pepper," orig box, c1930s, 7" h, 2.5" w 250
Koca Nola, wood, "Try A Bottle Of Koca Nola, The Great Tonic Drink, Invigorating, Exhilarating, Harmless," straight-sided diamond-label bottle image next to thermometer tube, 1905-15, 24" h, 7" w 465
Orange Crush, masonite, "Drink Orange-Crush Carbonated Beverage – And Feel Fresh!," bottle image next to thermometer tube, trademark Orange-Crush character below, 1943, 16" h, 4.5" w 385

7-Up, pam thermometer, "Fresh Clean Taste" on green and white vertical stripe ground, 7-Up logo below, white rim, 10" d 250

Sprite, pam thermometer, "Enjoy Sprite, Tart and Tingling!," green lettering and logo on white ground, gold trim, 1960s, 12" d 275

Whistle, chalkware, "anytime...any weather. Thirsty? Just Whistle," thermometer tube next to boy wearing polka-dot bowtie and holding oversized bottle, wintry sky in background, 1940s, 12" h, 12" w 415

Whistle, tin, "Thirsty? Just Whistle," 2 elves carrying oversized bottle next to thermometer tube, 21" h, 9" w 990

THIMBLES

A thimble was one of the few gifts considered appropriate for an unmarried man to give to a lady. Many of these fancy thimbles show little wear, possibly a result of both inappropriate sizing and the desire to preseve the memento.

Advertising thimbles were popular between 1920 and the mid-1950s. Early examples were made from celluloid or aluminum. Plastic was the popular post-war medium. The first political thimbles appeared shortly after ratification of the 19th amendment. They proved to be popular campaign giveaways through the early 1960s.

Clubs: Thimble Collectors' Club of America, 6130 Rampart Dr., Carmichael, CA 95608; Thimble Collectors International, 8289 Northgate Dr., Rome, NY 13440.

Bone China, Pepsi logo, England 5

Bone China, portrait and "100th Birthday of Her Majesty Queen Elizabeth the Queen Mother," Cottage Thimbles, England 4

China, American Fashion Circa 1900, orig box, Avon, 1982 7

China, American Fashion Circa 1947, orig box, Avon, 1982 15

China, "a stitch in time saves nine," Davenport, England 8

China, Baby Animals of the World, Baby Coyotes, World Wildlife Fund, Franklin Mint, 1981 10

China, Blomen Van Nederland, Freesia, Franklin Mint, 1978 10

China, Blomen Van Nederland, Gladiolus, Franklin Mint, 1978 10

China, floral design and "Blossom By Blossom the Spring Begins," Royal Grafton, England, 1970s 10

China, Friends of the Forest, Woodchuck, Franklin Mint, 1982 12

China, Sunbonnet Babies, cleaning, mkd "Downs Ltd Ed 2500" 26

Pewter, "Always Coca-Cola" 12

Pewter, hummingbird on top, raised flowers with Swarovski crystal center around sides, Comstock Creations 10

Pewter, locomotive on top, Lancaster area, PA 8

Porcelain, long-eared rabbit on top, gold trim, orig box, Avon 5

Porcelain, World's Greatest Porcelain Houses, Franciscan, Desert Rose, Franklin Mint, 1982 15

Porcelain, World's Greatest Porcelain Houses, Royal Doulton, Tea Roses and Blue Bonnets, Franklin Mint 12

Sterling Silver, emblem mark and "sterling," "12," Goldsmith, Stern & Co .28

Sterling Silver, gold band, mkd with thimble in star, "sterling," and "8," Waite Thresher .32

Sterling Silver, gold band, Simons Bros . . .20

Sterling Silver, Greek Key band, size 9 25

Sterling Silver, hallmarked with "JS&S" in block and anchor, lion, and "M" in shields, England, size 7 20
Sterling Silver, scrolled band, mkd with star and "sterling 9" 15

TIFFIN GLASS

A. J. Beatty and Sons built a large glass works in Tiffin, Ohio, in 1888. In 1892 Tiffin Glass Company became part of the U.S. Glass Company, a combine based in Pittsburgh, Pennsylvania.

During the Depression, Tiffin made hundreds of patterns, its output twice that of Cambridge and A. H. Heisey. Tiffin purchased Heisey blanks to meet its production requirements. The company's famed "Lady Stems" were made between 1939 and 1956.

Tiffin purchased the molds and equipment of the T. G. Hawkes Cut Glass Company, Corning, New York, in 1964. Continental Can purchased the Tiffin factory in 1966, selling it in 1968 to the Interpace Corporation, a holding company of Franciscan china. Tiffin was sold once again in 1980, this time to Towle Silversmiths. Towle began importing blanks from Eastern Europe. In 1984 Towle closed the Tiffin factory and donated the land and buildings to the city of Tiffin. Jim Maxwell, a former Tiffin glasscutter, bought the Tiffin molds and equipment. The Tiffin trademark is now a registered trademark of Maxwell Crystal, Inc. In 1992 Maxwell placed four Hawkes and Tiffin patterns back into production.

Club: Tiffin Glass Collectors' Club, P.O. Box 554, Tiffin, OH 44883.

Basket, black satin, 11" h 70
Basket, twilight, 3" h, 5" w 140
Bowl, Dolores, 3" h, 13" d 75
Bowl, handled, Modern, 4" h, 11.5" d 135
Bowl, pink, 2.75" h, 7" d 95
Candlestick, double, Fuchsia 70
Candlesticks, black satin glass, twist, 8.5" h 125
Candy Dish, cov, ftd, 6" h, 7.25" w 50
Cologne Bottle, 7" h 90
Compote, amberina satin finish, red, dark orange, 5" h, 7" d 75
Compote, black, 7" h, 9.5" w 65
Console Set, amethyst, blue, white, and green enamel around base of candlesticks and rim of bowl 150
Creamer, Old Gold, 3" h, 6" w 22
Creamer and Sugar, amberina satin, 3.25" h, 6" w 75
Creamer and Sugar, Dolores 50
Decanter, amber trim, 7" h 90
Flower Basket, Empress Modern, light blue glass wings, 17" w 150
Luncheon Plate, Cherokee Rose, 8" d 20
Mayonnaise and Ladle, pink, 2.75" h, 6" w 40
Pitcher, Wave Optic, 2 qt, 7.5" h 50
Puff Box, black, satin dec, 3.25" h, 6.25" d 150
Salad Plate, yellow, 8" d 20
Serving Plate, pink satin, 10" d 35
Sherbert Dish, dark green, 3.5" h, 4" d 8
Stemware, Elinor, grapefruit, green, pr ..150
Sugar Bowl, Vaseline Glass, 4.75" h 25
Tumbler, Laurel Wreath, 6 oz 8
Tumblers, Elinor, green, ftd, 5.5" h, set of 4 175
Urn, black amethyst, 10.5" h 115
Vase, Modern, Copen Blue, 12" h, 4"d ...140
Vase, Poppy, black amethyst, 8.75" h 145
Vase, Poppy, black satin amethyst, 5" h, 6.5" w 35
Vase, Poppy, blue satin, 8" h, 8" d 100
Vase, Swedish, Copen Blue, 7" h, 5" w 60
Vase, Wisteria, 4-ftd, 7.5" h, 4.25" d 145

TINS, ADVERTISING

The advertising tin has always been at the forefront of advertising collectibles. Look for examples with no deterioration to the decorated surfaces and little or no signs of rust on the insides or bottoms.

The theme sells the tin. Other collectors, especially individuals from the transportation fields, have long had their eyes on the tin market. Tins also play a major part in the Country Store decorating look. Prices for pre-1940 tins are still escalating. Before you pay a high price for a tin, do your homework and make certain it is difficult to find.

Club: Tin Container Collectors Assoc., P.O. Box 440101, Aurora, CO 80044.

Armour's Veribest Peanut Butter, litho tin, colorful nursery rhyme characters all around, 3.5" x 3.75" 275
Aspirin, slide top, dispenses one tablet at a time, 2.5" x 1.5" 30
Calcox Tooth Powder, 4.25" h, 2.5" d 85
Calumet Baking Powder, 5 lb, 7.5" h, 4.5" d 75
Cascarets Brand Laxative Tablets, Chocolate Flavor, 3.75" x 2.25" 22
Crisp-N-Good Potato Chips – IGA Big-Big Can, 20 oz, 11.25" h, 9.75" d 35
Forbe's Golden Cup Coffee, 3 lb, 9.25" h . . 215
Gold Flake Peanut Butter, bail handle, 5 lb, 6" h, 6" d 25
Gulf Lighter Fluid, lead spout, 5.5" x 2.5" . . 105
Italina Laxative Prepartion, 5" h, 3.75" d . . . 75
Kodak Developer, 3.5" h, 2" d 40

Log Cabin Syrup, 100th Anniversary, 4.75" l, 5" h 50
Lucky Strike, flat fifty, 5.5" x 4.25" 35
Maxwell House Coffee, with key-open lid, 1 lb 45
May's Glycerine and Menthol Lozenges, The May Drug Co, .75" x 2.5" 135
Mosquito Talcum Powder, Harmony of Boston, 4.5" x 2.5" 85
Nelson's Baby Powder, 5" h 165
Pineoleum Iron Tablets, .5" x 2.5" 95
Quaker Marjoram Spice, 1 oz, 2.5" h, 2.25" w 30
Red Pepper Silver Buckle Spices, Cayenne, 1.5 oz, 2.5" h 25
Royal Hawaiian Macadamia Nuts, 12 oz, 4" h, 4" d 35
Sir Walter Raleigh Tobacco, 7 oz, 4" h 55
Spartan Cream of Tartar, 1.5 oz, slide top . 20
Sportsman Tobacco, round, screw lid 30
State of Vermont Maple Syrup, 1 gal, 6.25" x 4.25" x 10" 22
Taxico Dandelion Coffee, screw lid, 1920s 25
Tetley Tea, 100 tea bags with tags, round, 1940s 45
Tuxedo Tobacco, green with gold lettering, 4.25" h, 3" w 35
Uncle Sam Shoe Polish, round, 3.5" d 75
Union Leader Cut Plug Tobacco, 7" x 5" x 4.5" 120
Watkins Petro-Carbo Salve, 1.25" h, 2.5" d . 28
William's Talc Powder, JB Williams Co, violet, 5" h 165
Witch Hazel Cream, Larkin Co, 3" x 2" 95
Yankee Wax Polish, Yankee Polish Co, round, 3.5" d 95
Zion Hard Candies, dark blue, 9.25" h 50

TOBACCO COLLECTIBLES

The tobacco industry is under siege. Fortunately, they have new frontiers to conquer in Russia, Eastern Europe, Asia, and Africa. The relics of America's smoking past, from ashtrays to humidors, are extremely collectible.

With each passing year, the price for tobacco-related material goes higher and higher. If it ever stabilizes and then drops, a number of collectors are going to see their collections go up in smoke.

Club: Society of Tobacco Jar Collectors, 3011 Falstaff Rd. #307, Baltimore, MD 21209.

Note: See the Cigarette & Cigar category for additional listings.

Humidor, devil, majolica, orange with glass eyes, 4.75" h 180
Humidor, dog head, wearing blue hat and smoking pipe, glazed terra cotta, mkd "4766" with signature, 6.25" h 165
Humidor, head of green man smoking pipe, majolica, incised "7060/67," 5.5" h 200
Humidor, Indian chief head, majolica, 8" h 250
Humidor, man with hands in pockets, Rockingham style glazed earthenware, 11.5" h 170
Humidor, owl standing on book, majolica, mkd "4963/52," 10.5" h 335
Humidor, pig in long coat holding sword and saluting, porcelain, ink stamp "Made in Czechoslovakia," 6" h 115
Humidor, seated man smoking pipe, Staffordshire, 8.5" h 335
Meerschaum Pipe, 2 bulldogs, orig case . 55
Meerschaum Pipe, 2 horses drinking from fountain, orig case 100
Meerschaum Pipe, claw holding bowl, orig case 60
Meerschaum Pipe, flora-form bowl with nude Art Nouveau woman on front, orig case 145
Meerschaum Pipe, lion's head, orig case 105
Meerschaum Pipe, long-bearded sultan, silver collar with names Wm Parsons from JB Sparrow, 1879, orig case 305

Meerschaum Pipe, mastiff, brass-mounted lid, flexible stem 48
Meerschaum Pipe, mother dog with puppy 72
Meerschaum Pipe, prancing horse with trees, orig case 75
Meerschaum Pipe, rabbit's head, glass eyes, orig case 110
Meerschaum Pipe, winged fairy on front of bowl with wrap-around wings 230
Smoking set, 5-pc set in orig fitted box, consisting of 2 Meerschaum pipes, 2 cigarette holders, and match holder . 165

TOKENS

Token collecting is an extremely diverse field. The listing below barely scratches the surface with respect to the types of tokens one might find.

The wonderful thing about tokens is that, on the whole, they are very inexpensive. You can build an impressive collection on a small budget. Like match cover and sugar packet collectors, token collectors have kept their objects outside the main collecting stream. This has resulted in stable, low prices over a long period of time in spite of an extensive literature base. There is no indication that this is going to change in the near future.

Clubs: American Numismatic Assoc., 818 N. Cascade Ave., Colorado Springs, CO 80903; Token and Medal Society, Inc., P.O. Box 366, Bryantown, MD 20617.

Boy Scout, good turn token 30
Bridge Token, Delaware River Joint Toll, 1934 5
CM May Steubenville, Ohio, 1863 Civil War 55
Cracker Jack, Woodrow Wilson 8
Fay Motor Bus Co, Good for One City Fare 5
Fountain of Youth, St Augustine, Florida . . 10
France Automobile 25
Gettone Telefonico, telephone token 5
Hollytex Carpet Mills, brass, emb N-S-E-W directional design 25
Hospital Parking 4
Landing of First Fleet Australia, cupro-nickel 15

Metropolitan Transit Authority, One Fare . .4
Narrows Bridge, Washington Toll Bridge Authority 4
North Carolina Prison, hard plastic 10
Old Golden Nugget Gaming, Laughlin, NV .15
Property of Mills Vendor, for Amusement Only 5
Rockford, Illinois Transit Company, Good for One City Fare .5
Royal Arch Masonic 1 Penny 10
Sales Tax Token, Alabama State Department of Revenue .5
Seattle Municipal Railway 10
Spokane United Railways, Good for School Fare 8
Sturgis Harley Davidson Gaming 5
Takoma, Washington Transit, Good for One Fare 4
US Army ROTC Dragon Batallion Leadership Excellence .10
US Constellation 20
US Marine Corp 10
Willie Wirehand, Silver Jubilee, aluminum .8

TOOLS

Every flea market has at least a half dozen tables loaded with tools. The majority are modern tools sold primarily for reuse. However, you may find some early tools thrown in the bunch. Dig through tool boxes and the boxes under the tables. Decorators like primitive tools for hanging on walls in old homes. Other desirable tools include those that are handwrought or heavily trimmed with brass. Names to look for include Stanley, Keen Kutter, and Winchester. Refer to the Stanley and Winchester listings for further information on these brand names.

Club: The Early American Industries Assoc., 167 Bakersville Rd., South Dartmouth, MA 02748.

Adjustable Wrench, Crescent, 4" 65
Bicycle Wrench 15
Blow Torch, Montgomery Ward 85
Bow Saw, wooden frame, 27" h, 35" w 45
Bullet Mold, Winchester 65
Combination Square, Bates 45
Double Square, Starrett #13 , 4" 35
Draw Knife, Greenlee, adjustable, 10" 95
Edging Tool, Miles Craft 65
End Nipper, Acme, forged steel, 12" 55
Felling Axe, double-edged 5" w cutting edge 60
Fencing Pliers 40
File, Nicholson, wooden handle, 8" l 20
Folding Rule, 24" l .25
Gouge Chisel, Buck Brothers, tanged crank neck 35
Hack Saw, Sterling, iron cast, 8" 35
Hammer, round, brass, leather handle 50
Hand Drill, Yankee, multi-setting 40
Hatchet, with inset nail puller, 1914 50
Lock Joint Caliper, Starrett, inside transfer 45
Measuring Tape, Lufkin, metal, 100' 65
Micrometer, Starrett #2c, orig box, 1"-2" 70
Molding Plane, Union Warranted by Chapin Stephens Co 50
Monkey Wrench, mkd "Coes Wrench Co Worchester Mass.," 8" 95
Pipe Wrench, Erie Tool Works #8, angled 65
Plumb Bob, cast iron, 4.75" l, 1.75" d 15
Pruning Shears, Bernard 110
Rule, Lufkin #879, brass bound 95
Screwdriver, H Hitchcock, wood handle . .40
Screwdriver, solid handle, brass ferrule . .45
Spiral Hand Drill, Goodell-Pratt, nickel plated, orig box .50
Taps, Bay State, boxed set 50
Tinner's Snips, red handle, 7" 25
Try Square, Keen Kutter 45
Upholstery Tack Hammer, Fairmount #22 .50
Wood Block Plane, 26" l, 3.25" w 55
Wood Rasp, American File Co, 16" x 1.75" .20

TOOTHBRUSH HOLDERS

Forget your standard bathroom cup or mounted wall toothbrush holders. They have no pizzazz. No one collects them.

Collectors want the wonderful ceramic figural toothbrush holders from the 1930s through the 1960s. Images are generation-driven, from a 1920s bisque boy seated in a fence and holding an umbrella to a 1950s high-glazed seated elephant. Licensed characters from comic strips, children's literature, and cartoons, especially Disney, are plentiful. Prices for pre-1940 examples begin around $60 and extend into the hundreds.

If you find these vintage toothbrush holders pricey, consider modern plastic examples, many of which are found in the shapes of licensed characters from children's television shows and comics. Do not overlook figural electrical toothbrush sets. I already have several in my collection.

Big Bird, Sesame Street, bisque, 1970s, 4.5" h 55
Doc, from Snow White, porcelain, 1950s, 4.25" h 175
Dog, crouching, lusterware, mkd "Made In Japan," 1940s-50s, 3" h 85
Donald Duck, cold-painted bisque, mkd "©Walt Disney, Made in Japan," 1940s-50s, 5.125" h 450
Elephant, white, porcelain, mkd "Made In Japan," 1940s-50s, 5" h 175
Kayo, standing with hands in pockets, porcelain, mkd "©F.A.S., Kayo, Made in Japan," stands or hangs on wall, 1940s-50s, 5.125" h 155
Kitten, porcelain, lusterware, mkd "Made In Japan," 1940s-50s, 3.25" h 90
Little Orphan Annie and Sandy, #1565, cold-painted bisque, #1565, 1940s-50s, 4" h 145
Mickey and Minnie Mouse, #C100, cold-painted bisque, Japan, 4.5" h 250
Mickey Mouse, yawning, porcelain, 1960s, 4.75" h 135
Moon Mullins and Kayo, #S1563, cold-painted bisque, FAS, Japan, 1940s-50s, 4" h 135
Puppy, spotted, porcelain, mkd "Made in Japan," 1940s-50s, 6" h 175
Skippy, movable arm, 1940s-50s, 5.75" h .145
Three Little Pigs, #5217, cold-painted bisque, Japan, 1940s-50s, 4" h 250
Three Little Pigs, #5336, cold-painted bisque, Japan, 1940s-50s, 3.5" h 250
Three Little Pigs, hp porcelain, Goldcastle, Japan, 1940s-50s, 4" h 165
Uncle Willie, porcelain, mkd "© F.A.S. Uncle Willie, Made in Japan," 1940s-50s, 5.25" h 145
Westie Dog, porcelain, mkd "Goldcastle, Hand Painted," made in Japan, 1940s-50s, 6" h 155

TOOTHPICK HOLDERS

During the Victorian era, the toothpick holder was an important table accessory. It is found in a wide range of materials and was manufactured by American and European firms. Toothpick holders also were popular souvenirs in the 1880 to 1920 period.

Do not confuse toothpick holders with match holders, shot glasses, miniature spoon holders in a child's dish set, mustard pots without lids, rose or violet bowls, individual open salts, or vases. A toothpick holder allows ample room for the toothpick and enough of an extension of the toothpick to allow easy access.

Club: National Toothpick Holder Collectors Society, P.O. Box 417, Safety Harbor, FL 34695.

Ceramic, cornucopia, Occupied Japan, 2.5" h 5
Ceramic, cow, white with black spots, 2.25" h, 3" l 10
Ceramic, Figaro and Pinocchio standing next to basket holder, Japan, 5" h 10
Ceramic, horse pulling cart, Occupied Japan, 2.25" l 5
Ceramic, pig, pink, 2.5" h 8
Ceramic, Scottie dog, red, mkd "EW 224" and "WG" under crown mark, 2.5" h ...40
Glass, amber, Colonial pattern, Fenton 8
Glass, amberina, Daisy and Button pattern, ftd 95
Glass, amethyst carnival, emb cherries, scalloped rim, flat bottom, 2.25" h 25

Glass, clear, top hat shape, hobnail pattern, 2.25" h 12
Glass, frosted, goblet shape, swirled body, flattened rim, Lalique, 1950s, 2.875" h, 2.5" d 70
Glass, ruby flashed, clear base with pressed crosshatched star pattern, etched "Alma Anderson," c1905, 2.625" h, 2" d 20
Glass, vaseline, Panel pattern, Mosser, 2.5" h 12
Milk Glass, blue, urn shaped, beaded rim, mkd "NYC Vogue Merc Co USA 5," Akro Agate, 3.5" h, 3" d 12

TOYS

The difference between men and boys is the price of their toys. At thirty one's childhood is affordable, at forty expensive, and at fifty out of reach. Check the following list for toys that you may have played with. You will see what I mean.

Clubs: Diecast Toy Collectors Assoc., P.O. Box 1824, Bend, OR 97701; The Antique Toy Collectors of America, Inc., 2 Wall St., 13th Flr., New York, NY 10005; Toy Car Collectors Club, 33290 W. 14 Mile Rd. #454, West Bloomfield, MI 48322.

Note: *Maloney's Antiques & Collectibles Resource Directory* by David J. Maloney, Jr., lists many collectors' clubs for specific types of toys. Check your local library for the most recent edition.

All toys listed are in working order. Refer to Battery Operated Toys and specific toy types or manufacturers for additional listings.

Alps, Pat My Party Doll, keywind, orig box, 8.5" h 100
Amazon Industries, Bob Hope Golfer, radio control, MIB 45
Arcade, Airflow Auto, white rubber wheels mkd "Arcade," 6.25" l 300
Arcade, McCormick-Deering Plow, decal label, orig paint, 7" l 225
Arcade, Pullman Railplane Railroad Transport, labeled inside body, orig paint, 8.75" l 75
Buddy L, Bell Telephone Truck 110

Buddy L, Ford Station Wagon 100
Buddy L, Jewel Home Shopping Service Delivery Truck 200
Buddy L, Repair-It Unit 285
Buddy L, Sand and Gravel Dump Truck . . .85
Buddy L, Towing Service Truck 325
Chein, Chipper Chipmunk, #270, tin and plastic, keywind, orig box 95
Chein, Playing Piano, 3 rolls 180
Cragstan, School Bus, Cragstan, litho tin, battery operated, forward and reverse action, orig box, c1950s, 11.25" l 100
Cragstan, Two-Gun Sheriff, fabric, plastic, and tin, battery operated, body sways as sheriff shuffles sideways and moves his arms and mouth, gun noise, c1950s, 11" h 215
H, Japan, Pan American Airways Bus, litho tin, friction, c1960s, 8.5" l 95
Horikawa, Space Fighter Robot, tin and plastic, battery operated, chest doors open to reveal a gun with sound and light mechanisms, toy walks forward, body bounces up and down, late 1960s, 9.5" h 235
Hubley, Bell Telephone Truck, mkd inside, orig paint, 5.25" l 225
Hubley, Crash Car Motorcycle, with cart, orig paint, nickel wheels, 4.75" l 220
Hubley, Duck, worn orig paint, 9.5" l 110
Hubley, Dump Truck, worn orig paint, 6.75" l 160
Hubley, Grasshopper, decal label, worn orig paint, antenna loose, wheels possibly replaced, 11.5" l 358
Hubley, Motorcycle Cop, electric lamp with possible orig battery, worn orig paint, very worn rubber tires, 6.25" l 75
Hubley, Patrol Wagon, worn orig paint, 6.75" l 120
Hubley, Racer, with driver, labeled inside body, worn orig paint, 7" l 165
Hubley, Studebaker Roadster, nickel trim, mkd with patent date, worn orig paint, 6.5" l 330

Hubley, Water Tower Fire Truck, worn orig paint, 10.75" l with tower 110
Japan, BOAC Jeep, tin, friction, c1960s, 6" l 65
Japan, F-9 Fire Engine, litho tin and plastic, friction, ladder extends, siren noise, orig box, c1970, 10.25" l 125
Japan, Ford Fairlane, litho tin, clockwork, c1970, 7" l 65
Japan, Greyhound Scenicruiser Bus, tin, friction, c1960s, 11" l 75
Japan, Horse and Jockey, litho tin, friction, galloping motion, c1960, 4.5" l 55
Japan, Mercedes Benz 250SE, tin, clockwork, orig box, c1970, 7" l 80
Japan, Mother Goose, tin, key-wind, goose moves forward and turns right, lowers head and turns it from side to side, c1960, 7" l 120
Japan, Speedboat, wood, battery operated, complete with deck fittings, working light on bow, and wooden stand, c1950, 13.5" l 145
Japan, Submarine #571, tin, battery operated, light on bow, 2 periscopes can be raised and lowered, deck gun lifts off to reveal battery compartment, c1960s, 13" l 180
Kaymar, Japan, JFK and Rocking Chair, mechanical musical movement, c1963, MIB 210
Kenkosha Toys, Occupied Japan, Lucky Sledge, boy on sled, plastic and metal, keywind, orig box, 4.5" 100
Kenton, Beer Wagon, with 2 horses and driver, worn orig paint, 15" l 415
Kenton, Hansom Cab, with horse, driver, and passenger, orig paint, 16" l 195
Kenton, Jaeger Cement Mixer, 7.5" l 275
Kenton, Overland Circus Wagon, with 2 horses with outriders, driver, and 6 musicians, worn original paint, 16" l .415
Kenton, Road Grader, labeled "Kenton Toys, Kenton, Ohio," worn old paint, very worn white rubber tires, 6" l 94
KO, Japan, Atom Robot, tin, hand-cranked friction motor, bump-and-go action, c1950s, 6.5" h 475
Marusan, Tugboat, litho tin, battery operated, moves through water, puffs smoke from funnel, engine noise, orig box, c1960, 13" l 185
Model Toys, Grain Elevator Scoop, green 160
Modern Toys, Japan, Mother Bear, fabric-cov tin, battery operated, eyes light up as mother bear rocks in rocker, knits with both hands, and moves her head back and forth, orig box, c1950s, 9.5" h 225
Northwestern Products, Knockout Electronic Boxing Game, #777 95
Occupied Japan, Cowboy on Horse, clockwork, tin horse, celluloid cowboy, 1945-52, 6" h 110
Smith Miller, 1947 Chevy Truck with Flatbed, #109, metal and wood, 23" l . . .360
Smith Miller, 1949 GMC Bank of America Truck, #1325, metal, Bank of America California's Statewide Bank decals on sides, 14" l 465
Smith Miller, 1949 Materials Truck, #1325, metal cab with wood bed, decals on door, wooden barrels and logs in bed, 14.25" l 300
Smith Miller, 1949 Silver Streak, #109, metal and wood, 23" l 225
Smith Miller, Dump Truck, #109, metal, red, crank-up, 11.75" l 415
TM, Japan, Broadway Trolley, tin, battery operated, bump-and-go action, bell rings, c1960, 12" l 110
TM, Japan, Mercedes Race Car, tin, battery operated, c1950s, 11" l 135
TN, Japan, Louis Armstrong, playing trumpet, rubber, tin, and plastic, keywind, 10" h 150
Toymaster, Japan, Concrete Mixer Truck, tin, friction, mixer spins as truck moves, lever tilts mixer, c1960, 8.5" l 100
TPS, Japan, Climbing Linesman, battery operated, MIB 450

US Zone, Germany, Fisherman, tin, keywind, orig box 45
US Zone, Germany, Turkey, litho tin, keywind 90
West Germany, Spring Powered Airplanes Circling Globe, litho tin 50
Yonezawa, Japan, Emergency Space Rocket, clockwork, tin police rocket, driver with vinyl head, orig box, c1970, 6" l 150
Yonezawa, Japan, Rolls Royce Silver Cloud, tin, friction, c1960, 9" l 175

TOY TRAINS

Toy train collectors and dealers exist in a world unto themselves. They have their own shows, trade publications, and price guides. The name you need to know is Greenberg Books, now a division of Kalmbach publishing, 21027 Crossroads Circle, Waukesha, WI 53187. If you decide to get involved with toy trains, write for a catalog. The two most recognized names are American Flyer and Lionel, and the two most popular gauges are S and O. Do not overlook other manufacturers and gauges.

The toy train market has gone through a number of crazes—first Lionel, then American Flyer. The current craze is boxed sets. Fortunately, the market is so broad that there will never be an end to subcategories to collect.

Clubs: American Flyer Collectors Club, P.O. Box 13269, Pittsburgh, PA 15243; Lionel Collector's Club of America, P.O. Box 479, La Salle, IL 61301; Train Collectors Assoc., P.O. Box 248, Strasburg, PA 17579.

Note: See the most recent edition of *Maloney's Antiques & Collectibles Resource Directory* by David J. Maloney, Jr., for additional information on other specialized train collector clubs.

American Flyer, Caboose, #930 25
American Flyer, Caboose, #938, 1955-56 ..15
American Flyer, Cattle Car, #929, S gauge, orig box 55
American Flyer, Cement Car, #924, S gauge, orig box 28
American Flyer, Coach Car, #975, animated, S gauge, red, orig box, 1955 ...100
American Flyer, Engine, Silver Streak ...100
American Flyer, Freight Set, #21100 steam engine with tender, #925 Gulf tank car, #805 gondola with 2 cylinders, #637 MKT box car, #807 Rio Grande box car with solid doors, #806 caboose 60
American Flyer, Girder Flat Car, C&NW RY #42597 25
American Flyer, Gondola, Texas & Pacific #931 20
American Flyer, Gulf Tanker, #24325, split tank 55
American Flyer, Hopper Car, #640, gray ...18
American Flyer, Hopper Car, CB&Q #921 ..45
American Flyer, Hopper Car, Pennsylvania #4-9205, orig box 45
American Flyer, Industrial Crane Car, #944 90
American Flyer, Operating Tie Ejector Car, #25071, with 2 track trips and 4 ties 80
American Flyer, Passenger Car, New Haven #650, lighted int 60
American Flyer, Silver Bullet Set, #356, 2-car set 65
American Flyer, Train Set, #303 steam engine and tender, #919 automatic dump car with controller, #942 Seaboard Silver Meteor box car, #938 caboose 125
American Flyer, Wrecking Crane Car, #24561 45
Lionel, Armour Stock Car, 3656, pen, 9 cattle, orange gates, no ramp, orig boxes 75
Lionel, B&A 4-6-4 Hudson Steam Locomotive and Tender, 8606, orig box 600
Lionel, B&O Budd RDC Passenger motorized unit, 400, orig box 190
Lionel, B&O Sentinel Boxcar, 6464-325, light blue and gray, orig box 325
Lionel, Caboose, 817, peacock and green .65
Lionel, Caboose, 2817, red, truck side frames painted black 50
Lionel, Carnation Milk Car, 19802, orig box 65
Lionel, Crane Car, 810, yellow cab, red roof, green boom 225
Lionel, Diner, 442 140
Lionel, Executive Inspection Car, 68 250

Lionel, Fire Car, 52, orig box 240
Lionel, Flatcar, 811, with reproduction lumber load, silver 55
Lionel, Flatcar, 3811, with log load 75
Lionel, Flood Light Car, 2820, light green, nickel lights 185
Lionel, GN Snow Blower, 58 350
Lionel, Gondola, 812, light green, 4 barrels 65
Lionel, Hopper, 2816, red 140
Lionel, Lionel Jr Passenger Set, 1700E diesel, 1701 coach, and 1702 observation, red and chrome, fluted roofs 130
Lionel, Locomotive and Tender, 2-6-2, 2026 locomotive, 6466W tender 55
Lionel, Locomotive and Tender, 4-6-4, 2065 locomotive, 6026W tender 110
Lionel, Merchandise Boxcar, 3814, brown 200
Lionel, Minuteman Locomotive, 59, orig box 350
Lionel, NYC Commodore Vanderbilt Locomotive and Tender, 18045, orig box 715
Lionel, Operating Burro Crane, 18402, orig box 75
Lionel, PRR Fire Car, 8378, tuscan, orig box 55
Lionel, Rio Grande Snow Blower, 8459, orig box 100
Lionel, Shell Tank Car, 2815, orange 150
Lionel, Side Dump Hopper, 5859, red tray, black base 65
Lionel, Sunoco Tank Car, 2815, silver 140
Lionel, Tank Car, 815, green with black base 85
Lionel, The Phantom, 18860, orig box with display case 275
Lionel, Train Set, #253 engine, 2 #607 Pullman cars, 608 observation car, #81 controlling Rheostat, O gauge track, orig box 850
Lionel, Traveling Aquarium Car, 3435, gold lettering, orig box 225

Lionel, Wanamaker RR Boxcar, 9466, orig box 45
Lionel, WP Boxcar, 6464-250, orange with blue feather, orig box 145

TRADING STAMPS & RELATED

Trading stamps were offered by retail stores to attract customers and increase sales. The more money spent, the more stamps you could earn. The stamps could be redeemed for merchandise, either from the store that issued the stamps or from redemption centers that offered catalog merchandise. The first independent trading stamp company was set up in 1896. The use of trading stamps has declined, but some companies still give them out to stimulate sales.

Redemption Brochure, S&H Green Stamps, Summer 1948 16
Redemption Catalog, Blue Chip Stamps, 1972 9
Redemption Catalog, Club Plan, 1950s 13
Redemption Catalog, EF MacDonald Plaid Stamps, 1967 8
Redemption Catalog, Gold Arrow Premium Stamps, 1950s 5
Redemption Catalog, Gunn Brothers Stamps, 1960s 5
Redemption Catalog, S&H Green Stamps, 1956 20
Redemption Catalog, S&H Green Stamps, 1978 9
Redemption Catalog, S&H Green Stamps, 1985 6
Redemption Catalog, Top Value Stamps, 1966 5
Redemption Catalog, World Green Stamps, 1957 5
Sign, Family Stamps, electric, plastic, light-up 32
Sign, Top Value Stamps, Kinduell Screen Products, KY, 1967, 47" h, 29" w 8
Stamp Saver Books, including Big Dollar Stamps, Family Stamps, Gift House Stamps, Gold Bond Stamps, King Korn Stamps, Plaid Stamps, S&H Green Stamps, and Top Value Stamps, mostly filled, 33 books 26

Stamp Saver Box, litho tin, rooster image, 7" h, 4.25" w 9

Stamp Saver Box/Shopping List, litho tin, fruit images on white ground, 14.625" h, 5" w 17

TRAMP ART

Tramp art refers to items made by itinerant artists, most of whom are unknown, who made objects out of old cigar boxes or fruit and vegetable crates. Edges of pieces are often chip-carved and layered. When an object was completed, it was often stained.

Box, hinged lid formed as a handle, painted red, 6.5" h, 14.5" w, 8" d 260

Cabinet, hanging, shaped crest above 2 pierced doors, each depicting a standing figure, 19" h, 11.5" w, 5" d 175

Chest of Drawers, miniature, rect framed mirror plate above a rect case with 2 stepped drawers over 3 long drawers, 13" h, 9" w, 5.5" d 350

Chest of Drawers, miniature, rect mirror in a shaped frame above 3 small drawers flanked by 2 narrow cabinet doors, over 1 long drawer, raised on shaped skirt and feet, set with layered diamond bosses, 29" h, 18" w, 7" d 350

Doll's Chair, puzzlework, arched crest incised with foliage, 14.5" h 350

Match Safe, double star-shaped back with a container for matches, above a grater for lighting, applied label on back sgd "Philip Weingard 1904," 11" h, 7" w, 2.5" d .690

Medicine Cabinet, mirrored door above drawer, sides with glass and foil panels, lower panel with a glass and foil panel mkd "Medicine Case," 22.5" h, 15.5" w, 9.5" d 460

Mirror, 3-part, center rect frame with circ corner bosses, flanked by 2 similar smaller frames, 15" h, 26.5" w 260

Mirror, Crown of Thorns, diamond-shaped frame with outset corners, 19" h, 19" w, 4" d 175

Mirror, rect frame composed of stacked, scalloped layers, painted orange, pink, red, yellow, and green, 25.5" h, 15" w, 5.5" d 460

Mirror, rect frame with outset leaf-shaped corners and layered geometric carving, 12" h, 16.5" w 175

Mirror, shaped rect frame with outset round corners applied with gold stars, gold-painted details, 24" h, 29" w 1,500

Umbrella Stand, 4 short drawers flanked by 2 compartments for umbrellas, angled skirt, raised on angled feet, painted, 26.5" h, 30" w, 9.5" d 635

Vase, Crown of Thorns, rect form, raised on sq base, 13" h, 6.5" w, 6.5" d 175

Wall Bracket, in the shape of a butterfly, painted, 14" h, 21" w, 4.5" d 115

Wall Pocket, arched back set with a star, pocket set with a heart, 8" h, 4.5" w, 2.5" d 430

Wall Pocket, arched crest above 2 pockets, painted red, tan, black, cream, and orange, 17" h, 9.5" w 175

Wall Pocket, diamond-shaped, pointed crest above a latticework back, single shelf and pocket, applied stars and hearts, painted blue, white, red, green, and brown 490

TRAPS

Although trapping is not a well thought-of occupation this day and age, we must admit the American trappers of bygone days were the men who opened the West and after whom many towns are named. Trap collecting today is a growing hobby and condition means everything on those old traps. A rusty old Victor trap has very little value, yet please don't sandblast or paint traps that you plan to sell. Let the buyer decide how he wants to clean it. Value is determined by the maker of the trap, condition, and readability of lettering on the pan (where the animal places its foot).

Trap collecting encompasses mouse and rat traps, glass fly and minnow traps, and steel traps from small to large bear traps, as well as paper ephemera such as fur company catalogs and trapping magazines.

Club: North American Trap Collectors Assoc., P.O. Box 94, Galloway, OH 43119.

Blake and Lamb, #21, small game, steel . . 15
Nash, mole trap, 7" x 9" 28
Oneida Victor, rabbit trap 20
Small Game Leg Traps, 1940s, set of 20 . . . 60
Triumph Ranger, #42, double long iron spring trap, 18.5" l 130
US Government Animal Trap, Standard #3 65
Victor, mouse trap, 2 traps, orig box 20
Victor, small animal trap, 8" l, 14" chain and ring 15
Wild Bird Trap, wood, painted forest green, catches 10 birds with 1 setting . 225

TRAYS

Tin lithographed advertising trays date back to the last quarter of the 19th century. They were popular at any location where beverages, alcoholic and nonalcoholic, were served.

Kitschy serving trays from the 1950s, '60s, and '70s have also become popular with collectors.

Abalone Shells, surrounded by black resin, chrome arrow handles, 12.5" x 12.5" 24
Advertising, Barbey's Sunshine Beer, blue and gold, 12" d 55
Advertising, Coors Beer, red, white, and gold, 13" d 8
Advertising, Coors Beer, yellow, white, and black, 1994, 13" d 15
Advertising, Duquesne Brewing Silver Top Beer, red, white, and green, 13" d . . 12
Advertising, Hires Root Beer, orange and yellow parrot on green ground, 14" x 9" 30
Advertising, Hornung Beer, Jacob Hornung Brewing, Phildelphia, PA, early 1950s, 12" d 65
Advertising, Iroquois Indian Head Beer and Ale, red, black, and white, 12" d . . . 70
Advertising, Kaiser's, "We Serve Kaiser's Star of Excellence Beer," red, white, and black, 12" d 25
Advertising, O'Keefe's Old Vienna Beer, Extra Old Stock Ale, 4.75" d 35
Advertising, Olympia Beer, oval, 1981, 15" x 12.5" 15
Advertising, Piel's Beer, 1940s-50s 40
Advertising, Royal Wrexham Border Barley Wine Beer, black, gold, and red, 10.5" d 20
Advertising, Satin Cigarettes, 14" d 10
Advertising, Schlitz Beer, "The Beer That Made Milwaukee Famous," 12.5" d 4
Advertising, Schmidt's Brewing, gold, red, and white, 13" d 5
Advertising, Schmidts of Philadelphia Light Beer, red, white, gold, and black, 13" d 10
Advertising, Scottish and Newcastle Breweries Ltd, "The Best Beers," blue, tan, and red, 12.5" d 25
Advertising, Valley Forge Beer, Washington and his men raising flag at headquarters, 12" d 36
Fabcraft, Rococo prints, 8.25" d, set of 4 . . 15
Fred Press, gray and black squares with gold leaf galloping horse weather vane in center, 19" x 19" 60

Fred Press, gray, black, and gold leaf diamonds with gold leaf rooster perched on sphere, 19.5" x 25" 60
Steiff, pewter and fiberglass with hp steeplechase rider jumping a fence, 14" x 14" 35
Toleware, metal, hp yellow roses on black ground, 7.75" d, set of 3 35
Trout Trays, wooden with trout design, 18.75" l, 12.75" w, set of 3 50

TROPHIES

There are trophies for virtually everything. Ever wonder what happens to them when the receiver grows up or dies? Most wind up in landfills. It is time to do something about this injustice. If you plan on collecting them, focus on shape and unusual nature of the award. Set a $5 limit—not much of a handicap when it comes to trophy collecting. Always check the metal content of trophies. A number of turn-of-the-century trophies are sterling silver. These obviously have monetary as well as historic value. Also consider sterling silver when the trophy is a plate.

Bowl, handled, pedestal base, mkd "Trophy-Craft Co, Los Angeles," early 1900s, 4" w, 3.75" h 10
Bowling, bowling ball and 3 engraved silver plaques, 1940-1947 45
Dog Show, Best Breed at Perth County Kennel Club, Canada, 1964, 5.5" h 18
Golf, Birmingham 1936, silver, British hallmarks, 3" h, 5" w 125
Golf, Calcutta Ladies Golf Club, SS, Indian hallmarks, 1938 235
Horse Breeding, SP hand-forged horseshoe, awarded to carriage horse, 5.5" w 50
Marksmanship, Plainfield Shooting Association of New York, SS, 8.5" h, 7.25" w 185
Occupational, Master Plumbers of US, 1915 Convention, SP, for most attractive exhibit 165
Tankard, inscribed "Presented to The Winning Owner Of The 1964 Melbourne Cup With Congratulations From Capers Restaurant" 100
Tennis, Bastrop Boys, "Smithville 1938-1939" engraved on front, "Elgin 1937, Bastrop 1938-1940" on back, 7" h 25

TUPPERWARE

Clean out those kitchen cabinets—Tupperware has found its niche in the secondary market!

Bar Set, ice bucket, tray, and 4 glasses, black 25
Bowls, orange and yellow, set of 3 18
Cake Carrier 15
Cake Taker, rect, white, 9.5" x 13" 22
Canister Set, flour, sugar, and tea, sky blue 25
Condiment Caddy, 8-pc set 20
Cookie Cutters, red, set of 5 6
Cream and Syrup Dispensers, hourglass shape, ivory and harvest gold, 7" h 15
Creamer and Sugar, flip lids, gold 14
Deviled Egg Carrier, ivory-colored tray, 2 white removable egg trays, and lid, holds 16 eggs 15
Figurine, Tupperware Lady, 7.75" h 65
Floral Arranger, Floralier, multiple levels . .16
Hamburger Keepers, set of 5 12
Ice Tea Spoons, pastel colors, 12" l 10
Jello Mold, green, 9.5" w, 3 pcs 15
Keeper, red, 1970s, 8.75" sq 5
Lettuce Crisper, light green 15
Mustard and Ketchup Dispensers, yellow and red with white pumps, 6" h .12
Pickle Keeper, avocado green 10
Pie Saver, divided, 6 triangular sections, 12.75" d 14
Salad Tongs, jadeite green, orig box, 1958 100
Salt and Pepper Shakers, hourglass shape, clear with white lids 14
Snack Trays, orange, yellow, and red, set of 6 12
Spice Containers, stackable, green, orange, brown, and yellow, set of 4 18
Stacking Cooking System, white, 3 qt, 9" d, 4" deep 30
Stacking Set, white, 13 pcs 15
Travel Condiment Set, gold and cream colored, 3 cov bowls and handled carrier 12
Wagon Wheel Coasters, blue, pink, green, peach, and yellow, 3" d, set of 6 18

TURTLE COLLECTIBLES

Turtle collectors are a slow and steady group who are patient about expanding their collection of objects relating to these funny little reptiles. Don't you believe it! My son is one of those collectors, and he's not at all slow when it comes to expanding his collection. Turtle collectibles are everywhere. Like all animal collectibles, they come in all shapes and sizes. Candles, toys, storybooks, jewelry, and ornaments featuring turtles can be found at almost any flea market. Watch out for tortoise shell items. This material is subject to the provisions of the Federal Endangered Species Act.

Bank, 6.5" l 22
Brooch, gold tone, pearl body surrounded by clear rhinestones, red rhinestone eyes, 1" x 1.5" 18
Brooch, purple and emerald enamel on goldtone, clear rhinestones accenting shell, 2.25" l 25
Coasters, yellow turtles with orange "Flower Power" inside, plastic, 5" l, set of 4 7
Cookie Jar, brown glaze with red, green, and yellow butterfly on top, McCoy 35
Dish, cov, green, 5" d 45
Dish, porcelain, pink and blue floral dec, 6.25" l, 3.25" h 70
Earrings, screwback, silver with blue stone shell, .75" l, .5" w 25
Earrings, SS, amethyst stone in middle, .5" x 1" 22
Fetish, turquoise, 4" l, 2.25" w 150
Figurine, Shawnee, 3.5" l, 1.5" h 30
Lamp, electric, glass and metal, 8.25" l, 4" h 45
Nodder, 3.5" l 25
Pendant, fuschia marbelized body, green rhinestone eyes, gold based alloy setting, 2.25" l, 2" w 35
Pendant, silvertone, 22 stones on back, 1.5" 25
Perfume Compact, goldtone, 1.75" l 25
Pie Bird, brown turtle sitting on black and blue stump, 4" h 55
Pin, clear rhinestones, green rhinestone eyes, 2" l 40
Pin, gold and black enamel, 1.5" x 1.25" . . .16
Pin, gold foil cabuchon back, gold plated, 1.5" l, 1" w 28
Pin, metal, green rhinestones on back, clear rhinestone eyes, 1930s 35
Pincushion, Lefton, 3" x 2" x 2.75" 18
Pincushion, nodder, metal and velvet, pink velvet back, pink rhinestone eyes, 3.25" l 28
Ring, SS, adjustable .15
Trinket Box, 6.5" l, 5" w, 1.75" h 35
Trinket Dish, souvenir of "Kirks Folly Turtle Island," gold finish, 3" x 1.25" 80
Watch Pendant, utopia quartz 65

TV LAMPS

What 1950s living room would be complete without a black ceramic gondola slowly drifting across the top of the television set? Long before the arrival of VCRs, Home Box, and Nintendo systems, figural lamps dominated the tops of televisions. The lamps were made of colorful high gloss ceramics and the subject matter ranged from the relatively mundane dog statue to the more exotic (tasteless?) hula dancer.

A collection of ten or more of these beauties will certainly lighten up the conversation at your next party. On second thought, it does not take ten. The pink poodle lamp on my TV is more than adequate.

Eland on Rocks, Art Deco, 9" h, 11" l 100
Gazelle, chalkware, red, brown and gold, c1950s 65

Horse, mkd "Lane & Co, ©1959 CALIF USA" .75
Horse Head, black, 13" h .65
Inverted Cone, simulated woodgrain finish, 8.25" h .20
Masks, Comedy and Tragedy, pale green with brown wash and gold highlights, Hedi Schoop, 12" h, 11.5" w .400
Mallard Duck, 10" h .50
Owl, mkd "Kron, Texas Inc B Bangs Texas," 10.5" h .145
Panther, emb on curved green panel, 8" h, 5" w .50
Pillar, chartreuse with gold trim, mkd "Kirkwood, Calif," 10" h .90
Planter Base, green and white drip glaze, 7.5" h, 10" w .35
Planter Base, mottled green with plastic ivy, inverted white cone shade, Cookson Pottery, Roseville, OH, 13" h .35
Stylized Rooster, glossy white with gold highlights, 11" h .150
Two Puppies, black cocker spaniels, c1950, 8" h .45

TYPEWRITERS

The number of typewriter collectors is small, but growing. Machines made after 1915 have little value, largely because they do not interest collectors. Do not use the patent date on a machine to date its manufacture. Many models were produced for decades. Do not overlook typewriter ephemera. Early catalogs are helpful in identifying and dating machines.

Clubs: Early Typewriter Collectors Assoc., P.O. Box 641824, Los Angeles, CA 90064; Internationales Forum Historishe Burowelt, Postfach 500 11 68, D-5000 Koln-50, Germany.

Blickensderfer No. 5, 1893 .325
Blickensderfer No. 7, 1897 .300
Corona Folding No. 3, 1912 .90
Densmore No. 4, 1898 .365
Empire, 1892 .200
Erika Folding, 1910 .35
Hammond Multiplex, 1913 .365
Hammond No. 12, 1893 .265
Harris Visible No. 4, c1913 .315
Imperial Model B, 1908 .250

Imperial Model B, 1914 .365
Imperial Model D, 1919 .215
International Electromatic, IBM, 1930 .120
LC Smith & Bros, 1904 .60
Mignon Model 2, 1905 .325
Monarch Pioneer, 1932 .100
National No. 5, c1920 .230
Rem-Blick, 1928 .325
Remie Scout, 1932 .200
Remington Monarch No. 3, 1906 .280
Remington No. 6, 1894 .365
Remington Noiseless No. 6, 1925 .130
Remington Standard No. 8, 1897 .120
Royal Model 1, 1906 .230
Smith Premier No. 1, 1889 .600
Smith Premier No. 10, 1907 .50
Underwood No. 4, 1900 .365
Woodstock, 1914 .45
Yost No. 1, 1887 .425

UMBRELLAS

Umbrellas suffer a sorry fate. They are generally forgotten and discarded. Their handles are removed and collected as separate entities or attached to magnifying glasses. Given the protection they have provided, they deserve better.

Look for umbrellas that have advertising on the fabric. Political candidates often gave away umbrellas to win votes. Today baseball teams have umbrella days to win fans.

Seek out unusual umbrellas in terms of action or shape. A collection of folding umbrellas, especially those from the 1950s, is worth considering.

Advertising, *The Morning Call,* Allentown, PA, newspaper, comic strip characters, unused .25
Beach .5
Davy Crockett, vinyl .85
Golf, metal shaft .3
Man's, black cloth, figural golf club handle .45
New York World's Fair, 1939, child's, multicolored, 28" d .40
Plastic, dome shaped, clear, 1960-70s .20
Silk, plastic handle .5

UNIVERSAL POTTERY

Universal Potteries of Cambridge, Ohio, was organized in 1934 by The Oxford Pottery Company.

Three of Universal's most popular lines were Ballerina, Calico Fruit, and Cattail. Unfortunately, the Calico Fruit decal has not held up well over time. Collectors may have to settle for less than perfect pieces.

Not all Universal pottery carried the Universal name as part of the backstamp. Wares marked "Harmony House," "Sweet William/Sears Roebuck and Co.," and "Wheelock Peoria" are part of the Universal production line. Wheelock was a department store in Peoria, Illinois, that controlled the Cattail pattern on the Old Holland shape.

Ballerina, bowl, 3.25" h, 9.25" w .20
Ballerina, creamer .10
Ballerina, cup and saucer .10

Ballerina, dinner plate .10
Ballerina, leftover, cov .40
Ballerina, lug bowl, 6.5" d .12
Ballerina, lug platter .20
Ballerina, Moss Rose, cup and saucer .15
Ballerina, sugar bowl, cov, 6.5" w .8
Ballerina, vegetable bowl .12
Ballerina Fruit, saucer .15
Ballerina Woodvine, cup and saucer .10
Ballerina Woodvine, dessert plate .6
Ballerina Woodvine, mixing bowl, 9.75" d .30
Ballerina Woodvine, salt and pepper shakers .16
Ballerina Woodvine, soup bowl .10
Bittersweet, casserole, cov, 8.5" d .42
Bittersweet, mixing bowls, set of 3 .35
Calico Fruit, jug, cov, 6.5" h .50
Calico Fruit, platter, oval .30
Cambridge, custard cup, 2.5" h .16
Cambridge, pitcher, cov, 6.75" h .100
Camwood Ivory, dinner plate, 10" d .15
Camwood Ivory, lug platter .12
Cattail, casserole, cov .50
Cattail, grill plates, set of 4 .75
Cattail, kitchen scale .55
Cattail, leftover lid, 6" d .20
Cattail, milk pitcher, 6" h .25
Cattail, pitcher .30
Cattail, platter, handled, 13.25" d .15
Cattail, serving bowl, handled .20
Cattail, teapot .50
Wood-Hyacinth, bread and butter plate .8
Wood-Hyacinth, cup and saucer .10
Wood-Hyacinth, dinner plate .12
Wood-Hyacinth, platter .18

URINALS

When you gotta go, you gotta go—any port in a storm. You have been in enough bathrooms to know that all plumbing fixtures are not equal.

The human mind has just begun to explore the recycling potential of hospital bedpans. Among the uses noted are flower planters, food serving utensils, and dispersal units at the bottom of down spouts. How have you used them? Send your ideas and pictures of them in action to the Bedpan Recycling Project, 5093 Vera Cruz Road, Emmaus, PA 18049.

U.S. GLASS

United States Glass resulted from the merger of eighteen different glass companies in 1891. The company's headquarters were in Pittsburgh, Pennsylvania. Plants were scattered throughout Indiana, Ohio, Pennslvania, and West Virginia.

Aunt Polly, berry bowl, blue, 4.75" d 18
Aunt Polly, bowl, 2 handles, blue, 7.25" d . .50
Aunt Polly, bowl, blue, 7.75" d 60
Aunt Polly, bowl, oval, blue, 8.25" l 150
Aunt Polly, butter, cov, blue 230
Aunt Polly, creamer, blue 55
Aunt Polly, pitcher, blue 275
Aunt Polly, sherbet plate, blue, 6" d 15
Aunt Polly, sugar, cov, blue 250
Aunt Polly, tumbler, blue 40
Aunt Polly, vase, blue 60
Cherryberry, bowl, green, 7.5" d 32
Cherryberry, bowl, pink, 4" d 12
Cherryberry, bowl, pink, 7.5" d 17
Cherryberry, sherbet, ftd, green 10
Primo/Paneled Aster, bowl, yellow, 4.5" d .18
Primo/Paneled Aster, cake plate, green . .30
Primo/Paneled Aster, creamer, yellow 16
Primo/Paneled Aster, cup, yellow 12
Primo/Paneled Aster, plate, yellow, 7.5" d .10
Primo/Paneled Aster, saucer, green 4
Strawberry, berry bowl, green, 4" d 15
Strawberry, butter, cov, green 225
Strawberry, comport, pink, 5.75" d 25
Strawberry, pitcher, pink, 7.75" h 225
Strawberry, sherbet, ftd, green 10
Strawberry, sugar lid, pink 80

VALENTINES

There is far too much emphasis placed on adult valentines from the 19th century through the 1930s. It's true they are lacy and loaded with romantic sentiment. But, are they fun? No!

Fun can be found in children's valentines, a much-neglected segment of the valentine market. Focus on the 1920 through 1960 period penny valentines. The artwork is bold, vibrant, exciting, and a tad corny. This is what makes them fun.

There is another good reason to collect 20th century children's valentines. They are affordable. Most sell for less than $2, with many good examples in the 50¢ range. They often show up at flea markets as a hoard. When you find them, make an offer for the whole lot. You won't regret it.

Club: National Valentine Collectors Assoc., P.O. Box 1404, Santa Ana, CA 92702.

Valentine, heart character knocking on door, knock-knock jokes, American Greetings 3
Valentine, mechanical, "With a heart full of love" on heart behind fold-down dove, "Greetings to my Valentine" below 10
Valentine, standup, little girl wearing pink dress and slippers and green bonnet with pink bow and roses around brim, "To My Valentine," 7" x 6.5" 15

VERNON KILNS

Founded in Vernon, California, in 1912, Poxon China was one of the many small potteries flourishing in southern California. By 1931 it was sold to Faye G. Bennison and renamed Vernon Kilns.

The high quality and versatility of its product made Vernon ware very popular. Besides a varied dinnerware line, Vernon Kilns also produced Walt Disney figurines and advertising, political, and fraternal items. Another popular line was historical and commemorative plates, which included several plate series featuring scenes from England, California missions, and the West.

Surviving the Depression, fires, earthquakes, and wars, Vernon Kilns could not compete with the influx of imports. In January, 1958, the factory was closed. Metlox Potteries of Manhattan Beach, California, bought the trade name, molds, and remaining stock.

Brown Eyed Susan, jumbo cup 45
Brown Eyed Susan, vegetable bowl, cov, 11" x 5.5" 45

Calico, casserole, tab handled, 4" w 50
Gingham, flowerpot saucer, 3" d 50
Gingham, mixing bowl, 8" d 45
Gingham, teapot 30
Homespun, dinner plate, 10.5" d 15
Homespun, salad bowl, 5.25" d 20
Homespun, tidbit, 2-tier 40
Organdie Plaid, butter, cov, rect 20
Organdie Plaid, casserole, 2-handled 40
Organdie Plaid, chop plate, 12" d 24
Organdie Plaid, creamer, round 12
Organdie Plaid, demitasse cup and saucer 25
Organdie Plaid, dinner plate, 9.5" d 7
Organdie Plaid, gravy boat 20
Organdie Plaid, mug, straight-sided 26
Organdie Plaid, pitcher, streamline, 2 qt ..45
Organdie Plaid, salad plate, 7" d 5
Organdie Plaid, salt and pepper shakers .18
Organdie Plaid, sugar lid 6
Organdie Plaid, teacup and saucer 7
Souvenir Plate, Albuquerque 18
Tickled Pink, chop plate, 13" d 30
Tickled Pink, vegetable bowl, 9" d 18
Tickled Pink, vegetable bowl, divided 55

VIDEO GAMES

At the moment, most video games sold at a flea market are being purchased for reuse. There are a few collectors, but their numbers are small.

It might be interesting to speculate at this point on the long-term collecting potential of electronic children's games, especially since the Atari system has come and gone. The key to any toy is playability. A video game cartridge has little collecting value unless it can be played. As a result, the long-term value of video games will rest on collectors' ability to keep the machines that use them in running order. Given today's tendency to scrap rather than repair a malfunctioning machine, one wonders if there will be any individuals in 2041 that will understand how video game machines work and, if so, be able to get the parts required to play them.

Next to playability, displayability is important to any collector. How do you display video games? Is the answer to leave the TV screen on twenty-four hours a day?

Video games are a fad waiting to be replaced by the next fad. There will always be a small cadre of players who will keep video games alive, just as there is a devoted group of adventure game players. But given the number of video game cartridges sold, they should be able to fill their collecting urges relatively easily.

What this means is that if you are going to buy video game cartridges at a flea market, buy them for reuse and do not pay more than a few dollars. The more recent the game, the more you will pay. Wait. Once a few years have passed, the sellers will just be glad to get rid of them.

VIEW-MASTER

William Gruber invented and Sawyer's Inc., of Portland, Oregon, manufactured and marketed the first View-Master viewers and reels in 1939. The company survived the shortages of World War II by supplying training materials in the View-Master format to the army and navy.

Immediately following World War II a 1,000-dealer network taxed the capacity of the Sawyer plant. In 1946 the Model C, the most common of the viewers, was introduced. Sawyer was purchased by General Aniline & Film Corporation in 1966. After passing through other hands, View-Master wound up as part of Ideal Toys.

Do not settle for any viewer or reel in less than near-mint condition. Original packaging, especially reel envelopes, is very important. The category is still in the process of defining which reels are valuable and which are not. Most older, pre-1975, reels sell in the 50¢ to $1 range.

Club: National Stereoscopic Assoc., P.O. Box 14801, Columbus, OH 43214.

Reel, #400, President Eisenhower 35
Reel, Glacier IV, Saddle Party on Piegan Pass Trail, Grinnell Glacier, Crossley Lake Camp, Sperry Glacier 4
Reel, Hot Springs National Park, Arkansas, Hot Springs, Spring Blossoms, Famous Bath House Row, DeSoto Room 4
Reel, Island of Hawaii 3
Reel, Mesa Verde Colorado 5
Reel, Montreal, Quebec, Canada, City of Mt Royal, St Joseph's Shrine, Beaver Lake, Montreal Cathedral, University of Montreal, Chateau de Ramezay 4
Reel, Northern Maine, typical Northern Maine country, Moosehead Lake, Logging Boom Piers in Kennebec River, Potato Field in Bloom, Potato House by St John River, Field of Flowers in Aroostook 10
Reel, Oklahoma Sooner State, State Capitol at Oklahoma City, Pensacola Dam, Rock Creek in Platte National Park, Turner Falls, Birthplace of Will Rogers, Will Roger's Tomb and Memorial, Civic Center 5
Reel, Rockefeller Center 10
Reel, San Juan Capistrano, the Patio, Old Arch and Gardens, Ruins of the Old Stone Church, Altar in Serra Chapel, Front Corridor, Famous 17th Century Bells, Father Junipero Serra Statue 5
Reel, Spider Man 15
Reel, Wild Animals of Africa, lion family, giraffe, hippopotamus, rhinoceros, spotted hyena, zebra, waterbuck 4
Reel and Booklet, Little Black Sambo, 1948 90
Reel Set, A Day at the Circus, scenes from Ringling Bros and Barnum & Bailey Circus 15
Reel Set, Disneyland's Main Street USA, Disneyland Entrance, Town Square, Horse-drawn Trolley, Disneyland Band, Ice Cream Parlor, and the Horse and Chemical Wagon 10
Reel Set, Easter Story, the Resurrection, the Appearance of Jesus, and the Ascension 15
Reel Set, scenes from Texas, the Alamo, Will Roger's Statue, Industrial Scenes, Neches River Bridge, Devil's Tombstone, El Captain Mountain, International Bridge, San Jacinto Monument 20
Reel Set, the Coronation of Queen Elizabeth II, includes story book 20
Viewer, Sawyer's, Bakelite 28
Viewer, Sawyers De Luxe Stereoscope, black Bakelite, brown and silver box, instruction card, and catalog, 1948, 4.25" w 35
View Master, Sawyer's 12

VIKING GLASS

The New Martinsville Glass Company was founded in West Virginia in 1901. Following the difficult years of the Great Depression and World War II, the company was renamed the Viking Glass Company in 1944.

Basket, blue, 7" x 5.5" x 6.5" 35
Bell, ruby red, mid "76," 3.5" h, 3.5" d 15
Bookend, shaggy dog, pink, 4.5" h 15
Bookend, teddy bear, frosted crystal, 7" h, 4.75" w 50
Bookends, pr, elephant, clear, 5.75" h 18
Bowl, amethyst, 1950s 25
Bowl, Epic, green satin, 6" d 8
Bowl, ftd, orange 30
Bowl, purple, 3.25" h, 5" w 15

Bowl, rooster, white, pink, and blue, 5" h, 8" l 40
Bowl, silver encrusted, 3-toed 20
Bowl, tangerine 40
Candleholders, pr, black, 5.5" h 35
Candleholders, pr, orange, 3.25" h, 6" w . . .32
Candleholders, pr, red, mushroom top, 3" h 25
Candy Dish, bird finial, orange, 12" h, 6.5" d 75
Celery Dish, swan, clear, 6" h, 8" l 15
Cigarette Lighter, amber, 7" h 35
Compote, amber, 8.25" w, 7" h 22
Compote, amber, ruffled edge, 4" h, 7" w . .18
Compote, blue, 6" x 5.25" 22
Compote, cov, ruby red, 8.25" h 65
Compote, yellow floral, 4" h, 5.25" d 12
Console Bowl, black, 19" x 7.5" 45
Dish, cov, teardrop, lime green, 8" h 15
Dish, handled, heart-shaped, 6.5" x 7" x 2.5" 40
Fairy Light, owl, ruby red, 7.5" h 60
Figurine, bird, red, 10" h 50
Figurine, horse, blue, 4.25" h, 4.5" l 60
Figurine, sail fish on pedestal, clear and amber, 10" h 75
Flower Bowl, with flowerlite frog, forest green, 4.5" h, 5.5" w 90
Goblet, Georgian, honeycomb design, cobalt blue, 9 oz, 5.75" h, 3.75" w 16
Relish Dish, red, 9.25" l, 6" w, 2" h 24
Server, open petal, emerald green, 13.25" w, 5.5" h 15
Swan Dish, forest green and clear, 5" l, 5.25" w, 4.75" h 15
Tidbit Tray, White Rose, 7.25" x 2.25" 15
Tumbler, honeycomb design, cobalt blue, 12 oz, 4.75" h, 3.5" w 18
Vase, amethyst, 8" h 35
Vase, Epic Ruby, 1968, 16.5" h 35

WADE CERAMICS

Red Rose Tea issued several series of small Wade figurines. I will not be happy until I have multiple sets. "Drink more tea" is the order of the day at my office. How much simpler it would be just to make a list of the missing Wades and pick them up at flea markets.

Club: Wade Watch, 8199 Pierson Ct., Arvada, CO 80005.

Ashtray, British Airways, 5.5" d 12
Basket, Flaxman, blue and green, 5.5" l, 5" h 36
Bud Vase, souvenir of Eros, Piccadilly Circus 8
Coddler, green with blue, mkd "Irish Porcelain, Wade Ireland" with a shamrock and "W" in a half sq, 2.5" h . .15
Decanter, turquoise, 9" h 20
Dish, hp pink and yellow flowers and green leaves 10
Figurine, Bactrian camel 25
Figurine, beagle 35
Figurine, black sheep 15
Figurine, Clown Throwing Custard Pie, Circus, 6th issue, pale blue, Red Rose Tea premium, 1996-98 5
Figurine, Clown with Water Bucket, Circus, 6th issue, light green, Red Rose Tea premium, 1996-98 5
Figurine, cobbler with red hat 10
Figurine, Jack, from Jack and Jill, 2.5" h . .18
Figurine, leaping fawn 20
Figurine, leprechaun on acorn, green hat .40
Figurine, leprechaun on pig, yellow hat . . .30
Figurine, llama 20
Figurine, mare, light brown 25
Figurine, Pex, fairy 250
Figurine, racoon 22
Figurine, Sebastian's Church, Whimsey on Why Series, 2.25" h, 3" l 30
Figurine, Si the Siamese cat (Disney's *Lady and the Tramp*), Hat Box Series, 1.75" h 35
Figurine, Simon, from "Bengo and His Puppy Friends," TV Pet Series, 2.5" h . . .30
Figurine, snowy owl 32
Figurine, squirrel 18
Figurine, tailor, blue hat 10
Figurine, tortoise, 6" l, 2" h 30

Figurine, Tramp, sitting (Disney's *Lady and the Tramp*) .25
Figurine, Viking ship .10
Jug, Orcadia, 7" h .25
Teapot, orange with chintz band, 6" h, 7.75" w .100
Tray, chestnut leaf-shaped .4
Vase, black frost with white flowers, 6.5" h .20
Vase, Viking ship shape, brown and green, 7" l, 3.5" h .15

WAGNER WARE

Wagner Manufacturing Company was established in Sidney, Ohio, in 1891.

Wagner Manufacturing made brass casting and cast-iron hollow ware, some of which was nickel plated. Wagner was one of the first companies to make aluminum cookware. The line included cake and ice cream molds, coffeepots, percolators, pitchers, scoops, spoons, and teapots. The company won numerous awards for its aluminum products between 1900 and 1940.

Ashtray, skillet shaped, 6.25" l, 3.5" d .15
Cornbread Pan, 13" l, 6" w .20
Dutch Oven, Magnalite, #4229, 6 qt .45
Dutch Oven and Trivet, 10" w, 7" h .40
Frying Pan, #5, 8" x 8.5" .15
Frying Pot, with basket, 7" d, 5" h .60
Long Spoon, #710, aluminum .35
Muffin Tray, 8.5" x 4.25" .65
Roaster, #4285, 15.75" l, 10" w .75
Roaster, Drip Drop, mkd "Round Roaster" 95
Scoop, mkd "Wagner Ware Scoop 912," 9.25" l .25
Sizzle Server, #1095 .25
Skillet, #2 .90
Skillet, #3 .15
Skillet, #3, pie logo .22
Skillet, #4, smooth bottom .55
Skillet, #6, 9" d .35
Skillet, #7, pie logo .125
Skillet, #9, with heat ring .65
Skillet, #11, pie logo .325
Skillet, #13 .375
Skillet, #1053E .50
Skillet, #1101A, sq .45
Skillet, National Wagner Ware, center logo, with heat ring .85
Skillet Lid, #9, 5-ring .40
Spoon, pistol grip, aluminum, 10.5" l .30
Steak Platter, 13" w .50
Tea Kettle, #0, stylized logo .160

WALLACE NUTTING

Wallace Nutting opened a photography studio in New York in 1904. Within a year, he moved to Southby, Connecticut and opened a larger studio. In 1907 he opened a branch office in Toronto, Canada. By 1913 Nutting's operation was located in Framingham, Massachusetts. At its peak, Nutting employed over 200 colorists, framers, salesmen, and support staff.

Although Nutting took all his own pictures, printing, coloring, framing, and even signing his name were the work of his employees. Over 10,000 photographs in an assortment of sizes have been identified.

Wallace Nutting died on July 19, 1941. His wife continued the business. When Mrs. Nutting died in 1944, she willed the business to Ernest John Donnelly and Esther Svenson. In 1946, Svenson bought out Donnelly. In 1971 Svenson entered a nursing home and ordered the destruction of all of the Nutting glass negatives. A few were not destroyed and are in the hands of private collectors.

Club: Wallace Nutting Collectors Club, P.O. Box 1536, Doylestown, PA 18901.

Book, *England Beautiful,* Garden City Publishing Co .25
Book, *Furniture of the Pilgrim Century 1620-1720,* Marshall Jones Company, 1921, 587 pgs .40
Book, *Furniture Treasury,* Vol III, illus by Ernest John Donnelly .175
Book, *Pennsylvania Beautiful,* Eastern, Old American Co, Framingham, MA, 1924 .25
Print, A Garden of Larkspur, summer cottage in the woods, 22.5" x 15" .125

Print, Charles River Elm, now extinct elm tree along the Charles River, 13.75" x 16.5" 280
Print, Confidences, 16" x 12" 75
Print, Home Lane, 1913 285
Print, Returning from a Walk, 9.75" x 7.5" 150
Print, The Coming Out of Rosa, 1912, 10" x 12" 180
Print, The Swimming Pool, 27" x 20" 170
Print, View from Casino, Funchal, Funchal Harbor, Madeira, 12" x 16" . . 1,500
Print, Without a Ripple, birch trees along a quiet pond, 7" x 9" 285

WALLACE NUTTING-TYPE PRINTS

The commercial success of Wallace Nutting's hand-colored, framed photographs spawned a series of imitators. David Davidson (1881-1967), Charles Higgins (1867-1930), Charles Sawyer (born 1904) and his Sawyer Picture Company, and Fred Thompson (1844-1923) are only a few of the dozens of individuals and businesses that attempted to ride Nutting's coattails.

Most of these photographers followed the same procedure as Nutting. They took their own photographs, usually with a glass plate camera. Prints were made on special platinum paper. Substitute paper was used during World War I. Each picture was titled and numbered, usually by the photographer. A model picture was colored. Colorists then finished the remainder of the prints. Finally, the print was matted, titled, signed, and sold.

Carlock, Close-Framed Lincoln Monument, large multi-columned Lincoln Memorial reflects in the blue Potomac River above pink blossoms and green tree-line, 8" x 10" 75
Carlock, Washington Monument, sun sets beyond large blue pond, pink apple blossoms, and distant Washington Monument, 5" x 7" 60
Davidson, Driving Home the Cows, little boy trails 4 cows walking in a blossom-bordered country road, 5" x 7" 135
Davidson, Easter Bonnet, girl in long paisley dress stands beside hallway mirror, 5" x 7" 110
Davidson, Echo Lake Drive, country road winds past tall trees and New Hampshire Echo Lake, 6" x 8" 95
Davidson, Meeting House Lane, 2 girls walking past colorful flower garden towards village Meeting House, 7" x 9" .85
Davidson, Old Ironsides, white waves crashing against large shoreline rocks, 7" x 9" 135
Davidson, Otter Cap Falls, 13" x 16" 100
Davidson, Snow Basin, Western Canada scene with tall snow-draped Rocky Mountains standing beside large blue lake, 5" x 7" 135
Davidson, The Falls, tall double waterfalls flowing down rocky cliff past leafless trees, 10" x 12" 125
Pease, Love's Blossom, infant boy with white toy lamb in hand sleeping beneath blue and white blanket, 11" x 14" 110

Sawyer, Ausable Chasm, narrow blue stream rushes between tall tree-lined rocky gorge, 7" x 9" 125
Sawyer, Cypress Point, Monterey, California seascape with tall tree standing upon rocky shoreline overlooking Pacific Ocean and rocky point with a cypress tree, 11" x 14" 265
Sawyer, Mt Ascutney, miniature, blue river ripples past green trees and fields towards Vermont's Mt Ascutney, 4" x 5" 125
Sawyer, Newfound Lake, close-frame scene with long rock-bordered country road winding around colorful Newfound Lake, 8" x 10" 125
Sawyer, San Juan, Capistrano, California scene with colorful flower and cactus garden beside old Spanish Mission, 10" x 13" 195
Standley, Pike's Peak From Near Colorado Springs, Colorado scene with hilltop view of tree-lined valley and tall distant snow-capped Rocky Mountains, 10" x 13" 135
Thompson, miniature, girl in white apron sitting beside red-brick fireplace, 3" x 4" 110
Thompson, Olde Tyme Way, girl arranges bed in bedroom with wreath-pattern wall paper, 7" x 9" 115
Thompson, The Arbor, girl in striped dress and blue cap enters flower arbor beside large house, 6" x 12" 125
Thompson, The Covered Bridge, country road winds towards covered bridge and blossom trees, 10" x 15" 135

WALL POCKETS

What is a wall pocket? My mother used them for plants. A "rooter" she called them. Now they are used as match holders and places for accumulating small junk.

Most common wall pockets were produced between the 1930s and 1960s; though there are some that date to the Victorian era. Wallpockets can be made of wood, tin, glass, or ceramic. Ceramic examples have been produced both domestically and abroad. Wall pockets come in all shapes and sizes, but all have a small hole on the back side for the insertion of the wall hook.

Club: Wall Pocket Collectors Club, 1356 Tahiti, St. Louis, MO 63128.

Acorn, majolica, 8" h .95
Apple on Leaves, McCoy, 7" h 65
Angel, Royal Copley, 6.25" h 25
Bird on Branch, majolica-style, red and yellow bird on branch, flowers, and blue basket, luster ware, mkd "Made In Japan," 7" h, 3.5" w 35
Butterfly, Occupied Japan, 5" x 6.5" 35
Canadian Geese, mkd "Made in Japan," set of 3 40
Chinese Faces, pr 35
Clock, c1950 45
Cockatiel, pastel colors, Morton Pottery, 8" h 35
Cuckoo Clock, mkd "Made in Japan," 5.5" h 40
Cup and Saucer, floral motif, c1950 35
Cup and Saucer, fruit decal, 8" d 35
Duck, mouth open, mkd "Maruhonware," 9.5" h 35
Dutch Children Scene, pr, 6" h 85
Flower, yellow, 10.5" h 18
House, Occupied Japan 15
Jam Jar, Pixieware, pink stripes, "Jam & Jelly," 5.25" h, 4.25" w 100
Lady with Full Skirt, Occupied Japan, 6" h 35
Parrot, Morgan Potteries, 7.75" h 18
Parrot, Occupied Japan 15
Peacock, blue, 6.5" h 28
Rose, pink rose on pale blue ground, 3.5" h 45

Scoop, pink, 7.5" l 35
Shell, small roses with gold leaves, gold trim, 6.5" h 65
Smiling Sunflowers, set of 3, large mama sunflower and 2 babies, Holt-Howard knockoffs, Japan 100
Sunflower, Holt-Howard, mkd "Made in Japan" 105
Teapot, 3.5" h, set of 3 40
Teapot, bail handle, "A Singing Kitchen Kettle and a Kitchen Bright Makes a Home Your Hearts Delight" 35
Teapot, hp, "Take Time For Tea," mkd "The California Cleminsons," c1950 ...40l
Violet, pr, Lenox, 5.5" l 20
Violin, speckled gold paint with gold trim, 9" h 20
Woman, parrot on her shoulder, Occupied Japan, 6" h 20

WARNER BROTHERS

The Warner Brothers Animation Studio, located initially in a bungalow dubbed Termite Terrace, produced over 1,000 six- and seven-minute theatrical cartoons between 1930 and 1969. Cartoon Hall of Fame characters who appeared in these shorts included Bugs Bunny, Daffy Duck, Elmer Fudd, Porky Pig, the Road Runner, Sylvester, the Tasmanian Devil, Tweety, Wile E. Coyote, and Yosemite Sam.

Although third in popularity behind Disney and Hanna-Barbera in cartoon collectibles, Warner Bros. collectibles have established a strong collecting niche. Collectors are advised to look beyond the superstars at characters such as Bosco, Foghorn Leghorn, Pepé Le Pew, and Speedy Gonzales.

Action Figure, Wile E Coyote/Charles Barkley, Space Jam, Playmates, 1996 ...7
Alarm Clock, Tweety in plastic nest, digital, Westclox, 1996, 5" x 5.5" 10
Bank, Porky Pig standing beside tree, metal, on base with name on front, 1947, 3.5" 175
Bank, Speedy standing on cheese, vinyl, Dakin, 1971, 6" h 40
Bank, Tweety, holding large hammer, plastic, Applause, orig box, 8" x 6" 8

Bendy Figure, Bugs Bunny, 1970, 3.75" h, MOC 15
Big Little Book, *Bugs Bunny: The Last Crusader,* Whitman, #5772-2 10
Bobbing Head, Scooby Doo, plastic, 1997 10
Book, *Bugs Bunny and the Secret of Storm Island,* Leon Schlesinger, Dell Fast Action Story, 1942 12
Book, Elmer Fudd, *Gone Fishin',* Dell, 1953 8
Coloring Book, Bugs Bunny, Whitman, #1147, 128 pgs, 1963 15
Comic Book, Elmer Fudd, Dell, #977, 1959 2
Cookie Cutters, Porky Pig, Bugs Bunny, Tweety, and Sylvester, red, Wilton Enterprises, 1988, set of 4 6
Cookie Jar, Bugs Bunny, "What's up Doc?," mkd "TM 1993 Warner Bros Inc, Certified International Corp, Taiwan," 11" h 40
Cup, Bugs Bunny, plastic 10
Doll, Speedy Gonzalez, stuffed, yellow hat, orange shirt, hands, and feet, red scarf, 1971, 14" h 35
Drinking Glass, Bugs Bunny, Welch's Looney Tunes Collector Series #1, 1994, 4" h 1
Drinking Glasses, Porky Pig, Bugs Bunny, Yosemite Sam, and Road Runner, Pepsi series, 1973, set of 4 10
Figure, Porky Pig, ceramic, smiling and waving, blue jacket, orange bow tie, light blue cap, orange base, mkd "©Warner Bros Inc, 1975 Japan," 4.25" h 15

Figure, Road Runner, hard plastic, soft rubber head, cheeks make beep-beep sound when pressed, "R Dakin & Co, San Francisco" tag, 1950s, 9" h 10

Figure, Speedy Gonzalez, vinyl, dark brown, yellow hat, red cloth kerchief, green shirt, and white pants, gray plastic base with black "Have A Speedy Recovery!," Dakin Goofy Grams series, 1970, 7.5" h 15

Figure, Taz, vinyl, WB store exclusive, 1995, 8" h 6

Gumball Machine, Bugs Bunny standing with carrot in hand, Superior Toy & Mfg, 1988, 9.5" h 4

Hot Water Bottle, Sylvester and Tweety Bird, Duarry, Spain, mid-20th C, 12.75" h 65

Lamp, Wile E Coyote and Road Runner figures, vinyl, 1977, 15" h 55

Lotion Dispenser, Taz, 1993 10

Lunch Box, Looney Tunes characters on TV screen with knobs, replaced handle, American Thermos, 1959 30

Mug, Bugs Bunny, blue, Homer Laughlin Fiestaware 8

Mug, Tasmanian Devil, ceramic, mkd "Warner Bros Inc, 1989, The Good Company, Woodland Hills CA 91367" 2

Neck Tie, child's, Elmer Fudd, wearing red pants, white vest, yellow jacket and hat on blue ground with "Elmer" below, 9" l 15

Night Light, Scooby Doo, ceramic, Warner Bros Studio, 7" h 20

Pie Bird, Bugs Bunny, ceramic, mkd "Made in Calif.," 4" h 28

Pinback Button, Bugs Bunny, "Help Crippled Children," smiling Bugs Bunny face on orange ground, purple lettering, 1958, 1.25" d 3

Planter, Bugs Bunny, holding hand to chest, smiling and standing next to brown log, blue with pink accents, 1940s, 3" x 6" x 7" 35

Plate, Scooby Doo, "Scooby Snacks," sea-mist green, Homer Laughlin Fiestaware, 10" d .18

Plate, Tweety, "Happy 50th Birthday Tweety," #Y7454, center Tweety surrounded by Looney Tunes characters in party scene, gold rim, 1993 40

Record, Bugs Bunny and Tweetie Bird, *I Taut I Taw A Puddy-Tat,* 78 rpm, yellow vinyl 20

Refrigerator Magnets, Bugs Bunny, Marvin the Martian, Sheriff Daffy Duck, Taz, and Tweety Bird, 1993, set of 5 8

Salt and Pepper Shakers, Bugs Bunny holding "Duck Season" sign, Elmer Fudd holding rifle, 5.5" h Bugs Bunny, 4.75" h Elmer 15

Salt and Pepper Shakers, Foghorn Leghorn and Little Chicken Hawk, Certified International Corp, 1993 25

Salt and Pepper Shakers, Wile E Coyote and Road Runner, ceramic, 1993, 5.5" h Wile E, 4.75" h Road Runner 25

Salt and Pepper Shakers, Yosemite Sam, ceramic 12

Snow Globe, Elmer Fudd, Daffy Duck, and Bugs Bunny, "Rabbit Season/Duck Season," plays *A Hunting We Will Go,* Goebel, 6" h, 7" d 15

Spoon Rest, Yosemite Sam, Certified International Corp, 1993 10

Squeak Toy, Sylvester, hands behind back, Reliance Prod Corp, 1978, 7" h 8

Thermos, Porky's Lunch Wagon, red plastic cap, 1959, 8" h 75

Tie Tack, Road Runner, cloisonné, Howard Eldon of California, 1970s, 1" h 5

Toy, Bugs Bunny in red biplane, die-cast, Ertl, 1988 5

Toy, Scooby Copter, Boley, 1996 12

Tray, Tweety and Sylvester, Bugs Bunny, Porky Pig, Roadrunner, and Daffy Duck on white ground, banded rim, Fabcraft, 1974, 11.75" d 6

View-Master Reel, Bugs Bunny and Elmer Fudd, "The Hunter," #800 8
Watch, Speedy Gonzalez, full figure smiling Speedy image, diecut yellow gloved hands, vinyl band, Hong Kong, 1970s 75

WASHDAY COLLECTIBLES

Washday material is a favorite of advertising collectors. Decorators have a habit of using it in bathroom decor. Is there a message here?

Advertisement, 1945 Maytag Washer Woman with little girl, black and white, 10" x 12" 10
Basin, European, brown, 14.75" d, 5" h 40
Clothes Pins, plastic, mkd "Storm Denmark," set of 30 12
Ironing Board, wooden sleeve, with pad and linen cover, 17" l 12
Ironing Board Cover Fasteners, Evertite, 5 metal spring-action fasteners, 1950s .10
Laundry Bag, appliqued cats 12
Laundry Bag, Peanuts characters on front, red pull string 15
Laundry Bag, Raggedy Ann and Andy, 1970s 30
Laundry Bag, Scottie dogs, 1920s, 31.5" l, 18" w 50
Laundry Basket, splint weave, wood handles 45
Laundry Basket, wicker, 16" x 12.5" 40
Laundry Sorter, #46, Crescent Laundry and Cleaners, brass 35
Plate, Royal Bayreuth, Sunbonnet Babies Washday, 6.25" d 150

Sadiron, #0, Colebrookdale Iron Co, wooden handle, 6.5" l, 3.25" w 40
Sadiron, cast iron, mkd "UXX5" 10
Salt and Pepper Shakers, old lady sitting on laundry basket 25
Toy Iron and Ironing Board, metal, 23.5" h, 27" l 25
Washboard, brass, hammered design, 24" l 30
Washboard, Columbus Washboard Co . . .40
Washboard, dec with pictures of women, 19th C 8
Washboard, glass, wooden frame, 13.5" x 26" 45

WASTEBASKETS

Wastebaskets are not just for garbage. Many collectors are just beginning to appreciate the great lithographed artwork found on many character cans.

Aluminum, dogwood pattern, Wendell August Forge, 10" h, 10" w 150
Brass, English pub scene, 14" h, 8" d 45
Chinoiserie, hand-cut and applied oriental scenes, 13" h, 10" w 100
Decoware, pink and yellow roses on maroon ground 30
Graniteware, white with black rim, 10" h, 9.5" w 30
Iron Mesh, wooden bottom, 9" d, 16" h 25
Litho Tin, Mickey and Minnie Mouse, Chein 30
Metal, brightly colored dishes, step-on opener, 9.75" w, 14" h 42
Metal, Governor's Palace at Colonial Williamsburg, sage green ground 20
Metal, leather-like cov, 10.25" x 7.25" x 12.5" 10
Metal, painted black paisley design on goldtone, 9.25" x 9.25" 12
Metal, perfume bottles on pink ground, 10.5" x 6.5" x 12.75" 12
Metal, roses, 9.5" x 7.25" x 9.25" 10
Metal, white daisies on green ground, 9.5" x 7" x 9" 10
Plastic, clear with gold metal scroll and flower dec around opening 25
Wicker, Amish, 2 leather handles, 9.5" x 12.5" 60
Wood, nesting set of 2, hp floral design on black ground, 12" h, 9.75" d 50

WATCHES

The pocket watch generations have been replaced by the wristwatch generations. This category became hot in the late 1980s and still is going strong. There is a great deal of speculation occurring, especially in the area of character and personality watches.

Since the category is relatively new as a collectible, no one is certain exactly how many watches have survived. I have almost a dozen that were handed down from my parents. If I am typical, the potential market supply is far greater than anyone realizes.

Clubs: National Assoc. of Watch & Clock Collectors, Inc., 514 Poplar St., Columbia, PA 17512; The Swatch Collectors Club, P.O. Box 7400, Melville, NY 11747.

Note: Watches are in working order unless noted otherwise.

POCKET WATCH

Addison, gold-filled floral-engraved hunter case with house vignette, white enameled dial, size 6 55

C Howard & Co., open-faced, Dueber silverine case, key wind, #40157, white enameled dial sgd and dated "Pat. Feb. 4th, 1868," chips on edge of glass, size 18 125

E Howard & Co, Boston, open-faced, silveroid case, #17316, white enameled dial with subsidiary seconds dial, size 18 125

Ekegren, moon phase calendar watch, sgd on bezel "H. R. Ekegren Geneve," 18K yg engine-turned hunter case, white porcelain dial with aperture for moon phase, calendar day arc below moon phase, day of the week aperture above "VI," subsidiary seconds dial, subsidiary month dial, display cuvette, stem wind, pin set, approx 52 mm, wear to engine turning 6,150

Elgin, hunter case engraved with flowers and house vignette, monogram medallion on reverse, #1870693, hinged dust cover, white enameled dial with subsidiary seconds dial, 15 j, lever set, size 8 200

Elgin, open-faced, gold-filled Wadsworth Revere case with monogram, #21039822, 7 j, white enamel dial with subsidiary seconds dial, size 10 35

English, gold, sgd "Beezley, Liverpool" on backplate, No. 6748, hunter case with geometric engraving, porcelain dial, key wind, c1825-35, approx 55 mm 190

Hampden, coin silver, open-faced, key wind, #131459, white dial with subsidiary seconds dial, size 18 120

Seth Thomas, railroad, white dial with locomotive and subsidiary seconds dial, engraved silveroid case with house, #226140, 15 j, size 18 130

Swiss, dust cov mkd "14K Mascot," engraved hunter case, lever set, white enameled dial with subsidiary seconds dial, dial edge flake, approx 34 mm 90

Swiss, Relion Watch Co, Art Deco design, gold-filled keystone form open-faced case 25

Waltham, Broadway, open-faced, silveroid case, key wind, #4903043, white dial with subsidiary seconds dial, size 18 35

Waltham, Keystone, gold-filled hunter case with geometrics, #1292601, white dial with subsidiary seconds dial, size 0 55

WRISTWATCH

Bulova, lady's, 10K rolled gold plate, round dial, flexible bracelet, c1950s 20

Character, Mickey Mouse, large Mickey and inset with 3 small Mickeys on dial, black leather straps, Ingersoll, 1933 . .350

Elgin, lady's 10K gold filled, square dial, narrow expanding bracelet, c1950s 20

Hamilton, lady's, 14K white gold case with 14K white gold filigree band, #E5318, pearlized dial, engraved case, 17 j 150

Hamilton, Savitar, electric, 14K yg asymmetrical case, pearlized dial with sweep second 465

Lady Hamilton, 14K white gold oval link band and case, band set with 12 diamonds, case set with 8 diamonds, 22 j, 761 series, approx 15 grams total weight 275

Ollendorf, lady's, 14K yg, hinged dial cov, gold mesh band, 17 j 165

Swiss, Alleman Sons & Co, AZO, lady's, platinum and diamond, rect case with tapered extensions set with 42 diamonds, 17 j, silvered dial, metal filligree band 275

Swiss, ball watch, engine-turned apple green enameling with floral dec 145

Swiss, Hofbros, lady's, platinum case set with 12 diamonds and 4 sapphires, 16 j, added metal band 225

Swiss, Orator Watch Co, pendant , blue enameled silver engine-turned ball case, 15 j, white enameled dial, silver watch chain with matching enameled links, small chip on medial band 130

WATCH FOBS

A watch fob is a useful and decorative item attached to a man's pocket watch by a strap. It assists him in removing the watch from his pocket. Fobs became popular during the last quarter of the 19th century.

Most fobs are made of metal and are struck from a steel die. Enameled fobs are scarce and sought after by collectors. If a fob was popular, a company would order restrikes. As a result, some fobs were issued for a period of twenty-five years or more. Watch fobs still are used today in promoting heavy industrial equipment.

The most popular fobs are those relating to old machinery, either farm, construction, or industrial. Advertising fobs rank second in popularity.

The back of a fob is helpful in identifying a genuine fob from a reproduction or restrike. Genuine fobs frequently have advertising or a union trademark on the back. Some genuine fobs do have blank backs but a blank back should be a warning to be cautious.

Club: International Watch Fob Assoc., Inc., 601 Patriot Place, Holmen, WI 54636.

"Dead Shot Powder," brass, full color celluloid center depicting duck on pale green ground, 1.25" h 235

DuPont Ammo Co, presentation, SS, classical woman with arm draped over shield, "For Greater Safety" cloisonne inlay in green and white, orig strap, unused in orig box, 1.5" x 1" 176

Mennen's Talcum Powder, "Mennen's For Mine," color image of infant on dark blue ground .35

"Our Choice Harding Coolidge," emb brass, spread-wing eagle and Capitol dome at top center with large oval portraits below, 1.5" h 70

RCA Victor, "His Master's Voice," gold-tone metal, raised lettering and Nipper image, 1.5" h, 2" w 85

Socony Polarine Brand Oil and Greases, emb metal, highly detailed trademark seated polar bear with wintry seascape in background, 1.5" x 1.25" 120

Taft, jugate, "Good Luck," portraits surrounded by horseshoe, "Our Choice Taft & Sherman," 1.5" h 70

Taft/Sherman 1908, brass, enameled red, white, and blue emb flag design, 1.5" h .40

Tudor Tea, Coffee & Cocoa, 2-sided celluloid, adv on front, baseball image and dial scorekeepers on back, orig leather strap, 2" x 1.75" 440

Vin Fiz, oval, celluloid with colorful graphic image of trademark woman in aviator's clothing sipping product, detailed emb metal frame, "Vin Fiz" on woman's coveralls and metal frame, emb adv on back, 2" x 1.5" 770

Washburn's Ice Cream, "A Health Food," rect ice cream carton with pink, white, and black striped cloisonne enameled porcelain front, emb adv on back, 1.25" x 1.5" 185

Wilson, "His Pen Mightier Than The Sword," copper lustre, Wilson's portrait at top, scale with quill pen outweighing a sword below, 1.75" h 35
Woodrow Wilson, celluloid with mirror back, 2.25" h 145

WATT POTTERY

Watt Pottery, located in Crooksville, Ohio, was founded in 1922. The company began producing kitchenware in 1935. Most Watt pottery is easily recognized by its simple underglaze decoration on a light tan base. The most commonly found pattern is the Red Apple pattern, introduced in 1950. Other patterns include Cherry, Pansy, Pennsylvania Dutch Tulip, Rooster, and Star Flower.

Club: Watt Collectors Assoc., P.O. Box 1995, Iowa City, IA 52244.

Apple, 2-leaf, refrigerator pitcher, #69 . . .300
Apple, 3-leaf, bowl, #7 70
Apple, 3-leaf, cookie jar, #503 225
Apple, 3-leaf, grease jar 40
Apple, 3-leaf, pie bird, 3.5" h 30
Apple, 3-leaf, pitcher, #16 120
Apple, 3-leaf, spoon rest 20
Apple, 3-leaf, tea bag rest 15
Apple, bowl, adv 125
Apple, grease jar 40
Apple, mixing bowl, #7, ribbed 110
Apple, mixing bowl, #9 175
Apple, mixing bowl, #64 125
Apple, mixing bowl, #65 145

Apple, pitcher, #15 .100
Apple, spaghetti bowl, #39 135
Autumn Foliage, bowl, #119 115
Autumn Foliage, pepper shaker 90
Autumn Foliage, pitcher, #5 110
Basketweave, bowl, 5" h, 9" d 30
Bleeding Heart, serving bowl, #75 30
Butterscotch, casserole, cov, #8 30
Cherry, cereal bowl .65
Loops, flat bowl, #8 30
Loops, mixing bowl, #6 20
Loops, mixing bowl, #8 30
Old Pansy, bowl, 13" d 110
Old Pansy, pie plate, 9" d 85
Orchard, bowl, #119 115
Pansy, cut leaf, bowl 88
Pansy, cut leaf, platter 105
Pansy, pie plate 85
Pansy, spaghetti bowl, #39 95
Rooster, ice bucket 325
Rooster, milk creamer, #62 265
Shaded Line, bean pot, #37 45
Silhouette, platter, #31 125
Starflower, bowl, #6 55
Starflower, bowl, #24 85
Starflower, casserole, cov 245
Starflower, cookie jar, #21 225
Starflower, creamer 75
Starflower, pitcher 110
Starflower, platter, #31 125
Starflower, salt and pepper shakers 150
Starflower, spaghetti bowl, #24 150
Tulip, bowl, #64 175
Tulip, bowl, #65 190
Tulip, salt shaker, 4" h 450

WEATHER VANES

Weather vanes indicate wind direction. In addition to being functional, weather vanes are decorative. Popular forms include horses, Indians, leaping stags, and patriotic emblems. Church vanes were often in the form of a fish or rooster. Buildings in coastal towns featured ships or sea creatures.

Sportsmen and others frequently used weather vanes for target practice. Bullet holes decrease the value of a vane.

Vintage weather vanes have skyrocketed in price, creating a market for affordable reproductions.

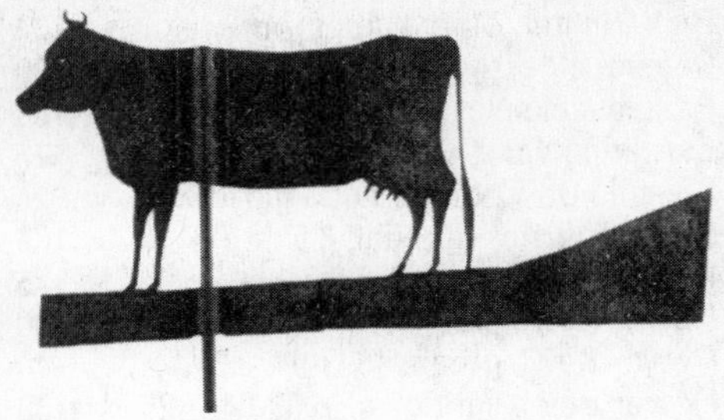

Angel Gabriel, copper, polished, 27" h, 18" w 215
Country Doctor, copper, green patina finish, 33" w 200
Cow Silhouette, sheet metal, 16" l 600
Deer, leaping, 29" h, 23" l 200
Duck, landing, 16" h, 22" l, 28" w 265
Fish, 9.5" h, 26" l 130
Golfer, copper, polished, 28" h, 27" w 215
Grasshopper, 12" h, 26" l 160
Heron, 18" h, 24" l, 30" w 275
Horse and Buggy, 3-D 800
National USA Eagle, polished 225
Osprey, antique finish, 16" h, 37" w, 17" l .310
Pegasus, wrought iron, 32" w, 18" h . . .1, 500
Pelican, 21" h, 24" w 225
Pig, copper, antiqued finish, 17" h, 26" l . .200
Rooster, copper, polished, 28" l, 25" h 225
Rooster, flat tail, antique finish, 25"h, 28" l 225
Rooster, wooden, 19.5" h, 12" w 1,275
Sailboat, copper, verdegris finish, 37" h, 27" w 230
Sailfish, copper, polished, 30" l, 21" h 190
Sloop, polished, 31" h, 31" w 260
Sloop, verdegris finish, 31" h, 31" w 230
Sperm Whale, copper, polished, 29" l 225
Stallion Race Horse, polished finish, 33" l, 20" h 250
Whale, copper, 36" l .70

WEDGWOOD

In 1759 Josiah Wedgwood established a pottery near Stoke-on-Trent in Burslem, England.

During the 1960s and 1970s Wedgwood acquired many English potteries, including William Adams & Sons, Coalport, Susie Cooper, Crown Staffordshire, Johnson Brothers, Mason's Ironstone, J. & G. Meakin, Midwinter Companies, Precision Studios and Royal Tuscan. In 1969 Wedgwood acquired King's Lynn Glass, renaming it Wedgwood Glass. The acquisition of Galway Crystal Company of Galway, Erie, followed in 1974.

In 1986 Waterford and Wedgwood merged. The Wedgwood Group, a division of Waterford Wedgwood, is one of the largest tabletop manufacturers in the world.

Ashtray, black jasperware, 3.5" d 10
Ashtray, green jasperware, 4.25" d 15
Bread and Butter Plate, Countryside 8
Casserole, Malverne, black and white, 5" h, 9.5" d 90
Child's Bowl, Peter Rabbit, 5.75" d 18
Creamer, Windbrush, white porcelain with blue flowers, 3.5" h, 2" d 42
Cup and Saucer, blue floral design 22
Cup and Saucer, Cathay 20
Cup and Saucer, Countryside 10
Cup and Saucer, gold leaves on cream ground 18
Cup and Saucer, Royal Blue 8
Cup and Saucer, Windbrush, blue flowers on white 32
Demitasse Set, Blue Willow, cup, saucer, and plate 35
Dinner Plate, Royal Blue, 1965 10
Pincushion, Florenza, blue and white, 2.5" x 2.5" 20
Pitcher, light blue jasperware, classical design, #36, imp "Wedgwood, Made in England, 1951," 4.75" h 75
Plate, blue jasperware, 4.5" d 20

Plate, blue jasperware, guide dog, leaf, and berry design, 4.5" d 25
Plate, Cathay, 8" d 10
Plate, cornucopia with fruit, rosettes, and filigree dec, 4.5" d 24
Plate, Countryside 12
Plate, "Early Morning Milk" 35
Plate, York Minster, Cathedrals of Britain Series, 1940, 6" d 65
Salad Plate, Devon Spray, gold trim rim, 8" d 12
Saucer, Patricia, 6" d 10
Smoking Set, blue jasperware, lighter and 2 ashtrays, grape and leaf design on ashtrays, Roman chariot on lighter, mkd "Wedgwood, Made in England" . . .80
Teacup, Windbrush, blue flowers on white 22
Urn, white, 3.5" h 20
Vase, cream and lavender, grape and leaf design, 10.75" h 125
Vase, white birds on blue ground, 5" h 12
Vase, white grape leaves on light blue, 6.5" h 95
Wall Plaque, portrait of Mary and Jesus, blue, 5.75" x 8" x 1.75" 12

WELLER POTTERY

Weller's origins date back to 1872 when Samuel Weller opened a factory in Fultonham, near Zanesville, Ohio. Louwelsa, Weller's art pottery line, was introduced in 1894. Among the famous art pottery designers employed by Weller were Charles Babcock Upjohn, Jacques Sicard, Frederick Rhead, and Gazo Fudji.

Weller survived on production of utilitarian wares, but always managed to produce some art pottery until cheap Japanese imports captured the market immediately following World War II. Operations at Weller ceased in 1948.

Club: American Art Pottery Assoc., P.O. Box 834, Westport, MA 02790.

Basket, Florence, 5.25" h, 7.5" w 145
Basket, Warwick, 7" h, 7" w 125
Bowl, Roma, 3" h, 6.25" d 95
Bud Vase, double, green and mauve flowers on ivory 220
Bud Vase, Woodland, 10.5" h 195
Bulb Planter, Marvo, log form, green 120
Candleholders, pr, 10" h 220
Candlesticks, pr, Warwick, 2" h, 5" d 100
Carnation Vase, Orris, Mayan motif 175
Console Bowl, matte aqua glaze with blackberries in relief, 3.5" h, 7.5" w 165
Figurine, seated frog, 6" h 175
Flower Bowl, blue, 1903-04, 12" d 90
Flower Bowl, green, 1903-04, 8.5" d 40
Flower Bowl, light blue, 1903-04, 7.25" d . .30
Flowerpot, hanging, Wild Rose, 5.5" h, 5.5" d 90
Jardiniere, Breton, matte green, 4" d 175
Jardiniere, Burntwood, 1910, 6.5" x 5" . . .135
Jardiniere, Clinton Ivory, fruit and flowers on bower, pre-1914, 8" x 9.25" 225
Jardiniere, Forest, 8.5" d 360
Mug, Aurilian Grape and Leaf, 8" h 160
Mug, child's, bird and rabbit on front, 3" x 3" 125
Mug, Claywood, 1910, 5" h 160
Pitcher, Panella, pastel shades of gray, green, and yellow, 6.5" h 125
Pitcher, Zona, 7" h, 8" w 95
Planter, Cameo, 4" x 4" 85
Planter, log, twig handle, green, 9.5" l . . .165
Planter, Warwick, frog lid, 5" h 185
Plaque, Robert E Lee in relief, 4.5" d 125
Stick Vase, marbelized, 1903 100
Swan Bowl, Knifewood, 3.25" h, 4.25" w . .150
Urn, cherub design, 8" h 175
Vase, Baldin, incised "Weller," 11" h 250
Vase, Flemish, rose with ribbon, c1915-28, 8" h 200
Vase, Floretta, 5.5" h, 4" w 100
Vase, Gloria, bulbous, tan with white flowers, 9.75" h 125

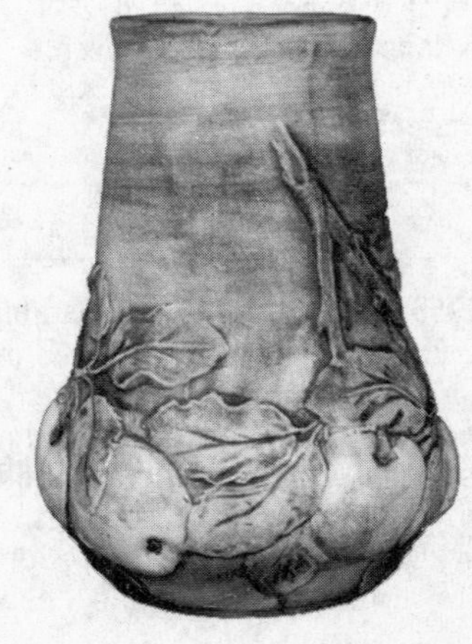

Vase, hp flowers on white ground, 4.25" h, 6.5" d 200
Vase, Louwelsa, #595, 6.5" h 170
Vase, Marvo, orange, 1920s-33, 8.5" h . . .120
Vase, Roma, 8.5" h .165
Vase, Tutone, green, late 1920s, 7.5" h . . .200
Vase, Wildrose, 14" h 175

WESTERN COLLECTIBLES

Yippy Kiyay, partner, let's get a move on and lasso up some Western goodies.

The Western collectible is a style or motif as it relates to the object. The Western theme presents itself in the decorative imagery of the item. The use of Western materials for construction of the item also defines it as a possible Western collectible; i.e. cattlehide carpets and wall hangings, or items constructed from bull horns. The Western motif may also be defined as any item that relates to the Western frontier culture. Native American Indian and Mexican cultures are also part of the Western collectible theme. It is these cultures that contribute so much of the color to the Western heritage.

Clubs: 101 Ranch Collectors, 10701 Timbergrove Ln., Corpus Christi, TX 78410; National Bit, Spur & Saddle Collectors Assoc., P.O. Box 3098, Colorado Springs, CO 80934.

Bar Rail Hardware, cast brass, horse head, 6.5" h 45
Book, *Roy Rogers and the Sure 'nough Cowpoke,* Whitman Tell-A-Tales, 1950 . .25
Book, *Tex,* Graphic Publishing Co, paperback, 1951 5
Eye Glass Case, hand-tooled leather, emb acorn and oak leaf, 6.5" l, 3.5" w 15
Figurine, horse wearing western saddle, metal, 2.5" h 8
Grill Plate, longhorn steer, spurs, rope and cattle brands, 11.25" d 95
Key Chain, cowboy boot, hard plastic, turquoise 14
Mug, white china, boy sitting by his mailbox with horse nearby, 4.25" h 8
Pitcher, plastic, figural cowboy, yellow, 10" h 145

Postcard, adv, Garners Jellies, Preserves, and Sauces, Cisco Kid on Horse, 1953 .12
Salt and Pepper Shakers, covered wagons, 2.75" h, 3.75" l 10
Salt and Pepper Shakers, Daffy Duck and Bugs Bunny dressed as cowboys, 5.5" h 55

WESTMORELAND GLASS

Westmoreland Glass Company made a large assortment of glass. Some early pieces were actually reproductions of earlier patterns and are now collectible in their own right. Other patterns have been produced for decades.

Expect to pay modest prices. Flea market prices are generally much lower than contemporary department store prices.

Clubs: National Westmoreland Glass Collectors Club, P.O. Box 100, Grapeville, PA 15634; Westmoreland Glass Society, 1144 42nd Ave., Vero Beach, FL 32960.

Note: All items are white unless noted otherwise.

Beaded Edge, bread and butter plate, 6" d .5
Beaded Eagle, cake stand, sq ft, 9.5" d . . .70
Beaded Eagle, cup, fruit dec 12
Beaded Eagle, cup and saucer 5
Beaded Eagle, plate, 7" d 5
Beaded Eagle, plate, fruit dec, 7" d 12
Beaded Eagle, salad plate, 8" d 4
Beaded Eagle, saucer, fruit dec 5
Beaded Eagle, tumbler, fruit dec 15

Beaded Eagle, wedding bowl, large, roses and bows dec 90
English Hobnail, electric lamp, crystal, 6" h 45
English Hobnail, ginger ale tumbler, sq ft, crystal 8
English Hobnail, goblet, round ft, crystal, 6" h 10
English Hobnail, plate, amber, 8" d 10
English Hobnail, plate, crystal, 5.5" d 5
English Hobnail, plate, crystal, 8" d 6
English Hobnail, puff box, cov, 6" d 20
English Hobnail, sherbet, high, round ft, crystal 9
Fan & File, child's punch cup, crystal 5
Fan & File, fairy light, 2-part, green mist ..75
Figurine, owl, glass eyes, dark blue frosted 35
Figurine, pouter pigeon, apricot mist, 2.5" h 35
Figurine, pouter pigeon, crystal, 2.5" h 25
Hobnail, powder jar, Belgian blue opalescent 145
Old Quilt, candy dish, cov 20
Old Quilt, celery, ftd 30
Old Quilt, cheese dish, cov 55
Old Quilt, shaker, squat, 3.5" h 12
Old Quilt, water goblet 18
Paneled Grape, 2-pc appetizer set 45
Paneled Grape, ashtray, 4" sq 20
Paneled Grape, basket, scalloped ft, 10.5" h 90
Paneled Grape, bowl, lipped, 8.5" d 90
Paneled Grape, bowl, ruffled 25
Paneled Grape, cake salver, pedestal ft, 11" d 50
Paneled Grape, candy dish, cov, roses and bows dec, 6.25" d 32
Paneled Grape, celery, 6" h 35
Paneled Grape, comport, cov, ftd 30
Paneled Grape, creamer and sugar 25

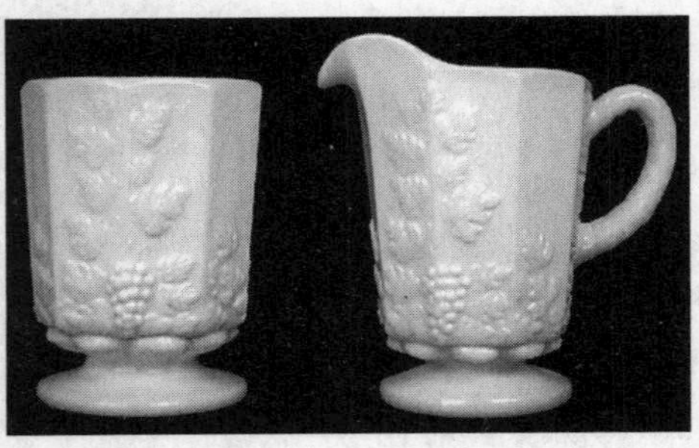

Paneled Grape, cruets, pr 40
Paneled Grape, cup and saucer 20
Paneled Grape, dresser tray, oval, 13" l ...55
Paneled Grape, gravy boat and liner 40
Paneled Grape, milk pitcher 20
Paneled Grape, pitcher, 16 oz 48
Paneled Grape, plate, 8.5" d 20
Paneled Grape, punch stand 135
Paneled Grape, salt and pepper shakers .25
Paneled Grape, soap dish 125
Paneled Grape, vase, bell-shaped, 11.5" h 45
Paneled Grape, vase, roses and bows dec, 8.5" h 32
Paneled Grape, wall pocket 135
Pillow and Sunburst, bowl, amethyst, 8" d 35
Princess Feather, bowl, 4.5" d 16
Princess Feather, plate, 8" d 80
Princess Plate, wine goblet, 1.5 oz 18
Woolworth, plate, pink, 8.5" d 15
Woolworth, sugar, pink 20

WHEATON

The Wheaton Glass Company, Millville, New Jersey, manufactured commemorative bottles, decanters, and flasks between 1967 and 1974. Series included Christmas, Great Americans, Movie Stars, Political Campaigns, and Space.

The Wheaton Historical Association continued production of the Christmas and Presidential series from 1975 to 1982. The Millville Art Glass Co. obtained a licensing agreement from the Wheaton Historical Association and added some additional bottles to the series.

The Wheaton Glass Company also manufactured copycats (stylistic copies) of 19th century bottles and flasks between 1971 and 1974. Most were marked "Nuline," "W," or "Wheaton, NJ" on the base. Amber, amethyst, blue, green, milk, and ruby were the colors used.

Club: Classic Wheaton Club, P.O. Box 59, Downingtown, PA 19335.

American Miniatures, A Lancaster's Indian Vegetable Jaundice Bitters, topaz 10

American Miniatures, Church Brand Ink, ruby 28
American Miniatures, Dr Fisch's Bitters, ruby 28
American Miniatures, EC Booz's Old Cabin Whiskey, blue 15
American Miniatures, Frank's Safe Kidney & Liver Cure, green 15
American Miniatures, McGiver's Bitters, army drum, green 15
American Miniatures, RIP, casket, poison, blue 40
American Miniatures, RIP, casket, poison, ruby 36
American Miniatures, RIP, casket, poison, topaz 31
American Miniatures, Straubmuller's Elixer, amber 10
Astronaut Decanter, Apollo 11, cobalt 15
Astronaut Decanter, Apollo 13, amber 9
Astronaut Decanter, Apollo 15, green 15
Bank, 1888 Wheaton Glass Factory Bldg, clear 45
Bank, Indian chief with headdress, blue ..23
Christmas Decanter, Poinsettia, blue 25
Colonial Antique Series II, Pocahontas, ruby 15
Great Americans, Benjamin Franklin, aqua 10
Great Americans, Billy Graham, green 9
Great Americans, Edison, cobalt 9
Great Americans, General George Patton, blue 18
Great Americans, Martin Luther King, Jr, topaz 10
Ink, Church Brand, ruby 12
Mini-Presidential Series, Ford, amber 25

Mini-Presidential Series, Reagan, green ..25
Political Campaign, 1968 Republican elephant, topaz 15
Presidential Series, Eisenhower, amethyst .9
Presidential Series, Ford, ruby 15
Presidential Series, Kennedy, blue 20
Presidential Series, Teddy Roosevelt, deep blue 18
Presidential Series, Washington, frosted .10
Special Commemorative, Liberty Bell, amethyst 10
Star Decanter Series, Humphrey Bogart, green 10

WHISKEY BOTTLES, COLLECTORS' EDITIONS

The Jim Beam Distillery issued its first novelty bottle for the 1953 Christmas market. By the 1960s the limited edition whiskey bottle craze was full blown. It was dying by the mid 1970s and was buried sometime around 1982 or 1983. Oversaturation by manufacturers and speculation by non-collectors killed the market.

Limited edition whiskey bottle collecting now rests in the hands of serious collectors. Their bible is H. F. Montague's *Montague's Modern Bottle Identification and Price Guide* (published by author, 1980). The book used to be revised frequently. Now five years or more pass between editions. The market is so stable that few prices change from one year to the next.

Before you buy or sell a full limited edition whiskey bottle, check state laws. Most states require a license to sell liquor and impose substantial penalties if you sell without one.

Clubs: International Assoc. of Jim Beam Bottle & Specialties Club, 2015 Burlington Ave., Kewanee, IL 61443; National Ski Country Bottle Club, 1224 Washington Ave., Golden, CO 80401.

Note: Bottles are empty unless noted otherwise.

Double Springs, 1911 Mercer 44
Double Springs, 1913 Cadillac 35
Double Springs, 1927 Bentley 45
Double Springs, 1940 Ford 40
Ezra Brooks, Iron Horse 10
Ezra Brooks, Quail 12
Ezra Brooks, Reno Heritage, 1968 25
***Jim Beam, 1935 Duesenburg Roadster* ..125**
Jim Beam, 1976 Bicentennial 25
Jim Beam, Bass Fish 20
Jim Beam, Cardinal 25
Jim Beam, Cat 25
Jim Beam, Chopin, screw-on lid 2
Jim Beam, Dog 40
Jim Beam, Elks Centennial 10
Jim Beam, Frans Hals 25
Jim Beam, German Shorthaired 25
Jim Beam, Irish Setter 25
Jim Beam, Kentucky Straight Bourbon ...10
Jim Beam, Labrador Retriever 25
Jim Beam, Largemouth Bass 20
Jim Beam, Lautrec 25
Jim Beam, Observation Car Train 85
Jim Beam, Order of the Blue Goose, 1971 .20
Jim Beam, Pony Express 28
Jim Beam, Raccoon 25
Jim Beam, Remington 25
Jim Beam, Renoir Painting 25
Jim Beam, Republican Elephant, 1972 35
Jim Beam, San Francisco Trolley 10
Jim Beam, Socrates 5
Jim Beam, Springer Spaniel 25
Jim Beam, Texas Jack Rabbit, 1971 8
Jim Beam, The Antique Trader 18
Jim Beam, Van Dyke 25
Lionstone, Engineer 40
Lionstone, Robin Red Breast 125
McCormick, Betsy Ross 25
McCormick, Calamity Jane 35
Ski Country, Ivory Billed Woodpecker 30
Ski Country, Mountain Goat, 1975 35
Ski Country, Political Donkey, 1976 35
Ski Country, Raccoon 30
Wild Turkey, Wild Turkey 35

WHISTLES

Webster defines a whistle as an instrument for making a clear, shrill sound. No wonder children love them. Collectors can whistle a happy tune at virtually every flea market. The most desirable whistles are those associated with well-known characters and personalities. They can command prices that are hardly child's play.

Club: Call & Whistle Collectors Assoc., 2839 E. 26th Place, Tulsa, OK 74114.

Acme Thunderer, all brass, nickel plated .40
BF Goodrich, bird, plastic, yellow 22
Boat, hard plastic, yellow and white 8
Boy Scout, 2" l 5
Charm, 14K yg, .5" l 20
Cracker Jack, metal 15
Dairy Queen, ice cream cone, hard plastic, 3.25" h 5
Foremost Dairy, horn, hard plastic, red and off-white, 1950s, 5" l 32
German, brass, pre-WWII, 2" l 15
Gun, hard plastic, red and blue, 3" h 14
Heinz Pickle, green, 3" l 5
Hopalong Cassidy, tin, 2.75" l 25
Nabisco, Mr Peanut, plastic, orange, 2.5" h 15
Police, mkd "Police Special" 15
Poll Parrot Shoes, litho tin, barrel type, parrot head on 1 end of barrel, red star symbol for "Red Star Shoes" on other end, green and red lettering on yellow ground, F L Rand Co, St Louis, 1930s 50

Souvenir, Santa's Village, banana, hard plastic, yellow, 6" l 5
Thimble, Landon/Knox, 1936 25
Train Engine, plastic, red, 1950s 12
Train Engine and Tender, plastic, red and yellow 14
Two Birds, hard plastic, red, 1950s, 3.5" h .16

WHITE-KNOB WINDUPS

White-Knob Windups are small, plastic mechanical toys. They arrived on the market in the mid-1970s. Their name is derived from the small white ridged knob found at the end of the metal rod that extends from the body and winds the motor.

Club: White Knob Wind-Up Collectors Club, 61 Garrow St., Auburn, NY 13021.

Baby Donald Duck 14
Bart Simpson 5
Bear, playing music with hand-tapping instrument 4
Bugs Bunny 12
Cabbage Patch Kid 8
California Raisin 10
Chuck E. Cheese 5
Chuckie, Nickelodeon's TV Rug Rats 4
Disney's Mickey Mouse Hat 4
Doozer, Fraggle Rock 20
ET 15
Fred Flintstone 5
French Fries, Burger King 15
Garfield 12
Gargamel, Smurfs .10
Genie, Disney's *Aladdin* 5
Hamburgler, McDonald's 10
Helicopter 5
Humpty-Dumpty 5
Ice Cream Cone 5
Lady Bug 5
Mother Goose 12
Oscar the Grouch 25
Pacman 10
Pink Panther 15
Pluto 25
Popeye 12
Sebastian, Disney's *The Little Mermaid* 4
Shark 5
Smurfette 5
Snoopy 5
Speedboat, #351 12
Spiderman 15
Stegosaurus 4
Sweating Pig 4
The Tick 10
Woody Woodpecker 20
Yogi Bear 5

WICKER

Wicker and rattan furniture enjoyed its first American craze during the late Victorian era. It was found on porches and summer cottages across America. It realized a second period of popularity in the 1920s and 1930s and a third period in the 1950s. In truth, wicker has been available continuously since the 1870s.

Early wicker has a lighter, airier feel than its later counterparts. Look for unusual forms, e.g., corner chairs or sewing stands. Most wicker was sold unpainted. However, it was common practice to paint it in order to preserve it, especially if it was going to be kept outside. Too many layers of paint decreases the value of a piece.

Armchair, woven back with geometric designs and latticework panels, 1920s 525
Basket, green plastic trim, 1960s, 15" w . . .25
Chest of Drawers, dark finish, 6 drawers 300
Creel, leather trim pouch and shoulder strap 475
Doll Stroller, green, metal frame, 1910s-20s, 26" l, 28" h 85
Fernery, 2 shelves framed by braiding, pattern woven into 2 sides of skirting, 1920s 475
Fernery, fishbowl center with 2 flower sections and woven bottom shelf, 1915 475
Fernery, handled, flared top, pedestal base, framed by braiding, latticework panels, c1900, 36.5" h 550
Funeral Baskets, pr, white, jack-in-pulpit shape, 25" h 25
Hamper, pale green with pink diamond on front, satin lining, 17.5" h, 17" w 125
Highchair, rattan frame, 44" h 125
Picnic Basket, with plastic tableware, 11.5" w, 20" l 25

Planter, with liner, 31.25" h, 27.5" w 225
Purse, black and white striped, gold metal closure, lined with black and white floral fabric 85
Purse, butterfly ornamentation, Princess Charming by Atlas, 8.5" h, 12.5" w 100
Rocking Chair, serpentine rolled back and arms, loop work and latticework panel in back, beaded front skirting, 1890s 495
Scale, baby, 1890 115
Sewing Basket, wooden beads, orange, 6.5" d 20
Sewing Stand, child's, woven top with diamond designs, cabriole turned legs, wood bottom shelf, cane-wrapped handle, 1900 395
Stool, Heywood-Wakefield, white 150
Table Lamp, 24" h, 18" d 175
Tables, nesting pr, dark brown finish 200
Tea Strainer, 5.25" l, 2.25" opening on strainer basket 5
Wall Shelf, with drawer, white, 22" h, 17" w 60
Wastebasket, tooled crocodile leather trim, 15" h, 12" w 90
Wine Rack, 26" h, 13" w 60

WILLOW WARE

The traditional Willow pattern, developed by Josiah Spode in 1810, is the most universally recognized china pattern. A typical piece contains the following elements in its motif: willow tree, "apple" tree, two pagodas, fence, two birds, and three figures crossing a bridge.

Willow pattern china was made in almost every country that produces ceramics. In the 1830s over 200 English companies offered Willow pattern china. Buffalo China was one of the first American companies to offer the pattern. Japanese production started about 1902, around the same time Buffalo made its first pieces.

Since the Willow pattern has been in continuous production, the term reproduction has little meaning. However, the Scio Pottery, Scio, Ohio, is currently producing an unmarked set that is being sold in variety stores. Because it lacks marks, some collectors have purchased it under the mistaken belief that it was made much earlier.

Club: International Willow Collectors, 503 Chestnut St., Perkasie, PA 18944.

Ashtray, blue, Royal China 18
Bowl, blue, tab handles, Royal China, 6.25" d 40
Bowl, green, Royal China, 10" d 40
Bowl, pink, tab handles, Royal China, 6.25" d 45
Bowl, red, Royal China, 6.5" w 8
Bread and Butter Plate, blue, Royal China, 6.25" d 5
Casserole, cov, blue, Royal China 90
Charger, pink, Royal China, 13.25" d 60
Chop Platter, blue, Royal China, 11.5" d . . .28
Chop Platter, green, Royal China, 13.25" d .80
Chop Platter, pink, Royal China, 12" d 32
Coffee Cup, blue, design on handle, Royal China 16

Creamer, blue, Japan 10
Creamer, pink, Royal China 12
Dinner Plate, black, Royal China, 9.25" d . .20
Dinner Plate, blue, Churchill, 10.375" d 12
Dinner Plate, blue, Homer Laughlin, 9" d . .16
Dinner Plate, blue, Japan, 9.5" d 12
Dinner Plate, blue, Royal China, 9" d 25
Dinner Plate, blue, Shenango 12
Dinner Plate, mulberry, 8.75" d 125
Gravy Boat, blue, Royal China 25
Gravy Boat, pink, Royal China 30
Gravy Ladle, white, Royal China 50
Grill Plate, brown, Royal China, 11.5" d . . .40
Oil and Vinegar Set, blue, Royal China . . .145
Pie Baker, blue, Royal China, 10" d 50
Pitcher, blue, Victoria Ware, 5" h 150
Platter, black, Royal China, 8.75" x 11" l . . .25
Platter, blue, Homer Laughlin, 11" l 28
Platter, blue, Japan, 9" x 12.5" 70
Platter, blue, Royal China, 13" x 10" 40
Platter, blue, tab handles, Royal China, 10.5" d 20
Platter, pink, Royal China, 13" x 10" 35
Salad Plate, blue, Japan, 7" d 10
Salad Plate, pink, Royal China, 7.25" d 18
Salt and Pepper Shakers, blue, design on handle, Royal China 40
Salt and Pepper Shaker, blue, no design on handle, Royal China 30
Vegetable Bowl, blue, Japan 15
Vegetable Bowl, blue, oval, Buffalo Pottery 20
Vegetable Bowl, blue, Royal China, 8.5" d .10
Vegetable Bowl, pink, Royal China, 10" d . .35
Snack Plate, blue, Royal China, 9" d 40
Soup Bowl, blue, Royal China, 8.25" d 12
Sugar Bowl, pink, cov, tab handles, Royal China 25
Teapot, blue, droop spout, Royal China . . .80
Teapot, blue, flat spout, Royal China 70
Tumbler, blue, Royal China, 5" h 40

WORLD'S FAIRS

It says a lot about the status of world's fairs when Americans cannot stage a fair in 1993–1994 that is even half as good as the 1893 Columbian Exposition in Chicago. Was the last great world's fair held in New York in 1964? Judging from recent fairs, the answer is an unqualified yes. Although it is important to stress three-dimensional objects for display purposes, do not overlook the wealth of paper that was given away to promote fairs and their participants.

Clubs: 1904 World's Fair Society, 12934 Windy Hill Dr., St. Louis, MO 63128; World's Fair Collectors' Society, P.O. Box 20806, Sarasota, FL 34276.

1933 Century of Progress, garrison cap, purple flannel, white symbols and title on 1 side, 4-color Travel Building, Sky Ride, and Fort Dearborn on other side, green felt inner crown 40
1933 Century of Progress, letter opener, mkd "A Century of Progress, Chicago, June 1st-Nov 1st, 1933," metal, 7.25" l .125
1933 Century of Progress, pinback button, blue and white Fair symbol 20
1933 Century of Progress, toy, "A Century of Progress, Chicago 1933, Greyhound Lines" Bus, mkd "AMC 1933," Arcade, 14.25" l 330
1939 New York, pennant, dark purple felt with orange end band, white lettering, and multicolor images, 27" l, 7.5" h 45
1939 New York, paperweight, Trylon and Perisphere, "Made in USA Syroco Wood Syracuse, NY" label, orig mailer box . . .40

1939 New York, pin, silvered metal, twin-engine plane, "World's Fair USA" on upper wing, "Flight 1939 NX18973" on lower wing, disk hanging from propeller inscribed "New York World's Fair 1939" around Trylon and Perisphere . . .35
1939 New York, thermometer, rect with Trylon and Perisphere, Syroco, 4" h, 2" w 15
1939 New York, toy, litho tin, "Greyhound Lines, New York World's Fair" Trolley, orig paint, 10.5" l 350
1964-65 New York, license plate attachment, litho tin, emb gold and white Unisphere at center, "Peace Through Understanding," 6" x 12" 18
1964-65 New York, pinback button, celluloid, multicolor, 22 participating nations' names around rim, "I Was There," 3.5" d 25
1964-65 New York, plate, white china, Pool of Industry, Heliport, Monorail, and Unisphere in center, emb floral dec on rim, gold trim, 9" d 15

WRESTLING MEMORABILIA

The names used in professioinal wrestling are almost as entertaining as the performances. No longer considered a "sport," wrestling still has a huge following of loyal fans.

Action Figure, Biz Ref, 5" h, 1999 4
Action Figure, Jakks Blue Blazer 15
Action Figure, Nikolai Volkoff, bendable arms and legs, Tilan Sports Inc, 1985 . . .25
Action Figure, Randy Savage, WCW, 7" h .25
Action Figure, Ric Flair, flexible arms and legs, 6" h 12
Action Figure, WCW Hak 15
Action Figure, WCW Vader 20
Action Figure, WWF Mankind, with ladder 15
Bean Bag Figure, Diamond Dallas Page . . .8
Belt Buckle, pewter with gold enameling, 1985, 5.5" x 4.25" .70
Big Head Figure, Buff Bagwell, WCW/NW, 1999, 8" h 5
Board Game, Milton Bradley, WWF Wrestling Stars Game, 1985 20
Book, *The Rock Says,* by the Rock, 2000 . .20
Comic Book, "Pro Wrestling's True Facts" .4
Doll, porcelain, Sumo Wrestler, Tanikaze Kajinosuke, 9" h .150
Medal, "4th 120LB 1948" on back, 1" h 5
Model Kit, The Undertaker, 10" h 8
Movie Poster, *The Greats of International Wrestling* 75
Photograph, Hulk Hogan, 8" x 10" 28
Pin, 1984 Olympics Wrestling, Coca-Cola . .4
Program, Dec 2, 1966 Championship
Program, Spectacle in Montevideo, Uruguay, Sep 1913, 11.5" x 8.75" 20
Shirt, Nash image, black 10
Snap-together Figure, Undertaker, WWF, 24 pcs, 10" h 25
Sweater, Hulk Hogan .6

WORLD WAR II

Although some World War II material was included in the militaria category, so much is available that a separate category is also warranted.

Blotter, multicolor, "Defend Your Country, Defend Your Car's Life," Sunoco Oil, 1943, 3.5" x 6.5" 20
Carnival Chalkware, baby wearing pistol belt, holster, and Navy cap, holding 2 pistols, "Remember Pearl Harbor," 1943 100
Comic Book, "I Was a Nazi Flier," German pilot's diary, Dell War Book, 1941 50
Greeting Card, Easter, "From Someone in the Service Who Loves You," large flowered "V" with gold eagle top, Gibson, 8" x 10" 25
License Plate Attachment, metal, "Remember Pearl Harbor," image of plane and battleship, black, red, and white, 3.5" x 8" 35
Magazine, *Warplanes of the World,* #1, 1943 annual, Dell Publishing, 100 pgs, red and white cover with center full color photo of blue "Grumman TBF-1 Avenger" in flight, black and white photos and articles related to air warfare, 8.5" x 11.25" 15
Matchcover, "Registered for National Defense," image of Iowa state seal, 1.5" x 4.75" 3

Milk Bottle Cap, wax cardboard insert, image of aircrafts, inscribed "Keep 'Em Flying/Buy Bonds," Raw Milk Products . . 8

Paper Dolls, Girl Pilots of the Ferry Command, Saalfield, 1943, 11" x 14" 75

Pennant, felt, "Let's Go Americans/ Remember Pearl Harbor," blue, white, and yellow, 8" x 30" 75

Pillow Cover, "Army Air Forces, Truax Army Air Field, Madison, Wis," silk, flocked planes and banner, dark blue ground, red fringe, 17.5" sq 25

Pinback Button, celluloid, "Jap Hunting License – Open Season, No Limit," 1.25" d 50

Poster, "A Careless Word...A Needless Sinking," full color art of wounded seamen in boat departing destroyed battleship, Anton Otto Fischer, Office of War Information #24, Government Printing Office #502219, 1942, 28" x 37" . . 50

Poster, "Deliver Us From Evil/Buy War Bonds," black and white, blue text at bottom with photo of war-torn refugee girl in center, large white swastika in background against storm clouds, Official US Treasury poster, 1943, 22" x 28" 35

Salt and Pepper Shakers, pr, bomb shape, "V" on 1, "Morse Code" on other, 3.5" h 45

Seed Packet, Victory Garden, Richfield Co 20

Toy, Army-Navy Junior Fighting Forces, 150 pcs, 45 units, DA Practer & Co, 1943, 18" x 24" 175

YARD-LONG PRINTS

Yard-long prints cover a wide variety of subject matter. Desirability rests not so much with subject as with illustrator. The more recognized the name, the higher the price.

Ben Austrian, "Battle of the Chicks," baby chicks fighting for a moth 100

CL Van Vredeburgh, "Yard Of Kittens," kittens in a field of white daisies 125

CW Henning, Pabst Extract, "American Girl," woman on horseback, 1911 175

F Earle Christy, "The Witching Hour," Pompeian Beauty Calendar, 1915, 4.5" x 18.5" 50

Grace Barton Allen, basket overflowing with red carnations 80

Grace Barton Allen, "Yard of Pansies" . . . 80

Gregson, NY, Cosmopolitan Lady, woman in long red dress holding a rose by her face, 1914 150

Guy Bedford, "A Yard of Mixed Flowers" . 90

Howard Chandler Christy, "She Held a Deep Red Rose," Victorian lady with long-stemmed rose, 1907, 9.5" x 7" 50

J Hoover & Son, "Swallows over Lilypads," 1897 150

Maud Humphrey, "Butterfly Time," 5 children in front of flowers and playing with butterflies, 1903 200

Newton A Wells, "American Beauty Roses," long-stemmed roses in glass vase 90

"The White Rabbit," floral print, wooden frame 60

YO-YOS

Yo-yos are the only collecting category I know of where the collector is sometimes accused of being what he collects! In recent years yo-yos have become increasingly recognized as one of the hottest new collectibles. Some makes and models of vintage yo-yos from the 1920s thorugh the 1960s are now worth hundreds of times their original retail price, depending on condition and rarity.

Baseball-Shaped 4
Buzz Lightyear, changes pictures as it moves, 2"d 32
Duncan, Butterfly, #3058NP, green, mail-in offer and instructions on back . . 15
Duncan, glow-in-the-dark 6
Duncan, key chain, red and white 6
Duncan, wooden, black and red, mkd "Genuine Duncan Yo-Yo," 1930s 25
Eleyo, battery operated, lights up, 1950s . . .5
Gorham, sterling repousse, 2.25" d 165
Grinch Who Stole Christmas, promotional, 2" d 45
Mark Martin, Nascar #6 5
Marsupilama, Disney character 4
Millennium 2000, wooden, black and gold 20
Pepsi-Cola, bottle cap, 2"d 2
Pez, plastic, red and blue, Germany, 1970s 20
Political, plastic, Jimmy Carter, white with black lettering, "Plains, Georgia. Home of President Jimmy Carter" 10
Poll Parrot Shoes, Leonard's Department Store 10
Pro Flash Boy, plastic, pink sparkles 8
Sea Rider, clear plastic with embedded specks of glitter 6
Smothers Brothers, Kodak, red 4
Star Trek, Deep Space Nine, Commander Data, 1993 Spectra Star 10
Sunbeam, lights up, 2.5" d 5
Thrasher, clear plastic with embedded specks of glitter and real shark teeth . . .8
Tiffany, Stockbroker's, SS, engraved "High Yield" 135
Wooden, design of circles within circles on each side, 1950s 8

ZOO COLLECTIBLES

I have been trying for years to find "Z" categories to end antiques and collectibles price guides. Finally, a book in which zoo collectibles are not out of place!

Bell, Brookfield Zoo, African Safari scene, porcelain, gold accents, 4" h 6
Candy Jar, koala, San Diego Zoo, glass, plastic lid, 6.5" h 5
Coaster, San Diego Zoo, metal, tiger in center, 3" w 4
Figurine, Berma the Elephant, Racine Zoo, plastic 4
Figurine, Crinoline Lady ballerina, Cincinnati Zoo, 4.75" h 25
Frame Tray Puzzle, cardboard, 1966 Whitman Zoo Friends, features tiger, monkey, bear, birds, zebra, hippo, and lion, 7 pcs, 8" x 10" 5
Magazine, *Saint Louis Zoo Album*, illus guide to St Louis Zoological Park and classes Mammalia, Aves, Reptilia, and Amphibia, 96 pgs 10
Plate, St Louis Zoo, vignettes of lion cub, zebras, elephant, Big Cat Country, Bear Pits, and Zoo Line, 7.25" d 6
Postcard, Carnivore House at the Philadelphia Zoo 2
Postcard, entrance to Overton Park Zoo, Memphis, TN, 1911 .5
Postcard, Philadelphia Zoo, lioness and her 5 cubs 5
Postcard, St Petersburg Alligator Farm and Zoo, FL 15
Postcard, Viennese Zoo, European boy embracing 2 black boys, 1898 22
Salt and Pepper Shakers, Cincinnati Zoo, parrots, 3" h 15
Snow Globe, Turtle Back Zoo, bottle, 1970s, 6.5" w, 2.75" h 12
Souvenir Spoon, San Diego Zoo, applied medallion of koala bears, SP, 4.5" l 5

Part Three

REFERENCE SOURCES

FLEA MARKETEER'S ANNOTATED REFERENCE LIBRARY

A typical flea market contains hundreds of thousands of objects. You cannot be expected to identify and know the correct price for everything off the top of your head. You need a good, basic reference library.

As a flea marketeer, there are two questions about every object that you want to know: "What is it?" and "How much is it worth?" A book that answers only the first question has little use in the field. Titles in the "Books About Objects" list contain both types of information.

This is a basic library, a starting point. Acquiring all the titles on the list will not be cheap. Expect to pay somewhere between $1,250 and $1,500. You can occasionally find some of these books at clearance prices—25% to 75% off—from the publishers or at discount booksellers.

The list contains a few books that are out-of-print. You will have to pursue their purchase through various used-book sources.

Many antiques and collectibles book dealers conduct book searches and maintain "wants" lists. It is common to find one or more of these specialized dealers set up at a flea market. Most advertise in the trade papers, especially ***The Antique Trader Weekly*** (700 E. State St., Iola, WI 54945) and "Books For Sale" in the classified section of ***AntiqueWeek*** (PO Box 90, Knightstown, IN 46148). One dealer that I have found particularly helpful in locating out-of-print books is Joslin Hall Rare Books, PO Box 516, Concord, MA 01742. Also check these web sites: www.bookfinder.com and www.abebooks.com.

Many reference books are revised every year or every other year. The editions listed are those as of Fall 2003. When you buy them, make certain that you get the most recent edition.

One final factor that I used in preparing this list was a desire to introduce you to the major publishers and imprints in the antiques and collectibles field. It is important that you become familiar with the Charlton Press, Collector Books, House of Collectibles, Krause Publications and its various imprints, L-W Book Sales, and Schiffer Publishing.

General Price Guides

Does a flea marketeer need a general antiques and collectibles price guide? The realistic answer is no. As each year passes, antiques play a smaller and smaller role in the flea market environment. General antiques and collectibles price guides tend to be heavily weighted toward the antiques portion of the market. Most flea marketeers, whether buyers or sellers, deal primarily in 20th century collectibles.

Yet, I believe every flea marketeer should maintain a multiple year run of one general antiques and collectibles price guide for the purposes of tracking market trends and researching and pricing objects that fall outside their knowledge level. The worst mistake a flea marketeer can make is to buy a different general antiques and collectibles price guide from one year to the next. Find the guide that best serves your need and stick to it.

The following price guides are listed in the order of frequency that I see them being used in the field. The order is not by my personal preference. However, I am putting aside personal feelings and reporting facts.

Huxford, Sharon and Bob, eds., ***Schroeder's Antiques Price Guide, 21st ed.*** (Paducah, KY: Collector Books, 2003).

Kovel, Ralph and Terry, eds., ***Kovels' Antiques & Collectibles Price List 2003, 35th ed.*** (New York: Three Rivers Press, 2002).

Husfloen, Kyle, ed., ***Antique Trader Antiques and Collectibles 2003 Price Guide,*** (Iola, WI: Krause Publications, 2002).

Identification of Reproductions and Fakes

Hammond, Dorothy, ***Confusing Collectibles: A Guide to the Identification of Reproductions*** (Leon, IA: Mid-America Book Company, 1969). This book provides information about reproductions, copycats, fantasy items, fakes, and contemporary crafts from the late 1950s through the 1960s. Much of this material appears regularly in today's flea markets. Some is collectible in its own right. The best defense against being taken is to know what was produced.

Hammond, Dorothy, ***More Confusing Collectibles, Vol. II*** (Wichita, KS: C.B.P. Publishing Company, 1972). Out-of-print. Confusing Collectibles took a broad approach to the market. *More Confusing Collectibles* focuses primarily on glass. It contains all new information, so you really do need both volumes.

Lee, Ruth Webb, ***Antique Fakes and Reproductions*** (published by author, 1938, 1950). Out-of-print. Note: This book went through eight editions. The later editions contain more information. A good rule is to buy only the fourth through eighth editions. Dorothy Hammond followed in Ruth Webb Lee's footsteps. Lee's book chronicles the reproductions, copycats, fantasy items, and fakes manufactured between 1920 and 1950. While heavily oriented toward glass, it contains an excellent chapter on metals, discussing and picturing in detail the products of Virginia Metalcrafters.

Antique & Collectors Reproduction News. This is not a book, yet it belongs on this list. This monthly publication tracks the latest reproductions, copycats, fantasy items, and fakes. An annual subscription costs $32, an amount you are certain to save several times over during the course of a year. Consider acquiring a full set of back issues. Write Antique & Collectors Reproduction News, PO Box 12130, Des Moines, IA 50312.

Krause has published three "best of" books containing articles that have appeared in ***Antique & Collectors Reproduction News—Antique Trader Guide to Fakes & Reproductions, 1st Edition*** (2001), ***2nd Edition*** (2002) and ***3rd Edition*** (2003). Also worth obtaining is the ***Antique Trader Guide to Fake & Forged Marks*** (2002).

Books About Objects

Austin, Richard J., ***The Official Price Guide to Military Collectibles, 7th ed.*** (New York: House of Collectibles, 2004). This book covers military collectibles from medieval to modern times. The book is organized topically, e.g., uniforms and footwear, helmets and headgear, etc. It also includes chapters on military images, military paper, military art, and homefront collectibles. It provides one-volume coverage of the material found in Ron Manion's three-volume set *American Military Collectibles Price* (1995), *Japanese & Other Foreign Military Collectibles* (1996), and *German Military Collectibles* (1995), all published by Antique Trader Books.

Bagdade, Susan and Al, ***Warman's American Pottery and Porcelain, 2nd ed.*** (Iola, WI: Krause Publications, 2000). Recommended because of its wide range of coverage. The category introductions provide a wealth of good information, including a large number of drawings of marks. Pricing that is auction based is clearly indicated. Use to cross-check information in Duke's *The Official Price Guide to Pottery and Porcelain*.

The Bagdades also authored ***Warman's English & Continental Pottery & Porcelain, 3rd ed.*** (Iola, WI: Krause Publications, 1998). While most ceramics found at American flea markets are American in origin, European pieces do slip into the mix. If you encounter English and Continental ceramics on a regular basis, consider adding this second Bagdade book to your library.

Baker, Mark, ***Auto Racing Memorabilia and Price Guide*** (Iola, WI: Krause Publications, 1996). Auto racing collectibles replaced baseball collectibles as the hot sport collecting category of the 1990s. Collecting auto racing memorabilia, from dirt track to Indy cars, has shed its regional cloak and become national in scope. Baker's book is the first off the starting line.

Barlow, Ronald S., ***The Antique Tool Collector's Guide to Value*** (Gas City, IN: L-W Book Sales, 1991, 1999 value update). This is the book for tools. Barlow has compiled auction and market prices from across the United States. Since this book is organized by tool type, you need to identify the type of tool that you have before you can look it up. There are plenty of illustrations to help. Treat the pricing with some caution.

Collectors' Information Bureau's Collectibles Market Guide & Price Index, 18th ed. (Barrington, IL: Collectors' Information Bureau, 2000). The best thing about this book is that it covers a wide range of limited edition types, from bells to steins. It serves as a collector's checklist. The worst thing is that it is industry-driven. Important negatives and warnings about the limited edition market are minimized. When the issue value and secondary value are identical or within a few dollars assume the real secondary market value is between 20% and 40% of the issue price.

Mary L. Seiber's (ed.) ***2003 Price Guide to Contemporary Collectibles and Limited Editions, 8th Edition*** (Iola, WI: Krause Publications, 2002) is an alternate choice.

Cornwell, Sue and Mike Kott, ***House of Collectibles Price Guide to Star Trek Collectibles, 4th ed.*** (New York: House of Collectibles, 1996). There is no question that Star Trek collectibles will "live long and prosper." This price guide covers over 5,000 items licensed for the initial Star Trek television program, the movies, and television spin-off series, Star Trek: The Next Generation, Star Trek: Voyager, and Deep Space 9. Includes some foreign licensed materials. Unfortunately, a chapter on convention souvenirs is nowhere to be found.

Cornwell, Sue and Mike Kott, ***House of Collectibles Price Guide to Star Wars Collectibles, 4th ed.*** (New York: House of Collectibles, 1997). Star Wars won the galactic battle over Star Trek for universal dominance in the field of space collectibles with Lucas' 1997 re-release of the Star Wars trilogy. When the first of the prequels premiered in May 1999, the world went Star Wars mad. Many, myself among them, predicted a major pricing jump in older Star Wars material. This book documents values prior to their jump to light speed. As an alternate reference source, see *The Galaxy's Greatest Star Wars Collectibles Price Guide,* 1999 Edition by Stuart W. Wells III (Dubuque, IA: Antique Trader Books, 1998).

Cunningham, Jo, ***The Collector's Encyclopedia of American Dinnerware*** (Paducah, KY: Collector Books, 1982, 1998 price update). This is a profusely illustrated guide to identifying 20th century American dinnerware. In spite of the fact that many new companies and patterns have been discovered since Cunningham prepared her book, it remains a valuable identification tool, especially since its pricing is updated periodically.

Dale, Jean, ***The Charlton Standard Catalogue of Royal Doulton Figurines, 8th ed.*** (Toronto, Canada: The Charlton Press, 2003). This is one in a series of four books edited by Dale covering the products of Royal Doulton Beswick. The others are: ***The Charlton Standard Catalogue of Royal Doulton Animals, 3rd Ed.*** (2002); ***Charlton Standard Catalogue Royal Doulton Beswick Jugs, 7th ed.*** (2003); and ***Charlton Standard Catalogue of Royal Doulton Beswick Storybook Figurines, 6th ed.*** (2000). A feature of each of these books is that pricing information is provided in English pounds, Canadian dollars, and American dollars. Americans should pay more attention to books published by The Charlton Press. The title list also includes books on chintz and hockey trading cards.

Florence, Gene, ***The Collector's Encyclopedia of Depression Glass, 15th ed.*** (Paducah, KY: Collector Books, 2002). This is the Depression glass collector's bible. Among its important features are a full listing of pieces found in each pattern and an extensive section on reproductions, copycats, and fakes. One difficulty is that there are hundreds of glass patterns manufactured between 1920 and 1940 that are not found in this book because they do not have the Depression Glass label. Supplement the book with Gene Florence's sixth editions of ***Kitchen Glassware of the Depression Years*** and ***Collectible Glassware from the 40s, 50s, 60s…,*** both published by Collector Books, ***Mauzy's Depression Glass, 3rd Edition*** (Schiffer Publishing, 2003) by Barbara and Jim Mauzy, and ***Warman's Depression Glass: A Value & Identification Guide, 3rd ed.*** (Krause Publications, 2003) by Ellen Schroy.

Foulke, Jan, ***16th Blue Book Dolls and Values*** (Grantsville, MD: Hobby House Press, 2003). Foulke is the first place doll collectors turn for information. The book is high-end, turning its back on many of the post–World War II and contemporary dolls. Within the doll field, it sets prices more than it reports them. Cross-check Foulke's prices in Dawn Herlocher's ***200 Years of Dolls, Second Edition: Identification and Price Guide*** (Iola, WI: Krause Publications, 2002).

Franklin, Linda Campbell, ***300 Years of Housekeeping Collectibles*** (Books Americana, now an imprint of Krause Publications, Iola, WI, 1993). Books Americana split the second edition of *300 Years of Kitchen Collectibles* into two separate volumes, albeit retaining the edition number for one of the spin-offs. Now, instead of paying $10.95 for a handy-to-use single source, you have to pay $47.90 for two volumes. Hopefully a publisher will see an opportunity and once again put this information in a single volume. Until such time, it makes sense to buy the two Franklin volumes.

Franklin, Linda Campbell, ***300 Years of Kitchen Collectibles, 5th ed.*** (Iola, WI: Krause Publications, 2003). The fifth edition's format is easy to use. The wealth of secondary material may is great for researchers and specialized collectors. Focus is primarily in 19th and early 20th century material. It is not the source to use if your kitchen item dates from the post-1945 era.

Hagan, Tere, ***Silverplated Flatware, Revised 4th ed.*** (Paducah, KY: Collector Books, 1990, 2002 value update). You do not see a great deal of sterling silver at flea markets because most dealers sell it for weight. Silver-plated items are in abundance. This book concentrates only on flatware, the most commonly found form. While you can research silver-plated hollowware in Jeri Schwartz's ***The Official Identification and Price Guide to Silver and Silverplate, 6th ed.*** (House of Collectibles, 1989, out-of-print), disregard the prices. The market has changed significantly.

Hake, Ted, ***Hake's Guide to …*** series (Radnor, PA, Wallace-Homestead). In the first half of the 1990s, Ted Hake authored a five-book priced picture-book series focusing on material sold in Hake's Americana & Collectibles Mail Auction. Each collecting category is introduced with a brief history, often containing information not readily available to the collector. The series consists of: ***Hake's Guide to Advertising Collectibles: 100 Years of Advertising From 100 Famous Companies*** (1992); ***Hake's Guide to Comic Character Collectibles: An Illustrated Price Guide to 100 Years of Comic Strip Characters*** (1993); ***Hake's Guide to Cowboy Character Collectibles: An Illustrated Price Guide Covering 50 Years of Movie and TV Cowboy Heroes*** (1994); ***Hake's Guide to Presidential Campaign Collectibles: An Illustrated Price Guide to Artifacts from 1789–1988*** (1992); and, ***Hake's Guide to TV Collectibles: An Illustrated Price Guide*** (1990). Several titles are out-of-print. Some are still available from Krause Publications.

Allowing this series to die was one in a long list of mistakes made by Chilton Books in the company's final years as publisher of Wallace-Homestead and Warman titles.

Hake, Ted, ***The Official Hake's Price Guide to Character Toys, 4th ed.*** (New York: Random House, 2002). Hake is the king of collectibles. If anyone knows, he does. This title covers 350 categories and more than 200 different characters. Its 6,000 plus listings range from common to one-of-a-kind premiums and each entry is accompanied by an illustration. The category introductions provide historical data not available elsewhere. Also be sure to read the front matter. It provides insights into the latest market trends.

Herlocher, Dawn, ***200 Years of Dolls, Second Edition: Identification and Price Guide*** (Iola, WI: Krause Publications, 2002). Doll identification and pricing information presented in an extremely usable format. Covering more than one hundred doll manufacturers, the book features a mix of antique and collectibles dolls. Use to cross-check the information and pricing in Foulke's ***Blue Book of Doll Values.*** See also ***Doll Makers & Marks: A Guide to Identification*** (Dubuque, IA: Antique Trader Books, 1999) by Dawn Herlocher.

Huxford, Bob, ***Huxford's Old Book Value Guide, 14th ed.*** (Paducah, KY: Collector Books, 2003). There are always piles of old books at any flea market. Most are valued at less than 50 cents. However, there are almost always sleepers in every pile. This book is a beginning. If you think that you have a really expensive tome, check it out in the most recent edition of ***American Book Prices Current,*** published by Bancroft-Parkman.

Huxford, Sharon and Bob (eds.), ***Shroeder's Collectible Toys: Antique to Modern Price Guide, 8th ed.*** (Paducah, KY: Collector Books, 2002). See also [O'Brien's] ***Collecting Toys: Identification & Value Guide, 10th ed.*** edited by Elizabeth A. Stephan (Iola, WI: Krause Publications, 2001) and ***2003 Toys & Prices, 10th ed.*** edited by Sharon Korbeck and Dan Stearns (Iola, WI: Krause Publications, 2002).

Malloy, Alex G., ***American Games: Comprehensive Collector's Guide*** (Iola, WI: Antique Trader Books/Krause Publications, 2000). There are a number of guides to games. Malloy's provides the most comprehensive listing. The descriptions are minimal. Always check a game's instructions for information on what playing pieces are needed to make the game complete. Harry L. Rinker's ***Antique Trader's Guide to Games & Puzzles*** (Antique Trader Books, 1997) offers a second opinion and expands the coverage to puzzles.

Martinus, Norman E., and Harry L. Rinker, ***Warman's Paper*** (Radnor, PA: Wallace-Homestead, 1994, out-of-print).The paper market is hot and getting hotter. Paper is available and affordable. The market already has dozens of specialized shows. ***Warman's Paper*** is organized into seventy-five collecting topics and over two hundred subject topics. Of all the books with which I have been involved, this title ranks number three on my "most proud" list, right behind ***The Official Rinker Price Guide to Collectibles, Post-1920s Memorabilia*** and ***Warman's Furniture*** (out-of-print).

Melillo, Marcie, ***The Ultimate Barbie Doll Book*** (Iola, WI: Krause Publications, 1997). Barbie—the vinyl goddess, the billion-dollar baby—has become so important she deserves a separate listing. There are dozens of Barbie price guides available. This is my favorite full coverage guide. When I want information on contemporary Barbies, my choice is the new edition of Jane Sarasohn-Kahn's ***Contemporary Barbie: Barbie Dolls 1980 and Beyond*** (Antique Trader Books, 1998). Also consider adding a Barbie price guide that includes information on costumes and accessories, two hot Barbie subcollecting categories in the late 1990s.

Morykan, Dana G., ***The Official Price Guide to Country Antiques and Collectibles, 4th ed.*** (New York: House of Collectibles, 1999). This is the bible for Country collectibles. In it, you'll find information on thousands of antiques and collectibles from nineteenth- and twentieth-century rural life. Published previously as part of the Warman series, it has found a new home in New York.

Osborne, Jerry, ***The Official Price Guide to Records, 16th ed.*** (New York: House of Collectibles, 2002). This is the book to which everyone refers. It lists every charted hit single and album from the 1950s through 1990. Alas, it provides minimal coverage for pre–1940 records. Today, record collecting is highly specialized. There are dozens of specialized price guides to records, many published by Krause Publications. See also ***Goldmine Records & Prices*** edited by Tim Neely (Iola, WI: Krause Publications, 2002).

Overstreet, Robert M., ***The Official Overstreet Comic Book Price Guide, 32nd ed.*** (New York: House of Collectibles, 2002). Long live the king. Although focused too heavily on the Golden and Silver Age of American comics and not heavily enough on contemporary American comics, foreign issues, and underground comics, Overstreet is clearly the price guide of choice among adult collectors. This book sets the market more than it reports it.

Petretti, Allan, ***Petretti's Soda Pop Collectibles Price Guide, 2nd Edition: The Encyclopedia of Soda Pop Collectibles*** (Norfolk, VA: Antique Trader Books, A Division of Landmark Specialties Publications, 1999). This is the latest offering from the king of Coca–Cola collectibles. This priced picture guide is organized first by object type and then alphabetically by soda company. Do not overlook Allan Petretti's ***Petretti's Coca-Cola Collectibles Price Guide, 11th ed.*** (Krause Publications, 2001). It utilizes the Petretti numbering system, an easy method to describe Coca-Cola collectibles.

Rinker, Harry L., ***Dinnerware of the Twentieth Century: Top 500 Patterns*** (New York: House of Collectibles, 1997). This book provides detailed information on the 500 most popular dinnerware patterns sought by replacement buyers. Each pattern has an illustration of the plate from the set and a comprehensive checklist of the forms available. There are two other titles in this series: ***Stemware of the Twentieth Century: Top 200 Patterns*** covers the 200 most popular stemware patterns and ***Silverware of the Twentieth Century: Top 250 Patterns*** includes the 250 most popular sterling, silver plated, and stainless flatware patterns. Buy all three.

Romero, Christie, ***Warman's Jewelry, 3rd ed.*** (Iola, WI: Krause Publications, 2002). The best general price guide to jewelry available. It utilizes a time period approach, is well illustrated, and features highly detailed listing descriptions. The book is loaded with historical information, hallmarks, manufacturer's marks, reference source referrals, and a time line chronicling the history of jewelry. Appendices include a listing of American costume jewelry manufacturers (with dates of operation) and a glossary.

Schroy, Ellen, ***Warman's Glass, 3rd ed.*** (Iola, WI: Krause Publications, 1999). A comprehensive guide to the traditional glass market. While heavily American focused, it does include information on major English and European glass collecting categories. It has a balanced approach, covering everything from the finest art glass to household utilitarian glass. Check out Mark Pickvett's ***The Official Price Guide to Glassware, 3rd ed.*** (New York: House of Collectibles, 2000), a challenger to ***Warman's Glass*** that gets better and better with each new edition.

Shugart, Cooksey, Tom Engle and Richard E. Gilbert, ***Complete Price Guide to Watches, No. 20*** (Cleveland, TN: Cooksey Shugart Publications, 2000). Although this book has been distributed by four different publishers during the past ten years, it has never failed to maintain its high quality. It is the best book available on pocket and wrist watches.

Slusser, John and the Staff of Radio Daze, ***Collector's Guide to Antique Radios, 5th ed.*** (Paducah, KY: Collector Books, 2001). There is a wealth of radio books in the market. This one is tuned in to a wide band of radios. Organization is by manufacturer and model number. Although heavily illustrated, the book does not picture the majority of the models listed. The book also covers radio parts and accessories.

Sports Collectors Digest, ***2003 Baseball Card Price Guide, 17th ed.*** (Iola, WI: Krause Publications, 2002). This book has become a superstar. It is more comprehensive and accurate than its competition. Supplement it with the ***2003 Standard Catalog of Baseball Cards, 12th Edition*** (Iola, WI: Krause Publications, 2002). The one-two hitting combination of these two books relegate James Beckett's ***Baseball Card Price Guide*** to benchwarmer status.

Swedberg, Robert W. and Harriett, ***Collector's Encyclopedia of American Furniture:*** three volumes: ***Volume 1—The Dark Woods of the Nineteenth Century: Cherry, Mahogany, Rosewood, and Walnut*** (1991, 1998 value update); ***Volume 2—Furniture of the Twentieth Century*** (1992, 1999 value update); and ***Volume 3—Country Furniture of the Eighteenth and Nineteenth Centuries*** (1994, 2000 value update). This series is published by Collector Books in Paducah, KY. The Swedbergs write about furniture. While their most recent work is done for Collector Books, Krause Publications still keeps their Wallace-Homestead series on oak furniture in print. It is worth a referral from time to time. Also do not ignore the Swedbergs' ***Furniture of the Depression Era: Furniture & Accessories of the 1920's, 1930's & 1940's*** (Collector Books, 1987, 1999 value update). All books utilize a priced-picture approach. Text information, including descriptions for individual pieces, is minimal. Sources are heavily Midwest. The plus factor is that the books feature pieces for sale in the field, not museum examples.

Wells, Stuart W., III and Jim Main, ***The Official Price Guide to Action Figures, 2nd ed.*** (New York: House of Collectibles, 1999). Finally, we have a price guide to action figures, and it is excellent. It provides background information and detailed listings for twenty-four major action figure groups such as the A-Team, Masters of the Universe, Marvel Superheroes, Spawn, Teenage Mutant Ninja Turtles, and X-Men. It even includes Star Trek and Star Wars figures. Its index is top of the line.

Mark Books

Lehner, Lois, Lehner's ***Encyclopedia of U.S. Marks on Pottery, Porcelain, and Clay*** (Paducah, KY: Collector Books, 1988). This is the best reference book for identifying the marks of United States pottery and porcelain manufacturers. It contains detailed company histories and all known marks and trade names used. Whenever possible, marks and trade names are dated.

Rainwater, Dorothy T., ***Encyclopedia of American Silver Manufacturers, Fourth ed.*** (Atglen, PA: Schiffer Publishing, 1998). This book focuses on hand-crafted and mass-produced factory–manufactured silver and silver plate from the mid-nineteenth century to the present. It is organized alphabetically by company. Each detailed company history is accompanied by carefully drawn and dated marks. A glossary of trademarks is another welcome feature.

Business References

Berg, Garry, ***The Art of Buying & Selling at Flea Markets*** (Grantsville, MD: Hobby House Press, 2003). The information is basic, the writing style chatty. Forget the cuteness and look for solid tips. One good tip will quickly earn back the $19.95 cost of the book.

Huxford, Sharon and Bob Huxford, ***Wanted to Buy, 7th ed.*** (Paducah, KY: Collector Books, 1999). This book lists individuals who want to buy things. If you are a serious collector, write to Collector Books and see if your name and interests can be included in subsequent editions. The book differs from Trash or Treasure because it contains several dozen listings and prices for most categories.

Hyman, Dr. Tony, ***Trash or Treasure Guide of Best Buyers: How and Where to Easily Sell Collectibles, Antiques & Other Treasures*** (Pismo Beach, CA: Treasure Hunt Publications, 2002). Tony Hyman is one of the most magnetic radio personalities that I have ever heard. He writes and compiles. Most importantly, he hustles what he has done. This is a another list of people who buy things. One good contact pays for the cost of the book. It is also a great place to get your collecting interests listed.

Johnson, Don, and Elizabeth Borland, ***Selling Antiques & Collectibles: 50 Ways To Improve Your Business*** (Radnor, PA: Wallace-Homestead, 1993). Out-of-print. In a flea market era when there is a proliferation of dealers and fierce competition for customers, this book gives you the competitive edge. It shows you how to stand out from the crowd, increase clientele, and keep customers coming back. The advice is practical and budget conscious.

Maloney, David, J., ***Maloney's Antiques and Collectibles Resource Directory, 6th ed.*** (Iola, WI: Krause Publications, 2001). This is the one reference book to buy if you are only going to buy one. It is a comprehensive directory to the antiques and collectibles market containing approximately 18,000 entries (names, addresses, telephone numbers, and a wealth of other information) in approximately 3,100 categories. It is fully cross-referenced. It covers buyers, sellers, appraisers, restorers, collectors' clubs, periodicals, museums and galleries, show promoters, shops and malls, and many other specialists.

Internet Buying & Selling

Boileau, Ray, ***The ABCs of Collecting Online, 3rd ed.*** (Grantsville, MD: Hobby House Press, 2000).

Hix, Nancy L., ***Collector's Guide to Buying, Selling and Trading on the Internet, 2nd ed.*** (Paducah, KY: Collector Books, 2000).

Heim, Judy and Gloria Hansen, ***Free Stuff for Collectors on the Internet*** (Lafayette, CA: C&T Publishing, 2000).

Books on buying and selling on the Internet are appearing as fast as publishers can publish them. Given the rapid changing nature of the Internet, they are outdated by the time they hit the bookstore shelves. Instead of using these books as "how-to" books, use them to hone the skills acquired by your own seat-of-the-pants experiences.

The problem with many "how-to" books is that they make it sound so simple. Buying and selling on the Internet is simple and time consuming. Few individuals factor in the cost of their time, equipment, and other expenses when determining how much they paid or made. After hauling the fiftieth box to the post office, selling or buying at an antiques mall or show is an attractive alternate way to do business.

General References

Long, Jane S. and Richard W. Long, ***Caring for Your Family Treasures*** (New York: Harry N. Abrams, 2000). You have a responsibility to care for the antiques, collectibles, and desirables in your possession. This book provides practical care tips. Many are nothing more than common sense, approaches that should be natural but not always are. My advice is to read the book once a year. Even if you do not learn something new, you have a chance to re-evaluate your care procedures to see if changes are warranted.

Rinker, Harry L., ***Rinker on Collectibles*** (Radnor, PA: Wallace–Homestead, 1988). Out-of-print. This book is a compilation of the first sixty text columns from my column, "Rinker on Collectibles." Many are now classics. The book allows you to delve into the mind-set of the collector. It deserves textbook status. I bought the remaining warehouse stock. If you would like a copy, send $10 to: Harry L. Rinker, 5093 Vera Cruz Road, Emmaus, PA 18049. I will even autograph it for you.

Werner, Kitty, ed., ***The Official Directory to U.S. Flea Markets, Eighth Edition*** (New York: House of Collectibles, 2002). My opinion of this book is clearly stated in Chapter 2. Take my suggestion and buy a copy.

Just for the Fun of It

Gash, Jonathan, ***The Sleepers of Erin*** (New York: Viking Penguin, 1983). If you are unfamiliar with Lovejoy the antiques dealer, it is time you make his acquaintance. You will not regret it. I had a hard time picking a favorite. I could have just as easily chosen ***The Judas Pair, Gold by Gemini, The Grail Tree, Spend Game, The Vatican Rip,*** and ***The Gondola Scam,*** all in paperback from Viking Penguin. I do not like the more recent Lovejoy novels, e.g., ***The Tartan Sell, Moonspender,*** and ***Pearlhanger.*** They do not read well.

Rinker, Harry L. ***The Joy of Collecting with Craven Moore*** (Radnor, PA: Wallace-Homestead, 1985). Out-of-print. Try never to become so serious about your collecting or dealing that you forget to laugh and have fun. Find out if you are Craven Moore, Anita Moore, Howie Bys, or Constance Lee Bys. Trust me, you are in *The Joy of Collecting with Craven Moore*. I guarantee it. Although out-of-print, I still have a few copies around. I will sell you one for $6. Send a check or money order to: Harry L. Rinker, 5093 Vera Cruz Road, Emmaus, PA 18049.

ANTIQUES & COLLECTIBLES TRADE NEWSPAPERS

NATIONAL MAGAZINES

Antique Trader's Collector Magazine & Price Guide
Krause Publications
700 E. State St.
Iola, WI 54990
(715) 445-2214
www.collect.com

Antiques & Collecting Magazine
1006 S. Michigan Ave.
Chicago, IL 60605
(800) 762-7576
e-mail: acm@interaccess.com

Collectors' Eye
6 Woodside Ave., Ste. 300
Northport, NY 11768
888-800-2588
e-mail: collectorseye@aol.com

Country Accents Collectibles Flea Market Finds
Goodman Media Group
419 Park Ave. South
New York, NY 10016
212-541-7100
www.newco.com

NATIONAL NEWSPAPERS

The Antique Trader Weekly
Krause Publications
700 E. State St.
Iola, WI 54945
715-445-2214
www.collect.com

Antique Week (Central and Eastern Editions)
P.O. Box 90
Knightstown, IN 46148
(800) 876-5133
www.antiqueweek.com
e-mail: dscott@antiqueweek.com

Antiques and the Arts Weekly
The Bee Publishing Co.
P.O. Box 5503
Newtown, CT 06470
(203) 426-8036
www.antiquesandthearts.com
e-mail: info@thebee.com

Collectors News
P.O. Box 306
506 Second St.
Grundy Center, IA 50638
(800) 352-8039
www.collectors-news.com
e-mail: collectors@collectorsnews.com

Maine Antique Digest
911 Main St.
P.O. Box 1429
Waldoboro, ME 04572-1429
(800) 752-8521
www.maineantiquedigest.com
e-mail: mad@maine.com

REGIONAL NEWSPAPERS

New England

The Fine Arts Trader
P.O. Box 1273
Randolph, MA 02368
(800) 332-5055
www.fineartstrader.com

The Journal of Antiques and Collectibles
P.O. Box 37
Hudson, NY 12534
518-828-5497

New England Antiques Journal
P.O. Box 120
4 Church St.
Ware, MA 01082
(800) 432-3505
www.antiquesjournal.com
e-mail: visit@antiquesjournal.com

Northeast Journal of Arts & Antiques
P.O. Box 37
Hudson, NY 12534
518-838-5497

UnRavel the Gavel
14 Hurricane Rd., #1
Belmont, NH 03220
(603) 524-4281
www.thegavel.net
e-mail: gavel96@worldpath.net

Middle Atlantic States

Antiques Tattler (Adamstown)
P.O. Box 938T
Adamstown, PA 19501
www.antiquescapital.com

Northeast Journal of Antiques & Art
P.O. Box 37
Hudson, NY 12534
(800) 836-4069
www.northeastjournal.com
e-mail: nejourl@mhonline.net

Renninger's Antique Guide
2 Cypress Place
P.O. Box 495
Lafayette Hill, PA 19444
877-385-0104
www.renningers.com

South

The Antique Shoppe
P.O. Box 2175
Keystone Heights, FL 32656
(352) 475-1679
www.antiqueshoppefl.com
e-mail: antshoppe@aol.com

Cotton & Quail Antique Gazette
Krause Publications
700 E. State St.
Iola, WI 54945
715-445-2214
www.collect.com

Country Register of Virginia
P.O. Box 365
New Market, MD 21774
(866) 825-9217
www.countryregister.com
e-mail: virginia@countryregister.com

The Old News Is Good News Antiques Gazette
P.O. Box 305
Hammond, LA 70404
985-429-0575
www.theantiquesgazette.com
e-mail: gazette@i–55.com

Southeastern Antiquing and Collecting Magazine
P.O. Box 510
Acworth, GA 30101-0510
(888) 388-7827
www.go-star.com
e-mail: antiquing@go-star.com

Southern Antiques
P.O. Box 1107
Decatur, GA 30031
888-800-4997
www.kaleden.com
e-mail: southernantiques@msn.com

Midwest

The American Antiquities Journal
126 East High St.
Springfield, OH 45502
(800) 557-6281
www.americanantiquites.com
e-mail: mail@americanantiquities.com

The Antique Collector and Auction Guide
c/o Farm and Dairy
185-205 E. State St.
P.O. Box 38
Salem, OH 44460
(330) 337-3419
www.farmanddairy.com

Auction Action Antique News
1404 E. Green Bay St.
Shawano, WI 54166-2258
(715) 524-3076
www.auctionactionnews.com
e-mail: auction@auctionactionnews.com

Auction World
8880 Ballentine
Overland Park, KS 66214
(888) 541-8084
www.auctioneers.org
e-mail: ryan@auctioneers.org

The Collector
P.O. Box 148
Heyworth, IL 61745-0148
(309) 473-2466
e-mail: collinc@mchsi.com

Collectors Journal
P.O. Box 601
Vinton, IA 52349
(800) 472-4006
www.collectorsjournal.com
e-mail: antiquescj@aol.com

Discover Mid-America
104 East 5th St. Ste. 201
Kansas City, MO 64106
(800) 899-9730
www.discoverypub.com
e-mail: publisher@discoverypub.com

Great Lakes Trader
132 S. Putnam
Williamstown, MI 48895
(800) 785-6367
e-mail: gltrader@aol.com

Indiana Antique Buyer's News, Inc.
P.O. Box 213
Silver Lake, IN 46982
574-893-4200
www.indianaantique.com
e-mail: iabn@hoosierlink.net

The Old Times Newspaper
P.O. Box 340
Maple Lake, MN 55358
(800) 539-1810
www.theoldtimes.com
e-mail: oldtimes@theoldtimes.com

Yesteryear
P.O. Box 2
Princeton, WI 54968
(920) 787-4808
e-mail: yesteryear@vbe.com

Northwest

Antique Browser
P.O. Box 1340
Kamiah, ID 83536
(208) 935-0866
e-mail: thecountrycourier@cybrquest.com

Southwest

The Antique Register
P.O. Box 84345
Phoenix, AZ 85071
(602) 942-8950
www.countryregister.com
e-mail: info@countryregister.com

West Coast

Antique & Collectables
500 Fesler, Ste. 201
P.O. Box 12589
El Cajon, CA 92022
800-445-4154
www.collect.com

Antique Journal
500 Fesler, Ste. 201
P.O. Box 12589
El Cajon, CA 92022
800-445-4154
www.collect.com
e-mail: antiquejournal@aol.com

Old Stuff
VBM Printers, Inc.
P.O. Box 449
McMinnville, OR 97128
(503) 434-5386
www.oldstuffnews.com
e-mail: oldstuff@onlinemac.com

West Coast Peddler
P.O. Box 5134
Whittier, CA 90607
(562) 698-1718
www.WestCoastPeddler.com
e-mail: westcoastpeddler@earthlink.net

INTERNATIONAL NEWSPAPERS

Australia

Carter's Antiques & Collectables
Carter's Pty. Ltd.
Locked Bag 502
Galston, NSW 2159
Australia
+61 2 9653 2755
www.carters.com.au
e-mail: info@carters.com.au

Canada

Antique Showcase
Trajan Publishing Corp.
103 Lakeshore Rd., Ste. 202
St. Catherines, Ontario
Canada L2N 2T6
(800) 408-0352
www.trajan.com
e-mail: office@trajan.com

Thompsons' Antiques Gazette
#50-39026 Range Rd. 275
Red Deer County, Alberta
Canada T4S 2A9
(403) 346-8791
www.antiquesalberta.com
e-mail: mdthompson@shaw.ca

The Upper Canadian
30 D Chambers St.
P.O. Box 653
Smiths Falls, Ontario
Canada K7A 4T6
(613) 283-1168
www.uppercanadian.com
e-mail: uppercanadian@recorder.ca

England

Antiques Trade Gazette
Circulation Dept.
115 Shaflesbury Ave.
London WC2H 8AD U.K.
020 7420 6600
www.atg-online.com
e-mail: subscriptions@antiquestradegazette.com

Antiques & Art Independent
P.O. Box 1945
Comely Bank
Edinburgh, EH4 1AB Scotland UK
+44 7000 268478
www.antiques-UK.co.UK/independent
e-mail: antiquesnews@hotmail.com

Finland

Keräilyn Maailma
Vuorikatu 22 B 65
00100 Helsinki
(09) 170090

France

France Antiquités
Château de Boisrigaud
63490 Usson
(04) 73 71 00 04
e-mail: France.Antiquites@wanadoo.fr

La Vie du Collectionneur
B. P. 77
77302 Fontainbleau Cedex
(01) 60 71 55 55

Germany

Antiquitäten Zeitung
Nymphenburger Str. 84
D-80636 München
(089) 12 69 90-0

Sammler Journal
Journal-Verlag Schwend GmbH
Schmollerstrasse 31
D-74523 Schwäbisch Hall
(0791) 404-500
e-mail: info.sj@t-online.de

Sammler Markt
Der Heisse Draht Verlagsgesellschaft mbH & Co.
Drostestr. 14-16
D-30161 Hannover
(0511) 390 91-0
www.dhd24.com

Spielzeug Antik
Verlag Christian Gärtner
Ubierring 4
D-50678 Köln
(0221) 9322266

Tin Toy Magazin
Verlag, Redaktion, Anzeigen, Vertrieb
Mannheimer Str. 5
D-68309 Mannheim
(0621) 739687

Trödler & Sammeln
Gemi Verlags GmbH
Pfaffenhofener Strasse 3
D-85293 Reichertschausen
(08441) 4022-0
www.ag-advertising.de

AUCTION HOUSES

The following auctioneers, auction companies, and antiques and collectibles dealers generously supply Rinker Enterprises, Inc., with copies of their auction/sales lists, press releases, catalogs, illustrations, and prices realized.

If you are an auctioneer, auction company, or antiques and collectibles dealer and would like your name and address to appear on this list in subsequent editions, please send copies of your auction lists, dealer sales lists, press releases, catalogs and illustrations, prices realized, and/or photographs or digital images to: **Rinker Enterprises, Inc., 5093 Vera Cruz Road, Emmaus, PA 18049.**

Auction Houses & Auctioneers

Alderfer Auction Company
501 Fairgrounds Rd.
Hatfield, PA 19440
215-393-3000
fax: 215-368-9055
www.alderferauction.com
e-mail: info@alderferauction.com

Arman Absentee Sales
P.O. Box 39
Portsmouth, RI 02871
401-539-4608
fax: 401-841-8403
e-mail: armans@mindspring.com

Arthur Auctioneering
563 Reed Rd.
Hughesville, PA 17737
800-ARTHUR-3
www.overshot1.com/waynearthur

Auction Team Köln
Breker – The Specialists
Postfach 50 11 19
D-50971 Köln, Germany
Tel: 0221/28 70 49
fax: 0221/37 48 78
www.breker.com
e-mail: auction@breker.com
Jane Herz, USA Representative
(941) 925-0385
fax: (941) 925-0487

Cerebro
612 State St.
Lancaster, PA 17608
800-69-LABEL
fax: 717-392-4468
www.cerebro.com
e-mail: sueupdike@comcast.net

Cohasco, Inc.
Postal 821
Yonkers, NY 10701
914-476-8500
fax: 914-476-8573
www.cohascodpc.com
e-mail: cohascodpc@mail.com

Cowan's Historic Americana Auctions
673 Wilmer Ave.
Cincinnati, OH 45226
513-871-1670
fax: 513-871-8670
www.historicamericana.com
e-mail: info@historicamericana.com

Craftsman Auctions
333 North Main St.
Lambertville, NJ 08530
609-397-9374
fax: 609-397-9377
www.ragoarts.com
e-mail: info@ragoarts.com

Doyle New York
175 E. 87th St.
New York, NY 10128
212-427-2730
fax: 212-369-0892
www.doylenewyork.com
e-mail: info@doylenewyork.com

Flomaton Antique Auction
P.O. Box 1017
Flomaton, AL 36441
205-296-3059
www.flomatonantiqueauction.com

Fontaines Auction Gallery
1485 W. Housatonic St.
Pittsfield, MA 10201
413-448-8922
fax: 413-442-1550

Garth's Auctions
2690 Stratford Rd.
P.O. Box 369
Delaware, OH 43015
740-362-4771
fax: 740-363-0164
www.garths.com
e-mail: info@garths.com

Glass Works Auctions
P.O. Box 180
East Greenville, PA 18041
215-679-5849
fax: 215-679-3068
www.glswrk–auction.com
e-mail: glswrk@enter.net

Greenberg Auctions
1393 Progress Way, Ste. 907
Eldersburg, MD 21784
410-795-7448
fax: 410-549-2553
www.greenbergshows.com
e-mail: auction@greenbergshows.com

Hake's Americana & Collectibles
P.O. Box 1444
York, PA 17405-1444
717-848-1333
fax: 717-852-0344
www.hakes.com
e-mail: auction@hakes.com

Tom Harris Auctions
203 S. 18th Ave.
Marshalltown, IA 50158
641-753-3865
fax: 641-753-3865
www.tomharrisauctions.com
e-mail: tomharris@tomharrisauctions.com

Norman C. Heckler & Company
79 Bradford Corner Rd.
Woodstock Valley, CT 06282
860-974-1634
fax: 860-974-2003
www.heckleraution.com
e-mail: info@hecklerauction.com

Michael Ivankovich Antiques & Auction Co., Inc.
P.O. Box 1536
Doylestown, PA 18901
215-345-6094
www.michaelivankovich.com
e-mail: ivankovich@wnutting.com

Jackson's Auctioneers & Appraisers
2229 Lincoln St.
Cedar Falls, IA 50613
319-277-2256
fax: 319-277-1252
www.jacksonsauction.com
e-mail: jacksons@jacksonsauction.com

James D. Julia, Inc.
P.O. Box 830
Fairfield, ME 04937
207-453-7125
fax: 207-453-2502
www.juliaauctions.com
e-mail: jjulia@juliaauctions.com

Kruse International
5540 County Road 11A
Auburn, IN 46706
800-968-4444
fax: 260-925-5467
www.kruse.com
e-mail: info@kruseinternational.com

Lang's Sporting Collectables, Inc.
663 Pleasant Valley Rd.
Waterville, NY 13480
315-841-4623
e-mail: langsauction@aol.com

Majolica Auctions
200 North Main
P.O.Box 332
Wolcottville, IN 46795
260-854-2859
fax: 260-854-3979
www.strawserauctions.com
e-mail: info@strawserauctions.com

Mark of Time
1128 8th Avenue West
Palmetto, FL 34221
800-277-5275
www.markoftime.com
e-mail: auction@markoftime.com

Mastro Net Inc.
1515 W. 22nd St., Ste. 125
Oak Brook, IL 60523
630-472-1200
fax: 630-472-1201
www.mastronet.com

Metz Superlatives Auction
P.O. Box 18185
Roanoke, VA 24014
540-344-7333
fax: 540-344-3014
www.muddyrivertrading.com
e-mail: metzauction@rbnet.com

Wm Morford
RD #2, Cobb Hill Rd.
Cazenovia, NY 13035
315-662-7625
fax: 315-662-3570
www.morfauction.com
e-mail: morf2bid@aol.com

Ray Morykan Auctions
1368 Spring Valley Rd.
Bethlehem, PA 18015
610-838-6634
e-mail: dmorykan@enter.net

Norton Auctioneers
Pearl at Monroe
Coldwater, MI 49036-1967
517-279-9063
fax: 517-279-9191
www.nortonauctioneers.com
e-mail: nortonsold@cbpu.com

Pook & Pook, Inc.
P.O. Box 268
Downingtown, PA 19335
610-269-4040
fax: 610-269-9274
www.pookandpook.com
e-mail: info@pookandpook.com

Rago Modern Auctions
333 N. Main St.
Lambertville, NJ 08530
609-397-9374
fax: 609-397-9377
www.ragoarts.com
e-mail: info@ragoarts.com

Railroad Memories
1903 S. Niagara St.
Denver, CO 80224
303-759-1290
fax: 303-757-6063
www.railroadmemories.com
e-mail: knous@railroadmemories.com

Red Baron's Antiques
6450 Roswell Rd.
Atlanta, GA 30328
404-252-3770
fax: 404-257-0268
www.redbaronsantiques.com

L. H. Selman Ltd.
123 Locust St.
Santa Cruz, CA 95060
800-538-0766
831-427-1177
fax: 831-427-0111
www.pwauction.com
e-mail: lselman@got.net

Shelley's Auction Gallery
429 N. Main St.
Hendersonville, NC 28792
828-698-8485
fax: 828-693-4305
www.shelleysauction.com
e-mail: sag@shelleysauction.com

Skinner, Inc.
Bolton Gallery
357 Main St.
Bolton, MA 01740
978-779-6241
978-779-5144
www.skinnerinc.com

Skinner, Inc.
Boston Gallery
The Heritage On The Garden
63 Park Plaza
Boston, MA 02116
617-350-5400
fax: 617-350-5429
www.skinnerinc.com

Slater's Americana, Inc.
5335 Tacoma Ave., Ste. 24
Indianapolis, IN 46220
317-257-0863
fax: 317-254-9167
www.slatersamericana.com
e-mail: slater@indy.net

Sloans & Kenyon
4605 Bradley Blvd.
Bethesda, MD 20815
301-634-2330
fax: 301-656-7074
www.sloansandkenyon.com
e-mail:
info@sloansandkenyon.com

Smith & Jones, Inc. Auctions
12 Clark Ln.
Sudbury, MA 01776
978-443-5517
fax: 978-443-2796
www.smithandjonesauctions.com
e-mail: smthjnes@gis.net

R. M. Smythe & Co., Inc.
26 Broadway, Ste. 973
New York, NY 10004-1703
800-622-1880
fax: 212-908-4047
www.smytheonline.com
e-mail:
dherzog@smytheonline.com

SoldUSA, Inc.
1418 Industrial Dr., Box 11
Matthews, NC 28105
704-815-1500
www.soldusa.com
e-mail: support@soldusa.com

Sotheby's New York
1334 York Ave.
New York, NY 10021
541-312-5682
www.sothebys.com

Swann Galleries, Inc.
104 E. 25th St.
New York, NY 10010
212-254-4710
fax: 212-979-1017
www.swanngalleries.com
e-mail:
swann@swanngalleries.com

Tool Shop Auctions
Tony Murland
78 High St.
Needham Market
Suffolk, 1P6 8AW England
Tel: 011-44-01449-722992
fax: 011-44-01449-722683
www.antiquetools.co.uk
e-mail: tony@antiquetools.co.uk

York Town Auction Inc.
1625 Haviland Rd.
York, PA 17404
717-751-0211
fax: 717-767-7729
www.yorktownauction.com
e-mail:
info@yorktownauction.com

INDEX

NARRAGANSETT PUBLIC LIBRARY
3 2298 00098 8065